THE GREAT TRIUMVIRATE

Webster Replying to Hayne. Painting by G. P. A. Healy. *Courtesy of the Boston Art Commission*

The Great Triumvirate

Webster, Clay, and Calhoun

MERRILL D. PETERSON

NEW YORK   OXFORD

Oxford University Press

1987

Oxford University Press

Oxford   New York   Toronto
Delhi   Bombay   Calcutta   Madras   Karachi
Petaling Jaya   Singapore   Hong Kong   Tokyo
Nairobi   Dar es Salaam   Cape Town
Melbourne   Auckland

and associated companies in
Beirut   Berlin   Ibadan   Nicosia

Published by Oxford University Press, Inc.,
200 Madison Avenue, New York, New York 10016

Oxford is a registered trademark of Oxford University Press

Library of Congress Cataloging-in-Publication Data
Peterson, Merrill D.
The great triumvirate.
Includes index. 1. Statesmen—United States—biography.
2. Webster, Daniel, 1782–1852. 3. Clay, Henry, 1777–1852.
4. Calhoun, John C. (John Caldwell), 1782–1850.
5. United States—Politics and government—1815–1861. I. Title.
E339.P47 1987   973.5′092′2   86-31254
ISBN 0-19-503877-0

7 9 8 6

Printed in the United States of America
on acid-free paper

TO

Colleagues, Students, and Staff

OF THE

CORCORAN DEPARTMENT OF HISTORY

UNIVERSITY OF VIRGINIA

1962–1987

PREFACE

This book has a dual character. On the one hand, it is a collective biography of three American statesmen—Henry Clay, Daniel Webster, and John C. Calhoun—whose careers were virtually coterminous and who because of their mutual eminence and power became known as The Great Triumvirate. On the other hand, it is a history of public policy and political leadership in the United States during the forty years, roughly 1812–1852, when these three men held the center of the stage. Coming to this work after many years of research and scholarship focused on Thomas Jefferson, it was perhaps inevitable that I should conceive of it as a study of the second generation of American statesmanship.

I began the book in 1971. For several years other projects took precedence, but by 1976 I was giving *The Great Triumvirate* major attention and it was well advanced five years later when I accepted a tour of duty as Dean of the Faculty of Arts and Sciences at the University of Virginia. The book was completed in the sabbatical year, 1985–86, following my retirement from this office. I am well aware that on subjects as large as mine true completeness is seldom attained, and it certainly has not been attained here. In this regard I take comfort from the wisdom of an earlier American historian, Woodrow Wilson, who remarked that were one to pursue the last scrap of evidence and to incorporate the last detail "it would take as long to write history as to enact it, and one should have to postpone reading it to the leisure of the next world."

Acknowledgments are owed first to the University of Virginia, including the Alderman Library, for aid and support that have been indispensable to the writing of this book. Scarcely less important have been the fellowship awards of the National Endowment for the Humanities and the National Humanities Center. Residence at the Center in 1980–81 provided me with nine months of uninterrupted time to write, along with the stimulation of a new environment and interesting colleagues. Grants from the American Philosophical Society and the American Council of Learned Societies have also aided my research. In the course of that research I have visited libraries, historical societies, and other depositories from Concord, New Hampshire, to

Baton Rouge, Louisiana, and Madison, Wisconsin; and I am indebted to all of them. I am especially grateful, however, to the editorial offices of the *Papers of John C. Calhoun*, at the University of South Carolina, and the *Papers of Henry Clay*, at the University of Kentucky, which extended to me the courtesy of consulting materials collected for these works. (With respect to the *Papers of Daniel Webster*, at Dartmouth College, this proved unnecessary because of the availability of a prior microfilm edition.) Some parts of Book Four appeared in another form in *Olive Branch and Sword—The Compromise of 1833*, published by Louisiana State University Press, in 1982, to which I make acknowledgment. I wish also to thank William W. Abbot for reading several of the early chapters; Amy Henderson, James Barber, Frederick Voss, and Ellen Miles at the National Portrait Gallery; Jessica Kitay, William Gilmore, Michael Holt, George Herring, Daniel Hollis and Richard Ellis for small favors; my wife Jean for patience and encouragement; and Sheldon Meyer, who has been my editor and counselor at Oxford University Press for almost thirty years.

In quoting from letters and manuscripts I have taken the liberty of modernizing peculiarities of spelling, punctuation, and capitalization.

Charlottesville, Virginia   M.D.P.
January 1, 1987

CONTENTS

THE GREAT TRIUMVIRATE

* *One* *

PATHS TO POWER

The Twelfth Congress of the United States, convening on November 4, 1811, was a watershed in the history of the republic. It marked the entry into national politics of a new generation of leaders who had had no part in the founding of the republic and whose highest aspiration was to preserve it. Preservation was not a task for sunshine patriots in 1811. President James Madison, in his opening message to Congress, issued a call to arms. He reported on the failure of the latest round of diplomacy with Great Britain and urged Congress to make the country ready for war. For seven years American peace and commerce had been held hostage to the European belligerents, Britain and France. There were grievances enough to justify war with either or both powers, but in the eyes of the administration and the ruling Jeffersonian Republican party Britain was the chief aggressor against American rights, honor, and independence. On the seas of trade, where she was supreme, Britain continued to treat the United States like colonies. Her cruisers hovered off the Atlantic coast and plundered American carriers in the neutral trade. Ships of His Majesty's Navy impressed thousands of American seamen into its service, thereby assaulting the very existence of American nationality and citizenship. The British government demanded that the United States cooperate in its commercial warfare against Napoleon's "continental system" as the price of protection for neutral carriers, cargoes, and profits. War was narrowly averted in 1807 after the *Chesapeake* Affair, in which a British frigate brutally fired on an American naval vessel, killing three and wounding eighteen. The president, Thomas Jefferson, pressed Britain for a negotiated settle-

3

ment, to no avail. Six months later he proposed an embargo of American commerce in order to avoid war and also to force justice on Britain by the denial of trade. In the latter aim the experiment failed, and the embargo was repealed when Madison became president, although he stuck to the policy of pursuing some form of commercial coercion as the means of securing American rights and interests without war. Now, after almost three years, the policy had come to a dead end. Pending the outcome of one last diplomatic overture, Madison was ready to go to war.

He was encouraged, if not driven, in this direction by the warlike spirit of the new Congress. Among some seventy new members was a small cadre of aggressive young leaders from the South and West, primarily, to whom John Randolph of Roanoke applied the epithet "war hawks." At their head was a thirty-four-year-old Kentuckian, Henry Clay. Clay was already known, from his brief prior service in the Senate, as a fiery nationalist and orator, who brought to politics a bold gambling spirit learned at the card table, and who was impatient with the timidity and pacifism of the Virginia presidents. He was promptly elected Speaker of the House of Representatives and from that post organized committees and inspired Congress for war. "What are we to gain by war?" Clay asked, answering, "What are we not to lose by peace? Commerce, character, a nation's best treasure, honor!"[1]

Among the War Hawks was a freshman congressman from the South Carolina upcountry, John C. Calhoun. Five years Clay's junior, he was equally ardent, if less flamboyant, in his nationalism. The Speaker appointed him to the Committee on Foreign Relations, and he soon succeeded to the chairmanship. Believing that he stood at "the commencement of a new era in our politics," Calhoun claimed that those previously in charge of the nation's affairs had sought to avoid or remove difficulties by a sort of management—commercial, diplomatic, political—that produced only distrust at home and contempt abroad. "We have said, we will change; we will defend ourselves by force."[2] When the president sent his war message to Congress on June 1, 1812, it was referred to Calhoun's committee, and he immediately returned a report on the causes and reasons for war. The report reviewed the long-standing issues with Britain, essentially those of "free trade and seamen's rights," but concluded by justifying the war on the loftier plane of freedom and independence. The "freeborn sons of America" must fight to preserve what their fathers had won with so much blood and treasure. In war, Calhoun declaimed in language reminiscent of the Declaration of Independence, "the Americans of the present day will prove . . . to the World, that we have not only inherited that liberty which our Fathers gave us, but also the will and power to maintain it."[3]

The minority party in Congress, the Federalists, and some of the majority as well, never accepted this Republican conception of the war as the Second War for American Independence. The vote on the declaration of war disclosed the strength of the opposition: 79–49 in the House, 19–13 in the Senate. The opposition was centered in the eastern states, ironically in that section of the country most interested in foreign commerce. But the true causes of the war lay not in "free trade and seamen's rights," the Federalists argued, but in Jeffersonian weakness and folly, subservience to France, and what Randolph, suspecting Republican designs on Canada, called "agrarian cupidity." A young champion of the Federalist cause, Daniel Webster, came into Congress from New Hampshire eleven months after war had been declared. At thirty-one, already touted as the "Yankee Demosthenes," Webster brought to the opposition some of the same vigor and spirit that animated the War Hawks.

Webster, Clay, and Calhoun: the destinies of these three men who met in Congress in May 1813 were intertwined. Their arrival on the political stage announced a new era of American statesmanship, and their departure forty years later brought it emphatically to a close. They were representatives, spokesmen, ultimately personifications, of their respective sections: East, West, and South. Intensely ambitious, they were more often political rivals than friends; and although each would be disappointed in his quest for the presidency, they were widely regarded at home and abroad as the foremost American statesmen of the age. In 1832, when they came together in the Senate for the first time and coalesced in opposition to the president, Andrew Jackson, the idea of "The Great Triumvirate" was born. It was the offspring of the feverish Jacksonian imagination, for the prospect was very small of these master spirits—Webster, Clay, and Calhoun—uniting in power like the famed Roman triumvirs who ruled after Caesar's death. Yet had they become a triumvirate in fact, what worlds they might have conquered!

The idea of "The Great Triumvirate" survived and eventually entered into the history books because for so long these three men divided so much of American politics between them. In 1847, when Webster made a heralded tour of the South, the Charleston *Daily Courier* called upon the people to honor him as an illustrious American.

> And ours is indeed a fortunate contry—Ireland has her O'Connell, England her Peel, France her Louis Philippe—but we can happily point on our roll of free citizenship to a triad of living greatness—Clay, Webster and Calhoun are the *three* GREAT MEN OF AMERICA—each in his section or sphere towering in colossal proportion and pyramidal eminence above all rivalry; and, when grouped on the national canvas, forming a picture and a spectacle of moral and intellectual grandeur, for the world's admiration and the nation's pride. They have each stood beyond compeer Senators in the State House . . . co-equals in greatness, but each having a greatness peculiarly his own . . . and each of whom, although he may never be destined to climb the Presidential steep, is crowned with a loftier, wider and more valuable fame than the Presidency can bestow—for they preside in the admiration and the hearts of their countrymen.[4]

Because each of these statesmen was deeply conscious of the interrelationship among them, he rarely made a move without calculating its effect on the others. Public opinion reinforced this sense of interrelationship. They were all celebrities, conscious of their public roles and of themselves as symbols of certain principles and policies in an age when the dramatic encounters of great men in politics claimed the nation's attention and, many thought, determined its future. They all became conservatives, each man's thought revealing a different facet of the conservative mind of the age.

Great men though they were, neither Webster nor Clay nor Calhoun ever realized his highest ambition. The popular preference for second- and third-rate men in the presidency was a cause of recrimination against republican government. It was notorious, said the *Edinburgh Review,* that in America men, like Milton's fiends, "must make themselves dwarfs, before they can enter the Pandemonium of political life."[5] And so Webster, Clay, and Calhoun, the legitimate successors of Washington, Adams, and Jefferson, never attained the presidency. When the last of this "second race of giants" passed away in 1852 nothing was left to challenge the sway of the Lilliputians. The republic lost its glory—the regalia of great statesmen.

The Great Triumvirate became part of the furniture of American memory. In 1957 a special committee of the United States Senate, under the chairmanship of John F. Kennedy, was charged with recommending the five preeminent senators in the history of that body, whose portraits should adorn the Senate Reception Room. After a survey of scholarly and political opinion, the committee recommended Clay, Webster, and Calhoun in that order, followed by Robert La Follette and Robert A. Taft. While thus remembered in the nation's capital, Webster, Clay, and Calhoun are also well remembered in their home states; and it is to them, to New Hampshire and Kentucky and South Carolina, that the historian must turn to search out their separate paths to power.

1. *"Star of the West"*

Kentucky was a fabled land when Henry Clay, a twenty-year-old Virginia lawyer, immigrated there in 1797. As the Indian tribes receded before the onrush of settlers that poured through the mountain gaps and down the Ohio River, the Dark and Bloody Ground of Daniel Boone and the pioneer adventurers became the Promised Land of American dreams. Clay's destination was the town of Lexington in the heart of the luxuriant Bluegrass, a high plane well south of the Ohio River, encircled by the Kentucky River, where the land was so rich and beautiful it could be described only in superlatives. "Everything here assumes a dignity and splendour I have never seen in any other part of the world," Gilbert Imlay rhapsodized. "You ascend a considerable distance from the shore of the Ohio, and when you would suppose you had arrived at the summit of a mountain, you find yourself upon an extensive level. Here an eternal verdure reigns, and the brilliant sun of latitude 39°, piercing through the azure heavens, produces, in this prolific soil, an early maturity that is truly astonishing. Flowers full and perfect. . . . Soft zephyrs. . . . The sweet songsters of the forest. . . .

Everything here gives delight." It was, as Clay himself would say, the most favored land of Providence.[1]

Lexington and Henry Clay were the same age, and given their reciprocal energies, the man and the place seemed meant for each other. With its swelling population of 1,600, its three hundred houses, many of them brick, fronting broad streets laid out in a checkerboard pattern, with its booming commerce and infant manufactures—rope walks, forges, tanyards, powder mills—on an extensive scale, with even an embryo university, Lexington was rapidly passing from a frontier village into the great metropolis of the Western world. It was still crude and raw, of course. Eastern travelers were shocked by the raucous behavior of hunters, boatmen, farmers, and drovers who arrived in Lexington to market or to court. These "untutored savages" crowded the public square, the taverns, the bawdy houses; drinking, gambling, whoring, wrestling, and horse swapping were their amusements. The city was dominated, however, by Virginia-born lawyers like Clay himself. They had transplanted the manners of the Virginia gentry and the ideals of Virginia republicanism to the Bluegrass. Representing the wealth and power of Kentucky, they controlled the city's future and in lesser measure the state's as well.[2] Young Clay became the newest recruit to the Jeffersonian lawyer-aristocracy.

Kentucky was a new land, the Kentuckians were a new people, separated from the Atlantic states by the Appalachian barrier, nurtured by the frontier, their fortunes tied not only to the new national government but to the westward flowing waters of the Ohio and the Mississippi; yet, as the offspring of the Old Dominion, Kentucky remained under Virginia's influence and bore the Virginia stamp. When in 1792, having received her independence, she was admitted to the Union as a sovereign state, the state agreed, as one of the conditions of independence, to abide by Virginia land laws and respect the claims of Virginia speculators. The mother state's power persisted, and with it the incredible confusion over land titles that made Kentucky a paradise for lawyers. The first constitution was framed primarily by the leader of the "court party," George Nicholas, who had come from Virginia only three years before; it contained several unique provisions—a strong executive, an elitist senate, a centralized judiciary—that checked the frontier democracy of Kentucky. From the beginning the constitution was a source of contention, and the rising party conflict in the United States, driven in part by democratic ideas, brought the constitution under attack even in respectable Jeffersonian quarters. Clay at once joined the movement for reform. The Virginia elite, firmly and fervently Republican in national affairs, was less united at home. Jeffersonian Republicanism was more than a matter of politics, however. It was a matter of intellectual temper and personal style—liberal, enlightened, progressive—and when it confronted the challenges of a youthful, brash, and venturesome society it became something different without ceasing to be Jeffersonian.[3]

Henry Clay would experience, then personify, this change. Kentucky was destined to be the western proving ground of the republican experiment born during the American Revolution; and Clay, casting his lot in this wide and un-predictable environment, would furnish the most interesting part of the proof. In his valedictory to the United States Senate in 1842, he recalled with deep emotion his immigration to Kentucky forty-five years before. "I went as an orphan, who had not yet attained the age of majority, who had never recognized a father's smile, nor felt his caresses—poor, penniless, without the favor of the great, with an imperfect and inadequate education, limited to the ordinary business and common pursuits of life. But scarce had I set my foot upon her generous soil, when I was seized and embraced with parental fondness, caressed as though I had been a favorite child, and patronized with liberal and unbounded munificence."[4] Whatever disappointments he suffered during his long career, Clay was never disappointed with Kentucky, nor Kentucky with him. The marriage of the man, the time, and the place was, indeed, one of the most fortunate in the annals of American politics.

In 1797 Clay was not the poor, orphaned, uneducated youth he later described so pathetically for the Senate. He had a genius for self-dramatization, and the idea that he was "the artificer of his own destiny" formed the core of his personal legend. Boasting of his deprivations became a habit. "I inherited only infancy, ignorance, and indigence," he said.[5] Political friends and biographers embroidered the legend of a child of nature. "He owes less of his greatness to education or to art than any man living," wrote a prominent Kentuckian after long observation. "He wears nature's patent of nobility forever on his brow. . . . He is independent alike of history, or the schools; he knows little of either and despises both. If he is like anybody, he does not know it. He has never studied models, and, if he had, his pride would have rescued him from the fault of imitation. He stands among men in towering and barbaric grandeur, in all the hardihood and rudeness of perfect originality, independent of the polish and beyond the reach of art."[6] When Calvin Colton, an early biographer, asked Clay for the family coat of arms, to be used as an emblem for the book, he replied that he had none and suggested the substitution of an insignia incorporating loom, plow, anvil, and other articles of national improvement, which he could rightfully claim as his own.[7]

Although the legend had the color of truth, Henry Clay owed more to his Virginia heritage and upbringing than he was inclined to admit. He was born on April 12, 1777, the seventh son of John Clay, in Hanover County "somewhere between Black Tom's Slash and Hanover Court-house." The first Clay came to Virginia not long after the settlement of Jamestown; Henry belonged to the fifth generation. They were Tidewater tobacco planters who reached the middle rungs of the social ladder but no higher. Henry's father had made a name for himself among the common people of Hanover as a crusading Baptist preacher. His mother, Elizabeth Hudson, sprang from the same hardy stock. The four-hundred-acre Hudson homestead where Henry was born and raised supported the large family. During the Revolutionary War, Simcoe's Rangers and Tarleton's Dragoons came to pay their respects. Clay would later claim he was "born a democrat—rocked in the cradle of the revolution." He remembered "a visit made by Tarleton's troops to the house of my mother [in 1781], and of their running their swords into the new made graves of my father and grandfather, thinking they contained hidden treasures."[8] Only four years old when his father died, he had no memory of him, nor of his grandfather. His widowed mother soon married Henry Watkins, who took over the farm and started another large family. The upset evidently inflicted no permanent emotional damage on the boy. He got a meager three years of schooling—the only formal education he ever received—in a typical "old field school" near the Hanover courthouse. It is hard to say what he may have learned from his dutiful mother and stepfather, for he seldom spoke of them or any of his family. He had little remembrance of his childhood and no sentimental associations with its people, places, and events. After he left Hanover he returned only once. Yet, decades later, the sentimental image of "The Millboy of the Slashes"—a tow-headed youth, ragged and barefoot, mounted on a pony, with a bag of corn thrown on either side, bound for the mill on Pamunkey River—was indelibly engraved on the public mind.

In 1791 the Watkins family caught the Kentucky fever and migrated, but Henry, who at fourteen had displayed talents beyond the ordinary, stayed behind. Watkins had arranged for him to become a deputy clerk in the High Court Chancery in the capital at Richmond. "Virginia's high courts and legislative halls were to be his preparatory school," as Bernard Mayo has said, "giving him a training far more congenial than that of musty books and studious drudgery."[9] He observed the great and near great who came to the capital; he learned the rounds of Richmond society, from its gambling taverns and racecourses to its fashionable balls and outings; and he embraced the city's ascendant Jeffersonian Republicanism as well as its moral and religious counterpart, deistic rationalism, so different from his father's faith.

After a year or so in the clerk's office, Henry had the good fortune to become secretary to the chancellor, George Wythe. Wythe was a man of exemplary character, a fine classical scholar, and Virginia's most learned jurist. He made the eager but untutored clerk his pupil, companion, and protégé. In the course of dictation the old judge would stop to explain a classical allusion, offer a comparison to Plutarch or Thucydides, or expound on Lord Coke. He guided Henry in his reading, and although that reading was neither broad nor deep, the pupil acquired at least a nodding acquaintance with ancient and modern authors. "To no man," Clay later said of Wythe, "was I more indebted by his instructions, his advice, and his example."[10] Clay, of course, was less a scholar than a man of action. His talents found an outlet in the debating society formed by ambitious young Richmonders like himself. Patrick Henry, "The Forest Demosthenes," who could still be heard in the ornate Roman-styled Capitol, was their model. Such was the force of his example that no aspirant for public acclaim in the rising generation could ignore oratory. "The Virginians," said a keen Yankee observer, "are the best orators I have ever heard." Clay began to declaim as a schoolboy; it was the only art he pursued methodically. In time he would be celebrated as "the greatest natural orator" of the age. And whatever the deficiencies of his learn-ing, it would be said, they were more than offset by "the abundance of his na-tive resources."[11]

In 1796 Chancellor Wythe handed his protégé over to Robert Brooke, At-torney General of the Commonwealth, in order to prepare him for the bar. The thirty-five-year-old Brooke, who had been educated at Edinburgh, had just completed a term as governor. He took Clay into his home—where he began a lifelong friendship with Brooke's younger brother Francis—spon-sored Clay's initiation into the Masonic fraternity, and introduced him to an influential political circle. The apprenticeship lasted only a year. In Novem-ber 1797, "Henry Clay, Gentleman," was admitted to the Virginia bar. He had already decided, however, to make his career in Kentucky. Within a few days of receiving his license, Clay packed up his belongings and set out for the Wilderness Road.

It was a wise decision. With all his talents, and with the aid of influential patrons and friends, Clay would surely have made his mark in the Old Do-minion. But her courts and forums were crowded with able aspirants, many of them well-educated, from patrician families, with much more powerful connections. He would have been expected to play by certain rules worked out to control the traffic, and to wait his turn, with the consequence that ei-ther his natural ardor would have been crushed or he would have become a martyr to decorum. Virginia was at her zenith and could only decline. The fu-ture lay in Kentucky. There Virginians still reigned, but the game was played under the free and open rules of the frontier. To twenty-year-old Henry Clay, grown to over six feet, slender and loose-jointed, with light features, a mischievous smile, and captivating manners, Kentucky must have repre-sented, more than an opportunity for success, the enchanting prospect of a society capable of satisfying his impetuous passions.

Within three months of his arrival in Lexington, Clay was admitted to the Kentucky bar and, as he later said, "immediately rushed into successful and lucrative practice."[12] The Bluegrass triumvirate of George Nicholas, John Breckinridge, and James Brown, all of them Virginia emigrants, graduates of William and Mary, and pupils of the distinguished Wythe, welcomed Clay into their circle. He formed a profitable connection with Colonel Thomas Hart, perhaps Lexington's most enterprising merchant, manufacturer, and speculator. Hart, who came from Maryland, was also a good Jeffersonian; he had, it was said, the only copy of Voltaire's works in Kentucky, and his house boasted the first piano in Lexington. Clay set his cap for the youngest of Hart's daughters, red-haired Lucretia, and after a brief courtship married her on April 11, 1799. All the informants agree that, though she possessed neither beauty nor intellect, Lucretia was a spirited woman with "strong, natural sense."[13] It was certainly a fortunate marriage for Clay. It placed him in the midst of Lexington's leadership in law, business, and politics, and inti-mately connected him not only with Colonel Hart but also with James Brown, who became his devoted brother-in-law, and several other promi-nent families.

There was enough litigation in Kentucky to employ an army of lawyers, largely because of the singular character of the state's land law. The original vice of Virginia laws which permitted capricious location of entries, without recorded surveys, resulted in single tracts being "shingled over" with as many as a dozen different claims of title. This produced endless litigation, along with an abstruse branch of jurisprudence, "an unknown code with a peculiar dialect," according to Joseph Story, so foreign to the common law that only Kentuckians could understand it. The problem was compounded when Kentucky courts and assemblies attempted to amend the Virginia laws. The principal beneficiaries of "this sad predicament" were lawyers, as Clay acknowledged.[14] He had more than his share of land-title suits, yet they were only part of a large and varied practice.

It was as a trial lawyer in capital cases, where his forensic talents had free reign, that Clay made his reputation. At the fall term of the Fayette County Court, in Lexington, in 1801, he entered the novel plea of "temporary insanity" in the defense of Doshey Phelps, charged with murdering his sister-in-law, and talked the jury into a verdict of manslaughter, punishable by imprisonment. By common report not one of the accused murderers he defended, though their guilt was plain as day, was ever sentenced to the gallows. In the case of Abner Willis, Clay, having won a new trial for the defendant on a technicality, turned around and pleaded double jeopardy to a jury that was like wax in his hands. Willis was discharged. Years later, when the culprit boisterously hailed him on the street as the man who had saved his life, Clay shook his head and replied, "Ah! Willis, poor fellow, I fear I have saved too many like you, who ought to be hanged."[15]

With many of the Lexington attorneys, Clay rode the circuit of the county courts and practiced, too, before the Court of Appeals and the United States District Court at the state capital in Frankfort. The camaraderie, merrymaking, and rollicking good times of this band of strolling lawyers led to the conception of Clay as "a wildish fellow" and "a gamester" who loved the law not less but the card table more. As a county clerk observed, "there were gentlemen, attending the courts, who studied Hoyle, more than they did Blackstone, and generally *won all the money*, made by others."[16] Clay was one of the winners. As he rose to fame, many stories were told of his romps and frolics, all doubtless exaggerated. Toward the end of one festive evening, Clay reportedly brought events to a close by "a great Terpsichorean performance" in which he executed "*a pas suel* from head to foot of the dining-table, sixty feet in length, amidst the loud applause of his companions, and to a crashing accompaniment of shivered glass and china," for which expensive music he paid the next morning, without demur, a bill for $120.[17] Not for nothing would be become known affectionately as "Prince Hal," after Shakespeare's "nimble-footed madcap."

Before long Clay stood at the top of the legal profession in Kentucky. Nicholas died in 1799; Brown, denied reelection to the United States Senate, moved to Louisiana in 1804; and the next year Breckinridge gave up his Senate seat to become attorney general in Washington. Clay fell heir to much of their practice as well as to their influence. His steady rise to affluence can be charted through the county tax bills. In 1799, the year of his marriage, Clay paid taxes on a single house, three slaves, and two horses. In 1805 he was assessed for 5,500 acres of land, his house and office on Mill Street, with some other town property, six slaves, fifteen horses, and a carriage. In 1810 he owned 7,380 acres of land (some of it acquired in lieu of fees), nineteen slaves, sixty horses, several carriages, and town lots worth approximately $15,000. He was proprietor of a Lexington hotel, part owner of a hemp company, a salt works, and of a favorite resort, Olympian Springs, in Bath County.[18] Emblematic of Clay's wealth, station, and aspirations was Ashland, one of the fine country estates that ringed Lexington. Henry, Lucretia, and their three children established themselves there in 1806. Soon they added to the acreage, laid out pleasure gardens, and built a roomy brick mansion. Even if he had never been the penniless orphan of song and story, Henry Clay had come a long way.

Whether or not he could have become a distinguished lawyer on a larger stage than the Kentucky hustings will never be known because politics intervened and became his profession. One of the first things he did upon arriving in Lexington was to join a debating society. He made his maiden public speech, a fiery attack on the Federalist Alien and Sedition Laws, at a meeting ground south of town in the summer of 1798. The crowd, which had listened stolidly to George Nicholas, was aroused by Clay's thunder. Some were reminded of Patrick Henry; one ardent Republican pronounced this upstart "the best three-year-old he had ever seen on the turf."[19] The Jeffersonian lawyer-aristocracy was united on national issues, and in November pushed through the legislature the Kentucky Resolutions declaring the Alien and Sedition Laws unconstitutional. The party was not united in state politics, however. Clay, a zealot for the radical democratic ideas of Thomas Paine and William Godwin, immediately found himself at odds with Nicholas, Breckinridge, and most of the moderate leaders on the raging issue of a state constitutional convention. The original constitution made provision for revision, should the people want it, after seven years. Two of the reforms most agitated involved direct popular election of the Senate (currently filtered through an electoral college) and a provision for the gradual emancipation of slavery. Under the pen name "Scaevola," which advertised his acquaintance with Plutarch, Livy, and Cicero, Clay warmly advocated both reforms. Indeed, with respect to the first, he went the whole length, calling for the abolition of the upper house, which would concentrate the popular will in a single democratic assembly.

Clay had lived with slavery all his life. (Hanover County had a larger population of black slaves than white people, and 38 percent of Kentucky households owned slaves.) Indeed Clay owned slaves from the age of five, having inherited two from his father. As he acquired property, he acquired slaves. Yet he hated the institution and in his first public letter championed gradual emancipation. In the land of liberty slavery was an unmixed evil, not only for blacks but also, as Thomas Jefferson had argued, for the white masters debauched and degraded by it.[20] In these views Clay was joined by his brother-in-law, by John Bradford—editor of the *Kentucky Gazette*—and by some other Lexington leaders, both civil and religious. Even so, it was not a popular position.

The convention referendum passed in 1798, but the reformers suffered a crushing defeat in the election of delegates a year later. The question of emancipation never surfaced in the convention, nor was anything done to lift the bar to legislative action without the consent and cooperation of slaveholders. Slavery was more firmly entrenched in Kentucky than before. In the spirit of accommodation, the moderates led by Breckingridge conceded to a popularly elected Senate and relaxed the centralized judicial control of the first constitution.[21] Clay, too, made his accommodation with the establishment, not only by marrying into it but by retreating from the boldly democratic ideas he had brought from Virginia and by accepting the balance of the 1799 constitution.

Elected to the state legislature in 1803, Clay promptly became the spokesman and protector of the Lexington-centered lawyer-aristocracy. The arts of electioneering were already well developed in Kentucky. A candidate ran around the district with "the velocity of a race horse," it was said; on the stump, he employed "the whole comedy of tricks and maneuvers," "the whole dictionary of inspired jokes;" "a pack of cards, a keg of whiskey, and a game cock" were commonly part of his apparatus. Despite the constitution's ban on treating, whiskey and toddy flowed through the cities and villages during an election "like the Euphrates through ancient Babylon."[22] Clay became a master of these arts. For several years he was annually reelected to the legislature, and there proved himself a masterly legislative tactician.

Frankfort, the seat of government on the Kentucky River, was only a village, "the dullest place that the Lord ever made in the six days work."[23] Like the lawyers on circuit, the legislators, who were often the same persons, made their own entertainment. The closeness of living arrangements in this "great penitentiary," as Clay called the infant capital, put a premium on friendship and good humor that transcended political enmities. These enmities were, nevertheless, very real. In the legislature Clay faced the helpless minority of Federalists on the right and the swelling ranks of Republican "radicals" on the left. The latter, representing the small-farming interest of the backcountry, were capably led by young Felix Grundy.

Clay locked horns with Grundy in 1804 when the "southside" lawyer attempted to repeal the two-year-old charter of the Kentucky Insurance Company. The Lexington company had been granted the exclusive privilege of insuring the cargoes on the Mississippi and its tributaries; moreover, by an obscure clause that may have escaped Grundy's attention in 1802, the company was authorized to issue negotiable bank notes on its capital. The Lexington Insurance Company promptly erected itself into the Lexington Bank— Kentucky's first and only bank—and it did a whopping business. Clay could claim no credit for this maneuver, but at once he became a stockholder in the company and now defended it against attackers who railed against capitalistic monopoly and privilege. Repeal of the charter, he argued, would violate the sanctity of contract and undermine all confidence in the government of Kentucky. Regardless of the law of the matter, Kentucky needed capital and credit to finance its growing trade and manufactures. The conflict between Clay and Grundy focused the opposing economic forces of Jeffersonian republicanism on the frontier. It was the entrepreneurial progressivism of the metropolis versus the individualistic democracy of the countryside. The metropolis prevailed in 1804 by a single vote, only after amendments curbed the powers of the company. Clay professed astonishment at the "ignorance" and "the most unheard of prejudices" of the lawmakers on this vital subject. In Lexington he was hailed as a savior, while Grundy was denounced as an unprincipled demagogue. At the succeeding session Grundy returned with reinforcements. First he elected his candidate, John Adair, who had been defeated by "the artful management of H. Clay" in 1804, to the United States Senate.[24] Then he pushed through repeal of the Kentucky Insurance Company charter. The governor vetoed the bill but was promptly overridden by the House; as the Senate prepared to vote, and gloom descended in Lexington, Clay introduced in the House a bill to compel payment of long-standing debts on the Green River lands. Settlers and speculators on these lands south of Green River, purchased from the state, had evaded payment for years by the notorious logrolling in the assembly of the "Green River Band," the core of Grundy's following. Clay, with this bill, adroitly turned the tables on his opponents. Faced with ruin, the Green River delegates reversed their position and went into the Senate to lobby for sustaining the veto. And so it happened: the Lexington Bank was saved, the Green River interests won another reprieve. Politically, Clay became the hero of the Bluegrass, and when Grundy retired the next year, then moved to Tennessee, there was no one to challenge his leadership in the legislature.[25]

Clay had a brush with political disaster when he agreed to defend Aaron Burr against the charge of treasonable conspiracy in 1806. The former vice president, wanted in the East for the murder of Alexander Hamilton, had set out to recoup power and fortune in the West. His project was veiled in obscurity when he first appeared in Lexington the previous August; it was not much clearer when he returned to execute it thirteen months later. With charms that disguised deceit, Burr led Clay and many others to believe his designs were perfectly innocent, indeed even sanctioned by the president himself. In his eagerness to obtain the Floridas from Spain, Jefferson had raised apprehensions of war in the West. The West must have the Floridas; and if in a war to get them Burr went fillibustering into Mexico, not many Kentuckians were inclined to object. The United States Attorney for Kentucky, Joseph W. Daveiss, however, believed that Burr aimed to separate the West from the Union. Daveiss was a Federalist whose continued incumbency testified to Jefferson's tolerance of political dissent. Just at this time, as he moved against Burr, Daveiss and his political friends launched a newspaper, *Western World*, which, after reviving the old "Spanish Conspiracy," linked this new project to the long history of disunionist plots alleged against Kentucky's early leaders, many of whom were now prominent Republicans, and so used Burr as an instrument of revenge against the Jeffersonian party. Viewing Daveiss's motives in this light, and hearing Burr's profession of innocence, Clay agreed to act as his chief counsel when the attorney general sought indictment from the grand jury in the federal court at Frankfort. Backed by Judge Innes, Clay held Daveiss to a strict line of proceeding. His evidence, it soon became obvious, consisted of nothing more than rumor, conjecture, and gossip. In December, the jury not only threw out the indictment but, in an unprecedented step, declared Burr "innocent of any conduct injurious to the United States." "A scene was presented in the Court-room which I had never before witnessed in Kentucky," Clay later wrote. "There were shouts of applause from the audience, not one of whom, I am persuaded, would have hesitated to level a rifle against Colonel Burr, if he believed that he aimed to dismember the Union, or sought to violate its peace, or overturn its Constitution."[26]

Clay, meanwhile, had been elected to the United States Senate to fill the three-month vacancy created by the resignation of John Adair. On the road to Washington, Clay learned of the president's proclamation warning the country of the western conspiracy. This was the first intimation he had that in the eyes of the Jefferson administration Burr was a traitor. Taking his seat in the Senate (it went unnoticed by him, and everyone else, that he was four months short of the constitutionally prescribed age for senators) he continued to believe that Burr was "unjustly accused." Only after Jefferson invited him to the President's House and laid before him the incriminating reports and dispatches from various quarters did he become convinced that Burr was, indeed, a would-be Catiline.[27] Jefferson's special message to Congress soon convinced the West. Burr's capture in February ended the conspiracy, but its shock waves reverberated in Kentucky politics for several years. The junto that revived the "Spanish Conspiracy," making Burr's plot its culmination, sought to discredit the entire Republican leadership. Suits for libel, calls for impeachment, were the order of the day. Clay could not escape. He was, if not himself a conspirator, one of the party of conspirators, said Humphrey Marshall, the Federalist chieftain. His confession of honest error in defending Burr at Frankfort was dismissed with contempt by the *Western World*. He knew all along of Burr's guilt, the newspaper charged, yet emerged unscathed. Writing as "Scaevola" and "Regulus," Clay treated the charge as pure political slander and showed less interest in defending himself than Republican friends, like Judge Innes, who were not as lucky.[28]

It was in this embittered political climate that Clay issued his first challenge and fought his first duel. Returning from Washington under a cloud in 1807, he was triumphantly reelected to the assembly, then chosen speaker by his colleagues. Humphrey Marshall, after several years in the political wilderness, had been returned to the legislature. Pursuing the junto's campaign against the Republicans, he sponsored a resolution calling for Judge Innes's impeachment by Congress. Clay opposed the resolution and was indignant when it passed. (Congress subsequently decided against impeachment.) At the next session the long simmering conflict between these party leaders,

Clay and Marshall, boiled over on the issue of legislative support for the Jefferson administration's commercial hostilities against Great Britain. In the wake of the *Chesapeake* Affair, Kentuckians loudly denounced Britain as a murderous aggressor and some, like Clay, were ready for war. But Jefferson was devoted to peace. He called for a trade embargo, and Congress quickly complied. Now, at Frankfort, after a year's experience with the famous embargo, Clay introduced resolutions endorsing the administration's policy. Marshall assailed the embargo as tyrannical and dishonorable. When the vote came, he stood alone against the resolutions. Clay then introduced a resolution that called upon the legislators "to clothe themselves in the production of American manufactures." Attacking this patriotic artifice, Marshall made the mistake of calling Clay "a liar." Ready to take his revenge on the spot, Clay rushed toward Marshall, but was restrained, and then offered a weak apology. "It is the apology of a poltroon!" the Federalist declared. Clay promptly wrote his challenge, and Marshall accepted. The duel with pistols, at ten paces, occurred across the river in Ohio. Both men were wounded—though Marshall walked off the field as if untouched—and both were dutifully censured by the legislature. But the duel, even in the face of censure, added a new dimension to Clay's popularity. "Your firmness and courage is admitted now by all parties," a lawmaker wrote to him while he nursed his wound at home. "I feel happy to hear of the heroism with which you acted."[29] The duel was the final ordeal in his rise to fame in Kentucky.

In January 1810, Clay was again elected to serve out an unexpired term in the Senate. Had he no interest in a full term? Perhaps not. In 1806, clearly, he had entertained no thought of beginning a national career. He had gone to the Senate, as he told Senator Plumer of New Hampshire, because several of his clients with suits pending in the Supreme Court had got up a purse of $3,000 for him to handle them. So it was "a very convenient, and a money getting business to him." Nor was Clay's only business at the court. He boasted to Plumer of winning $1,500 at cards in a single sitting. "He is a great favorite with the ladies—gambles much here—reads but little. Indeed he said he meant this session to be a tour of pleasure."[30] Young and dashing, Clay cut "a considerable figure" in the Potomac capital. He spoke for western interests, and taking his cue from the president's advocacy of federal internal improvements (roads and canals especially) made his maiden speech in behalf of this policy. None of his early speeches was reported, but he was described as "a damn good speaker," bold, animated, eloquent, whose only weakness was one of logical reasoning. "He declaims more than he reasons," Plumer observed. John Quincy Adams, impressed by Clay's enthusiasm, called him "a republican of the first fire."[31]

By 1810 Clay felt a stronger interest in national service. Both his family and his law practice were flourishing, permitting him to indulge the luxury of long absences in Washington. He had built an enviable political base in Kentucky. He had come to understand the heavy dependence of western wealth and welfare on the policies of the federal government. And in the boiling foreign crisis he realized how much the power of Great Britain—on land in Canada, among the Indians, on the seas of trade—strangled western pride and prosperity. The western patriot had become a super-nationalist. In February he astonished the Senate with a speech heaping scorn on the feeble weapons of commercial resistance to British tyranny and summoning "a new race of heroes," fired by martial spirit, to preserve the nation's Revolutionary heritage.[32] Again, as in 1807, when he spoke for internal improvements, he struck a theme with which he would ever be identified, the encouragement of domestic manufactures. Clay's "patriotic wound" testified to the strength of his conviction in this matter. National independence was his aim, but in advocating manufactures Clay advocated the interests of Lexington, where new factories sprang up every year, and more particularly of the Hart family, which had large investments in hemp, rope walks, and cotton bagging. In fact, it was on the specific question of a congressional mandate to the Navy to purchase, so far as possible, American-made cordage and sail cloth that Clay first declared his protectionist principles. Western interests, as he perceived them, buttressed the great patriotic goal.[33]

In these early congressional speeches, Clay sounded only one false note: his vigorous opposition to rechartering the Bank of the United States. Here he backed away from liberal nationalism and retreated to the sanctity of Republican dogma, condemning the bank as unconstitutional, as a transgressor against state rights, and an all-powerful monopolistic corporation. He thought the banking needs of the country were better left to local banks, like the Bank of Kentucky, which he had defended locally against the same arguments that now came from his own mouth.[34] No doubt his association, and the association of his Lexington constituents, with that bank influenced his opposition to the national bank. In the main, however, this was a rare instance in which he was misled by the Jeffersonian principles he had imbibed in his youth. Generally he adapted these principles to new conditions and new demands. But in opposing the national bank, he spoke more as a Virginian than a Kentuckian, as a state-rightist rather than a nationalist. In retrospect, his speech against recharter—his most ambitious to date—would seem the most incongruous of his political career.

When Clay returned to Lexington in May 1810, he promptly announced his candidacy for the Fayette district seat in the House of Representatives. (He attended the short session of the Senate in the winter—it was then that he made his speech against the bank.) Saying he preferred the "turbulence" of the popular body to "the solemn stillness of the Senate Chamber," Clay also revealed a good deal about the political style he had matured over a decade or longer. It was a style that thrived on turbulence. It prized action over thought, will over intellect, energy over sagacity. It expressed in politics the very traits that were already being identified as Kentuckian: "an enthusiasm, a vivacity, and ardor of character, courage, frankness, generosity, that have developed with the peculiar circumstances under which they [the Kentuckians] have been placed."[35] Clay, as he became known to the American people, would be seen as the consummate Kentuckian. The Virginia breeding continued to tell, but chiefly as a veneer of taste and refinement. The mature

Clay possessed the manners of the Virginian without the reticence and repose; his pride and self-assurance were inflated with the robustness of the West. But Clay eluded simple stereotypes. "He stalks among men with an unanswerable and never doubting air of command. His sweeping and imperial pride, his indomitable will, his unfailing courage, challenges from all, submission or combat," Tom Marshall later wrote. "Great in speech, great in action, his greatness is all his own."[36]

Clay's apprenticeship was over in 1811. Elected without opposition to the crucial Twelfth Congress, he took with him to Washington a bold spirit of nationalism and enterprise that gradually reshaped the timid Republicanism of Jefferson and Madison and the Virginia school. As if in recognition of his ascendancy, "the Star of the West" was at once propelled into the speaker's chair.

2. "Young Hercules"

One of the War Hawks in the Twelfth Congress was a tall, stiff, and earnest South Carolinian, John C. Calhoun. Only twenty-nine years old, he represented, along with two other youthful members of the delegation, Langdon Cheves and William Lowndes, the coming of age of a new generation of leaders in the Palmetto State. By fate or design the three became part of the dominant "War Mess" in the capital, its other members being Felix Grundy, now in his first term from Tennessee, Kentucky senator George M. Bibb, and Henry Clay. Lowndes, who represented the state's lowcountry planters, had never met his colleague from the western hills. "I had heard a very favorable character of him," he wrote home the day after Calhoun took his seat in the House, "but [was not prepared] for the pleasure of an acquaintance with a man well informed, easy in his manners, and I think amiable in his disposition. I like him already better than any other member of the mess and I give his politics the same preference."[1] Calhoun soon made a spectacular debut in debate; and becoming an administration leader second only to Clay, he found himself celebrated as "the young Hercules who carried the war on his shoulders."[2]

Calhoun was a product of the great migration that took possession of the southern backcountry in the decades before the American Revolution. The Calhoun clan came from Ireland in 1733 and dwelled in western Pennsylvania. They were Scotch-Irish, taught by Calvinistic Presbyterianism to regard life as a battle against evil. Growing up on the frontier, fighting Indians most of his life, Calhoun's father Patrick embodied the rough and resolute character of the race. Driven by Indian warfare and drawn by the vision of a land of plenty over the horizon, the Calhouns moved steadily southward along the mountain barrier, down the Shenandoah Valley to Augusta, then to the New River in southwest Virginia, then to the Waxhaws at the border separating the Carolinas. There they heard hunters' tales of a rich land, abounding with game, only recently ceded by the Cherokee to the royal government, one hundred or more miles farther west in South Carolina. The saga of the Calhoun migration ended in 1756 when Patrick, his brothers, and their families settled in the Long Canes Creek region bordering Cherokee country.[3]

The present-day traveler to John C. Calhoun's birthplace takes the southwesterly road from Abbeville eight or nine miles, almost to the Little River. A historical marker informs him that the place was settled by Patrick Calhoun and defended against both Cherokee and British warriors. Walking perhaps two hundred yards through field and shrub, past what must have been the homesite, the traveler comes to a burial ground dominated by a stone monument—pedestal and obelisk—erected by the statesman-son in 1844 to the memory of his mother and father. A quiet place even today, it was primitive when the Calhouns raised the first Scotch-Irish cabins in the region; and instead of the present forest of walnut, cedar, oak, and pine, it presented the prospect of "an extended tract of prairie country, waving under a rich growth of cane, from five to thirty feet in height."[4] The height of the cane, greatest along the river bank, was thought to be an index of the fertility of the soil. "Calhoun's Settlement," as it came to be called, was on a stream, "Calhoun Creek," flowing into Little River.

The family not only inscribed its name but shed its blood upon the land. This pioneer heritage was always a source of pride in the son. Growing up, he heard the stories of his father's exploits. In 1760, during the French and Indian War, Patrick Calhoun and a handful of companions fought off a Cherokee raiding party for many hours, until finally forced to retreat before overwhelming numbers. Returning to bury the dead three days later, Patrick found among the massacred bodies his widowed mother and eldest brother. Several women and children of the settlement had been carried into captivity. When peace came, Patrick gave up fighting for surveying and farming. He also played a part in the struggle of the backcountry for political power at Charleston. In the centralized provincial government, power was monopolized by the planter-aristocracy of the lowcountry parishes. With the rapid growth of the west, this became intolerable. At last, in 1769, a court of justice was erected in the backcountry; and a small coonskin army marched one hundred and fifty miles to the nearest polling place, not far from Charleston, to elect their leader, Patrick Calhoun, to the provincial assembly. The first backcountry representative, he served twenty-seven years, took an active role in the movement for independence, and marshaled the libertarian principles of the Revolution in the continuing struggle of western farmers against Charleston grandees. This, too, belonged to the son's heritage.[5]

Born on March 18, 1782, he was named for his maternal uncle, Major John Caldwell, who had been murdered in cold blood by Tories only a few months before. Martha Caldwell, of the same Scotch-Irish stock as Patrick, was his second, possibly third, wife, and she gave him five children. John, the fourth, and the last survivor, inherited the stern character of his father, already old when he was born, but added a strain of his mother's tenderness. Life at the Calhoun homestead was strenuous and severe. Until cotton came to the rescue in the 1790s, farming in the red hills was mostly of subsistence crops, which provided a livelihood but little else. Patrick Calhoun was among the most prosperous farmers in the region, with a fine frame house, several hundred acres of land, and sufficient slaves to work them; he journeyed to Charleston, or later to Columbia, every year, and, of course, was the leading citizen of the community. In all this, John was favored, but it did not relieve the humdrum isolation of his childhood. His father was uneducated and cared not a shilling for books or learning. There were no schools in the upcountry. The child grew up virtually illiterate, knowing little more than the rod and gun, the ax and the plow, until his thirteenth year.[6]

In that year, 1795, he was sent to a fledgling academy, across the Savannah River in Georgia, kept by his brother-in-law, Moses Waddel, a Presbyterian clergyman with a missionary zeal for educating boys, although, as it happened, the school was discontinued soon after young Calhoun's arrival. Left to his own devices, he discovered Waddel's library and began a voracious course of reading. "His taste, although undirected, led him to history, to the neglect of novels and other light reading," Calhoun himself later recalled in a third-person narrative, "and so deeply was he interested, that in a short time he read the whole of the small stock of historical works . . . , consisting of Rollin's Ancient History, Robertson's Charles V, his South America, and Voltaire's Charles XII. After dispatching these, he turned with eagerness to Cook's Voyages (the large edition), a small volume of Essays by Brown, and Locke on the Understanding. . . . All this was the work of but fourteen weeks."[7] It was his intellectual awakening. Having skipped the slow, hesitant, dreamy learning of childhood, with all its innocent fantasies and pleasures, Calhoun suddenly vaulted into the realm of the philosophers.

The youth's health failed under the strain of study, it was said, and his mother called him home. At the same time, his father died, leaving the widow and younger sons to care for the farm. For five years John plowed and hoed and picked cotton. "We worked the field," said his slave and childhood playmate Sawney, "and many's the time in the brilin' sun me and Mars John has plowed together."[8] During this halt in his education, John learned to manage a large farm and, in retrospect, he judged that hard labor and rural sports were responsible for his own good health as well as his lifelong love of agriculture. As he became known in the community, people thought that he "ought to be educated." His older brother James concurred. Visiting from Charleston in 1800, he urged John to prepare for one of the learned professions. John replied that he could not leave his mother to run the farm alone; besides, "he would far rather be a planter than a half-informed physician or lawyer." If he was to be educated, he went on, nothing less than seven years of study in the best schools and colleges would satisfy him. The condition was agreed to, and James undertook to manage the farm in order to finance an extraordinarily ambitious education for an eighteen-year-old farmer from the Carolina upcountry.[9]

Meanwhile, Moses Waddel had reopened his academy. For two years John studied Greek and Latin and got as sound a classical education as the southern states afforded. Several years later, after its relocation in Willington, near Abbeville, the academy became famous. It boasted many distinguised graduates—James L. Petigru, George McDuffie, Hugh S. Legaré, to name only three. Waddel, a glum-looking man with a warm heart, was a remarkable teacher who employed remarkable methods. At Willington the boys were expected to study in the woods, in crude huts of their own construction in winter, in the open air in summer; and they were goaded to compete strenuously in recitations, debates, and examinations. "In this manner the classics are taught 190 miles from the sea-coast . . . ," wrote South Carolina's first historian in 1809. "The melody and majesty of Homer delight the ear and charm the understanding in the very spot and under the identical trees, which sixty years ago resounded with the war whoop and horrid yellings of savage Indians."[10] The classics broadened Calhoun's intellect, while the rigorous instruction toughened a temperament already firm and unbending.

In the fall of 1802, the twenty-year-old youth "straight from the backwoods" journeyed eight hundred miles northward to New Haven, Connecticut, to attend Yale College. Admitted to junior standing, he had almost, but not quite, compensated for his delayed start up the educational ladder. Just why he chose Yale—and it was *his* choice—is a mystery. Its president, Timothy Dwight, was a notorious Federalist. All of Calhoun's political associations were Jeffersonian. Hardly more attractive, it would seem, was Yale's religious character, with still a strong odor of Puritanism. Calhoun, despite his Presbyterian upbringing, belonged to no church and had no obvious religious convictions. South Carolina still had no college, of course, so he had to go away to school. And in education, as in commerce, the state had stronger ties to New York and New England than to Virginia. But Calhoun chose Yale apparently because he thought he could get a better education there than anywhere else, and he wanted the best. The college was flourishing. "Pope" Dwight had pulled in his political horns, and had begun to modernize the curriculum, a move highlighted the preceding year by the election of young Benjamin Silliman as Professor of Chemistry; and while riot and vice seemed to reign at other colleges, Dwight had managed to maintain order and decorum at Yale. In his class of sixty-six, Calhoun was not the only student from South Carolina; but the overwhelming number were from "The Land of Steady Habits," and most were bound for the ministry. Calhoun felt like the outlander he was. He liked Yale's strict moral climate, however. It helped complete a character already well formed. As to Yale's conservative teachings about God, man, and society, distilled in the president's senior-year course in moral philosophy, Calhoun appropriated the nut but rejected the shell.

Yale's select body of students, every one of whom had much more schooling than he, became a critical testing ground for Calhoun. He soon became aware not only of his abilities but of his superiority, and he never doubted it thereafter. His academic record has not survived, but all the testimony suggests it was outstanding. Years later a classmate recalled that Calhoun had excelled in Latin and mathematics, especially the latter, and said he had looked up to him as a scholar even though they differed in politics. Silliman remembered him as "a first-rate young man, both for scholarship and talent, and for pure and gentlemanly conduct." He was elected to Phi Beta Kappa and named to deliver the English oration at commencement. It was not delivered because of illness, but the choice of topic, "The qualifications necessary to constitute a perfect statesman," was unusually revealing.[11] Later in life, after he had become a statesman and had taken aim at the presidency, Calhoun often told the story of a classroom encounter with Dwight on the legitimate sources of political authority, in which the pupil so forcefully maintained his opinion that Dwight, though he thought him in error, remarked admiringly to a friend, "That young man has talents enough to be President of the United States," and predicted he would one day attain that station. Calhoun, hearing those words, took them as prophecy. Later he cleverly embroidered the story for political effect. It became part of his personal legend, and like all such stories passed into the realm of myth and fable.*

Graduating from Yale in September 1804, Calhoun spent the fall in fashionable Newport, Rhode Island, the guest of the widow of his late cousin and former United States senator, John Ewing Colhoun. This was the lowcountry branch of the family, and it kept the old spelling of the name. Introduced to the Charleston *beau monde* at Newport, the youth also met a thirteen-year-old girl, Floride Colhoun, who would one day become his bride. That winter he began reading law in the Charleston office of Henry W. De Saussure, a leader of the bar and of the declining Federalist party. Calhoun had heard no summons to the law but felt it offered the surest entree to the political career he desperately wanted. He impressed De Saussure, who described him in a letter of introduction to Robert Goodloe Harper, formerly a congressman from South Carolina but now a Baltimore lawyer, as "the son of old Patrick Calhoun," a young man who possessed "more knowledge than is usual at his age," and who gave "indications of a superior mind."[13] Calhoun had decided to return to New England to pursue law studies at Judge Tapping Reeve's famous school in Litchfield, Connecticut. Arriving in July, he settled into the study of law for a solid year.

The little New England village of Litchfield with its central green, white steepled church, tree-lined streets, and Federal houses today preserves the quiet serenity of a bygone era. Not far from the green, next to the fine old home of Judge Reeve, stands a weathered one-room building, utterly unadorned within or without, that was once the law school. Every morning, six

*A campaign ditty from the 1840s runs as follows:

John C. Calhoun, my Jo, John,
When first we were acquaint
You were my chum at Yale, John—
And something of a saint.
And Dr. Dwight, God bless him, John,
Predicted as you know,
You'd be the Nation's President,
John C. Calhoun, my Jo![12]

days a week, twenty or more students crowded into the room to hear the lectures of Judge Reeve or his young assistant, James Gould, and to dispute the law. Afternoons were devoted to reading in philosophy, history, and literature, which was the sideboard of the lawyer's liberal learning. Calhoun liked the study, the discipline, and the disputation. "No period of my life of equal duration has been spent more advantageously to myself," he later wrote.[14] The crisp logic of Gould's lectures, in particular, set a standard for him. In their debates the students were taught to prepare closely, to speak without notes, and to rely upon memory. These severe rules became Calhoun's habit.[15]

At Litchfield, as at Yale, he felt alien and alone. In this orthodox Congregational community, the young man who absented himself from church on Sunday morning was a sabbath breaker and probably a Jeffersonian infidel as well. A certain amount of social unpleasantness went with this stigma. It was a tempestuous time politically in Connecticut. Jefferson's Republican followers were beating at the doors of the establishment. When one of them, Selleck Osbourne, was thrown into the Litchfield jail for seditious libel, Calhoun, alone of the law students, marched in a procession to salute him in his cell. The Republicans retaliated through the federal courts. Judge Reeve himself was indicted for libeling President Jefferson. As Calhoun wrote home in a letter, "This place is so much agitated by party feelings, that both Mr. Felder [a South Carolina classmate, also of the Yale class of '04] and myself find it prudent to form few connections in town. This, though somewhat disagreeable, is not unfavorable to our studies." Calhoun's diploma stated he "has attended diligently and faithfully to the study of law." Apparently it spoke the truth.[16]

He returned to Charleston and resumed his place in De Saussure's office. In no time at all, however, he developed an aversion both to Charleston and the law. The lowland city between the Ashley and Cooper rivers, with its sumptuous houses, fancy balls, and teeming wharves, its penetrating sensuality, bothered Calhoun. Although back in his native state, he again felt like "a recluse." He formed the habit of daily three-mile walks, usually solitary, during which he attempted to focus his mind on some particular idea or problem. The Presbyterian heritage, for all his intellectual rejection of it, entered deeply into his character. The "sickly fevers" of Charleston were not, he thought, to be ascribed to the climate alone; they were "a curse" levied for the "intemperance and debaucheries" of the inhabitants. Young Calhoun felt as many of his upcountry compatriots felt about the city then and for generations after: "It was Cavalier from the start; we were Puritan."[17]

Calhoun longed to settle on a farm in Abbeville. It represented to him health, industry, and moral improvement. Farming was in his blood, and his roots were firmly planted in the Carolina upcountry. Remarkably, in an age when most Americans were on the move, Calhoun lived nearly all his life within a few miles of where he was born. Returning to Abbeville in 1807, he opened a law office and began a lucrative practice. Lawyers were not popular among the Scotch-Irish farmers; Calhoun was only the third in the district.

But he found plenty of business and in a short time was generally considered the most promising young advocate west of Columbia.[18] Like Henry Clay in Kentucky, and Daniel Webster in New Hampshire, Calhoun rode the circuit of the neighboring counties—Pendleton, Newberry, Edgefield—but unlike them he took no pleasure in it. He had no sense of humor, certainly a failing in a frontier lawyer and likely to prove fatal in a statesman. He rarely, if ever, swore, smoked, drank, or jested. The boisterous, lusty style of speech and bearing popularized by Charles James Fox in England, and emulated by Clay, held no attraction for Calhoun, who harked back to the gravity of Lord Chatham.[19] As an abstract discipline, the law challenged his mind; as a profession, practiced before county court judges and juries, it was all pettifoggery. So distasteful did the law become that, after a year he was "determined to forsake it" as soon as he could obtain "a decent independence" on a small plantation of his own.[20]

"But," as an intimate biographer wrote, "the fates were spinning for him a different destiny."[21] When news of the barbarous British attack on the *Chesapeake* reached Abbeville in the summer of 1807 some of the local citizens called a public meeting, and showing their esteem for the young lawyer—old Patrick's son—who had just returned to the community, they asked him to prepare and introduce suitable patriotic resolutions. No report of the speech, Calhoun's public debut, or of the resolutions, has survived, but before long the people of Abbeville elected him to the legislative seat held so long by his father. This was bound to happen, but it happened sooner than he, or anyone else, expected. The *Chesapeake* Affair brought him forcefully before the public, enabling him to inaugurate his political career on the stirring issue of national pride and honor.

The legislature Calhoun entered in the fall of 1808 was the first since "the compromise of 1808" finally closed the great sectional rift in South Carolina politics and gave the government the character it maintained until the Civil War. Calhoun's political fortunes, including his mature political thought, were profoundly shaped by this development. The upper country and the lower, with their different origins and interests, had been like two different civilizations. The Circuit Court Act of 1769, coincident with Patrick Calhoun's election to the assembly, had been only the first concession Charleston made to the rapidly populating interior. The Revolutionary constitution of 1776 extended representation to the western districts, but under grossly inequitable arrangements that left coastal planters and merchants in control. The unequal representation of the upcountry brought on the constitutional convention of 1790. What was then defined as the "upper division" (the scrubby middle pine belt above the coastal plain, together with the piedmont above the fall line) possessed four times the white population of the "lower division," which, conversely, had over four times as many slaves. The principal western gain was more symbolic than real: the low country was left in control of both legislative houses, and the capital was transferred from Charleston to Columbia on the fall line. The situation of the state, with its white population concentrated in the west, its wealth and property in the east, posed a dilemma for republicans. Westerners demanded equal representation, not only as a matter of right but in order to advance their diversified agricultural interests. The planter-aristocracy of the eastern parishes, on the other hand, feared destruction from an unchecked democratic majority. The "compromise of 1808" finally resolved the dilemma by basing representation on wealth and numbers combined. Of 124 representatives, one-half would be apportioned according to white population, one-half according to taxable property. By this formula the "upper division" came into control of the dominant lower house and even gained a single-vote margin in the senate.

Calhoun rejoiced in the "compromise of 1808," though there is no reason to believe he saw any philosophical genius in it at the time. Only in later years would it become one of the building blocks of his theory of the concurrent majority. The compromise, he wrote in 1846, saved the state from the tyranny of the majority and from the conflicts and discords of political parties. By giving each of the great divisions the power to protect itself, the compromise made the government "the concurrent and joint organ of both, and thereby the true and faithful representative of the whole state."[22] In fact, of course, the compromise proved a condition, not a theory. It was a product of the consolidation of interests, of peoples, and of cultures in South Carolina at the turn of the century. Illustrative of the movement was the opening in 1804 of South Carolina College. Located in the state capital, Columbia, it soon became the common school of eastern and western youths. The swift decline of Federalism, and of the once powerful Charleston mercantile interest, along with the Jeffersonian ascendancy in the state at large was another indicator of this change. Most important, however, was the astonishing rise of cotton production in the piedmont, and the parallel rise of slave labor and plantation ideals. Already in 1808, the middle country, though classified as "upper division," had become part of the plantation economy, and it was destined to spread all the way to Abbeville. "Low-country ideals by the grace of white cotton and black slaves . . . conquered the State." As South Carolina united around *one* interest, a concurrent majority became irrelevant.[23]

Calhoun's career in the legislature was brief and uneventful. He called attention to his talents, however, and after two sessions won election to Congress from the old Ninety-Six district. It was later said that his was the only great reputation in the state during the antebellum years not founded on service in the legislature.[24] Although elected in October 1810, he would not take his seat until the commencement of the Twelfth Congress fourteen months hence. Meanwhile, he acquired a small plantation above the Savannah River and married his cousin, Floride Bonneau Colhoun, whom he had been courting from afar, primarily through the agency of her mother, for at least a year. Mrs. Colhoun was anxious to make the best possible match for her daughter, now eighteen years old, and parried Calhoun's advances until she could be sure he was worthy of her. The wedding took place at Bonneau's Ferry, near Charleston, in January 1810. Floride was a Charleston belle. She grew up in a mansion on the Cooper River, gazed upon portraits of Huguenot ancestors, danced at St. Cecilia assemblies, worshiped at St. Michael's, summered at Newport. In short, she embodied Charleston, which Calhoun hated but with which he knew he must come to terms if he intended to exercise leadership in South Carolina. However honorable his ambition, however heartfelt his love of Floride, he must have calculated the political advantage of the marriage. Instantly, it gave him position in Charleston. By it, indeed, Calhoun himself physically advanced the unification of the state.

This pertained to the future. In any assessment of the resources Calhoun brought to Congress, first place must be given to his upcountry heritage. The hardy, persevering enterprise of Scotch-Irish frontiersmen entered into his flesh and blood and permeated his politics. He had learned at his father's knee to prize individual liberty and to distrust government. Patrick Calhoun had been an Antifederalist who opposed ratification of the United States Constitution. The statesman-son liked to recall a conversation from his ninth year "in which his father maintained that government to be best which allowed the largest amount of individual liberty compatible with social order and tranquility, and insisted that the improvements in political science would be found to consist in throwing off many of the restraints then imposed by law, and deemed necessary to an organized society."[25] This struck a pungent Jeffersonian note, surely more appropriate to Calhoun's politics in 1843, when the recollection was published, than in 1811. His political admirers and early biographers liked to see him as the spiritual heir of Jefferson. It would even be maintained that, as among the ancient Greeks, the torch had been passed from the elder Virginian to the youthful Carolinian during a nocturnal interview at Monticello in 1805.[26] There is, alas, no record of such a meeting. More to the point, the story seriously misrepresents the young Calhoun's politics.

The individualism and provincialism of Calhoun's upcountry heritage had, in fact, been modified by his education in Federalist New England. That education had broadened his outlook, softened his prejudices, extended his sympathies. He entered Congress as a fervent nationalist who took the whole country as his constituency. In his first important speech, he boldly rejected the system of "commercial coercion" so long practiced by the Virginia presidents, so long traduced by New England, and beseeched the American people to rally behind the war policy. "There is, sir, but one principle necessary to make us a great people—to produce, not the form, but the real spirit of union, and that is to protect every citizen in the lawful pursuit of his business. He will then feel that he is backed by the government—that its arm is his arm. He then will rejoice in its increased strength and prosperity. Protection and patriotism are reciprocal. This is the way which has led nations to greatness."[27] It was this speech that prompted Thomas Ritchie, editor of the influential Richmond *Enquirer*, to "hail the young South Carolinian as one of the master-spirits who stamp their name upon the age in which they live."[28]

Calhoun was at once a celebrity. The dazzling rapidity of his rise—the farm boy who went to school at eighteen, graduated from college at twenty-two, began to practice law at twenty-five, entered the legislature at twenty-six, and won election to Congress at twenty-eight—seemed to defy explanation. Some men, trying to explain it, resorted to notions of natural genius or, like James H. Hammond in his eulogy in 1850, gave him an immaculate conception. "But Mr. Calhoun had no youth, to our knowledge," Hammond said. "He sprang into the arena like Minerva from the head of Jove, fully grown and clothed in armor: a man every inch himself, and able to contend with any other man."[29] In truth, however obscure the sources of Calhoun's character, it had been formed by tenacious self-discipline and driving ambition. Gradually, diffidence and self-doubt had been replaced by unshakable self-esteem. By studied effort he had fashioned his mind into an instrument, "clear and precise in his reasoning," as Ritchie noted, and remorseless in its logic. He was not eloquent by usual standards, and lacked a vivid imagination, but his powers of reasoning were applauded from the first. His speeches, barren of tropes and figures, were rich in thought. Intensely serious and severe, he could never write a love poem, though he often tried, it was later said, because every line began with "whereas." To a commanding intellect he united a character of almost Doric simplicity. Mind and character—hard, grave, inflexible—were all one. Morally and temperamentally, he was more Puritan than the Puritans. The purity of his private life, conceded by all, tended to elevate his public life, placing it above suspicion of mere selfishness, at least in the eyes of his admirers. He soon attracted many of them, not by the weight of his talents alone but also by his engaging manners and brilliant conversation. All considered, despite his limited experience, Calhoun entered the national arena with powers of mind and character, of reason and sensibility, unsurpassed in his generation.

3. "Yankee Demosthenes"

Daniel Webster was born on January 18, 1782, in the same year as Calhoun but on the northern frontier. Four generations of Websters, all of them plain, God-fearing farmers, had come before him in New England. His father, Ebenezer, had enlisted in Rogers' Rangers while still a youth and fought in the French and Indian War, returning with the rank of captain. When Canada was conquered at last and peace came, he joined the rush of pioneers up the Merrimack River valley. Pressing into the densely forested and granite scarred hill country west of the river, Webster located his 225-acre grant in the new township of Salisbury, promptly cleared a tract for planting, and reared a log cabin. The smoke from his clearing, his famous son would later say, "ascended nearer to the North Star than that of any other of His Majesty's New England subjects."[1] Captain Webster, a tall, strongly built man with a swarthy complexion, black hair, and deep, dark eyes, became a prominent citizen in the town. When news arrived of the Battle of Lexington in April 1775, he marched a company of volunteers to the outskirts of beleaguered Boston. From dozens of inland towns, New Hampshire farmers, clad in homespun, their coats as variously colored "as the barks of oak, sumach, and other trees of our hills could make them," and carrying whatever weapons they could lay their hands on, streamed into Boston.[2] Webster was later with General Washington at White Plains; he commanded a company under General Stark at Bennington. The son cherished a pair of silver buttons Captain Webster had clipped from a fallen Redcoat on the battlefield at Bennington. "If I thought either of my boys would not value them, fifty years hence . . . ," he wrote in 1828, "I believe I should begin to flag him, now."[3]

Daniel was the fourth child, and last son, of Eben Webster and his second wife, Abigail, or "Nabby." Many years after the event, when the log cabin had become a talisman of democracy, Daniel Webster had occasion to regret that, though his elder brother and sister had been born in a log cabin, he was not. The pioneer's cabin had been replaced by the still simple but more comfortable frame house of the settled farmer. A replica of the house—two rooms divided by a chimney, with an attached shed—stands today in the shadow of a great elm planted by Eben Webster. Punch Brook, where he operated a sawmill and a gristmill, flows cheerfully just below the house. Daniel often returned there after the family moved to Salisbury Lower Village, now Franklin, on the west bank of the Merrimack in 1784. This was a more fertile farm, with its fields and meadows running up from the valley floor; and Eben turned part of the large two-story white house into a tavern, for which he had been granted a license by the town selectmen in recognition of his merit and services.

Daniel Webster adored his father, and all his life felt nostalgic for the people, scenes, and events of his boyhood. Long after he joined the great migration of New Hampshire's sons to Boston, long after the waters of the Merrimack were harnessed to power the spindles and looms of the mill towns that rose on the once verdant landscape, Webster rhapsodized about his native land. "This is a very picturesque country," he wrote from the Franklin farm during a visit in 1845. "The hills are high, numerous, and irregular; some with wooded summits, and some with rocky heads as white as snow." From an upper pasture he viewed the White Mountains to the northeast, the crest of the Vermont hills to the west, and within these points "mountains and dales, lakes and streams, farms and forests . . . the true Switzerland of the United States." The sophisticated statesman cultivated a rustic image; and it became part of his legend that he had not been born but sprang up like some noble tree between the clefts of New Hampshire granite. But there can be no doubt of the genuineness of his pastoral idyll or—what was part of it—his ancestral piety. "White stones, visible from the window, and close by," he wrote, "mark the graves of my father, my mother, one brother, and three sisters. Here are the same fields, the same hills, the same beautiful river, as in the days of my childhood."[4]

The child heard from his father tales of pioneer hardship and Revolutionary bravery that hung in his memory all his days. Eben Webster had taught himself to read and write; he was a good Christian, indeed an elder of the Congregational church in Salisbury, and with his Puritan forebears got a respect for learning out of devotion to the Scriptures. "My father had a sonorous voice, an untaught yet correct ear, and a keen perception of all that was beautiful or sublime in thought," Webster recalled. "How often after the labors of the day, before twilight had deepened into obscurity, would he read to me his favorite portions of the Bible, the Book of Job, the Prayer of Habukkuk, and extracts from Isaiah!"[5] The son supposed his own taste for literature, perhaps even his rhetorical style, owed something to his father's impressive manner on such occasions. He could never remember a time when he could not read. He loved poetry, and at an early age learned by heart Dr. Watts's psalms and hymns. Little Dan Webster, it was said, recited Watts's verses to the teamsters and hawkers who stopped at his father's tavern.[6] Books were scarce in the village, so scarce, so precious, that Daniel thought they were not merely to be read but memorized. "I remember that my father one day brought home a pamphlet copy of Pope's Essay on Man. . . . I read, reread, and then commenced again; nor did I give up the book till I could recite every word of it from beginning to end."[7] And so the classics of English literature as well as the Scriptures were engraved in his memory. Decades later, sharing a stagecoach with his learned friend Rufus Choate, Webster, hoping to relieve the tedium of the journey, asked Choate what he had been reading of late. He mentioned Milton. Webster replied, "As you are so recently out of Paradise, won't you tell us something about the talk that Adam and Eve had before the fall?" "Do you intend that to be a challenge?" Choate, the younger man, asked. "Yes, I do," said Webster. After Choate recited long passages from the conversation of Adam and Eve, Webster, not to be outdone, sonorously declaimed the debate between Gabriel and Satan from another book of *Paradise Lost*.[8]

It soon became apparent to everyone that Daniel had more talent for books than farming. "Somehow I could never learn how to hang a scythe. I had not wit enough," he said. "My brother Jos[eph] used to say, that my father sent me to college in order to make me equal to the rest of the children!"[9] He was a frail, sickly lad, with none of the robustness of his father or his brothers. The idea that he was indolent became the theme of countless anecdotes. Even at boyish sports like sledding, a companion said, Daniel "had a knack of making us draw the sled up the hill," which suggests the larger truth that he was less lazy than clever.[10] He got most of his early education at home. But in the New England backcountry, unlike the southern, the schoolmaster followed in the footsteps of the pioneer. For several years during the winter months Daniel attended a school kept by an itinerant schoolmaster either in Salisbury or a neighboring village.[11] This soon ceased to be satisfactory, however, and in 1796, encouraged by a young village lawyer, Thomas W. Thompson, a Harvard graduate who had loaned books to Daniel, Eben decided to send his son to Phillips Exeter Academy, where he could study to become a teacher. Exeter, in the state capital, was about the same age as Daniel, fourteen, and under the guidance of Dr. Benjamin W. Abbot was already earning a reputation for excellence. Daniel met the minimum entrance requirement by reading the Book of Luke for the examiners. Lacking

Latin, he was placed at the bottom of the lowest class. Most of the ninety boys in the school knew more and had seen more of the world than he; he felt inferior, uncouth in his rustic dress and manners, weak and timid in his mind. Disheartened, he was unable to make the usual declamation before his classmates, despite years of practice before a different audience in Salisbury. But this was his only failure. At the end of the spring quarter he stood first in his class, and in the fall quarter rose to the next class. Soon after that, in December, his father called him home to take charge of the Salisbury school. There he might have remained for some time but for the intervention of the Reverend Samuel Wood in neighboring Boscawen. He believed Daniel had a higher destiny, and he offered to take him into his home and prepare him for college for the fee of one dollar a week. When his father consented and packed him in a sleigh for Boscawen, Daniel cried for joy.[12]

No other college but Dartmouth was ever considered. Chartered in 1769 by the royal government of the province, the college had grown until, a quarter century later, it enrolled approximately 140 students. After the Revolutionary War, Boscawen and several other towns along the Merrimack had petitioned the legislature to lay out a road to the Connecticut River at or near Hanover, the seat of the college. This was done, and the completion of the "College Road" turned many of New Hampshire's sons toward Dartmouth. Few, of course, went to college at all or, if they did, graduated. Webster was only the third native of Salisbury to obtain a college degree; the two who preceded him, both lawyers, also went to Dartmouth.[13] In August 1797, after six months of Latin and considerably less of Greek, under the Reverend Wood's tutelage, Webster rode horseback to Hanover and took his entrance examination, probably in Greek, Latin, English, and mathematics. Distinguishing himself in none, he was nevertheless admitted to the class of 1801. Greek was his chief deficiency. Apparently it was never repaired. "Would that I had pursued Greek, till I could read and understand Demosthenes in his own language!" Webster later lamented.[14]

Webster performed creditably at Dartmouth from the first and excelled in his junior and senior years when the balance of the curriculum shifted from mathematics and ancient languages to English, history, and philosophy. He was not a close scholar, but neither was he, as some supposed, a careless one. "Many other students read more than I did, and knew more than I did," he observed. "But so much as I read I made my own."[15] He developed powers of concentration equal to his powers of memory. And with his "intuitive and comprehensive talent," he easily mastered subjects which slower students labored over in vain. Webster evidently was unpopular with most of his classmates, who thought him arrogant and assuming; but he was flattered by a small circle of admirers centered in the United Fraternity, one of the two campus literary societies, in which he was the shining light. A student who followed him at Dartmouth, and distinguished himself in the same way, pointedly observed, "The truth is that at a university of this kind, a few glowing pieces of composition, with one or two public declamations, written and spoken with spirit, have more effect in raising the reputation of a student than the reasoning of a Locke, the application of a Newton, or the wisdom of a Solomon."[16] Webster was the United Fraternity's leading debater; he wrote a dramatic dialogue, made political speeches and occasional addresses, and delivered at least three orations. Every trace of shyness or timidity was gone by his junior year; applause for his forensic and literary efforts bolstered his self-esteem. "He had unbounded self-confidence," a classmate recalled, "seemed to feel that a good deal belonged to him, and evidently intended to be a great man in public life." By the time the class graduated in 1801, Webster was generally acknowledged as "our ablest man."[17]

In the ordinary course of things Webster had every reason to expect that he would be chosen to pronounce the valedictory of his class at commencement. Because of a squabble the previous year, however, the faculty had taken the election from the students, and guided by strict academic performance rather than by distinction on the platform, the professors awarded the honor to the top-ranking scholar.[18] Webster was angry, so angry, it was later said, that after receiving his diploma he tore it up before his friends, declaring, "My industry may make me a great man, but this miserable parchment cannot."[19] Alas, the story was invented, perhaps by Webster himself, to dramatize his feelings. No disappointment of his life, he once told Choate, ever affected him more keenly.[20] Still he was not silent at commencement. He delivered a remarkably sensitive funeral oration on one of his classmates and, before the United Fraternity, an oration on "The Influence and Instability of Opinion," an epitome of his political thought in 1801. Exalting George Washington, less than two years in the grave, Webster called upon his auditors to stand firm on the bedrock of principle against the *ignis fatuus* of "those opinionated philosophers"—Paine, Godwin, Wollstonecraft—"who mistake the fantastic dreams of their own minds for the oracles of philosophy."[21] The youthful orator never mentioned Thomas Jefferson, that "visionary philosopher" who had just been elected president of the United States; but the barbs were clearly intended for him and his followers.

During the next several years Webster prepared to become a lawyer. He had no enthusiasm for the law but turned to it because it was his father's wish, because most of his classmates were inclined that way, and because he felt no call to the ministry or any other profession. What was the extent of his ambition? It is difficult to say, for though he certainly had ambition, and talked about it, conscience told him to confine it within the limits of the "rational and necessary." "So much ambition," he wrote to a friend, "as shall prompt to laudable exertion and industry; so much as is consistent with the duties and the honest pleasures of life, . . . and, on the score of property, so much ambition as instigates to the acquirement of a decent, competent estate"—so much ambition, in short, as would make an honest country lawyer.[22] Growing up in a community where lawyers were generally distrusted, Webster worried lest he fall victim to the profession's vices—to avarice, cunning, hypocrisy, and insensibility. "I pray God to fortify me against its temptations," he confided to another friend.[23] While the law thus appeared as a wicked temptress, it also appeared, as it did to Calhoun, a singularly unattractive one. "The language of the law is dry, hard, and stubborn as an old maid. Murdered Latin bleeds through every page, and if Tully and Virgil could rise from their graves, they would soon be at fisticuffs with Coke, Hale, and Blackstone, for massacring their language."[24] Webster believed his true talent lay in literature, where he could fly like Pegasus over the field of drudgery. Law, unlike poetry and oratory, was artificial; it was learned, not inspired; its genius consisted in application, not in nature. Webster, of course, gradually quelled this youthful discontentment, coming to terms with his chosen profession as well as with the deeper stirrings of personal ambition.

In January 1802, after four months of desultory reading in lawyer Thompson's office, Webster took a teaching position at Fryeburg Academy, just over the Granite State's eastern border in Massachusetts (now Maine). This was a diversion, undertaken to earn money to help his father and contribute to his older brother Ezekiel's education. At Fryeburg he borrowed a copy of Blackstone's *Commentaries*, understanding it much better than *Coke on Littleton*, which Thompson had started him on, read any other books he could lay his hands on, and in the evenings, after teaching all day, copied deeds for twenty-five cents apiece in the office of the county recorder. Asked once to describe his appearance as a twenty-year-old schoolmaster, he replied, "Long, slender, pale, and all eyes; indeed, I went by the name of *all eyes* the county round." On Saturday afternoons he went fishing, rod in hand, Shakespeare in his pocket.[25] Returning to Salisbury in the fall, Webster resumed reading in Thompson's office, but was still unable to take himself seriously as a student of law and found himself hoping for "something like a miracle" to spring him loose from "this smokey village." Poverty was rapidly becoming the goad of ambition. "Money, Daniel, money," Ezekial preached in his letters.[26] In the spring of 1804 Ezekial, who had gone to Boston to teach school, provided the miracle. Suddenly finding himself with more pupils than he could handle, he offered the surplus tuitions to Daniel, thinking he would be able to support himself with ninety minutes of labor a day and devote the rest of his time to law study in the New England metropolis. Daniel seized the opportunity.

He was fortunate to find a place in the office of Christopher Gore, a prominent Federalist who had just returned from England as a commissioner under the Jay Treaty and was resuming his practice. "He has great amenity of manners, is easy, accessible, and communicative, and, take him all in all, I could not wish a better preceptor," Webster wrote.[27] Gore was also "a deep and voracious scholar." The struggling apprentice obtained, for the first time, an elevated view of the law that united intellectual distinction with social refinement and practical influence. He read generously—Vattel, Gibbon, Boswell, Paley, Moore—in Gore's library, but focused on the common law, and within that made himself a master of the intricacies of special pleading by taking the old folio edition of the standard work, *Saunders Reports*, translating the Latin and Norman French into English, and abstracting every case in the book. When the Massachusetts high courts commenced in the fall, Webster was an attentive observer, finding other professional models in such eminent lawyers as Theophilus Parsons and Samuel Dexter, whose characters he sketched in a diary kept at this time.[28]

During the course of study, Webster was offered the clerkship of the Court of Common Pleas in his New Hampshire county, Hillsborough. The post was meant as a political favor to old Ebenezer Webster, who had served the county long and well as militia captain, selectman, town clerk, state assemblyman, and justice of the peace. Daniel was delighted. "My brother and I were both in debt, our father was old, and his estate mortgaged," he recalled twenty years later. "I had been looking to this office, but hardly with hope, and here it was—here was the appointment to what, as I may say, had been the ambition of the family ever since the Revolution. It was fifteen hundred a year. Why, I could pay all the debts of the family, could help Ezekial—in short, I was independent." The next morning he went to Gore in the flush of triumph and was dumbfounded when he shrugged his shoulders at the clerkship. "Go on and finish your studies," Gore advised.[29] And Webster acted on the advice, though he knew that the rejection of so great a prize would strike his father like a thunderbolt. It was, in fact, his declaration of independence from his father; and with it he extended the horizon of his ambition beyond the Merrimack valley.

In March 1805, Webster was admitted to practice in Boston. He intended to settle in Portsmouth, New Hampshire, developing a commercial practice similar to Gore's, but his plans were upset by his father's illness. Returning home he opened an office in Boscawen, and for the next two years he was the pettifogging country lawyer he disdained. His air of superiority gave him a reputation for "haughty, cold, and overbearing" manners. But slowly he built a respectable practice in Hillsborough and two neighboring counties.[30] With a loftier ambition, he continued his studies, investing his meager profits in books. Counseling a young aspirant years later, Webster said he owed his eminence to his poverty. "When I commenced practice, I was without fortune or friends. I went into an interior town in New Hampshire, hired two rooms of a broken merchant and paid him nine shillings a week, made my own fire and bed and brushed my own boots and lived almost literally for two years on bread and milk, and for a whole time went not into a single party. I had little to do; and only a small library which I read over and over on the principle of *multum non multa*."[31] While he was not, in fact, a recluse, he looked upon this country practice as a temporary expedient. When his father died the following year, Webster surrendered the practice, along with management of the family farm, The Elms, in Franklin, to his brother, and as soon as he could gracefully do so set out for Portsmouth.

Portsmouth was still a thriving seaport, the shipbuilding capital of the United States, when Webster went there in his twenty-fifth year. The choice of the East over the West, of a coastal city at its zenith over a rising inland town, reflected Webster's caution and conservatism. After a few months he returned home to marry Grace Fletcher, the daughter of a Congregational minister in another town. She was by all accounts a lovely young woman, as gentle as a dove, and deeply religious.[32] It was probably because of her that Webster, before his marriage, united with the church in which he had been baptized. Her piety warmed but never succeeded in igniting his faith. Entering rapidly upon a lucrative practice in Portsmouth, earning upward of two thousand dollars a year, Webster rose to the front rank of the New Hampshire bar. In chaise or sleigh or on horseback, he followed the sessions of the superior court through six New Hampshire counties. His more or less constant companion was Jeremiah Mason, a man fourteen years older, whose towering physical presence was matched by his reputation as a lawyer. The two men commonly found themselves in opposition. Their courtroom duels were celebrated. Naturally, they came to admire each other. Webster was influenced by the strength and lucidity of Mason's style as well as by his mastery of the common law. In the fine points of the law Mason was judged superior, but the New Hampshire courts had never seen a better forensic lawyer than Daniel Webster. Mason, who delighted in his friend's conversation and good humor, once remarked, "there never was such an actor lost to the stage as he would have made had he chosen to turn his talents in that direction."[33]

While establishing his reputation at the bar, Webster was also rising to leadership in the Federalist party. His earliest political memory dated from his seventh or eighth year when he purchased from a village shopkeeper a cotton handkerchief printed, in the manner of the time, with the Constitution. He thus learned of the existence of the Union that became his apotheosis. While John C. Calhoun's father in South Carolina opposed ratification of the Constitution, Webster's, in New Hampshire, advocated it and then cast one of his state's electoral votes for George Washington to be president. The Merrimack towns, unlike most of the interior between Portsmouth and the rich Connecticut River valley, tended to be Federalist. Daniel grew up in a Federalist household; he went to a Federalist college; all his mentors in the law—Thompson, Gore, Mason—were Federalist leaders. His youthful political outlook had already been suggested by the oration upon his graduation from Dartmouth. He felt about the Jeffersonian "revolution of 1800" much as Edmund Burke felt about the French Revolution: that licentiousness, tyranny, death, and destruction lay at the end of its fantastic visions. "The path to despotism leads through the mire and dirt of uncontrolled democracy," he declared in 1802, then adduced Jefferson's administration to prove the proposition.[34] In light satiric verse, he prayed for Federalist return to power in Washington.

> Thou *Federal Orb* again return
> And up the sparkling Orient burn,
> Shoot o'er our land a ray of light
> And banish hence this noxious blight.[35]

The Republicans swept to victory across the nation in 1804, carrying even New Hampshire for Jefferson. The next year they won the governorship and control of the state. In that campaign Webster's pen was enlisted for the Federalist standard-bearer and perennial governor, Nicholas Gilman, against the

Republican challenger, John Langdon. *An Appeal to the Old Whigs of New Hampshire* was a typical Federalist diatribe. Associating the Jeffersonian Republicans with immorality, infidelity, and hostility to the Constitution, Webster denounced all the principal measures of the administration.[36] He was part of a movement led by younger Federalists to make the party not just the voice of conservatism but an effective electoral machine in competition with the popular party. After settling in Portsmouth he helped redeem the city and surrounding Rockingham County from the Republicans. The torrent of opposition to Jefferson's embargo swept the Federalists back into power in the state in 1809. Thereafter, through the war years, every election was bitterly contested, and neither party was long in control at Concord.

On the platform, in the courtroom, and in occasional writings, Webster developed a public character and voice unmistakably his own. Steeped in the Bible, in Shakespeare and Milton, he knew the power of eloquence and sought to attain it himself. He still aspired to a literary reputation as well as a juristic one. While in Boston he had been invited to contribute to the *Monthly Anthology,* the literary review of the Federalist elite. His topics ranged from the law of seditious libel to the bearing of language on national character. Today the articles seem less important for what they say than for the evidence they provide of Webster's membership in an intellectual circle devoted to the Ciceronian ideal of high thought and leadership in what they perceived as a dangerously democratic and money-loving society. This was the theme, coincidentally, of Webster's Phi Beta Kappa address, "The State of Our Literature," delivered at Dartmouth in 1809. There were two great impediments, he said, to literary and moral improvement in the country. First, "the love of gold," and second, "the pursuit of politics." "To warm the apathy, to subdue the avarice, to soften the political asperity, of the nation, are the objects for the prosecution of which every man of letters stands pledged," the orator declared.[37] There was a special poignancy in the message, for gold and politics were the two demons perched on Webster's shoulders.

The ideal of "the man of letters," though receding, remained a fixture of Webster's consciousness and, of course, of his public reputation. Its principal medium of expression, oratory, was also the embodiment of what became the Websterian style. In the course of a dozen years, Webster delivered at least four Fourth of July orations. The first, at Hanover, in 1800, was exceedingly florid; pretending to eloquence, it achieved empty bombast and little else. Recalling the Revolution, Webster imaged America as an eagle "springing from the torturing fangs of the British Lion," spoke of "the spiral frames of burning Charlestown," and of Bunker Hill as "the grand theatre of New England bravery." (Even at his worst, however, Webster could be good. From this oration came the often-quoted line in praise of the forefathers: "For us they fought! for us they bled! for us they conquered!")[38] Criticism of the address when it appeared in print led Webster to study British authors, like Addison, known for chaste and fluent styles. He learned the difference between eloquence and ornament. Each successive oration marked an improvement in the direction of strength and simplicity. The law, too, oddly enough, contributed to this. Good speaking, he came to understand, was like good pleading; it consisted in penetration, terseness, and perspicuity. "Besides," Webster once reflected in conversation, "I remembered that I had my bread to earn by addressing the understanding of common men—by convincing juries—and that I must use language perfectly intelligible to them. You will therefore find, in my speeches to juries, no hard words, no Latin phrases, no *fieri facias;* and that is the secret of my style if I have any."[39] Mason was his example in this regard. It carried over to all his speech making. He aimed, as he said, "to allow nothing to words but as they are signs of ideas."[40] Needless to say, he did not always succeed.

The early writings and speeches repeatedly struck the chords that would resound through the public discourse of the rising statesman. Most of these have already been suggested, but they bear summary repetition. One was adherence to values and principles received from the past. "We come to take counsel of the dead": thus began a Fourth of July oration. The act meant more, much more, to Webster than mere ancestral piety. It meant preserving at all hazards the "great experiment" launched in 1776. The rock of principle was the Constitution, its hero George Washington, its guardians the Federalist party. A quarter century before his famous encounter with Senator Hayne of South Carolina, Webster was hymning praises to the Constitution as "the sacred and inviolable palladium" of American liberty. Another theme concerned religion. Webster spoke much of religion as necessary to the support of good government. He defended the tax-supported Congregational church in New Hampshire against attack from dissenters and Republicans alike. "The altar of our freedom should be placed near the altar of our religion," he intoned in the manner of Puritan forebears. Webster believed, too, as he said in his Phi Beta Kappa address, that it was the duty of the government to elevate, refine, and liberalize private passions and interests by politics that blended them with the public good. Thus the pursuit of wealth might be legitimated, the pursuit of power redeemed. Still another recurrent argument in these early speeches and writings was that the Constitution and the Union came into existence primarily to protect and promote commerce. "It is the essence of the national compact," he said. The miracle of peace and commerce under President Washington was the source of the nation's wealth, the redeemer of its credit, and the bond of the Union. Under the Republicans both commerce and peace were destroyed. In 1812, Webster would argue, the nation went to war on principles that betrayed its very existence.[41]

Webster's "first halo of political glory," in the words of an early biographer, was the Rockingham Memorial of August 5, 1812.[42] This, in turn, grew out of a stirring Fourth of July address to the Washington Benevolent Society. The Society functioned as an arm of the Federalist party, which, in New Hampshire as elsewhere, draped itself in the mantle of George Washington. Webster had often spoken at its meetings. With the war scarcely two weeks old, he seized the occasion to define the Federalist position. The war was unjust, immoral, inexpedient; nevertheless, patriots must yield to it. "It is now the law of the land; and as such we are bound to regard it. Resistance and insur-

rection form no parts of our creed. The disciples of Washington are neither ty-
rants in power, nor rebels out of it."[43] Resistance, in sum, would be confined
to normal political channels. The address quickly ran through two printings.
Elected a delegate to the Federalist county convention in August, Webster
was appointed chairman of a committee to draft a protest against the war.
The paper, which was later signed by fifteen hundred citizens of Rockingham, took the form of a memorial to President Madison. It repeated, with
some elaboration, the argument of the Washington address. The war, and
the years of commercial restriction preceding it, broke the contract of 1787
for the protection of commerce. Although trumpeted as a war for "free trade
and seamen's rights," it was undertaken in the face of bitter opposition by the
seafaring interests of New England. In fact, the war looked to the annihilation of commerce and to a Franco-American alliance against Britain. We are
attached to the Union, the memorialists declared, but to its substance, not to
its form; and if we are deprived of its blessings, separation will be forced
upon us. "If a separation of the states shall ever take place, it will be, on some
occasion, when one portion of the country undertakes to control, to regulate,
and to sacrifice the interest of another."[44] The words would return to haunt
Webster long after the war ended.

Thrust into prominence as the spokesman of New Hampshire Federalism,
Webster was nominated for Congress by this same convention, on the "Peace
Ticket." The state chose its six congressmen at large, on a "general ticket,"
and the Federalists swept the field in the fall election. Webster ran second.
Except for being elected moderator of the Portsmouth town meeting earlier
in the year, he had never run for or served in any office. He skipped all the
lower rungs of the political ladder and began his career near the top, in Congress. He never sat in a state legislature, but for ten stray days in 1823. Of
course, having labored for seven years in the precincts of the Federalist
party, he had a claim on its suffrages. But it was an unpopular war addressed
by brilliant rhetoric that brought Webster, at thirty, to the threshold of
fame.

Webster differed from Clay and Calhoun, whom he would meet in the
Thirteenth Congress, most obviously in his Federalism and in his opposition
to the war. He was on the losing side, as it turned out—some said the side of
treason—and this cast a long shadow over his political career. Other differences are less obvious. But any accounting of the young Webster must begin
with several dominant characteristics. He was a man of deep sentiment, so excessive at times that it bordered on sentimentality. He was sentimental
about the past, ancestors, the common law, hearth and home, his college,
Washington, and the Constitution. To strangers he seemed haughty and
cold, doubtless an expression of the superiority he felt; but he had an inordinate need for love and friendship and admiration, and a knack for inspiring it
within his social circle. Webster had pretensions to learning. Indeed, among
the statesmen of the second generation, only he, after John Quincy Adams,
could claim some of the literary and philosophical distinction of the first. In
time, of course, as he pursued money and power, the learning became a

mere gloss; although it may have continued to fool others, it no longer fooled Webster. His mind was immensely receptive but contained no originality. In nothing he wrote or said in his youth—and the record is much fuller for him than for Clay or Calhoun—was there the trace of an original idea. Observers would later say, correctly, that his mind possessed neither the strength of Calhoun's nor the comprehensiveness of Clay's, yet was more luminous than either. This quality came from his rigorous training in courts of law. His thought, his style, his rhetoric were all profoundly influenced by his forensic experience. Alone among his illustrious contemporaries, Webster would attain double fame, in law as well as in politics. His conservatism, like his keen historical sensibility, stemmed in large part from his Burkian enchantment with English institutions and the common law, "the original block of marble," in his view, from which the American republic was carved.[45]

In New Hampshire towns and courthouses, where he had countless admirers, Daniel Webster was already a figure larger than life when he went to Congress. "He was a black, raven-haired fellow," one of those early admirers recalled him on the circuit, "with an eye as black as death, and as heavy as a lion's—and no lion in Africa ever had a voice like him, and his look was like a lion's—that same heavy look, not sleepy, but as if he didn't care about any thing that was going on about any thing; but as if he would think like a hurricane if he once got worked up to it."[46] Here was the beginning of the Webster whose name was a byword for Yankee knowledge, who sprang from the granite, "nature's own child," in Emerson's phrase, and could outwit the devil himself. His political enemies sensed his mythmaking power at the same time they lampooned him as "the great man." Even Isaac Hill, the New Hampshire Republican leader, was finally convinced. Webster, he said not long before the statesman's death, "is the greatest man who ever lived in America." "He was all," the state's later poet laureate, Robert Frost, would write, "The Daniel Webster ever was or shall be."[47]

4. War and Peace

Southern and western congressmen were usually delighted with the federal city on the Potomac and entered freely into its social life; those from the North generally hated it and were miserable together. Politics had something to do with the contrasting attitudes. Washington was a southern city, presided over by a Virginia president, and ruled by the Republican party. When Daniel Webster, who had never before ventured outside New England, finally arrived for the special session of the Thirteenth Congress in May 1813, he complained of the worsening roads as he traveled southward, said the capital was surrounded by a "desert," and about the city itself, "this Great Dismal," had nothing good to say.[1] He took up residence in a boardinghouse in nearby Georgetown, where he enjoyed the congenial company of Christopher Gore, his mentor in the law, now a Massachusetts senator; Jeremiah Mason, his Portsmouth friend, now a New Hampshire senator; and Rufus King, the distinguished senator from New York. The day after Congress convened, Webster went to the White House to make his bow to the president. Madison, his ashen countenance etched in solemn blackness, had more the appearance of a Roman cardinal than an American chief executive. "I did not like his looks, any better than I like his Administration," Webster remarked.[2]

Madison had reason to be glum. The war had been going badly. Hopes for the quick conquest of Canada had been crushed as American forces were defeated at every point along the wide front from Michilimackinac to Montreal. Striking back, "the flower of Kentucky youth," whipped into action by Henry Clay and his friends to avenge treachery and humiliation in the Northwest, had been massacred at the River Raisin below Detroit. Early victories at sea had offered some compensation for the defeats on land; but the Americans had lost control of Lake Champlain, and the news in June of the destruction of the frigate *Chesapeake*, with its captain and crew, only deepened Madison's gloom. The British blockade from New York to New Orleans disrupted the economy, deprived the treasury of customs receipts to finance the war, and invited illicit trading with the enemy, which shattered morale and reached epidemic proportions in New England. Hoping to exploit New England disaffection, the British left the northern ports open. The governments of Massachusetts and Connecticut steadfastly refused to furnish militia for "Mr. Madison's War." News of Russian victories in Europe, of Napoleon's winter retreat from Moscow, boded ill for the fortunes of American arms. Of course, many Federalists believed the American war was undertaken to aid the French, perhaps even at Napoleon's bidding. Not long after Congress convened, three hundred people attended a dinner in Georgetown to celebrate the Russian triumph. Webster was presumably among the Federalist congressmen present. No Republican could be observed.[3]

The Republican leaders in Congress, Clay and Calhoun at the head, were disappointed but not discouraged after a year of war. They laid some of the blame for failure at the door of the administration. "Mr. Madison is wholly unfit for the storms of war," Clay reluctantly confessed.[4] The very traits that made him a great statesman—his coolness, prudence, and benevolence—incapacitated him for the conduct of war. The incompetence of the executive officers in Washington, to say nothing of the generals in the field, was a public scandal. After the disasters of the first military campaign, Madison moved to strengthen the cabinet. The good effects of this change had worn thin by May. Regardless of administrative failings, congressional leaders laid most of the blame on the Federalist party. Not only did it oppose the war; it sought in every possible way to distract the country and embarrass the administration in order to climb back into power. Some of the foremost Federalist leaders, Republicans believed, carried their opposition to the verge of treason and were, in fact, guilty of "moral treason," as Felix Grundy named this brand of disloyalty. In January, during debate on a bill to raise troops, Clay had descended from his speaker's chair and in a three-day harangue castigated the

Federalists as never before. They appeared to forget, he said, that "they stand on American soil," as members of the House of Representatives, and instead imagined themselves little Burkes and Pitts declaiming in the House of Commons. Clay singled out "the coarse assaults of party malevolence" by Josiah Quincy of Massachusetts. He had described the administration as "little less than a despotism" and Clay and his friends as "sycophants, fawning reptiles, who crowded at the feet of the president, and left their filthy slime upon the carpet of the palace." Quincy's attack on Thomas Jefferson, the retired president, whom he had tried to impeach at the time of the embargo, drew from Clay a eulogy of the Republican hero that would be lisped by schoolboys for decades to come.*[5] Every Federalist eye, it was said, bent with shame to the floor. "Never was a man more severely castigated or one who more richly deserved it." Clay went on to offer the best defense of the war yet heard in Congress, against Federalist demands to end it as a bad cause and a lost one. "In conception he was forcible. In diction sublime. In eloquence impressive and in action great."[6] The speech electrified the country and had a chastening effect on the Federalist opposition in Congress.

In the special session Clay was again elected Speaker, by a margin, eighty-nine to fifty-four (with five scattered votes), that showed the strength of the two parties. Calhoun had succeeded to the chairmanship of the Committee on Foreign Relations, and the Speaker, recognizing the merits of the new member from New Hampshire, placed him on the committee. Webster did not wait long to make his presence felt. On June 10 he introduced a series of resolutions, presumably backed by the Federalist leadership, directing the president to explain when he and other officers learned of the so-called Trent Decree, dated April 28, 1811, purporting to repeal the sanctions of the Berlin and Milan decrees against American neutral trade. From the first month of the war, when the decree came to light, Federalists suspected that Madison had deliberately concealed knowledge of the French action lest it prompt the British ministry to lift its orders in council and thereby remove the pretext for war on Britain. The suspicion was unfounded. The decree had been manufactured by Napoleon a year after its assigned date; it was unknown in the United States until after the declaration of war. But many Federalists, seeking to justify their opposition to the war, grasped at straws to prove that

---

*"When the gentleman [Quincy] to whom I have been compelled to allude, shall have mingled his dust with that of his abused ancestors, when he shall have been consigned to oblivion, or, if he lives at all, shall live only in the treasonable annals of a certain junto, the name Jefferson will be hailed with gratitude, his memory honored, and cherished as the second father of the liberties of the people, and the period of his administration will be looked back to, as one of the happiest and brightest epochs of American history—an oasis in the midst of a sandy desert. But I beg the gentleman's pardon; he had indeed secured to himself a more imperishable fame than I had supposed: I think it was about four years ago that he submitted to House of Representatives, an initiative proposition for the impeachment of Mr. Jefferson. The house condescended to consider it. The gentleman debated it with his usual *temper, moderation,* and *urbanity.* The house decided it in the most solemn manner, and, although the gentleman had somehow obtained a second, the final vote stood, ONE for, and *one hundred and seventeen against,* the proposition!"

French artifice was behind it. Madison supposed he had answered Federalist cavils on this subject in response to a Senate inquiry at the previous session. Webster either was not satisfied with the explanation or chose to revive the issue in hopes of further embarrassing the administration. What distinguished the "Websterian Attack" from the earlier inquiry was the presumption that the president himself had secretly suppressed information that, if known, would have prevented war. The arrogance of the attack was unprecedented. Search the annals of Parliament, said the *National Intelligencer*, the Republican press in Washington, and no example of such rudeness toward a chief magistrate could be found. After several days of heated debate, Calhoun and his friends, eager to get on with pending tax bills, chose to let the resolutions pass. Clay appointed the author of the resolutions to present them to the president. Finding him sick in bed, Webster gloated that he would get no relief from his prescription. Madison's reply, about three weeks later, took the form of a six-thousand-word letter, with supporting documents, from Secretary of State James Monroe. It vindicated the president's conduct, showed the French decree to have been of no importance, and offered additional proof for the justice and necessity of war. Calhoun promptly reported a resolution of his committee approving the report. Another debate was averted because Webster and several of his colleagues had already gone home, and the leadership had agreed not to force a vote in their absence.[7]

The issue thus left in suspension, both sides could claim a tactical victory. The "Websterian Attack" revived "the sun of Federalism," sent Madison to bed with a fever, and drove another nail into the administration's coffin, said the Federalists. Republicans argued, on the contrary, that the attack recoiled on its authors by presenting the administration an opportunity to defend itself and the war. The House printed five thousand copies of Monroe's report. Timothy Pickering called it "trash," all sophistry and misrepresentation, but even he believed the people would be swayed by it.[8] One thing is certain: attack and counterattack called attention to the freshman congressman from New Hampshire. The New York *Herald* interpreted passage of the resolutions as an overwhelming victory and praised Webster as "second to none" in the House of Representatives. Isaac Hill contended that though Webster had made a splash, he had been blinded by the overweening confidence he got from arguing petty lawsuits and falsely supposed his malignant attack dishonored the government when, in fact, said Hill, it only disgraced himself.[9] Returning to Washington in the fall, Webster attempted to revive the issue, without success.

Much later Webster remarked that "it better suits my temper and feelings to be able to support the measures of government" than to oppose them.[10] He had in mind Andrew Jackson, but he might have said the same thing about James Madison. Opposing the war, Webster placed himself in a false position, as advocate of strict versus broad construction of the Constitution, of state rights against the Union, of revolt rather than authority. To oppose the war was awkward for Federalists like himself who, as he kept apologizing, "are not of a school in which insurrection is taught as a virtue."[11] The line he took was that because the war originated in an unjust cause, it could never be effectively prosecuted or won. The failure rested not with bad generals or a disloyal opposition; it rested with the Republican leadership. If the war was purely defensive, waged on the ocean for "free trade and seamen's rights," as Republicans claimed, the Federalists would support it, he said; but the mainspring of every measure was Canada, and commerce, far from being defended, had been annihilated. Unfortunately, only a fine line separated opposition to the war on these grounds from aiding and abetting the enemy. Even if the conflict began in error or folly, did that justify the attempt to paralyze the nation's will? And was not the quarrel over the ways and means of conducting the war really an excuse for opposition on other grounds? Calhoun, answering Webster in January 1814, tore away the mask of patriotism and denounced the Federalists as a "factious opposition." Every reader of Demosthenes and Cicero knew this was the most dangerous of all evils in a republican government, since it set loyalty to party above loyalty to country.[12] Some Federalists, such as Rufus King, regularly voted for revenue and appropriation bills to support the war despite their opposition to it. Webster generally did not. In the darkest days of the war, after the British burned the capital, he refused to vote for or against an increase of the direct tax, having somehow persuaded himself that this evasion was the morally responsible position.[13]

On one matter, the repeal of the restrictive system, Webster and Calhoun were in basic agreement. War Hawk though he was, Calhoun had not hesitated to attack embargo, non-importation, and the principles of economic coercion which remained a touchstone of Republican fidelity even after war was declared. He assailed the whole system as founded on dishonor and delusion. "It does not suit the genius of our people," he said. "We are a people essentially active. . . . Distance and difficulties are less to us than any other people on earth. Our schemes and prospects extend every where and to every thing. No passive system can suit such a people. . . . Nor does it suit the genius of our government. Our government is founded on freedom and hates coercion."[14] By striking the shackles from commerce, Calhoun hoped to reconcile eastern trading interests to the war and thus unite the people in the flames of heroism and patriotism. Doubtless he hoped also to cultivate northern Federalist influence and to establish a character for political independence. Bristling at Calhoun's defection, Clay used his casting vote as speaker to block repeal of the two-year-old Non-Importation Act in 1812.

The system of commercial sanctions, including a short-lived embargo, had been converted from its original purpose of keeping the nation at peace to an auxiliary of the war machine. In 1814, after Napoleon collapsed and the liberated nations on the continent resumed trading with Britain, these measures were self-defeating, and Madison, for many years their leading advocate, requested repeal. Webster gloated over the death of this "system of politics." "I have not for a long time seen the Federalists look in so good humor," wrote one old Republican, who confessed to "feel a little sore under Webster's rubs." The system was abandoned in "the twinkling of an eye" upon the downfall of France, Webster noted. What better proof that it had been all along the American counterpart of Napoleon's "continental system."?[15] Calhoun did not gloat. He had acquiesced in the war embargo. He refuted the stale charge of French influence, and tactfully pleaded the case for repeal on the ground that circumstances had changed. Although he and Webster both opposed the restrictive system, they did so for different reasons, Webster because it was part of a system antagonistic to New England commercial interests, Calhoun mainly because it clashed with his heroic nation-building conception of the war. For Calhoun the war was the ordeal of American nationality. "It is the war of the Revolution revived—we are again struggling for our liberty and independence."[16] This, of course, was just ranting nonsense to Webster and his friends. Nevertheless, Calhoun's rejection of the leading policy of Jefferson and Madison, his advocacy of free trade as the true American system, endeared him to northern Federalists, some of whom afterward became his political followers. At the same time he and Webster were burying the restrictive system, they found themselves working together against the administration's plan for a national bank. Here was another manifestation of Calhoun's vaunted independence.

Webster might have lived down his opposition to a war that, in retrospect, was the pride of American glory and patriotism had it not been for the Hartford Convention. New Hampshire politics were in turmoil in 1814. The Federalists, having returned to power the preceding year, abolished the existing courts with their Republican judges and set up new courts manned by Federalists under the head of Jeremiah Smith, who, with Webster and Mason, was one of the party's triumvirs. Controversy over the Judiciary Act further inflamed partisan feelings about the war. While the Portsmouth *Oracle* lauded Webster for giving luster to the state, the New Hampshire *Patriot* ridiculed his talents and lumped him with "the sharks of the green bag," "the high-tone Jackals in Portsmouth"—the lawyer-aristocracy that tyrannized over the people.[17] Webster led the "American Peace Ticket" that swept the congressional election in the fall. He had already decided to make the second term his last. Disgust with "Mr. Madison's War" and Republican hegemony in Washington had something to do with the decision, but so did personal misfortunes, such as the loss of his home to fire, and his ambitions to make money in the law.

Hill, the *Patriot's* editor, spread suspicion that Webster's opposition to the war was not only unpatriotic but treasonable. "Of all the men in the State, he is the fittest to be the tool of our enemy; and if he has not already been rewarded he probably expects some portion of 'secret service money' for prating long and loud about *French influence*, about the justice and magnanimity of Britain, and the wickedness and corruption of the American government."[18] When the "second Daniel" arrived late for Congress in the fall of 1814, Hill said it was because he "tarried in Boston" until he could be sure the Massachusetts government was ready to proceed with the "New England Convention" that had been bruited for several months.[19] On October 17 the Massachusetts legislature did, in fact, issue the call for the convention, to be held at Hartford two months hence. But so little did Webster know of its man-

agement that on that same October day, reaching the war-ravaged capital—
the British had burned it in August—he had to write to Boston to learn what
had been decided. He was dismayed by rumors that the convention would
be put off. There was no prospect of peace; the government could not protect
New England; the five states must unite to protect themselves.[20] While saying nothing of disunion, Webster was obviously eager for the convention.
His actions in Congress tended to support the movement toward resistance.
Speaking against the administration's conscription bill, recommended in part
because of the failure of the New England states to furnish militia for the
army, Webster denounced the measure as unconstitutional and warned that,
should it pass, the state governments would be solemnly bound "to interpose
between their citizens and arbitrary power." He disavowed, for himself and
New England, any disunionist intentions. "Those who cry out that the Union
is in danger are themselves the authors of that danger," he declared.[21] That
was all very well, but by advocating state interposition against the Republican administration in Washington he had turned the party creeds inside out
and wrapped beleaguered Federalism in the Jeffersonian "principles of '98."

In the years to come, every dusty archive, every nook and corner of New
Hampshire, would be ransacked in search of evidence linking Webster to
the Hartford Convention. The convention, as it turned out, was controlled
by moderate Federalists, and their report, while founded on state rights
principles, avoided the heresy of disunion. But the nation read the report
in the light of bonfires raised for General Jackson's glorious victory at New
Orleans and for the Peace of Ghent. The Hartford Convention, so somberly
against the war, became the butt of ridicule, and a synonym for treachery,
defeat, and disunion. Webster never rid himself of the stain. What did it
matter that he was not actually among the delegates to Hartford? it would
be asked. "He was their Magnus Apollo! To him they looked for guidance in
every movement; he had only to wave his hand and they obeyed his signal."[22] This characterization by a congressman a dozen years later was not
only malicious but false, for it attributed to Webster political power and fi-
nesse he did not possess in 1814. Nonetheless, though he neither caused
nor counseled the convention, Webster imbibed its spirit, which sufficed to
fix its stigma upon him.

Henry Clay shared in the glory of the peace as well as in the dubious glo-
ries of the war. In January 1814, responding to overtures from the British government, Madison appointed Clay, John Quincy Adams, James A. Bayard,
and Jonathan Russell commissioners to negotiate peace. (Albert Gallatin was
subsequently added to the commission.) Federalists were appalled by Clay's
appointment. A fire-breathing westerner, he was as diplomatic as a game-
cock; no one in the government, except perhaps the president himself, had a
greater personal stake in a victorious outcome to the war. (The London press
also took a dim view of Clay. One newspaper confused him with "the man
that killed Tecumseh," and said "that he cut several razor strops out of his
[Tecumseh's] back after he was dead." When a British peace commissioner
remarkable for his beard later inquired about the report, Clay offered to pres-

ent him with one of the razor strops.)²³ He was appointed, of course, because he spoke for the West and because of his unrivaled influence in Congress. He was sent to Europe, as Irving Brant has said, not as a negotiator but "as an intrepid athlete who would cede the smallest ground possible."²⁴

The cession of territory, rather than its acquisition or even recognition of the maritime claims that had caused the war, was the grim prospect facing the commissioners when they sat down with their British counterparts at the Flemish town of Ghent in August. Clay alone refused to be dismayed. While the others saw the British triumph in Europe as a bad omen for America, Clay thought, "It is impossible that Europe, liberated as it is from the despotism of Buonaparte, should be indifferent to the enormous power and the enormous pretensions of Great Britain on the ocean." He looked to Vienna— the Congress of Vienna—for help at Ghent. He dismissed the dissensions in the New England states as "a game of swaggering and gasconade."²⁵ Above all, he prayed for American victories. Clay's optimism, it has been said, "though a personal asset . . . was not a factor in the situation," and it savored more of "a natural exuberance of temper rather than of political insight."²⁶ It savored also of Clay's gambling instincts, which were very good. At a later stage of the negotiations, after the British retreated from their initial demands, Clay announced that as they had been playing brag with us, it was time to begin playing brag with them. "He asked me if I knew how to play *brag*," Adams jotted in his diary. "I had forgotten how. He said the art of it was to beat your adversary by holding your hand with a solemn and confident phiz, and outbragging him."²⁷

The victories finally came—at Erie, Plattsburg, and Baltimore—and the British prudently agreed to the American *projet* for a peace based on the *status quo ante bellum*. This meant, on the American side, abandoning the neutral rights and seamen's rights which, for Clay more than the others, had been the moral hinge of the war; but he swallowed his pride and accepted the principle. He then waged a prolonged, ill-tempered duel with Adams over the interlocked issues of the Newfoundland fisheries and the navigation of the Mississippi. The British insisted that the American "liberty" to catch and dry fish in British waters, confirmed by the peace of 1783, was terminated by the war. As compensation for this loss, the British government would give up its right, also a legacy of the earlier treaty, to navigate the Mississippi, seemingly an empty right, since the Mississippi, though once an international waterway, had become Americanized from its headwaters below the 49th parallel to the mouth of New Orleans. Yankee fishermen still swarmed over the Newfoundland coast, however, and Adams refused to yield the traditional right. Gallatin offered to break the impasse by including the renewal of both rights in the American proposal. But Clay, joined by Russell, declared he would sign no treaty that restored the right to navigate the Mississippi to Great Britain. Considering that one right was real, the other unreal, Bayard accused Clay of "bragging a million against a cent."²⁸ Real or unreal, the Mississippi claim had great symbolic significance for Clay. It was the remnant of British pretensions, since 1763, to control the future of the

American West. The apparent indifference of three of his colleagues (Adams, Bayard, and Gallatin) demonstrated once again how little easterners understood, or cared about, western interests. The formal abandonment of the right became, in the end, the last shred of vindication Clay could take from the peace. And in the dawning age of the steamboat, the British right to navigate the Mississippi was far from empty. Although this calculation never entered into Clay's thinking, he had the fortitude to see that the perpetuation of any British claim or influence in the Mississippi valley was intolerable. Still, unable to convince the majority of his colleagues, he finally acceded to Gallatin's proposition. Fortunately for him, for the peace, and the country, the British commissioners rejected the bargain. The peace that was finally signed on Christmas Eve mentioned neither the fisheries nor the Mississippi, but left them, with many other issues, to be resolved at some future time.[29]

By any objective standard, the Peace of Ghent should have been a disappointment to Henry Clay. No neutral rights, no Canada, no indemnities, no secure boundaries, no abandonment of the Mississippi—none of the goals for which he, the president, and the War Hawks had led the country into war were achieved in the peace. But the exuberant Kentuckian quickly put a victorious face upon the peace. The fact that it was considered a defeat in respectable British circles lent validity to his claim. All Europe must reflect, said the London *Times*, "that we have retired from the combat with the stripes yet bleeding on our backs—with the recent defeats at Plattsburgh, and on Lake Champlain, unavenged."[30] And New Orleans had not yet been heard from. Jackson's astounding victory, two weeks after the signing at Ghent, prepared the way for a jubilant American reception of the peace. Clay returned home the following summer, after negotiating a tentative commercial agreement with Britain, to a hero's welcome. Feted from the moment he stepped off the boat in New York, a final banquet awaited him at Lexington. Responding to the unfailing congratulatory resolutions, Clay harped on three points. First, that it was the British, not the Americans, whose reputation suffered at Ghent. Second, by standing up singlehandedly to the mightiest power on earth, the United States had established its national character. And third, in the ordeal of the war and the peace, the republican government born of the Revolution had met the crucial test.[31] The question, "What have we gained from the war?" was asked all over the country in 1815. The answer, as summed up in a Vermont newspaper, underscored Clay's recurrent theme:

> The fear of our late enemy;
> The respect of the world; and
> The confidence we have acquired in ourselves.[32]

* *Two* *

DIMENSIONS OF NATIONALISM

The American people confronted a new political world in 1815. For a quarter century they had directed their industry and commerce toward a Europe ravaged by war and revolution; now that era had ended, and with it the opportunity of rearing American prosperity on the misfortunes of the Old World. For almost as long, government had been carried on by party spirit; now one of the the two parties, the Federalist, around which the rivalry of men and principles had turned, virtually disappeared from the national stage, and it was by no means clear what force—patriotic or Caesarian, ideological or imperial, uniting or disuniting—would replace the force of party. A country that had hugged the Atlantic seaboard and sought its prosperity in foreign trade was about to spill into the Transappalachian West. During the next six years five new western states would enter the Union, raising serious questions both of economic development and of constitutional principle; and the rise of the West as a self-conscious section added a disturbing new element to the political balance. The nation, since its Revolutionary birth, had enjoyed an astonishing continuity of leadership. The author of the Declaration of Independence was a gray eminence at Monticello; the father of the Constitution was the president who had finally, irrevocably, secured independence in a second war with Great Britain. But as the Revolutionary fathers passed from the scene, there were apprehensions that the sons, while more showy, might be unworthy of the trust reposed in them. Fundamental changes set the terms of the new political world opened by the Peace of Ghent. New ideas, new policies, new leaders, and new directions were needed to meet the challenges of the new world.

Uplifted by the patriotic *elan* of 1815, nearly all Republicans, and most Federalists, united on the program of national improvement and consolidation laid before the Fourteenth Congress in December by President Madison. The "Madisonian Platform," as it would later be named, formed the basis of every effort during these years to increase the responsibility of the government for the nation's welfare.[1] Madison called for legislation to strengthen American arms even as the army and navy reverted to a peacetime footing. The war had taught no lesson more pointed than the need for military preparedness; and while the coalition of restored kings, the Holy Alliance, trampled on the ruins of liberty in Europe it was no time for the United States, the only republic in the world, to lower its defenses. A national bank had previously been recommended to Congress as an agency for financing the war. Now, facing the chaos of runaway state banking, Madison recommended it as a permanent institution to secure a stable and uniform national currency. The new Republican platform was thus reared on the broad constitutional principles that the party and Madison himself had once opposed. He urged Congress, in adjusting the high wartime duties on imports, to protect the infant manufactures that had grown up under the aegis of war and embargo. He underscored "the great importance of establishing throughout our country the roads and canals which can best be executed under the national authority." Any deficiency of constitutional power for internal improvements should be overcome by amendment. In a final appeal to the liberality of American patriotism, Madison proposed establishing a national university, located in the capital, that would be "a central resort of youth and genius from every part of their country, diffusing on their return examples of those national feelings, those liberal sentiments, and those congenial manners which contribute cement to our Union and strength to [its] great political fabric."

Congress, engaged for so long in averting disaster, turned earnestly to debating policies that would promote growth and development. Before adjourning it enacted a series of measures that constituted, said the *National Intelligencer*, "an era in legislation" of immerse importance for the American future.[2] National defense was strengthened by the creation of a general staff for the army, by improved militia organization, by appropriations for forts, and by assigning $1 million a year for building nine ships-of-the-line and twelve frigates. Congress thus practiced the maxim, "In peace, prepare for war." "These Halcyon days of peace, this calm will yield to the storms of war," Henry Clay advised, "and when that comes I am for being prepared to breast it."[3] The tariff of 1816, although it provided a schedule lower than the wartime double duties—about 25 percent *ad valorem* on the average—and lower than the administration wanted, established the principle of moderate protection incident to the revenue needs of the government. John C. Calhoun collaborated with Secretary of Treasury Alexander J. Dallas to devise a bank charter that won general support. Clay, in a dramatic reversal, voted for the bill, while Webster, the Federalist disciple of Alexander Hamilton, voted against it. His objections went to two of the bank's technical features, however, not to its national character; and with the passage of a supplementary bill, on which he joined forces with Calhoun, mandating the payment of taxes and other government dues in the legal currency of the country (gold and silver) or in bank notes redeemable in specie, thereby forcing "the true remedy" of a specie-based currency, Webster became the advocate of the Second Bank of the United States. An internal improvements bill was deferred to the second session. Here, too, Calhoun took the lead, proposing that the $1.5-million bonus paid by the B.U.S. for its charter be constituted a permanent fund for the support of internal improvements. Congress passed the Bonus Bill, but Madison, in the last act of his presidency, vetoed it on constitutional grounds.

Despite this surprising retreat to Old Republican dogma, there was every expectation that the progress of consolidation and improvement would continue under the new president, James Monroe, the last of the Virginia Dynasty. Shortly after his inauguration Monroe toured the northern states and everywhere met with public rejoicing. The tour became a vehicle of political reconciliation. When the president reached Boston the *Columbian Centinel*, long a leading voice of Federalism, hailed the administration so auspiciously launched as an "Era of Good Feelings." The dissolution of old party ties and sympathies was part of the Republican consensus upon which the Madisonian Platform rested. Its measures threw men into new associations and divided them along new lines that, however, assumed no definite form. The Republican party survived, of course. It had become the grand party of the nation. Old Federalists no longer opposed it but sought rank within it. Monroe would run for reelection in 1820 unopposed, with only one erratic electoral vote cast against him. But his success had nothing to do with party. Indeed, by the end of his first term the Republican consensus had been shattered and "good feelings" had vanished on the winds of change. Personal factions rose up to challenge the administration, then sundered it from within. Great issues, like the Missouri Compromise, split the nationalizing Republican party along its sectional seams. The Panic of 1819, which led to the first great depression in the country's history, released powerful political currents that shriveled the bright hopes of 1815.[4]

At the center of these events stood Henry Clay. Returning to the Fourteenth Congress, again elected Speaker, Clay embarked on the most brilliant period of his career. As in 1811, he shared the honors of eagle-pinioned nationalism with Calhoun, "the Young Hercules" from South Carolina, whose wide and magnificent views inspired both awe and dread in Congress. The third member of the trio, Daniel Webster, was also in Congress. Still a Federalist, he nevertheless worked with Calhoun on the bank bill and currency reform, and in other ways pointed a course toward political reconciliation. All three men added to their fame and raised public anticipations of an illustrious era of legislative leadership. In retrospect, it seemed they had "but to form a triumvirate and divide the world between them"; and had they done so, in succession filling the presidential chair for twenty-four years, the United

States might have enjoyed an era of national power and greatness unparalleled in ancient or modern times.[5] In 1817, however, Webster, Clay, and Calhoun went their separate ways. Clay remained in the House, where his leadership, while undeniably brilliant, was so much imbued with personal whim and ambition that it became one of the forces disrupting the unity and calm of the Monroe administration. Calhoun chose to join the administration, and as secretary of war for eight years he developed the administrative resources of nationalism, in contrast to the political-economic dimension that absorbed Clay. Webster retired from government altogether in order to secure fame and fortune at the bar. But in his practice the law was so deeply blended with public questions that he was never really retired; and in his career on the platform, as well as at the bar, Webster gave substance and form to the national ideal. "We are a young nation," one of Webster's New England contemporaries observed; "a great man easily gives us the impression of his hand; we shall harden in the fire for centuries, and keep the mark."[6] In the years after Ghent all three men laid their hand on the nation and left their mark.

1. Clay and the Disruption of Republicanism

Alone among the leading Republicans in Washington, Henry Clay declined to attend the inauguration of James Monroe. Indeed, if the press reports may be credited, the ceremony was held outdoors for the first time, before the burned-out Capitol, only because the Speaker refused to let the senators bring their elegantly velveted chairs into the makeshift House chamber furnished with ordinary wooden seats.[1] Clay's dander was up because Monroe had passed over him in favor of John Quincy Adams for the top cabinet post of secretary of state. Clay might have had the War Department, but having declined it when earlier tendered by Madison, whom he idolized, he considered it an insult coming from a respectable timeserver like Monroe. However genuine his interest in foreign affairs, Clay's zeal for the State Department was mainly political. Both Madison and Monroe had succeeded to the presidency from that post; it was becoming such a habit that upon his appointment Adams, with virtually no following in the Republican party, instantly became a contender for the first office in the land. He had just completed two years' service at the Court of St. James; he had, of course, abundant experience in the avenues of American diplomacy. He was further recommended to Monroe on political grounds. Adams's appointment gave New England prominent representation in the administration, thereby contributing to the spirit of harmony and conciliation. Although Clay was jealous of Adams, whom he had come to view as a rival at Ghent, his quarrel was not with him, nor with the political objective, but with Monroe. Clay felt that he, and the West, had a better claim. No westerner held cabinet rank in the new administration which, as usual, was dominated by southerners.

Monroe went out of his way to appease Clay, but to no avail. The arrogance that spurred his ambition was also its greatest enemy. He struggled constantly to control it, sometimes with marvelous results, though usually it was a losing battle. Congressional colleagues, while they stood in awe of his talents, bristled at his domineering manner. "His disgusting vanity and inordinate ambition were fast destroying his influence and his usefulness as a public man," wrote a Virginian who seemed to mistake pride for vanity.[2] He was not sorry to see that Clay had to fight for his political life in the Fayette district congressional election in 1816. This was the "salary grab" election, in which public outrage over a law that doubled congressional salaries retroactively caused the retirement or defeat of two-thirds of the incumbents. Clay's advocacy of the Compensation Act, together with his turnabout on the national bank, had made him vulnerable. (The new law was especially awkward for Clay who, as Speaker, received twice the pay of ordinary congressmen, hence twice the benefit from the law, increasing his salary for the two years from approximately $3,000 to $6,000.) An old political foe, John Pope, entered the field against him. Pope was still a formidable figure, despite former Federalist connections and the stigma of voting against the war. He was no match for Clay on the stump, however.* After conceding the wrong of the "salary grab," promising to work for its repeal, and offering a popular explanation for his switch on the bank, Clay went on to win reelection by a comfortable margin. Never again would he be seriously challenged in Kentucky.[3] In 1817 he returned to Congress with enhanced strength and prestige.

Clay promptly determined to test his power as a congressional leader against the Monroe administration. The focal point of his power was, of course, the speakership. Since 1811 Clay had transformed the office from that of a passive moderator to one of policy-making leadership. While Madison was president he used the speakership to rally Congress behind the administration. Now, with Monroe, he used it to raise opposition. Clay's popularity in the office was about the only thing that could be taken for granted in American politics. Elected Speaker six different times, always on the first ballot, he was never really contested, and only handfuls of votes were cast against him. When he resigned in 1820, twenty-two ballots were required to elect a successor; yet when he returned in 1823, despite his presidential candidacy, Clay was reelected Speaker by a first-ballot vote of 139 to 42. Obviously he would not have been so popular had he been guided by merely personal or partisan motives. Although sometimes accused of mounting an "odious tyranny" or of manipulating the rules to secure personal objectives, Clay was much more often praised for his firmness and impartiality. Men might differ on his qualifications for the presidency, said the *National Intelligencer* in 1823, "but all will

*In his defense Clay told the story of encountering an old hunter who had always before voted for him but was now opposed because of the Compensation Act. "Have you a good rifle, my friend?" asked Clay. "Yes." "Does it ever flash?" "Once only," the hunter replied. "What did you do with it—throw it away?" "No, I picked the flint, tried it again, and brought down the game." "Have I ever flashed but upon the compensation bill?" Clay demanded. "No." "Will you throw me away?" "No, no!" the hunter exclaimed. "I will pick the flint and try you again!" No anecdote about Clay was told as often as this one.

acknowledge that, as *Speaker,* no one ever did, and it is hardly expected that any one ever will, more ably or more 'impartially' perform the arduous duties of the statesman."[4]

To an extent, certainly, the duties of the speakership disarmed Clay as a party leader and presidential aspirant. But they did not prevent him from using the influence and prestige of the position to shape policy in the House and opinion in the country. As Speaker he appointed all committees, including chairmen; he set the tone and temper of the House, enforced the rules, and governed the flow of business; by making the committee of the whole the principal forum of debate, he ensured an active role for himself, further secured by his unprecedented claim to vote, as well as to speak, as an ordinary member. Because of the dearth of experienced leadership in the House (in the Fifteenth Congress only six of 184 members had served ten years or longer), Clay's authority, eloquence, and deportment—patience without anger, decision without dogmatism, power mixed with amiability—were immensely important. It is too much to say, as the historian of the speakership has said, that Clay was the most powerful man in the United States between 1811 and 1825; but he, more than anyone, was responsible for the rising reputation of the lower house and for filling the leadership vacuum left by waning presidential influence. "The House of Representatives," Justice Joseph Story observed, "has absorbed all the popular feeling and all the effective power of the country."[5] Opposing the Monroe administration, Clay undertook in 1817 to center policy-making in the lower house under his command.[6]

Clay opposed the Monroe administration on almost everything, but the dominant issue was Latin American independence. The colonies of the southern hemisphere had broken the shackles of oppression after the collapse of the Spanish empire during the Napoleonic wars. They refused to put them on again during the restoration, and revolt swept the continent from Caracas to Buenos Aires. The rebels took advantage of loopholes in American neutrality laws to obtain arms—especially armed ships—from the United States. Early in 1816 the Madison administration, responding to official Spanish protests, sought to close the loopholes. Clay strenuously objected, partly on the grounds of infringement of the liberties of American citizens but mainly in the name of Latin American independence. Congress nevertheless enacted the bill for enforcing neutrality. Clay labeled it "an act for the benefit of his majesty the king of Spain," and set out to overturn it.[7] He had, therefore, staked out his position on this matter at least a year before Monroe became president. By then the Latin American revolutionaries, with their friends and agents, looked upon Clay as the leading spokesman of their cause in the United States.

Months before the new Congress convened in temporary quarters on Capitol Hill, in November 1817, it was well understood that Clay "considered himself pledged" to move for a "friendly" American neutrality and official recognition of the new Latin American republics. He had, said William H. Crawford, the secretary of treasury, announced his determination to force this issue, which rightly belonged to the executive, upon Congress.[8] The only question in dispute concerned Clay's motive. Crawford traced it to dissatisfaction over Adams's appointment, and supposed that by connecting his popularity with the revolutionary cause Clay hoped to raise up a new party.[9] Adams held the same opinion even more strongly. He asserted that the quixotic Kentuckian mounted his "South American great horse" and rode forth to attain the presidency on the ruins of the administration. Since Ghent, Clay had marked Adams as "the principal rival in his way," and so made a foreign affairs issue "the apple of discord."[10] Adams, for his part, hoped to immortalize his ministry by diplomatic triumph in Spanish affairs, including the acquisition of Florida, which was jeopardized by Clay's Latin American policy. In the view of the secretary of state, and of the administration, Clay cared very little for Latin American independence and was simply using it as a political hobby.

It would be naive to suppose Clay was innocent of political or personal motives, but no one who reads his many speeches or surveys the whole ground can doubt the republican idealism that inspired him. He was, again, committed to the Latin American cause before Monroe's election or Adams's appointment. Moreover, the fact that he chose this political vehicle, if that is what it was, rather than another attests to his values and goals. Monroe had hoped to take the wind out of Clay's sails before Congress met by the appointment of a fact-finding commission to Buenos Aires, seat of the United Provinces of Rio de la Plata, the most secure of the new republics. But Clay plunged ahead, trying first to overturn the unfriendly neutrality bill of the previous session, then, in March, proposing to appropriate funds to send a minister to the United Provinces. This would be tantamount to recognition. In these matters decisions had always been left to the executive. Clay conceded the point but archly observed that a congressional appropriation for a foreign envoy, even if unasked and unwanted, was no intrusion on executive prerogative.

"We behold," said Clay in the major speech on his motion, "the glorious spectacle of eighteen millions of people, struggling to burst their chains and to be free."[11] He argued that the United Provinces, like all the rebellious colonies, were struggling not only for independence but for liberty and self-government on the American model. The Latin American revolutions were a continuation of the American Revolution; indeed, after the return of despotism in Europe, they offered the last great hope of liberty outside the United States. There was rampant skepticism on this point. Adams, for instance, dismissed the whole affair as a tragicomedy of hapless desperadoes. He thought that the Latin Americans, for centuries sunk in ignorance and superstition and oppression, were incapable of self-government.[12] Clay, preferring to act on hope, viewed independence as the necessary first step on the road to free government and took delight in pointing out that in at least one respect, slavery emancipation, most of the Latin American republics were in advance of the United States. Because American principles were at stake in the contest, Clay said, the country had a responsibility, transcending all selfish and timid motives, to assist the revolutionaries. Whatever doubts could be entertained about them, none could be entertained about their oppressors, "the combination of despots" in the European Holy Alliance. Clay had not only "sniffed the carnage at Waterloo," as he remarked upon his return from Europe, clutching the sword as a result; he had also, it now seemed, "lit a torch there."[13] One reason why the government ought to declare itself on behalf of Latin American independence, he always insisted, was "that it would give additional tone, and hope, and confidence, to the friends of liberty throughout the world."[14]

American interests followed the march of American principles, Clay maintained. The Manifesto of the United Provinces made the same claim to liberty as the Declaration of Independence. "I would not disturb the repose even of a detestable depotism," Clay said. "But, if an abused and oppressed people will their freedom; if they seek to establish it; if, in truth, they have established it; we have a right, as a sovereign power, to notice the fact, and to act as circumstances and our interest require."[15] No one could deny that the commerce and navigation of Latin America, which Britain coveted, was an important American interest. By acting boldly the government might create a hemispheric commercial system with the United States, rather than Britain, at the center. While Clay preached protectionism against Europe, he preached free trade and reciprocity in the Western Hemisphere, where the United States could exploit its economic superiority. But Clay went further, envisioning a New World system outside the vortex of European politics and under the leadership of the United States. He elaborated this idea of an "American system"—"a sort of counterpoise of the Holy Alliance"—over the next several years. "We should become the center of a system which would constitute the rallying point of human freedom against the despotism of the Old World," he declared in 1820.[16] The system would operate, not by military force, but by "the force of example." Clay insisted on the peacefulness of his policy. Far from violating neutrality, it would tend to equalize the workings of neutrality in a situation where one of the parties was powerfully represented in the United States and the other not even recognized. He dismissed any dangerous repercussions from American intervention, since Spain and her allies had their hands full in Europe. There was no novelty in the country's recognition of *de facto* regimes substantially representative of the people; it had acted on this rule since its recognition of the French republic in 1792. Indeed, the rule followed inevitably from the right of revolution upon which American independence was founded. "Are we not bound, then, upon our own principles, to acknowledge this new republic?" Clay asked. "If we do not, who will? Are we to expect that kings will set us the example of acknowledging the only republic on earth, except our own?"[17] The moral influence of diplomatic recognition would be incalculable, he thought. Administration spokesmen, answering Clay, shared neither his enthusiasm for the Latin American revolutions nor his confidence that the United States could defy Spain with impunity. The proposal to fund a minister to Buenos Aires was soundly defeated, 113–43.

It was a calculated loss. Latin American independence was not a popular issue in 1818, as Clay appreciated. Most congressmen—probably most of the

Henry Clay, Speaker of the House. Painting by Matthew Harris Jouett. *Courtesy of the Henry Clay Memorial Foundation*

Daniel Webster, New Hampshire Congressman. Painting by Charles Bird King. *Courtesy of the Redwood Library and Athenaeum*

John C. Calhoun, Secretary of War. Painting by Charles Bird King. *Courtesy of the Redwood Library and Athenaeum*

Clay and Latin American Independence. Engraving by Peter Maverick, after painting by Charles Bird King. *Courtesy of the National Portrait Gallery, Smithsonian Institution*

Webster at Forty-five Years of Age. Miniature by Sarah Goodridge. *Courtesy of the Massachusetts Historical Society*

Calhoun while Vice President. Painting by Chester Harding. *Courtesy of the University of North Carolina at Chapel Hill*

Signature Pages of Letters Written by Clay, Calhoun, and Webster. *Courtesy of the University of Virginia Library*

American people—approved the cautious policy of the Monroe administration. Clay hoped not for immediate recognition but, rather, to arouse public opinion and gradually force a change of policy. Here he had some success. In Fourth of July celebrations throughout the country in 1818, Americans toasted Latin American independence. Clay was acclaimed, as at Cincinnati, "the independent and enlightened statesman, and the eloquent defender of South American liberty and the best interests of our country."[18] Still, Clay was hurt by the attack on his motives. In speeches and public letters he repeatedly denied any personal or factious ambition, any hostility to the president, any jealousy of his first secretary. "I had rather have my present station than any appointment in the gift of any executive under heaven," he declared. "I court no favors."[19] Returning to Congress for the short session in the fall, Clay seemed quite subdued. "He appears rather downcast and as if he regretted his premature measure at the last session," one legislator observed.[20] Clay expressed renewed astonishment at the administration's coldness and timidity toward the Latin American countries. All the evidence, including the reports of at least two of the president's own commissioners, pointed to the rout of the Spanish and the establishment of secure republican governments. Clay refrained, however, from resubmitting the proposal that looked to the recognition of the United Provinces. The announcement in February of the long-awaited treaty with Spain reinforced the decision. The Spanish minister, Don Luis de Onís, had signed the treaty with the tacit understanding that the United States would go slow in Latin America. Clay felt that Adams had conceded too much to Spain; he had obtained Florida but given up the greater prize, Texas, in which the West was much more interested. Nevertheless, to endanger approval of the treaty in Madrid by rash actions toward Latin America was a responsibility too great even for the ardent spirit of Henry Clay.

In the same session Clay suffered a stinging defeat at the hands of the administration in the celebrated case of Andrew Jackson and the Seminole Campaign in Florida. Indian troubles along the Florida border had long been a sore point in American relations with Spain. General Jackson, who in 1814 had vanquished the Creeks in the Battle of Horseshoe Bend, was ordered in 1818 to pursue the hostile Seminoles to the outer limits of the Spanish posts in Florida. But Jackson, whether by design, confusion, or misunderstanding, exceeded his orders. He marched his troops to the forts at Pensacola and St. Marks, executed two British traders among the Indians, Alexander Arbuthnot and Robert Ambrister, and proceeded to establish military control of the province which the secretary of state, in Washington, was negotiating to buy from Spain. Monroe laid the matter before Congress. The House Committee on Military Affairs returned a majority report condemning Jackson's behavior. In the course of debate, Clay proposed to censure the general, and he lit up the House in a blaze of eloquence on January 20.

This was the first of the great oratorical displays in the capital that captivated the age. Clay's speech, in which he became Jackson's accuser, was billed in advance. The Senate adjourned to hear him; strangers, foreign min-

isters, and fashionable ladies crowded into the chamber.[21] Clay traced the
cause of recent Indian troubles to the humiliating treaty of Fort Jackson, imposed on the Creeks by the victorious general in 1814; he denounced Jackson for conducting unauthorized war on Spain and for the brutal murder of
two British subjects; closing, he warned the nation against the dangers of a
new Caesar. This was no mere affair of an errant general in Florida—it struck
at the hopes of mankind in the American republic.

> We are fighting a great moral battle, for the benefit, not only of our country,
> but of all mankind. The eyes of the world are in fixed attention upon us.
> One, and the largest portion of it, is gazing with contempt, with jealousy,
> and with envy; the other portion, with hope, with confidence, and with affec-
> tion. Everywhere the black cloud of legitimacy is suspended over the world,
> save only one bright spot, which breaks out from the political hemisphere of
> the west, to enlighten, and animate, and gladden the human heart. Obscure
> that, by the downfall of liberty here, and all mankind are enshrouded in the
> pall of universal darkness. . . . Beware how you give a fatal sanction, in this
> infant period of our republic, scarcely yet two-score years old, to military in-
> subordination. Remember that Greece had her Alexander, Rome her Cae-
> sar, England her Cromwell, France her Bonaparte, and that if we would es-
> cape the rock on which they split, we must avoid their errors.[22]

Clay was acclaimed for argument and eloquence rarely surpassed, not even
by Burke and Sheridan in the famous trial of Warren Hastings, whose
crimes, some said, were no worse than Jackson's. Scarcely anyone questioned the patriotism of Clay's motives; even his enemies praised his moral
courage.[23] Monroe and every member of his cabinet except Adams condemned Jackson in council, yet sustained him before Congress, the country,
and the world. Clay's warning, his call for censure, went unheeded. Jackson
would never forgive him. He arrived in Washington the day after the
speech. Clay promptly called on him, explained he had meant nothing personal, and trusted their friendly relations would continue. Jackson was astounded by this aplomb. Nothing personal indeed. Clay had ascribed to him
the ambitions of Caesar. He had maliciously twisted the facts of the Pensacola campaign in order to drag the general into his private war on the administration. "[A] man who would exalt himself upon his country's ruin ought to
fall never to rise again," Jackson said.[24] Needless to say, he did not return
Clay's call.

When the new Congress convened in December 1819, the president sent
notice that Ferdinand VII refused to ratify the Adams-Onís Treaty until the
United States agreed not to recognize the rebel governments in Latin America. (Jackson's invasion of Florida was no longer a problem, since the forts
had been returned to Spain.) Clay took the setback as proof of the bankruptcy of the administration's Spanish policy. In April, after the president
begged Congress to desist from any action that might further upset diplomacy in Madrid, Clay proposed that the United States abandon the treaty
and start over. Instead of arguing strict neutrality toward the Latin American
republics in order to get a treaty with the mother country, which was the ad-

ministration policy, the United States ought to appeal to Spain's fears by recognition of the republics. The treaty, by sacrificing Texas, long claimed as part of the Louisiana Purchase, was a bad bargain in any event. Congress listened to Clay but acquiesced in administration policy. The next month, again pleading for recognition, he offered a cut-rate version of the old resolution that declared it was expedient to send ministers to the countries that had established their independence of Spain but omitted appropriation for salaries and outfits. The House, surprisingly, passed the resolution by a margin of five votes. Clay was elated. But it proved, as has been said, "a barren triumph."[25] At the short session—Clay's last before going into retirement—he attempted once more to force recognition, ministers, salaries, and outfits on the administration. Monroe's failure to act on the House's deliberate expression of opinion was more in keeping with a European monarch than an American president, he said. Again, he met with defeat. In February 1821, while he was laboring to resolve the Missouri crisis, the House voted a second empty resolution in support of recognition. It was immediately followed by news of Spain's ratification of the treaty, which took the last wind out of Clay's sails. Adams noted in his diary that three of the only four dissenting votes on the Senate's second ratification of the treaty were cast by Clay's bosom friends. The secretary gloated over the treaty. It ended the Clayites' "snickering at the simplicity with which I had been bamboozled by the crafty Spaniard."[26] Making the best of it, Clay had a long conciliatory talk with Adams before going into retirement in Lexington.

In retirement, Clay continued to be the paramount American voice of the Latin American patriots. At a public dinner in his honor at Lexington, he again advocated a hemispheric "American system" as "a rallying-point and an asylum . . . for freemen and freedom" around the globe.[27] Adams answered him in a Fourth of July address in Washington. America was the friend of freedom and independence, he acknowledged. "But she goes not abroad in search of monsters to destroy. She is the well-wisher to the freedom and independence of all. She is the champion and vindicator only of her own."[28] The address was widely criticized as jingoistic. Clay said it confirmed his opinion of Adams's "total want of judgment and discretion." The secretary's intentions were quite different. He said he meant the address as a reply "both to Edinburgh and to Lexington," that is, to the writers in the Edinburgh Review who wished the United States to take an active part in the political reformation of Europe, and to Henry Clay who wished the United States to intervene in Latin America.[29] Actually, Clay had never advocated intervention; indeed the two men were united on the principle of liberty everywhere but intervention nowhere.

At last, on March 8, 1822, seven years after Clay launched his campaign, President Monroe declared the time had come to recognize the Latin American republics and called upon Congress to vote the necessary funds. Clay, of course, was not in the House to claim credit for this volte-face. Had he been, knowing politicians suspected, it would not have occurred. His friends claimed it for him. When the recognition resolution passed with only one dissenting vote, it was hailed as Clay's "monument of imperishable fame—a monument as broad as the continent whose cause he advocated, as high as the towering Andes."[30] Whether recognition finally came because of Clay or in spite of him is an interesting question. Calhoun, no more generous toward Clay than his colleague at the state department, exclaimed upon Monroe's message, "Yes! The fruit has now become ripe and may be safely plucked." He was reminded of the story of a cantankerous farmer who insisted his neighbors sow their grain in January; they said it was too early, but he persisted month after month; in the spring, at the proper time, the neighbors sowed, and soon had a bumper crop; and the cantankerous farmer claimed all the credit because he had been the first to tell them to sow.[31] The point was well made. There were good reasons for recognizing Latin American independence in 1822—and the United States was the first nation to do so—that were absent six or three years earlier. But timing was not everything. Sowing the seed, Clay prepared the way for recognition; and the champion of a great cause ought not be denied the laurels of victory by prudent statesmen who may become its executors.

In the longer perspective of history, Clay's advocacy of this cause had a profound influence. First, as to his American fame. The earliest widely known likeness of Clay was an engraving by Peter Maverick, published in May 1822, in celebration of the recognition of Latin American independence. Clay is represented holding in his hand a scroll upon which the independence resolution is written.[32] It would generally be remembered as the most gallant chapter of the statesman's life. Second, as to Latin America. Clay's speeches, which were translated into Spanish, his friendly counsel to agents and others laboring in the cause, his impact on opinion not only in America but abroad, lifted the hopes of the revolutionary patriots. Several years after these events, when Clay had become secretary of state, Simon Bolivar, the Liberator, wrote a moving tribute of gratitude: "All America, Columbia, and myself, owe your excellency our purest gratitude for the incomparable services you have rendered to us, by sustaining our course with a sublime enthusiasm."[33] On the one hundred and fiftieth anniversary of Clay's birth, although it passed virtually unnoticed by the American people, the diplomatic chiefs of twenty Latin American republics assembled in Washington to pay homage to Clay, both as the champion of liberty and independence and as the prophet of Pan-American union.[34] Venezuela raised a statue of Clay in Caracas. Third, as to the United States, particularly its foreign policy. Clay's "American system"—"a sort of counterpoise of the Holy Alliance"—was one of a congeries of ideas and sentiments and interests that led to the proclamation of the Monroe Doctrine in 1823. In a celebrated speech George Canning, the British foreign minister, declared that *he* himself "called the New World into existence to redress the balance of the Old."[35] In fact, little credit belonged to Canning, or to the British government. Richard Rush, the United States minister to Great Britain when Canning finally decided for recognition in 1824, observed that, on the contrary, it was Clay who "called the

New World into existence." "This is truth: this is history."[36] Clay never made the boast, but it was certainly part of the truth and would not be forgotten.

If Clay created division and discord with his Latin American policy, he won an enviable reputation for conciliation and union because of his leadership in behalf of the Missouri Compromise. The admission of Missouri to the Union became an issue in February 1819, when Representative James Tallmadge, Jr., of New York, proposed a two-part amendment to the enabling legislation. The further introduction of slaves into Missouri was prohibited and all slaves henceforth born in the state would be emancipated at the age of twenty-five. The amendment started a political storm. It raised serious questions about the constitutional authority of Congress, the nature of the Union, the future of the West, the morality of slavery, and the sectional balance of power. From the first many southerners felt that Tallmadge and his supporters at the North were less interested in freedom for the slaves than in hoisting a popular banner under which they might march back into political power. The fact that Rufus King, the former Federalist presidential candidate, now a New York senator, was the most prominent advocate of the Missouri restriction lent credence to suspicions of a political plot. King had a reputation for opposition to western growth and development. Further, as a member of the Federal Convention in 1787 he had opposed adoption of the three-fifths clause of the Constitution, and with many of his northern friends he still groaned under this compromise that gave slaveholders 60 percent more political representation than non-slaveholders. Missouri was the first portion, after Louisiana, of the vast Trans-Mississippi territory to seek admission to the Union. By checking the expansion of slavery there, the North could substantially control the destiny of this great heartland, as it had already done in the Northwest above the Ohio River.

No politician could regard the Missouri Question as simply a moral issue. Clay did not. His own anti-slavery principles enabled him to appreciate the higher motives of the restrictionists, however. As a personal matter, he told the restrictionists, he not only opposed slavery in Missouri but would be willing for Congress to confer freedom on any slave henceforth imported into the new state provided there was authority to enforce the decree. The Constitution gave no such authority. Under the Constitution the decision between slavery and no slavery belonged exclusively to the people of Missouri. Congress could not intervene. Attempting to do so would only array section against section, state against state, jeopardizing the peace and harmony of the Union.[37]

The Tallmadge amendment passed the House but failed in the Senate; in the ensuing deadlock, the enabling bill was lost and the Missouri Question was referred to the country. In northern cities the movement for restriction bore the character of an organized campaign, adding fuel to southern suspicions of a plot "for the erection of a northern party, the triumph of Federalism, or the separation of the Union." Suspicions were further aroused by the publication at this time of a detailed defense of the Hartford Convention from the pen of Harrison Gray Otis, the putative father of that notorious assemblage. Daniel Webster was associated with the northern movement and may have written the influential Boston Memorial, which adopted King's views on the constitutionality as well as on the justice of restriction.[38]

The Sixteenth Congress convened in a state of anxiety over Missouri. "It is a most unhappy question, awakening sectional feelings, and exasperating them to the highest degree," Clay reported. "The words, civil war, and disunion, are uttered almost without emotion."[39] The grandeur of the new House chamber, occupied for the first time, enhanced the dignity of the occasion. The great domed semi-circular hall—modeled on a Greek theater—with its twenty-six massive columns of Potomac marble and white Corinthian capitals, was elegantly finished throughout. Over the entrance was the allegorical figure of History, poised in a winged chariot, recording the proceedings of the nation. Over the Speaker's chair, from which Clay gazed at the moving hand of History, rose a colossal statue of Liberty, supported on one side by an American eagle and on the other by Roman fasces in the coil of a serpent.[40] Clay had acted with the South against restriction in the previous session. Now, without abandoning his opposition, he decided to throw his influence, and the influence of the speakership, behind conciliation and compromise.[41] On this question there was no executive leadership; it was legislative altogether, and if leadership was to come from anyone it would have to come from Clay. Fortuitously, the people of Maine, heretofore a district under Massachusetts jurisdiction, petitioned Congress for admission to the Union as a state. Clay hastened committee action on a Maine enabling bill and when it reached the floor declared that its fate depended on the unconditional admission of Missouri. He cited the analogous case of Vermont and Kentucky, the first two states, one free, one slave, admitted to the Union under the Constitution. Because of the preponderate restrictionism of the House, Clay made no attempt to join Maine with Missouri there, but predicted they would be joined, irrevocably, in the Senate. And so they were.

Clay made his major speech against the Missouri restriction on February 8. Unfortunately, like every other speech he made on this question, it was not reported. Careless of fame, Clay never wrote out or even scribbled notes for his speeches before or after delivery, as if acknowledging the inadequacy of the printed page to convey the power of his oratory. The speeches are known to history only to the extent and in the form they were reported. And the reporting of congressional debates was notoriously erratic in 1820. This speech of February 8 was called "incomparably great" by one who heard it. It would be remembered as a masterpiece. "Everyone felt the electricity of his mind," wrote a newspaperman. "His elocution was so rapid, his argumentation so resistless, and his manner so vehement and impetuous, that I believe none were unmoved, and but few retired unconvinced." It was like "continued peals of thunder, interrupted by repeated flashes of lightning."[42] Regrettably, the orator's actions—the shrugs, contortions, scowls, foot stompings, snuff takings, and so on—were better remembered than his words, though scattered hints and allusions give some suggestion of his argument. Clay ad-

vanced the idea of the diffusion of slavery in the hope of reconciling all but
the most determined opponents of the institution to its geographical extension. The spread of slaves into fertile new lands would improve their well-
being, lighten the fears of emancipation in overcrowded southern states, and
enlist western support in efforts, like African colonization, to alleviate slavery. In the course of time, Clay theorized, the country would be well populated with whites, driving down the price of free labor, until slave labor, unable to compete, would be eliminated. Black slavery, therefore, was only a
transient phenomenon. The laws of economic development, together with
the national commitment to freedom, would gradually end it. The Union, on
the other hand, was the great permanent interest of all the people; still at
peril, it should not be risked by wanton attacks on slavery that, while they
freed no slaves, drove the sections apart. This argument founded on the idea
of diffusion was popular among liberal-minded southerners, who, like Clay,
sought to rub humanitarian balm over the problem of slavery. To the northern enemies of slavery, diffusion was a fraud. To them its proponents were
like the physician who supposed he could cure the disease by spreading the
seeds throughout the system. It would not work; and Clay's speech, for all its
power, probably changed not a single vote.

Given the stalemate between the House and the Senate, any resolution of
the question depended on maneuver and management, in which the resources of the Speaker were well known. The Senate adopted the Maine-Missouri bill on February 16. The next day it added an amendment introduced
by Illinois Senator Jesse Thomas, excluding slavery from all the Louisiana
Purchase territory above 36°30' north latitude, except for Missouri. The idea
of a geographical line between slave and free states first had been proposed
in 1819 by John W. Taylor, the New York congressman who now led the
House anti-slavery forces, in connection with a territorial government bill for
Arkansas. But it attracted no interest then, and Taylor withdrew it.[43] Now offered as an appendix to the Maine-Missouri bill, which everyone considered
"a southern measure," it was easily adopted as a sweetener for the North.
Clay welcomed passage of the compromise by the Senate, though it stood no
chance of passage in the House. The House proceeded to adopt its anti-slavery Missouri bill. The Senate declined to yield, and the matter was referred
to a conference committee stacked with conciliatory members. The deadlock
was broken, the resistance of the house crumbling, when the Senate agreed
to separate the various elements of its bill. The majority that was not available for the bill as a whole—Maine, Missouri, Thomas amendment—was
available for each of its parts. Whether or not Clay was the author of this "parliamentary *coup de main*," as the Richmond *Enquirer* called it, is unknown,
but it bore his imprint.[44]

Following House approval of the compromise, John Randolph, the eccen-
tric Virginian who thrived on discord, and who opposed any congressional
meddling with slavery, moved for reconsideration. The hour was late, and
the motion was deferred to the next morning. When Randolph rose at the appointed time, the Speaker ruled him out of order and proceeded with the

usual business of routine petitions; that done, Randolph again rose to make his motion only to be told by Clay that the bill had been signed and dispatched to the Senate and could not be retrieved. The Virginian was outraged. He had been badly treated by Clay before, but never so arrogantly. Cheated of his right to move a reconsideration, Randolph pleaded with the House to overrule the Speaker. Before this motion could be voted on, the clerk returned from the Senate with the enacted bill. Reconsideration would probably have changed nothing, but Clay would not risk it; more important, he could not allow Randolph to control the business of the House. One of Clay's biographers, Carl Schurz, who knew whereof he spoke, said of his action, "The history of the House probably records no sharper trick."[45]

The Missouri bill became law with the president's signature on March 6. Monroe had kept his silence. The cabinet, to whom he referred the bill for opinion, was divided on the question whether the prohibition of slavery in the *territory* above 36°30' could be extended to *states* upon their admission to the Union; but all agreed on the constitutionality of the territorial bar and approved the compromise. Calhoun approved because, like Clay, he thought the compromise would bank the sectional fires started by the Missouri Question and permit the country to return to the work of consolidation and improvement. The Boston Memorial, which undoubtedly expressed Webster's opinion, held that Congress was constitutionally empowered to exclude slavery in new states. Whether or not he approved of the 36°30' line is unclear. But as finally enacted, the Missouri Compromise in no way damaged the Constitution, always a key point with Webster, and could be interpreted as a partial vindication of anti-slavery principles.[46]

The danger was not over. Maine was admitted to the Union without further incident. The Missouri constitution, drafted during the summer, however, contained a provision to exclude "free negroes and mulattoes" from the state. And this furnished a handle for the renewal of opposition of Missouri as a slave state. A fundamental condition of the enabling act was that nothing in the proposed constitution should be repugnant to the Constitution of the United States. Among the latter's provisions was the following: "The Citizens of each State shall be entitled to all the Privileges and Immunities of the Citizens of the several States" (Article IV, Section 2). In the northern states free Negroes were commonly citizens, and so, it was argued, could not be deprived of citizenship if they went to Missouri. Immediately, a mighty chorus demanded that Congress bar the admission of Missouri, which, of course, would unravel the compromise.

Clay, as earlier noted, had resigned as Speaker. The division in the House on a successor was sharpened by the Missouri crisis. The election of Taylor, co-parent of the restriction resolution, over William Lowndes, the southern candidate, was the opening round of the renewed contest. When Clay finally arrived on the scene the middle of January, he found the House wandering without a thread in the labyrinth Missouri had become. The Senate had adopted a resolution approving statehood with the proviso—named "the Pontius Pilate proviso" by the historian of the compromise[47]—that it should not be construed as the assent of Congress to any provision of the Missouri constitution supposed to violate Article IV, Section 2 of the United States Constitution. In the House a select committee headed by Lowndes took the position that Missouri was already a sovereign and independent state; accordingly, no condition could be attached to her admission to the Union, and if anything in her constitution violated the supreme law of the land the courts would declare it void. But the House had firmly rejected the Lowndes resolution. Since then it had tried every possible avenue and alley to resolve the moral and constitutional difficulties presented by the Missouri constitution. Fervent restrictionists proposed to deny admission and let Missouri remain a territory. But would she then be a territory or an independent state? Moderates proposed to admit Missouri on condition that the offensive clause in the constitution be expunged. But how would Congress enforce the condition? From the other side could be heard threats of disunion if Missouri was rejected, and there was talk of repealing the eighth section of the compromise act fixing the status of slavery in the Trans-Mississippi West. "Unhappy subject!" Clay exclaimed. "Every attempt to settle it has yet failed." The issue was the most stubborn he had ever faced. Never, he thought, were the consequences of failure greater.[48]

Talking to congressmen in search of a consensus, Clay found among those who had voted against Missouri's admission a number who were in agony about disunion. These he made the point of operations. William Plumer, Jr., an anxious New Englander, said that Clay had assumed a new character. "He uses no threats, or abuse—but all is mild, humble, and persuasive—he begs, instructs, adjures, supplicates, and beseeches us to have mercy on the people of Missouri."[49] On January 29 Clay moved acceptance of the Senate resolution. Without expecting passage, he hoped the motion would furnish an opening to a negotiated settlement of the crisis. He declared his support of the Senate measure and seemed untroubled by its shameless evasion of the rights of black citizens. But Clay was interested in preserving the Union, not in securing the rights of rare free blacks in Missouri. The latter struck him as a spurious cause in any event, since there were few places in the United States, north or south, east or west, where free blacks actually enjoyed the privileges and immunities of white citizens. Any solution was worthy that would end in Missouri's admission to the Union. Desperately searching for a solution more palatable than Clay's, the House took up five substitutes by five different movers, and rejected them one by one. Finally, early in February, believing the opportune moment had arrived, Clay moved to refer his (and the Senate's) resolution to a special committee of thirteen. The Speaker appointed a conciliatory committee, five (counting Clay as chairman) from slave states and eight from free states.

In the eyes of Congress, Clay alone seemed capable of achieving a settlement of the crisis. Forceful, eloquent, indefatigable, magnanimous, he pursued his object, it was said, "with a zeal which does equal honor to his heart and head, as though he desired to earn for himself, in the last days of his service in Congress, the laurel, peacefully won, which never fades."[50] After a week's labor, the committee reported. It called for Missouri's admission on the condition that the legislature never pass a law barring settlement by any description of persons who are or who may become citizens of the United States. Whenever the legislature signified its assent to the condition, the president would proclaim Missouri a state without further ado. The proposition went some way toward meeting anti-slavery objections. Neither side got what it wanted, but neither was compelled to yield its principle. Clay, leading off the debate, appealed to "that spirit of compromise which is occasionally necessary to the existence of all societies."[51] But the proposition was defeated in committee of the whole, 64–73; and when the House refused to concur, it moved to a third reading before going down to defeat, 80–83. On the next day, February 13, Clay and his friends—over Randolph's protest—successfully moved for reconsideration. Clay spoke for one hour, making a majestic appeal for conciliation thought by one observer worth all of Burke, Pitt, Fox, and Sheridan.[52] Again he was defeated.

The next day the question took another turn as Congress met in joint session to count the electoral votes for president and vice president. Three Missouri electors had voted. Their votes alone would have no bearing on the outcome. But should they be counted? Yes, said those congressmen, mainly southerners and westerners, who believed Missouri was already a state. No, said those who were still fighting Missouri's admission to the Union. Clay offered an ingenious solution that avoided the nettle of Missouri's status: let the electoral vote be counted with Missouri and counted without Missouri, and the announcement made that, in either event, A and B are elected. Randolph vehemently objected. Congress had no authority to tamper with the electoral college. He was right, of course, but being right was no solution. Congress adopted Clay's rule, and though there was some mishap in the execution, James Monroe and Daniel D. Tompkins were declared elected by two different votes amid tumultous cries of "Order! Order!"[53]

A fresh initiative was necessary to resolve the crisis over Missouri. On February 22 Clay moved the appointment of a special committee to meet jointly with a corresponding Senate committee and to report on the expediency of providing for admission of the new state. The motion passed easily. Clay called, further, for this committee of twenty-three to be elected, which was unprecedented in the House. He sought in this way to obtain a committee of the most respected and influential members. Seventeen were elected on the first ballot, and Clay was allowed to name the others from the list of nominees. The so-called "joint committee," elected on Friday, February 23, met on Saturday and again on Sunday. The chairman converted several members to his views. The committee, while not unanimous, agreed overwhelmingly to a slightly modified version of his resolution for conditional admission. Before adjourning, he exacted a pledge from every member of the majority to stand by the resolution. And in order that no time be lost, he undertook to have the resolution printed overnight and laid on the representatives' desks without the usual order of the House. "It was Sunday evening," Clay later recalled, "and he had now to take a walk of three miles to dine with the Russian minister . . . , and never, no never did he move with more buoyant step . . . than on that occasion."[54] The next morning Clay reported to the House. The resolution passed through all the forms in record time and was approved on the same day, 87–81.[55] Most southerners were unhappy with this second compromise; in the end, however, only one, Randolph of Roanoke, voted against it. Eighteen northern votes—none from the Northwest—were cast for it. In June, almost four months later, the Missouri legislature accepted the "fundamental condition" for admission, insisting at the same time that Congress had no right to bind the state. The pledge was equivocal, but Monroe accepted it; and the twenty-fourth state entered the Union.

Clay was lavishly praised for the Second Missouri Compromise. "No other man could have effected it," it was commonly said. The Kentucky congressman was "a second Washington," "the savior of his country," and in the accolade of Thomas Hart Benton of Missouri, "the *Pacificator* of ten millions of Brothers."[56] In the future Clay would be extolled as the author of the first Missouri Compromise, a title he did not deserve, as he was quick to acknowledge, but forgotten for the second, which was itself soon forgotten, though it resolved an even more perilous crisis of the Union.[57] As a westerner, and as a nationalist whose legislative program required sectional balance and harmony, Clay was deeply interested in cutting the Gordian knot of the Missouri constitution. His sleight-of-hand solution, upholding the supremacy of the federal Constitution in the face of the Missouri provision that flagrantly violated it, surrendered moral and legal niceties to the imperatives of the Union. The "fundamental condition" was got up to win a handful of northern votes; no one, certainly not Clay, ever imagined Congress would enforce it. Missouri acquiesced, however, sparing Congress the embarrassment. Clay could not fairly be accused of indifference to the fate of free blacks. He was the most prominent leader of the American Colonization Society, indeed had presided over its birth in Washington in 1816. The society (its full name was the American Society for Colonizing the Free People of Color of the United States) had its own solution to the problem and well-being of these distressed people, and Missouri was no part of it. They would be returned to "the land of their fathers."[58]

Both Missouri compromises were considered measures in the southern interest and passed into law primarily on southern votes. In the long run, however, they worked to the advantage of the North. Only one or, at most, two slave states could be carved from the territory south of the compromise line, while many free states could, and would, enter the Union from the great domain to the north. The South accepted a bad bargain because slavery was on the defensive, and it could hope for no better. Some congressmen, too, may have acted under the delusion, still prevalent, that the northern territory was a "great desert" destined to remain barren for generations to come. While the South lived to regret the compromise, and the North came to cherish it, the whole Union was relieved in 1820–21 by the legal determination of the fate of slavery in every inch of territory owned by the United States. No repetition of the Missouri crisis could occur. To that extent, certainly, the two Missouri compromises contributed to the peace and harmony of the Union. Yet they also disclosed divisions compromise could neither calm nor resolve and introduced slavery as an element in the balance of power. The Missouri Compromise, it has been well said, "summoned the South into being."[59] Its effect on the Republican consensus of the postwar years was devastating. To Thomas Jefferson at Monticello it was "like a fire-bell in the night," sounding "the knell of the Union." "It is hushed, indeed, for the moment. But this is a reprieve only, not a final sentence. A geographical line, once conceived and held up to the angry passions of men, will never be obliterated; and every new irritation will mark it deeper and deeper."[60] Every Republican was chastened by this prophecy from one of the last of the fathers.

Clay retired from Congress to attend to his private affairs. In the crash of personal fortunes brought on by the Panic of 1819, he found himself liable for tens of thousands of dollars as the endorser of notes of defaulting debtors. He sold some property at sacrifice prices, mortgaged other property to the hilt, worked hard, and practiced rigid economy. In 1820 he accepted the position of chief counsel of the Bank of the United States in Ohio and Kentucky. He hoped, as he told Adams upon his departure from Washington, to rebuild his once flourishing law practice with the aid of this agency, itself worth $5,000 a year, and after several years reenter Congress financially independent.[61]

The Lexington to which Clay returned had been badly damaged by the depression. The city was still the cultural capital of the West, but its population, about five thousand, grew very little after 1819, and its wealth and industry never recovered. The steamboat, a godsend to river towns like Louisville and Cincinnati, doomed Lexington's commercial ambitions. Following the path marked out earlier, Lexington businessmen invested heavily in manufacturing after the war and in 1817 formed the Kentucky Society for the Encouragement of Domestic Manufactures. Textile, paper, iron, hemp and cordage mills, some employing over a hundred workers, invaded the verdant landscape. But British policies aimed at smothering American infant manufactures, backed by Congress' rejection of higher protection in 1820, blighted these hopes as well. When the tariff bill was defeated, a Lexington newspaper bordered its pages in black: "Mourn, oh, ye sons and daughters of Kentucky . . . put on sackcloth and ashes. . . . You must still remain tributary to the workshops of Europe." Most factories closed their doors. Only one cotton-bagging plant survived in 1820.[62]

Many westerners impulsively blamed the panic and the depression, with all their woeful effects, on the Bank of the United States. Local banks fell and their paper became worthless because of pressure from the B.U.S. and its branches. One failure led to another until a whole society was caught in a whirl of bankruptcy. "The Monster" gobbled up what was left. Everybody—farmers, merchants, bankers—was in debt to it; none seemed able to gratify its voracious appetite. As chief counsel for the B.U.S. in the Ohio valley Clay would not win any popularity contests. He appeared as the Bank's Shylock, heartlessly preying upon poor, innocent debtors. The business was very large. In February 1821, for instance, he had about four hundred suits on the dockets of the federal courts in the two states; they involved debts of nearly $2 million to the B.U.S. By such suits, the Bank acquired a large portion of the property of Cincinnati and some fifty thousand acres of prize farmland in Ohio and Kentucky.[63] All these suits, it was commonly said, had been brought on Clay's advice and counsel. The hapless debtors, one Cincinnatian wrote, "would seem justified, whenever in their power, to remunerate the author of this mischief with a coat of Tar and Feathers."[64]

Clay was also retained in the celebrated case of *Osborn v. the Bank of the United States*. Ohio had levied a prohibitive tax on the resident branches of the B.U.S.; when it refused to pay, the state auditor, Osborn, seized $100,000 of the Bank's funds and locked them in a vault. Lawyers from all over Ohio descended on the capital at Columbus to hear Clay argue the case. He lost the initial round, but prevailed in the federal circuit court, then successfully reargued the case on appeal before the United States Supreme Court.[65] Like the court's earlier decision in *McCulloch v. Maryland*, the ruling in the Osborn case was an important victory for national over state authority.

The Kentuckian appeared often before the Supreme Court during these years, usually but not always as counsel for the B.U.S. He was retained by the state to defend its Occupying Claimants' Law—a legacy of Kentucky's chaotic land system—which gave color of title to squatters after seven years' occupancy and improvement of lands. In 1821 the Supreme Court ruled unanimously that the law, which dated from the 1790s, violated Kentucky's compact with Virginia at the time of separation as well as the contract clause of the Constitution. The decision threw into question titles to one-third of the lands in the state. Appointed one of two commissioners to work out a settlement with Virginia, Clay accomplished this in 1822, only to see the Virginia legislature reject the agreement. He then reargued the Kentucky cause, *Green v. Biddle*, before the Supreme Court, but without success. Justice Story, although he strongly opposed the Kentucky law, was impressed by Clay. Did he not prefer the fame of popular talents, Story remarked, "he might attain great eminence at the Bar."[66]

Clay's association with the B.U.S. identified him ever more closely with the Bluegrass aristocracy of the state. Economic discontent widened into severe political conflict in the 1820s, and Clay for the first time faced rampant popular opposition that viewed banks and courts as symbols of oppression. He disputed the popular analysis that traced western hardships to the B.U.S. It was only a collector of western debts owed to eastern merchants and the general government; and in performing this service it put wholesome restraints on state banks. "It has been badly administered," Clay conceded. "But shall we give up the Ship because the crew have misbehaved?" The Bank had, in fact, become indispensable to the economic health of the country. The problem of the West was not the Bank but the section's debtor status.[67] And the cure for that was a more dynamic national economy driven by domestic manufactures. When Clay returned to Congress in 1823, having rid himself of most of his debts, plans for economic growth and development headed his legislative agenda.

2. *The American System*

Almost from his entrance into Congress, Henry Clay was an advocate of national policies of economic development. They were grounded initially in western needs and interests, but the war exposed the larger interest of the nation in internal development and made it a mission of patriotism. After the war these policies were embodied in the Madisonian Platform, which might as well have been named the Clay and Calhoun Platform, for they were its movers and shapers in Congress. The Panic of 1819, the depression and demoralization it produced, turned some Americans, particularly in the South, away from the economic nationalism of the postwar years; for Clay and his followers, on the other hand, these events simply showed that the government had not gone far enough. Upon returning to Congress, he placed himself at the head of a growing movement which combined specific national policies— protective tariff, internal improvements, national bank, and so on—into an integrated system of political economy. In the Eighteenth Congress' great debate on the tariff, Clay baptized it "the American System." And "Father of the American System" became his political motto as well as his principal title to fame.[1]

This glossy phrase had had various usages from the American Revolution onward. For Thomas Jefferson it meant a set of political principles and interests separate and distinct from those of Europe. With the Latin American revolutions, Jefferson, Clay, and others had extended this conception to the entire hemisphere; and in this guise it was embodied in the Monroe Doctrine. Political independence and protection had its counterpart in economic independence and protection. Alexander Hamilton, dwelling in *The Federalist* on the scope and diversity of economic enterprise open to the United States, had formed the idea of "one great American system, superior to the control of all transatlantic force or influence."[2] Three years later, as secretary of treasury, Hamilton laid the cornerstone of the system in his celebrated Report on Manufactures. Hamilton's plan of industrial empire never got off the drawing board, however. His own financial system, to which he gave priority, and which depended on the revenue of imports at the customs houses, actually had the effect of increasing the country's subservience to British industry; and with the wars of the French Revolution, American enterprise embarked on the seas of trade. The country became, as Jefferson said despairingly, "a city of Amsterdam," carrying on the trade of half the world, importing its own needed goods at the cost finally of breakdown and war.

The American System was sometimes mistaken for a renascent Hamiltonian Federalism; and by association with Hamilton's political designs, it triggered old fears about the survival of the republic. But whatever its policy debt to the Hamiltonian tradition, as in the encouragement of domestic manufactures, the American System was the legitimate outcome of Jeffersonian experience at the helm of government since 1800. It was the positive counterpart of the Jeffersonian revulsion from Europe, further intensified after Ghent by monarchical restoration and reaction. It expressed a broad national movement on behalf of American character and independence, casting off the trammels of the mind as well as the trammels of industry. Politically, as Jefferson had predicted, the Republicans had *become* the nation, and so could be inspired more by their hopes than by their fears of governmental power. Jefferson himself, who had once thought to keep American workshops in Europe, called for placing the manufacturer beside the cultivator and looked to a balanced national economy of agriculture, commerce, and manufactures.[3] It never occurred to Clay, or to Calhoun and many other Republicans, that in advocating an enlarged role for the government in the promotion of economic development he was surrendering Jeffersonian principles for Hamiltonian ones. On the contrary, he believed he was adapting Jeffersonian principles to new economic imperatives resulting from a historic change in the country's relations with Europe. What was the great cause of distress? Clay asked in 1824. "It is to be found in the fact that, during almost the whole existence of this government, we have shaped our industry, our navigation, and our commerce, in reference to an extraordinary war in Europe, and to foreign markets, which no longer exist."[4] Peace wiped out the markets, while political reaction revived policies of monopoly and restriction. This circumstance, particularly when viewed in conjunction with the rapid growth of population and productivity in the United States, practically demanded the reorientation of American political economy to the home market.

The American System was not so much a philosophy seeking embodiment in public policy as it was a set of policies, with distinct interests behind them, seeking the dignity of a philosophy. Yet the ideas, whatever their sources, were important. Viewed as a theory of political economy, the American System disputed the fundamental "free market" premises of the classical school. It believed that a youthful economy, like the American, required the fostering hand of government; it believed a republican government responsive to the interests of the people ought to promote employment, productivity, and wealth; it believed that national government, in particular, should assume a positive role in opening up promising lines of economic growth in advance of market forces. "The great desideratum of political economy," Clay asserted in 1824, ". . . is, What is the best application of the aggregate industry of a nation, that can be honestly made to produce the largest sum of national wealth?" This, said one of the opponents, was the "true doctrine" of the system, and it converted man "from a natural being . . . into a mere governmental machine."[5] This new system of political economy, which proposed to divert capital from its accustomed channels and to place human skill and industry under the tutelage of government, received theoretical form less from Clay and his allies in Congress than from a group of writers and publicists in Philadelphia and Baltimore. The most important of them were Mathew Carey, an indefatigable pamphleteer and leader of the Pennsylvania Society for the Encouragement of Manufactures, the first large, organized pressure group in the history of the republic; Friedrich List, an exiled German professor imported by Carey to give academic *éclat* to the movement; Daniel Raymond, a Baltimore lawyer, whose *Thoughts on Political Economy*, published in 1820, expounded corporative and interventionist principles; and Hezekiah Niles, editor of the influential *Niles' Weekly Register*, who built his nationalism on statistics and common sense without once consulting Adam Smith or J. B. Say.[6]

The central measure, the *primum mobile*, of the system was the protective tariff. Although the protection and encouragement of domestic manufactures was an object of the government's first tariff laws, it did not become the primary object, overriding considerations of revenue, until after the war. Many infant manufactures had been nurtured under the Jeffersonian guardianship of embargo and war. Now they could survive only by a tariff that allowed sale of the domestic product at a profit. Protectionist ideology was freighted with the old rhetoric of American independence, which held that the country was still vulnerable economically to Great Britain, who in her jealousy of "the youthful Hercules," aimed to strangle American manufactures in the cradle, thereby monopolizing the market for herself. And she was succeeding. "The truth is, and it is vain to disguise it," Clay said in 1820, "that we are . . . independent colonies of England—politically free, commercially slaves."[7] The pillars of this domination were the free trade and *laissez-faire* principles of the ascendant school of political economists. While everywhere proclaimed, these principles were nowhere practiced—not even in Britain, where economic liberalism was the natural ally of industrial supremacy—and to impose them on a young and developing country like the United States was to condemn it to permanent weakness, poverty, and inferiority.* In the books of the economists a protec-

---

*That a young country might present an exception to the rule was sometimes acknowledged by the classical economists. Clay would surely have welcomed in 1820 the concession later made so clearly by John Stuart Mill: "The only case in which, on mere principles of political economy, protective duties can be defensible, is when they are imposed temporarily (especially in a young and rising nation) in hopes of naturalizing a foreign industry, in itself perfectly suited to the circumstances of the country. The superiority of one country over another in a branch of production, often arises only from having begun it sooner. There may be no inherent advantage on one part, or disadvantage on the other, but only a present superiority of acquired skill and experience. A country which has this skill and experience yet to acquire, may in other respects be better adapted to the production than those which were earlier in the field: and besides, it is just to remark, that nothing has a greater tendency to promote improvements in any branch of production, than its trial under a new set of conditions. But it cannot be expected that individuals should, at their own risk, or rather to their certain loss, introduce a new manufacture, and bear the burden of carrying it on, until the producers have been educated up to the level of those with whom the processes are traditional. A protective duty, continued for a reasonable time, will sometimes be the least inconvenient mode in which a nation can tax itself for the support of such an experiment." *Principles of Political Economy* (London, n.d.), 593–94.

tive tariff constituted not only unwarranted interference with the natural balance of the market but an unjust tax on consumers for the exclusive benefit of the producers. It constituted, in short, an arbitrary and wholly selfish redistribution of wealth. But in the dynamic "growth model" of Clay and the protectionists, any temporary inconveniences and inequities were offset by valuable long-term gains in capital formation, rising employment, acquisition of skills, technological innovation, and so on. The protective tariff was an "inducement mechanism" in this growth. Once it had done its work, once all the latent industrial energies were released, once the infant manufactures had matured and gained the strength to withstand the rigors of the free market, protection would die away.[8] This would not alter the fundamental premise that government had a responsibility to promote the national wealth, though it would, of course, change the means and the objects.

In the philosophy of the American System, national wealth was an aggregate interest, paramount to the interests of individuals or of other nations; and in the United States its prospects were wonderful to behold. The first generation of American statesmen had worked out the implications of a large territory for free government under the Constitution, and found them good. Now statesmen of the second generation worked out the implications for the American economy, with the same positive result. A country of continental proportions, a vast and wonderfully varied landed empire with almost limitless room to grow, was potentially "a world within itself."[9] It need not, like Britain—an island nation—look to far-flung markets, which might be conquered under a regime of free trade; it could look instead to a "territorial division of labor," founded in climate and geography, and to a protected "home market" for the productions of its diverse industry. Even Adam Smith conceded the economic superiority of the "home trade" to the foreign. From his free-trade point of view, the principal objection to protection was its interference with the natural division of labor among nations, through which each would fully realize its competitive advantage. But this was the rule for an island, not for a continent. In the United States the territorial division of labor was, or at least promised to be, sufficiently extensive to overcome the supposed disadvantages of protectionism. Indeed, intercourse between the parts of the American Union might be considered a species of foreign commerce.[10] Given to homely simile, Clay imagined a nation conducted with the same virtuous industry and harmony as the farm of his Kentucky friend Isaac Shelby—no giddy wives and daughters, no going into debt for imported fineries, no haunting of grog shops, no hovering sheriffs and preying lawyers, but every family member usefully employed, at the plow, the spinning-wheel, the forge, and the churn. "What the individual family of Isaac Shelby is, I wish to see the nation in the aggregate become."[11] Of course, if this were to occur, the Isaac Shelbys would disappear, for the diverse industry of his family would be parceled out across the nation. Without quite realizing the implications, Clay and his associates fashioned a model of the "home market" in which each great section of the country concentrated on the productions for which it was best suited: the South on staples like cotton, the West on grains and livestock, the Northeast on manufacturing.[12] A mutually supporting and balanced economy of agriculture, manufactures, and commerce would thus be established; and although founded on sectional interests, the sum of the parts would be exceeded by the sum of the whole, the national interest.

The tariff laws recorded the rise of protectionism. The tariff of 1816 was designed by its author, Secretary of Treasury Dallas, to offer moderate protection for infant manufactures. The Ways and Means Committee reported a bill with generally lower rates than the secretary proposed, however. Clay was defeated in his attempt on the floor to raise the *ad valorem* duty on cotton textiles from 25 to 33⅓ percent. Congress finally settled on 30 percent for two years, 25 percent for two more, ending finally in 20 percent, the hypothetical revenue standard. This proposal came from Daniel Webster, an opponent of the protective tariff, and represented the opinion that, while there might be a short-term obligation to the manufacturers, the benefits should be terminated as soon as possible. Undoubtedly, the same opinion contributed to generous southern support of the bill. Calhoun, Lowndes, and other representatives of cotton-growing interests were, in fact, responsible for inclusion of the *minimum* principle devised and pushed by Francis Cabot Lowell, head of the Boston Manufacturing Company, the country's largest producer of cotton cloth. The purpose of the minimum, which would tax all cottons at a base of 25 cents regardless of lower values on the invoice, was to protect both the grower and the manufacturer from cheap India cottons. Except for this provision, Calhoun paid little attention to the bill. In the course of debate he remarked that if the United States had naval ascendancy in the Atlantic the policy of the bill would be highly questionable. As it was, the need for revenue to build up the nation's defenses in a perilous world amply justified the measure. Years later Calhoun had some difficulty accounting for his protectionist vote in 1816. In fact, his vote, though tainted by protectionism at this time, rested less on considerations of political economy than on considerations of national defense.[13]

The initiative for tariff reform in 1819–20 came from Pennsylvania, the leading manufacturing state, soon to be named by Clay "the keystone state" of the Union. The depression bankrupted factories from Philadelphia to Pittsburgh and threw tens of thousands of workers into unemployment. Organized protectionist agitation began, led by Mathew Carey. In Congress, exercising his prerogative as Speaker, Clay brought about the separation of the Committee on Commerce and Manufactures, whose very title was a contradiction, and packed the new Committee on Manufactures with protectionists under the chairmanship of Henry Baldwin of Pittsburgh. The previous Congress had repealed the last of the internal taxes, leaving the government dependent on the revenue of the customs houses for its support. Every nationalist deplored this action. Calhoun, for instance, denounced "the contracted idea, that taxes were so much money taken from the people," and compared this "old imbecile mode" with "a liberal and enlightened policy . . . to raise the nation to that elevation to which we ought to aspire."[14] But the internal taxes were gone, and no one had any hope of reviving them, not even after plummeting revenues in 1819 showed the hazards of supporting government on such a narrow and uncertain basis as foreign imports. Treasury Secretary Crawford projected a $5-million deficit in 1820. He thought higher duties would only reduce imports further and also encourage smuggling. Protection and revenue were thus arrayed in opposition. The Baldwin tariff, nevertheless, attempted to meet both objectives. Higher duties on sugar, coffee, tea, salt, and so on would fill the treasury coffers, while an increase of approximately 10 percent on a broad range of manufactures would furnish the necessary protection without risk to the revenue. The bill would continue the protective duty on textiles, and although the Boston Manufacturing Company, with profits of 20 to 25 percent, no longer needed it, other companies were less fortunate. Significantly higher duties would be levied on hemp, linen, iron, glass, and several other products. Baldwin's committee also sought a number of changes in customs regulations intended to favor the domestic over the foreign producer, such as the requirement of cash duties in place of a system allowing credit for up to twenty-four months.[15]

In the prolonged debate on the tariff bill, which followed the Missouri debate, Clay, according to Baldwin, "discharged the triple duties of a rank-and-file man, captain, and general-in-chief."[16] His speech for the bill—his first important protectionist speech—contained several of the key ideas of the American System. Contrasting the "manufacturing system" with the "agricultural system" advocated by his opponents, Clay underscored "the avidity for improvement" of the former and the habitual inertia of the latter. The agricultural system, moreover, rose and fell with the fluctuations of foreign commerce. The depleted treasury was proof of its capriciousness. Even when prosperous it added nothing to the inner strength and vitality of the nation. "Now our connexion is merely political," Clay observed. "For the sake of the surplus of the produce of our agricultural labor, all eyes are constantly turned upon the markets of Liverpool. There is scarcely any of that beneficial intercourse, the best basis of political connexion, which consists of the exchange of the produce of our labor. On our maritime frontier there has been too much stimulus, an unnatural activity; in the great interior of the country there exists a perfect paralysis. Encourage fabrication at home, and there would instantly arise animation and a healthful circulation throughout all the parts of the Republic."[17] The protective tariff, as this statement suggests, was more than an economic policy. Through the magic of the home market it sought to harmonize the Union; through the modernizing stimulus of industrial innovation it sought moral and intellectual improvement; through the dynamics of new economic activity it sought to increase national wealth and power. "No country on earth," Clay said, ". . . contains within its own limits more abundant facilities for supplying our national wants, than ours does." The time had come to throw off the last vestiges of colonial bondage. "The war of our Revolution effected our political emancipation. The last war contributed greatly toward our achieving commercial freedom. But our entire independence will only be consummated after the policy of this bill shall be recognized and adopted."[18]

The Baldwin tariff bill passed the House but died in the Senate. (The House vote showed New England divided, the Middle States all but unanimously for the bill, the Northwest strongly for it, and the South overwhelmingly opposed.) Efforts to revive it during the next three years failed, in part because of the hostility of the Speaker, Philip P. Barbour of Virginia. Resuming the chair upon his return to Congress, Clay provided the leadership that culminated in the passage of the tariff of 1824. It was a year of presidential politics. Clay was one of the major candidates, and the American System was his platform. He received unexpected assistance from James Monroe, who recommended higher protective duties in his annual message to Congress. The Committee on Manufactures under another Pennsylvania congressman, John Tod, reported its bill in January.[19] The first that looked to protection alone, regardless of the revenue, the bill would raise the *ad valorem* rates on many articles, including those denied in 1820, and extend the benefits of the tariff to some sixty or more new articles. The generous application of *specific* instead of *ad valorem* duties would substantially raise the effective level of protection. The bill was unusual, too, in proposing to extend protection to a range of agricultural commodities—beef, pork, wheat, wool. The Committee on Agriculture, reportedly with Clay's connivance, endorsed the bill. Peculiarly western manufacturing interests, such as whiskey distilling and cotton bagging, would reap rewards. The proposed duty on the latter (six cents per square yard) equaled two-thirds of the value of the product and amounted, according to a New York congressman, to an annual tribute of $200,000 to the Kentucky manufacturers. It is impossible to say how much Clay had to do with the outlines and details of the committee bill. But the plan of covering Pennsylvania and Kentucky, East and West, manufacturing and agriculture under the same mantle of protection suggested his political artistry. In his grand design domestic manufactures would contribute to the relief of agriculture by absorbing the surplus labor and the surplus products of the farm. Himself a hemp grower, Clay's own economic interest agreed with the interest of his Kentucky constituents, who had struggled for many years to establish hemp growing and hemp manufacture as a major industry. Russian hemp was a superior product for rope and cordage; after the war, Scottish makers of cotton bagging flooded the market and destroyed this branch of the industry in Kentucky. It could be reestablished only by a high tariff.[20] Clay finally had to settle for a lower duty than the one proposed, but by virtue of his casting vote as Speaker he got the protection necessary to revive the cotton bagging industry in Kentucky. In the end, a unanimous western vote, north of Tennessee, secured passage of the tariff bill in the House, while the votes of the senators of the two states Clay had helped bring into the Union in 1820–21 guaranteed its passage in the Senate.

The fact that southern congressmen voted 70–6 against the bill points up the deepening sectional division on the tariff. In the past, the commercial and navigation interests centered in the Northeast had spearheaded the opposition. Daniel Webster, who also returned to the House at this session, continued to speak for the merchants, the shippers, and others involved in foreign trade. More and more, however, it was the planters of the South—above all the cotton planters of the lower South—who tilted against the tariff. The change was already evident in 1820 when Lowndes, one of the architects of the postwar tariff, attacked Baldwin's bill. Now the cadre of young South Carolinians, men like George McDuffie, Robert Y. Hayne, and James Hamilton, Jr.—all nationalists of the Calhoun stamp—breathed defiance of the tariff. Whether or not they spoke for their leader, the secretary of war, was a secret never divulged to the public. Most southern congressmen felt no interest in manufacturing. The South lived on its exports; indeed, these exports paid for American imports which, in turn, supported the government. The burden of the South's complaint was that the tariff levied an unequal and unjust tax on its capital and industry. Protection was not simply a tax on the consumer for the benefit of the producer; it was a tax laid upon one class of producers, one section, one interest, for the benefit of another. Justice as well as policy was at issue. Barbour, in a powerful speech, attacked the constitutionality of the tariff for the first time. The tax powers were given to raise revenue, not to support a favorite branch of industry. While acknowledging that "the sensibility of the pocket nerve," rather than "political metaphysic," was at the bottom of the opposition, the Virginia Old Republican nevertheless poured out his metaphysics of state rights, *laissez-faire*, and free trade. It was a maxim, he said, "that Government should never interfere but in matters of State; that, in relation to the internal police of a country, it has done all that is required of it, all that it ought to do, when it has secured to its citizens their personal liberty and private property, and an impartial administration of justice."[21]

Clay's reply to Barbour—the most elaborate of his protectionist speeches—displayed his usual ardor but was also impressively informed by economic understanding. He began by painting a melancholy picture of the country's condition, attributed the decline to economic weakness and imbalance, then prescribed "a genuine American System" as the remedy. "We must naturalize the arts in our country," Clay said, "and we must naturalize these by the only means which the wisdom of nations has yet discovered to be effectual—by adequate protection against the overwhelming influence of foreign industry."[22] Clay developed his argument in answer to a long string of objections to the system. To the southern objection that it was a system of privilege, taking money from the planter's pocket and putting it in the manufacturer's, Clay asked, Were the majority of Americans to sit on their hands and submit to the planter minority? "That, in effect, would be to make us the slaves of slaves," he said. The present policy, which sacrificed everything to keep up markets abroad, represented in fact "a sort of tacit compact between the cotton grower and the British manufacturer," holding the rest of the nation in tribute. There were, he maintained, benefits for the South in the new policy, for instance the creation of a competing American market for cotton. To the same basic objection urged on behalf of foreign commerce, Clay made no apology for its loss of favor. For many years, as he had often said, foreign commerce was the "spoilt daughter" of the republic. American shipping profited from a discriminatory tonnage law; the navy protected foreign trade; shipbuilding subsidies and promotion of the fisheries aided commerce; the nation had even gone to war to defend it. Indeed, the protective system would extend to manufacturing only the benefits government had heretofore bestowed with a lavish hand on foreign commerce. Clay sought, nevertheless, to reassure commercial interests. The coastal trade would increase under his system; in time a prosperous home market would stimulate foreign trade as American manufacturers successfully competed with the British in world markets. Clay saw his Latin American policy as a first step toward this goal.

In the textbooks of the economists, protective tariffs must reduce revenue and, of course, raise prices. Clay disputed both points. To the stereotyped objections to state interference with natural economic forces, Clay returned what were becoming stereotyped answers. Americans could control their economic destiny as they already controlled their political destiny: this was the task of the second generation. Clay discovered a symbol of the process in the steamboat's mastery of the torrent of the Mississippi. In a similar fashion, industrial machinery would overcome the principal natural obstacle to progress cited by proponents of the American System: land abundance and labor shortage. Critics said that it was, in fact, "the British System," adverse to the condition as well as the genius of the American people. Protectionism would convert America into "a city of Manchester," degrading the people, corrupting their morals, and endangering republican government. Clay thought these fears groundless. Industrial cities would scarcely be noticed on the vast agricultural landscape of the United States; many of the new factories, rising in the countryside, would be free of the iniquities of coastal cities. Besides, said Clay, employment was the best security against demoralization. There was the further objection that Britain was about to abandon old mercantilist policies and take up the liberal and enlightened system of free trade. Clay vigorously disputed this. But what if it were true? It would only signify that those policies had achieved their purpose and that Britain, with her great industrial power, could now conquer the markets of the world under a regime of free trade. "The object of the most perfect freedom of trade, with such a nation as Britain, and of the most rigorous system of prohibition, with a nation whose arts are in their infancy, may be precisely the same. In both cases, it is to give greater protection to native industry." Finally, Clay addressed the constitutional question. He disagreed with Barbour's narrow interpretation of the tax power, yet rested his case on another power, the power of Congress to regulate commerce, which had been liberally construed since the time of Jefferson's embargo. In closing, he appealed to the authorities of Jefferson and Hamilton, of Henry VIII and Colbert and "the master spirit of the age," Napoleon, to sustain the American System.

Clay was at once answered at length by Daniel Webster. The two speeches together, it has been said, "are as interesting an economic study as can be found in our parliamentary history."[23] In an even greater debate six years later, Senator Hayne recalled the April day when Webster "like a mighty giant bore away upon his shoulders the pillars of the temple of error and delusion" and "erected to free trade a beautiful and enduring monument," from which unfortunately he soon turned away.[24] Webster astounded everyone by the knowledge he displayed of intricate questions of political economy. Actually he was a tyro in this new science, although he had the mental resources to appear as a master. When the bill was reported, he obtained fifty copies, sent them to the best-informed merchants in the East, requesting their observations, and thus acquired the mass of information that gave such an aura of authority to his speech.* Despite this advantage, no less real because it was borrowed, one New England congressman who listened attentively to both Clay and Webster thought the former maintained his superiority "in popular address, in the skillful adaptation of means to ends, in the contagious enthusiasm which leaves no time for hesitation or doubt, in promptness, in confidence of power or success."[25] Early in the session Webster had made a speech—one of the most splendid ever heard in Congress—on Greek Independence, and Clay had rushed to his aid. Observing that much of the opposition to Webster's resolution of support for the Greek patriots was personal, Clay rebuked these old party feelings and embraced the Federalist as a better Republican than boastful sentinels of party principle like John Randolph.[26] On the tariff, however, the two men were still at odds in 1824.

Coming from New England, which was enjoying unprecedented prosperity and progress, Webster took an entirely different view of the economic condition of the country. The cause of the recent depression had nothing to do with tariff levels. It was experienced in Britain as well as in America, and it was most felt in those parts of the country where banking and currency were in disarray. While Clay saw bank closings and rag money as symptoms of a deeper disease, remediable by protectionism, Webster saw them as the true cause of the difficulties. Clay and his protectionist friends proceeded on false economic principles. Ignoring the simple truth taught by David Ricardo that labor was the chief cost of production, ignoring comparative labor costs between Britain and the United States, they sought to rear manufacturing industry on no other foundation than government patronage. It would not work. They were misled, too, said Webster, by the fallacy of "the balance of trade." Clay, for instance, had held that because the country's imports exceeded its exports, causing an "unfavorable" balance, precious metals were drained abroad, damaging the internal trade and releasing all the evils of worthless paper, debt, bankruptcy, unemployment, and so on. Webster's refutation of this doctrine—one of the pillars of protectionism—was masterly. "The excess of imports over exports, in truth," he said, "usually shows the gains, not the losses of trade; or, in a country that not only buys and sells goods, but employs ships in carrying goods, also, it shows the profits of commerce, and the earnings of navigation." There were problems with this

---

*Webster once offered this advise to his elder son: "If, on a given occasion, a man can, gracefully, and without the air of a pedant, show a little more knowledge than the occasion requires, the world will give him credit for eminent attainments. It is an honest quackery. I have practiced it, and sometimes with success." *Private Correspondence*, II, 16.

theory as well, but it demolished the fallacy that descended from mercantilism. Webster tried to convince Clay that Britain was, in fact, abandoning protectionism. If the United States were to take it up, he said, "we will be attempting to ornament ourselves with cast-off apparel." In 1824 the evidence on this point was ambiguous. Under the leadership of William Huskisson, president of the Board of Trade, the British government was moving toward a more liberal policy. But the heralded reform, when it came a year later, proved to be "a piece of mere politico-economical juggling," as Friedrich List said.[27] Clay remained skeptical of British policy, believing in any event that the coming imperialism of free trade would be as injurious to American interests as the old imperialism of prohibition and monopoly. Webster chose not to challenge the constitutionality of protection. His private opinion, repeatedly stated, was that it was constitutional only as an incident to raising revenue. Despite the fundamental importance of the commerce power in his conception of the Constitution, he could not admit protectionism under that power because of free market preferences and because it would ratify retroactively the whole chapter of Jeffersonian embargo and restriction.[28]

Webster was never doctrinaire in his economic views, however. Even at this time he regarded the tariff as a matter of interest and expediency rather than of principle. Wishing to settle the business on terms the entire country could live with, Webster was ready to support a moderately protectionist bill in 1824. He did, in fact, support higher tariffs on woolens, glass, fine cottons, and certain other articles; and had it been more a New England and less a Pennsylvania and Kentucky bill, he might have finally voted for it. Clay sensed this, remarking that the famous speech was "on both sides" so as to enable the congressman to jump either way.[29] When the bill passed the House after two months debate, Webster voted with a small majority of New England congressmen in opposition. Although somewhat weakened by Senate amendments, the bill that became law in May provided substantially increased protection at an average *ad valorem* level of about 35 percent. Clay, though dissatisfied with several of the concessions made to reconcile conflicting interests, believed the 1824 tariff placed the American System on a firm foundation.[30]

Congress also enacted in 1824 the General Survey Act, the culmination of the long struggle for national internal improvements. The protective tariff, with the idea of the home market, presupposed a system of internal improvements. Roads and canals would lower costs of transportation, circulate goods and services over a larger territory, and unite the country around one common interest. How grand, how harmonious, how felicitous the promised "new epoch" would be is suggested by the report of a congressional committee in 1816: "Different sections of the union will according to their positions, the climate, the populations, the habits of the people, and the nature of the soil, strike into that line of industry which is best adapted to their interest and the good of the whole; an active and free intercourse, promoted and facilitated by roads and canals, will ensue; prejudices which are generated by distance . . . will be removed; information will be extended; the union will acquire strength and solidity, and the Constitution of the United States, and that of each state, will be regarded as fountains from which flow numerous streams of public and private prosperity."[31] The policy of centrally planned and supported internal improvements had its beginnings in Jefferson's administration, when Clay was among the first advocates. Albert Gallatin's celebrated report to Congress in 1808 provided both the plan and the rationale for a national system. The treasury surplus that was supposed to fund the improvements suddenly vanished, however; and the report was laid aside during eight years of foreign crisis and war. With the peace a rage for improvements swept the nation. New York matured its great project, the Erie Canal. Virginia created its Board of Public Works to plan and manage projects beneficial to the commonwealth but beyond the capabilities of private enterprise; and the Virginia system became the model for other states.[32]

It was the model too, perhaps, for Calhoun's Bonus Bill in 1816. Speaking for it, Calhoun made a powerful case for national aid and direction in building roads and canals, improving the navigation of rivers and every accessory of internal commerce. As Gallatin had earlier, he argued that in a country as large as the United States leadership from the center was necessary to form the arteries of traffic into a system and to overcome the deficiency of private capital. Regardless of economic considerations, a comprehensive system of roads and canals was essential to secure "the strength and political prosperity of the Republic." National defense and national unity: these were Calhoun's overriding concerns. The extension of the republic over such a prodigious surface was a marvel. It could survive only by counteracting relentlessly the centrifugal tendencies toward disunion. "We are great, and rapidly, I was about to say fearfully, growing. This," Calhoun declared, ". . . is our pride and danger—our weakness and our strength. . . . We are under the most imperious obligation to counteract every tendency to disunion. . . . The more enlarged the sphere of commercial circulation, the more extended the social intercourse; the more strongly we are bound together, the more inseparable are our destinies. . . . Let us then bind the Republic together with a perfect system of roads and canals. Let us conquer space."[33] The constitutionality of the policy had been questioned by the Virginia Republicans and by New England Federalists, though not by Daniel Webster. Calhoun rebuked these grumblers and doubters. The largeness of the country, with its varied interests, required an enlarged and liberal statesmanship, one that subordinated all low, sordid, and selfish views to the common good. "It must be submitted to as the condition of our greatness." The constitutional question was to become a labyrinth of perplexity, but it gave no trouble to Calhoun in 1817. He was no advocate of refined arguments on the Constitution. "The instrument was not intended as a thesis for the logician to exercise his ingenuity on. It ought to be construed with plain, good sense. . . ." With that assertion he threw caution to the winds and claimed the "general welfare" clause was a distinct power of Congress to raise and appropriate money for the general welfare.[34] In the end, however, Calhoun was forced to accept two amendments to allay constitutional fears about his bill. One required the consent of a state to federal internal improvements within its borders; the other mandated that the expenditures be prorated among the states. These local ideas, as Webster later remarked, threatened to undermine legislation founded on the broadest nationalism.[35]

But Madison had constitutional objections of his own and vetoed the Bonus Bill on March 3, 1817. Forewarned of the veto, Clay sent an eleventh-hour appeal to Madison to leave the bill on his desk for Monroe's action within the allotted ten days. Madison was adamant. When he returned the bill, Clay demanded that his name—the name of the Speaker—be called first on the vote to override.[36] The vote—Clay, Calhoun, and Webster on the same side—fell short of the required two-thirds. The Madisonian Platform had been deserted by its author, delivering the first shock to postwar nationalism. New York, a disappointed petitioner for national aid, now set out to build the Erie Canal on its own. Henceforth, New York Republicans opposed federal internal improvements. Other states, too, became preoccupied with their own projects; as they went forward, prospects for an integrated national plan receded. Clay had hoped Monroe would rise above outmoded Virginia dogmas and support a liberal policy. But in his first message to congress, Monroe adopted his predecessor's opinion and called for a constitutional amendment. Clay responded angrily that the president had no right to attempt to control congressional opinion on this matter. The Senate proceeded to consider an amendment. Not to be outdone Clay appointed a select committee friendly to internal improvements. It recommended reenactment of Calhoun's Bonus Bill, with the requirement of state consent but omitting *pro rata* distribution. There was no defect of constitutional power. Congress could, if it chose, construct roads as well as appropriate money for them. The committee conceded that no constitutional amendment could be obtained. Everyone knew this; indeed, as Clay said, the demand for an amendment was simply the expedient way to kill the policy. Moreover, every unnecessary amendment narrowed and circumscribed the Constitution, making it more a hindrance than a help to the tasks of government.[37]

Clay placed the internal improvements power on very broad grounds.[38] It was contained in both the commerce and post road clauses of the Constitution; it embraced construction as well as appropriation; it was in no way answerable to state authority. He protested against "the water-gruel regimen" that would reduce the Constitution to a skeleton of itself. When his adversaries invoked the Republican "doctrines of '98," Clay responded that these jealous principles were declared to preserve personal liberty against an oppressive government, while the present danger came from weakness and atrophy of the Constitution. Continuing to profess state rights principles, Clay disagreed with their new champions, who seemed to regard the general government as a foreign nation and to believe that the only security against abuse of power lay in the negation of power. Were there no other ways of controlling power? "Yes," Clay answered, "there is such security in the fact of our being members of the same society, equally affected ourselves by the laws we promulgate. . . . There is the further security in the oath which is taken to sup-

port the Constitution. . . . There is the yet further security, that, at the end
of every two years, the members [of Congress] must be answerable to the
people for the manner in which their trust has been performed. And there remains also that further though awful security . . . the right of revolution."
Clay, in sum, was willing to trust reputation, representation, and politics—
"forebearance, liberality, practical good sense, and mutual concession"—to
keep the Constitution in order, while the fears and jealousies of his opponents allowed them to trust nothing but the restraints of the Constitution.[39]

The tendency for every question of policy to turn into a question of constitutionality, which the 1818 debate disclosed, suited neither Clay's methods
nor his objectives. For a westerner, of course, and one who traveled every
year some six hundred miles to and from the capital, most of it over slow
and treacherous roads, the idea that Congress could not act to improve
roads was ridiculous. The issue ought to be decided as one of union and political economy. Clay liked to dwell on the example of Roman roads. As
they had diffused civilization and sustained a great empire in ancient times,
so might a similar system of roads, supplemented by modern wonders of canal construction, sustain the American empire of liberty. The economic development of the West, indeed of the entire nation, depended on it. Clay
implicitly made the distinction that has since been emphasized by economic historians between *exploitative* and *developmental* enterprise in
transportation. The former occurs in a situation that offers an opportunity
for early return on invested capital; in the latter that opportunity does not
exist, though improvements will stimulate economic activity and produce
great rewards in the course of time. The former was the British case, amenable to the rule of *laissez-faire;* the latter was generally the case of the
United States. Public initiative and public investment were essential to
prime the pump of economic growth over large, thinly populated areas without capital and scarcely even involved in the market economy.[40]

But Clay and the West were defeated in 1818. In the course of debate,
Lowndes proposed to test the principles of the committee report by a series of resolutions on the constitutional authority of Congress. The House
rejected the power to *construct* under any provision; it approved the power
to *appropriate,* yet voted down creation of a permanent internal improvements fund from the bonus and dividends of the B. U. S.[41] The issue continued to come regularly before Congress in connection with appropriations
for the repair and extension of the Cumberland, or National, Road. This
great enterprise, born in Jefferson's administration, was designed to unite
Ohio, the seventeenth state, to the national government. By the terms of a
compact between the two, 2 percent of the proceeds from the sale of public
lands in Ohio were committed to building a road from Cumberland, Maryland, to the new state. The government later entered into similar compacts
with Indiana and Illinois. By 1819 the road had reached Wheeling, on the
Ohio River; it then became a question whether it would reach any farther.
Clay considered the road nothing less than the umbilical cord of the Union.
The villages that had sprung up all along the route from Cumberland to

Wheeling, until it resembled "one continued street," offered visible proof of the prosperity generated by internal improvements. The road was supposed to be a western project, yet, as Clay observed, not one stone had yet been broken, not one spade of dirt turned, not one dollar spent in the West. Constantly championing the National Road, Clay became identified with it. A monument was erected to him near the Wheeling terminus in 1820.[42] Although he was not in Congress two years later, his hand, it was believed, directed the effort of western friends to raise money for the road by means of tolls. The bill passed, only to be vetoed by Monroe because it implied the power of Congress to execute a complete system of roads and canals.

Monroe's opposition was weakening, however. He had been shaken by Clay's attacks. Politically, he dared not yield to the Kentuckian. Fortunately for him, the retrenchment forced on the treasury in 1819 gave Monroe several years' reprieve on this thorny question. Now, however, he followed up the veto message with a long exposition of his views in which, by a tortuous line of reasoning, he conceded the unlimited power of Congress to appropriate money for internal improvements of national importance. He had very likely been drawn to this view by Secretary of War Calhoun.[43] Never suspected of intellectual profundity, the president offered his solution as a compromise with Virginia Republicanism, though it was obviously in direct collision with that straitlaced political faith. As Clay pointed out, the general power of Congress to spend money was "of infinitely greater magnitude" than specific powers to establish post roads, regulate commerce, and so on.[44]

Nationalists in Congress moved at once to test Monroe's opinion, first by an appropriation to repair the National Road, then, in 1824, by the General Survey Bill. The latter, signed in April, authorized planning and surveys and appropriated money for this purpose. Clay could trumpet the act as a victory for the American System. It was, in fact, the closest he ever came to triumph over Monroe. Yet, for all this, Clay firmly rejected the constitutional basis of the act. "If the power can be traced to no more legitimate source than that of appropriating the public treasury," Clay acknowledged to an old adversary, Philip Barbour, "he yielded the question."[45] The power to spend must be drawn from the power to legislate, he insisted, which, in turn, required liberal construction of the enumerated powers. Clay happily took the benefits even as he rejected the reasoning, however, and considered the principle of internal improvements under the general government settled by the bill. Western congressmen cast a unanimous vote for it. With generous support in every other section as well, the General Survey Act transcended its sectional origins. During the next four years ninety projects would be commenced under the act. One of the greatest, the Chesapeake and Ohio Canal, would be acclaimed at the groundbreaking by President John Quincy Adams as the third great step, after the Declaration of Independence and the Constitution, toward the realization of the old dream of an empire of liberty and enlightenment in the New World. "It is the adaptation of the powers, physical, moral, and intellectual to the whole union, to the improvement of its condition . . . by the pursuit and patronage of learning and the arts."[46]

In the theory of the American System internal improvements should be financed, as they were at their inception, by income from the sale of the public lands. Since the creation of the national domain during the Confederation, everyone understood that these lands were held in trust for the common benefit of the Union. After the war they were pledged to the payment of the national debt; and as long as the debt was formidable little thought was given to shaping land policy to further the goals of economic development. There was broad consensus on the system of disposing of the lands. (In 1820 land could be purchased at auction at federal land offices for the minimum price of $1.25 an acre in the minimum quantity of eighty acres.) This did not mitigate the continuing tension between the two objects of settlement and revenue. Settlement was uppermost in the western mind, while revenue was the primary concern in the East. In the eyes of many easterners, above all the economic nationalists, public lands were at best a mixed blessing. They drained off labor and capital from the East, where both were wanted for the growth of manufactures—indeed, for the whole complex of arts and industries of advancing civilization—and dispersed them in the slow and exhausting work of frontier development. Richard Rush, Adams's secretary of treasury, summarized the argument in one of his annual reports: "It is a proposition, too plain to require elucidation, that the creation of capital is retarded, rather than accelerated, by the diffusion of a thin population over a great surface of soil. Any thing that may serve to hold back this tendency to diffusion from racing too far, and too long, into an extreme, can scarcely prove otherwise than salutary."[47] Perhaps the most effective check on this potentially crippling dispersal of national energies was the protective tariff. The redundant farm population in the East, instead of going west and adding to the agricultural surplus, would be absorbed into factories and become consumers of that surplus. Opponents criticized the tariff on grounds of equity, but from this point of view the support it extended to manufacturing was more than offset by the bounty of public lands policy to western agriculture. Another means of counteracting the natural pull of the frontier—"the barbarizing tendency of dispersion" in the opinion of an English political economist[48]—was a land policy slanted to revenue.

As a westerner Clay would never act consciously to stem the growth of his section in order to facilitate the concentration of labor and capital in the East. But he opposed turning public lands policy into a vehicle for sectional aggrandizement. The lands were a national trust; revenue should be an object of policy; speculative, unregulated, and scattered dispersal should be avoided; and policy should countervail the excessive predisposition of the American people toward agricultural employment. At the same time, Clay believed the western lands offered a safety valve from the apprehended excesses of eastern manufactures—from the vices and oppressions of American Manchesters and Birminghams—and so should relieve anxieties on that score.[49] Once land

policy became a fighting political issue, Clay would be hard-pressed to balance national and sectional claims. In 1824 Senator Thomas Hart Benton of
Missouri launched his crusade for cheap land, squatter rights, and rapid westward settlement. Rising eastern dissatisfaction with public lands policy was
reflected in a movement begun by the Maryland legislature in 1821 to distribute millions of acres of lands to all the states for education or other purposes.
Since Congress had already appropriated some eight million acres for such
purposes to new western states—the very ones complaining of niggardly
treatment by Washington—it seemed only fair to extend the largess to the Atlantic states (plus Vermont and Kentucky) which had contributed their people and wealth to the West but had received neither land nor other compensation in return. Nine eastern states quickly endorsed the Maryland plan;
and although Congress rejected it outright in 1822, it started in motion the
idea of distribution in public lands policy, which would not soon be stilled.[50]
As the economy revived and statesmen began to contemplate the prospect of
a government liberated from debt, distribution of the proceeds of the public
lands (rather than the lands themselves, as in the Maryland plan) became an
attactive means of aiding internal improvements in the states; moreover, as it
would take money from the treasury, distribution would help keep up the
protective tariff. Clay's political fortunes, and the future of the American System, were thus bound up with public lands policy.

A national bank, perhaps the leading measure in the Madisonian Platform
of 1815, became an integral part of the American System. Under the expert
direction of Nicholas Biddle, beginning in 1822, the Bank of the United
States came to be considered an essential, as well as a highly successful, instrument of centralized and controlled economic development. It provided
the entire country with a stable and uniform currency, a fundamental condition of the home market; it also regulated credit expansion and managed the
complex domestic exchanges among the sections. Prejudice against the Bank
died hard, however. Opponents of the American System, for whatever reason, made the Bank into a monstrous symbol of its supposed evils. Clay,
Webster, and Calhoun had all been involved in one way or another with the
B.U.S.; it was one great measure all three men supported. Webster had yet
to embrace protectionism in 1824, while Calhoun was beginning to recoil
from it; neither matched Clay's enthusiasm for internal improvements. But
on the Bank these men of such different backgrounds, with such different
constituencies, were allied in their nationalism.

3. Calhoun at the War Department

President Monroe's search for a secretary of war had become desperate when
in October 1817, seven months into his administration, he offered the post to
John C. Calhoun. The fact that it had been previously offered to Henry Clay
and two others, and been declined by all, was no disgrace to Calhoun. Mon-

roe had wanted a westerner in this third-ranking cabinet post, and he had counted on the support of Calhoun's brilliant talents in the House of Representatives. His reelection to Congress was a personal triumph achieved in the face of popular outrage against the Compensation Act, which Calhoun had manfully defended, while Clay, with so many others, had bent to the torrent of public opinion. Monroe respected Calhoun. As Madison's sometime secretary of war he had worked closely with the South Carolinian. He had reason to be grateful to him as well, for Calhoun had helped put down William H. Crawford's challenge to his nomination in 1816.

It was easy enough to understand why Monroe finally turned to Calhoun to complete his cabinet. But why did Calhoun accept the invitation? His closest political friends, including William Lowndes, the last to decline the post, advised against it. Calhoun's talents, they said, were more legislative than administrative, more theoretical than practical, more feverish than calm and deliberate. "Mr. Calhoun . . . is a man of genius," Langdon Cheves observed, "and has the temptation of such men to leap to conclusions boldly, perhaps hastily."[1] Besides, War was an inferior ministry; more reputations had been lost than gained in it; its affairs were in disarray, and with the return of peace it was sure to decline in importance. Calhoun, however, turned these reasons for rejection into reasons for acceptance. If it was true—and he did not admit it—that his mind was too "metaphysical" or his feelings too warm, then he should strive to overcome these weaknesses in administrative office. And if the future of the War Department was as poor as his friends said, he ought to do everything in his power to make it strong.[2] For Calhoun was not only an ardent patriot; he also believed that war was an inescapable part of the nation's destiny. He had learned perhaps too well the lessons of the last war. If Britain did not give the United States cause for another war, then the despots united in the Holy Alliance surely would. "They have power and union, and can we suppose that this country claims no part of their attention?" Calhoun asked. "Neither our distance from Europe, nor our pacific policy, will secure us from great disasters."[3] So he adopted the old maxim, "in peace prepare for war," and supposed that the war desk, instead of losing, might gain importance. The magnitude of the department's responsibilities, as wide and varied as the continent, also appealed to Calhoun. In its brief history the republic had produced two models of ministerial leadership, Alexander Hamilton's, which was honored even when disapproved, and Albert Gallatin's, which was little recognized. Both were in the treasury, of course. Entering the Augean stable that was the War Department, Young Hercules set out to create a model of his own.

Among the statesmen of his generation Calhoun was remarkable for the unmitigated conviction, inseparable from his sense of honor, of acting always on high principles regardless of personal or partisan interest. It was the same spirit that made "principles not men" the boasted motto of the Monroe administration. In reality, no administration was ruled less by principles or dominated more by the ambition and caprice of commanding personalities. Monroe himself was a lackluster figure. "No man, perhaps," a Washingtonian observed, "ever succeeded so well with powers so moderate."[4] Whether he had the political wit and cunning to keep his eager secretaries in harness was a difficult question from the outset. Adams, for all his learning and experience in foreign affairs, was a stiff Puritan wholly lacking in political tact and suspicious of everyone's motives but his own. Knowing well that he had "no powers of fascination," hence could never be "a popular man," he was a particularly harsh judge of anyone who shone in the public eye.[5] He had been favored for the first office in the cabinet because he was a New Englander, because he was the most distinguished of all the Federalist converts to Republicanism, and because of his eminent abilities. Lowndes suggested another reason for the appointment. Seeing that both Clay and Crawford panted for it, and not wishing to side with either, Monroe chose Adams because "it was impossible he should ever be President."[6] Crawford, a legacy from the Madison administration in the Treasury Department, had both the ambition and the following to be president. A product, like Calhoun, of the southern Scotch-Irish frontier, Crawford ruled the roost in Georgia; and in his career as senator, minister to France, and treasury secretary he had demonstrated a remarkable capacity for public business as well as a fine talent for political maneuver and intrigue. "He is a hardy, bold, resolute man, with the *appearance* of great frankness and openness of character," observed a skeptical Yankee, "unpolished and somewhat rude in his manner, and very far inferior to Mr. Adams in learning and attainments. He has, however, a strong, vigorous mind, and has made himself what he is by his own active efforts."[7] William Wirt, the attorney general, long a leader at the Virginia bar, was basking in the celebrity of his newly published biography of Patrick Henry. The Navy Department continued to be led, for a time, by Benjamin Crowninshield, who belonged to the first family of Massachusetts Republicanism. Monroe ran his administration through the cabinet. There every important issue was discussed and decided. Adams, Crawford, and Calhoun were the principal actors, of course; even before Monroe's second term began they were competing for the presidential succession. No less important than these three to the fate of the administration, and the succession, were Henry Clay, Speaker of the House, and Andrew Jackson, then in command of the southern department of the U.S. Army.

Calhoun, at thirty-five, was the youngest member of the cabinet, and in the view of some its "only great man." His exemplary private character, his "manly independence, aloof from party views and local prejudices," his strong and active mind, his large vision, his captivating manners and conversation— in the eyes of his admirers Calhoun was, indeed, a paragon of virtue.[8] Adams, who met Calhoun for the first time when he took up his duties in December, liked him from the opening cabinet session. "Calhoun thinks for himself, independently of all the rest, with sound judgment, quick discrimination, and keen observation. He supports his opinions, too, with powerful eloquence." Adams did not soon change his opinion. Four years later he wrote in his diary: "Calhoun is a man of fair and candid mind, of honorable principles, of clear and quick understanding, of cool self-possession, of enlarged philosophical views, and of ardent patriotism. He is above all sectional and factious prejudices more than any other statesman of the Union with whom I have ever acted."[9] Coming from Adams this was high praise indeed. Although they sometimes differed on important issues, such as on the censure of General Jackson, Calhoun felt perfectly congenial with Adams. In their moral and mental temper they were, in fact, more alike than Calhoun and Crawford, who shared a common frontier culture. Adams thought Calhoun was overly sensitive to the whims of public opinion; some thought he was too sanguine in his views of popular government, while others criticized his impatience before obstacles in the path of his great projects. Everyone agreed he was too subtle, too ingenious, too metaphysical in his thinking. Even the criticisms were well meant, however, since they looked to the realization of the statesman's high destiny. The portraits of Calhoun from this period—Charles Bird King's, for instance—reveal a striking face, too pallid to be beautiful, but with clear features and eager, searching eyes above high cheekbones. "There was a glare, a fire in his eyes, the fire of a soul that seemed to burn within him," wrote a keen observer. "It fascinated the beholder and riveted his gaze."[10]

Calhoun brought his family to Washington and moved into a big house above Pennsylvania Avenue midway between the Capitol and the White House. He quickly realized that his salary of $4,500 a year was insufficient to support the standard of living and the social obligations expected of a cabinet secretary. In Washington, "this great watering place," amusement was a business to which almost everybody gave himself up from five o'clock until bedtime. The President's House, previously the center of gaity, lost its glow under the Monroes. The president dutifully gave dinners every Friday, dull, tasteless affairs; even the rooms were cold, which led Clay to promise the guests at one dinner "they would be better warmed in his tenure." The first lady, sickly and retiring—a pale contrast to Dolley Madison—seldom appeared publicly and never entertained.[11] The cabinet secretaries helped fill the void, even if they couldn't afford it. Calhoun received financial assistance from his brother-in-law at home. He did not gamble or play cards and was no one's drinking companion, yet he loved to entertain, to be surrounded by admiring guests, and to talk in his dazzling fashion on some great subject—never on trivia—that took his fancy. Floride, the mother of two children when he entered the War Department, of five when he left it, was a clever and charming hostess. The Calhouns were popular socially. And a dinner or ball at their house was sure to be a lively occasion.[12]

Plunging into the work of the War Department, Calhoun soon realized the full measure of its responsibilities. Its combined budget, exceeding $7 million in 1818, was by far the largest in the government. In addition to overseeing the army, the department was responsible for coastal fortifications, the military academy at West Point, for administering pensions, land warrants, and Indian affairs. All this business, with its multitudinous details and regulations spread throughout the statutes, was handled by a civilian staff of thirty-four clerks and two chief clerks. "The department was almost literally without organization," Calhoun wrote in retrospect, "and everything in a state of confusion."[13] He had little acquaintance with any of the duties; he had never so much as read a treatise on military science. Yet after three hard months of investigation he began to overhaul the work of the department. The army had already fallen several thousand men under its authorized peacetime strength of 12,000 and was dwindling rapidly. It was wretchedly organized, its command and staff divided between northern and southern departments, its supply services so badly disordered that there were some $40 million of unsettled accounts. The first thing Calhoun did was to develop a plan to reorganize the general staff. This became the basis of a bill passed by Congress in April. The staff was enlarged, centralized in Washington, and organized into six bureaus according to function. The system of supply through private contractors, the source of so much waste and fraud, was abolished and a commissary general, with a bureau in Washington, assumed the responsibility. The reorganization, though founded on a novel and untried principle, endured. Calhoun gradually extended the principle to the department as a whole, until there was a Land Warrant Bureau, a Pension Bureau, and a Bureau of Indian Affairs.[14]

Calhoun aimed at more than administrative efficiency, of course. The urgent necessity was to close the gap, as he perceived it, between the defensive requirements of the country and its military capabilities. With a long exposed coastline and extensive land frontiers, the Spanish to the south, the British to the north, and the Indians to the west, the United States remained dangerously vulnerable to enemy penetration. In proportion to wealth, population, and extent of territory, Calhoun told Congress, the military establishment was smaller than in 1802 under the austere Jeffersonian standard.[15] Combating traditional republican fears of a standing army, he maintained that a small professional force was necessary both to defend the frontiers and to form the rallying point for the militia in time of war. The army was rapidly rebuilt to its authorized strength. For coastal defense Calhoun proposed constructing a series of forts at strategic points from the New England waters to the Gulf of Mexico. Supported by the navy, manned by army garrisons, these forts would repel British invasion by sea. The bulk of the twelve-thousand-man army would be stationed on the land frontiers, especially along the Canadian border and among the so-called "uncivilized" tribes of the upper Mississippi valley. The British continued to curry favor with these tribes. Although the privilege of trading below the border supposedly ended with the Peace of Ghent, British traders kept up their intercourse with the Indians and diverted much of the profitable traffic in furs to Canadian posts from Lake Erie westward to the Columbia River. Calhoun moved to check this insidious influence by the westward expansion of American military power.[16]

His most ambitious enterprise in this regard was an expedition eighteen hundred miles up the Missouri River to plant the American flag at the mouth of the Yellowstone. "The world will behold in it," Calhoun wrote grandly, "the mighty growth of our republic, which but a few years since, was limited to the Allegany; but now is ready to push its civilization and laws to the western confines of the continent."[17] The expedition was mounted at St. Louis in the spring of 1818. Unforeseen difficulties, a crucial change of plan to substitute steamboats for keelboats, and towering expenses delayed the expedition for more than a year. Finally, the four steamboats (named *Expedition, Jefferson, Calhoun,* and *Johnson*) were built, and three of them (the *Calhoun,* forebodingly, was incapacitated) set forth on the Missouri in July 1819. In St. Louis, Calhoun was toasted as the worthy successor of Jefferson in the promotion of western empire: "The Secretary of War—The new line of defense from the Yellow Stone River to the Falls of St. Anthony, is a conception worthy of that eminent statesman—the honors and interests of the West have received his peculiar attention—British encroachments, at least on our inland waters, will meet with a proper check."[18] Calhoun had already, by another expedition, placed an American regiment at the headwaters of the Mississippi, and he would send still another up the Platte and the Arkansas. Military objectives were of primary importance, but all this enterprise was part of the ongoing effort begun by the Lewis and Clark Expedition to explore the Trans-Mississippi West. For guidance Calhoun had only to refer his commanders to the instructions Jefferson had written for Captain Meriwether Lewis in 1803.

It was axiomatic that no adequate defense over such a large territory was possible without an improved transportation network for the movement of troops and supplies. One of the results of the House debate on internal improvements in 1818 was a resolution calling on the secretaries of treasury and war to submit recommendations on the subject. Crawford, averse to meddling in these troubled political waters, made no response. Calhoun submitted a comprehensive report, in which he dodged the question of constitutionality, thereby avoiding conflict with the president, and viewed roads and canals mainly from the standpoint of the country's defense. The eastern states, in their race for western markets, might be expected to carry the primary responsibility for these connections. The north–south trunk of the system, consisting of a coastal highway as well as an inter-coastal waterway from Maine to Louisiana, ought to be a federal responsibility, however. The waterway could be completed, Calhoun estimated, by digging one hundred miles of canals between bays and rivers at a cost of $3 million. A canal linking Lake Michigan to the Illinois River would open passage to the Mississippi, while roads and canals would both be built to connect the Ohio River to the Great Lakes. Such a facility of intercourse, all within the country's means, Calhoun said, would ensure its security along with its prosperity. He recommended that Congress designate the Army Corps of Engineers to make the surveys on a comprehensive plan, that the army be employed in building roads and canals, and that the War Department be the principal agency for executing the whole. The corps, the department, and the army were, in fact, already building military roads surreptitiously. Clay complained of this in order to show the hypocrisy of Monroe's constitutional opposition, and in 1819 he forced the president to approve a specific item appropriation for military roads. Calhoun, with a statesman's eye for power, aimed to make the War Department the head of an internal improvements empire.[19] The General Survey Act, finally approved in 1824, lodged in the War Department most of the authority for carrying it into effect.

Calhoun's passion for order and system extended to Indian affairs, but no area of responsibility proved more taxing or more frustrating. Part of the difficulty was the fragmentation of authority between the secretary, the superintendent of the Indian trade, the various territorial governors, and numerous Indian agents and factors. Calhoun sought and finally achieved centralization of authority in the Bureau of Indian Affairs. The competing interests of traders, settlers, and politicians inevitably got in the way of efficient conduct of Indian affairs. This was the basic problem. Calhoun could not cancel or avoid the pressures thus generated, but he managed to moderate them; and believing that the reputation of the United States was involved in this matter, he mixed a good deal of humanitarian principle into a realistic policy. Fundamentally, the policy traced back to Washington and Jefferson and to the first secretary of war, Henry Knox. Its main features were, first, the peaceful acquisition of Indian lands through negotiation with the tribes as if they were independent nations; second, control of the Indians through control of trade with them; third, by these means gradually drawing them from the chase and the hunt into the paths of civilization, ending eventually in their amalgamation with the dominant race. The policy assumed, in every respect, the supremacy of national authority in Indian affairs.[20]

When Calhoun entered office the system of trade with the Indians on the frontier through government-owned and -operated trading houses, or factories, was the target of attack from John Jacob Astor's American Fur Company and its political friends. The factory system dated from 1796. Now there were eight houses with a combined capital of $300,000. Private traders, though allowed to compete under license, wanted to eliminate government from the business. The factory law was due to expire in 1819, and the House directed the new secretary to report a plan of Indian trade premised on the abolition of the factories. Backed by Thomas L. McKenney, superintendent of the Indian trade, Calhoun defended the system but said that if the factories must be given up, control of the trade should remain in government hands as the only effective means of protecting the Indians and bringing them to civilization. In the East, where the Indians lived in proximity to whites and were already in the paths of civilization, private trade might be allowed under strict license of a few large businessmen subject to government surveillance. In the West, where the savages were scattered and nomadic, where British and Spanish companies competed with the Americans, where the tribes were prey to unscrupulous traders, Calhoun proposed the creation of a chartered trading monopoly. He acknowledged the objection, well entrenched in republican belief, against monopoly and privilege, and the general preference for *laissez-faire*, but he argued that exceptional circumstances justified exceptional solutions. "A nation discovers its wisdom no less in departing from general maxims, when it is no longer wise to adhere to them, than in an adherence to them in ordinary circumstances. In fact," said Calhoun, "it evinces a greater effort of reason. The first advance of a nation is marked by the establishment of maxims, which are deemed universal, but which further experience and reflection teach to be only general, admitting of occasional modifications and exceptions."[21] There spoke the anti-ideologue, the creative statesman, the nationalist. The factory system survived in 1819. The assault continued, however; and although Calhoun and McKenney defended it ever more vigorously, Congress voted in 1822 to abolish the government trading houses, then grown to nine, and to throw the trade wide open to private enterprise.[22]

The ultimate goal of government Indian policy was, of course, the incorporation of the natives into white society. With his enlightened predecessors Calhoun believed this was the only alternative to extinction; and he looked forward to the day when bounty and protection would cease, when millions of acres of tribal lands would be divided among the Indians as private property—the bulk of the lands having been ceded to the United States—when they would become independent farmers as well as free American citizens. "It is impossible, with their customs," Calhoun wrote, "that they should exist as independent communities in the midst of civilized societies."[23] He looked to the education of Indian children to effect this change. In 1819, and annually thereafter, Congress appropriated $10,000 for the work of civilizing Indian tribes near the frontiers. Calhoun chose to devote this "civilization fund" to schools conducted by Protestant missionaries under the direction, and with the partial support, of the American Board of Commissioners for Foreign Missions. Most of the appropriation went unused in 1819, when only four schools existed in the Indians' country. Three years later there were fourteen schools with over five hundred pupils.[24] Calhoun was encouraged. The case of the Cherokee proved that the most educated tribe was also closest to the ultimate goal. Nevertheless, he worried whether there was enough time—at least a generation was necessary—for education to accomplish its work. For the course of degradation and extinction continued apace. Indeed, in too many instances, the white man's civilization brought nothing but misery to the Indians. "They lose the lofty spirit and heroic courage of the savage state, without acquiring the virtues which belong to the civilized. Depressed in spirit, and debauched in morals, they dwindle away through a wretched existence, a nuisance to the surrounding country."[25]

This dilemma led Calhoun, along with other men of good will, to conclude that in order to save the Indians it was necessary to remove them out of the way of the white man, to buy time, as it were, in the isolation of reservations beyond the frontier, where the slow processes of education and civilization could do their work. The policy of Indian removal, taking form during these years, would be fully implemented in Andrew Jackson's administration. Jackson was already an advocate. He had no patience with "the farce of treating with Indian tribes," thought that they should be considered "subjects" rather than nations, and would use whatever measures of force, cajolery, and chicane might be necessary to remove the eastern tribes west of the Mississippi.[26] Hearing this advice from an old Indian-hater, Calhoun came to realize that it was also the voice of the frontier. Westerners made no humanitarian fuss. But in the East, wherever white men pressed on Indian lands, removal offered itself not only as the realistic solution but as the humanitarian one as well. Calhoun himself, although he could never agree with Jackson's iron-fisted approach to the Indians, favored giving the policy a trial under fair and moderate rules.

The Choctaws, in Mississippi, became the test case.[27] One of the five civilized tribes, the Choctaws were peaceful, friendly, and relatively advanced under good leadership. They claimed in excess of fifteen million acres in central and western Mississippi. Nowhere, except in Georgia where Creeks and Cherokees were the problem, was there stronger pressure for cession and removal. In 1818 Calhoun appointed a commission to negotiate for a large tract on the Mississippi in exchange for lands in the western reaches of the Arkansas Territory. The Choctaws stubbornly refused to consider the proposition. Next year a second commission, of which Jackson was a member, met with the same fate. Angry Mississippians led by Governor George Poindexter demanded that Calhoun get tough with the Choctaws. The political consequences of a third failure would be severe, yet the secretary had little choice but to risk it. And he succeeded. The Treaty of Doak's Stand, in October 1820, provided for the Mississippi cession in exchange for lands in Arkansas. Unfortunately, the jubilation was spoiled when the Choctaws discovered that some of the new lands were already occupied by whites. Arkansas, at the same time, protested against being turned into a Botany Bay for the refuse of Mississippi. Nevertheless, the treaty was ratified, and Calhoun plunged ahead. Immediately, the Choctaws, feeling betrayed, repudiated the treaty; and in 1822, knowing he courted new outrage in Mississippi, Calhoun conceded the justice of the tribe's complaint and halted removal. Finally, in 1824, a Choctaw delegation under Chief Pushmataha visited Washington to negotiate a new treaty. Signed only a month before Calhoun left office, the treaty of 1825 arranged a settlement satisfactory to the Choctaws at considerable expense to the government. Under it the Indians were encouraged to emigrate, but were not compelled to do so. And as long as Calhoun's moderate and voluntary policy prevailed very few did—no more than fifty by 1830. But then a new treaty imposed by President Jackson took most of the remaining Choctaw lands in Mississippi and forced some twelve thousand to emigrate in three years. Calhoun also tried to induce the Eastern Cherokee to move to Arkansas and the old tribes of the Six Nations to move to Wisconsin. He was no more successful in these efforts, however, than he was with the Choctaw.

Disappointed by his inability to control Indian affairs, Calhoun suffered his worst defeat in the main arena of military policy. The gloomy treasury forecast in December 1819 gave rise to a party in Congress called "Radicals," whose principal demand was for retrenchment and economy. The War Department presented the most inviting target. Calhoun suspected that Crawford had purposely shaded his report in order to provoke budget-slashing mania in Congress, looking to the relief of the treasury at the expense of the

War Department—in sum, that the treasury report proceeded more from political than fiscal calculations. His suspicion was not groundless. The rivalry between the two secretaries contributed to the increasingly partisan division in Congress. Not all Radicals were Crawfordites, or vice versa; but they tended to converge, and through the election of 1824 and beyond Crawford and his followers were Calhoun's bitter enemies. They were not his only ones, however, nor was retrenchment the only basis for the congressional attack on the War Department. It actually began two years earlier when Lewis Williams, of North Carolina, dredged up old republican fears of a standing army. This was followed by Jackson's adventure in Florida, which offered a textbook case of the dangers of Caesarism to the republic. Calhoun himself had wanted to censure Jackson because he realized that the integrity of the army as a republican institution depended on prompt compliance by generals in the field to the orders of the commander-in-chief. But regardless of these other influences, the secretary believed Crawford was behind the attack on his department; moreover, that the Speaker of the House cooperated with him.[28]

The attack covered a wide front. Pensions were drastically reduced. Two years earlier Congress had voted Revolutionary War pensions with a lavish hand. The Pension Bureau, after screening tens of thousands of applications, extended its rolls to over eighteen thousand persons. Now, by congressional decree, it was required to lop off one-third of the pensioners. The Yellowstone Expedition, in winter quarters at Council Bluffs in 1820, was ordered to go no farther. The expedition had been undertaken without congressional authorization; costs had got out of hand, and it was learned that $300,000 had been advanced on credit to the principal contractor, James Johnson, brother of Kentucky congressman Richard M. Johnson. No one suspected Calhoun of wrongdoing, but the troubles of the expedition suggested want of judgment and moderation. "His schemes are too grand and magnificent, and he labors too much for show and effect," wrote one congressman who was neither friend nor foe. "If we had a revenue of a hundred million, he would be at no loss how to spend it."[29] Fortifications, for which expenditures had exceeded appropriations, were slated for reduction. Some Radicals, with a flurry of democratic rhetoric, denounced the academy at West Point and moved to abolish this "dangerous aristocratic" institution.

The army itself survived the Radical assault in 1820, but only because there was no agreement on how the proposed 50-percent reduction in force should be made. In this situation Clay offered a resolution requesting the secretary of war to report a plan to the next session to reduce the army to six thousand men, plus the present two-thousand-man Corps of Engineers. "For himself," Clay remarked, lest his own position be misunderstood, "he could not vote to reduce a man of the Army in the present posture of our affairs."[30] The Florida treaty lay in the balance. Clay continued to support a strong military posture for the nation. The intent of his resolution was, by postponement, to avoid reckless and ruinous action against the army. But retrenchment was unavoidable, in Clay's opinion, once defeat of the tariff bill doomed the prospect of more revenue. And he was increasingly disgusted by the president's passivity. Monroe looked on as "an unconcerned spectator," the secretaries quarreled, and the budget was abandoned to the passions of Congress.[31] Although unsure of the Speaker's intentions in this matter, Calhoun took his usual dim view of Clay's political disposition. "Mr. Clay has undoubtedly his own personal views," Calhoun wrote, "and his friendship will be much regulated towards most public characters, as they may be supposed favorable, or opposed to his personal views." This was the opposite of his own system—his own ambition—founded on high principles. "I do not view politics as a scramble between eminent men; but as a science by which the lasting interest of the country may be advanced."[32] Clay's resolution was adopted, gaining a reprieve for the army, though the secretary was contemptuous of the scrambling politics that produced it.

Calhoun was ready with his report in December. As expected, he argued for keeping the army at its present strength, taunted those who trumpeted the virtues of militias and the vice of standing armies, and insisted that he had already achieved great economies—$1 million by the reorganization of the general staff alone—along with improvements in strength and efficiency. But on the supposition that Congress would persist in its demand, Calhoun offered a plan which, while shrinking the size of the army, would keep it entire and intact. The staff, the officer corps, the number of battalions and companies would remain the same; only the number of enlisted personnel would be reduced. Thus the nucleus of skill and experience would be maintained; the bones and sinew of a skeleton army would be continued, ready to take on flesh and blood in any national emergency.[33] The plan was certainly ingenious. Some congressmen applauded it. The Radicals, however, thought the report impudent and ridiculed the conception of an army which, by one estimate, would have one officer for every two enlisted men.[34] The plan was buried in committee, and the House proceeded to adopt by a lopsided vote an army bill that mandated drastic reductions all through the ranks. Senate amendments made it only a little more palatable to Calhoun. More than the army was hurt. The appropriation for coastal fortifications was cut from $800,000 to $200,000. The Indian affairs budget was sliced in half. (A companion bill retired one-half of the naval vessels in service.) When the Sixteenth Congress adjourned the total budget of the War Department had been cut almost in half to $5 million. Surveying the wreckage, Calhoun reflected sadly on the results of four years' labor to raise the army to a state of perfection unknown in its history. He blamed the disaster on narrow-minded politicians, stealthily maneuvered by Crawford, who seized upon the temporary embarrassment of the treasury "to disorganize and cast down" his best work.[35]

The secretary proceeded in 1821 with the painful task of making the reductions mandated by Congress. Even after the work was done, and done conscientiously, he continued to be harassed by the Crawford faction in Congress. They complained of the demotion of this brigadier general or that one, the dismissal of this captain or another, every one of whom seemed to have political connections. In Clay's absence, the Radicals installed one of their own, Philip P. Barbour, in the Speaker's chair; and while exposed to their fury in the House, Calhoun had also to contend with the growing opposition of Thomas Hart Benton and his friends in the Senate. It was perhaps a small victory, owing in part to economic recovery, that Calhoun was able to maintain the War Department for the balance of his tenure at the appropriation level established in 1821.[36]

At this point Calhoun became, in John Randolph's derisive comment, "the Army candidate for the Presidency," and ambition eclipsed the administrative nationalism he brought into the department.[37] The secretaryship proved a chastening experience. The ideal of making the War Department not only an agency of national power but also an agency of national progress and enlightenment—a center of energy radiating across the continent—was defeated. The army fell victim to old prejudices, personal politics, and untoward circumstances. Few of the forts would ever be constructed. Exploration of the continent was stopped in its tracks. Internal improvements were hobbled. Indian affairs began to slip altogether from the control of the government. Of course, Calhoun did not admit defeat—he later wrote a glowing account of his ministry—and close associates were lavish in their praise. "If ever there was perfection carried into any branch of the public service it was that which Mr. Calhoun carried into the War Department," wrote McKenney in his *Memoirs*. "Father of the War Department" became a title of the statesman's fame.[38] To impressive managerial talents, which in another era might have made him a captain of industry, Calhoun united bold and comprehensive views of public policy. Even in small things he showed breadth and vision. He inaugurated a great collection of Indian portraits in the War Department. He directed surgeons at military posts across the country to keep minute records of the diseases they treated, with what results, and of the weather, to be forwarded regularly to the surgeon general in Washington. Compilations of these statistics, among the first gathered by the government on subjects other than population and trade, were later published.[39]

Science and statecraft went together in Calhoun's conception of government. But the conception was too grand for its time, unpopular with Congress, and vulnerable to political assault. His experience at the head of the War Department became another chapter in the disruption of the Republican party. As he recovered from disappointment and defeat, and made his own bid to control the destiny of the party, Calhoun became notably more cautious and also opened himself to that "scramble" of personal, sectional, and factional politics he deplored. The ultimate irony was that this leader of the "Prodigals," as Calhoun and company were dubbed by the Radicals, would later boast, not of the boldness and liberality that distinguished his ministry, but of the regimen of economy and retrenchment that, in fact, was forced upon him.[40]

4. *Webster at the Bar, on the Platform*

Daniel Webster moved to Boston in August 1816, several months before he retired from Congress, and began to practice law in this flourishing city—the financial, commercial, and literary capital of New England—he had first known as an apprentice twelve years before. He had outgrown Portsmouth, the New Hampshire seaport, which had gone into decline since the war. There his political prospects appeared no brighter than his professional prospects. Not even Portsmouth, for years the Federalist stronghold, escaped the political revolution of 1816 that swept the Republicans into power in New Hampshire. They promptly emulated the proscription practiced against them in 1813, throwing out all the Federalist judges and packing the courts with Republicans. The Granite State was no longer a hospitable place for a Federalist lawyer and politician, and although Webster retained familial and proprietary interests there, he cheerfully left its political fortunes, and those of his beleagured party, to old leaders like Jeremiah Mason and Jeremiah Smith and to younger ones like his brother Ezekial.[1]

Webster's reputation had preceded him to Boston. He quickly moved to the head of the bar and acquired the usual badges of the Boston aristocracy, from a seat in the Athenaeum to a pew in the Brattle Square Church. Man and city seemed made for each other. Webster possessed the cool reason, the conservative values, the literary culture, and the pride of heritage so much admired in the New England capital, together with the personal force and eloquence to represent its interests before the nation. To Webster Boston offered everything. A city of forty thousand—six times the size of Portsmouth—it boasted wealth without ostentation, the manners and tastes of aristocratic society along with the profit-making habits of bourgeois capitalism. Oddly, it was still being governed by town meeting, and, as in a country village, "the character of every man [is] open to the observation of every other."[2] Webster settled his family in the fashionable residential area on Beacon Hill, near the splendid new State House, and built his practice in the business hub, State Street. His practice ran the gamut of cases: civil and criminal, law and equity, trial and appellate, from lowly county courts to the majesty of the United States Supreme Court. By 1819 Webster was earning $15–$20,000 a year, a handsome income.[3] But no matter how much Webster earned, it was never enough to support his extravagant habits and wasteful ways. He was already borrowing from his friends before he left Congress. He had assumed his father's debts; he had not yet recovered from the loss of his Portsmouth house, which was uninsured, to fire; and, of course, he incurred large expenses during his move to Boston. Whether he had at this early date sold himself to his new Boston clients, as one biographer has suggested, is doubtful; but even if no purse was dropped into his lap, even if no bills were paid, he knew by whom he was retained and what was expected of him. He had met Francis Cabot Lowell in Washington, lobbying for the tariff. Lowell, the chief of the textile manufacturers, failed to convert the congressman to protectionism, but he encouraged him to move to Boston, then helped him get started and offered the opportunity to invest in the great new venture of the Boston Associates at the town called Lowell.[4] The Boston merchant princes, having made their money in foreign trade, were now investing heavily in industrial manufactures. Webster watched this shift of capital, and when the balance of financial interest changed in State Street in the 1820s, he changed with it.

Webster focused his talents and energies for six years on making money, yet he was never out of the public eye or removed from politics. He continued to act as a Federalist, which was not immediately suicidal in Massachusetts; realizing that the party was doomed, however, and wholly without influence nationally, Webster sought to make the "good feelings" of the Monroe era a prelude to the end of old party distinctions and to the amalgamation of the Federalists into a transcendent party of the Union, at once national and republican. He adopted the slogan, "measures, not men," in this connection. Boston Federalists seemed to believe he was responsible for President Monroe's grand tour of the northern states in 1817. Before leaving Washington, it was said, Webster had called on the new president and, after dwelling on the need to allay party feelings, overcame Monroe's fears that he would be unwelcome in New England. "The country," Webster had supposedly assured him, "was much too busy and too eager in its prosperity, to give much time to quarreling about things chiefly bygone."[5] Monroe, although he made the tour, disappointed Webster. He refused to lift the proscription of Federalists lest he shock his Republican friends. Locally, and in the state, the Federalist party split between those who sought to keep up opposition and those who sought conciliation at any price. Webster deplored this division, "this miserable, dirty squabble of local politics," which was depriving Massachusetts of character and consequence in national affairs, most strikingly demonstrated by the Missouri Compromise. "What has sickened me beyond remedy is the tone and temper of these disputes," Webster wrote in 1823. "We are disgraced beyond help or hope by these things. There is a Federal interest, a Democratic interest, a Bankrupt interest, an Orthodox interest, and a Middling interest, but I see no national interest, nor any national feeling in the whole matter."[6] He had, at this time, just been elected to Congress as the "Goliath" of the Federalist establishment in Boston over the candidate of the "Middling interest," a coalition of dissenting Federalists and Republicans. Returning to Congress, Webster continued to seek Republican acceptance of reformed yet unrepentant Federalists, but he made little headway. As the party shrank into insignificance, losing even its bargaining power, he tried to overcome his Federalist past and enter the Republican ranks under the banner of reconciliation. And he succeeded by virtue of a reputation too formidable to be denied. He was twice reelected to Congress, once without opposition, once overwhelmingly; and in 1827 he was elevated to the Senate by the Republican-dominated legislature of Massachusetts.[7]

The mass of Webster's law business, like that of his colleagues at the bar, was neither edifying nor important in the history of the nation; but in his advocacy before the United States Supreme Court, Webster turned ordinary law cases into vehicles of statesmanship with profound effects. In this he epitomized the glory of the American legal profession so much celebrated during these years. The unique right of judicial tribunals to decide constitutional questions, enabling the humblest citizen in the humblest case to appeal to the supreme law, widened the scope of American law and invested it with the utmost dignity of state. As Justice Story, Webster's good friend, declared in 1821, "The discussion of constitutional questions throws a lustre round the bar, and gives a dignity to its function, which can rarely belong to the profession in any other country." He went on to draw the conservative implications. "Lawyers here are emphatically placed as sentinels upon the outposts of the constitution; and no nobler end can be proposed for their ambition or patriotism, than to stand as faithful guardians of the constitution, ready to defend its legitimate powers, and to stay the arm of legislative, executive, or popular oppression."[8] Webster came to embody this ideal, attaining an eminence unrivaled in his time, indeed never surpassed, as "guardian of the constitution." In this role he often appeared before the First Federal Circuit Court, in Boston, and the Supreme Judicial Court of Massachusetts, but the United States Supreme Court was his great tribunal, as it was the nation's. He first appeared there in 1814 as counsel in a prize case. Soon he had four or five cases a term; by the middle of the next decade he had as many as sixteen a term, after which he allowed his practice to decline, though he revived it toward the end of his life. Altogether from 1814 to 1852 Webster argued 168 cases before the Supreme Court. He won only half of them; as many of the cases involved high constitutional questions, however, he exerted great influence through his advocacy, win or lose.[9]

It was his argument in the Dartmouth College Case, in 1818, that established Webster's eminence before the court. His *alma mater* had fallen on baneful times. The president, John Wheelock, son of the founder, had always ruled the college as a benevolent despot, even in Webster's day; as he grew older his running quarrel with the trustees escalated until, in 1815, he invited the New Hampshire legislature to intervene and take control of the college. The trustees fought back, removed Wheelock, and appointed a new president. Inevitably the issue between the president and the trustees entered into the state's fiercely partisan politics. All the trustees—the "Octagon," as they came to be called—were Federalists, including some of Webster's close political friends. Wheelock, too, was a Federalist. Alienated from the orthodox church and the party leadership, however, he allied himself with Isaac Hill and the Republicans, in whose eyes the college was the citadel of a haughty aristocracy. When the Republicans returned to power in Concord in 1816, they proceeded to transform the private college into a state university. Governor William Plumer contended that, although Dartmouth was founded by a royal charter, the state had become the principal benefactor, hence could legislate for the college in the public interest. The governor's university bill abolished the old charter, condemned as a vestige of monarchy, and created a publicly appointed board of trustees. The issue was now between the state and the old board, the Octagon, which refused to submit. The new board eventually prevailed in this contest. Meanwhile, the Octagon brought suit against the secretary-treasurer, William H. Woodward, for the records and seal of the college. Thus the case of *Dartmouth College* v. *Woodward* was born.[10]

Webster had lobbied against the university bill at Concord, but he was not one of the original counsel for the college when the case was argued before the superior court at Exeter in 1817. The two Jeremiahs, Mason and Smith, were the counsel. Their brief introduced several pleas under the common law, the constitution of New Hampshire, and the United States Constitution. A principal issue was whether Dartmouth was a *private* corporation, immune from public supervision, or a *public* corporation subject to the will of the people of New Hampshire. Mason was apparently responsible for the argument that in the end proved decisive: the charter of 1769 not only created a private corporation but constituted a *contract* within the meaning of the clause of the federal Constitution (Article I, Section 10) prohibiting the states from violating "the Obligation of Contracts." Webster was brought in to summarize for the plaintiff at the close of the trial at Exeter. No record of his speech has survived, but it was said that his emotional peroration "left the whole courtroom in tears."[11] The solidly Republican court returned the expected verdict. Dartmouth was ruled to be a public corporation, created for the benefit of the people of New Hampshire; as for the contract clause, it applied only to the private rights of individuals, hence imposed no bar to legislative discretion with regard to the civil institutions of the state. The college immediately appealed to the United States Supreme Court on writ of error. Since neither Mason nor Smith wished to go to Washington, Webster was asked to take the case, which he agreed to do for $1,000, bringing in Joseph Hopkinson, of Philadelphia, as his associate.

The case was heard in the cramped temporary quarters of the Supreme Court during three days, March 10–12, 1818. Opening the argument for the plaintiff in error, Webster spoke in his calm, deliberate manner for over four hours. "It was hardly eloquence in any strict sense of the term," an observer later wrote. "It was pure reason. Now and then for a sentence, his eyes flashed and his voice swelled into a bolder note as he uttered some emphatic thought, but he instantly fell back into the tone of earnest conversation which ran throughout the whole body of his speech."[12] The argument was not original. Webster simply repeated the case developed by Mason and Smith at Exeter; in fact, he scarcely bothered to recast in in terms of the single plea, involving the contract clause, on which the suit was appealed to the Supreme Court. Undertaking to prove that Dartmouth was a private, eleemosynary institution, a creature of the founder, Eleazer Wheelock, rather than of the sovereign, Webster drew on English law dating back to Queen Elizabeth's time. This was edifying, perhaps, but beside the point; yet it served Webster's basic purpose, to place the rights and property of private corporations beyond legislative interference. If Dartmouth College could be destroyed by legislative fiat, so could Harvard, Yale, and every other educational institution founded by private benevolence. "It will be a dangerous, a most dangerous experiment, to hold these institutions subject to the rise and fall of popular parties, and the fluctuations of public opinion."[3] By extending the bar of the contract clause to corporate charters, this, and much more, would be prevented. Webster marshaled the mere handful of precedents in American law to support his position. The counsel for the university, John Holmes and William Wirt, relied entirely on the New Hampshire opinion, which was much admired and thought to be correct by so distinguished a jurist as Chancellor James Kent of New York.

In the end it may not have been Webster's legal argument that persuaded Chief Justice John Marshall and his associates to decide in favor of the college. Observers in Washington reported that Webster closed his speech "with a very pathetic address to the Court, apparently too much affected by apprehensions of the certain and inevitable ruin of the institution [the college], to express himself without tears of sorrow and regret."[4] Oddly, in view of the interest taken in the case, that "very pathetic address," Webster's peroration, would not be furnished to the public until after his death. It was only then that Chauncey Goodrich, a Yale professor and student of oratory, who had journeyed to Washington in 1818 to hear Webster in "the college case," published his recollection. For four hours he had sat enthralled by Webster's luminous reasoning, then, following a dramatic pause heard him address the court as follows:

> This, sir, is my case. It is the case, not merely of that humble institution, it is the case of every college in our land. It is more. It is the case of every eleemosynary institution throughout our country—of all those great charities founded by the piety of our ancestors, to alleviate human misery, and scatter blessings along the pathway of life. It is more! It is, in some sense, the case of every man among us who has property of which he may be stripped, for the question is simply is this: Shall our State Legislatures be allowed to take that which is not their own, to turn it from its original use, and apply it to such ends or purposes as they in their discretion shall see fit?
> Sir, you may destroy this institution; it is weak; it is in your hands! I know it is one of the lesser lights in the literary horizon of our country. You may put it out. But, if you do so, you must carry through your work! You must extinguish, one after another, all those greater lights of science which, for more than a century, have thrown their radiance over our land!
> It is, sir, as I have said, a small college. And yet there are those who love it—[15]

Here Webster was overcome with emotion. "The whole seemed to be mingled throughout with the recollection of father, mother, brother, and all the privations and trials through which he had made his life," Goodrich thought. In view of the similar pathetic appeal at Exeter, it seemed unlikely the peroration was "wholly unpremeditated," however, or its effects uncalculated by Webster. The courtroom, at any rate, presented an extraordinary spectacle. Tears suffused the eyes of the Chief Justice; all the associates, deeply moved, gazed intently on the speaker, while the audience sat spellbound. Webster, regaining his composure, then closed.

> Sir, I know not how others may feel [glancing at the opponents of the college before him], but, for myself, when I see my Alma Mater surrounded like Caesar in the senate-house, by those who are reiterating stab after stab, I would not, for this right hand, have her to turn to me, and say, *Et tu quoque mi fili! And thou too, my son!*

He sat down, said Goodrich, amid "deathlike stillness."

Although Goodrich's account of the address stands alone, it has the ring of truth and agrees with contemporary reports of Webster's impact upon the court. George Ticknor, his literary friend, and fellow alumnus of Dartmouth, said the heartfelt remembrance imparted a "sort of religious sensibility" to the logic of the law and, in this extraordinary state of excitement, made the logic irresistible. Only those who heard Webster, he thought, truly understood how he had given life to "the dry skeleton" of the college case.[16] Webster, however, confessed more embarrassment than pride in the peroration. When a decision in the case was deferred to the next term, both sides actively sought to influence the court, believed to be closely divided. Webster shrewdly had copies of his argument printed for circulation among prominent judges. "All the nonsense is left out," he told Mason, referring to the pathetic address which he knew, whatever its power in the courtroom, was beneath the dignity of the law.[17] The copy sent to Chancellor Kent not only converted him to the college side but may have prompted him, as intended, to use his influence with one or more of the justices in Washington.[18]

On February 2, 1819, without the reargument that had been expected, the Supreme Court delivered its decision. Only one justice dissented from Marshall's opinion that the college was a private, charitable institution protected from state interference by the contract clause of the United States Constitution. Webster had hoped that the court would go beyond this narrow ground and, appealing to "the general principles of our governments," condemn all legislative infringements of "vested rights."[19] The decision, even if narrow, went on his argument and substantially increased the protection of all corporations, whether in education or in business. "The decision in that case," Kent would assert, "did more than any other single act proceeding from the authority of the United States, to throw an impregnable barrier around all the rights and franchises derived from the grant of government."[20] Webster was satisfied with it. Friends of Dartmouth wished to publish a book on the case in order to attract support for the struggling college. He showed some hesitation. "I shall stand well enough in the Washington Report [Wheaton's official report of Supreme Court decisions] and if the Book should be published, the world would know where I borrowed my plumes."[21] But this was by way of apology to Mason. Webster knew that he had become thoroughly identified with the case, that it had already sent his reputation soaring, and would add to his fame in the future. "This is a work you must do for *reputa-*

tion," he told Hopkinson in urging him to write out his argument for the book. "Our college cause will be known to our children's children."[22] Even in *The Report of the Case,* however, Webster omitted the peroration that in time eclipsed the fame of the argument. The book, edited by his Portsmouth law partner, Timothy Farrar, Jr., appeared in August while Webster was attending the Dartmouth commencement. On the day when the college decision was announced, six months before, Hopkinson had written to the president, "I would have an inscription over the door of your building, 'Founded by Eleaszer Wheelock, Refounded by Daniel Webster.' "[23] The tribute was apt. It would, in fact, later be carved in bronze before Webster Hall, becoming no less a part of the history of the college than it was part of the legend of Daniel Webster.

"Great things have been done in this session," Webster wrote at the end of the court's term in 1819, its first in the elegantly refinished chamber of the Capitol.[24] Two weeks after the opinion in *Dartmouth College* v. *Woodward,* Marshall employed the contract clause to strike down a New York statute for the relief of debtors, further fortifying the protection of private property against government. Webster did not appear in this important case, *Sturges* v. *Crowninshield,* but he was a deeply interested spectator, as he must have been also of the great debate in Congress on Jackson and the Seminole campaign. He appeared as an advocate in four other cases during the term, the most important being *McCulloch* v. *Maryland.* Two points were at issue: the constitutionality of the congressional act chartering the Bank of the United States and of the Maryland law imposing a prohibitive tax on the Baltimore branch of the Bank. Here the Boston lawyer stood in the shadow of William Pinkney, the flamboyant Marylander who was the acknowledged old master before the Supreme Court, as Webster was the rising star. Pinkney was employed as senior counsel for the Bank, Webster as a junior associate; and the contrast between the torrential eloquence of the former and the calm deliberation of the latter was a remarkable study.[25] The question of the constitutionality of a national bank had been exhausted, as Webster said, by Alexander Hamilton in his famous opinion of 1791 invoking the doctrine of implied powers. Proceeding on that ground, the only question was whether a state could tax a legitimate instrument of the general government. If it could, the Constitution existed at the sufferance of the state legislatures. "An unlimited power to tax involves, necessarily, a power to destroy," Webster declared. In ruling for the Bank, Marshall relied primarily on Pinkney's closing argument, but in asserting that "the power to tax involves the power to destroy," he raised Webster's logic to an axiom of constitutional law.[26]

Webster vied with the chief justice himself as a proponent of the judicial nationalism that burst upon the country in 1819. And when Pinkney died three years later, there was no one to challenge his preeminence before the Supreme Court. As he invoked judicial power to strengthen the national authority, he also exalted the dignity and authority of the court. "Sir," he said, "there exists not upon earth, and there never did exist, a judicial tribunal clothed with powers so various, and so important." It was "the great arbitrator between contending sovereignties"—mightier than sovereigns! "I am persuaded that the Union could not exist without it."[27] Influence before the court was influence before the country, and Webster rejoiced in it. Even in the law he conceived of himself as a statesman. Like all lawyers he submitted his talents to a motley clientele; personal belief, therefore, cannot be automatically inferred from courtroom arguments. But there was a high correlation between the two in his professional career; in cases of constitutional law he was almost always on the side of vested property rights or of national power. *Dartmouth* and *McCulloch* set the course. The two were not always compatible, but like Hamilton before him Webster used property interests as the fulcrum of national power and that power as the protector of property.

Two additional cases in which he distinguished himself during these years may be offered as examples. *Gibbons* v. *Ogden,* in 1824, involved the constitutional validity of laws of New York granting a monopoly of steamboat navigation in the waters of the state to Robert Fulton and Robert R. Livingston. The monopoly had repeatedly withstood challenge in state courts; now it was brought before the Supreme Court on the plaintiff's appeal of an injunction restraining him from operating a steamboat between New York City and the New Jersey shore. Webster was retained by the plaintiff, Gibbons, though he had no prior connection with the question. The case was then called up suddenly, allowing him, it later was said, less than twenty-four hours to prepare his brief.[28] Setting up the claim of the *exclusive* power of Congress to regulate interstate commerce, Webster made perhaps the boldest and most original argument of his career. Since his youth he had believed that the Constitution owed its existence to the movement to rescue commerce from the embarrassments of state legislation by placing it under the care of a national and uniform system. The regulation of such a system, he now maintained, must be exclusive. The prevalent idea of a concurrent regulating power in the states, as advocated by the defendant, was "insidious and dangerous" even where congressional power lay dormant, as in this case. The report offers only an outline of Webster's five-hour argument, but it suggests the plain and luminous statement of the issue, the keenness of analysis, and the vigor of generalization that, as Ticknor said, "were no small part of the secret of his power before the court."[29] Striking down the steamboat monopoly, Marshall again extended the limits of national power. He did not, however, follow Webster and assert exclusive congressional jurisdiction; rather, he found the New York legislation in conflict with the federal Coastal Licensing Act of 1793, a plea Webster had introduced as little more than an afterthought.

In the case of *Ogden* v. *Saunders* (1827), Webster again entered the claim of exclusive national jurisdiction in a matter of vital importance to the trade and property of the country. At issue was the validity of a New York bankruptcy statute with respect to contracts made after its enactment. Earlier, in the *Sturges* case, the court had declared a similar New York act unconstitutional because it retroactively discharged debts contracted before passage. Now Webster, for the plaintiff, asked for reconsideration of that decision and the extension of the prohibition on state legislation to future contracts. When the case was first argued in 1824, Henry Clay appeared for the defendant. The record of the confrontation—the only one between the two men before the Supreme Court—is meager, but Clay challenged Webster's application of the contract clause to this subject, upon which there was a mass of state legislation, and held that in the absence of congressional bankruptcy legislation the states were free to act.[30] Before leaving the House of Representatives in 1817, Webster had attempted to breathe life into the constitutional provision empowering Congress to establish "uniform laws on the subject of Bankruptcies throughout the United States" (Article I, Section 8). He renewed the effort upon his return to Congress. This was an instance where Webster's activities in the House and before the Court overlapped. A national bankruptcy law would, of course, take precedence over the dissonance of state laws and ensure the same protection for the property of debtors and creditors wherever it lay. But most congressmen felt little interest in a bankruptcy law, supposed to be primarily for the benefit of merchants; indeed, Webster's bill met defeat in the Senate while decision in *Ogden* v. *Saunders* was pending before the court. It therefore became imperative, in Webster's view, for the court to deprive the states of any right to decide how debts should be discharged. He argued brilliantly that the two clauses, contract and bankruptcy, were correlatives: the states were barred from interference with the former; Congress alone could legislate on the latter. Once the court ruled definitively, the states would retire from the field and Congress would take rightful possession.[31] But the court ruled narrowly, four to three, that the New York statute was constitutional. Webster took what consolation he could from the fact that the chief justice, and also his friend Story, agreed with him.

In the winter of 1820–21, Webster was a delegate to the Massachusetts convention, assembled in Boston, to revise the constitution of 1780. "His all-important services in this body," one of his friends later wrote in a newspaper biography, "introduced him to the people of Massachusetts most auspiciously as a legislator, and prepared his way for reentering Congress."[32] It was a distinguished body, beginning with old John Adams, the father of the original constitution, and counting Josiah Quincy, Chief Justice Isaac Parker, and Justice Story who, with Webster and two or three others, composed the conservative cadre in the convention. The reformers, led by the sons of the first Bay State Jeffersonians—Levi Lincoln, James T. Austin, and Henry Dearborn, among others—were more numerous but neither as distinguished nor as well led. The conservatives pursued a defensive strategy, conciliatory on minor points but obstinate on major ones. Thus Webster yielded the oath of religion for officeholders but saved state-supported religion in Massachusetts; yielded the freehold suffrage but secured a taxpaying qualification; and while he failed in his effort to strengthen the independence of judges, he successfully defended the judiciary against democratic attack. As Story wrote, "It was no small thing to prevent sad mischiefs to the Constitution."[33]

Webster made his most memorable speech in opposition to Dearborn's resolution to change the basis of representation in the senate from property to population. The historic principle of proportioning the senate according to the taxable property of the districts was an "aristocratical" survival in the eyes of reformers, and had no place in a government committed to equal rights. Vigorously defending the propertied basis of the senate as a prudent check on the popular lower house, Webster demonstrated his learning in political philosophy and revealed his conservatism.[34] He spoke as John Adams had spoken in 1780; drawing his ideas from the same well, chiefly from James Harrington, the seventeenth-century English "commonwealthman," he seemed to say that the Americans had made no advance in political science since the Revolution. In reality, of course, they had overcome Old World fears of democracy trampling on the rights of property—fears that had haunted John Adams. Discarding the notion of a legislative balance between property and numbers, American constitution-makers had moved rapidly toward adoption of a uniformly democratic system of representation. This had happened, in part, for reasons that Webster himself underscored in his speech. The laws of property, founded on fee simple and allodial tenure, worked for its wide distribution, for a rough equality, for giving the great majority of the people an interest in its preservation. Society was not divided between the rich and the poor, so there was no call to secure property against numbers in government. Webster knew this logic, indeed thought it the genius of New England institutions, yet defended the principle rooted in the old logic of balanced government. Why, he asked, if so great a portion of the people of Massachusetts owns property, should there be any objection to its protection in the constitution of the senate? But why, it could as well be asked, did property need special protection, if it was so widely distributed? Webster's argument, for all its brilliant passages, simply did not hang together. This suggests the intellectual defect of a conservative whose attachment to traditional values and institutions hobbled his response to an increasingly egalitarian society. Nonetheless, Webster and his friends prevailed on this issue, turning the original majority for the Dearborn resolution into a majority for maintaining the 1780 rule. In practice, the difference between the two rules, property and numbers, was not great—the old one tended to favor Boston and the eastern cities—but the "aristocratical principle" of senatorial representation remained an affront to Massachusetts democracy until after Webster's death.

Several days before Christmas, Webster took leave of the convention and journeyed to Plymouth, two days' drive from Boston, to join in the commemoration of the two-hundredth anniversary of the landing of the Pilgrims. There had been Pilgrim celebrations since 1770; for the past twenty years they had occurred more or less regularly at Plymouth. The bicentennial was a special occasion, of course; and the newly organized Pilgrim Society hoped to make it memorable by having Daniel Webster deliver the oration. The weather turned mild, and a great crowd descended on Plymouth. Among the visitors who sat down to dinner, then attended the gala ball, on Thursday, December 21, were President John T. Kirkland and Professors Edward Everett and George Ticknor of Harvard College; Massachusetts judges John Davis and Isaac P. Davis; merchants Thomas H. Perkins and Amos Lawrence;

Thomas Bulfinch, the architect; many Boston lawyers, and a veritable conclave of ministers. The next day Webster delivered his oration, "The First Settlement of New England," before an audience of fifteen hundred in the First Parish Church.[35]

The oration was in perfect harmony with the place and the occasion. At the outset Webster conjured up "the *genius of the place*."

> We cast our eyes abroad on the ocean, and we see where the little bark, with the interesting group upon its deck, made its slow progress to the shore. We look around us, and behold the hills and promontories, where the anxious eyes of our fathers first saw the places of habitation and of rest. We feel the cold which benumbed, and listen to the winds which pierced them. Beneath us is the Rock, on which New England received the feet of the Pilgrims. We seem even to behold them, as they struggle with the elements, and, with toilsome efforts, gain the shore. We listen to the chiefs in council. . . . All of these seem to belong to this place, and to be present upon this occasion, to fill us with reverence and admiration.

Having invested the historical event with an almost religious sensibility, the orator sought to attach the feelings thus aroused in his audience to the ideas and institutions received from the Puritan forefathers. He spoke of that "moral and philosophical respect for our ancestors, which elevates the character and improves the heart"; in obedience to it we are—he continued to paraphrase Edmund Burke—"but links in the great chain of being, which begins with the origin of our race, runs onward through its successive generations, binding together the past, the present, and the future, and terminating at last, with the consummation of all things earthly, at the throne of God."

As spokesman for the collective wisdom of the people of New England, connecting their origins to their destiny, Webster surveyed the country's history from the founding to the Revolution. The colony quickly became a homeland, which was unprecedented in the annals of colonization; and unique institutions of religion, society, and government arose, fixing the future of the country. Here Webster repeated the theme of his speech, only a week before, in the Massachusetts convention. The laws of property reflected the comparative equality of social condition, and largely determined the republican character of government. In fact, the Pilgrims' laws of property bore little resemblance to the theory; it scarcely mattered, for Webster was addressing the sons, not the forefathers, who were only a sentiment. At Plymouth, however, because there was no cause to enlist the theory in the defense of inequality, it possessed an integrity missing from the Boston speech. "With property divided, as we have it, no other government than that of a republic could be maintained, even were we foolish enough to desire it," Webster declared. "There is reason, therefore, to expect a long continuance of our system." He went on to hymn the praise of other ancient institutions, such as free schools and support of religious instruction. The reign of public liberty in New England proved to the world that law and order, learning, religion, and morality were secure in a purely elective government. But lest New Englanders fall victim to the sin of pride, Webster concluded his discourse with a solemn arraignment of an old evil, the African slave trade.

> It is not fit that the land of the Pilgrims should bear the shame longer. I hear the sound of the hammer, I see the smoke of the furnace, where the manacles and fetters are still forged for human limbs. I see the visages of those, who by stealth, and at midnight, labor in this work of hell, foul and dark, as may become the artificers of such instruments of misery and torture. Let that spot be purified, or let it cease to be of New England.

And he called down the denunciations of the pulpit on these crimes. "Advance, then, ye future generations!" The orator spread his arms as if to embrace them. "We would hail you, as you rise in your long succession, to fill the places which we now fill. . . . We bid you welcome to this pleasant land of our fathers."[36]

"I was never so excited by public speaking before in my life," the scholarly Ticknor wrote that evening. "Three or four times I thought my temples would burst with the gush of blood. . . . I am aware it is no connected and compacted whole, but a collection of wonderful fragments of burning eloquence, to which his manner gave tenfold force. When I came out I was almost afraid to come near him. It seemed to me as if he was like the mount that might not be touched, and that burned with fire. I was beside myself, and am so still."[37] It is impossible to say how many were similarly affected; but Webster succeeded on this occasion in making his mind the mind of his audience, his feelings their feelings, his will their will. Oratory could go no further. Almost a year passed before he was ready to publish the discourse. The delay diminished its impact nationally but not in New England. The *North American Review* devoted an article to "Mr. Webster's Discourse," calling it the work of a great mind and a noble exemplification of patriotism. John Adams told Webster he had surpassed Burke as "the most consummate orator of modern times" and said he had entered perfectly into the spirit of New England. "This oration will be read five hundred years hence, with as much rapture as it was heard," he predicted. "It ought to be read at the end of every century, and read at the end of every year, for ever and ever."[38] Many orations, including some of Webster's, scarcely bore the light of print. But this one became a literary classic, long celebrated for its soul-stirring passages, recited by generations of schoolboys, and cherished as a primer of New England principles.

The Plymouth discourse marked Webster's debut on the stage of literary eminence and the commencement of a remarkable career in commemorative oratory. The ancients defined three types of oratory: forensic, deliberative, and epideictic or panegyrical. Webster, like Cicero, excelled in all three. In the third he was the first of the moderns, "the founder of his own school," for there were no models of commemorative oratory in England or on the Continent, and in the United States only a popular tradition of Fourth of July oratory, in which he had trained.[39] After 1820 Webster's eloquence was in constant demand—at the bar, in the assembly, on the patriotic platform. Hearing Webster, Josiah Quincy later recalled, marked an epoch in the lives of young New Englanders. From him they got their first idea of "the electric force" wielded by a master of speech. That force gained much from Webster's magnificent presence. "What a figurehead was there for the Ship of State!" Quincy exclaimed.[40] Ralph Waldo Emerson, growing up in Concord, going to Harvard, preaching in Boston, followed that majestic figurehead all his youthful days, "from the court to senate-chamber, from caucus to street," and never escaped its spell.[41] In his journal Emerson recorded a detailed characterization, not his own, though "very truly drawn" by a Boston lawyer:

> Webster is a very large man, about five feet, seven, or nine, in height, and thirty-nine or forty years old—he has a long head, very large black eyes, bushy eyebrows, a commanding expression—and his hair is coal-black and coarse as a crow's nest. His voice is sepulchral—there is not the least variety or the least harmony of tone—it commands, it fills, it echoes, but is harsh and discordant. He possesses an admirable readiness, a fine memory and a faculty of perfect abstraction, an unparalleled impudence and a tremendous faculty of concentration. . . . He knows his strength, has perfect confidence in his own powers, and is distinguished by a spirit of fixed determination; he marks his part out, and will cut off fifty heads rather than turn out of it; but is generous and free from malice, and will never move a step to make a severe remark. . . . He has no wit and never laughs, though he is very shrewd and sarcastic, and sometimes sets the whole court in a roar by the singularity or pointedness of a remark. His imagination is what the light of a furnace is to its heat, a necessary attendant—nothing sparkling or agreeable, but dreadful and gloomy.[42]

On June 17, 1825, the fiftieth anniversary of the Battle of Bunker Hill, Webster delivered the oration on laying the cornerstone of the monument at the historic site in Charleston, across the river from Boston. A charter member of the Bunker Hill Monument Association, he was now its president and had consented to deliver the anniversary address at the request of the trustees. General Lafayette, nearing the close of his triumphal tour of the United States, would be present along with many surviving veterans of the Revolutionary War. It was a fitting occasion to summon the spirit of the Revolution and shine it on the nation's future. The hillside where the battle had been fought formed an amphitheater; the platform, embowered with evergreen and roses, lay at the bottom of the hill. Webster, with his gown flowing in the breeze, conveyed to at least one spectator the idea of a Roman orator, in toga, sending his clarion voice to the far reaches of some ancient theater. Directly before him were Lafayette and the two hundred grizzled veterans, while all around on the rising hillside were an estimated twenty thousand people.[43]

"We are among the sepulchres of our father," Webster intoned.[44] The monument, which would be a granite obelisk rising to the heavens, was conceived as an emblem of gratitude to the Revolutionary forefathers and of the liberty and glory of the country: "Let it rise, till it meet the sun in its coming; let the earliest light of the morning gild it, and parting day linger and play on its summit." Webster brilliantly fused sentiment with symbol, then asked when or where had history recorded such momentous achievements as the first fifty years of the United States. "Venerable men!" he addressed the soldiers of the Revolution, "you have come down to us, from a former generation." (He had, he later said, composed this moving address while fishing for trout in the Mashpee River south of Boston.)[45] There were also eloquent tributes to General Warren, who perished at Bunker Hill, and to Lafayette, who planted the tree of liberty in Europe. Progress was everywhere—in the arts and sciences, in commerce and manufactures, in self-respect, refinement, and education, in the "vast commerce of ideas" across national boundaries. Most of all, there was progress in government. The Revolution, although an earth-shaking event, had succeeded only in the United States, leading Webster to reflect on the fortunate circumstances that produced it and the sober heads that guided it: "We had no domestic throne to overturn, no privileged orders to cast down, no violent changes of property to encounter. In the American Revolution, no man sought or wished for more than to defend and enjoy his own." But liberty was like a volcano, Webster said. Although suppressed for a time in other lands, it would "break out and flame up to heaven," as it had most recently in Greece. The United States remained the bright example to mankind. The sacred obligation to keep it free and pure devolved upon the sons of the fathers.

> The great trust now descends to new hands. . . . We can win no laurels in a war for independence. Earlier and worthier hands have gathered them all. Nor are there places for us by the side of Solon, and Alfred, and other founders of states. Our fathers have filled them. But there remains to us a great duty of defense and preservation, and there is opened to us, also, a noble pursuit, to which the spirit of the times strangely invites us. Our proper business is improvement. Let our age be the age of improvement.

And so the oration that began with the commemoration of one generation terminated in the exhortation of another.

The oration was a triumph. One man who had listened spellbound from beginning to end—about two hours—turned to his companion after Webster sat down and remarked with Yankee acuity, "Well, that was good, every word seemed to weigh a pound."[46] As with the Plymouth discourse, Webster had written out the speech, then committed it to memory, so that upon delivery he rarely glanced at the notes on the table beside him, indeed seemed to speak from the depths of his soul. The oration was immediately published. Webster gave the copyright to the Monument Association, which then sold it to a Boston publisher for, reportedly, the "enormous sum" of $600. His friend Ticknor, who prepared the copy for publication while Webster went off with his wife and friends on an excursion to Niagara Falls, said the amount was only half that. At any rate, it was probably the most ever paid to an orator to publish his work. Some readers thought the style of the oration too plain and severe, like the style of the monument it consecrated; others thought this accounted for its grandeur.[47]

The third of the great trilogy of commemorative orations by the young Webster was his eulogy on the lives and services of John Adams and Thomas Jefferson, delivered in Boston's famed Faneuil Hall on August 2, 1826. In this "age of commemoration," nothing so dramatically punctuated the end of the founding era of the republic as the passing of these two civic heroes in the midst of national jubilee, within hours of each other, on the fiftieth anniversary of American independence. The event, so extraordinary it was automatically pronounced providential, produced a flood of oratory all across the country, very little of it memorable. Webster's eulogy was the rare exception. It was, in fact, his most polished oration; like a fine symphony, it possessed unity of feeling and form throughout its various parts. Edward Everett, Webster's friendly rival in commemorative discourse, offered the *ex cathedra* judgment that "no similar effort of oratory was ever more completely successful." The setting was sublime. Faneuil Hall was shrouded in black; an organ placed in the gallery furnished the music; and the President of the United States led four thousand mourners in an imposing funeral service. Webster then rose. He spoke for just under two hours, never glancing at his manuscript, in perfect command of the multitude.[48]

"The tears which flow, and the honors that are paid, when the founders of the republic die," he began, "give hope that the republic itself may be immortal." The elegiac refrain "Adams and Jefferson are no more" punctuated the exordium, then gave way to the reflection that they yet lived in the remembrance of their countrymen and the homage of mankind. Webster traced the careers of the two men, one in Massachusetts, the other in Virginia, until they came together in the Continental Congress, where Jefferson was the author of the Declaration of Independence and Adams its leading advocate. Boldly recreating the scene in Congress, Webster borrowed the technique of Carlo Botta, the Italian historian of the American Revolution, improvising a debate between the two sides, in which Adams spoke with divine eloquence. "Sink or swim, live or die, survive or perish, I give my hand and my heart, to this vote." These were the first words of the imaginary speech that many Americans took to be genuine, and that would be recited so often in coming generations that it might as well have been.* Webster then resumed the biographical record, following the lives of the two statesmen to conclusion. In his peroration he returned to the dominant idea of the Bunker Hill oration; abandoning the solemn tone of the eulogy, he enjoined the sons of the fathers to faithful performance of the duties devolved upon them. "This lovely land, this glorious liberty, these benign institutions, the dear purchase of our

---

*Richard Rush wrote to Webster after reading the oration: "The speech . . . made my hair rise. It wears the character of a startling historical discovery. . . . Nothing of Livy's ever moved me so much. Certainly your attempt to pass the doors of that most august sanctuary, the congress of '76, and become a historian and reporter of its immortal debates, was extraordinarily bold, extremely hazardous. Nothing but success could have justified it, and you have succeeded." (*Papers of Daniel Webster*, II, 129.)

fathers, are ours; ours to enjoy, ours to preserve, ours to transmit. Generations past and generations to come, hold us responsible for this sacred trust." He went on in this vein for several minutes, finally drawing the moral:

> If we cherish the virtues and the principles of our fathers, Heaven will assist us to carry on the work of human liberty and human happiness. Auspicious omens cheer us. Great examples are before us. Our own firmament now shines brightly upon our path. Washington is in the clear upper sky. These other stars have now joined the American constellation; they circle round the centre, and the heavens beam with new light.

When the orator closed, the pitch of excitement he had wrought was such that three tremendous cheers roared through the hall, "inappropriate indeed for the occasion," Ticknor remarked, "but as inevitable as any great movement of nature."[49]

Three days later an obscure temperance journal in Boston commented, "To say of this production that it was eloquent, would be too common an expression to apply to such a performance. It was profound—it was sublime—it was godlike."[50] Thus originated, apparently, the appellation "Godlike Daniel." It was meant as the ultimate accolade, of course, and to Webster's New England admirers was nothing less than the solemn truth; but among his political enemies it would also become an epithet, a theme of party jest and ridicule. The adjective "godlike" had been Webster's own in one of the most interesting passages of the eulogy. As if in apology for the speech he was about to put in the mouth of John Adams, who was not known for his eloquence, Webster spoke of "the eloquence of action," which was especially appropriate to public bodies on great occasions:

> True eloquence, indeed, does not consist in speech. It cannot be brought from afar. Labor and learning may toil for it, but they will toil in vain. Words and phrases may be marshalled in every way, but they cannot compass it. It must exist in the man, in the subject, and in the occasion. Affected passion, intense expression, the pomp of declamation, all may aspire to it; they cannot reach it. It comes, if it comes at all, like the outbreaking of a fountain from the earth, or the bursting forth of volcanic fires, with spontaneous, original, native force. The graces taught in the schools, the costly ornaments and studied contrivances of speech, shock and disgust men, when their own lives, and the fate of their wives, their children, and their country, hang on the decision of the hour. . . . Then, patriotism is eloquent; then self-devotion is eloquent. The clear conception, outrunning the deductions of logic, the high purpose, the firm resolve, the dauntless spirit, speaking on the tongue, beaming from the eye, informing every feature, and urging the whole man onward, right onward to his object—this, this is eloquence, or rather it is something greater and higher than all eloquence, it is action, noble, sublime, godlike action.[51]

Concluding, said Ticknor, who never beheld grander presence or power in Webster, "he stamped his foot repeatedly on the stage"—an unusual gesture from him—"his form seemed to dilate, and he stood, as that whole audience saw and felt, the personification of what he so perfectly described."[52] Never, certainly, did he give more luminous statement to his own ideal of eloquence. It had nothing to do with the vehement declamation or the tinseled ornament so often admired in the oratory of the age and, indeed, supposed to characterize Webster's.

The three orations between 1819 and 1826 existed in the occasions, in the subjects, and also in the man.

> Immortal man! whose eloquence outstrips
> Rome's, Athens', England's, ancient, modern, all.[53]

They rapidly entered the classical literature of the young nation. "In the study of the scholar, and the cottage of the farmer, the old read them with delight and instruction," Caleb Cushing later wrote, "in our schools and colleges the young recur to them as the oracles of political wisdom, and in the recitation of their chosen passages, mould the boy to the destinies of the future patriot and statesman."[54] It was rare for an American statesman to attain the double fame of a lawyer; it was rarer still for one to attain the triple fame of a man of letters. But so it was with Godlike Daniel.

*   *Three*   *

THE POLITICAL CROSSROADS

When Daniel Webster reentered Congress in December 1823, the Monroe administration was in disarray and the presidential sweepstakes at full tilt. "We have no administration," Rufus King, the distinguished senator from New York observed. "Mr. Monroe tho' not buried, is dead, as respects direction or control."[1] For two years or longer the chief cabinet officers— John Quincy Adams, William H. Crawford, and John C. Calhoun—had been in the race for the succession, and they had been joined by Henry Clay and Andrew Jackson. No one, no agency, could control it. In the absence of a single dominant leader or a clear line of succession, such as the Virginia Dynasty had afforded, the Republican party split into personal followings and factions. The congressional caucus of the party, the mechanism for nominating candidates for the presidency and vice presidency, could no longer be relied on—the caucus itself had become an issue. In an increasingly democratic political environment it was assailed as a closed, elitist institution. Yet politicians saw no satisfactory alternative. "We are putting to the proof the most delicate part of our system, the election of the Executive," Webster remarked.[2] What was especially disturbing about the present contest, among Republicans nourished on traditional whig fears of executive power, was that it tended to make the presidency the center of gravity in the government. Great issues of public policy were submitted to the artifice and caprice of presidential politics; and senators and representatives, if elected on the basis of presidential loyalties, must submit their votes to the interest of one candidate or another. "It is an inversion of the natural order of things," editorialized the *National Intelligencer* in the capital. "The Third power in the government is thus made the first—the *only one* indeed, because all others are made subordinate to it in fact, when they become so in popular estimation. We cannot conceive, under our government, an evil more to be deprecated than this."[3] The worst was yet to come, of course. For with a multiplicity of candidates, each with his own ardent following, and none able to command a majority of votes, the election of the president must finally be made in Congress.

Nationalism was still in vogue when the Eighteenth Congress convened. It was this Congress, after all, that passed the 1824 tariff and the General Survey Bill. But the Republican consensus of 1815 had vanished. The Missouri Question had raised fears of sectional parties and politics, and these were not dispelled by the compromise. The growth of the West, with a sectional consciousness of its own, the multiplication of states, the scramble of economic interests and groups for the bounty and favor of the general government put the political system under heavy strain. While nationalists continued to feel that the Union would survive only through measures of consolidation, growing numbers of Republicans, inspired by the Virginia "Old Republicans," believed consolidation must tear the Union apart. They called for a return to Jeffersonian austerity. The vision of harmony and balance and reciprocity among the sections, which animated the American System, was becoming blurred. As each of the sections grew more and more conscious of its particular economic interest and committed to its pursuit, national politics was reduced to a struggle for power among great geographical interests. This would be clearer in 1828, or in 1832, than it was in 1824, when nothing appeared to be at stake but the political fortunes of the candidates; but behind the men were differences of principle, clashing ideas and policies, contrasting political styles, all of which gave a more significant cast to the contest.

Webster was full of apprehension for the future. Surveying the candidates, he thought all the prospects bad. A division had occurred in Congress between Republicans and Radicals that would, he supposed, become the basis of a new party division, and his sympathies lay with the former faction. He was scarcely at liberty to entertain presidential ambitions of his own. The odor of Federalism was still too strong. "I believe," he wrote to his lawyer friend Joseph Hopkinson, "we are to have a day of small things, and of bitter things; more small, and more bitter, by much, than the state of things which was introduced in 1801."[4] Combating this downward tendency, he spoke in Congress in the lofty cadences of his commemorative orations. His brilliant speech on the revolution in Greece was more than an indictment of the Holy Alliance, it was a declaration of American duty and purpose. "What do *we* not owe to the cause of civil and religious liberty? to the principle of lawful resistance? to the principle that society has a right to partake in its own government?"[5] These were "large things," the burden of that "sacred trust" Webster imposed on the new generation and made the motif of his own career. William Plumer, Jr., recalled a nocturnal stroll on the Capitol grounds during which Webster cursed the pettiness of law and politics and broke out in passionate aspirations for glory. "At thirty, Alexander had conquered the world; and I am forty." Plumer reminded him that Caesar had done nothing at forty, so there was still hope. "You laugh at me, Plumer!" Webster retorted. "Your quiet way of looking at things may be best, after all; but I have sometimes such glorious dreams! And sometimes too, I half believe they will wake into glorious realities."[6] Meanwhile, Webster was bound to "small things." For several years he had been chief counsel for the prosecution of Spanish spoliation claims on behalf of northern merchants and underwriters before the commission established under the Florida Treaty of 1819. This proved to be the most profitable business he had ever had at the bar, finally worth some $70,000 in legal fees; and he frankly confessed that he had returned to Congress mainly with the intention of obtaining passage of an appropriation bill to pay the awards handed down by the commission.[7]

Crawford and Adams were generally thought to be leading the presidential race, followed by Calhoun, then Clay, with Jackson in the rear. "But," as Webster said, "the moon does not change so often as the prospects of these candidates."[8] He was committed to no one, and intended to remain aloof until an opportunity arrived to strike a bargain for the proscribed Federalists. He ought, it would seem, to have supported Adams, who was not only a Bay Stater but the only northerner in the race. Adams was an apostate from Federalism, however; and Webster, with many others, had never forgiven him. Webster also was shrewd enough to recognize that Adams, if elected, must be on guard against the imputation of Federalism. Webster could not support Crawford, the candidate most closely identified with Virginia Republicanism, though Crawfordites courted and flattered him.[9] Of Jackson he knew nothing—nothing beyond the legend of frontier heroism and violence that every American knew. Calhoun was his favorite among the candidates. He had known the South Carolinian since 1813. In his opposition to commercial coercion, in his concern for mercantile interests, in his opinions of currency and banking, Calhoun had early proved to be a southern Republican whom Webster, the Federalist, could support. He admired his intellect and character, and shared his enlarged views of the powers and capacities of government. In 1820, when Calhoun made a tour of northern military posts, Webster was his host in Boston. So completely agreeable did they appear, some observers thought even then that Webster wished Calhoun to be the next president.[10] He had known Clay as long, though not as well or as agreeably. Like many congressman, he was daunted by the Speaker. Doubtless he was gratified to be named the head of the Judiciary Committee in 1823, and gratified too by Clay's warm support of his resolution to send a commission to Greece. But Clay maintained his reputation as a Federalist-hater. Webster opposed his leading measure, the protective tariff; and before the session ended, they would quarrel bitterly over Webster's Spanish Claims Bill. "That damned yellow coward is to have $70,000 of the money," Clay protested to a friend. (The idea of Webster's cowardice stemmed from his refusal several years earlier of John Randolph's challenge to a duel.) And Webster supposedly complained, in turn, "that damned rascal Clay meant to oppose the bill because he, Webster, had an interest in it."[1] Clay would never overcome his belief in Webster's venality; the Yankee, in turn, always despised Clay's pride and vehemence. Nevertheless, before the election of 1824 terminated they were political intimates, while Webster and Calhoun drifted into opposite camps.

1. *The Election of 1824*

It was not until December 1821 that Calhoun decided to seek the presidency. And when he did both Crawford and Adams, the acknowledged front-runners, felt betrayed. According to the Georgian, Calhoun had assured him in October that there could be only one candidate from the South and "*he was young enough to wait*."[1] He had offered similar assurances to Adams. For the good of the country, he had said repeatedly, the next president should come from the North. Adams, of course, was the only northern candidate. The two secretaries had cooperated closely in the Monroe administration. They gave it whatever strength or character it had; and after Crawford commenced his "war in disguise" on the administration—above all on the War Department—Calhoun seemed to have no alternative but to get behind Adams.[2] Such was the political logic of the situation. But Calhoun yearned to be president, and, though not yet forty years old, he was little inclined to wait his turn in a profession as unpredictable as politics. His nationalist ardor was at full tide; his confidence in his own powers and in those of the country was unlimited. With much more than the ordinary politician's capacity for self-delusion, he convinced himself that the people agreed with his principles and policies, that he had a large following in all sections, and that he could be elected president as the nationalist candidate. Ambition ruled his judgment, too, in his assessment of Adams and Crawford. The former, he came to believe, could not be elected. During his tour of the northern states, where Adams should have been strong, Calhoun found him weak. Even if by chance Adams prevailed, he would be a weak president, abused from the south for his antislavery opinions and from the north as a political apostate. "With bitter temper and views, the dread of insinuations, growing out of his political opinions would render his policy feeble and timid."[3] A Crawford administration would be just as feeble, though for different reasons, Calhoun thought. The secretary of treasury was a political intriguer, without character or principles, who offered himself as a national Republican in the North and as a state rights Republican in the South. Crawford was "the southern candidate," of course, but Calhoun wondered if, in fact, he was only the Virginia candidate. Crawford could not even control Georgia. The proof of this came in November 1821 with the reelection of John Clark, Crawford's old enemy, and Calhoun's friend, to the governorship.[4]

Calhoun's candidacy got off to an awkward start. He arranged for his name to be "*protruded* on the publick notice" by his Pennsylvania backers. In August he had made a tour of defense facilities in the state and won the support of the "Family party" (so called because of the marital connections among its leading members), which descended from the moderate Republican faction in the state. These men—George M. Dallas, Samuel Ingham, and Thomas J. Rogers, among others—were economic nationalists, like Calhoun, and they envisioned a political alliance between Pennsylvania and South Carolina that would challenge the dominant Virginia–New York axis in national politics.[5] Nomination from this source would bolster Calhoun's image as a national leader independent of the Republican caucus, which Crawford commanded, and as a leader called out not by the people of his own state and section but of another. Meanwhile, however, on December 18 the South Carolina legislature nominated William Lowndes for the presidency. Calhoun's friends at Columbia had attempted to block any nomination, knowing that Lowndes would be the choice. He might not be Calhoun's intellectual equal, but he was older, wiser, and more deserving in the opinion of most legislators. Word of the nomination had not reached Washington on December 28 when a congressional delegation headed by the Pennsylvanians called on Calhoun to ask him to accept their endorsement and support. Lowndes himself expected to support Calhoun until he learned of his own nomination a day or two later. The two men had a friendly discussion after which neither volunteered to withdraw. Calhoun, for his part, thought the nomination at Columbia "very rash and foolish," and through young friends like George McDuffie may have tried to overturn it.[6] His candidacy was embarrassed by the evidence of weakness in his own state. Lowndes made it clear that he, at least, was not seeking the presidency. "It is not in my opinion an office to be either solicited or declined," he declared.[7] In contrast to this old-fashioned stance, Calhoun appeared brash and pushy. His claims of widespread support simply were not believed in South Carolina. Obviously, two native sons in the field would split the opposition against Crawford, and so defeat the common goal. Of the two Calhoun could retire the more gracefully. The state would degrade itself by withdrawing Lowndes's name and substituting one of inferior pretensions.[8] But Calhoun stood firm. Then in May 1822 the problem was resolved in his favor by Lowndes's death.

Calhoun's strategy from the first was to concentrate his opposition on Crawford while maintaining a friendly posture toward the other candidates with the expectation of gaining their followings as the campaign progressed. He assumed that the contest was between the Republicans and the Radicals—that they were the nascent national parties—and so as the election drew near there could be only one champion against Crawford. "The struggle is between cunning and wisdom; and political virtue and vice."[9] Through an intermediary, young Plumer, he told Adams that his candidacy was purely defensive, to defeat Crawford. He dwelled on the political objections to Adams, upon his lack of popularity in such key states as New York and Pennsylvania, even in New England. "He said much," Plumer reported, "of his own friendship for the North—that his education had been northern, his politics, his feelings, his views, and his sympathies were all northern." He offered himself, therefore, as the rallying point against Crawford. This was sophistry, Plumer thought.

He left the interview convinced that Calhoun was as much a candidate against Adams as against Crawford.[10] Adams drew the same conclusion. The relationship of the secretaries, formerly warm and trustful, deteriorated into one of cool civility. Within a year the friends of the two men were publicly attacking each other as well as Crawford. Each had his own newspaper in the capital. In Philadelphia the *Franklin Gazette,* which had been supporting Adams, suddenly took up Calhoun's cause. The man who had earlier appeared as fair, honorable, enlightened, above all personal or factional prejudice, assumed an entirely different character in Adams's eyes: a man of burning ambition, unprincipled, undiscerning, and the dupe of every knave and flatterer.[11]

Running for the presidency in the fluid political environment of the 1820s was largely a matter of arousing the zeal of political friends and opinion makers in key states, and through this network creating a favorable image of the candidate in the public mind.[12] Calhoun made no speeches; although he occasionally wrote for the press, his principal activity was writing letters intended to inform and excite his friends. Who were they? Next to the Pennsylvanians, who were crucial, was the nucleus of army officers, beginning with General Jacob Brown, the commanding general of the army, and including General Winfield Scott—even General Jackson for a time—with many officers of lesser rank, all intensely loyal to Calhoun. Retired General Joseph G. Swift, now surveyor of the port of New York, wrote the premier pamphlet, *Principles, Not Men,* of the Calhoun campaign. No wonder that Crawfordites tagged him "the Army candidate." Among Calhoun's backers were several vigorous leaders in state politics, for instance Senator Ninian Edwards of Illinois and Judge John McLean in Ohio. Edwards was the anonymous author of the notorious "A. B. Letters" charging Crawford with gross mismanagement of treasury funds. The secretary believed the letters were part of a plot engineered by Calhoun to destroy him. A congressional investigation, in which Webster played a part, eventually discredited Edwards, whose authorship had been revealed, and vindicated Crawford, yet could not undo the injury. McLean, a former congressman, was Calhoun's leading advocate in Ohio. In 1822 the president appointed him Commissioner of the Land Office, which placed thirty-nine district offices under his control. (The next year McLean was made head of the Post Office, which had an enormous patronage.) This was taken as evidence that Monroe, after hovering above the battle for two years, had swung his support to the South Carolinian.[13]

The patronage of the War Department itself—clerkships, cadet commissions, pensions, contracts, and so on—was considerable. Calhoun was not reluctant to use it. Enemies called him "a greedy pretender" who, unable to command popular votes, hoped to mount to the presidency on jobs and contracts.[14] Identifying his cause with the administration, Calhoun sought to place his friends in influential posts throughout the government. Senator Samuel Southard, who carried his banner in New Jersey, was flattered with the promise of appointment to the Supreme Court, and when this failed Calhoun successfully backed his appointment as secretary of the navy.[15] The candidate's entourage included a number of former classmates at Yale and

Litchfield. Micah Sterling was now a congressman; Virgil Maxcy, Calhoun's unofficial campaign manager, was a prominent Maryland lawyer and politician. Some of these friends were current or former Federalists. Calhoun recruited Federalists avidly. So did the other candidates. "One thing is observable," Webster wrote. "They are all, just now, very civil toward Federalists. We see and hear no abuse of us except in some places in New England."[16] Webster himself was courted by Calhoun; so were former Federalist leaders like Robert Goodloe Harper, of Maryland, and William Gaston of North Carolina. "Mr. Calhoun takes great pains to secure the support of the Federal Party," Plumer noted, "and the leaders are said to be generally in his favour."[17] Calhoun's eagerness in this regard was either a mark of desperation or, as some thought, proof that his political character and principles were "more ultra than those of Alexander Hamilton himself."[18]

Calhoun remained optimistic to the end, long after it became obvious to most observers that his political base was as thin as December ice. He could not compete with Crawford in the South. McDuffie fought a duel—and was crippled for life—in the futile effort. Although he could count on South Carolina's electoral votes, Calhoun faced formidable opposition even in his native state. In 1823 his friends managed to secure the election of Robert Y. Hayne, Calhoun's handpicked candidate, to the United States Senate, defeating the Radical incumbent, William Smith. But Smith remained a thorn in Calhoun's side, and his state rights following grew stronger year by year. In Virginia the party was already in the hands of state rights Republicans: Spencer Roane, Thomas Ritchie, Philip P. Barbour, and others. The South Carolinian struck Republicans of this persuasion as doubly dangerous, not only as ultra as Hamilton but as ambitious as Aaron Burr. "Ambition is his ruling passion," wrote one of the Virginians, "and, if I mistake him not, he will never be scrupulous as to the means of gratifying it."[19] Occasionally, when accused of extreme nationalism, Calhoun denied it, protested his innocence of protectionism and other alleged heresies, and pledged his adherence to state rights principles.[20] More often, however, he was content to run on his record from 1811 forward and present himself as an unabashed nationalist. "I belong to no section or particular interest. It has been my pride to be above all sectional or party feelings and to be devoted to the great interests of the country."[21] Because only New York and Pennsylvania, with their comprehensive interests, offered a sure basis for sustained "national policy," one or the other was essential to his candidacy. He made a bid for New York but withdrew before the strength of the old alliance, "the Constitutionalists of Virginia and the political managers of New York," which favored Crawford.[22] Everything thus came to depend on Pennsylvania. Even there his strength was more apparent than real, hinging on little cliques which exchanged congratulatory letters and kept up what Thomas Ritchie derided as "a regular system of puffery." "Calhoun's praise has been elaborately spread over the country in the pages of pamphlets. Letters seem to be continually written for publication to swell his pretensions and his chances." Tactics so self-centered became a species of self-deceit. "The enthusiasm of [army] officers; the zeal of personal friends; the panegyrics in the newspapers and the puffs of letter writers, cannot prevail upon the people to prefer Mr. Calhoun."[23]

That Henry Clay aimed for the presidency in 1824 was never in doubt. His design was first disclosed, Adams thought, when he quietly maneuvered in the congressional caucus of 1820 to wrest the vice presidential nomination from the incumbent, Daniel D. Tompkins.[24] He was blocked then, but many believed he still hoped to control the caucus decision in 1824, and for this reason he initially spurned Calhoun's example of seeking to mobilize the caucus machinery in the states. In November 1822, however, Clay too embarked on this popular route, starting with the nomination of the Republican members of the Kentucky legislature. Similar nominations quickly followed in Missouri, Ohio, and Louisiana. Clay was put forth as the *western* candidate. In the words of the Kentucky resolution nominating him, "the time has arrived when the people of the West may, with some confidence, appeal to the magnanimity of the whole Union, for a favorable consideration of their equal and just claim to a fair participation in the Executive Government of these states."[25] The resolution went on to portray Clay as the leading statesman not only of the West but of the entire Union. The patriot leader of 1812, the eloquent champion of human liberty, the father of the American System was not a sectionalist, of course. And for all his opposition to the Monroe administration, he had more principles in common with Calhoun than with Crawford. But unlike Calhoun, Clay had an undisputed claim on the affections of his section. He was the patron of internal improvements, the friend of western farmers and manufacturers, the champion of the Mississippi at Ghent, and the opponent of the sacrifice of Texas.[26] "Great Hal" thus claimed the suffrages of Kentucky, Ohio, Indiana, Illinois, Missouri, and Louisiana—a total of forty-six electoral votes. He did not claim Tennessee, where in July the legislative caucus suddenly, surprisingly, nominated General Jackson. A second western candidate threatened to split the sectional vote; but neither Clay nor anyone else at first took Jackson's nomination seriously. It was believed to be either an empty compliment to the Old Hero or a cynical deployment of his name in a game of state politics without national implications.[27]

What Calhoun saw as a contest between Republicans and Radicals, Clay tended to see as a three-cornered contest between sectional candidates: Adams, Crawford, and himself. Calhoun did not count except as he might prostrate Crawford, turning the election into a choice between the easterner of Federalist lineage and the westerner whose roots were in Virginia Republicanism. In 1822, at least, this was Clay's preferred scenario. The episode of the "Duplicate Letters" in the spring of that year helped to dramatize the sectional clash between Adams and Clay. Jonathan Russell, who had sided with Clay at Ghent, arranged for a Crawfordite in the House to call upon the president for a private letter Russell had written home after negotiation of the treaty; and since the original was supposed to be missing, Russell happily furnished a "true copy." In this electioneering maneuver against Adams, Russell portrayed the New Englander at Ghent as one who "would barter the patriotic blood of the West for blubber, and exchange ultra-Allegheny scalps for codfish."[28] He was outsmarted by Adams, however, who recovered the original letter and by a close comparison with the alleged duplicate annihilated Russell for a base forgery. (So overwhelming was the destruction that the phrase "to be Jonathan Russelled" entered into the language.) Adams defended the Ghent commission's position on the issue of the fisheries and Mississippi navigation, insisting that the British right to the latter was as inconsequential as it was specious, while the American right to the former was both solid and fundamental.[29] Russell replied, Adams rejoined, and the controversy widened into a review of Ghent from the perspective of sectional interests and candidates in the election of 1824. Adams voiced no public anger at Clay. Indeed, he pointed out that Clay had finally adopted a position little different from his own on the fisheries. But privately he believed that Clay was at the bottom of this "miserable plot" against him. "He has been for seven years circulating this poison against me in the West," Adams confided to his diary in August. ". . . Russell has all along performed for him the part of a jackal."[30] His suspicions were not unfounded. Clay and his western friends had, and did, spread "this poison"; still he protested his innocence in the matter of the Duplicate Letters and fumed at Russell, a Crawford partisan, for drawing him into it. In November, at the time of the Kentucky nomination, he said as much in a public letter. Candor compelled him to add, however, that there were errors in Adams's account of the controversy at Ghent to which he would reply at another time.[31] He never did, though for the next four months the Frankfort *Argus* labored futilely to prove that Clay had been misrepresented and injured by Adams.[32] What began as a ploy to incriminate Adams in the eyes of the West ended, in the judgment of some observers, in raising the New Englander's presidential stature by enabling him to score a forensic victory over his opponents.

One of the problems of the western candidate was which West, free or slave, did he represent and with which of the older sections, North or South, would he construct a political alliance. From the beginning there were two objections to Clay above the Ohio River: first, he had helped the Bank of the United States ravage the country; second, he was a slaveholder and the architect of the Missouri Compromise. He made no apology for his employment as B.U.S. counsel. While the association hurt him badly in some places, Cincinnati for instance, it was far from fatal. In Kentucky, where the backwash of the depression gave rise to a Relief party espousing replevin laws and other debtor legislation, Clay stood with the Lexington lawyers in opposition and still commanded the suffrages of the state. As to slavery, Clay's friends did their best to present him in a favorable light. They emphasized his youthful advocacy of gradual emancipation and his leadership of the American Colonization Society. Further, in the whole course of his law practice, it was said, Clay had never appeared against a slave suing for freedom, except once when investigation proved the claim fraudulent; on the other hand, he had acted as counsel without fee for a large number of slaves in such suits and had obtained the liberty of ten or twelve blacks. As to Missouri, he had disapproved in principle of the establishment of slavery in the state.[33]

In every race he would make for the presidency, Clay—not only a westerner but the Great Compromiser from the typical border state—had to decide whether to turn to the North or to the South for support. The decision gave him no difficulty in the 1824 election. The South was a crowded political field. The American System, the main pillar of Clay's "platform," led him to seek backing in the middle states, above the Potomac and west of the Hudson. He aimed at the union of the western and middle states, leaving the South, as he remarked to a Virginian, "a little squad to itself to carp and complain."[34] He hoped to anchor the alliance in New York. Both Adams and Crawford already, in 1822, had large followings in the state. DeWitt Clinton, the governor, was an uncertain force. But with the Erie Canal, New York was preparing to unite its economic destiny with the West. It had everything to gain from political union as well, Clay maintained. "Whereas, by lending its support either to New England or to the South, it will not advance its own pretensions one inch."[35] Western New Yorkers, in particular, listened sympathetically. The leaders of Clay's campaign in the state were western politicians and entrepreneurs, men like Peter B. Porter and William B. Rochester, whose interests were closely identified with the canal. In Albany, downstate, and in the commercial metropolis, New York City, Clay found little support. In 1823 Martin Van Buren, the head of the Clintonian opposition, the Bucktails, declared for Crawford and proceeded to reconstruct the old alliance of New York and Virginia—"the plain republicans of the North and the planters of the South." Although he failed to secure endorsement of Crawford by the legislative caucus—Adams's followers blocked that—Van Buren's decision ended Clay's chances in the state. But he refused to accept this, and indeed, never understood the political significance of Van Buren's maneuver. How could New York think to hazard her great interests and policies by becoming the "humble satellite" of Virginia?[36] But economic interest or policy had nothing to do with it. The Little Magician contrived to make party itself the dominant interest.

Clay would probably have returned to Congress in 1823 regardless of his presidential candidacy, and despite poor health, though he seemed to think that occupancy of the Speaker's chair would work to his advantage if the election finally went to the House. His triumph in the speakership contest had a deceptive appearance. After Adams's New York friend John W. Taylor withdrew, the choice lay between Barbour, Speaker in the previous Congress, and Clay. Barbour, the Virginia Radical, expected to win the votes of Crawford's New York followers. Surprisingly, all but one of them went to Clay, apparently on the theory that he would return the kindness by withdrawing from the presidential race. Every Pennsylvania congressman, it was said, voted for Clay for this reason. When some of Calhoun's friends sought to strike a bargain for their votes, Clay laughed and said they were too few to worry about.[37] Despite the rumors, he had no intention of withdrawing, of course, nor did he bargain himself into the speakership. But he seemed to think that his wide margin of victory, 139 votes to 42 for Barbour, accurately measured his strength as a presidential candidate. In fact, it was based on cal-culations of his weakness.

This was the last non-partisan speakership election in the history of the House. True to that non-partisan spirit, Clay went on to name Crawfordites to chair Ways and Means and Foreign Affairs, a Calhounite to chair Military Af-fairs, and an unrepentant Federalist, Webster, to chair Judiciary. The Ken-tuckian's popularity with Congress, as a freshman member observed, was of an unenviable species. "It is a high admiration of his talents in debate, and his adroitness in the management of individuals and deliberative bodies—all of which is sustained and enforced with manners the most dignified, and yet the most fascinating and popular. . . . All admire him—but this admiration wants an indispensable requisite. The column that presents so beautiful a Corinthian capital does not rest upon a broad basis of Moral confidence."[38] Calhoun, many believed, was "wildly extravagant" in his ideas; Clay was commonly seen as ex-travagant, even dangerous, in his moral character. "Ardent, bold, and adven-turous . . . , he would be, as is feared, rash in enterprise, and inconsiderate and regardless of consequences" in executive office.[39] The objection ran less to the supposed impurity of his private character, as exhibited in stories of gam-bling and carousing, than to the impetuosity of the public man.

In the early months of 1824 Adams's candidacy, with its New England base, held steady, Jackson's soared, Clays's and Crawford's declined, and Calhoun's ended ingloriously. General Jackson had been elected to the Sen-ate, where he charmed everyone with his soft manners, allaying prejudices based on his reputation for rough border warfare. Crawford, despite a debili-tating stroke, was nominated by the congressional caucus in February. Only sixty-six congressmen, almost all Crawfordites, attended the caucus. The nomination was worse than worthless. Four days later, at a meeting in Phila-delphia held prior to the state nominating convention in Harrisburg, Dallas struck Calhoun's flag and called upon Republicans to unite behind Jackson. Calhoun, who had not been consulted, was stunned; but Dallas was bowing to the inevitable. Jackson had taken Pennsylvania by storm. The legislative caucus endorsed him. Calhoun and his managers, having failed to turn the party machinery to their advantage in Pennsylvania or in other states, joined the rising popular attack on the caucus. "The people claim their Constitu-tional right of choosing electors; the political managers . . . will use every ef-fort to evade or defeat their right. In such a contest, our advantage is im-mense," Calhoun wrote to Swift. ". . . In opposing the Radical party, it is now manifest, that we are contending under the same banner, under which contested the heroes of the Revolution, and the Republicans of '98 and 1812; the banner of the people."[40] In Congress McDuffie introduced a constitu-tional amendment providing for the uniform choice of electors in congres-sional districts by the people themselves. This would take the election out of the hands of the bosses and the cliques in the legislatures, McDuffie ar-gued.[41] But the maneuver was of no use to Calhoun, who simply could not compete with Jackson as a democratic candidate. Of that Pennsylvania exhibited convincing proof, although Calhoun closed his eyes to it and accused Dallas of betrayal. "Taking the U.S. together," he wrote, "I never had a fairer prospect than on the day we lost the state."[42]

Calhoun had jumped before he came to the stile; the only question now was whether he would resume his place in the procession or be turned out forever. The Harrisburg convention nominated him for vice president on the Jackson ticket. The office had been a political dead end since Jefferson, but Calhoun acquiesced. Because he had been everybody's "second choice," the nomination was appropriate, perhaps even unavoidable. Only the Radicals were disturbed by it. Albert Gallatin, the caucus nominee on the Crawford ticket, thought that for all the danger posed by Jackson the greater danger was posed by Calhoun. The adroit political jockeys in "the family faction" had succeeded in making Old Hickory "the horse on whom Calhoun is to ride and to reach the Presidential chair, after the next term; and they have done it against the will of Calhoun who was going headlong to destruction by aiming at what [was] impossible, viz being elected at the next election." The Jackson ticket in Pennsylvania ought to be named the "*Calhoun ticket,*" Gallatin declared.[43] But if Jackson was to be Calhoun's horse, he was quite unaware of it. Adams's followers also took him up. He became the vice presidential front-runner while at the same time remaining neutral between these two contenders, either one of whom he could support for the presidency.[44] This was some consolation, as was the belief that he had stopped Crawford, which in retrospect became the justification of his candidacy from the beginning.

Clay sought his running mate in New York. Jackson's rise, cutting into his western support, underscored the importance of the middle states for Clay. He did not expect a president to emerge from the electoral college. In the absence of a majority vote, the top three candidates would be returned to the House of Representatives, which would choose the president as provided by the Constitution. Clay's game now was to be one of these finalists, for if returned to the House he expected to be elected.[45] Passage of the General Survey Bill followed by the Tariff of 1824 enhanced Clay's prestige as the masterly statesman of a system of public policy geared to the interests of the middle states. "Our manufacturers feel the debt of gratitude due to their great patron," a fellow protectionist assured Clay.[46] A surge of support for him in New England suggested that he might successfully challenge Adams there. "Our people are full of fire and zeal—the Jenniers and Wool Growers are rallying, and the tariff is the word," wrote a Bay State campaigner. Clay's great tariff speech had been scattered through the state by the thousands.[47] Both the weekly *New England Galaxy* and the daily Boston *Courier* came out for Clay, perhaps less because of the American System than because of old Federalist feelings against Adams; and in Boston, Worcester, and other cities manufacturers rallied to Clay.[48] The trail of good fortune ended in the legislature, however, where his friends lost the fight for a district ticket (as opposed to a general, or statewide, ticket) with which they might have split the electoral vote for Adams.

In the summer an old friend, Josiah S. Johnston, newly elected to the Senate from Louisiana, took charge of Clay's faltering campaign in the middle states. Newspapers were finally acquired in New York City and Philadelphia. A great public meeting in the latter place, chaired by Mathew Carey, hailed Clay as "the great champion of the American System."[49] This was followed by the first organized activity for Clay in Pennsylvania. It was, of course, too late. Johnston wondered if the East was ready for a western president, if Clay's section, regardless of the nationalism of his program, was not an insurmountable obstacle. Still he was frank with Clay about the crucial weakness of his campaign: the want of presses, money, management, and zeal.[50] Clay had profited from the warfare among his adversaries, especially Crawford and Calhoun, but he never matched their resources of patronage and press, and he won over few of their followers in the final stages of the campaign. Calhoun's friends in Pennsylvania went mostly to Jackson, while in New York they went to Adams. Even Clay's strongest appeal in the East, his economic nationalism, was blunted by the espousal of the same doctrines, the same policies, by Jackson and Adams, both of whom commanded greater public confidence.

One of Clay's problems was the widespread opinion that he would withdraw and coalesce with Crawford. Rumors of a deal with the Georgian persisted in the face of repeated denials. In the spring Crawford's managers began to consider moving Gallatin off the ticket. Gallatin, for all his abilities and services, had never been popular; the residuary legatee of much old political hatred, he was proving a liability to Crawford. Van Buren and Ritchie, with Gallatin's concurrence, sought to substitute Clay, not because they approved of his politics but because of the strength he would bring to the ticket. Clay and his friends rebuffed these overtures, finally and decisively in October.[51] By then they were concentrating on excluding Crawford, perceived as "a living death" in any event, from the House and returning Clay along with the leaders, Adams and Jackson. New York was the main battleground.

In New York, as in five other states, the law provided for the choice of electors by the state legislature. Efforts to change the law, to give the election to the people, were thwarted by Van Buren's Bucktails, who controlled the state senate. When the legislature met in November each house at first balloted separately for the thirty-six electors. The senate quickly chose the Crawford ticket. The assembly was deadlocked. For three days the vote stood fifty for Adams, forty-three for Crawford, and thirty-two for Clay. The Clay men thus held the balance of power. Their object was to defeat Crawford. Only the Adams party, their leader already assured of returning to the House of Representatives, could offer Clay enough New York electors to bring him in ahead of Crawford. The Adamsites pledged those electors, seven in number, in return for Clayite support of the Adams ticket in the assembly. The disagreement between the two houses forced a joint session. There, too, the Clay men held the balance: thirty-nine votes between sixty for Crawford and fifty-seven for Adams. During three tumultuous days in the Albany capital, the slate of electors was finally chosen: twenty-five for Adams, seven for Clay, and four for Crawford. Adams prevailed because of the votes of the Clay party—the result of the bargain it had made to get the votes necessary to enter their leader in the final contest. Unfortunately for Clay, the Adams people failed to keep their side of the bargain. When the New York electors met on December 1 to cast their ballots, Clay actually got fewer votes than Crawford. After that his only chance lay with the Louisiana legislature. When several pro-Clay lawmakers failed to appear, either by accident or design, he was shut out and the state's five votes were split between Adams and Jackson.[52]

The electoral vote would not be counted officially until February 9, but the result was known in Washington by mid-December: ninety-nine for Jackson, eighty-four for Adams, forty-one for Crawford, thirty-seven for Clay. (Clay had won three western states—Kentucky, Ohio, and Missouri—and picked up four votes in New York.) With the choice now between the first three, the Kentuckian was cast in the role of kingmaker. He immediately eliminated Crawford from consideration on grounds of health. Thomas Hart Benton, with many others, later argued that Clay should have been guided by "the *demos kraeto* principle" and supported Jackson because he received the most popular votes and the most electoral votes.[53] No one argued this in the winter of 1824–25, however. The election of the president was not a democratic process, nor was it ever intended to be. The popular vote, very low wherever it occurred, reflected so many variables and contingencies that even a reliable estimate of it was impossible. The electoral college was constituted on the majority principle. In the absence of a majority there, the House of Representatives was to choose from among the three leaders, each state having but one vote and a majority of the states, thirteen in 1824, being necessary to election. The single representative of Illinois was thus equal to the thirty-four of New York; and what mattered was not the previous division of the electoral vote but the division among the three candidates within the congressional delegations of twenty-four states. The rules were well understood. Once before, in 1800, the House had chosen the president; ever since Congress had done so, in effect, through the nominating caucus. In 1824 the circumstances were different, but they were neither unprecedented nor unexpected; and all concerned seemed ready to play by the rules.

Arriving in Washington in December, Clay found himself courted and flattered by the partisans of both Adams and Jackson. In the privacy of his own mind he soon decided, indeed very probably had decided before he left Lexington, to support Adams. It was a choice between political evils, of course, but one evil was dangerous, the other was not. "The principal difference between them is that in the election of Mr. Adams we shall not by the example inflict any wound upon the character of our institutions; but," Clay explained, "I should much fear hereafter, if not during the present generation, that the election of the General would give to the Military Spirit a stimulus, and a confidence, that might lead to the most pernicious results."[54] This opinion of Jackson was firmly held. It traced back to 1819 when Clay had demanded censure of the general for his lawless conduct in the Seminole campaign. Hearing of the Old Hero's nomination in Pennsylvania, which first made him a serious candidate, Clay had voiced his disgust at seeing "the people so intoxicated and deluded by a little military glory, that a man totally unknown to the civil history of the country—who knew nothing of the constitution, or laws of the land—and who, in short, had no other recommendation than that which grew out of his fortunate campaign at New Orleans, should be thought of for president of the United States, and even preferred to . . . men who had grown gray in the civil departments of government."[55] Knowing Clay's feelings in the matter, congressmen were not surprised by the theme of his eloquent address to another old hero, General Lafayette, on the occasion of his reception in the House in December. The speaker dwelled on Lafayette's civic virtues, on his devotion to ordered liberty, saying it was in this character that the American people honored him.[56] Jackson may not have understood this, as some did, as a side blow at him. The two gentlemen had clasped hands and sat down to dinner together at the previous session. It was strictly a personal reconciliation, however, which neither man was inclined to transfer to the political arena.[57]

From the beginning of the session, Clay let Adams know through intermediaries of his intentions and attempted to remove any ill feelings left by the unfortunate Russell affair.[58] Clay had sometimes complained of the New Englander's "want of judgment and discretion," but he admired him as a statesman who, like himself, "had grown gray in the civil departments of the government."[59] He believed, too, that Adams, with his eastern constituency, was finally wedded to the American System. Clay's friends asked nothing in return for his support. They did not have to. They knew, and Clay knew, that he could have any cabinet position he wanted in any administration. Friends of both leading candidates held out the promise of secretary of state. Clay blithely remarked that he "would not cross Pennsylvania Avenue to be in any office under any Administration which lies before us."[60] At the same time, however, his followers were lining up behind Adams to ensure Clay's appointment at the head of the cabinet. The two men met at the congressional dinner for Lafayette on the first day of the new year. It was a gala occasion. Clay arrived in high spirits, took the main seat between Adams and Jackson and joked, "Well, gentlemen, since you are both too near the chair, but neither can occupy it, I will slip in between you, and take it myself!"[61] Before the dinner ended, Clay requested an interview with Adams. They met at the latter's home on Sunday evening, January 9. After a three-hour conversation that roamed over the past and glanced into the future, Clay denounced Jackson and avowed his support for Adams.[62] Some days later, as if to seal the alliance, Clay brought forward in the House an appropriation bill to extend the National Road. The issue was doubtful, but Clay risked it in order to show the West that most of the Jacksonians, southern and eastern, opposed this great highway, while most of Adams's followers favored it. The greatest Yankee of them all, Daniel Webster, spoke forcefully for the bill. Passing by a slender margin, it helped to swing four western states into the Adams column and offered, as Plumer observed, "new proof of Clay's boldness and address."[63]

Jacksonians and Crawfordites turned on Clay when his position in the contest became known. "I am a deserter of Democracy: A giant at intrigue; have sold the West, sold myself—defeating General Jackson's election to leave open the Western pretensions that I may hereafter fill them myself—blasting all my fair prospects, etc etc etc . . . ," Clay summarized the complaint. "The Knaves cannot comprehend how a man can be dishonest."[64] Some of Kentucky's representatives were shaken by resolutions by the state legislature calling upon them to vote for Jackson as the favored western candidate. Clay denied any right of the legislature to control his vote or that of the delegation. The legislature's claim was, in fact, unprecedented. Most of the Kentucky delegation, eight to four, followed Clay in supporting Adams.[65]

At the end of January the Jackson managers, staring at defeat, made a desperation move. The *Columbian Observer*, a party newspaper in Philadelphia, published a Washington report from an unnamed congressman charging bargain and corruption in the election. "For some time past, the friends of Clay have hinted that they, like the Swiss, would fight for those who pay best," the report said. When overtures to the Jackson leaders were unsuccessful, Clay transferred his interest to Adams. "As a consideration for this abandonment of duty to his constituents, it is said and believed, should this unholy alliance prevail, Clay is to be appointed secretary of state."[66] Clay promptly, on February 1, published his "card" in the *National Intelligencer* denouncing the author of the letter "a base and infamous calumniator, a dastard, and a liar," and declared that, if he dared reveal himself, Clay would hold him responsible to the laws governing men of honor.[67] This challenge to a duel appeared ludicrous in Clay's eyes two days later when George Kremer, a timid and inept congressman from Pennsylvania, came forward and, without actually acknowledging authorship of the letter, said he would undertake to prove the truth of its charges. *The School for Scandal*, playing at the local theater, moved into the House chamber. Clay indignantly demanded the appointment of a select committee to investigate the charges. Quickly concluding that Kremer was not the author of the letter, but only a tool of more proficient intriguers high in the ranks of the Jackson party, he directed his suspicions at Major John Eaton, one of the general's inner circle, at Samuel Ingham, George McDuffie, and even Jackson himself.[68] On February 9, the day set for the presidential election, the committee headed by Philip P. Barbour submitted its report. Since Kremer, the accuser, declined to appear, saying he could not submit to the authority of the House in such a matter, the committee was unable to investigate the charges and asked to be discharged. Obviously the authors of the bargain and corruption story wanted no investigation. What was their purpose? Immediately, they may have hoped to frighten Clay out of supporting Adams; if so they were very poor judges of his character. It seems more likely, since they could not influence the result of the impending election, that they sought to sow the seeds of bargain and corruption in the public mind with the intent of reaping the harvest at the next election. That, at any rate, is what the authors of this atrocity succeeded in doing.

The election itself was anticlimactic. As Clay and his friends had predicted for two months, Adams was elected with the necessary thirteen states on the first ballot. Careful examination of the votes in the House shows that, regardless of preferences or deals, the only winning coalition was the Adams-Clay coalition. Adams brought to it ten states, Clay three (Kentucky, Ohio, Missouri). Had Clay followed the wishes of the Kentucky legislature, adding his votes to Jackson's, the general would have had only ten states. It would then have become the Crawfordites' turn to bargain with their four states (Delaware, Virginia, North Carolina, and Georgia). A Jackson-Crawford coalition could not prevail, and it would have been folly for Clay to become a junior partner in this coalition. Clay's course was, therefore, the only reasonable and responsible one, the only one that could avert a long drawn-out battle leading to constitutional crisis.[69]

Either of two state delegations might have upset things. In January the nine Maryland congressmen were supposed to be divided as follows: three for Jackson, three for Adams, two for Clay, one for Crawford. The two Clay men together could control the majority vote of the state. Webster sought to turn this situation to his advantage. One of the Marylanders was an old Federalist, Henry Warfield, who shared Webster's concern for the admission of the party brethren into the next administration. Webster himself had his heart set on an appointment to the Court of St. James. He had just returned from a visit to Monticello, and, though he had no taste for Thomas Jefferson's politics, freely repeated his warning against the election of Jackson whom he called "a dangerous man."[70] Webster expected to vote for Adams, but he, like Warfield, wanted ironclad assurances on the appointment of Federalists. So he artfully extracted a pledge from Adams. The "Webster pledge," as it would be named after disclosure several years later, drew Maryland along with Webster into the Adams camp.[71] In the case of New York, the vote stood seventeen for Adams, sixteen for Crawford, and one for Jackson. The single vote Adams needed for a majority was furnished by silver-haired General Stephen Van Rensselaer, "The Patroon" of the great Hudson River estates. He, too, had been a Federalist; he disliked Adams, and was counted for Crawford. But Clay and Webster worked on him, and when the roll of the states was called, Van Rensselaer bowed his head in prayer, saw an Adams ballot at his feet, picked it up and stuffed it in the box. Such, at least, was the common story.[72]

Three days after his election, Adams offered Clay the post of secretary of state. The Kentuckian took several days to consider it; most of his friends, including a number in the Crawford and Jackson camps, urged him to accept, and he did so on February 20. It turned out to be the worst error of his political life. Crawford, who never credited the "corrupt bargain" charge, and who approved of Clay's vote for Adams, accused him of no higher crime than political stupidity. The bargain charge might be a dastardly lie, said James Buchanan, who knew it was, yet nothing could prevent the people from believing it once Clay accepted Adams's appointment. "They will judge the *cause*, from the *effects*."[73] Neither Clay nor his friends foresaw this in February 1825. He believed he would add strength to the Adams administration, that it would receive a fair trial, that the cloud of party malice would blow over, and that after four years the administration would be judged on its merits. As secretary of state, he hoped to advance the foreign policy goals—above all, consolidating the hemispheric American system—he had advocated in the House. And he calculated the value of the office for the realization of his presidential ambition. Whatever the risks of acceptance, they were over-matched by the risks of declining the office, since that must appear as submission to calumny and intimidation. In the end Clay's character, his reputation as a man of honor and independence, demanded that he defy his accusers and accept what they had publicly ticketed as a bribe.[74] In March the nomination was confirmed by the Senate with thirteen votes in opposition. Only one senator, John Branch of North Carolina, offered any remarks. Whether or not a bargain had occurred, he thought the suspicion of it enough to warrant rejection of the nomination. Clay's friends on the floor heard nothing that called for response or inquiry. Several of the nay votes, old Nathaniel Macon's for instance, were cast against Clay's principles; others, like Jackson's, were cast from malice.[75]

Party malice, like death, prefers a shining mark. Clay, while innocent of bargain and corruption, had done something worse for a politician; he had, as Talleyrand might have said, committed a great blunder. The conspirators wove a web of criminality around Clay the logic of which was very simple: Clay said to Adams, "I will make you president if you will make me secretary of state." And it was done. Guilt was inferred from the circumstance. Clay was doomed to the impossible task of proving a negative, that he had not entered into a bargain. The charge was made to injure him and the Adams administration. But it was made also to promote the political fortunes of Andrew Jackson and his party. Jackson himself was among the first to draw the damning conclusion, writing on February 14, "So you see the Judas of the West has closed the contract and will receive the thirty pieces of silver."[76] The next month he went public with a letter to a New York follower. Turning Clay's epithet, "military chieftain," into a title of patriotic glory, the gray-haired hero presented himself as wholly submissive to the will of the people; he, unlike Clay, had engaged in no secret conclaves, made no bargains, nor prostrated democracy.[77] Clay replied to Jackson and the pack of accusers in a long address to his constituents at the end of March.[78] Were truth the issue, it would have been a triumphant vindication. But the issue was political power; and the more Clay protested his innocence the more guilty he seemed.

Senator Jackson soon returned to Tennessee to resign. One of his last public acts was to administer the oath of office to the new vice president. Calhoun ended his neutrality after Clay declared for Adams. He would probably have coalesced with the Jacksonians in any event. South Carolina had voted for Jackson, as had Pennsylvania. Calhoun's political base was shifting, and as the new administration would occupy the nationalist pole, he would be drawn to the opposite. He saw at once that the administration was doomed to failure from the circumstances of its birth. It would destroy his great rival,

Clay, for it would be impossible for him to succeed to the presidency behind Adams; Calhoun, on the other hand, might in time succeed behind Jackson. From a lofty seat—one of the privileges of the vice presidency—he had only to watch Clay sink into the pit of bargain and corruption. "I see in the fact that Mr. Clay has made the President against the voice of his constituents, and that he has been rewarded by the man elevated by him to the first office in his gift, the most dangerous stab, which the liberty of the country has ever received," Calhoun wrote as he prepared to return to South Carolina. "I will not be on that side. I am with the people, and will remain so."[79]

2. Adams and Clay

No administration ever began under conditions more crippling than those facing John Quincy Adams. His inaugural address lauded the national spirit and pleaded for the extermination of rancor and strife and the final realization of the ideal of union and concord—"We are all federalists, all republicans"— voiced by Thomas Jefferson a quarter century before. Adams's own career, now crowned by his election as chief magistrate, was a living monument to this ideal. Unfortunately, it had little relationship to the political realities of 1825. The seeds of new party strife had been sown among the dying weeds of the old.

Neither Adams nor his first minister, Henry Clay, was daunted by the scandal that ushered them into power. They had no consciousness of guilt or error and believed the lurid glow would quickly disappear. "We shall have no serious opposition," Clay wrote optimistically. "The power of the malcontents is already beginning to fail, and their guns are heard weaker and weaker."[1] From Daniel Webster, who hailed the new administration in a speech at Faneuil Hall, Clay learned that the charge of bargain and corruption had made no impression in New England. From John Tyler, in Virginia, he was assured that instead of earning the curses of his country, the country owed him, as it must recognize, a debt of gratitude for speedily resolving the presidential crisis.[2] On May 15 Clay set out for Kentucky. Two months earlier he might have traveled all the way home by the light of his burning effigies. Now it was almost a triumphal procession. At home, while he wound up his private affairs—sold his livestock, rented the house at Ashland, paid his debts—he was feted in a dozen Kentucky counties and across the river in Ohio. "Lafayette's transit through the Country has hardly occasioned more excitement than my return," he boasted to Adams. "There is not a murmur existing against me."[3] In numerous speeches and replies Clay not only vindicated his own conduct but, as in his Lexington address, turned charges of combination and conspiracy against his accusers. A young Cincinnati lawyer would remember Clay's speech—at the largest public dinner on record in that city—as the most eloquent he ever heard. When he came, after speaking of foreign policy, to the defense of his vote in the House, Clay seemed to grow taller, his head and face took a lofty bearing, his foot advanced, his arm upraised, and his eyes flashed defiance to the pack of conspirators in pursuit of him.[4] Clay returned to Washington in August convinced that he and Adams would prevail over their enemies.

Adams formed his cabinet on non-partisan principles. Most of the members had, in fact, opposed his candidacy. Samuel Southard, one of Calhoun's friends, continued in the Navy Department, while another, John McLean, remained in the office of postmaster general which, though not of cabinet rank, was immensely influential. William Wirt stayed on as attorney general. Treasury was offered to Crawford, partly as a matter of courtesy but also with a view to courting his followers in Congress and the country. When he declined, the post went to Richard Rush, of Pennsylvania, who had won Adams's admiration as minister to Great Britain. The Crawford interest came to be represented in James Barbour, the attractive Virginia senator who was a friend of Clay's and was put at the head of the War Department. Acknowledging his political debt to New York, Adams offered Governor Clinton appointment to the Court of St. James; and when he declined, Senator Rufus King was named to the post. This pleased most Federalists, but neither King nor Clinton had any claim on Adams's political affections. Those who did, like young Thurlow Weed, who had fashioned Adams's victory in New York, felt neglected. With Clay at its head, the cabinet stood for the American System of political economy at home and policies of liberal nationalism abroad, with as much political harmony and conciliation as the factions would tolerate.

Adams and Clay, for all their differences in manner and temperament— one austere, the other exuberant; one circumspect, the other impulsive; one moralistic, the other opportunistic—enjoyed a happy working relationship. It might have been expected that Adams, after eight years in the state department, and half a lifetime in foreign affairs, would have perched himself on Clay's shoulder; but this was not the case. Clay had a mind of his own in foreign affairs, and the president respected it. If in the end his tenure as secretary of the state was disappointing, it was not because Clay lacked clear views or failed in his duty.[5] The duty of day-to-day administration, for which Clay was temperamentally ill-suited, was performed under severe handicaps of a private as well as a public nature. Clay's health, though on the mend when he entered the State Department, soon deteriorated; after three years many wondered if he would leave it alive. On his return to the capital in August 1825, one of his younger daughters became ill and died. Only a month later he learned of the death from fever of a favorite older daughter in New Orleans. Of six daughters, only one survived. Three of his sons were a constant torment. Lucretia Clay, already withdrawn from society, and sorry to return to Washington after an absence of several years, was devastated by these blows. Henry soon regained his natural buoyancy, which nothing seemed capable of suppressing for long, not even the load of slander and obloquy under which he labored. He knew, of course, most of that was political, not personal, and discounted it accordingly.

Society was untroubled by it. Indeed, Washington society was seldom gayer than during the Adams years. The president and first lady led the way with splendid levees. "Gravity is natural to him, and a smile looks ill at home," it was said.[6] Yet this Puritan was as grave and earnest about play as he was about work or religion or physical exercise. Clay took a leisurely evening stroll, but Adams jogged four and a half miles every day, more or less, or during the summer swam in the Potomac River. His Maryland-born wife, Louisa Catherine, was a charming hostess. The dinners and drawing rooms at the White House—even large dinners in the East Room, unheard of before—provided the warmth Clay had promised, but could not himself deliver, during the frigid reign of the Monroes. The Clays did their part with regular Wednesday evening parties. Early in 1827 they moved from indifferent quarters on F Street to the elegant Decatur House on the square across Pennsylvania Avenue from the President's House. Spacious, with a fine garden, Clay called it "the best house . . . in the city," and filled it with furnishings sent from Paris by James Brown, his rich brother-in-law and the United States Minister to France.[7] Adams could never erase from his mind the conception of Clay as "a political gamester," just as he could never admit to himself that he, too, played political games. And Clay believed that Adams, even at his most relaxed, was too stiff and unbending, inclined to view politics as an arena for the assertion of conscience rather than as a field for the brokerage of conflicting interests. But these two men thrown together by the fates of politics respected each other; and the loyalty of the secretary to the chief executive, under the trying circumstances of the administration, showed the better side of Clay's nature.[8]

Adams ran up the flag of the administration in his first message to Congress.[9] Reading the draft, discussing it in cabinet, Clay was astounded by its bold design. Adams proposed to unite the country behind a great program of national improvement, one which took conventional internal improvements—roads and canals, rivers and harbors—only as a starting point. A national university, an astronomical observatory—"lighthouses of the skies," in Adams's unfortunate phrase—scientific expeditions, a uniform system of weights and measures all were elements of the design. None of the proposals was without precedent. Every president, beginning with the first, had recommended establishment of a national university. Jefferson had written the first report—Adams as secretary of state the second—calling for a national system of weights and measures. Jefferson had sent Lewis and Clark to the Pacific and inaugurated the coastal survey. There had even been earlier proposals for a national observatory. Adams was inspired, in part, by Jefferson's dream of an "empire of science," and like Clay he had charted his political course from the Madisonian Platform of 1815. Nevertheless Clay, the champion of internal improvements, was jolted by Adams's message. The two men seemed to change places: Adams now bold, Clay turning cautious. It was not the specific measures Clay objected to, though he thought some of them, like a national university, had been proved utterly impracticable, but the philosophy that was thrown around all the measures and the glowing, even passionate, rhetoric with which they were advocated. A decade earlier national sentiment would have sustained the program; now nationalism was on the defensive, and projects that once seemed patriotic were assailed as heretical. Clay's political instincts led him to object to crucial elements of the message, but seeing the president's heart was set on it he acquiesced along with other members of the cabinet.

The message was a hymn to "the spirit of improvement . . . abroad upon the earth." Only a month before, the waters of Lake Erie and the Atlantic Ocean had been joined by the Erie Canal. This establishment of dominion over physical nature, this consolidation of the Union, this application of republican energies to the benefit of mankind was a mighty illustration of that "spirit of improvement" Clay, Webster, and Calhoun had all identified in their different ways as the motif of their American generation. The great object of civil government, Adams declared, is "the improvement of those who are parties to the social compact." Echoing Bacon, he said "that liberty is power; that the nation blessed with the largest portion of liberty must in proportion to its numbers be the most powerful nation upon earth, and that the tenure of the power of man is, in the moral purposes of his Creator, upon condition that it should be exercised to ends of beneficence, to improve the condition of himself and his fellow-men." The Constitution presented no obstacle. Adams could not believe that the Founding Fathers had denied the country the means of bettering its condition. To refrain from exercising powers for good would be a sin against God and treachery to the people. "While foreign nations less blessed with that freedom which is power . . . are advancing with gigantic strides in the career of public improvement, were we to slumber in indolence or to fold up our arms and proclaim to the world that we are palsied by the will of our constituents, would it not be to cast away the bounties of Providence and doom ourselves to perpetual inferiority?" The question had generally been asked by protectionists. Adams was silent on the tariff. However, Secretary of Treasury Rush, in his annual report, acclaimed the prosperity diffused by manufactures, which he traced to protectionism, and endorsed government policies to animate the industry of the country.[10] The administration was thus fully identified with the American System.

The message immediately exposed Adams to attack as "the son of Federalism" who, like his father before him, sought to "monarchize" the Constitution. All the Old Republican artillery, first hauled out against the American System, was turned on the administration. "Liberty is power?" What dangerous nonsense. Liberty consisted in the jealous restraint of power, indeed in palsying the government. Individuals, not governments, were the best judges of their own interests; and there was no national interest beyond the aggregate of individual interests.[11] The metaphor "lighthouses of the skies" was perhaps more damaging than all the president's measures, which only threatened tyranny, for it provoked derision and ridicule. In Virginia, where Ritchie's *Enquirer* led the attack, the General Assembly elected John Randolph, the splenetic satirist and acid-tongued orator, to fill out Barbour's term in the Senate. In South Carolina, Judge William Smith seized the occa-

sion to drive through the legislature resolutions declaring the protective tariff and federal internal improvements unconstitutional. Smith was the leading Radical in the state. A year earlier the same resolutions had been defeated; a year before that, Smith had been turned out of the Senate by Calhoun and his party.

The "revolution of 1825," as this turnabout in the legislature came to be
known, not only pointed up the rising state rights frenzy in South Carolina
but showed how far out of step Calhoun was with the opinion of the state.
The doctrine of Adams's first message was substantially Calhoun's doctrine.
He had, in fact, reiterated his nationalist views in speeches at home during
the summer. Thomas Cooper, president of South Carolina College, had
lumped Calhoun with Adams, Clay, and old Federalism in his powerful pamphlet, *Consolidation,* in behalf of Crawford in 1824. Now the vice president
was held up as the advocate, even the author, of the system of measures condemned as unconstitutional by the legislature of his state. "He was the adviser of that fool Monroe," Cooper wrote, "he is a national internal improvements man; he is a fortification man; he spends the money of the South to
buy up influence in the North. . . . He is active, shewy, fluent, superficial,
and conceited."[12] The revolution in the legislature came about, interestingly
enough, when Calhoun's principal complaint against the new administration
was its courting of the Radicals. As for Adams's message, he did not know
who had a better right to grumble: the state rights party because of its
ultraism or friends of the Monroe administration, like himself, who favored
liberal measures but prudently guarded against the backlash of extravagant
doctrine. Adams had gained nothing, at any rate, and added numbers and
zeal to the opposition.[13]

Calhoun quietly expressed his dissatisfaction with the administration upon
returning to Washington in the fall. In his new post of "dignified inaction,"
he could, if he chose, remain neutral; but he was too much of a political ani-
mal for that. Jefferson, and John Adams before him, had used the second office as a stepping-stone to the first; for Aaron Burr it had led to disaster; since
then no incumbent had gained stature or influence in the office. For the retiring Daniel D. Tompkins it had been virtually a sinecure, since he seldom performed the only official duty of presiding over the Senate. Calhoun, with a
scrupulous regard for duty as well as a keen interest in the unfolding political
drama, was determined to reverse this downward course. He assumed the
chair from the first day of the session and never left it until the close. Returning to Dumbarton Oaks, the great house in the hills behind Georgetown his
mother-in-law had purchased in 1824, Calhoun and his wife were no less scrupulous in meeting their social obligations. At their dinner parties, where the
vice president was always the center of attention, he dazzled the guests with
the brilliance of his conversation. Young men were charmed by him. He
made a point of cultivating them. The freshman senator from North Carolina
reported that, on leaving, Calhoun stood at the door with him, holding his
hand, and said in the most imposing manner: "Mangum—Mangum do—do
Sir call and see me frequently and spend some of your evenings with us—

without ceremony. Come Sir, we shall always be glad to see you and bring a friend with you." Willie Mangum commented to his correspondent, "Ah Sir! he knows a thing or two. It is that way he sweeps the young fellows."[14]

Calhoun had an unusual opportunity at the start to turn his office to political advantage. In the previous Congress the Senate had adopted a rule conferring on the presiding officer the appointment of standing committees, heretofore elected by ballot. Since the vice president was usually absent, especially at the beginning of a session, senators supposed the duty would fall upon the president pro tempore, who was elected by them. But Calhoun, in a move some thought adroit, others brazen, took the chair the first day and proceeded to appoint the committees. Political alignments in the Senate were unclear; Calhoun, nevertheless, made an honest effort to divide control of the committees between friends and enemies of the administration. Of course, the administration saw this as hostile. In the instance of the Committee on Foreign Relations the vice president patently stacked the cards against the secretary of state. John Binns's *Democratic Press*, the administration newspaper in Philadelphia, at once made this charge, and it was copied around the country.[15] Two of the five committee members, Nathaniel Macon and Littleton Tazewell, had voted against Clay's confirmation; of the other three only one could be considered friendly to the administration. Calhoun found many defenders, but the *Democratic Press* kept up its attack. In February it reported that the vice president had made overtures before the session began to support the administration if it would dump Clay and his friends, and only when refused did he turn against it.[16] The report lacked substance. Nevertheless, Calhoun's hostility to Clay grew blatant as the session advanced; and before it ended the Senate, in an implied rebuke, repealed the new rule for the appointment of committees and returned to the tedious practice of election by ballot.[17]

It did not really matter who the aggressor was in this fight, but each man blamed the other. By February it was obvious, Calhoun wrote, that the whole weight of the administration would be thrown against him. Why? "Mr. Clay governs the President," he answered. "The latter is in his power. He has thought proper to consider me as his rival; and while Mr. Adams is left to struggle with General Jackson as he can, the weight of the Executive is made to bear, as Mr. Clay desires, and for his own ends."[18] He thus pleaded self-defense in justification for going into opposition. Actually, of course, his move was influenced by weightier political considerations. The state rights revolution in South Carolina, the vulnerability of the administration, the prospects of the emerging Jacksonian coalition—all were important. They were not self-justifying, however. An issue, one that resonated as a clash of principle, was needed. It was provided by the Panama Congress.

Adams had mentioned American participation in this first Pan-American conference—an idea originated by the Liberator, Bolivar—in his annual message. A special message followed, along with the nomination of two ministers plenipotentiary to attend the Assembly of American Nations at Panama in June 1826. Calhoun later said that upon first hearing of the proposed mission he voiced his opposition to a member of the cabinet, probably Southard, and asked that his views be communicated to cabinet colleagues. He was told, however, that it was too late; the invitations from Columbia and Mexico had already been accepted.[19] Calhoun had never been sympathetic to Clay's Latin American policy. He seemed to regard the Panama project as further evidence of Clay's ascendancy in the administration and for that reason, if for no other, opposed it.

As secretary of state Clay sought to implement the Latin American policy he had championed in Congress. How were the seven or eight new states on the southern continent to be incorporated into the American system, liberal, pacific, and independent of the Old World? Monroe's celebrated declaration of December 1823 had recognized this hemispheric system and, in a sense, written its principles into national policy. The wheels of diplomacy—the exchange of envoys, the negotiation of treaties, and so on—had just begun to turn when Clay took office. He was anxious to move rapidly in order to counteract British influence and to secure American interests in the new republics. Recognition of these republics immediately doubled the foreign business of the State Department. The president proposed to separate its miscellaneous domestic business by the creation of a home, or interior, department. Congress demured, though it agreed to a substantial increase of staff in 1827.

All danger from Spain had passed, but after seventeen years of war she had yet to make peace with her former colonies, and there were alarming trouble spots, like Cuba, which Daniel Webster gravely declared was "the most delicate and vastly the most important point in all our foreign relations."[20] It was rumored that Columbia and Mexico planned to attack Cuba. This could not be allowed, Clay instructed the American minister to Mexico, Joel R. Poinsett, within three weeks of taking office. The United States had no designs on the island, but if it was to be attached to any American state it must, from "the law of its position," be attached to the United States.[21] The greater danger, as Clay recognized in urging Czar Alexander to prevail upon King Ferdinand VII to make peace, was that any Bolivarian expedition would provoke European intervention and the transfer of Cuba to a stronger power. George Canning, the British foreign secretary, proposed that the United States join with Britain and France to guarantee Cuba's status. Clay dodged the proposal, which violated the spirit of the American system and might prove embarrassing in the future. He breathed a sigh of relief when France formally rejected it.[22]

Toward the new republics Clay pursued the basic principles of American diplomacy since 1776: peace, neutrality, and maximum liberty of trade. The treaty negotiated with the United Provinces of Central America was the first based upon complete reciprocity of navigation. Through such liberal arrangements Clay hoped to achieve a competitive advantage for American ships and cargoes, including manufactured goods, in Latin American markets. Another, but less liberal, treaty was negotiated with Brazil, still another with Mexico, though its ratification was delayed for several years because of a controversial provision for the return of fugitive slaves to the United States. Clay was particularly disappointed in his Mexican diplomacy. Britain remained the dominant influence in Mexico City. Never reconciled to the loss of Texas under the Adams-Onís Treaty of 1819, Clay instructed Poinsett to obtain from the Mexican government what the former Spanish government had refused, a boundary at the Rio Grande or some other river south of the Sabine. But Mexico would not hear of it, and the more Poinsett pressed the proposition the more restive the Mexicans became.[23]

Clay envisioned the Panama Congress as a unique opportunity for the assertion of American leadership in the hemisphere. There was a certain awkwardness in the affair from the beginning, however. The convening nations hoped to erect a hemispheric alliance upon the principles of the Monroe Doctrine. Could the United States accept the invitation without seeming to countenance this objective or, indeed, since the nations were technically still at war with Spain, without violating American neutrality? Adams was cool to the project from the beginning but, carried along by Clay's enthusiasm, he advocated participation with the understanding, clearly stated in the special message, that the United States would abstain from any discussions of belligerency and would enter into no alliance. Clay offered the same assurances to Congress.

Nevertheless, opponents of the administration in Congress quickly seized on the alliance bugaboo to attack the Panama mission. The real object of attack was not the mission, of course, but the administration. No one doubted that the mission would be approved eventually. Approval, with an appropriation for the envoys, was held up for four months, however, as the issue was kicked around Congress, scoring impressively for the rallying Jacksonian coalition. Aside from the alliance horror, Adams had raised the old horror of monarchical prerogative by assuming in the message that he could send ministers to Panama without the consent of the Senate. Hearing this, Van Buren, the wily New York senator, went to the vice president, and the two men agreed there could be no better issue for uniting the jarring elements of the opposition. None had anything to gain from the Panama mission. Henceforth, Van Buren later said, there was "agreement in action" with Calhoun on everything but the tariff.[24] Clay recognized that Calhoun, if he had not already gone over, was "up to the hub with the opposition" on Panama. "One of the main inducements with him, and those whom he can influence, is that they suppose, if they can defeat or, by delay, cripple the measure, it will affect me."[25] Webster, too, believed Calhoun orchestrated the opposition to Panama, and mainly with a view to injuring Clay. The *Democratic Press* accused the vice president of sacrificing the national interest on the altar of political ambition. Calhoun himself later rejoiced in his fame as "the adviser and the author of the attack" on the Panama mission.[26]

Predictably, the Senate Foreign Relations Committee reported adversely on the mission. It was legislative rather than executive in character, said the committee, and it presaged the abandonment of the principle of "no entangling alliances" enshrined in Washington's Farewell Address. In the ensuing debate it was assailed as unconstitutional and un-American. Southerners, among them Calhoun's young friend Robert Y. Hayne, took the lead in opposition. In addition to Old Republican fears of executive tyranny, they played upon racial fears associated with the example of black Haiti, with a rumored concert against the slave trade, with racial intermingling at Panama, and with the prospect of receiving black and tan consuls and ambassadors in Washington. But the Senate finally voted approval of the two envoys, Richard Anderson and John Sergeant, 27–17.

Now the Jacksonian pugilists in the House took their turn. Webster masterfully argued that the House, having no authority in foreign affairs, ought not debate the measure at all but should simply vote the $40,000 appropriation to carry it out. Answering those who traced this policy of "unholy alliance" to the baneful influence of Henry Clay, Webster praised the secretary for his love of liberty and for the sagacity to foresee that the Latin American revolutions would not only succeed but give rise to a great "American family of nations." Clay ought to be esteemed among the foremost statesmen of the age, but instead, Webster said, "it is made matter of imputation and of reproach to have been first to reach forth the hand of welcome and of succor to new-born nations, struggling to obtain and enjoy the blessings of liberty."[27] Until this speech some southern politicians clung to the hope, derived from his free-trade opinions and his supposed "whitewash" of Crawford in the congressional report of 1824 on the "A.B. Letters," that Webster would add his remarkable talents to the opposition. The speech blasted that chimera and, at the same time, established Webster as the administration leader in the House. On April 22 the House voted overwhelmingly to approve the Panama appropriation, 134–66.

It was a costly victory. Politically, the Panama mission opened the administration to withering attack and furnished the issue around which a faction-ridden opposition could cohere. Diplomatically, as the vehicle of Clay's hopes, the mission came to nought. After the prolonged delay, one of the envoys, Anderson, died en route, while the other, Sergeant, arrived only for the postmortems in Mexico in 1827. Several preliminary agreements had been reached by four governments at Panama, but as the Congress never reconvened they were abortive. American absence and timidity contributed to the failure, which was, conversely, a victory for British policy in Latin American. Clay was disappointed, of course. For ten years he had given his heart to the cause of liberty in Latin America. The Panama Congress opened, he had hoped, "a new epoch in human affairs." Yet the people of his own country seemed indifferent to the fate of the new republics. Their leaders, in turn, beginning with the Liberator himself, were proving unworthy of the trust Clay had placed in them. The instructions he penned for the envoys reiterated his commitment to the "American system" ideal. The Senate rudely refused to publish this state paper; it would finally be published only after Clay left office, when it won the admiration even of his enemies. The instructions directed that nothing should be done to compromise American peace and neutrality. He urged the envoys to obtain commitments to American principles of free trade and freedom of the seas. He extended a warning to the new republics against granting exclusive commercial favors to any country, meaning Britain in particular. Seeking to embody Monroe's doctrine in the new Pan-American system, Clay called upon the nations at Panama for a joint declaration against European colonization. He called, too, for cooperation in planning a canal across the isthmus—a canal that would be open to all nations. And, while reiterating the pledge of non-intervention, Clay instructed the envoys to press upon the ministers of the other American states the principles of freedom and self-government that lay at the foundation of the government of the United States.[28]

On March 30, 1826, two weeks after the Senate concluded debate on the Panama mission, John Randolph delivered perhaps the most offensive speech ever heard in that body. The fifty-two-year-old Virginian, whose gaunt, emaciated frame gave dramatic point to the political degeneration and decay that was his constant theme, launched one of the "elaborate salmagundis and zigzags" with which he had alternately entertained and terrorized Congress for years. Once a master of Swiftian satire, he was now too consumed by malice for that and spoke only in sneers and sarcasms. Some thought him insane, others only demoniacal, but all dreaded the poison of his tongue. On this day Randolph touched on the doctrines of the First Message, recalled the "monarchism" of old John Adams, which the son had inherited, denounced the American System, scorned the Panama Congress, where Americans would be forced to commingle with mulatto generals, and accused the secretary of state of fraudulently manufacturing the invitations to this assembly. Several senators were shocked by this charge, but none called the speaker to order, and the vice president listened impassively. Concluding his harangue, Randolph recurred to the source of all these evils, the corrupt bargain between Adams and Clay, which he then bitingly characterized as "the coalition of Blifil and Black George . . . the combination, unheard of till then, of the puritan with the blackleg."[29]

Even Henry Clay, with his spotty education, had read Fielding's *Tom Jones* and understood the allusion: Blifil was a sanctimonious hypocrite, Black George a worthless knave.* In the previous session, when they were together in the House, Randolph had taunted Clay about his literary deficiencies. The Kentuckian, in reply, freely confessed them and, mocking Randolph's pride, gloried in his humble birthright. "I was born to no proud patrimonial estate. I inherited only infancy, ignorance, and indigence." At

---

*An eyewitness, John K. Kane of Philadelphia, later said that the published account of Randolph's outburst was but a poor caricature of the original. During the speech he drew a book from his desk, remarking, "Yes, Sir, the Bible!" The volume proved to be Shakespeare. No matter. He drew again. "Yes, Sir, the Bible!—and Shakespeare!—and," drawing once more, "and—Tom Jones. Good books, all of them, Sir, though oddly sorted." He then asked the vice president if he had read *Tom Jones* lately, saying one of the chapters showed how fiction may anticipate history. "It is where Blifil the puritan and Black George the poacher combine to swindle the hero of his right. Sir, Chaucer sang of it before it was chronicled, that snowbeard January from Old Massachusetts had mingled in espousals with the blooming May, the eldest daughter of Virginia. But we were the first to see on the stage of real life the blue-bonneted puritan of New England sharing the profits of the shuffle with the political Black Legs of the West!"[30]

this Randolph was heard to mutter, "The gentleman might continue the alliteration, and add *insolence*."[31] This was only the most recent of a series of clashes between Clay and Randolph that commenced in 1812 when Clay, the Speaker of the House, refused to entertain the Virginian's resolution against a declaration of war. It was sometimes said that Clay's popularity in that office rested on the belief that he was the only man in Congress who could control John Randolph. Obviously Calhoun could not or would not. Nor could Clay defend himself. Under the circumstances he felt he had no alternative but to challenge Randolph to a duel, and he did so the next day.

Like nearly everyone else, Clay opposed dueling in principle; but he had grown up in a society where it was an accepted practice among gentlemen in affairs of honor and had, of course, resorted to it himself, as had Andrew Jackson, Thomas Hart Benton, George McDuffie, and many men of prominence. Since 1811 dueling had been a crime in Kentucky. But no one had ever been punished—nor would anyone for the next quarter of a century—for taking part, or even killing an antagonist, in a duel. Clay had not challenged other accusers of "bargain and corruption," however. Why did he challenge John Randolph? Apparently because the accuser *was* Randolph, because the attack was unprovoked, because the attacker escaped reprimand, because of the grossness of the charge of forgery and the odium of swindling that went with the word "blackleg." Randolph's speech coincided with a full-page editorial blast, "Bargain, Management, and Intrigue," in the *United States Telegraph*, the opposition newspaper in the capital. Acting more from instinct than from reason, Clay hoped to place himself beyond the reach of similar attacks in the future by standing up to Randolph. Only one consideration gave him pause: the general opinion that the Virginian was mad, hence not responsible for his tongue. In this regard Clay decided to be governed by the opinion of the Virginia legislature, which presumably would not have elected a madman to the United States Senate.[32]

Randolph, having provoked the challenge, could not decline it. As much as he hated Clay's politics he had a sneaking admiration for him personally— Black George, after all, was a good-natured knave—and had been heard to say, "I prefer to be killed by Clay to any other death."[33] The two men met, with their seconds, on the Virginia side of the Potomac on April 8. Neither was experienced with dueling pistols. Both missed on the first exchange of shots at ten paces. This was enough to satisfy the code duello, but it did not satisfy Clay. He insisted on another round, and Randolph consented. Clay then put his bullet through the long, voluminous white coat Randolph wore for the occasion. Uninjured, and drained of any desire to injure Clay, he fired into the air, dropped his pistol, came forward, extended his hand and said, "You owe me a coat, Mr. Clay." Taking his hand, Clay replied, "I am glad the debt is no greater." (Rebecca Gratz, one of Clay's friends, remarked, "It would be well if he gave him [Randolph] a strait jacket.")[34] In the sensation produced by the duel no one blamed Clay but many, including some of his best friends, felt he should have consulted his discretion rather than his courage and found some other way of dealing with Randolph. Clay's sense of honor was never in question; the duel, while unnecessary to prove that, dramatized the very traits of anger and unruliness that he most needed to erase from the public image. It did not quiet Randolph. He liked Clay too much to kill him, yet continued his shrill attack; and when he died seven years later left instructions that he be buried facing west—not east as customary—so as to keep an eye on Henry Clay.[35]

Reports of Clay's duel with Randolph were followed by reports of a similar meeting with Calhoun in which he, the vice president, was killed.[36] They were credible because of the opinion that Calhoun, not Randolph, was responsible for the affair by his criminal negligence as presiding officer in the Senate. "Had either man fallen I should have considered, not the survivor, but Calhoun as the murderer," wrote Massachusetts congressman Edward Everett.[37] On May 1 there appeared in the *National Journal*, the administration newspaper in the capital, the first of a series of articles, signed "Patrick Henry," criticizing the vice president for prostrating the dignity of the Senate. The writer was thought to be the president himself. (In fact, it was a young friend of Clay's, Philip R. Fendall, who would later be appointed to a clerkship in the State Department.) He argued that, although the rules did not explicitly confer on the presiding officer the authority to call a senator to order, he possessed that authority by virtue of his office and by the responsibility laid down in *Jefferson's Manual* to maintain order. No one before Calhoun had ever doubted it. His passivity before Randolph's slanderous attack could only be explained by political enmity and ambition, said Patrick Henry. He was promptly answered by "Onslow," whom everyone recognized as Calhoun. Turning the issue into one of freedom of debate, he argued that the assumption of power by the vice president to call a senator to order would be despotic. As the war of words continued, it became evident that the narrow issue of parliamentary procedure involved the larger conflict between two nascent political parties. While Patrick Henry interpreted the vice president's conduct, beginning with the packing of the Senate committees, as part of an experiment, unprecedented in the United States, "of opposition to men without regard to principles," Onslow viewed the attack on the vice president as part of an administration conspiracy to create a monarchical executive dangerous to the liberties of Congress and the people. In 1828 the Senate amended its rules to sanction explicitly the authority of the presiding officer to call a senator to order. The change was, in fact, a repudiation of Calhoun for his conduct in the Randolph affair, although he chose to interpret it as a vindication of his position.[38]

Politics submerged Clay's diplomacy. He was not inactive. More treaties—twelve—were negotiated during his tenure than by any previous secretary of state. Most of these were commercial treaties favorable to American shipping and navigation which, having earlier been protected, could now flourish best, Clay thought, under conditions of reciprocity and freedom. Several of the treaties concerned boundaries and other old issues with Britain. Yet it was in Anglo-American relations that Clay's diplomacy suffered a second critical defeat. At issue was the long-standing American demand for free trade with the

British West Indies. After Ghent, when Britain restored the system of monopoly and restriction, closing the islands to alien carriers, the United States retaliated with a law barring its ports to British vessels coming from any colonial ports closed to American vessels. The West Indian trade was of declining importance for the American economy. But the British system—a remnant of the commercial imperialism that antedated the Revolution—was peculiarly galling to American statesmen, and thus had great symbolic importance. "The whole of this colonial system . . . is an outrage upon the first principles of civil society," Adams had said. Although it was not confined to Britain, she was the principal culprit. The exclusion from her colonies "is nothing less than a commercial conspiracy against the United States, the only nation whom it materially injures, and the only nation extensively commercial and maritime which possesses no colonies."[39] Retaliation worked. Britain opened the colonial ports to American carriers in 1822. The United States responded by lifting its bar, on the condition, demanded by Secretary of State Adams, that American vessels and cargoes be admitted into colonial ports on an equal basis with those of the mother country or her colonies. Britain refused the condition, standing on the right to regulate colonial trade and to impose "colonial preferences."

Things were at a stalemate when Clay became secretary of state. He was not deceived by the vaunted liberality of William Huskisson's trade reforms, which, he supposed, were designed to squelch American manufactures; nor did he expect Great Albion to drop mercantilist privileges and restrictions in her colonies. Once the United States receded from the unrealistic demand for equality in the colonial trade, Clay believed that matters could be easily adjusted. Several months after taking office he consulted a number of merchants and legislators experienced in foreign commerce; all of them, including Webster, who reckoned the West Indian trade "trifling" in any event, recommended backing away from Adams's demand.[40] Adams himself apparently acquiesced. Unfortunately, for the next nine months Clay was preoccupied with Latin American affairs, the Panama mission, and its political repercussions. No instructions on this issue ever reached Rufus King. By the time Albert Gallatin arrived as King's successor at the Court of St. James in July 1826, British colonial trade policy had swung back into the old restrictive orbit, and Canning, the foreign minister, refused to negotiate. Blaming Britain for the impasse, Adams and Clay sought to obtain a face-saving measure from Congress in 1827. But they had lost control of the Senate; the measure failed, leaving the president no recourse under the law but to return to the restrictions of 1818, closing American ports to British vessels in the colonial trade. Wherever the blame rightfully lay—and many Jacksonians along with merchants in foreign commerce laid it squarely at the administration's feet—it was a devastating defeat for Adams and Clay.[41]

With the formation of an organized opposition dedicated to the election of Andrew Jackson, nothing the administration attempted was free from partisan attack. Adams supposed his administration would be a continuation of Monroe's, with the same sort of political friends and foes; but this did not happen, for many reasons, mostly because of Clay's presence. "Every prominent public man feels, that he has been thrown into a new attitude," said Calhoun, trying to explain the change to Monroe, ". . . as if by some mighty political revolution."[42] For Calhoun, of course, principle and patriotism were on the side of the opposition. The popular will had been assaulted in the choice of the president; the corrupt coalition, unable to rule by American principles, was running the government back into a tyrannical British system. In this Adams was only an instrument. Clay was the prime mover. "The impulse . . . is from the West," Calhoun wrote. "It is a union of the bold and gambling spirit, which has sprung up in the West, and the old '98 Federal spirit of New England."[43] For Adams and Clay, on the other hand, the rhetoric of Old Republican principle was political humbug got up for no other purpose than to raise the Jacksonian coalition to power. While the coalition was forming in 1826, Kentucky Senator Richard M. Johnson accosted William W. Seaton, one of the publishers of the *National Intelligencer*, with the proposition to join the opposition. The newspaper had been deprived of the public printing by the Adams administration, which set up the *National Journal* as its mouthpiece; still Seaton thought it ought to be opposed or supported on its merits and wondered how Johnson could justify an opposition without regard to principle. "I don't care," the senator fumed, "for, by the Eternal, if they act as pure as the angels that stand at the right hand of the throne of God, we'll put them down." It was "the Moloch of party," of which Van Buren was "the master spirit," Seaton came to believe, that destroyed the Adams administration.[44]

If this was, indeed, the situation—if men, not principles, were the issue—the administration must look to its friends in order to survive. But for a president who set out to govern as if parties did not exist, this was bound to prove difficult. From the early months of the administration there were complaints that in matters of patronage Adams seemed more interested in appeasing his enemies, such as the Clintonians in New York, than in rewarding his friends. A Baltimore editor told Clay of the massive alienation of affections from the president: "hundreds of his former friends, in Maryland, would not turn on their heels to promote his reelection."[45] Answering such complaints, Clay defended the president, while at the same time working quietly to overcome his repugnance to removals and appointments made on political grounds. Under the Four-Year Law enacted by Congress in 1820 the term of every collecting or disbursing officer expired automatically every four years. The intent of the law was not to create a spoils system in the federal service but to achieve better accountability. Adams, nevertheless, believed that the law had been inspired by the former secretary of treasury, Crawford, to aid his election as president; and, holding the law vicious in principle, he would not employ it.[46] Not surprisingly, as Clay told Adams, many of his friends, finding no support at court, turned away in disgust.[47] John McLean, the postmaster general, with a vast patronage and lucrative mail contracts at his disposal, was devoted to the vice president and opposed to the secretary of state; yet Adams kept him in office and watched hundreds of local postmasters become Jackson partisans.[48] Webster, although he continued to tout amalgamation in Massachusetts, woke up to the realities of the new partisanship on his journey home in March 1827. In Philadelphia he met "one continued din of complaint" on the point of patronage. "Enemies laugh, and friends hang down their heads, whenever the subject is mentioned." Jacksonians manned the customs house; the federal attorney was politically suspect; only one newspaper supported the administration. Little honors, like appointment of visitors to West Point, went to opposition men, Webster reported to Clay, "so that it would seem our friends cannot even have *feathers*." "In short," his dolorous epistle concluded, "all protection, all proof of regard, all patronages . . . must be given to friends, or otherwise it is impossible to give any general or cordial support to the Administration before the people." And where better to begin than Pennsylvania, where the policies of the administration commanded strong support?[49]

Nothing was stranger in the Nineteenth Congress than the attack on the administration for using executive patronage to subvert the government. A Senate committee, packed with opposition members and chaired by Missouri's Benton, issued a lengthy report charging, among other things, perversion of the Four-Year Law that, in fact, Adams refused to pervert.[50] In the House, Clay was skewered and roasted for abuse of the principal patronage at his command, the appointment of newspapers to publish the laws of the United States. There were eighty or more of these, normally three newspapers in each state and territory (one in the District); and although the annual payment averaged only $200, it was not insignificant at a time when most newspapers operated on a shoestring and when public appointment of any kind carried influence. By January 1826 Clay had made ten changes in publishers of the laws. Compared to the standard that soon came to prevail, this was an exhibition of moderation and restraint; but it was unprecedented in 1826, and some of the changes, such as supplanting the Nashville *Republican*, ardently Jacksonian, by the Nashville *Whig*, which belonged to a family nearly related to Clay, were peculiarly sensitive. Romulus M. Saunders, of North Carolina, opened the attack on the secretary, charging that he used the power of his office to corrupt the press. Saunders proposed, as would Benton as well, to give Congress a check on the secretary's choice of newspapers. He resumed the attack at the second session, as Clay kept up his patently political use of this patronage power, dropping such prominent newspapers as Isaac Hill's *New Hampshire Patriot* and Amos Kendall's *Argus of Western America*, published at the Kentucky capital.[51]

Meanwhile, the new opposition press in Washington, the *United States Telegraph*, joined the campaign. The editor, Duff Green, had been taught to hate Henry Clay from an early age by his family's lawyer and friend, Humphrey Marshall, and his education was finished by Calhoun, to whom he tendered his services. Green portrayed Clay as a Machiavelli, plotting to obtain the presidency by bargain and sale. It was Green who broadcast the riposte Clay supposedly delivered to a Virginian rebuking him for sinking his popularity by going with Adams: "Give us the patronage of the Government and we will make ourselves popular!"[52] It naturally followed that the hired press would be the engine of popularity. The Jacksonians made no real effort to check this patronage, or any other, mainly because it would tie their own hands when they came to power. The object of the attack was not reform but further defamation of the administration. It was said of Green, the chief of the defamers, that he could teach lying tricks to the devil himself.[53] When the Jacksonians came into control of the upper house in 1827, they ousted Peter Force, editor of the *National Journal,* and elected Green printer of the Senate. Not only was this a lucrative and influential position; the election was, ironically, sweet revenge against Henry Clay, the architect of the 1819 law that made every newspaper in Washington a solicitor for congressional favor.[54]

If Clay had hoped to reap political advantage from that law, he must have been sadly disappointed in 1827. Green's success, together with the crescendo of criticism from the administration's friends, forced on every member of the cabinet, and finally on the president himself, the reality of two parties contending for control of the government and, therefore, the political necessity of rewarding friends and punishing enemies. It was too late, however. In retrospect Adams supposed his administration was doomed by "the Sable Genius of the South."[55] More accurately, it was doomed by his appalling lack of political leadership, beginning with congressional relations and extending to such mundane matters as customs house appointments. An anecdote that entered into American political folklore had Adams toasted, "May he strike confusion to his foes . . ."—at which point Webster interjected "as he has already done to his friends." Clay, although he loyally defended his chief, must have nodded assent. Through all the political difficulties he remained popular among the National Republicans, as they began to call themselves, and was regarded almost everywhere as the true head of the party.

3. Bargain and Abominations

Andrew Jackson was again placed in nomination for the presidency by the legislature of Tennessee in October 1825. He hastened to Murfreesborough, and in a carefully staged ceremony that Clay called "a miserable compound imitation of the august event at Annapolis, when Washington resigned the sword of Liberty, and the late legislative receptions of Lafayette," resigned from the Senate, where he had filled but two years of his term, and accepted the nomination. "Well," Clay further remarked, "the General having tried to be elected president by going into the Senate, now means to make the experiment by going out of it."[1] Jackson voiced approval of a constitutional amendment limiting the president to a single term, then in an obvious slap at Clay advocated another amendment that would make any member of Congress ineligible for executive office until two years after the expiration of his elected term. Intriguers would thus be foiled and the morals of the country saved. "But if this change in the Constitution is not obtained," Jackson said, ". . . it required no depth of thought to see that corruption will become the order of the day."[2] He thus gave notice that "bargain and corruption" would be the banner issue in the coming campaign.

Since Clay's personal vindication before his constituents in March 1825, no one had assumed responsibility for the "corrupt bargain" charge or undertaken to prove it. It floated on the wings of rumor and innuendo. In Congress irascible George McDuffie was the point-man on the issue. It was "but too obvious," he maintained, that the Kentucky gamester had sacrificed himself and his country at "the unhallowed shrine of ambition." "Yes, sir, ambition—corrupting ambition—that sin by which the 'Angels fell.' " In the circumstances of Adams's election and Clay's appointment, proof was established by the result. "Can any thing be more plain?" McDuffie asked. "It is the common case, sir, of a sale in market overt; and none but a man of the most consummate boldness and effrontery could hold up his head in society after such a transaction."[3] Jackson himself had not again come before the public as Clay's accuser. However, in March 1827 a North Carolina newspaper published the letter of an anonymous Virginian, soon revealed as Carter Beverley, reporting Jackson's statement at the Hermitage "that Mr. Clay's *friends* made a proposition to *his* friends, that, if they would promise, for him [General Jackson] *not* to put Mr. Adams into the seat of secretary of state, Mr. Clay and his friends would, *in one hour,* make *him* [Jackson] the president."[4] What was charged here was not collusion between Adams and Clay, the evidence of which apparently lay locked in their hearts, but the proposition of a bargain on Clay's part to Jackson. When a Washington reporter took the Beverley letter to Clay, he promptly branded the charge a lie and refused to believe Jackson had made it.[5] The epistle provoked other indignant denials as it went the round of the nation's press. Beverley, therefore, asked Jackson to confirm the truth of his report. The general replied at length on June 6. The proposition had been made to him by a member of Congress, unnamed, whom he supposed acted with Clay's knowledge and with the view to making him secretary of state in a Jackson administration. He instantly rejected it, of course, telling the congressman "that before I would reach the presidential chair by such means of bargain and corruption, I would see the earth open and swallow both Mr. Clay and his friends, and myself with them."[6] Clay met with this letter at Wheeling on the way home. He issued another denial and called upon Jackson to substantiate the charge. Why Jackson had waited over two years to make it, why he had been silent during the Kremer letter scandal, was a mystery; but Clay expressed relief that "a responsible accuser" had at last appeared and seemed confident he could turn events to his advantage. "I could not have wished the affair to take a more favorable turn," he wrote. "If it does not end in degrading General Jackson, I am greatly deceived as to the character of the American public."[7]

Clay offered a second personal vindication at a great public dinner in Lexington on July 12. This was followed by similar entertainments and speeches at Woodford, at Paris, and several other places. His speeches were by no means limited to the bargain and corruption issue. Clay advocated the policies of the American System, which he identified with the administration, and assailed the unprincipled opportunism of the opposition in Congress. In the main, however, it was a replay of Demosthenes against Philip. Not surprisingly, some compared Clay's speeches in moral grandeur and eloquence to Demosthenes' Oration on the Crown.[8] Others thought the speech making undignified. Robert Walsh, the acerbic editor of *The National Gazette*, in Philadelphia, named Clay "the table orator," and while he may have meant no harm, it was quickly taken up as a term of derision. Jackson boasted that he, at least, had confined his political talk to his own dinner table; he had not "gone into the highways and market-places . . . , even at public dinner-tables," to proclaim his opinions. A popular cartoon showed Clay sewing up Jackson's mouth.[9] Clay's speech making, on the dinner circuit in Kentucky and en route between Lexington and the capital, was unprecedented for a high official. He thus broke a new path in the practice of American politics. Interestingly, there also appeared at this time *The Speeches of Henry Clay, With a Biographical Memoir*. Assembled by a Lexington journalist principally from newspaper reports of congressional speeches, it was the first such volume to be published in the United States and showed the importance parliamentary eloquence had attained in the nation's life.[10]

On July 18, in a second letter to Beverley, Jackson responded to Clay's demand for proof by naming James Buchanan as the bearer of the incriminating proposition in January 1825. The Pennsylvania congressman was thus put on the spot as Jackson's star witness. In a public letter to the *Lancaster Journal*, Buchanan recalled his interview with Jackson, saying that he had sought assurance of at least the hope of office for Clay, that he had tried in this way to promote Jackson's election, and throughout had acted entirely on his own responsibility. Clay hailed this testimony as a complete exoneration. Indeed, by disclosing negotiations to secure Jackson's election, the letter turned the tables on his accusers. "Instead of any intrigues on my part and that of my friends, they were altogether on the side of General Jackson and his friends." Webster doubted Jackson would ever recover from the blow.[11]

Mortified by the testimony of his Pennsylvania friend, Jackson retired from the controversy without another word. Of course, he never admitted publicly that Buchanan's letter changed anything, and the pertinacious crew of Jacksonian editors led by Duff Green actually claimed the testimony sustained their leader and everything Kremer, Eaton, Ingham, *et al*. had said.[12] Clay undertook to lay the matter to rest by gathering, then publishing, the testimony of congressmen and others, such as Lafayette, who were privy to his thoughts and actions in the presidential contest. He showed his draft address, with its weighty appendix, to Adams, who had no hope it would succeed. "When suspicion has been kindled into popular delusion, truth and reason and justice spoke as to the ears of an adder—the sacrifice must be consummated before they can be heard. General Jackson will therefore be elected [president]," he wrote in his diary.[13] Other counsel, that of his Kentucky friend John J. Crittenden, for instance, held that Clay should say no more, that his innocence had been established by the excessive zeal of his enemies. "They grow weary of the subject, and find that the stone which they have so ignominiously labored to roll up the hill, is likely to return upon their own heads. As far as proof can go—proof called out by your accusers—given by your opponents— you stand triumphant," said Crittenden. "All that is wanting is a little silence."[14] But Clay did not know the meaning of silence. His *Address to the Public*—thirty tightly packed pages—appeared in December 1827; a supplement was published six months later.[15]

Early in the new year, several of Clay's Kentucky friends, apparently acting without his consent, moved to get the legislature to exonerate him. This proved to be a blunder, for while no conclusive action was taken on the resolution, it led to an investigation that produced several disclosures embarrassing to the secretary. Amos Kendall, editor of the *Argus of Western America*, earlier devoted to Clay but now a leading Jacksonian press, testified that Clay had paid him to publish in pamphlet form the anti-Adams articles he had written on the Mississippi issue under the pseudonym "Wayne"; further, and more recently, Clay had tried to bribe him with a clerkship in the State Department in order to silence his voice in Kentucky politics. Francis Preston Blair, another young Kentucky friend fallen from political grace, refused to disclose the contents of confidential letters from Clay at the time of the presidential contest in Washington. Some, like Kendall, supposed these letters were "the smoking gun"—to borrow a term of later coinage—that would convict Clay of bargain and corruption. Blair's refusal to testify was alternately interpreted as a point of honor or as presumptive proof of Clay's guilt. Clay himself opposed disclosure, though not from any fear of self-incrimination. The letters were written with much levity—Adams was portrayed as coming begging with tears in his eyes. Their publication would be embarrassing, as Clay candidly told Adams. Finally, after the investigation ended, he agreed to let one of the letters be inspected by interested parties; and Kendall, granted this indulgence, promptly published the letter. It contained nothing incriminating.[16]

Politically, Clay's quest for vindication was doubtless an act of folly. Had he simply ignored the "bargain and corruption" lie, it would probably have receded from public view, as his friends tried to tell him; in any event, he could not possibly prove his innocence, "*acquit* himself," as Jackson's code of jurisprudence seemed to demand. Nor could he establish his innocence in the eyes of men who chose to infer guilt from appearances. "Sir, are we children?" John Randolph would ask. "Are we babies? Can't we make out apple-pie without spelling and putting the words together—a-p, ap, p-l-e, ple, apple, p-i-e, pie, apple-pie?"[17] Even the Jackson leaders—Van Buren, Benton, Buchanan—who rejected this insidious logic, who never believed a corrupt bargain had occurred, were unwilling to deny it in public. Jackson himself, believing Henry Clay "the basest, meanest scoundrel that ever disgraced the image of his god," would carry his hatred into the grave.[18]

Kentucky was on the verge of anarchy during Clay's years at the State Department. The rash of relief legislation—stay lews, replevin laws, paper money laws—that had been passed in the wake of panic and depression to aid ordinary farmers and other hard-pressed debtors ran into difficulty in the

Court of Appeals. In the ensuing struggle the relief crowd won control of the legislature and created a new court to uphold its program. For two years, from 1824 to 1826, the New Court party controlled the executive and legislative branches of government, while the judiciary was hopelessly split between two high courts. The New Court leaders claimed to represent the popular will, which, they said, was opposed by the old alliance of the banks, particularly the two branches of the Bank of the United States, and the courts. Naturally, they exploited the issue of the popular will defied in the national government in order to recruit followers in the state campaign. Clay tried to stay out of this conflict in Kentucky politics. It was, as Crittenden told him, "a mighty quicksand" for the Adams administration.[19] Unfortunately, he could not avoid it. He had friends in both parties, but his interests with his affections were centered in the Bluegrass, whose lawyers, merchants, and bankers constituted the core of the Old Court party. Not only was it the party of law and order; it also embodied the old dream, now little more than a glimmer, of Lexington as the Athens of the West. Transylvania University, under the liberal leadership of Horace Holley, a Unitarian from Boston, was the educational bearer of the dream. Clay was closely associated with Transylvania, sometimes known as "the University of Kentucky"; as a trustee he had been instrumental in the appointment of Holley in 1818. The Presbyterians, who sought control of the institution, were furious. Waging a decade-long campaign that culminated in Holley's resignation in 1827, the Presbyterians did not hesitate to exploit popular prejudice against the university, which was of a piece with popular prejudice against banks, courts, and lawyer-aristocrats. Some even charged that Holley had been brought to the Bluegrass to aid Clay's presidential prospects by strengthening his liaison with New England; and when at a Lexington dinner honoring Clay in 1826, Holley compared the Jacksonian opposition to the infamous Jack Cade, he exposed the university to the furies of Kentucky politics. Sober Presbyterians joined the alliance of New Court radicals and Jacksonian politicians against the university, Holley, and Clay.[20]

The Jackson party in Kentucky emerged from the Old Court–New Court battle. Some of its leaders, like John Pope, were old political enemies of Clay. But most had been his friends; in some instances the splits were personally wrenching. Young Blair was the son of a prominent family, a graduate of Transylvania, and protégé of Clay's. Blair backed Clay's decision to become secretary of state in 1825 and fully expected him to succeed Adams as president. Becoming a leader of the New Court party, however, he was gradually alienated from Clay. Amos Kendall, fresh from Massachusetts, had joined Clay's family as tutor of the children when their father was in Europe; through this connection he hoped to launch a political career in Kentucky. Ten years later, as editor of the *Argus* at Frankfort, he was among Clay's warmest advocates. At first he wanted an office in the new administration in Washington, but then discovered that his attachment to Clay was incompatible with his Kentucky political interest, which lay with the New Court party. Both Kendall and Blair urged Clay to abandon the Old Court clique and rally to the popular standard, warning that if he did not they must take up General Jackson, not from any love of him but to uphold their cause in state politics.[21] For a time Kendall professed neutrality in the simmering presidential contest; but his attacks on the administration, even on Clay himself, for betraying the West, and his strident role in the state, led the secretary to deprive the *Argus* of public printing at the end of 1826. This mark of official disfavor proved a godsend to Kendall. It absolved him of an old obligation to Clay, permitted him to attack the administration without restraint and to become a Jacksonian in earnest.[22] Later he had the temerity, in the state senate's investigation, to accuse Clay of attempting to bribe him by the offer of a public office he himself had sought. The change in Kendall's political allegiance coincided with the return of the Old Court party to control of the government and the destruction of "the new court" with all its work. Leaders of the radical cause, finding it no longer viable at home, climbed on the Jackson bandwagon. Now they took aim at the Clay party in national affairs. In June 1827 the Jacksonians took over the oldest newspaper in the state, the *Kentucky Gazette*, published on Clay's turf at Lexington. The August election resulted in a sharp increase of Jacksonian representation in both Frankfort and Washington. Two of Clay's most trusted allies in Congress met defeat. "These are the darkest pages of our history," Clay wrote mournfully. "Every man should awaken to the impending danger."[23] Still, ever the optimist, he could not believe that Kentucky and the nation would prove faithless in 1828.

The vice president, having gravitated to the opposition during the Panama session, offered himself as Jackson's running mate in the election of 1828. In retrospect this appeared to be a fateful decision. At the time it seemed to make good political sense. The caucus of the South Carolina legislature endorsed Jackson. The Old Hero would be just shy of sixty-two years of age when he became president in 1829; moreover, he had pledged himself to serve but one term. By cultivating his friendship, by aiding in the defeat of Adams and Clay, Calhoun could look forward to the succession four years hence when, in all likelihood, Clay would be his opponent. The contest between them would, in Calhoun's eyes, mark a return to the main political arena after the diverting Jacksonian sideshow. Until then he had more need for the Jacksonians than they for him. Some elements of the coalition, above all the Crawfordites, wanted to dump him. But the New Yorker, Van Buren, sealed his union with the Carolinian when they were both guests at the home of a Virginia planter during the 1826 Christmas recess. Calhoun gave statesmanlike dignity to the ticket; as vice president he lent the weight of his office to the opposition; and any other candidate, DeWitt Clinton for instance, was sure to be more controversial. He was supported by Jackson himself, who was still under the illusion that Calhoun had defended his conduct in the Seminole campaign. This skeleton in the closet began to rattle in 1827, but Calhoun managed to turn off all inquiries by pleading the secrecy of cabinet proceedings.[24] Regardless of his opinion of Jackson, or of his prospects with the coalition, Calhoun had nowhere else to go in 1828. Some of his friends believed he had lost political ground since becoming vice president;

indeed, he conceded to one of them he would gladly give $10,000 not to have done so.[25] The error might yet be reversed if he continued in the second office under Jackson, however.

From the standpoint of principle or ideology, Calhoun's decision to go with the Jacksonians made no sense at all. For years he had been attempting to force a division of parties between *national* republicans, like himself, and *radical* republicans like Crawford. Now he found that the Adams administration usurped the leadership, even the name, of National Republicans, while the opposition he had joined was dominated by his former enemies, the Radicals. Van Buren, the adroit political jockey of New York, Ritchie, Randolph, and the Virginia Republicans—Calhoun had little in common with these parts of the motley coalition that were remolding Andrew Jackson in their own image. Principles of state rights and strict construction, opposition to banks, tariffs, and internal improvements had yet to figure significantly in his politics. When Governor George M. Troup raised the flag of state sovereignty in behalf of Georgia's claim to deal with the Creek Indians as it pleased, Calhoun denounced the project as "mad and wicked." Troup was a Crawfordite, of course, and this contributed to Calhoun's hostility. The feeling was mutual. When the electoral votes came to be counted in 1828, Georgia would give seven of its nine votes for vice president to William Smith, Calhoun's inveterate rival in South Carolina. Smith, it may be recalled, had led "the revolution of 1825" that started the state on the track of resistance to national consolidation; and it was Smith who, in a stunning defeat for Calhoun, was elected to fill a vacancy in the Senate the following year. Smith's opposition to the Adams administration was perfectly consistent. Calhoun's required explanation. He said, of course, that liberty and self-government were in danger. Working with issues of "bargain and corruption," of patronage, separation of powers, and freedom of debate, he conjured up the idea of a tyrannical administration and argued that the coming contest, like that of 1776 and that of 1798, was between the rulers and the ruled.[26] This was metaphysical shadow boxing. It had nothing to do with the reality of the administration or of the opposition.

Calhoun's tendency to turn his feelings into intellectual speculations, to become obsessed with his ideas, and to push them to their ultimate conclusions, no matter how absurd, may have been encouraged by the vice presidential office. Accustomed to a life of action, he was thrust into "a post of dignified inaction," hearing everything, responding to nothing, and therefore plowing ideas into the furrows of his own mind.[27] At home during long periods of the year, he became a serious farmer again and, as in Washington, was both blessed and cursed with time to think. He resettled his family on one of old Mrs. Colhoun's properties, Clergy Hall, near the village of Pendleton. Calhoun later remodeled the simple white frame house perched on a hill overlooking six hundred acres rolling down to the Seneca River, and renamed the place Fort Hill. Upcountry cotton planters still suffered hard times. No sooner had prices rebounded from the Panic of 1819 than they plummeted to record lows. From an average of 25 cents a pound in 1825, the price fell to 9 cents in 1827. He and nine-tenths of the planters, Calhoun said, operated at a loss.[28] Many were leaving the state, striking out for raw lands in the southwest. Within a few years South Carolina, long the leading cotton producer, would fall behind Mississippi, Alabama, and Georgia. Among the causes of the state's decline were the overproduction of cotton and the higher yields of new lands, which placed South Carolina at a competitive disadvantage with the southwest. The planters, however, increasingly blamed their misfortunes on the protective tariff. It enriched northern manufacturers and impoverished southern producers, they said. The agitation against the tariff, indeed against the American System generally, having produced the revolution in the legislature, now swirled around Calhoun, and he began to view public policy from the standpoint of the South Carolina planter.

In December 1826, just after he returned to Washington for the session of Congress, Calhoun was faced with revival of the old charge that he had, as secretary of war, profited from a fortifications contract awarded to Elijah Mix. The guilt of his chief clerk in this matter had been established. Hardly anyone suspected Calhoun of complicity in the crime; nevertheless, he promptly demanded an investigation by the House. Earlier the scandal of "Castle Calhoun," as they dubbed it, had been exploited by the Crawfordites; now, the vice president believed, it was the handle seized by Henry Clay to destroy him. Clay reportedly rushed to the House when he learned of Calhoun's demand, talked to Webster, and closeted himself with the Speaker in the hope of controlling composition of the investigating committee. Apparently he succeeded, for the committee was stacked against Calhoun, at least in the opinion of his friends. While Duff Green penned editorials on "Mr. Clay's Mix Conspiracy," McDuffie, who represented Calhoun before the committee, accused it of drawing out the investigation and admitting irrelevant testimony in order to create the impression of wrongdoing. It was, said Calhoun, an inquisition.[29] The committee finally returned not one but two reports: both acquitted Calhoun but one raised serious questions of impropriety and error, suggesting that the "Augean stable" had not been cleaned after all. Calhoun's pride was injured. He felt besieged, persecuted, despondent. He was, Clay remarked, "nearly as low as ever Burr was."[30] Assailed by old rivals like Clay, Calhoun still had little reason for trust or confidence in his new political friends.

The revision and redirection of Calhoun's politics in response to the new situation in which he found himself turned upon the protective tariff. In February the Woolens Bill passed by the House came before the Senate. The woolens industry had been slighted by the tariff of 1824. Seeing the opportunity to strangle this infant, Britain slashed the duty on raw wool, thereby conferring upon her own industry a great competitive advantage. Clay backed the cause of the woolen manufacturers; the bill that cleared the House with a margin of eleven votes in February 1827 was a leading administration measure. Fewer than three weeks of the session remained. Hayne, in the Senate, moved to table the bill. A tie vote, supposedly contrived by Van Buren,

placed the fate of the measure in Calhoun's hands. He might have equivocated and let the bill run its uncertain course—it could not pass on a tie
vote—but Calhoun unhesitatingly provided the majority to kill it.[31] This was
the first public signal he had ever given of opposition to the protective tariff.
It was not a Jacksonian vote, for the Jacksonian opposition was divided on the
tariff. It was an anti-administration vote. Above all, it disclosed Calhoun's willingness to risk his political following in the North in order to secure his ascendancy at home and in the South. Loss of the Woolens Bill raised a political storm from Ohio to Maine, wherever wool was grown and wherever it
was manufactured, for both grower and manufacturer would have profited
from the bill. The upshot was the Harrisburg Convention, the first important
use of an old extra-constitutional device by special economic interests. Over
a hundred delegates elected in thirteen states met at Harrisburg during five
summer days, concluding with a series of resolutions that embraced wool and
woolens in a larger program of protectionism.

Observing the simultaneous agitation of the tariff at Harrisburg and at Columbia, North and South, Calhoun said it threatened "to make two of one nation." In his letters to political friends he spoke with a new voice. Without
dropping the "*constituents against rulers*" idea, which was at the heart of
American republicanism, he directed his attention to "*another* point," the
permanent injurious operation of the system of national legislation upon the
agricultural interests of the South. The impending presidential election, formerly viewed as the means of vindicating the popular will, began to appear
as a means of saving the South from ruin. "I hold it certain, that at present,
we are the only contributors to the national Treasury. *We alone pay without
indemnity,* while other sections are more than indemnified for all their contribution, in their character of monopolists and receivers."[32] This was the doctrine of Senator Smith, of Dr. Cooper at Columbia, of Robert J. Turnbull at
Charleston: the tariff was a tax not on consumers, as political economists had
always said, but on the producers at the South, who paid for it with their exports, while the manufacturers at the North "recharged" their liability
through the American System upon the community. Formerly Calhoun had
said the great danger to the republic lay in the tyranny of rulers; now he said
it lay in the economic exploitation of one section or interest by another. "This
is the point of greatest danger, and, if not guarded with the greatest vigilance, combinations will be formed on separate and opposing interests,
which will end in despotism, as complete as that of a single and irresponsible
ruler."[33] The Harrisburg Convention was the terrifying example. The separate representation and association of one great geographical interest to promote its prosperity at the expense of other interests was well calculated "to
make two of one nation."[34] Calhoun thus shifted the focus of his political
theory from the conflict of rulers and ruled to the conflict of sectional economic interests. The corrupt coalition at the head of government was sustained by the tariff system; reform it and the country would be made whole
again. Calhoun was careful not to publish these new views. The first hint of
them appeared, without his consent, in the *Telegraph* in July 1828. By then

he had decided the protective tariff was unconstitutional as well as oppressive and unjust.[35] If he still lagged behind the South Carolina radicals, he was catching up very fast and, with them, extending his opposition to the American System as a whole.

As Calhoun commenced a long retreat from nationalism, Daniel Webster moved rapidly to occupy this political ground. In the spring of 1827, having finished his second term in the House as Boston's congressman, Webster made the momentous decision to go into the Senate. The term of Elijah H. Mills had expired. He might retire voluntarily, but if he did not his declining health provided the excuse for the legislature to replace him with a man of more commanding talents and one less burdened with the legacy of Massachusetts Federalism. The obvious choice was Governor Levi Lincoln, a birthright Republican and the most popular politician in the state. Adams, Clay, and Webster, too, urged the office upon him. But Lincoln refused to consider it. When the legislature tried to elect a senator in January, the lower house supported Elijah Mills, while the upper house supported John Mills, its president; and thus divided between the upper and nether Mills, the legislature failed to elect anyone.[36] The state election came on in April. Webster took a prominent part in putting together the "Union ticket," which united Federalists and Republicans behind both national and state administrations. Speaking at Faneuil Hall, "the idol of New England," whose "eye would shame an eagle's," in the words of an awestruck William Lloyd Garrison, lashed out at the unscrupulous opposition in Washington, characterizing it as chiefly southern, and appealed to all men of good will to rally behind the Adams administration regardless of old prejudices and antiquated party distinctions.[37] With four tickets in the field, the election produced no clear winner, though the Union party fared best. The new legislature would meet in June.

Webster, meanwhile, was pressed by many of his friends to accept the Senate seat. In January his name had not even been mentioned. A year before, when Nathaniel Silsbee had been elected to the Senate, Webster had been nominated as the Federalist candidate without his consent; and he seemed no more interested now in changing his seat from one wing of the Capitol to the other. "My habits are formed for the House, and I doubt if I should feel so much at home elsewhere," he wrote.[38] The lower house was still the chief forum of legislative leadership. The Senate was the more dignified body, of course (or was until the appearance of John Randolph) and had weighty responsibilities in foreign affairs and in executive appointments. One of Webster's habits likely to be upset by senatorial service was his practice before the Supreme Court during sessions of Congress. Regardless of personal preferences, Adams and Clay were reluctant to lose Webster's services in the House. So were his Boston constituents. Whatever his deficiencies as a leader, he was clearly the dominant figure on the administration side of the House. It was a case of sheer intellectual superiority. "No man is listened to in debate with such attention," wrote a freshman congressman in 1826. "No man is so certain to convince his hearers and no man is so sure to carry the house with him. He . . . puts out his strength only occasionally, but when it is exerted it is almost as destructive to his adversaries as that of Samson. . . . The boasted statesmen of the South are mere pigmies to him."[39] He did not always carry the House with him; yet the Senate, not the House, was the graveyard of most administration measures. There, before the array of opposition talent, the administration cut a poor figure. It was a nice question, then, where the balance lay between keeping Webster in the House and transferring him to the Senate. In truth, he was wanted in both. "It is difficult to see how we can get along in either house without you," wrote an Ohio congressman.[40] When final efforts to change Lincoln's mind failed in May, Webster put himself at the disposal of Adams and Clay. They settled his destiny on the Senate, "the weak point in the Citadel," in Lincoln's concurring opinion.[41] The success of the Union ticket, together with the manifest evidence of Webster's adherence to the emerging National Republican party, made his election a foregone conclusion. When the legislature balloted in June, the lower house gave Webster 202 of 328 votes, the upper house 26 of 39. Anti-amalgamation Federalists stuck with Elijah Mills, while John Mills received most of the Jacksonian votes, about one-quarter of the whole. The Jacksonian Republicans, centered in a faction led by David Henshaw, had been courting Adams's favor. Now they went into business for themselves.[42]

Webster had distinguished himself in the House, as he would in the Senate, by his work on judicial and constitutional questions. As chairman of the Judiciary Committee, he secured passage of the Crimes Act in 1825, the first federal criminal code since the original law of 1790. His friend Justice Story had been advocating this legislation for many years; he, in fact, was the principal author of the code. The two men were not only bosom friends but collaborators in law and legislation. This was recognized at the time, though not to its full extent. To some observers, like Louis McLane of Delaware, it seemed that Story was "but a wretched tool of Webster," while to others the relationship was just the reverse. "Mr. Justice Story," Theodore Parker would say, "was the Jupiter Pluvius from whom Mr. Webster often sought to elicit political thunder for his speeches, and private rain for his own public tanks of the law."[43] Parker was nearer the truth. Although Webster contributed to Story's opinions on the court, the congressman was the debtor in the intellectual account between them. In 1826 Webster reported a bill for a national system of bankruptcy. Story had a hand in this, too. Both men wished to establish preemptive national authority in this area. Simultaneously, Webster argued this position before the Supreme Court in the case of *Ogden* v. *Saunders*. But he could muster a majority neither in Congress nor of the court.[44]

Acting as a watchdog of the federal judiciary, Webster fended off attacks from western agrarians, who sought to curb its authority, and from southern radicals, some of whom still advocated repeal of the twenty-fifth section of the Judiciary Act of 1789 giving the Supreme Court appellate jurisdiction over the decisions of state courts. The supreme tribunal was, in Webster's opinion, "the great arbitrator between contending sovereignties." It was the main pillar of the government. "I am persuaded," he declared, "that the Union could not exist without it."[45] The case of Georgia and the Creeks was just such a case of "contending sovereignties," and Webster told Georgia, in a remarkable prelude to the Reply to Hayne three years hence, that she acted *at peril* in taking jurisdiction over Indian lands under the protection of the United States. Georgia congressman John Forsyth, while conceding the weight of Webster's character, the vigor of his mind, and "the great and commanding influence which he of late too often exercises here," interpreted Webster's remarks as threatening coercion of a sovereign state. In reply, the Bay Stater declined to amend or withdraw his remarks, though he acknowledged that the proper tribunal in such cases was the Supreme Court.[46] Webster took care not only to protect the judiciary but to ensure that it was capable of administering justice in a rapidly growing country. His reorganization bill in 1826 proposed to add three circuit courts in the West, where there was still only one, and at the same time to increase the complement of the Supreme Court from seven to ten. The merits of the bill were not in question. After clearing the House, however, it met with defeat in the Senate mainly, Webster thought, because the opposition did "not wish to give so many important appointments to the President."[47]

Webster and Clay never acted in greater harmony than during these years. Faithfully championing administration measures in Congress, Webster won Clay's gratitude and respect. Becoming a zealot for internal improvements, which New England votes had generally opposed, Webster also won favor in the West and helped to strengthen the sectional alliance that underlay the alliance between Adams and Clay. Leading advocates of internal improvements in the past had generally supposed that the policy could be limited to aiding works of a *national* character, excluding those of essentially local interest. But Webster saw clearly that the national-local distinction was insupportable, for it was mainly by the assemblage and interconnection of local works that the national interest was advanced. He repudiated the principle of *pro rata* distribution of internal improvement dollars to the states, which descended from the Bonus Bill, as both parochial and impractical. "The country," he said, "was to be considered as if there were no State lines—as if the legislation was for one unit."[48] The question of equality among the states was irrelevant. A breakwater in Delaware Bay, a road in Kentucky, a canal in Illinois—all benefited the entire nation. "There are no Alleghenies in my politics," Webster declared. Once asked how he, a Massachusetts senator, could vote funds to remove snags from rivers in Illinois or Missouri, he replied, "Is not *our* commerce floating on those western rivers?"[49] Disagreeing with this outlook, the vice president provided the casting vote to defeat a favorite administration project for a canal linking Lake Michigan and the Illinois River.[50] On the whole, however, the administration was successful in its support of internal improvements. More money was appropriated than in all the preceding years of the government. The Chesapeake and Ohio Canal, launched with much fanfare in 1828, was a gigantic undertaking, comparable in the president's opinion, to the Declaration of Independence and the Constitution in the realization of the nation's destiny.[51]

For all their cooperation in legislative matters, there remained a residue of distrust between Webster and Clay. Clay had finally accepted amalgamation as a political necessity, but he remained jealous of the appointment of Federalists to office. Webster blamed him, more than the president, for thus thwarting a principal object that had led him into the coalition. Many disappointed Federalists, especially in the middle states, joined the Jackson party. Webster urged Clay to mend political fences in Philadelphia, for instance, by high appointment of his lawyer friend Joseph Hopkinson and by attaching Robert Walsh, the Federalist journalist, to the administration. But Clay had no fondness for either one. Hopkinson was ultra; Walsh was a pedant and a prig who not only refused to support the administration, in part because of alleged proscription of Federalists, but spoke contemptuously of Clay.[52] Yet it was with this bilious character that Webster had contracted, and even raised a purse, to write a history of the government from the Federalist point of view. Political folly could go no further. Mercifully, the project was allowed to die after word of it leaked to the opposition press.[53] In the fall of 1827 reports of "the Webster Pledge" made their appearance. Some newspaper editors thought the charge of bargain against him more damning than the one against Clay. As it happened, the embassy to Great Britain became vacant at this time. The tempting post had been out of Webster's grasp before; it was within reach now, and he seemed to want it. Knowledgeable men expected he would get it. Clay told the president he was not averse to Webster's nomination, but he much preferred James Barbour. Appointment of the secretary of war would open the way to bring Clay's New York friend, Peter B. Porter, into the cabinet, thereby strengthening the administration in a key state. Barbour, moreover, was uncontroversial; his nomination would provoke no damaging fight over confirmation. Webster's, on the other hand, would be assailed as the payoff to the Bay State senator for Federalist votes in the election of Adams.[54] The president acted on Clay's advice.

Webster went to the Senate in 1827 a doubting free trader and came home six months later a hero of protectionism. In retrospect, his conversion was neither sudden nor surprising. He had never, not even in 1824, submitted his politics to the theory of free trade. The flow of eastern trading capital from land and commerce to manufactures, which had begun slowly a dozen years earlier, became a torrent after passage of the tariff of 1824. "A more complete revolution in public opinion upon any single topic has never been witnessed," wrote Joseph T. Buckingham in 1826, "than has taken place in the last three or four years in relation to the manufactures and commerce of our country." Only yesterday Yankee farmers and merchants had opposed the rise of industrial manufactures; now they saw that it lifted the prosperity of the entire community.[55] Saluting that prosperity, Governor Lincoln congratulated the people of Massachusetts upon the explosion of old moral and social prejudices against industrial manufactures. Derived mainly from English experience—specifically from the examples of Manchester and Birmingham—these fears and prejudices found no support in New England, said Lincoln, "and we have the delightful witness of every day's observation, that the richest sources of wealth to our country may be cultivated without danger to the moral habits and chaste manners of a numerous class of our population."[56] Webster went with this revolution. His principal clients, after all, were the Boston capitalists who inaugurated it. When the Woolens Bill was before the House in 1827, he spoke on neither side; but he knew that $50 million had been sunk in the woolens industry in New England, and that its claim to protection, as with cottons earlier, could not fairly be denied. Behind the scenes he worked for passage of the bill. The New York *Evening Post* was one of the few newspapers to notice Webster's "silent vote" for the tariff. "There he stands," said the *Post*, "boldly staring himself, as he was in 1824, directly in the face."[57] Webster wrote to the publisher, William Coleman, an old Federalist war horse, denying inconsistency and pleading force of circumstances. He offered a homely analogy: "You and I are going into the country. I propose the saddle and open air, but you insist on a carriage, and I submit to your pleasure. On our way, the wheel, at my corner of the coach flies off, and I am dragged along with the axle tree in the mud. Shall I refuse to stop, and have the wheel put on, because I was originally against the confinement and the close air of a coach, and in favor of a more free and unrestrained manner of motion?" Such was the situation of the woolens industry in the light of the tariff of 1824.[58]

Webster's initiation in the Senate was marred by the death of his wife, Grace. The self-deprecating "daughter of a poor country clergyman," she had been uncomfortable with her husband's fame and begun to worry that they were growing apart. In the fall of 1827, resolving to brave the limelight, Grace set forth with her husband for Washington. She became ill on the road, however, and Webster left her under the care of a physician in New York. No sooner had he taken his seat in the Senate than he was called back to New York as Grace's condition worsened. He was at her bedside when she died, apparently of cancer, on January 21, 1828. Webster dutifully returned her body to Boston for burial, made arrangements for the children, and resumed his Senate seat near the end of February. Story described him as "the sick lion," exhausted and despondent, yet capable of rousing himself if occasion demanded.[59]

The leading measure of the session was a tariff bill which, in John Randolph's famous line, pertained "to manufactures of no sort, but the manufacture of a President of the United States."[60] The spirit of the Harrisburg Convention invaded Congress. Rollin Mallary of Vermont, who had written the Woollens Bill of 1827, was again chairman of the Committee on Manufactures, but the new Jacksonian majority reported a bill that was a clever political strategem rather than a serious piece of economic legislation. Its author, Silas Wright, was one of Van Buren's henchmen. Aimed to set the Jacksonians right with the prevailing protectionism of the middle states and the West, the bill levied high duties on such agricultural products as wool and hemp, and also on iron, but maintained comparatively low duties on woolens. Although Van Buren, Wright, and company hoped the bill would pass, they persuaded their southern political allies to go along with it in the confidence it would fail, thereby enabling northern Jacksonians to claim credit for their protectionist efforts without afflicting further injury on the

South. It was easy enough to imagine the bill's defeat, first because it drove a wedge between wool growers and woolens manufacturers, and second because it was loaded with provisions sure to trigger New England opposition. With its high duties on iron, hemp, and molasses, the bill struck not only at woolens manufacturers but at merchants, shipbuilders, and rum distillers. Divide and conquer was the strategy. When debate began in March, Mallary tried to amend the bill in accordance with the Harrisburg resolutions, but every amendment was turned aside, mainly by southern votes. Led by George McDuffie, House southerners acquiesced in the passage of a bill they supposed would, from the pressure of its internal contradictions, be blown to pieces in the Senate.

In the Senate old Samuel Smith gave the measure its infamous name, "a bill of abominations." Van Buren took command of it as a friend. Whether or not he deliberately deceived the southerners is still in dispute among historians, but he was not such a fool as to go into an enterprise of this magnitude merely to engineer its defeat.[61] Seeing that the bill could not pass without a fair share of New England's senatorial votes, the Little Magician offered an amendment levying higher duties on woolens and extending to this infant industry the system of minimums that had been so effective with cottons since 1816. The amendment passed. The South felt betrayed. New England found the measure much less objectionable than before. On May 9 Webster rose to speak in favor of the bill. This left-handed legislation made a mockery of government, he declared. Public policy was submitted to the expediencies of presidential politics. The tariff bill was framed in hostility to New England, yet "a loud and ceaseless cry has been raised against what is called the cupidity, the avarice, the monopolizing spirit, of New England manufactures!"[62] He then entered into a defense of his section with regard to the tariff, pointing out that protectionism had become the settled policy of the country over the opposition of New England. "What, then, was New England to do?" he asked. "Was she to hold out for ever against the course of the government, and see herself losing on one side [to the commercial ascendancy of New York], and yet make no effort to sustain herself on the other? No, Sir. Nothing was left to New England, after the act of 1824, but to conform herself to the will of others."[63] He sought to reduce the abominable molasses duty, doubled in the bill, and the duty on hemp that protected Kentucky's inferior product at the expense of northern shippers. These efforts were defeated. Nevertheless, spokesmen for Massachusetts manufacturing interests urged the senator to vote for the amended bill. "New England would reap a great harvest," Abbott Lawrence said.[64] The bill passed, 26–21. Five of the nay votes came from the twelve New England senators, and included Webster's colleague; but he stood with the majority. A bad bill, as long as it protected the woolens industry, was better than no bill at all. The House accepted the amendments and Adams signed the bill into law on May 19.

If Calhoun and his friends were not suspicious of their northern partners before enactment of the Tariff of Abominations, they could hardly fail to be thereafter. They had been tricked into supporting this bill upon assurances that it would be defeated. They had, to use Calhoun's metaphor some years later, grabbed at the bait without seeing the hook under it.[65] In 1828, of course, it was unseemly to blame the northern Jacksonians. Instead, the southerners blamed Webster and Clay. According to Green's *Telegraph*, Webster owned $50,000 of stock in a New Hampshire woolens mill and had become a protectionist because of it.[66] This was untrue, though it was the kind of reckless falsehood that Webster's association with Yankee captains of industry provoked. Clay had no direct connection with the Tariff of Abominations, but as father of the American System he could not escape responsibility. A rash of protest meetings broke out in South Carolina. Flags on the vessels in Charleston harbor were lowered to half mast, while in Columbia, Clay and Webster were publicly burned in effigy.[67] In Washington members of the state delegation met at Senator Hayne's house to plot strategy. There was talk of vacating Congress. Counsels of prudence prevailed, however, as the delegation refrained from action that might imperil General Jackson's election.[68] Calhoun, if he did not advise this course, certainly concurred in it.

Webster returned to Boston in triumph. Boston, indeed Massachusetts and New England generally, approved of his course on the tariff. He was honored with a great public dinner at Faneuil Hall. It was, according to Edward Everett, "without exception, the most splendid public entertainment ever seen in Boston." The Jacksonian Boston *Statesman* heaped abuse on Webster, calling the dinner "an affair of the Hartford Convention nobility."[69] One of that nobility, Thomas Handasyd Perkins, presided. He was the epitome of the merchant prince who became an industrial magnate. As if to underscore the bipartisan basis of the new manufacturing aristocracy, however, many Republicans from Jefferson's time—Benjamin Austin, Henry Dearborn, George Blake—were also present. After a parade of speakers, including Everett and Story, Webster rose to vindicate his vote on the tariff, basically repeating what he had said in the Senate. In further apology to the shipping and navigation interest, still formidable in Boston, he spoke of his responsibility as a senator to represent the entire commonwealth, in which manufacturing was the ascendant interest. He went on to advocate an enlarged system of policy, "as wide and broad as the country over which it extends," for the United States government. "If there be any doubts, whether so many republics, covering so vast a territory, can be long held together under this Constitution," Webster declared, "there is no doubt in my judgment of the impossibility of so holding them together by any narrow, local, or selfish system of legislation. To render the Constitution perpetual . . . it is necessary that its benefits shall be practically felt by all parts of the country and all interests in the country."[70] Webster thus enunciated a philosophy of liberal and positive government in harmony with the principles of Clay and Adams and the spirit of the National Republican party.

Neither Calhoun nor Webster played a prominent part in the presidential campaign. The Carolinian went home to ponder what constitutional means could be devised to save the country from the twin dangers of despotism and disunion. The Bay Stater was a favorite whipping boy of Jacksonian propagan-

dists, of course. Finally, in October, he decided to take one of them to court
on the charge of criminal libel. In the course of the campaign there had appeared in the newspapers a letter Jefferson wrote in 1825 about disclosures
Adams made to him in the winter of 1807–08, when he was a Massachusetts
senator, of the treasonist and disunionist designs of "leading Federalists" in
New England. Adams's going over to the Republicans had long been a sore
point with the Federalists, but he had not previously been suspected of carrying tales of treachery to Jefferson. He publicly denied that now, yet admitted
the truth of disclosures to the Jefferson administration. In the ensuing controversy, the breach between Adams and many New England Federalists widened into a chasm.[71] The Jacksonians tried to make the most of it. One of
their electioneering sheets, *The Jackson Republican*, published an article
naming Daniel Webster one of the "leading Federalists," unnamed by Adams, charged with treasonable designs. Webster immediately learned the
identity of the author, Theodore Lyman, Jr., a prominent Bostonian, himself
a former Federalist as well as a personal friend, and sued him for libel. He
sought indictment and criminal prosecution in order to place the case
promptly before the highest tribunal of the commonwealth, from which he
hoped to obtain a kind of exculpation. "Webster wants a chance to narrate his
political career," Everett said, "and shake himself as free as he can of the
odor of the Essex Junto."[72] He got an indictment under the curious law of
scandalum magnatum—the slander of great men. It derived from the Star
Chamber, and although adopted into English common law, had never been
used in the United States. The solicitor general argued that as Webster was
the representative of the commonwealth in Washington, the protection of his
good name and character was a matter of public obligation. He could not perform his duty if he stood accused of treason. Called to testify, he was asked if
he had ever entered into a plot to dissolve the Union, and he replied, "I did
not, sir."[73] Of course, the charge against him was absurd. He was a New
Hampshire county court lawyer in 1807–08. The defense conceded that Adams had not named Webster, but argued lamely that Lyman was warranted
in naming him under the rubric "leading Federalists." Moreover, said Lyman, Adams, not Webster, was the target of the article. Chief Justice Parker's charge to the jury pointed to conviction. But the jury could not agree
(ten were for conviction, two for acquittal), and although the case was twice
continued, it was dropped a year later.

   Clay, the pillar of the Adams administration, was also the pillar of the president's campaign for reelection. Adams was despondent, but Clay, characteristically sanguine, sniffed victory in every political breeze. His devotion to a
lost cause made no sense to many of his friends. They wanted him to resign
and let Adams take the brunt of defeat. He had the perfect excuse in the
spring when his health became desperate. George Ticknor, who called on
Clay in April, portrayed him as "care-worn, wrinkled, haggard, and wearing
out." His doctor described the disease as a nervous torpidity, a neuralgia that
proceeded upward from his feet; although not paralyzing, it was exceedingly
debilitating. Near the end of the month Southard wondered if Clay would

live; his resignation was expected any day. On Adams's advice, however, Clay went to Philadelphia to consult the eminent Dr. Physick; and, while he experienced no miraculous recovery, he soon returned to Washington in good spirits.[74] Margaret Smith, the doyenne of Washington society, who knew every president and secretary from Jefferson on, said that Clay had "a *natural* power and force of mind beyond any I have ever witnessed." Considering the troubles of the administration, torpidity was a natural response for one in the secretary's position. But Clay fought it off. "He has an elasticity and buoyancy of spirit, that no pressure of external circumstances can confine or keep down," Mrs. Smith observed.[75]

The Jacksonian press kept up the drumbeat of "bargain and corruption" and punctuated it with other slanders both old and new. In the former category were dueling, gambling, and wenching. Timothy Fuller's portrayal of Clay in an 1824 pamphlet was revived: "he who spends his night at the gaming table, or in the revels of a brothel, in contempt of the laws of God and man."[76] There was also the old charge of complicity in the Burr Conspiracy, which Clay answered at length. To the image of the profligate it was easy to add the broad strokes of financial adventurer and bankrupt. Jackson underlings ransacked the Fayette County Court House for evidence of debts and misdeeds. They found none of the latter but charged that Clay was hopelessly in debt to the tune of $50,000 and had stayed afloat the past four years only because of his $6,000 salary as secretary of state. Again Clay refuted the charge. In a candid disclosure of his financial condition—perhaps the first in American politics—he said that the once formidable debt on his estate had been reduced to $10,000. Furthermore, he had never been sued for debt.[77] Duff Green started the story that Clay had embezzled a legacy of $20,000 to Transylvania University in the estate of James Morrison, of which he was executor. Although widely circulated, this was such a gross lie that even the Kentucky Jacksonians lacked the hardiness to print it. Authentic reports from Lexington showed that Clay's handling of the Morrison estate had been scrupulously correct. Translyvania was a residuary legatee, and had not yet received the $20,000 for this reason; meanwhile, annual interest in the amount of $1,200 was supporting a professorship.[78] (Interestingly, a bronze plaque on "Old Morrison," on the university grounds, states that Henry Clay supervised construction of this notable Greek Revival building, designed by Kentucky architect Gideon Shryock, and dedicated in 1833.) Clay could answer but not stop these libels.

Robert Wickliffe, one of Clay's Lexington supporters, said that the object of the Jackson propagandists was "the destruction of Henry Clay." On that the heterogeneous coalition could unite. He alone among the National Republicans represented a threat to them in the future.[79] Whatever the truth of this, there could be no doubt that the Jacksonians made the non-candidate Clay, more than Adams, the issue of the campaign. He was active; Adams was not. He was, in Jacksonian eyes, the architect of the campaign against Old Hickory, including such notorious smears as the "coffin handbill," which accused Jackson of murdering six militiamen during the war, and of adultery with his wife Rachel. In fact, these charges were the work of National Republican editors trying to stay abreast of their opposition. Clay, while not responsible for this character assassination, was gratified by it. No cabinet officer before him had taken a leading part, in the press, on the stump, in a presidential election. This was grating and earned him the derisive title "The Traveling Secretary."[80] Clay was active because, after Jackson's conduct toward him, he feared more than ever for the fate of the republic should this "military chieftain" be elected president. In May, as he was returning from his medical visit to Philadelphia, Clay stopped in Baltimore for a National Republican rally. Called to the platform, he spoke with overpowering emotion of the dangers to be apprehended from a new Philip or Caesar or Cromwell. Patriots must be aroused from their slumbers. If only he could carry his message to every town and hamlet in the country. After a long pause, he looked over the precipice. "If, indeed, we have increased the divine displeasure, and it be necessary to chastise the people with the rod of vengence," Clay declared, "I would humbly prostrate myself before HIM, and implore his mercy, to visit our favored land with war, with pestilence, with famine, with any scourge other than military rule, or blind and heedless enthusiasm for mere military renown."[81] Until August, when the Jacksonians carried Kentucky, Clay continued to hope the disaster might be averted. After that all the news was bad. Jackson won the popular vote, of course; and in the electoral vote carried Pennsylvania, the West, and the South solidly. A new political era was about to begin.

* *Four* *

LIBERTY AND UNION

A great multitude descended on Washington for the inauguration of Andrew Jackson, seventh president of the United States. "I never saw such a crowd here before," Daniel Webster observed. "Persons have come five hundred miles to see General Jackson, and they really seem to think the country is rescued from some dreadful danger." The danger, if there was one, came from Jackson and the horde behind him, Webster thought. It was too early to predict the course of the new administration, however. "His friends have no common principle—they are held together by no common tie." Weakness, dissension, and vacillation was the immediate prospect. In time, Jackson might impress his own resolute character on the administration, though the Massachusetts senator thought it more likely that one faction or another—western agrarians, southern planters, northern democrats—would gain the upper hand.[1] The inaugural address contained no surprises and, in a sense, reflected the ambivalence of the president who had yet to decide whether he was "a second Washington" dedicated to national glory or "a second Jefferson" dedicated to democratic reform. The former comported with his heroic image as well as with his earlier advocacy of the Madisonian Platform and the amalgamation of parties. The latter projected conflict rather than consensus. It was the image contrived by partisans who wished to tear down the national platform and rear a new party on specious Jeffersonian principles. Jackson bowed to these principles, but nothing in his address foreshadowed an attack on the American System. More ominous, at least to Webster's ears, was the pledge to reform alleged abuses of patronage, which could only be a prelude to partisan despoliation of public offices.[2]

Henry Clay took leave of his Washington friends at a public dinner on March 7. He spoke of Jackson's great injustice to him and, although wishing the administration well, voiced apprehensions for the future. He concluded with the toast, "Let us never despair of the American republic."[3] Unlike Webster, who feared most the men around the president, Clay feared most the president himself. In character and background, the two men had much in common. Jackson, at sixty-two ten years Clay's senior, had also once been an impecunious young lawyer seeking fame and fortune in the West. He had attached himself to the dominant party in Tennessee, as Clay had done in Kentucky; he, too, had speculated in lands, built a fine country mansion—the Hermitage, near Nashville—fought duels, and earned a reputation for wild and reckless behavior. He had, of course, exhibited his bravado on the battlefield, Clay in the forum. And while both men asserted themselves *fortiter in re*, they also acted *suaviter in modo*, the combination that, according to Lord Chesterfield's prescription, engaged the hearts of men. Jackson and Clay seemed to project onto each other the vehemence of their own characters. Clay had begun the cry of "military chieftain," and he meant now to rally an opposition with it. (Interestingly, when the Duke of Wellington became prime minister of Great Britain a year earlier, Henry Brougham, the Whig statesman with whom Clay was often compared, raised the same cry.)[4] Some of his friends had advised him to retire from politics and accept the place Adams offered him on the Supreme Court. But this suited neither his pride nor his ambition. Besides, he said, "he would not provide for himself and leave his friends in the mud."[5] He thought Jackson's election to the presidency, which in retrospect would appear as the product of an elemental democratic force, was an aberration brought about by Adams's dullness and timidity and Jackson's military charisma. It was not, certainly, a repudiation of the American System. The majority was for the man, not against measures. Even before he left Washington, Clay decided to place himself at the head of the opposition and to reclaim the presidency for the National Republicans in 1832.[6]

Clay's journey home was like the procession of a returning lord through his estates. "Dinners, Suppers, Balls etc. I have had literally a free passage," he wrote.[7] Lexington gave him a public dinner on May 16. Despite pouring rain, three thousand people crowded the picnic grounds at Fowler's Garden and washed down huge quantities of food with two hundred gallons of whiskey, rum, brandy, and punch. Clay's speech was the opening salvo of the opposition. Jackson's patronage policy—his removal of many civil servants and appointment of devoted partisans in their places—was the point of attack. The policy threatened to turn republican government into "one universal scramble for the public offices," Clay declared. "And on the conclusion of each [presidential election] we should behold the victor distributing the prizes and applying the punishments, like a military commander, immediately after he had won a great victory. Congress corrupted, and the press corrupted, general corruption would ensue, until the substance of free government having disappeared, some pretorian band would arise, and with the general concurrence of a distracted people, put an end to useless forms."[8] Such was Clay's frightful scenario. Some of Jackson's removals and appointments stabbed at his personal feelings. The cabinet, as James Parton later observed, revealed no principle except an aversion to Henry Clay. John Randolph was honored with the Russian ministry. Clay's political enemies in Kentucky, the core of the state's Jacksonian leadership—John Pope, Amos Kendall, William T. Barry, and others—were well provided for. Party feelings flared into violence in Lexington. The "butcher knife boys," both Clayites and Jacksonians, were not content to settle their differences by ballots. In the eastern press Prince Hal himself was rumored killed in a duel with Pope.[9] One of the first things he did upon returning to Lexington was to defend Charles Wickliffe in the shooting death of Thomas R. Benning, editor of the Jacksonian *Kentucky Gazette*. The Wickliffes belonged to the original Bluegrass aristocracy; Robert Wickliffe, father of the defendant, was reputedly the wealthiest man in the state and one of Clay's staunchest supporters. Clay had not appeared in a courtroom for four years; but he could still hypnotize a jury, and he won young Wickliffe's acquittal. Three months later another Jacksonian editor, after another political argument, killed Wickliffe in a duel.[10]

Despite the long arm of the Jackson administration, Clay and his party quickly regained ascendancy in Kentucky. The August election returned control of both houses of the legislature to the National Republicans. The legislature could be used, therefore, to launch Clay's presidential candidacy when the time was ripe. As he resumed farming, stockbreeding, and hemp making at Ashland, Clay regained his health and became almost euphoric about his political prospects. In September he embarked on a speaking tour in the southern part of the state, which had once been enemy country, and met with large crowds everywhere. The "Barbecue Orator," it was said, "depopulated the fields and forests of the West." An excursion across the Ohio caused a sensation. In the six months since his return to Kentucky, the Frankfort *Argus* charged in the fall, "The Gastronomic Cicero" had debauched thirty thousand people with his electioneering system combining speeches, victuals, and whiskey.[11] Easily misled by the cheers of the crowd, Clay became convinced he could regain the West Adams had lost and, whether or not Jackson was a candidate, lead the National Republicans to victory in 1832.[12]

Webster gave no thought to challenging the Kentuckian's leadership. While never fond of Clay personally, he agreed with his politics and, like most National Republicans, doubted anyone but Clay could run against Jackson with hope of success. Sometime after he returned to Boston, Webster was prevailed upon, perhaps by Josiah Johnston, who was managing Clay's campaign in the East, to write an article recommending him to New Englanders. The article, which appeared in the new *American Monthly Magazine*, praised Clay for the frankness of his character, for knowledge well beyond the limits of his education, for unmatched oratorical powers, marred only by excessive warmth and vehemence; and it applauded his assault on the humbug of Jacksonian "reform."[13] Webster's political despondency was influenced by continuing gloom over the loss of his wife. In the spring he received the terrible news of the death of his brother Ezekiel. A Federalist to the bitter end, Ezekial had just been defeated in a race for Congress. He died suddenly of a heart attack while pleading before a jury in New Hampshire. Webster adored his older brother, depended on him for counsel, and through him kept in touch with his Granite State origins. Now this rock was removed, and Webster, who had grown up the weakling of the family, found himself the sole survivor. Before long, as his spirits revived, he began looking for a wife who could help him politically and also be a mother to his three children. During the summer, as had been his habit for several years, he vacationed at a picturesque salt-water farm at Marshfield, south of Boston. Three years later he would buy it and make it his home. In the fall he was in Boston acting as counsel in the celebrated Charles River Bridge case. Arguing for the inviolability of the corporate charter of this toll bridge company, and against the claims of a proposed free bridge over the same river at the same place, Webster built upon the doctrine of the Dartmouth College case and, it was said, scaled new heights as a courtroom orator. The price of shares in the Charles River Bridge Company, which had been falling, soared.[14]

On December 12, in New York City, Webster married Caroline Le Roy, the thirty-one-year-old daughter of a wealthy merchant who had been a client. There was obviously, as a biographer has said, "more calculation than romance" in this marriage.[15] Quite aside from the dowry of $25,000 that went with Caroline's hand, she was a suitably sophisticated wife for the mature Webster. The marriage instantly placed him in the midst of New York society. Some of his Boston friends worried that he would follow the trail of money and fashion to New York. For the present, at least, such a move was not in Webster's plans. Immediately after the marriage he and his bride and eleven-year-old Julia journeyed to Washington for the meeting of Congress and court. Caroline, while lacking the delicate beauty of Grace Webster, was a well-bred lady of fashion, tall and stately, who adapted easily to the Washington scene. Happy in his marriage, the senator remained unhappy about politics. The republic was in peril, he believed, from party malice, the debasement of public morality, and the vauntings of state rights. "Mr. Webster foresees all that Alexander Hamilton foresaw thirty years ago," George M. Dallas acidly remarked of this assessment, "and his foresight will be just as wise."[16]

Calhoun spent the summer farming at Pendleton. Although a leading member of the victorious coalition, he, too, was uneasy with the administration. In the cabinet only Samuel Ingham, secretary of treasury, could be considered friendly to him. He had wanted Littleton Tazewell, the scrupulous Virginia senator, appointed secretary of state, and either James Hamilton, Jr., or George McDuffie secretary of war.[17] They were passed over. Another friend, John McLean, the postmaster general, was kicked upstairs to the Supreme Court when he declined to make the post office subservient to the

Jackson party. Not only was the cabinet weak, in Calhoun's opinion, it was dominated by Martin Van Buren, the secretary of state. As heir to the Crawford following, the elegant little New Yorker was Calhoun's natural rival for ascendancy in the administration. Politicians looked at the new president's every hint of policy in order to learn which of these rivals stood closer to the throne. But in this contest the vice president was crippled from the start. Suspicions of Calhoun growing out of his condemnation of Jackson's Florida adventure in the Monroe cabinet had been planted in the general's breast and were already germinating when he became president. Calhoun knew this. What in the end overwhelmed him, however, was not Jackson, not Van Buren, neither Webster nor Clay, but his commitment to the movement of resistance to the tariff in South Carolina.

In 1828, at the time of the presidential election, Calhoun had become the semi-official philosopher of the movement by drafting the South Carolina Exposition. A special committee of the legislature, charged with the preparation of an exposition of wrongs and remedies, had asked Calhoun to undertake the work. He consented, provided that his authorship remain secret.[18] Given his fears of political degeneration, Calhoun's consent was not surprising. But for him to place himself at the service of the state, to make himself the philosopher of "nullification," as it was called—this was a break with Calhoun's political past. He could not, of course, understand the implications of it himself. The Exposition repeated, with some elaboration, the litany of arguments against the tariff Carolina radicals had been urging for several years. Its constitutional theory was grounded in the Virginia and Kentucky Resolutions of 1798. These were the sacred texts of state rights, yet Calhoun was so little conversant with this tradition that he did not even own a copy in 1828 and had to send for one.[19] The Exposition departed from these famous resolutions in two crucial respects. First, it transformed a theory devised to secure the rule of the majority into a theory to protect an aggrieved minority. Second, it proposed a remedy, more precise and far-reaching than any Jefferson and Madison had offered, which invoked the constitution-making authority of three-fourths of the states to grant by amendment a power disputed by a single state.[20] After several alterations in committee, the Exposition was reported and the legislature ordered the printing of four thousand copies. Although never formally adopted, the Exposition was widely accepted as the authoritative statement of "the Carolina doctrine." It signified, moreover, Calhoun's rise to paramountcy in the politics of his native state.

In the Exposition, as in private letters, Calhoun emphasized that the state aimed at reformation, not revolution. If its intimidating tactics proved successful, nullification would be unnecessary; indeed, putting the theory to the test of practice, incurring all the dangers of disunion, would constitute defeat in Calhoun's eyes. The hope of reform, of healing the wounds of the Constitution and restoring the balance of the federal union, lay with the new administration in Washington. Let it have time, Calhoun pleaded with eager Nullifiers at Columbia, to show its good will toward the South.[21] Hope waned rapidly in 1829, however. Returning to Washington in December, Calhoun found Van Buren "cock of the walk." The president's "State of the Union" message further alarmed Calhoun. With regard to the tariff it offered only the possibility of gradual reform. Most of its other proposals—on patronage, Indian removal, management of the debt, and the national bank—were unacceptable to Calhoun. Jackson expressed impatience with him. And Calhoun, although he made no demonstration of opposition, could scarcely disguise his disappointment. "Judging from his appearance," one of Clay's informants wrote, "I should say, he considers everything lost. . . . The South is exceedingly dissatisfied with the Message."[22] From the vice president's chair, where he was about to preside over the greatest debate in the history of the Senate, Calhoun had ample time to contemplate the disheartening prospect.

1. *Webster and Hayne*

The administration had nothing to do with the debate. It was provoked by the rivalry among Senate leaders for the control of public policy on a range of issues beginning with the public lands. Calling attention to the disclosure in a report of the Commissioner of the Land Office that seventy-two million acres of land already surveyed remained unsold, Samuel A. Foot of Connecticut asked for an inquiry into the wisdom of suspending the surveys, abolishing the surveyor general's office, and closing some of the land offices. As a routine motion of inquiry, it was not expected to provoke debate. But the "blustering, bullying, and hectoring" senator from Missouri, Thomas Hart Benton, fell upon Foot's Resolution as the latest act in a sinister eastern conspiracy to check the growth of the West. By a tightfisted public land policy, backed by the protective tariff, the East sought to curb emigration, preserving "the vast and magnificent valley of the Mississippi for the haunts of beasts and savages," create a pauperized labor force for its mills and factories, and maintain its political power. The tariff was similarly exploitative of the South. Benton referred caustically to the 1827 report of Richard Rush, then secretary of treasury, which advocated the encouragement of manufacturing industry as a salutary check on the wasteful diffusion of capital and labor over a vast undeveloped terrain. "A most complex scheme of injustice, which taxes the South to injure the West, to pauperize the poor of the North!" Benton exclaimed.[1] Lauding the South as "the ancient defender and savior of the West," he begged her again, as in Thomas Jefferson's time, to stretch forth the protecting arm. His object, plainly, was to split the West from the East and consolidate in Congress the sectional alliance with the South that had already been achieved in presidential politics. This was awkward, however. For regardless of historic ties between the two sections, westerners continued to support American System measures, above all internal improvements, while the South was rallying to the old Republican standard of state rights. Politicians of this faith had never accepted the constitutionality of federal internal improvements; spokesmen for the South believed the policy survived mainly to keep up the tariff, whose Pactolian riches were drained into great projects for roads and canals. Nevertheless, South Carolina's senior senator, Robert Y. Hayne, responded to Benton's plea. Federal land policy had indeed been hard, grasping, and selfish. Why? Because it was part of the American System, said Hayne, which required "a low and degraded population" such as infested European cities. The root cause of western exploitation was thus the exploitation of the South by the protective tariff. The South stood to the United States as Ireland stood to England. "The rank grass grows in our streets; our very fields are scathed by the hand of injustice and oppression." The tariff and the revenue-producing public land law were "parallel oppressions," Hayne declared, one fatal to the South, the other to the West, and both fatal to the Union.[2]

Public land policy had become an urgent question mainly because of its connection with the public debt.[3] Revenue from the sale of public lands— over $2 million in 1830 and climbing—was pledged to the retirement of the debt. The debt had shrunk from $120 million at the end of the war to about $48 million. Favored with an overflowing treasury, Jackson was determined to distinguish his administration by sinking the debt. Ironically, the blessed state of debt freedom, so long dreamed of, threatened to levy a curse on the country. Regardless of one's opinion of the debt—whether one saw it as a bond of union or as an intolerable burden on the citizenry—everyone could agree on its retirement; but hardly anyone could agree on what to do with the projected surplus. Compared to the tariff, public land sales contributed very little to the revenue. They were, however, a crucial element in any plan for handling the projected surplus because of their special character, coexistent with the Revolutionary creation of the western domain, as a national trust.

Three different public land policies, each corresponding to the prevailing interest of a major section, had emerged by 1830. Westerners like Benton wanted the lands sold on exceedingly generous terms and, of course, no restriction on the survey. The senator's Graduation Bill, first introduced in 1824, would annually lower the price of unsold lands on the market until, finally, they would go for a few cents an acre. Brought to a vote in 1828, the bill was defeated. Some knowing politicians thought that Benton provoked the debate on Foot's Resolution in order to drive a bargain for the southern votes necessary to secure passage of the Graduation Bill. Other westerners, led by Governor Ninian Edwards of Illinois, called for federal cession of the public lands to the states where they lay. Since ownership of the lands was an incident of sovereignty, Edwards argued, public-land states like Illinois were little more than tenants of the national overlord. The Illinois legislature agreed and in 1829 sent a memorial to Congress demanding cession of the lands to the states.[4] This radical solution might have been expected to appeal to southern advocates of state sovereignty; and Hayne did, in fact, endorse the principle, though he would delay implementation until extinction of the debt.

The basic southern policy on the surplus was perfectly straightforward: drastic reduction of the tariff to the level that would produce the revenue necessary for the economical administration of the government and no more. The solution appealed to Jackson, who worried about the corrupting influence of a treasury surplus, yet he pointedly rejected it in his first message because it imperiled domestic manufactures. Instead he endorsed, much to Calhoun's disgust, the policy of distributing the surplus among the states according to the ratio of congressional representation. The idea of distribution traced back to Jefferson's administration, when the prospect of a debt-free government first appeared on the horizon, only to be dashed by foreign crisis and war. Revived in the 1820s, it took various forms, always in the service of eastern interests. In 1826 Senator Mahlon Dickerson of New Jersey proposed a four-year experiment, in anticipation of a permanent treasury surplus, to distribute $5 million annually among the states for support of education and internal improvements. The plan appealed to protectionists—Dickerson himself was one—since it would tend to keep up the tariff. The bill was tabled in successive congresses. A similar plan founded on the proceeds of public land sales got a thorough airing in the House of Representatives at the time of the great debate in the Senate. Its sponsors were Vermont protectionists. Benton denounced the scheme as the "twin brother" of Foot's Resolution, while the Charleston *Mercury* called it "a system of public robbery devised by Yankee headwork to plunder the South . . . the perfection of the American System."[5] None of the sectional policies could command a majority in Congress.

The public lands was not a favorite subject of Webster's. He had opposed the Graduation Bill in the previous Congress mainly because it would deluge the market with cheap land that would destroy property values. He much preferred Foot's approach to the problem of a surplus of surveyed land, but he had taken no part in framing the resolution. On January 19, while waiting to try a case in the Supreme Court, he strolled into the Senate chamber and was surprised to hear Hayne flaying the eastern states for consolidation, oppression, and pauperism. Only the day before, at Hayne's request, Webster had presented the petition of a South Carolina company for federal aid to build a railroad connecting Charleston with the Savannah River. The petition trespassed on Hayne's principles, yet he wanted the railroad. It was important both to cotton planters and to Charleston merchants; and the senator was not averse to requesting through Webster's agency what he would not request himself.[6] Now, when Hayne had finished, Webster rose on what he described as "an instantaneous impulse" to reply.[7] The Senate adjourned, however, deferring his speech to the next day. The first reply to Hayne was not therefore entirely extempory, although that claim was later made as further testimony of Webster's genius, while Hayne made it a matter of detraction that the senator had "slept on his speech." That night or, more likely, the next morning, as he was an early riser, Webster undertook some hurried research into the history of public lands policy and filled three sheets of paper with headings and notes.[8] The notes give scarcely a hint of the range, brilliance, and mastery of the speech.

Webster defended the historic policy for the national domain as both liberal and wise. Even before the lands were pledged to the retirement of the debt, they constituted a common fund for the common benefit, not just for western states or for settlers or speculators. The policy had been a resounding success. Webster portrayed for the senators Ohio as it was thirty-five years ago, after the Battle of Fallen Timbers—"fresh, untouched, unbounded, magnificent wilderness"—and Ohio in 1830, more populous than all but two or three of the original states. Obviously the West had grown and prospered under the parental care of the national government. Webster vigorously repelled the charge of eastern hostility to the West. "The East! the obnoxious, the rebuked, the always reproached East! . . . Sir, I rise to defend the East."[9] The protective tariff, the subject of so much reproach, actually began as a southern policy, and although finally forced on New England, it was not a policy from which hostility to the West naturally flowed. New England votes had carried many appropriations for the National Road. New England, said Webster, was the benefactor of the West. The system of land survey prior to sale originated in New England. Nathan Dane, a Bay Stater, framed the Northwest Ordinance of 1787 and was deservedly honored as the Solon of the West. Lauding the no-slavery proviso of the famous ordinance, Webster contrasted the prosperity of the states north of the Ohio River with the impecunious condition of those to the south. By thus identifying eastern policy with anti-slavery, and the interests of the West with both, Webster struck at the basic contradiction in the alliance of South and West.

The orator's purpose, of course, was to make his issue with the South rather than the West and, having vindicated New England, to carry the campaign into enemy country. Benton was ignored. To Hayne's wail of "Consolidation!" Webster responded with a fervent plea for the Union. There were, he knew, men in Hayne's part of the country who considered the Union a question of expediency, a mere matter of profit and loss, and who believed, in Thomas Cooper's notorious phrase, "it is time to calculate the value of the Union." To politicians of this school the Union was a means of good or a means of evil but never a good in itself. "Sir," Webster declared,

> I deprecate and deplore this tone of thinking and acting. I deem far otherwise the Union of the States; and so did the framers of the Constitution themselves. What they said, I believe, fully and sincerely believe, that the union of the States is essential to the prosperity and safety of the States. I am a unionist, and, in this sense, a national republican. I would strengthen the ties that hold us together. Far, indeed, in my wishes, very far distant be the day, when our associated and fraternal stripes shall be severed asunder, and when that happy constellation under which we have risen to so much renown shall be broken up, and sink, star after star, into obscurity and night![10]

Not only was the Union exalted; its strength and preservation were made to depend on the very consolidation that Hayne condemned. Turning to the issue of "corruption," which was the twin of consolidation in Hayne's state rights philosophy, and which he had decried in the government's public land system, Webster asked a series of rhetorical questions that reduced the charge to absurdity.

> These lands are sold at public auction, or taken up at fixed prices, to form farms and freeholds. Whom does this corrupt? According to the system of sale, a fixed proportion is everywhere reserved as a fund for education. Does education corrupt? . . . Can there be nothing in government except the exercise of mere control? Can nothing be done without corruption, but the impositions of penalty and restraint? Whatever is positively beneficent, whatever is actively good, whatever spreads about benefits and blessings which all can see and all can feel, whatever opens channels of intercourse, augments population, enhances the value of property, and diffuses knowledge—must all this be rejected and reprobated as a dangerous and obnoxious policy, hurrying us to the double ruin of a government, turned into despotism by the mere exercise of acts of beneficence, and of a people, corrupted, beyond the hope of rescue, by the improvement of their condition?[11]

In this breathtaking passage, Webster expanded the narrow issue of public land policy into an issue between two philosophies of government—one negative, the other positive; one founded in fear, the other in hope; one turning on *laissez-faire*, the other active and promotional in the manner of the American System.

Hayne's reply to Webster consumed most of two days, interrupted by a long weekend. The South Carolina senator was a small, slender man, with delicate features, graceful manners, and "a seductive eloquence," normally mild and amiable but shrill when his pride and the pride of his state were attacked.[12] Confessing at the outset that Webster's speech had "rankled here," clutching his hand to his breast, Hayne replied with scarcely suppressed bitterness and rage. Public land policy was left behind as the senator acquiesced in Webster's reformulation of the question in debate. He refuted the eastern claim to the affections of the West. It could bear no earlier date than February 1825, the date of the infamous coalition of Adams and Clay; the prior political history of New England, Hayne said, was epitomized by Hartford Convention Federalism, which the Massachusetts senator himself imbibed, and it was in this spirit that he now attacked the South. For Hayne interpreted Webster's defense of New England as, in fact, a veiled attack on the South. "He has crossed the border, he has invaded the State of South Carolina, is making war upon her citizens, and endeavoring to overthrow her principles and institutions." If indeed this was Webster's game, Hayne fell for it. He defended slavery, and made Webster's philosophy responsible for northern abolitionism. He denounced "the spirit of false philanthropy," the "visionary enthusiasts," and the "meddling statesmen" who, having discovered that "liberty is power," set out to improve the human race. "It is this spirit which has filled the land with thousands of wild and visionary projects, which can have no effect but to waste the energies and dissipate the resources of the country."[13] Under one of these projects especially, the protective tariff, the South groaned. Six years earlier Webster had "erected to free trade a beautiful and enduring monument." "Like a mighty giant [he] bore away upon his shoulders the pillars of the temple of error and delusion." Now, mounted on these same pillars, he estimated the Union at so low a price that he would concede nothing to save it. Concluding with a vindication of South Carolina on the score of liberty and union, Hayne also defended "the Carolina doctrine" as it had been expounded by Calhoun. The vice president, it was said, frequently passed notes to Hayne during the speech.[14] Everyone understood that he spoke for the vice president as well as himself and this heightened the significance of the debate.

Webster rose to reply, but the hour was late, so he yielded the floor for a motion to adjourn. Some thought, among them the vice president, that Hayne's scathing eloquence had annihilated Webster. But at home that evening he was completely at ease. "I never saw him more calm and self-possessed nor in better spirits," Edward Everett later recalled. Asked by a visitor who found him playing with Julia if he should not be at his desk, Webster replied, "Time enough for that in the morning."[15] As with the first speech, he scribbled several sheets of notes. They give little idea of the majesty of the speech, however, which runs to seventy pages in the National Edition of Webster's writings, or even hint at the celebrated peroration or other fine passages. The main ideas, drawn from the stock of National Republicanism, were so indelibly imprinted on Webster's mind that he felt no need to research or rehearse them.

The debate, now nearing its climax, had aroused unusual interest. Many came great distances to hear Godlike Daniel. The domed and colonnaded chamber, with its four rows of desks rising one above the other in a half circle and a long curving gallery above, was filled to overflowing an hour before Calhoun sounded the gavel. "A debate on political principles would have no such attraction," wrote one observer. "But personalities are irresistible. It is a kind of moral gladiatorship," with the Senate chamber taking the place of a Roman coliseum. "Every seat, every inch of ground, even the steps were compactly filled."[16] The scene is marvelously preserved, with small inaccuracies of detail, in G. P. A. Healy's mammoth painting. The audience stilled as Webster rose from his seat at the front and to the right of the vice president. He was clad in what would become his oratorical costume—blue dress coat with brass buttons, buff vest, and white cravat.[17] "I never spoke in the presence of an audience so eager and so sympathetic," he later remarked.[18] This was manifest in the power of his speech. For all his bravura, Webster's performances often proved listless and disappointing. Under the incitement of this great occasion, however, he rose to heights seldom attained by any orator and never surpassed by himself. He spoke for three hours the first day, for almost as long the second. Throughout he was in full command of himself, the language, and the subject. A Virginian, reporting to James Madison, said that in Hayne he had seen "nothing but country court *headlongness*," but that Webster spoke with the vigor, clarity, and effect of Shakespeare. "It was really the Mammoth deliberately treading the cane brake."[19] The speech was a stunning personal triumph, of course. It was also a political triumph, for after the Second Reply to Hayne the East stood vindicated while the South, above all South Carolina, was thrown on the defensive. Finally, and most importantly, it was the triumph of an idea: the supremacy and permanency of the Union.

At the outset Webster, as playful as a kitten, jested with Hayne. Nothing the honorable gentleman had said "rankled" him; he had, indeed, slept on his speech, "and slept soundly." Hayne had made a mistaken allusion to *Macbeth*. "Was it the ghost of the murdered Coalition," he had exclaimed, "which haunted the member from Massachusetts; and which, like the ghost of Banquo would never down?" Quite aside from the stale calumny, Hayne erred in supposing it was the friends rather than the enemies of the murdered Banquo at whose bidding the ghost would not down. Banquo was "an honest ghost," an innocent ghost, like the libeled coalition; and Webster, having taught Hayne a lesson in Shakespeare, turned Banquo's ghost into a prophecy of defeat for Calhoun and his friends at the hands of their Jacksonian allies. "Those who murdered Banquo, what did they win by it? Substantial good? Permanent power? Or disappointment, rather, and sore mortification; dust and ashes, the common fate of vaulting ambition overleaping itself . . . ? Did they not soon find that for another they had 'filed their mind'? that their ambition, though apparently for the moment successful, had but put a barren sceptre in their grasp? Ay, Sir," he continued

> a barren sceptre in their gripe,
> *Thence to be wrenched with an unlineal hand,*
> *No son of theirs succeeding.*

Saying this, Webster glanced at Calhoun, who, if he took in the force of the parallel, could run it out at his leisure.[20]

In the course of answering Hayne point by point, Webster unfolded a conception of the Union and the Constitution that stood in stark contrast to that of the South Carolinians. He denied ever attacking slavery, or uttering a word against it, except in praise of the Northwest Ordinance. Hayne was the fanatical one, imagining a northern conspiracy against slavery where none existed. In the North slavery had always been considered a local matter, part of the original bargain; and the Union was too full of benefits to be jeopardized by propositions to disturb slavery. "I go for the Constitution as it is, and for the Union as it is."[21] With regard to the American System, Webster again disclosed the wide gulf between two systems of politics, two philosophies of the Union. "What interest," Hayne had asked "has South Carolina in a canal in Ohio?" None at all on his system, Webster conceded, for in it South Carolina and Ohio were essentially different countries with different interests; but everything in the system founded on the principle of one nation. "We look upon the States, not as separated, but as united. . . . We do not impose geographical limits to our patriotic feelings or regard." Webster continued in a vein reminiscent of Burke. "We who come here . . . consider ourselves bound to regard with an equal eye the good of the whole, in whatever is within our power of legislation. Sir, if a railroad or canal beginning in South

Carolina and ending in South Carolina, appeared to me to be of national importance . . . [and] if I were to stand up here and ask, What interest has Massachusetts in a railroad in South Carolina? I should not be willing to face my constituents."[22] In view of the petition of the South Carolina Canal and Rail Road Company, which Hayne had declined to present, this was cutting. And so was the succeeding argument in which Webster insisted he had learned the doctrine of internal improvements, not from New England, but from South Carolina. "I repeat that, up to 1824, I for one followed South Carolina; but when that star, in its ascension, veered off in an unexpected direction, I relied on its light no longer." Here the vice president interrupted to ask if the reference was to him. Webster brushed the question aside, saying he referred to South Carolina at large.[23]

The accusation of Hartford Convention Federalism, the basis of Hayne's "new crusade against New England," after abandoning the original ground of the public lands, was ancient history, and Webster made light work of it. Of what consequence was it in 1830 whether men or states or sections had once been Federalist or Republican? "I see enough of the violence of our own times, to be very anxious to rescue from forgetfulness the extravagances of times past." Hayne's history of old Federalism was not worth the pains of refutation, the senator said, since anyone nowadays suffering the sins of Federalism could easily obtain remission, even a pristine new political parentage. "We all know a process, Sir, by which the whole Essex Junto could, in one hour, be all washed white from their ancient Federalism, and come out, every one of them, original Democrats, dyed in the wool!"[24] After this riposte, Webster delivered an encomium on Massachusetts: "There she is. Behold her, and judge for yourselves. There is her history; the world knows it by heart. The past, at least, is secure. There is Boston, and Concord, and Lexington, and Bunker Hill; and there they will remain forever. . . ."[25]

The orator turned finally to "the most grave and important duty" he had to perform, the explanation of the true principles of the Union and the Constitution. He was familiar with the South Carolina doctrine not only from Hayne's speech but from various publications including *The South Carolina Exposition*, whose true author he suspected.[26] His statement of the doctrine was basically correct: the general government is a creature of the sovereign states, and, when it exceeds the authority conferred by the Constitution, there being no common arbiter, a single state may interpose and nullify the action. Webster questioned whether this was actually, as Hayne claimed, the doctrine of the Virginia and Kentucky Resolutions. Regardless, he denied the authority of a state to decide constitutional questions. "It is, Sir, the people's Constitution, the people's government, made for the people, made by the people, and answerable to the people."[27] In thus stating the theory of the Constitution as the fundamental law of one people, rather than a compact of sovereign states, Webster drew upon a strain of Supreme Court interpretation, to which he had himself contributed, and upon a body of nationalist thought that included, perhaps most significantly for him, Nathan Dane's 1829 *Appendix* to his *General Abridgment and Digest of American Law*.

Dane, whose claim to authorship of the Northwest Ordinance was championed by Webster, held that the Union was older than the Constitution and the states were its creatures rather than the reverse.[28] While Webster did not go this far, he found ample basis for the nationalist theory in two provisions of the Constitution, one declaring it to be "the supreme law of the land," the other vesting in the Supreme Court the power to decide "all cases arising under the Constitution and laws of the United States." This, he said, was "the keystone of the arch." The Carolinians, holding that there was no ultimate arbiter, were wrong in principle and in law. The Supreme Court was the ultimate arbiter, Webster asserted. He went on to portray the disastrous consequences of proceeding on the nullification theory. "To resist by force the exertion of a law, generally, is treason. Can the courts of the United States take notice of the indulgence of a State to commit treason? Talk about it as we will," Webster solemnly declared, "these doctrines go to the length of revolution."[29]

The idea of a supreme and permanent Union was still something of a novelty in 1830. Free of the embarrassments of nullification, the Carolinians' view of the Union as only a partnership, which might be dissolved when it became inconvenient, was closer to the prevailing conception than Webster's doctrine. Almost every politician acknowledged "the sovereignty of the states." Liberty was supposed to depend more on the rights of states than on the powers of the general government. Even the leading textbook on the Constitution maintained the right of a state to secede peacefully from the Union.[30] But Webster consecrated the Union:

> While the Union lasts, we have high, exciting, gratifying prospects spread out before us; for us and our children. Beyond that I seek not to penetrate the veil. God grant that in my day, at least, that curtain may not rise. God grant that on my vision never may be opened what lies behind! When my eyes shall be turned to behold for the last time the sun in heaven, may I not see him shining on the broken and dishonored fragments of a once glorious Union; on States dissevered, discordant, belligerent; on a land rent with civil feuds, or drenched, it may be, in fraternal blood! Let their last feeble and lingering glance rather behold the gorgeous ensign of the republic, now known and honored throughout the earth, still full high advanced, its arms and trophies streaming in their original lustre, not a stripe erased or polluted, nor a single star obscured, bearing for its motto, no such miserable interrogatory as "What is all this worth?" nor those other words of delusion and folly, "Liberty first and Union afterwards"; but everywhere, spread all over in characters of living light, blazing on all its ample folds, as they float over the sea and over the land, and in every wind under the whole heavens, that other sentiment, dear to every true American heart,—Liberty *and* Union, now and forever, one and inseparable![31]

In this peroration Webster, who had turned to face Hayne directly, raised the idea of Union above contract or expediency and enshrined it in the American heart. Liberty was identified with the Union, the Union with Liberty; together they defined American nationhood. "The Union is part of the religion of this people," Ralph Waldo Emerson would say. And Webster, as he knew, had made it so.[32]

The speech touched the craving of the American imagination for the heroic and the fabulous. Webster demolished at a blow, "as with the club of Hercules, the monster of Nullification and Disunion"; he appeared "like a mammoth . . . crushing obstacles in his path"; like Antaeus, "the fabulous giant of antiquity, he gathered [strength] from the very earth that produced him" and claimed his empire.[33] The Reply to Hayne was often compared, with more justice than is usual in such matters, to the oration of Demosthenes on the Crown. Hayne himself, after the passage of years, paid Webster the supreme compliment, calling him "the most consummate orator of either ancient or modern times." Like Eshines, who was driven into exile at Rhodes because of Demosthenes' triumph, and who was there applauded when he declaimed his rival's oration, he could say, "Ah! If you had only heard it from Demosthenes."[34]

The debate on Foot's Resolution continued intermittently for five months. The hawks had flown, but the buzzards descended to feast on the carrion. Webster prepared a pamphlet edition of his speech, and it was read everywhere with the same interest as a Waverly novel. That the speech got reported, almost verbatim, was a lucky accident. Joseph Gales, one of the proprietors of the National Intelligencer, had gone to the Senate to hear Webster, not to report him; but, trained in shorthand, he decided on the spur of the moment to take down the speech and did not stop until the end. When he shrank from the task of transcribing it, Mrs. Gales came to the rescue. Webster read her manuscript with care, and made but few changes, most of them stylistic.[35] (Edward Everett, who also reviewed the manuscript, called Webster's attention to the phrase, "behold the standard of Union," in the peroration and suggested that he check Milton's description of the unfurling of "the imperial ensign . . . full high advanced" in the lower depths, thinking it probably the image in the orator's mind. Webster checked and changed the language to "the gorgeous ensign of the republic . . .")[36] There were earlier reports, of course, but the speech itself did not appear in the press until four weeks after delivery. Gales and Seaton published the first pamphlet edition; soon there were twenty or more in as many cities, numbering in excess of one hundred thousand copies. Webster was anxious to spread the pamphlet through the western states. His wealthy Boston friend, Abbott Lawrence, raised a fund for this purpose, which was apparently accomplished.[37] In Tennessee, it was said, each copy "has probably been read by as many as fifty different gentlemen" and "the name of Daniel Webster is familiar to the inmates of every log house on this side [of the] mountains."[38] "The time favored its impression," as Webster observed.[39] In May, when the Senate finally tabled Foot's Resolution, Benton expressed dismay at the outcome of the debate. Webster's speech, the cry of a defeated party, had been "multiplied into a myriad of copies, poured into the country under the franking privilege, [and] placed as a manual in every hand."[40] No speech in the English language, perhaps no speech in modern times, had ever been as widely diffused and widely read as the Reply to Hayne.

Webster returned to Massachusetts with a national reputation. As the hero of the Union and the Constitution, he had, it seemed, at last exorcised the demon of Federalism and won the patriotic heart of the country. Boston friends were eager to honor him with a lavish dinner or ball, in appreciation for his vindication of New England, but Webster declined lest it break the spell of national acclaim. If gentlemen were so inclined, however, he unblushingly suggested that they subscribe to a gift of plate. Which they did, making the presentation in October.[41]

During the summer and fall Webster's name was prominently before the country not only as a statesman but as a lawyer in the celebrated Salem murder case. In April, Captain Joseph White, a wealthy Salem merchant of eighty-two years, was found murdered in his bed. No motive could be discovered, and for a long time investigators turned up no clue to the perpetrators of the crime. Joseph Story, who was related to the victim by marriage, informed Webster of the "universal dread . . . as if we lived in the midst of Banditti," that pervaded the community.[42] At length the police arrested Richard Crowninshield, a local desperado, for the murder. Then, in a bizzare twist, suspicion turned toward two brothers, Frank and Joseph Knapp, Jr., sons of another prominent merchant, and they were arrested. Joseph Knapp, Jr., who was related to Captain White by marriage, made a full confession in return for immunity. Expecting a large inheritance from White, Joseph, evidently through his brother's agency, had hired Crowninshield to murder the old man. Ordinarily, Crowninshield would have been tried for the murder and Frank Knapp as accessory. But Crowninshield committed suicide in prison. Thereupon the state decided to prosecute Frank Knapp as principal and Joseph, who retracted his confession, as accessory. The attorney general, recognizing he was on slippery legal grounds, asked Webster to aid the prosecution. Frank Knapp's defense counsel filed no objection to this unusual maneuver, but put the jury on guard: "The most distinguished orator of our time . . . with his green and fresh-gained laurels wreathed upon his brow, comes here to aid the host already pressing down the hope and life of the prisoner, to overpower the jury with his eloquence and to 'nullify' the prisoner's defense. . . . The cry of the people is for blood."[43] In the later trial of Joseph Knapp, defense counsel did formally object to Webster's appearance and repeated the rumor he was being compensated for his services. Stephen White, the supposed client, was Webster's friend as well as the nephew and principal heir of the murder victim. Webster told the court that he appeared solely at the request of the attorney general and without fee. The court ruled to admit him. Whether or not he received a fee, in this case or in the earlier one, the "Salem lie," as Emerson called it, became a fixture of the Webster legend. Going on the theory that "a great man is always entitled to the most liberal interpretation" of his words and deeds, Emerson believed the lie belonged not to Webster but to his enemies.[44]

There were actually three trials at Salem during that summer and fall, and

Webster figured in all three. The first trial of Frank Knapp ended in a hung jury. He was immediately tried again and convicted. Webster's five-hour summation for the prosecution in the second trial is rightly regarded as one of his best speeches, certainly unsurpassed at the bar of criminal justice. "I never before, nor have I since, felt human power—power of mind and circumstance—equal to it or like it," said one spectator, a lawyer. "His voice, his logic, his gloomy descriptions, beautiful and terrific by turns, his language, his eloquence, with the ever-varying shades of his countenance, took perfect possession of my powers and sensibilities."[45] To prove that Frank Knapp was, more than an accessory, a principal and abettor in the crime, it was necessary to show that he was near enough to lend assistance to the assassin should it be required. Dramatically reconstructing the crime, Webster placed Knapp in the street below while Crowninshield struck the fatal blow and hung the abettor's guilt on the argument of "constructive presence." Never did Webster demonstrate to better advantage his uncanny ability to marshal a mass of confusing facts and inferences into a perfectly intelligible chain of reasoning leading to an inexorable conclusion. Some of the lawyers who crowded the courtroom worried that the argument broke down legal safeguards by extending to accomplices the crimes that belonged to perpetrators. Apparently untroubled by this consideration, the jury quickly returned a guilty verdict. The community rejoiced that, thanks to Webster, justice had triumphed over legal niceties and forms. At the end of September eight to ten thousand people witnessed the hanging of Frank Knapp.[46] In the case of Joseph Knapp, charged as accessory before the fact, Webster had also to struggle against legal safeguards, since conviction depended on admission of the defendant's repudiated confession. The court decided for the prosecution. Joseph Knapp, too, was convicted and sentenced to hang.

The popularity Webster gained as a public prosecutor was altogether different from that which he attained as a senator, but it similarly enhanced his reputation. A volume of his *Speeches and Forensic Arguments* appeared in Boston in the fall. Charles B. Haddock, his nephew and Professor of Rhetoric at Dartmouth College, was principally responsible for it. The volume, which opened with the Plymouth oration and closed with the address to the Salem jury, proved to be the first of a series that at Webster's death ran to six volumes. It was offered to the world, Haddock said, because the speeches of distinguished American statesmen were a "national treasure," constituting "the nearest approximation to conservative principles in our political institutions." Webster himself presented "at once a splendid model of the character developed under our republican institutions, and an illustrious instance of the power of character, thus developed, to preserve and improve those institutions."[47] It was in this spirit that George Ticknor, Webster's Brahmin friend, reviewed the speeches in the *American Quarterly Review*. The objections so often felt against productions of the American mind, that they want "a national air, tone, and temper," could not be brought here. Webster's speeches both formed and expressed the principles of American nationality. "He is the child of our free institutions," Ticknor said. "None other could have produced or reared him—

none other can now sustain or advance him."[48] In the new year, at the urging of friends, Ticknor among them, Webster wrote an account of his early life, before he became a public figure. Nothing was published, but the memoir furnished much of the information drawn upon by boosters of his fame. Samuel L. Knapp, a Dartmouth alumnus like Ticknor and Haddock, wrote the first book-length biography of Webster in 1831. Knapp had earlier known Webster at the Boston bar, then, while editing the *National Journal* as a Bay State representative and senator in Washington. Knapp's laudatory *Life of Daniel Webster* was not undiscerning, and it escaped the fate of most first lives, or "campaign lives," of American statesmen.

Collected speeches, biography, panegyric—these were indicia of a presidential candidacy. Boosted by his triumph over Hayne, Webster turned his ambition in that direction. William Wirt remarked that the applause lavished on the senator "destroyed his balance entirely" and he secretly desired "that Clay should be dropped and he should be substituted as the candidate against General Jackson."[49] This may have put it too strongly. Webster was, of course, sniffing the political winds, which were more swirling and unpredictable than usual in 1831. He grew restive under Clay's leadership and grasped at every hint of his political weakness; he tried to delay popular or caucus nominations of Clay; and he quietly courted the favor of the new Anti-Masonic party centered in New York. But throughout all this maneuvering, Webster remained in friendly correspondence with Clay, repeatedly acknowledged that he was the only man who could challenge Jackson, and never openly opposed him.

In March 1831, after Congress adjourned, Webster addressed a public dinner in his honor in New York. Some knowing politicians speculated it was a trial balloon for his presidential candidacy. Chancellor James Kent, introducing Webster, acclaimed his defense of the Union and the Constitution. "Socrates was said to have drawn down philosophy from the skies and scattered it among the schools," Kent said. "It may with equal truth be said that constitutional law, by means of these senatorial discussions and the master genius that guided them, was rescued from the archives of our tribunals and the libraries of lawyers, and placed under the eye, and submitted to the judgment, of the American people. *Their verdict is with us, and from it there lies no appeal*." To this brilliant tribute Webster responded with yet another hymn to the American republic.[50] The speech was wildly applauded; but as a trial balloon, if such it was, it never lifted off the ground.

Webster intended to make a personal tour of the western states in the spring. A political following in the West was essential to future presidential aspirations; and now, in the aftermath of the senatorial triumph, was the opportune time to plant his flag beyond the Appalachians. He was dissuaded from the trip, however, by advisers who feared it would be viewed as unfriendly to Clay. Wherever he turned, Webster came to realize Clay was in his way. Among National Republicans he was the undisputed chief; Webster dared not run the risk of alienating him or his followers. Joseph Gales, surprised to learn of Webster's sly moves, told him frankly that regardless of personal preference

Godlike Daniel, about 1830. Painting by Chester Harding. *Courtesy of the National Portrait Gallery, Smithsonian Institution*

Calhoun, Seated at Table. Painting by William James Hubard. *In the Collection of The Corcoran Gallery of Art, Museum Purchase, 1889*

Clay, Seated at Table. Painting by William James Hubard. *Courtesy of the University of Virginia Art Museum*

Black Dan. Painting by Francis Alexander. *Courtesy of Dartmouth College*

Calhoun the Senator—A Favored Likeness. Miniature by Washington Blanchard. *Courtesy of The New-York Historical Society. New York*

Webster as a Roman Orator. Marble sculpture by John Frazee. *Courtesy of the Boston Athenaeum Library*

The Kentucky Gentleman. Marble sculpture by Joel Tanner Hart. *In the Collection of The Corcoran Gallery of Art, Museum Purchase, Gallery Fund, 1878*

Two Busts of Calhoun. *(Left)* Plaster by Hiram Powers in 1835. *Yale University Art Gallery, Gift to Calhoun College of the Fellows and Associated Fellows in memory of Stanley T. Williams, B.A. 1911 (Right)* Plaster by Clark Mills in 1845. *Courtesy of the Boston Athenaeum Library*

he was committed to Clay, as were the mass of National Republicans everywhere, and that any division in the ranks would be disastrous. Webster heard the same advice from Judge Ambrose Spencer, one of his New York champions.[51] Clay was doubtless annoyed by Webster's little game behind his back but, sure it would come to nothing, chose to ignore it. Time ran out on the senator when the National Republican convention met at Baltimore in December. With less confidence than ever that Clay could be elected, Webster nevertheless fell into line behind him.

2. *Calhoun and Jackson*

In the political drama that ended in the rupture between Jackson and Calhoun, with heroes and villains in deadly earnest, comic relief was provided by the Peggy Eaton affair. The vivacious twenty-nine-year-old daughter of a Washington tavern keeper and recent widow of a navy purser, Margaret O'Neale Timberlake married Major John Eaton, the incoming secretary of war, in January 1829. Gossip gathered around Peggy like honey gathered on a bee. She was supposed to have been Eaton's mistress; and he married her with President Jackson's blessing, it was said, in order to silence wagging tongues. Of course, they were not silenced. Mrs. Eaton might be the wife of a cabinet officer, but Washington society refused to admit her into its circle. Jackson was enraged. Eaton was a special favorite, one of his Tennessee cronies and his principal biographer. The persecution of Mrs. Eaton was exactly parallel, in his eyes, to the persecution that had driven his beloved Rachel into the grave only a few months before. The zeal with which he set out to establish the innocence of Peggy Eaton had its source in his anguish over the death of Rachel who, the slanderers said, had wed Jackson before her first marriage terminated in divorce. At first he traced the new persecution, like the old, to his inveterate enemy, Henry Clay. It was Clay's "project" to injure him, sow tares in his young cabinet, and destroy John Eaton.[1] Jackson therefore proceeded to elevate a social spat into political warfare.

The true instigators of the affair were the ladies of the new administration, led by Floride Calhoun. Just what happened is unclear, but according to the vice president the Eatons made the appropriate first call and, though Calhoun himself was not at home, were received in a civil manner by his wife. The next morning she announced that, in view of Mrs. Eaton's questionable character, she would not return the visit. Hearing this, Calhoun felt like a drowning man. But knowing he could not change Floride's mind and believing, in any event, that women were the proper arbiters of social respectability, he approved her decision. The matter transcended politics. All must acknowledge, he later said in his defense, that "the purity and dignity of the female character mainly depend" on the censorship the sex exercises over itself.[2] He was undoubtedly familiar with William Paley's popular text, *The Principles of Moral and Political Philosophy*, in which the virtue of ostracism was clearly stated: "The confederacy among women of character, to exclude from their society kept mistresses and prostitutes, contributes more perhaps to discourage that condition of life, and prevents greater numbers from entering it, than all the considerations of prudence and religion put together."[3] Jackson did not dispute the principle. Base women ought to be shunned as a pestilence. But virtuous women ought to be defended, and in this instance, he thought, innocence was assailed by malice, envy, and ambition.[4] Disregarding the president's opinion, the cabinet wives and most of official Washington followed Floride Calhoun and shunned Peggy Eaton.

After supposedly conducting his own investigation, Jackson pronounced Peggy Eaton "chaste as a virgin," and demanded she be admitted into society before Calhoun returned to Washington near the end of the year. The ostracism continued, however. More significantly, "the Eaton Malaria" invested the struggle for supremacy in the administration. Seriously ill in December and distressed that in case of death Calhoun would succeed him, Jackson drafted a secret political will and testament naming Van Buren his heir and successor. The New Yorker had earned his trust and the trust of the nation, Jackson wrote. "Instead of being selfish and intriguing, as has been reputed . . . , I have ever found him frank, open, candid, and manly." Of Calhoun, in whom he had once had complete confidence, he had formed a different opinion, believing, in fact, "that most of the troubles, vexations, and difficulties" he had encountered in public life were caused by Calhoun and his friends.[5] The secretary of state, whose tact was exceeded only by his cunning, had lost no time working his way into Jackson's affections. Wifeless and daughterless, he was not embarrassed to pay court to the Eatons, thereby winning the president's gratitude. Webster reported the impression in Congress that Van Buren was the rising star. "He controls all the pages on the backstairs, and flatters what seems to be at present the Aaron's serpent among the President's desires, a settled purpose of making out the lady, of whom so much has been said, a person of reputation. It is odd enough, but too evident to be doubted, that . . . this dispute in the social and fashionable world, is producing great political effects, and may very probably determine who shall be the successor to the present chief magistrate."[6] This was astute, but Webster erred in supposing the Eaton affair was the cause of the split in the administration rather than, more accurately, an incident of it.

In his rising anger against Calhoun, the president blamed him for the Eaton affair. He was supported, indeed prompted in this, Calhoun believed, by Eaton and Van Buren, who were conspiring to destroy him. Eaton represented the western branch of the Jacksonian coalition, Van Buren the eastern. Both were protectionists and close allies in the distribution of the spoils. Behind Peggy Eaton's petticoats they sought to advance their own personal and political goals at the expense of Calhoun and the South.[7] Van Buren and his friends, on the other hand, charged that Calhoun, at his wife's prompting, created "the feminine controversy" in order to drive Eaton from the cabinet and isolate Van Buren. On this theory Peggy Eaton was the innocent victim of Calhoun's unhallowed ambition.[8] Wherever the truth lay between these alleged plots—actually there was little truth in either—it is evident that the outcome gave Calhoun the moral victory, Van Buren the political one. For a year and a half after the president ordered the acceptance of Peggy Eaton, three cabinet families (Ingham, Branch, and Berrien) stood defiantly with the Calhouns. Van Buren, Postmaster General William T. Barry, and Eaton, of course, stood with the president, who, in this situation, refused to consult with the cabinet. As the split in the administration became common knowledge, it was decried as a national disgrace. Finally, in April 1831 the entire cabinet resigned. Calhoun publicly hailed the stand of the cabinet officers and their wives as a "great victory . . . in favor of the morals of the country."[9] Van Buren must have smiled at this. Accused of plotting the succession, he had actually initiated the cabinet breakup, thereby enabling himself to withdraw from the theater of contention, purging the Calhoun remnant, ridding Washington of "the Eaton malaria," and placing Jackson in command of his own house at last.

Because of the Eaton affair Jackson was more willing to believe the worst of Calhoun. And the worst, as it turned out, struck at the nation's existence. When Calhoun joined the Jackson camp, the two men not only felt high regard for each other but shared a common background. Both were southerners and planters, and they even bore a marked physical resemblance, as contemporaries sometimes noticed: "They were of the same Scotch Irish stock and exhibited its characteristic traits. In both were seen the long face, the hollow jaws, the thick bristling hair, the tall, gaunt, erect figure, which belong to the race."[10] Each boasted an iron will and, however gracious his manners, brooked no opposition. It is tempting, therefore, to interpret the conflict between them as a clash of strong-willed personalities, neither of whom could stand in the light of the other. There were also, of course, as Calhoun's response to Jackson's First Message suggested, differences between them on issues and policies, for instance on the tariff and distribution. But the differences were not irresolvable; each had proved himself quite capable of altering position on such issues. More impressive was their common commitment to reversing the progress of consolidation and weakening the spring of the national government. This was the main thrust of the Jackson administration. It was blurred at the outset, however; and unfortunately for Calhoun, his own theory of nullification provoked an angry nationalist response from Jackson that obscured the direction almost to the end.

Unequivocal evidence that Jackson and Calhoun were divided on the nature of the Union was provided by the Jefferson Birthday Dinner in the capital on April 13, 1830. Although the affair originated with Benton, Hayne, and their friends with a view to bolstering the intersectional alliance under the sanction of Jefferson's name, most of the twenty-four programmed toasts gave aid and comfort to nullification. This caused consternation at the President's House. The president planned to attend the banquet. He would be embarrassed by the use of the Apostle of Liberty as "a mask or stalking horse" for the Carolina doctrine. Van Buren and two of Jackson's Tennessee cronies convinced him that this was, indeed, the purpose of the dinner; and so he prepared a toast of his own that had much less to do with the commemoration of Thomas Jefferson than with the destruction of John C. Calhoun. The dinner was large and boisterous. The capital had seen nothing like it before. Hayne, the principal speaker, drew an extended parallel between the Virginians of '98 and the South Carolina nullifiers. After the speeches and the regular toasts, the president was recognized for being the first of the volunteers. His message was simple and direct: "Our Federal Union: It must be preserved." The vice president was next. With trembling hand, Calhoun held up his glass and declared, "The Union: Next to our Liberty the most dear."[11]

Thus the celebration intended to rally the party under the Jeffersonian state-rights shibboleth reproduced within it, and within the administration, the conflict between Webster and Hayne. No one who had followed the great debate could have been misled by the meaning of these toasts, however innocuous or cryptic they seemed. It would be unnatural for the President of the United States to entertain any other sentiment, as the editors of the *Intelligencer* observed, "but there is something emphatic in it, under the circumstances that preceded and attended it." Duff Green, Calhoun's friend and editor of the administration daily, the *United States Telegraph*, denied that the president's toast was meant to place him in opposition to the vice president, the South, or the anti-tariff movement.[12] At this stage, certainly, Calhoun was anxious to avoid even the hint of conflict with Jackson. In the Senate he was usually supportive, providing, for instance, the casting vote for Amos Kendall's confirmation as an auditor in the Treasury Department. In May he applauded Jackson's Maysville Road Veto—a critical blow to internal improvements. He had not, in short, abandoned hope in the president or the administration. His quarrel was with Van Buren, who he feared was making Jackson his "dupe." He had been careful to conceal his association, still very limited, with the South Carolina movement lest open support foreclose his political options. Jackson, moreover, was not yet viewed as hostile to him; appearances to the contrary at the Jefferson Birthday Dinner were ascribed to Van Buren's influence.

One of Calhoun's options, to run for the presidency in 1832, was tightly circumscribed by events in the spring. Earlier everybody in Washington, as Josiah Johnston told Clay, seemed convinced that Jackson would honor his one-term pledge and not seek reelection.[13] The contest for the succession would be between Calhoun and Van Buren. Even before the Jefferson dinner, however, an address of the Jacksonian legislative caucus in Pennsylvania called for the president's reelection. It had, in fact, been invited by the White House. According to Major William B. Lewis, one of the "kitchen cabinet," as it came to be known, the object was to defeat "the machinations of Mr. Calhoun and his friends, who were resolved on forcing General Jackson from the presidential chair after one term."[14] The peculiar situation of the vice president had made this necessary, said Lewis, for after two successive terms in the second office, it would hardly do for him to seek a third; yet he dared not challenge Jackson for the first office and was little inclined to stand aside for Van Buren. Already the heir apparent in Jackson's eyes, Van Buren not only enjoyed the luxury of procrastination but won additional merit by pandering to the president's desires. "The President means to be re-elected. He has meant so all along," Webster wrote to Clay in April.[15] In good time Van Buren would be tapped as his running mate.

The final nail in Calhoun's coffin was the old affair of Jackson and the Seminoles. In May Jackson was given a copy of a letter William H. Crawford had written to a fellow Georgian, John Forsyth, confirming earlier statements about Calhoun's response to the attack on the Spanish ports in Florida. Crawford's assertion that Calhoun, in the cabinet, had advocated condemnation and punishment of the general for exceeding his orders was so different from what he had earlier been led to believe that he immediately laid the letter before Calhoun and asked for an explanation. Actually, Jackson had known of Calhoun's supposed treachery since before the presidential election. It had not been pursued then lest it damage the Jacksonian coalition on the threshold of victory. Making Crawford's letter his pretext, Jackson pressed the issue now, one month after the Jefferson dinner, because he wanted to put down Calhoun. And Calhoun, realizing he could no longer dodge the issue on the old apology of preserving the secrecy of cabinet deliberations, replied at length.[16] Coolly defending his position in 1818, Calhoun cited official orders to show that Jackson had had no authority to seize the posts. He went on to say that he had never doubted the honesty and patriotism of Jackson's motives, that he had finally concurred in the cabinet decision not to press charges, and that he had never intentionally deceived Jackson as to his position. This, the question of deception, was the sticking point. Jackson had counted Crawford as his enemy, Calhoun as his friend—his only true friend in the Monroe cabinet—indeed had publicly hailed him as "an honest man, 'the noblest work of God.'" It now appeared, however, that the recipient of his trust had concealed the truth in order to save himself and injure his enemies, the Crawfordites. As a contemporary framed the question of honor: "Could a man of nice sensibility permit another [Crawford] to be hated and himself to be held in honour with the knowledge that the disclosure of a single fact would reverse their position?"[17] Regardless of Jackson's other and deeper motives, there could be no doubt of *his* "nice sensibility" on the point of honor. He read Calhoun's letter as an admission of guilt, not only of the original offense but of twelve years of calculated duplicity toward himself. Exclaiming in reply, *Et tu Brute*, he declared the correspondence closed. But Calhoun persisted. Why had the president allowed his mind to be poisoned toward him? Did Jackson not realize that he was the dupe, Calhoun the victim, of the political conspirators around him? In all this he never cast blame on Jackson himself. He still hoped, with an odd mixture of desperation and naivete, to separate the president from the conspirators. Although unnamed, they surely included Eaton, Lewis, and, above all, Van Buren.

During the summer and fall Calhoun filled out the Seminole correspondence with letters solicited in his defense, and upon his return to Washington was led, against all prior inclination, to publish it. The correspondence had become the subject of gossip, he discovered. Some of the rumors about it, for instance that Van Buren had obtained John Quincy Adams's secret notes on the cabinet debate and dispatched them to Crawford and Jackson, were utterly unfounded. Believing the correspondence vindicated him, Calhoun hoped by publication to correct ignorant or malicious lies.[18] More importantly, his confidence in Jackson and the administration had eroded almost to the vanishing point. In the recent election of a senator in South Carolina, Jackson and Van Buren had backed the Radical incumbent, William Smith, against the Calhoun favorite, Stephen Miller, a Nullifier. The contest, in which Miller prevailed, further embittered relations between the president and the vice president.[19] At the same time, the administration withdrew its patronage of the *United States Telegraph,* whose editor was Calhoun's staunch friend, and started a new press, the *Washington Globe,* under the editorship of Frank Blair. Jackson's second message to Congress in December 1830 offered no more encouragement than the first for thoroughgoing tariff reform, and he again advocated "that most oppressive, most unjust, unconstitutional and dangerous of all projects," in Calhoun's estimation, the distribution of surplus revenue to the states.[20] When Calhoun's plan to publish the Seminole correspondence became known, friends of the administration tried to head him off. That failing, they urged him to tone down his accompanying explanatory address, making it as inoffensive as possible to the president. Felix Grundy, who was active in these efforts, showed the manuscript to Eaton, who, in turn, agreed to show it to Jackson. For some reason, perhaps to revenge himself against Calhoun, Eaton did not, although Grundy was led to understand that the president had seen the production and raised no objection to publication.[21] The *Correspondence between General Andrew Jackson and John C. Calhoun*—fifty-two pages in the pamphlet edition—first appeared in the *Telegraph* on February 17, 1831.

"They have cut their own throats!" Jackson exclaimed.[22] Fearing no political damage to himself from the *Correspondence,* he made no answer. Anxious for his reputation at the bar of history, however, he proceeded to fabricate the story—the so-called "Rhea letter hoax"—of having received secret orders from Monroe authorizing the attack on the Spanish posts.[23] The administration press represented the *Correspondence* as a wanton and unprovoked attack on the president. And so it must seem. But Calhoun's real target was Van Buren. He suspected, with many Washington politicians, that "The Little Magician" had manipulated the Seminole affair as part of the plot to destroy him. Van Buren protested his innocence till the end of his days. The plot was all on the side of Calhoun, "a most implacable man," said he, who sought to remove the rival in his way.[24] Doubtless the *Correspondence* revealed feelings so factious and jealous that it lowered public opinion of both men. Within the Jacksonian coalition, however, it worked entirely to Van Buren's advantage. Calhoun and his friends were read out of the party. "Calhoun was a very strong man in Maryland, until he came out against Jackson," one local party leader reported. "That killed him dead."[25] The president believed that the *Correspondence* was

Calhoun's last desperate gamble to wreck the administration and pronounced him "fit for any act of human depravity."[26] The next order of business was to purge the cabinet of officers loyal to Calhoun. Van Buren made this easy for the president by first tendering his own resignation as secretary of state. Eaton's followed, after which Jackson obtained the resignation of Ingham, Branch, and Berrien. The new cabinet formed in the spring was markedly cordial to Van Buren. Learning of this event after he had returned to Fort Hill, Calhoun lashed out at Jackson for the first time. "It confirms me, in what I have long believed, that General Jackson is unworthy of his station," he wrote to Ingham; and he called for a movement to unseat him in the coming election.[27]

Calhoun, of course, intended to be the candidate at the head of the anti-Jackson movement. Always at the whip of his emotions, he seemed to think that his manly defense against Jacksonian persecution and profligacy, combined with the erosion of Jacksonian support, especially in the South, favored his candidacy. After talking to Calhoun at the end of the congressional session, Matthew L. Davis, the well-known Washington newspaper correspondent, was certain the vice president would enter the field against Jackson. Webster was not so sure but told Clay that Calhoun was sanguine enough to run if encouraged by his friends, and that he could challenge or even defeat the president in Pennsylvania, Virginia, South Carolina, and possibly North Carolina. Clay, the front-running opposition candidate, supposed Calhoun was so angry with Jackson and Van Buren that he would finally submit to the movement most likely to defeat them. The breakup of the Jacksonian coalition was welcome news to Clay, and he expected to capitalize on it, though he was wary of cooperating with Calhoun.[28] How the vice president meant to cope with Clay is unclear, but there was no limit to his political delusion; he even supposed Clay might withdraw in his favor. Stopping at Richmond on the way home in March, Calhoun dined with the governor and visited with prominent Virginia Republicans who were also disillusioned with Jackson and angry at the settlement of the succession on Van Buren. Not only the governor, John Floyd, but both United States senators, Littleton Tazewell and John Tyler, had defected. As state rights Republicans, they could not support Clay. Quietly, in April, they began to organize Calhoun's candidacy in Virginia.[29] At the same time Virgil Maxcy's biography of him—the fullest to date—appeared in Green's *Telegraph*.[30]

The plan collided head-on with the course of Calhoun's political associates in South Carolina. They considered his presidential prospects hopeless, unless he bargained with the enemy, and they believed the only salvation for the state, and for the South, lay in nullification. It was impossible for Calhoun, or the state, to pursue nullification and the presidency at the same time. One strategy called for resistance, the other for conciliation; one invoked state sovereignty to overcome the bankruptcy of national politics, the other looked for salvation through the electoral system. Which should Calhoun choose? This was his dilemma in 1831. The movement to nullify the tariff had swept over the state, uniting lowcountry gentry with upcountry farmers, since Calhoun had secretly furnished it with a political philosophy. The

end of interposition, or nullification, in his conception, was to save the Union
in conformity with the Virginia model of 1798; and Calhoun may have imagined that he could repeat Jefferson's performance and march into the presidency. But the movement was not under his control. Some of its leaders
cared not a whit for the Union; others, including the prominent trio of Hamilton, Hayne, and McDuffie—all long-time associates of the vice president—
were more interested in forcing a confrontation with the general government
than with employing nullification as a lever of conciliation, which was
Calhoun's avowed purpose. To his northern friends who wanted him to
check "the ultra measures proposed by the Charleston Hotspurs," Calhoun
disclaimed responsibility for the movement but said it would be "an act of
madness" for him to attempt to arrest it.[31] The Hotspurs had turned the legislative election of the previous fall into a referendum on the question of a state
convention empowered to nullify the tariff. South Carolina became, in the
language of a keen observer, "a great talking and eating machine" for debating the pros and cons of nullification. Two parties, Unionists and Nullifiers,
were born; and wherever men gathered, at court days, militia musters, and
mammoth barbecues, "the appetites and lungs of the conflicting parties
never failed nor faltered."[32] The Nullifiers won a narrow victory. They went
on, when the legislature met, to elect Miller to the Senate and Hamilton governor. But they could not muster the two-thirds vote necessary to initiate the
convention process.

Calhoun's dilemma pulled him in opposite directions. He could not oppose nullification, to which he was committed in principle; neither could he
endorse the program of immediate action, certainly not as long as he entertained presidential ambitions. Unless he assumed control of the movement,
he risked being overrun by it. Partly for this reason he drew to the verge of
joining the Nullifiers during the final stage of the break with Jackson. It was
not only the tariff that concerned him. "I consider the Tariff act as the occasion, rather than the real cause of the present unhappy state of things," he
told Maxcy.[33] Resistance to the tariff was but the outer line of defense of
southern industry and southern slavery, which could not survive, tariff or no
tariff, under the government of an unchecked popular majority. "Under its
baneful influence, the noble, high-minded, chivalric spirit of the South
would be beat down in low and base subserviency."[34] He was, therefore, concerned with the section as well as the state. The South, as the oppressed minority, ought to unite against the majority power of the North. But Jackson
cleverly distracted the South with popular policies like Indian removal and
opposition to internal improvements, as in the Maysville Road Veto. Calhoun had no confidence in a wider southern strategy and concluded with the
Nullifiers that South Carolina should stand alone on its sovereignty.[35]

He was still not prepared for this test, however. At his last stop on his journey home, at Columbia, Calhoun had a long conversation with James H.
Hammond, editor of a radical newspaper, The Southern Times. Scarcely
touching on nullification, Calhoun spoke optimistically of the breakup of the
coalition, the shrinkage of Jackson's support, and also of Clay's weakness as

an opposition candidate. In this state of affairs, South Carolina ought to bide its time, he said, hinting at his own candidacy. He then unveiled to the astonished editor his "plan of reconciliation" of the different sections. The West would get its internal improvements with the sanction of a constitutional amendment and the creation of a great fund founded on the proceeds from the sale of public lands. With the East he would strike a compromise on the principles of the moderate tariff of 1816, retaining high duties on some of the most important articles. With this plan of sectional compromise Calhoun imagined he could win the presidency. And if he should fail, disunion was inevitable. "He is much less disposed to harangue than usual," Hammond wrote. "There is a listlessness about him which shows that his mind is deeply engaged and no doubt that it is on the subject of the Presidency. He is unquestionably quite feverish under the present excitement, and his hopes."[36]

Hammond, like most of Calhoun's South Carolina friends, rejected his "plan of reconciliation" and considered his presidential prospects hopeless. In their view the only viable strategy after the disappointment of the Jackson administration was nullification. Calhoun must either submit to this great cause or bear the political consequences. The Nullifiers were tired of his brooding, his vacillation, and his public silence. As the contest heated up, the Unionists, too, challenged him to declare himself. "The Vice President of the United States," he was toasted at a Unionist celebration. "His political intimates have declared their sentiments on Nullification—will *he shrink* from an *open* exposition of his own?"[37] Partly with a view to forcing Calhoun's hand, Governor Hamilton, the generalissimo of the Nullifiers, brought McDuffie to Charleston in May for a patented oration of fire and fury. The congressman expounded his favorite "forty-bale theory" (the tariff was equivalent to a 40-percent export tax on the cotton planters), denounced the Union as a foul monster, invoked the revolutionary example of 1776, and called on the patriots of South Carolina to rise up and break their chains.[38] The speech was widely reported in the press. Duff Green candidly inquired if Hamilton, McDuffie, and company "were all crazy." They were ruining Calhoun as a presidential candidate. But that, of course, was precisely the Nullifiers' intention. They wished to attach Calhoun unequivocally to their cause. His ruin as a presidential candidate was nothing, Hamilton told Green, compared to the ruin that must result from the surrender of principle in a Janus-faced compact between cotton planters and manufacturers, as practical, and as fatal, as a confederation of Poles and Cossacks.[39]

Between these feuding friends Calhoun kept his own counsel at Fort Hill. McDuffie's tirade took him by surprise. The presidential fever was still upon him, and he had hoped for restraint from the Nullifiers. "If Mr. McDuffie had been your bitterest political enemy," Green told him, "he could not have [done] you half the injury, no not a tithe of that which this speech has inflicted."[40] The indomitable editor, already besieged by charges in the administration press that the vice president was secretly a Nullifier, begged Calhoun to draw a line between himself and the radicals. Let him appear at a Fourth of July celebration, make a patriotic speech, and propose compromising the tariff question, Green suggested.[41] Calhoun rejected the advice. Without either aid or resistance from him, the Fourth of July celebrations of the rival parties escalated the contest. As much as he preferred to maintain "a silent and retired position," he realized this was no longer possible. McDuffie's rousing appeal to the pride and patriotism of South Carolina had moved the clock ahead dramatically. "I see clearly that it brings matters to a crisis," Calhoun wrote, "and that I must meet it promptly and manfully."[42]

The upshot was the Fort Hill Address.[43] In it he committed himself publicly to nullification and elaborated the theory of the 1828 *Exposition,* which he was now known to have authored. The right of "state interposition," the terminology he favored since it was more clearly founded than "nullification" in the Virginia and Kentucky Resolutions, was "the fundamental principle of our system" and "the only solid formation" of the Union. The protective tariff had divided the country into two great geographical sections, North and South, "so much so, that no two distinct nations ever entertained more opposite views of policy," and meetings of Congress had become "an annual struggle between the two sections . . . a struggle in which all the noble and generous feelings of patriotism are gradually subsiding into sectional and selfish attachments." (Calhoun omitted the West as a section in large part because a threefold division did not suit his model of majority tyranny.) Founded on opposing interests, the conflict was as inevitable as that between the rich and the poor in other societies; it must end in the total subjection, including the political disfranchisement, of the minority South. The only remedy was to give the minority a check on the majority; and Calhoun went on to expound the process of nullification, which he insisted was the constitutional remedy for the problem.

The address removed uncertainty about Calhoun's true political colors. The editors of the *Intelligencer,* recalling Calhoun's distinguished career as a national statesman, voiced "extreme surprise and deep mortification" upon learning he was a Nullifier. The editor of the *Telegraph* said the address "was like a shock produced by the cold bath." And a New Yorker eager to challenge Van Buren's Albany Regency behind Calhoun's presidential candidacy declared it had "totally destroyed his prospects."[44] To his northern friends Calhoun said he had written "with a sacred regard to truth, and in that spirit of attachment to our institutions and the Union . . . I have ever felt." The presidential question was necessarily subordinate to this. "Had my love of the Union and the Constitution been less, or ambition greater, I certainly would not have ventured the step," he wrote. While not expecting to be sustained in the North, where he supposed all regard for principle had been lost in the pursuit of gain, Calhoun hoped at least to obtain credit for valor and patriotism.[45] The notion of noble sacrifice to the principle and pride of his native state entered deeply into his public persona. With courage and high resolve, it would be written in the authorized *Life* of 1843, "Mr. Calhoun fearlessly assumed the responsibility of the movement in the great issue which South Carolina was preparing to make with the General Government; and, in obedience to the calls on him from various quarters, he unhesitatingly avowed his opinions on the complex and difficult questions arising out of it. It would be difficult to imagine a situation of more peril, or a greater example of self-abandonment and moral intrepidity. He and the state now stood alone in open, bold, and undaunted resistance."[46]

Conceding some portion of truth to this conception, the question remains, why did Calhoun openly declare himself for nullification in July 1831? First, because other political avenues were closed to him. He had been forced out of the Jackson party. Duff Green nourished his presidential delusions, courting support wherever he could find it, now among National Republicans, now with the new Anti-Masonic party in the eastern states, quite regardless of political principle. At the moment of truth following McDuffie's speech, however, Calhoun recognized the softness of his presidential support; and compelled to act, he resolved his dilemma in favor of nullification. Not surprisingly, South Carolina Unionists attributed his behavior to disappointment over his presidential prospects.[47] Second, Calhoun came to realize that nullification might grow into a political monster in South Carolina, swallowing him up and releasing violent forces, possibly ending in disunion. His political influence nationally rested on his leadership in the state. He must, therefore, take control of the movement and hold it to a moderate course. Adams remarked that Calhoun "veers round in his politics, to be always before the wind."[48] He got before the Carolina wind in the summer of 1831, although he had some way to go to establish his dominance. Third, lest Calhoun be dismissed as a mere opportunist, it is important to recognize the strength of his convictions and principles. He really believed that the South groaned under the tyranny of a corrupt northern majority, that nullification would bring relief, that it was not only correct in theory but, in practice, would work to save the Constitution and the Union, no matter that *his* Constitution and Union had ceased to have much resemblance to Webster's or Clay's or Jackson's. Of course, Calhoun was never at a loss for principle. When everything else failed, some high principle or theory became his refuge of order and virtue—the rock of his, and the country's, political salvation. It took possession of him, transfixed his political vision, and justified all his actions. In his public statements Calhoun emphasized the conservative tendency of nullification. By forcing the general government back within narrow constitutional boundaries it would further peace and harmony. In private letters, however, Calhoun confessed his belief that the system was so deeply diseased it could be cured only by something approaching a revolution. "The ardent pursuit of gain, and the squabbles of politics have been long drawing off our attention from the higher principles of government, till they are almost forgotten," he wrote, "and nothing but calamity, or its near approach, can move the country to a sense of the danger, always attendant on great and radical errors of policy."[49]

With the Fort Hill Address, it was generally agreed, Calhoun crossed the Rubicon, though opinion was divided on whether he should be admired for his valor or pitied for his folly. The act, said the *Raleigh Register*, "places an insurmountable barrier between him and the Presidential chair." This was echoed by the *New York American:* "This exposition closes the door forever

upon Mr. Calhoun's advance to the Presidency. He has . . . in fact 'disfranchised' himself."[50] His undeclared candidacy in the coming contest became
the solitary preoccupation of Duff Green. Calhoun, the irrepressible editor
continued to preach, was the only man who could defeat Jackson; and on the
eve of the Anti-Masonic convention in September, he was still trying to put
together a ticket of Calhoun and McLean. But the convention dared not
even think of the man who wrote the Fort Hill Address.[51] Calhoun himself
neither countenanced nor discountenanced these efforts. He never assumed
that the presidency and nullification were absolutely incompatible with each
other. Nearing the edge of the political abyss, the people might yet regain
their senses, at least in the South, and turn to him. He ceased to believe in
miracles in 1832, however, and instead consigned the presidential election to
the limbo of political degeneracy. Exchanging one delusion for another, he
entered heart and soul into the South Carolina crusade.

3. *Clay and Jackson*

Henry Clay's opposition to the administration, beginning on issues of executive patronage and prerogative, had spread by 1831 to the broad front of the
American System. Defending it, he was equally at odds with Jackson and Calhoun who, despite their personal quarrel, seemed united on its destruction.
In his first message to Congress, Jackson criticized the Bank of the United
States. Although its charter had seven long years to run, the president raised
questions of policy and constitutionality, and suggested it was not too early
for Congress to consider them. He raised the same questions about internal
improvements. The tariff escaped attack, even received guarded support,
but Clay worried about the fate of protectionism at the president's hands.
His ardor for paying off the debt and ridding the treasury of the surplus
threatened to sink the tariff. Distribution might save it, of course; but the coalition of western and southern Jacksonians in the debate on Foot's Resolution disclosed a political design hostile to distribution, Clay thought. The Jefferson Day Dinner then confirmed it. "It is," he wrote, "to cry down old con-
structions of the Constitution; to cry up State rights, to make all Mr. Jefferson's opinions the articles of faith of the new Church; to hold out the notion
of preserving the Union by conciliating the South, and to catch at popularity
by repealing taxes etc."[1]

The veto of the Maysville Road Bill the following month exhibited the new
policy in a manner that was a personal affront to Clay. The Maysville and Lexington Turnpike Road Company had been chartered by the Kentucky legislature in 1817; failing in its mission within the allotted time, it expired, but was
rechartered in 1827. A good McAdamized road from Maysville, on the Ohio
River opposite Cincinnati, would go far toward overcoming the handicap of
Lexington's inland situation. Clay had been interested in this and similar
Kentucky road projects for several years. The condition of Kentucky roads

was a public scandal. The steamboat journey from Baton Rouge to Louisville actually took less time than the overland journey from Louisville to Lexington. The Corps of Engineers had recommended the Maysville Road to Congress in 1827. It was envisioned as a section of a major highway from the National Road in Ohio southward through Lexington and Nashville to the Gulf of Mexico. The Kentucky legislature endorsed the project. Like many large public works in this era, it was a "mixed enterprise" combining private and public resources. The private subscription to the stock of the company was already full in 1830; the governor had asked the legislature for its portion; and $150,000 was sought from Congress.[2] Except for improvements on the Ohio River, Kentucky had not yet received a single dollar of federal money. This fact, combined with the merits of the project and strong bipartisan support in the state, augured well for congressional approval. Clay's friend Robert Letcher, introducing the bill in the House, spoke about it almost perfunctorily, as if passage was assured. And it was, though the vote on the Maysville Road Bill, 105–86, was one of the first signs of emerging party division on internal improvements. (On a simultaneous motion in the Senate to table a bill authorizing government purchase of stock in the new Baltimore and Ohio Railroad, every Jacksonian senator except the gentleman from Baltimore, Samuel Smith, was recorded in the 21–19 majority.)

In May, after clearing the Senate, the Maysville Road Bill went to the president, only to be returned with his negative. Reviewing the history of internal improvements legislation, conceding that millions had been appropriated and every president since Jefferson had approved these measures, Jackson said they had always been held to the test of *national* character; and the present bill for a road between two points in Kentucky failed to meet this test. He went on to express opposition to any general system of internal improvements.[3] The message jarred Congress. It threw the government back half a century, said the *Intelligencer*.[4] It placed in jeopardy the system finally established by the General Survey Act and liberally supported during the Adams administration. Jackson adroitly held back the veto until the day after the House narrowly passed his Indian Removal Bill, which carried an appropriation of half a million dollars. This had been made a party measure, and some Jacksonians had cause to regret their votes for Indian removal when they learned the fate of internal improvements under the president's decree.[5] But the Maysville veto was sustained by a party-line vote of 96–90, well short of the two-thirds required to override.

Clay and Kentucky were outraged by the veto. The leadership of both was identified with internal improvements. Jackson's contention that the Maysville Road was local rather than national in character was pronounced absurd. The same argument could be made against every coastal lighthouse and every segment of the National Road. The local-national distinction was unworkable, as Webster had repeatedly shown. (Sometime later, alluding to the veto message in a speech at Faneuil Hall, Webster remarked, "There is no road leading everywhere, except . . . ," at which point an auditor interjected, "except the road to ruin." And Webster roared, "Except the road to ruin, and that's an administration road!")[6] How, then, was the veto, so unprecedented since it was on grounds of policy rather than constitutionality, to be explained? Some thought that Jackson was motivated by personal hostility to Clay. (Jackson's suspicions of Clay were boundless. He was convinced, for instance, that Martin's *History of Louisiana*, which contained some censure of the general, was written at Clay's instigation to blacken his fame.) Politically, of course, the veto struck at Clay's prestige to the West. He fought back, organizing meetings of protest at Fayette Court House and in other counties, and proposing a constitutional amendment to allow a majority of the two houses to override an executive veto. This proposition, by which Clay hoped to get a weather gauge on the Jacksonians, was pressed on the legislature, on friendly newspapers, and on congressional leaders like Webster.[7]

The veto reinforced Clay's opinion of Jackson. He could hardly doubt that personal feelings, more than considerations of the public good, produced it. He supposed, too, that the veto was part of the policy of conciliating the South, perhaps even the payoff for Calhoun's casting vote, utterly unprincipled in Clay's opinion, confirming Kendall's appointment as an auditor.[8] In fact, though unsuspected by Clay, the man behind the veto was Martin Van Buren, who had been irrevocably opposed to federal internal improvements since New York built its Erie Canal. Moreover, as Clay soon learned, Jackson withheld his signature from two other internal improvement bills passed in the waning hours of Congress, thereby exercising for the first time in history the constitutional power of "pocket veto." One of these was for lighthouses, which had been routinely funded in the past; the other was for the Louisville and Portland Canal Company. This project for a canal around the falls of the Ohio River had also been previously funded. Neither project could be dismissed as local in character. Explaining these vetoes in the ensuing annual message to Congress, the president disclosed the broad ideological underpinings of the new policy. He called for "radical change in the action of the government" to remedy the evils of consolidation, the "sinister influence" of logrolling politics, and the inequities that must occur in any system of internal improvements. The government ought not dabble in matters that were properly the concern of states and individuals, he said; it should be entirely divorced from the economy and confined to a few simple objects.[9] It became Jackson's proud boast at the conclusion of his presidency that he had "overthrown . . . this plan of unconstitutional expenditure for the purpose of corrupt influence."[10] The truth was more complex. Actually, he signed more internal improvement bills than any predecessor, but many were for rivers and harbors and for projects in the territories, not the states. In 1831 Jackson abolished the board of engineers set up under the General Survey Act; later he turned over the National Road—the premier federal enterprise—to the separate states through which it passed. What Jackson overthrew was internal improvements on a coherent national plan, as envisioned by Jefferson and Gallatin, reformulated by Clay and Calhoun, and carried into execution by President Adams.[11]

The Maysville Road veto with the proposed override amendment was the springboard of Clay's presidential campaign. From Fourth of July platforms in 1830 orators denounced the veto and lauded the "Father of the American System." "The Lexington and Maysville Turnpike," ran a toast at a mechanics' dinner. "Though the President has refused to McAdamize it, the Kentuckians can make it *out of Clay*."[12] And so they did. The turnpike would finally be completed without federal subsidy; other means were found, too, to finance the canal around the falls of the Ohio; and Clay turned his attention to the new project of the Lexington and Ohio Railroad. In mid-summer he visited several cities north of the Ohio. Speaking in Cincinnati and elsewhere, he raised the flag of the American System, obviously intending to march into the presidency under its folds. He was eager to become a declared candidate, with nominations in the old manner by legislative caucuses as well as by conventions and mass meetings. But he was put off, first, by other opposition leaders, Webster among them, who wanted to keep alive their own quiet candidacies, and second, by political intimates who sought to shield him from the hazards of early exposure. Nevertheless, beginning in Delaware and Connecticut in September, state conventions of National Republicans, emulating the process initiated by the followers of Calhoun and Jackson several years earlier, placed Clay's name in nomination. He was pleased. "It is essentially a proceeding of the people; and as they have been pleased to take up this matter, against the present incumbent, it had better continue in their hands," Clay wrote to a Marylander in November.[13] Before long he endorsed a national nominating convention as well.

Outside the West, the main impulse of Clay's candidacy came from New England. Indeed, western Jacksonians commonly charged he had sold out to Yankee industrialists. Admirers in Hartford, Connecticut, doubtless influenced by the phenomenal success of Major Eaton's *Life of Andrew Jackson*, wished to publish a popular biography of Clay. They arranged for George D. Prentice, editor of the popular *New England Weekly Review*, to write it, and he journeyed to Lexington in the spring. Clay agreed to cooperate, but to Prentice's surprise found the idea of a biography distasteful. Although a great showman, he seemed to have no conception of the political importance of a vibrant public persona in this new age of democracy; and for all the boldness of his civic character, he was oddly diffident about his personal life and feelings. Drawing information from Clay's friends and acquaintances in Lexington and across the nation, Prentice finished the biography in November. His hand gave definite form to the maturing legend of the orphaned boy who was the artificer of his own destiny. Prentice wrote in the conviction that Clay was one of the master spirits of the age. Despite its idolatrous tone, however, this campaign biography, like Knapp's little life of Webster at the same time, offered an astute characterization of the man. Prentice did not return to Connecticut, where the *Biography of Henry Clay* was published, but went to Louisville to edit a struggling National Republican newspaper, the *Focus*, which he soon made into one of the leading newspapers of the time, under a new name, the Louisville *Daily Journal*.[14]

In 1831 it became obvious that Clay's candidacy was in serious trouble. Ex-

pected gains from Jackson's embarrassments, such as the rupture with Calhoun, did not materialize. The president remained immensely popular in
the South, in part because of Indian removal and opposition to the B. U. S.;
and with a flourish of the pen—vetoing the Maysville Road Bill—he won
many more southern votes than he lost by adherence to the tariff and distribution. In the West "Harrah for Jackson" drowned out dissent. Even in Kentucky, Jacksonians gave Clay and his party a hard time. The August election,
always the bellwether of Clay's political fortunes nationally, produced only a
bare legislative majority in 1830. When the legislature met the National Republicans were unable, after fourteen exhausting ballots, to elect their candidate, John J. Crittenden, to the United States Senate. Clay was in New Orleans during this struggle. He backed Crittenden, whose reputation among
Kentuckians was second only to his own, and he could not be blamed for the
defeat. But it reflected badly on his leadership and contributed to dissension
in the party.[15]

What devastated Clay's candidacy, however, was the sudden rise of the
Anti-Masonic party in the eastern states. The party had its birth in the outrage against Freemasonry that spread like wildfire through upstate New
York, then into Vermont and Pennsylvania, in the aftermath of the mysteri-
ous disappearance and presumed murder of a man, William Morgan, who
had threatened to expose the secret order. The popularity of Anti-Masonry
undercut Clay's support in the major eastern states essential to his success.
In New York the party was led by a new breed of daring democratic politicians who were as hostile to the ruling Albany Regency as to the vestiges of
aristocratic conservatism in the state. The opportunity existed, therefore, for
concert between the National Republicans and Anti-Masonry. This would
prove particularly advantageous to Clay, since his party had no organization
in New York, while Thurlow Weed, Francis Granger, and William H. Seward, the Anti-Masonic leaders, had assembled a formidable political machine. But Clay was contemptuous of Anti-Masonry and declined to seek its
support. Like many prominent men, including Andrew Jackson, he was a Mason, though he had been inactive for many years and felt quite indifferent toward the brotherhood. He was appalled by the channeling of popular fears
and prejudices about Masonry into a political party. What bearing had that
on the great issues before the citizens of the republic? He was, furthermore,
shocked by the demand that he renounce the Masonic order as the price of
the party's support for the presidency. Again and again he refused. "I tell
them that Masonry or Anti-Masonry has, legitimately . . . nothing to do with
politics."[16] This may have been true, but by failing to recognize the democratic and reformist character of Anti-Masonry, Clay cut himself off from powerful new political forces. His former cabinet colleague Richard Rush, having
joined the Anti-Masonic crusade in Pennsylvania, pleaded with Clay to bend
a little. "Anti-Masonry means, in effect, anti-Jacksonism . . . ," Rush wrote.
"Pray, then, for your country's sake, let me implore you to conciliate this interest."[17] Rush, who published a highly wrought pamphlet on Anti-Masonry,
said he championed the new party only in order to capture its suffrages for

Clay, thereby making his triumph certain.[18] Clay did not appreciate the favor and thought Rush deranged. Anti-Masonry also swept up John Quincy Adams, who might have liked the party's presidential nomination, yet was reluctant to injure Clay's chances against Jackson.[19]

Rebuffed by Clay, the Anti-Masons looked elsewhere for a presidential candidate. Supreme Court Justice John McLean, Calhoun's old friend and Clay's perennial adversary in Ohio, was often mentioned. So was Calhoun. He was not a Mason, and although much too proud to seek the party's nomination, he made it perfectly clear he was available.[20] Anti-Masonry might revive Calhoun's old following in Pennsylvania and the eastern states. "The Antimasonic nomination is all that is wanting to put Clay out of the field and to elect Calhoun," Green blustered in 1831. But the Fort Hill Address eliminated consideration of Calhoun as the party's standard-bearer.[21] When the Anti-Masons convened in Baltimore in September, in what was the very first national nominating convention, they surprised everyone, including themselves, by choosing William Wirt of Maryland. Himself a Mason, the portly Wirt was only an eleventh-hour convert to the cause. He had served as attorney general in the two previous administrations, stood next to Webster at the bar of the Supreme Court, and was currently in the public eye as counsel for the Cherokee nation in its case against Georgia. But Wirt had no political following and had never shown a spark of political leadership. The folly of the nomination was exceeded only by the folly of his acceptance. Wirt's motives remain a mystery. He sometimes talked as if he expected, as the Anti-Masonic candidate, to promote Clay's election, perhaps even finally withdrawing in his favor. At other times Wirt seemed to say that the only hope of defeating Jackson was by Clay's withdrawal and the coalescence of opposition forces behind his candidacy.[22] Whatever Wirt's motives, Clay felt betrayed by someone he had counted a friend. Wirt's candidacy could only take votes from him and thereby ensure Jackson's reelection. Webster agreed, as did most of the opposition press.[23] Wirt's discomfort increased as the campaign progressed. He would have withdrawn happily if Clay had only given him an excuse by, for instance, denouncing Masonry. But by this time the hearts of most Anti-Masons had hardened against Clay. It was not only that he refused to denounce the abominable order; many Anti-Masons believed he continued secretly to espouse the brotherhood and, if this were not enough, to live in defiance of the moral laws of God and man.[24]

Several weeks before the Anti-Masonic convention, Clay suffered a mortifying defeat in the Kentucky election. The National Republicans held their own in the congressional races, winning four to the Jacksonians' eight, and they maintained a narrow majority in both houses of the legislature—large enough to elect a senator. But having predicted a great victory, one that would instill national confidence in his presidential candidacy, Clay was chagrined by the result, the more so because it was soon repeated in other western states.[25] Was the "Star of the West" fading? In the East there was talk of Clay's withdrawing. Webster was again mentioned. But he showed no eagerness to run after the Anti-Masonic nomination. The National Republicans went through the motions of nominating Clay at Baltimore in December, but few entertained hopes for his election. Clay, too, recognized the overwhelming odds against him; he would have preferred to withdraw, but acquiesced in the nomination so as to offer a rallying point for the National Republicans in state elections.[26] In the wake of the western defeats, Webster had urged Clay to come into the Senate in the new Congress. "Everything valuable in the Government is to be fought for, and we need your arm in the fight," he wrote.[27] Hearing the same sentiment from different quarters, Clay agreed to run for the Senate, provided Crittenden, the leading candidate, would step aside. Crittenden could have been elected, and he must have resented Clay's claim to the office by a kind of seignorial right. But he was a good soldier and withdrew gracefully. In November Clay was elected to the Senate over Richard M. Johnson, the Jacksonian candidate, by a margin of nine votes.[28]

Of all the things to be fought for in the Twenty-Second Congress, nothing was as important to Clay as the protective tariff. The southern attack received northern reinforcement at the great Free Trade Convention in Philadelphia in October. Soon the press teemed with rumors that Clay would seek a political accommodation on a moderate tariff. A long article in the *American Quarterly Review*, purporting to be a review of the Address of the Free Trade Convention, defended protectionism but argued that the impending surplus of perhaps $10 million annually required "a modification that will compromise the different interests, conciliate all parties, and . . . preserve the Union." This could be accomplished without injury, it was suggested, by taking off the duties from imports not in competition with domestic productions. The article was supposedly written by Clay's close adviser, Senator Johnston of Louisiana.[29] The Richmond *Whig*, considered a reliable spokesman, went further, saying that Clay wished to reduce the revenue to the actual wants of the treasury, with the duties so arranged as to give only *incidental* protection to the home product. Had Virginia, or Calhoun, asked for more? "It is thus manifest," the *Whig* editorialized, "that the progress of events and the changed condition of the exchequer have produced a striking coincidence of thought and view between men of supposed different schools, and a near approach of conformity even between extremes."[30]

This was a fair, if not completely accurate, representation of Clay's position, and it correctly traced the change to the surplus. He told his old friend Judge Brooke, in Virginia, the time had come to meet with Calhoun on tariff adjustments that might be called for by impending retirement of the debt. Since $10 million was regularly devoted to that, the duties on non-competitive articles should be reduced in this amount. He opposed distribution and said he would rely on public land sales for the support of internal improvements.[31] The editor of the Richmond *Enquirer* rubbed his eyes in disbelief. The "Father of the American System" had put himself forward as "The Mediator of the South." Inevitably, Clay's shift on the tariff was attributed to the erosion of his political base in the North. A coalition between Clay and Calhoun, which had seemed impossible only months before, was now freely predicted. Free traders, however, denounced the reported plan as a fraud. It would lift taxes from luxuries, and it made no concession of the principle of protection. Editor Thomas Ritchie concluded after careful examination that the conception of Clay as a conciliator and mediator was a delusion.[32]

When Congress convened, Jackson acted at once to check the threatened union of Clay and Calhoun and keep the game in his own hands. He took pride in announcing that the debt would be extinguished at the end of his first term. It therefore became possible, even essential, to reduce the revenue to the costs of an economical administration of the government.[33] (The secretary of treasury, in his companion report, placed this at $15 million a year.) Tariff reform, looking to a revenue standard, became administration policy. Cheered by this, Nullifiers and other foes of the American System also noted with satisfaction the president's silent omission from the message of the plan to distribute the surplus. Jackson, it seemed, proposed to "annihilate the nullifiers" by removing the pretext of complaint.

From an ideological standpoint, Jackson's third annual message signaled full-scale retreat from the Madisonian Platform toward the denationalization and devolution of public policy that came to characterize the so-called Age of Jackson. Thus far it had shown itself most clearly in Indian affairs. The protecting arm of the federal government had been withdrawn and removal west of the Mississippi was forced upon the civilized tribes, like the Cherokee in Georgia, at the pain of subjection to callous state authorities. The change was manifested as well by the rejection of comprehensive aid and planning for internal improvements. Before the end of the present session of Congress the change would become a revolution in the opinion of opposition leaders. It would be dramatized by Jackson's veto of the bill to recharter the Bank of the United States. It would show itself further in land policy (the treasury report proposed to cede a great part of the national domain to the states) and in lesser matters, until it seemed that Jackson was destined to realize his ideal of government as "a simple machine."

Clay quickly clashed with his old chief, John Quincy Adams, on tariff reform. Just now beginning an astonishing new career as a Massachusetts congressman, Adams found himself, to everyone's surprise, placed at the head of the House Committee on Manufactures. Apparently the speaker, Andrew Stevenson of Virginia, intended to use Adams to baffle the Nullifiers, especially McDuffie, chairman of the Ways and Means Committee. Adams's sentiments were protectionist, of course; but he had never been bold on the issue and had no knowledge of the mysteries of tariff schedules. Seeing, moreover, that his committee had been formed to disagree, he thought it best to await the lead of Secretary of Treasury Louis McLane, himself a moderate protectionist.[34] Clay disapproved. In meetings he arranged with Adams and other opposition leaders, the newly elected senator was as arrogant as he was charming. "Mr. Clay's manner, with many courtesies of personal politeness, was exceedingly peremptory and dogmatical," Adams noted in his diary.[35] He had never approved of the smiling Kentuckian's manners or morals, and in 1831 the former colleagues had fallen out over the issue of Freemasonry.

Adams hated nullification, thought Calhoun "but a pupil of the Hartford Convention," but he would not be obliged to defeat it at the cannon's mouth for the sake of the protective tariff. "I tell gentlemen they must relieve the South or fight them," he declared. The South hailed him as a convert.[36] Instinctively a gambler, Clay dismissed nullification as bluff; and despite recent conciliatory statements, he spoke determinedly of maintaining the American System. Jackson and the Nullifiers had seized upon the burgeoning surplus as an excuse for destroying it. The way to beat them and save the system was to reduce the revenue immediately, regardless of debt or surplus, by lifting the duties on non-protected articles. Adams objected that this defied both South Carolina and the administration. "I do not care who it defies," Clay grandly replied. "To preserve, maintain, and strengthen the American System I would defy the South, the President, and the devil."[37] The two men, unable to agree, went their separate ways. Adams believed Great Hal placed his presidential ambitions ahead of the national interest. Always the politician, he sought first to satisfy his constituents in protectionist states. And to allow Jackson the glory of resolving the conflict with South Carolina was unthinkable. "It is an electioneering movement, and this was the secret of these meetings," Adams wrote, "as well as of the desperate effort to take the whole business of the tariff reduction into his own hands." He was convinced, finally, that if Clay succeeded "blood would flow."[38]

Early in January Clay introduced in the Senate a resolution for abolishing duties on all non-competitive imports, except wine and silk, which would only be reduced, and instructing the Committee on Finance to report a bill accordingly. Ignoring the southern threat, as well as objections to protectionism, he said that the advent of a surplus alone made necessary reduction of the tariff. His mode of accomplishing the reduction was "undebatable ground," Clay argued. "It exacts no sacrifice of principle from the opponents of the American System, it comprehends none on the part of its friends." On his inflated estimate the plan would reduce the annual revenue by $7 million, or less than half the projected surplus. The reduction would be less if Congress also passed two changes in the revenue laws proposed by Clay, one to substitute "home valuation" for the often fraudulently low foreign valuation on the invoices, the other to curtail sharply the long credits allowed on payment of duties. These measures connected with enforcement of the customs laws had long been favored by most protectionists, who considered them as important as the duties themselves.[39] Hayne answered Clay with a counter-resolution calling for reduction of the tariff to the revenue level, which he put at 15 percent. Samuel Smith, the octogenarian chairman of the Finance Committee, rushed to his support. Clay's proposal to resolve the crisis at no cost to anybody, without touching protection, was both shallow and wicked, he declared.[40] Six or seven weeks earlier, when the session began, talk of compromise had filled the air, and Clay had been cast in the role of mediator. These hopes had become desperate in January.

The supposed coalition of Clay and Calhoun—and Webster, too—to defeat the president's nomination of Van Buren as minister to Great Britain, whatever else it portended, had little bearing on the critical issue in Congress. Nominated months earlier as a consequence of cabinet reorganization, Van Buren was already on duty in London when his name came before the executive session of the Senate. He was opposed for his role in the cabinet crisis. The South Carolinians held him responsible for blasting their fond hopes for the Jackson administration. Clay, in particular, held him responsible for introducing "the odious system of proscription" borrowed from New York. It was in reply to this charge that William Marcy of that state stunned the Senate by candidly defending, indeed championing, the system. "To the victor belong the spoils of the enemy," Marcy declared.[41] Finally, Clay, Webster, and other National Republicans argued that Van Buren, as secretary of state, had sacrificed the honor of the United States by repudiating the position of the previous administration against Britain in the controversy over the West Indian trade. Renewed negotiations had been successful, and Jackson, by proclamation, reopened the trade on terms that many Americans thought both demeaning and unprofitable. Van Buren, who had actually had little to do with the terms or the settlement, thought the charge of official misconduct a subterfuge for a proceeding that was political through and through.[42] In the end the nomination failed on the casting vote of the vice president. "It will kill him, sir, kill him dead," Calhoun reportedly gloated. "He will never kick, sir, never kick." In fact, as the future would disclose, it was Calhoun who, in John Randolph's phrase, "like the Fanatic . . . emasculated himself." He had killed a minister, but he had also crowned Van Buren a political martyr, which was the next best thing to being a general and would help make him president.[43]

The idea of "the Janus-faced coalition"—the coalition of Nationals and Nullifiers—was floated by the administration mouthpiece, the Washington *Globe*, in response to the Senate rejection of Van Buren. Sometimes Webster's name was added to the combination, giving birth to the idea of "the triumvirate." Resolutions of an Albany mass meeting called to vindicate Van Buren declared, "That Daniel Webster, Henry Clay and John C. Calhoun were not only the instigators to, but the prominent and responsible actors in this rejection," and referred to them collectively as "this triumvirate."[44] Regardless of the implications of this development, the rejection of Van Buren was a piece of opportunism. Not even the *Globe*, though it cried "Coalition!" supposed Clay and Calhoun could unite on a tariff settlement. Its argument was that, while opposed on every issue, they were united in wishing to keep up the agitation. "Mr. Clay and his system is essential to Mr. Calhoun and his system." And *vice versa*.[45] At this time the prospect of cooperation between them in the coming election had ceased to concern even the *Globe*. It certainly did not concern Calhoun, who felt no interest in the election, or Clay, who would not risk a brush with nullification.

Clay delivered his masterly speech, "In Defense of the American System," during three days in February.[46] It was his maiden oration in the Senate. The chamber was packed to hear the man whose powers of persuasion— now charming, now badgering; now beseeching, now deprecating; now subdued, now vehement—were legendary, and who, if he did not command assent by the strength of his views, won it with his captivating manner and seductive voice. "Time has not yet robbed him of any of his ardour," an admiring congressman observed. "His eyes still blazed as in youth, and as passion impels or imagination prompts him, you perceive in his fine countenance all the workings of his soul."[47]

Clay began by contrasting the present prosperity of the country with its calamitous condition in the years after 1818. The protective tariff was the agent of this change, he said. From 1824 it had been settled policy. Property and fortune had been staked on it; it could not be disturbed without violence to the public faith and economic ruin. In defense of the system, Clay gathered up all the arguments he had been making for fifteen years. Free trade was a delusion; if adopted, he warned, calling up republican fears half a century in the past, "it will lead substantially to the recolonization of these states, under the commercial dominion of Great Britain." He underscored the economic benefits of the system: giving employment to labor, maintaining agricultural prices by the creation of a home market, reducing the prices of manufactured goods. Paradoxically, the duty levied to encourage the domestic article did not raise the price to the consumer, as logic seemed to dictate, and as free traders charged, but after a time lowered it by making possible improvements of skill and technology and by stimulating competition and supply in the American manufacture. (Clay's Kentucky associate, Crittenden, carrying the argument to its conclusion, namely that many domestic manufactures could now stand on their own, urged him to proclaim the victory of the American System and submit to lower tariffs.)[48] Replying to South Carolina cotton planters, Clay denied that the tariff was responsible for their distress (the main cause was competition from fresh lands in the Gulf states), that it imposed an unjust tax burden on them (the tax was borne equally by all consumers), that it reduced their exports (without injuring exports it created a large home market for cotton), and so on. Thus disposing of the economic grievance, Clay went on to berate South Carolina's leaders for attacking the democratic rule of the majority and practicing intimidation and blackmail on the Union. "The danger to our Union," he declared, "does not lie on the side of persistence in the American system, but in its abandonment." For in the latter event the industry of the northern states would be paralyzed, their prosperity blighted, "and then, indeed, might we tremble for the continuance and safety of the Union!" With this startling statement Clay warned South Carolina that two could play its game. And holding to "no compromise" between protectionism and free trade, he placed the government in the predicament of risking disunion from either policy.

Adoption of Clay's resolution was a foregone conclusion. The administration, although it had called for tariff reform, held back, as if afraid of opening itself to the charge of yielding to nullification. McLane's illness was part of the explanation. But Calhoun glumly complained of "an ignominious and criminal silence" by the president.[49] Clay, backed by the host of manufacturing lobbyists, seemed to hold the Senate in his grasp. By a clever parliamentary maneuver he got the reference of his resolution switched from Smith's committee to the Committee on Manufactures, of which he was himself a member and Mahlon Dickerson the chairman. At this point several western senators, thinking to extort a price for support of the tariff, moved to charge the committee also to look into the expediency of reducing the price of public lands and transferring them to the states. A new effort to join these two great issues offered no surprises, but the proposal by western politicians to commit public land policy to a body entrusted with the care of manufactures was scarcely credible, even absurd, as Senator Benton waggishly acknowledged. But there was, after all, a westerner on the committee, Henry Clay. Let him say he would keep up the price of public lands so as to force workers into eastern factories maintained by the protective tariff.[50]

The committee promptly reported Clay's resolution in the form of a bill that would reduce the revenue by some $5 million. After turning back a move to kill the bill, Clay deferred further action pending developments in the House, where revenue bills were supposed to originate according to the Constitution. Several weeks later he submitted his report, with an accompanying bill, on the public lands resolution.[51] Rejecting preemption, graduation, cession, and similar proposals as wasteful misappropriations of a precious resource, Clay extolled the national domain as a "sacred trust" sealed by the blood of the Revolution, not only a bond of union but, under the present land system, a guarantor of freedom and progress for countless generations to come. He would have preferred to make no change in the system, but the looming surplus suggested the wisdom of a five-year experiment in distribution, under which the states would receive the income from the sale of western lands (about $3 million in 1831) for purposes of education, internal improvements, and the colonization of free blacks. The constitutional objection he had voiced earlier to distribution of the surplus revenue from taxes did not apply to distributing the proceeds of the public lands since they were in the nature of a trust. Clay's plan would award large bonuses to the seven new states, with millions of federal acres and few people; the rest of the income would be shared by all twenty-four states on the basis of federal population.

With this report Clay believed he had turned a flagitious scheme to embarrass him into a political triumph. The basic idea of the Land Bill did not originate with Clay, but he matured it into a comprehensive and practical plan. A pragmatic response to new imperatives of public policy, it offered further proof, if any were needed, of Clay's resourcefulness and adaptability. In part, of course, his motives were narrowly political: to turn back the challenge, spearheaded by Benton, to his claim on western suffrages. In this respect, said a leading Jacksonian newspaper, the report was "the boldest move that ever was made by a candidate for the Presidency."[52] The senator was equally concerned for his eastern constituency and the preservation of the American System, however. Not only would the eastern states share in the annual dividends of the trust; they would be the principal beneficiaries of the indirect payoff through the protective tariff, which would be kept up by draining the treasury of income from the public lands. "It is a tariff bill; it is an ultra tariff

measure . . . ," Benton fumed. "Tariff is stamped upon its face, tariff is emblazoned upon its borders, tariff is proclaimed in all its features."[53] The
doughty Missourian even complained of the impropriety of the Committee
on Manufactures originating such a bill. The Senate tabled the bill and referred the subject to the Public Lands Committee. It subsequently reported
a measure lowering the minimum price (from $1.25 to $1.00 an acre) and
adopting the graduation principle. The issue was thus clearly drawn. Near
the end of the session the Senate passed Clay's bill, but the pressure of other
business caused its postponement in the House.*

Part of this other business was the bill to renew the charter of the Bank of
the United States. Jackson had pressed the subject on Congress from the
first year of the administration. Without revealing the depth of his hostility to
the Bank, he gradually made known his determination either to convert the
institution into a branch of the treasury or to overthrow it. But the Bank was
popular with Congress. Under Nicholas Biddle's brilliant leadership it had
met its fiscal obligations to the government, provided the country with a
sound and uniform currency, facilitated transactions in domestic and foreign
exchange, and regulated the supply of credit so as to stimulate economic
growth without inflationary excess. In 1830 investigating committees in both
houses of Congress gave the Bank a clean bill of health. Neither Biddle nor
any of the Bank's friends wished to force the issue of recharter before the
presidential election. Clay, although he had no particular influence with
Biddle, who had twice cast his presidential ballot for Jackson and hoped to do
so again, pointedly advised him to delay the recharter petition until after the
election. Clay believed a plan had been hatched by Van Buren, Ritchie, and
their circle to make destruction of the Bank the big issue in the election, and
that this explained Jackson's demand for action. The Bank would only play
into their hands by applying now, for if the question was blended into the
election, becoming mixed up with Jackson's popularity, and he prevailed, it
would be impossible for him to sign a recharter bill; on the other hand, if he
was reelected free of any mandate on the Bank, he would be disposed to conciliation.[55] Clay underestimated the fervent ideological basis of Jackson's opposition to the Bank; he erred, too, in supposing that Van Buren and his
friends led the anti-Bank attack. Even so, it was good advice, and Biddle
took it. He knew he had the votes in Congress for recharter. He still hoped

---

*In the Senate debate, Clay traced the raid on the public lands to Benton's Graduation Bill,
which would give away the "refuse lands"; and in a memorable satirical flourish compared that to
the claim of Governor Edwards of Illinois to all the lands within the state's limits. "The senator
from Missouri was chanting most sweetly to the tune, 'refuse lands,' 'refuse lands,' 'refuse
lands,' on the Missouri side of the Mississippi, and the soft strains of his music, having caught
the ear of his excellency, on the Illinois side, he joined in chorus, and struck an octave higher.
The senator from Missouri wished only to pick up some crumbs which fell from Uncle Sam's table, but the governor resolved to grasp the whole loaf. The senator modestly claimed only an
old, smoked, rejected joint; but the stomach of his excellency yearned after the whole hog! The
governor peeped over the Mississippi into Missouri, and saw the senator leisurely roaming in
some rich pastures, on bits of refuse lands. He returned to Illinois, and, springing into the grand
prairie, determined to claim and occupy it, in all its boundless extent."[54]

to change Jackson's opinion; and to that end he was agreeable to certain amendments. The problem lay, Biddle thought, with demagogic politicians who played upon popular prejudices against the Bank, arousing old fears of monopoly, corruption, and privilege, in order to subvert it to their own designs. The pattern was set at the Portsmouth branch soon after Jackson became president. The New Hampshire party bosses, Isaac Hill and Levi Woodbury, with the concurrence of Treasury Secretary Ingham, charged that the branch catered to rich merchants and unfairly restrained credit to farmers. They sought the removal of the director, Jeremiah Mason, Webster's old friend. Biddle himself went to Portsmouth to investigate. He sustained Mason and the other officers, and labeled the attack on them "a paltry intrigue got up by a combination of small bankrupts and smaller demagogues."[56] This did not sit well with Jackson. Biddle believed, of course, he had kept the B.U.S. out of politics; to do so, he said, was "the first law of its existence."[57] But the Jacksonians, whether because they wanted to control it or to destroy it, were making political abstinence more and more difficult for the Bank.

So were the National Republicans. At the opening of the new Congress Clay reversed himself and advocated recharter before the election. He had become convinced, he said, that President Jackson would not now veto a recharter bill but would do so if reelected. Pro-Bank Jacksonians with whom Clay discussed legislative strategy demurred, saying that a recharter bill in 1832 would be considered an electioneering attack on the president, inevitably provoking a veto. Biddle sent his personal emissary to the capital. He reported that Webster, the Bank's counsel, was decidedly for action. Jackson would bluster but finally yield to the will of Congress. McDuffie, who would guide the bill through the House, also called for action.[58] Reaching the decision to go ahead early in the new year, Biddle was motivated solely by what he deemed best for the institution over which he ruled like a petty prince. Neither he nor Clay, nor Webster, nor anyone else thought that the outcome of the recharter fight would have much bearing on the presidential election. It was only a question of whether Jackson would more likely approve of recharter before or after his reelection.[59]

As a candidate Clay had nothing to gain from recharter. He may have hoped for divine intervention in his favor following a Jacksonian veto. More likely, however, he hoped the Bank issue would spread dissension among the Jacksonians and further cooperation between opposition elements, for instance protectionists and Nullifiers. Outside of Pennsylvania, more B.U.S. stock was held in South Carolina than in any other state. McDuffie was only the most prominent Palmetto State advocate of the Bank. Calhoun, chief architect of the Bank in 1816, took refuge in the vast silence of the vice presidency, but he was believed to be friendly.[60] In March, another of Biddle's emissaries suggested to the secretary of state, Edward Livingston, a compromise on the two great issues of Bank and tariff. The North would yield on protection in exchange for southern votes on recharter. Livingston liked the proposition. He was pro-Bank, like every other member of the cabinet except Attorney General Roger B. Taney. The trouble was, as Biddle averred, that "the Kitchen"—the so-called "Kitchen Cabinet" made up of western agrarians such as Kendall and Blair—had come to predominate over "the Parlor." Livingston and McLane could do nothing. The emissary, Charles Jared Ingersoll, tried to get the Pennsylvania senators, George M. Dallas and William Wilkins, both Jacksonians, both pro-Bank and pro-tariff, to take up the compromise; but they declined. Ingersoll never approached Clay or Calhoun. If he had the proposition would surely have been rejected. No such compromise ever occurred to either of them. Nor was either in any mood to compromise in 1832.[61]

The two measures passed through Congress together, offering the opportunity for trade and bargain to anyone brave enough to seize it; indeed, in the House, both measures were for several months in the control of the same man, the stern and forbidding McDuffie. He was obsessed with the tariff. The ultraist bill he drove through the Ways and Means Committee would slash duties on the principal protected articles to 12.5 percent *ad valorem* in two years and admit everything else duty free. McDuffie demanded precedence for tariff legislation lest votes be lost during the debate on recharter of the Bank; and whether by accident or design he acquiesced in the appointment of a special committee to investigate the Bank once again. During the delay occasioned by the investigation, the administration stepped up its barrage against the Bank. The committee report, when it finally came, was hostile. Although it generated more heat than light, the report so aggravated feelings against the Bank that it ended all prospect of agreement on an amended charter.[62] In May Dallas presented the recharter bill to the Senate. Webster made one of the main speeches in its behalf.[63] He also helped defeat a crippling amendment, which he considered unconstitutional, that would permit the states to exclude or tax a branch of the B.U.S. Clay took no part in the debate. This did not keep Jacksonian senators from charging that the Bank had been made an engine of party; indeed the charge was made out of Clay's own mouth, from his indictment of the first bank as an engine of Federalism in 1811. The bill passed the Senate, 28–10, in mid-June. A cholera epidemic had broken out in New York. Fearing the session would end in panic, without Bank, tariff, or other legislation, Clay appealed to his friends in the House to move the recharter bill immediately to the floor, bypassing normal committee procedures. This was done. Told that even if the bill passed the House (as it did, 107–86, on July 3) Jackson would veto it, Clay snapped, "Should Jackson veto it, I will veto him!"[64]

The critical issue, involving the fate of the Union as well as of parties, was still the tariff. Clay's suspended measure in the Senate was unacceptable to southern leaders who said it offered but a shallow "pretense at settlement." In June the House killed McDuffie's ultraist bill in the face of a solemn warning that, unless Congress provided relief, South Carolina would nullify the tariff within five months of adjournment.[65] Meanwhile, the administration bestirred itself. McLane, recovered from a long and violent attack of gout, submitted a plan of tariff reform that was seen to occupy "middle ground." "It is a southern judicious tariff," Clay remarked.[66] It offered enough concessions to rally the Carolina Unionists and hold the loyalty of other planting states, thereby isolating the Nullifiers. By its moderation the plan also sought to reassure northern manufacturing interests. Indeed, the bill with its accompanying report was written as if Clay had been looking over McLane's shoulder. It made no across-the-board reduction of duties. It retained the odious minimum on cheap cotton textiles. Most protected articles suffered only slight reductions, if any. The main cuts were on non-protected articles: tea, coffee, tropical produce generally, tin, flax, dyes, and so on. The main reform occurred on wool and woolens, the most perplexing problem of the system, which had given rise to the Tariff of Abominations. Duties were slashed and the minimum abolished. McLane's plan became the basis of the bill that Adams reported from the Committee on Manufactures near the end of May.

The bill satisfied neither protectionists nor free traders. The fabled passage between Scylla and Charybdis was not more treacherous for the ancient navigator than the task of negotiating a passage between these interests. The Charleston *Mercury* denounced the bill as a scheme not to relieve the South, though that was pretended, but to save northern manufacturers in the face of the surplus.[67] If the measure were passed, McDuffie warned, "the door of hope will be forever closed upon the South." "Friends of the American System" held protest meetings in northern cities. One of these, in Massachusetts, declared, as if to back up Clay's warning, that secession from the Union was "preferable to the sacrifice of the principle of the protective system." The bill was seen as ruinous to woolen manufacturers, in which large investments had only recently been made. Mills were already closing, it was said. "Not one *manufacturer* believes we can live under it," Rufus Choate remarked, summing up the New England reaction to the bill.[68] Nevertheless, the House passed the McLane-Adams measure by a two-to-one margin (132–65) at the end of June, a victory of the broad middle over the extremes. The nay votes were almost equally divided between North and South, protectionists and free traders, National and Nullifiers. Significantly, the three South Carolina Unionists voted for the bill.[69]

Clay tried to regain control of the legislation in the Senate. Many protectionist amendments were debated in the torrid July heat of the capital, and many were adopted. Although the effort to restore the woolens minimum was defeated, and although Clay failed to get the protection he wanted for Kentucky's cotton-bagging, he was satisfied with the amended bill. It had become *his* bill, settled basically on the principles he had announced six months earlier. Hayne concurred, sadly, in this judgment. "It is neither more nor less than the resolution of the gentleman from Kentucky reduced to the form of law," he said.[70] The Senate adopted the amended bill 32–16. But then in the conference committee the amendments were yielded one by one to the utter disgust of Clay, Webster, and their friends. They blamed Wilkins, the head of the Senate conferees, for this betrayal. He was a protectionist, especially where Pennsylvania iron was concerned, but he was also a Jacksonian Democrat who harbored vice presidential ambitions; and it was to this that his shameful appeal to the South and betrayal of the Senate were attributed. "Clay was furious . . . ," Dallas wrote, "his defeat and mortification were signal and manifest."[71] Exhausted, the Senate voted to recede from its amendments. Even so, every protectionist beginning with Clay and Webster voted for the final bill. Wherever the honors, such as they were, for the tariff of 1832 properly lay, with McLane, or Adams, or the Pennsylvanians—and all registered claims—Clay arrogated them for himself. Again furnishing proof of his extraordinary boldness of address, he boasted to have smashed nullification and saved the American System.[72] It was primarily on this claim that he rested his faint hopes in the presidential election.

In the final throes of tariff legislation, Congress had also to deal with Jackson's veto of the recharter bill. The general's response when cornered was to attack. The veto came as no surprise, but the message announcing it was unprecedented for its vehemence. "It has all the fury of a chained panther biting the bars of his cage," Biddle fumed.[73] Never before had a president adopted such an imperious tone toward Congress. Its opinion, or the judgment of the Supreme Court on the constitutionality of the B.U.S., carried no authority with him. "Each public officer who takes an oath to support the Constitution swears that he will support it as he understands it, and not as it is understood by others," Jackson declared. "The opinion of the judges has no more authority over Congress than the opinion of Congress has over the judges, and on that point the President is independent of both." Jackson assailed the Bank as a monopolistic and corrupt money power which served "to make the rich richer and the potent more powerful," all at the expense of "the humble members of society." He assailed as well the fundamental premises—constitutional, political, economic—of National Republican policy from its formulation in the Madisonian Platform, through Clay's American System and the Adams administration. The ideal evoked in its place was that of a Jeffersonian arcadia where banking and related mysteries of modernity were unknown, where simple values and hard money reigned, where enterprise was free and equal to all, where government was jealously guarded and its powers widely diffused. Although drafted by Amos Kendall, with an assist from Taney, the message was, as his friend Blair said, "but a perfect transcription of the President's own mind."[74] It adroitly combined the democratic appeals of western agrarianism with the southern prejudices of state rights. "You will be astounded by the contents of the message," Dallas wrote after the clerk completed its reading in the Senate. "It irreparably throws the Government into the arms of the South." How Pennsylvania Democracy could absorb it, along with the blows to protection, to internal improvements, and other favorite measures, he did not know.[75]

The next day, July 11, Webster delivered a systematic rebuttal of the veto message. The termination of the B.U.S., he predicted, would plunge the country into economic depression. The president's reasoning on matters of currency, credit, banking, and exchange was "such miserable stuff" the senator was embarrassed to notice it.[76] His reasoning on the Constitution, rejecting the result of forty years' experience and setting his own independent judgment above that of Congress and the Court, presaged a government of men, not of laws. "If the opinions of the President be maintained," Webster roundly declared, "there is an end of all law and all judicial authority. Statutes are but recommendations, judgments no more than opinions. . . . If conceded to him, it makes him at once what Louis the Fourteenth proclaimed himself to be when he said, 'I am the State.'" Webster assailed the demagoguery of the message. It inflamed the poor against the rich, appealed to sectional prejudices, conjured up monsters to frighten the people, and raised the cry "liberty in danger" to divert attention from an act of despotism. "Mr. President," he gravely concluded, "we have arrived at a new epoch." Speaking the next day, Clay seconded these views. He branded the president's constitutional doctrine "universal nullification," nothing less than the doctrine of South Carolina extended to the entire nation.[77] Actually, the president had nullified nothing but the will of Congress. The attempt to override the veto failed, of course.

The issue of the B. U. S. was thoroughly politicized by the veto. This was part of Jackson's intention. From an object of hatred for him, the Bank was made into a common object of hatred for the diverse elements of his party. Justice McLean recalled Lord Bolingbroke's cynical remark about Walpole's parliament: "You know the nature of that assembly. They grow like hounds fond of the man that shows them game, and by whose hallos they are used to be fed."[78] Biddle, if he had not taken sides before, did so blatantly now, throwing money and influence behind Clay, "the instrument of deliverance" of Bank and country.[79] At Biddle's urging Webster "wrote off" his speech on the veto; it was subsequently printed and widely circulated. The Massachusetts senator's credibility as an advocate of the Bank was damaged by revelations in Blair's *Globe* that portrayed him as Biddle's mercenary. He had, it was reported, hurried to Philadelphia upon the adjournment of Congress and received from the B. U. S. an easy loan of $10-$15,000 for his services.[80] The more serious question, however, was whether Webster's speech, for all its persuasive reasoning, offered an effective answer to Jackson's flaming rhetoric. Thurlow Weed, the Anti-Masonic editor of the Albany *Journal,* refused even to print the speech; when questioned about it he answered that two or three demagogical sentences of the veto message were worth ten votes for every one secured by Webster's speech.[81] This was shrewd, yet it made no impression on Webster, Clay, and the National Republican leadership.

The veto lifted Clay's hopes. He appreciated Jackson's personal popularity but imagined that principles and issues—the American System issues so long identified with his name—could carry the election. So did a young politician in Illinois, Abraham Lincoln, who delivered his first campaign speech for Clay. "My politics are short and sweet, like an old woman's dance," he said. "I am in favor of a national bank. I am in favor of the internal improvements system and a high protective tariff."[82] Clay placed false hopes, as it turned out, in the efforts of his followers in the East to negotiate a deal with the Anti-Masons, whereby he would receive their electoral votes, and in the South to bridge the gulf with Calhoun and his friends. The Anti-Masons adhered to Wirt; Calhoun, and South Carolina, remained neutral. Although Duff Green held a finger to his nose and published a campaign newspaper for Clay, his pleas to join the anti-Jackson coalition went unheeded by Calhoun, who continued to insist that nullification was a greater issue than Jackson or Clay.[83] Some of Clay's eastern friends, already tasting defeat, would have welcomed his withdrawal. One of them, Edward Everett, remarked in October that people had ceased talking about the presidential election in Massachusetts. And Webster, speaking at the National Republican state convention in Worcester, arraigned the administration for two and a half hours without ever mentioning the name of Henry Clay.[84]

Clay did not give up easily, but after the August canvass in Kentucky, when the Jacksonians won the governorship, he knew the campaign was lost. The president had the termerity to visit Lexington in October. There was the usual barbecue at Fowler's Garden and a great torchlight parade into town where, it was said, the president slept in a hotel because no respectable home was open to him. The next morning he was escorted out of town on the Richmond Road passing right in front of Ashland. There, on Clay's manicured acres, no living thing stirred except one of his prize jackasses, and it sent up a tremendous bray as Jackson passed.[85] That was the only laugh Clay had on Jackson that fall. He won but five states (Kentucky, Massachusetts, Rhode Island, Connecticut, Delaware) and a piece of another (Maryland) in the election. The rest, omitting Vermont, which voted for Wirt, and South Carolina, which did not vote at all, went to Jackson. It was an even more stunning defeat than Adams's four years earlier. A "new epoch" had arrived indeed.

4. The Compromise of 1833

Day after day in the spring, as he presided over the Senate and listened to the tariff debate, John C. Calhoun felt mounting frustration. The two sides, instead of converging, as they ought to do in the deliberative process, were driven farther and farther apart. "It is, in truth, hard to find a middle position," he observed philosophically, "where the principle of protection is asserted to be essential on one side, and fatal on the other. It involves not the question of concession, but surrender, on one side or the other."[1] Even before the Senate passed the amended tariff bill, Calhoun set out for South Carolina. "The question is no longer one of free trade, but of liberty and despotism," he wrote to a compatriot at home. "The hope of the country now rests on our gallant little state. Let every Carolinian do his duty."[2] The message sounded like a communiqué—and a declaration of war.

The tariff of 1832 became the firebrand of agitation for the South Carolina Nullifiers. After this defeat, they told the people, it was hopeless for the state to look to the federal government for justice. The declared aim of the Nullifiers, who sported the blue-and-orange cockade of the State Rights and Free Trade party, was to annul and arrest the tariff within the state's borders, thence to force a constitutional revolution in the Union along the lines of Calhoun's theory. The South Carolina Unionists, along with many political observers throughout the country, were skeptical of these professions, however. Some believed the real object of the agitation was secession and the birth of a southern confederacy. Most thought that nullification was political bluff, part of an elaborate strategy of confrontation to extort concessions from the government and gratify the craven ambitions of Calhoun and his friends, but nothing else. The Unionists defended the new tariff as a step in the right direction, though short of a final settlement. They, too, generally were free traders, and supposed other steps would follow once the protectionist pressures of the presidential contest between Jackson and Clay were lifted. The election would also diminish the motive of Calhoun and his clique to embarrass the administration.[3] In the Unionist view the rhetoric *ad terrorem* of the South Carolina agitation had a conventional political goal, not the revolutionary one conjured up in Calhoun's theory, and certainly not the disunionist one of a few Hotspurs. Unionist complacency stemmed, in part, from inability to credit nullification as a constitutional theory. Professing to save the Union, it would destroy it. Professing to secure peace and concord, by restoring the niggardly government of the Constitution, it would provoke civil war. Yet the establishment of a fanatical constitutional theory, premised on the tyranny of a northern majority, had eclipsed the importance of the original grievance for many Nullifiers, with potentially dangerous consequences for state and nation.

In August, in another public letter to Governor Hamilton, Calhoun undertook to refute objections to the theory and explain its practical workings in some detail. Insisting that nullification was embedded in the Constitution itself, he held that it was the right and duty of a sovereign state to annul an unconstitutional act of the general government. One of two courses must follow. First, the government would acquiesce and yield the disputed power. That government, being only an "agent," had no authority to coerce one of the "principals" to the contract that established it. Second, more or less in accordance with Article V, a convention of the states would be called; if three-fourths of them granted the disputed power by constitutional amendment the nullifying state would acquiesce or, in the last extremity, secede from the Union. But the aim was to prevent secession. The process of nullification would in fact, Calhoun argued, preserve the Union by giving ascendancy to the constitution-making authority over the law-making authority. The latter operated on the rule of an "absolute majority" which, left to itself, must end in consolidation and tyranny; the former operated on the rule of a "concurring majority," in which the states were the active elements and amendment the means of preserving the Constitution.[4] The theory was ingenious, as Unionists acknowledged, and speciously laid in the groundwork of the Virginia and Kentucky Resolutions; but it was at war with reason, republicanism, and the Constitution. By what right, they asked, could one state stop the wheels of government and demand a convention of all the states? Why, in convention, should one-quarter of the states be allowed to dictate to three-quarters? Why, if each state is sovereign, should it submit to the decision of a convention? The result of the whole, as Webster observed, was "that though it requires three-fourths of the states to insert any thing in the Constitution, yet any one can strike any thing out of it." The theory stood exposed, said the Charleston *Courier,* "in all the deformity of anarchy and misrule."[5] Although trumpeted as a peaceful and constitutional remedy, nullification was a fraud against the people of South Carolina.

Whether it was or not would largely depend on President Jackson. He was a violent man, as Calhoun well knew. A year before, writing to a Fourth of July Unionist rally in Charleston, Jackson had vowed to enforce the law at all hazards. Now he seemed pleased with the new tariff, considering it a true compromise and the basis of a permanent settlement. His signature on that bill together with his veto of the Bank bill had, he said, broken the dangerous coalition of Clay, Webster, and Calhoun; and if the third member of the triumvirate persisted in nullification after the concessions of the new tariff, even his own people would see it for what it was, a scheme of "disappointed ambition." The South Carolina movement was incomprehensible to Jackson on any terms other than personal malice, ambition, and conspiratorial design—"unprincipled men who would rather rule in hell than be subordinate in heaven"—and this ensured a violent response.[6] The Nullifiers were apprehensive, as suggested by a disquieting Fourth of July toast: "Andrew Jackson: On the soil of South Carolina he received an humble birthplace. May he not find in it a traitor's grave!"[7]

Other signs pointed to a different outcome. During four years the president had steadily retreated from the moderately nationalist platform on which he began. In the spring he backed Georgia's meditated resistance to the decision of the Supreme Court in the case of *Worcester* v. *Georgia.* Even if he never uttered the provocative line later attributed to him—"Well, John Marshall has made his decision: now let him enforce it!"—Jackson said other things in the same spirit.[8] The case concerned Georgia's sovereign claim, which the court rejected, to jurisdiction over the Cherokee territory within the state's limits. The claim was a corollary of Jackson's policy of Indian removal, so his support of Georgia was hardly surprising and did not automatically implicate him in a radical state rights position. Still it encouraged the Nullifiers and embarrassed their opponents. If Jackson acquiesced in Georgia, on what basis could he enforce the laws of the United States in South Carolina? Some Unionists were alarmed. "The *old man,*" one observed, "seems to be more than half a Nullifier himself."[9]

Such was the main theme of Webster's address to the National Republican convention in Massachusetts. Appearing in the dual role of party leader and Defender of the Constitution, he declared that the Constitution was in "imminent peril" from President Jackson. Alluding to the problems in Georgia and South Carolina, he said the administration had renounced most of the Constitution's leading powers, matured over forty years. And so the national bank had been put on the road to extinction, national planning and support of internal improvements had withered, even the protective tariff faced an uncertain future. In vetoing the recharter bill Jackson had denounced not only the B.U.S. but all national legislation that, in his words, "arrayed section against section, interest against interest, and man against man, in a fearful commotion which threatens the foundations of our Union." Here, in false fears mixed with false principles, said Webster, was the whole creed. Like Calhoun's, it would preserve the Union by weakening the government. Jackson had also set himself up as co-equal with the Supreme Court in the interpretation of the Constitution. Webster was amazed by the assertion at a critical time of this "wild and disorganizing" doctrine. "Are we not threatened with dissolution of the Union?" he pleaded. "Are we not told that the laws of the government shall be openly and directly resisted? . . . Mr. President, I have very little regard for the law, or the logic of nullification. But there is not an individual in its ranks, capable of putting two ideas together, who, if you will grant him the principles of the veto message, can not defend all that nullification ever threatened." There was unfortunately, he concluded, no evidence that Jackson opposed nullification. And if he should oppose it in the event, he lacked the principles to oppose it successfully.[10]

In the fall South Carolina advanced with measured strides toward nullification. The legislative election, fiercely contested by Nullifiers and Unionists, amounted to a referendum on the question. The Nullifiers won an impressive victory; Governor Hamilton called the new legislature into session; the legislature, on the necessary two-thirds vote, quickly authorized election of a convention, the embodiment of the state's sovereignty. After a quiet two-week campaign, in which the Unionists conceded the outcome, the elected delegates gathered at Columbia. On November 24 they enacted an ordinance nullifying the tariff acts of 1828 and 1832. Its effective date, when the collection of duties would be prohibited, was put off until February. Resistance, meanwhile, would be voluntary and along lawful avenues. This was a victory for prudence, suggesting that South Carolina had not yet slammed the door on a political solution at the national level. The ordinance further decreed that any effort by the general government to coerce the state would be just cause for secession. A separate resolution called for a convention of all the states to decide the constitutional question of protection. The legislature promptly reconvened to enact the laws necessary to implement the ordinance: to raise an army, purchase arms, impose an oath of allegiance to the state, and so on.[11] The legislators also elected a new governor, Robert Hayne, and as his successor in the United States Senate, John C. Calhoun, who resigned from the office of vice president.

In this enveloping crisis Congress came into session. The president's annual message, following on the heels of his victory at the polls, was eagerly awaited. In an apparent bow to the South, Jackson called for further reduction of the tariff to the revenue standard. The advantages of protectionism, as in the encouragement of manufactures, were offset by the attendant evils of jealousy, discontentment, and disunionism. He thought its benefits should be limited ultimately to articles of military necessity. The report of the secretary of treasury, echoing these views, recommended lopping off an additional

$6 million of revenue, the estimated amount of the annual surplus that would remain under the tariff of 1832. Nullification was only one factor in this recommendation. Setting forth the goal of a government reduced to "that simple machine which the Constitution created," Jackson embraced the tariff in a general plan of denationalization, which included government divestiture of Bank stock, abandonment of internal improvements, and a new policy for rapid disposal of public lands, ending in their surrender to the states.[12] These negative clauses of the Jacksonian creed, more than the remarkable complacency of the message before the challenge of South Carolina, disturbed the National Republicans. Congressman Adams thought it the most deadly blow ever struck against the Union: "It goes to dissolve the Union into its original elements, and is in substance a complete surrender to the Nullifiers of South Carolina."[13] Could Webster have been right? Many thought so. A Washington correspondent summed up the gloomy response of the opposition press: "All—all is gone if the President's views are carried into effect. The Bank is gone! The American System is gone! Internal Improvements are gone! The public lands are gone! All is gone which the General Government was instituted to create and preserve.' "[14]

The appearance only six days later of the president's Proclamation to the People of South Carolina surprised nearly everyone. It was boldly nationalistic—a complete turnabout from the message. Jackson never explained the change, or acknowledged its existence. In theory, of course, there was no contradiction between belief in the supremacy and indivisibility of the Union and belief in a general government of severely limited powers. That the Union could be destroyed by consolidation and preserved by adherence to state rights and strict construction of the Constitution was an old republican philosophy, apparently as congenial to Jackson as to Calhoun. Practically, he had wanted to make a show of forbearance and conciliation so as to hold the loyalty of South Carolina's sister states; and when none rushed to her aid he knew that the South—the whole country—was ready for the rigors of the Proclamation. Scorning the claims of nullification, Jackson espoused a theory of the Constitution and Union associated with nationalists such as Webster and Marshall. The people of the United States, although acting through conventions, had created a national union, a government of "one people," to which they had committed sovereign powers heretofore belonging to the state governments; and no state could violate this union or secede from it without dissolving the whole. It was, in short, a binding compact, not a terminable one. Concluding with a paternalistic plea to his native state, Jackson sought to separate the people from their leaders who were rushing the state to certain ruin. "Disunion by armed force is treason," he warned. Force would be met by force. The laws of the United States would be executed. The Union would be preserved.[15]

The doctrines of the Proclamation caused uneasiness among Jackson's closest advisers, including Martin Van Buren, the vice president–elect, who had labored for years to restore the Jeffersonian alliance of "southern planters and plain republicans of the North." It mandated a state rights platform for the

Democratic party. But every "National" from Maine to Louisiana endorsed the Proclamation. Webster, at a Boston "union meeting," hailed it as a vindication of his own preaching and pledged unqualified support of the president. Jackson was delighted with the senator's speech. But the prospect of an old Federalist like Webster—a Hartford Convention "nullifying" Federalist at that—becoming Jackson's political bedfellow under cover of nullification was exceedingly mortifying to Van Buren and his friends.[16]

The administration moved quickly to resolve the crisis through tariff reform. The olive branch, it was hoped, would obviate the sword. McLane collaborated with the new chairman of the House Ways and Means Committee, Gulian C. Verplanck, to produce an acceptable bill. A fourth-term congressman from New York, one of Van Buren's Bucktails, Verplanck was a committed free trader who succeeded naturally to the chairmanship when McDuffie turned up absent. The bill he reported at the end of December would get rid of the surplus and return the tariff to the general level of 1816 when the present system began. Although backed by the administration, the Verplanck Bill was everywhere considered Van Buren's, rather than Jackson's, bid to settle the crisis. "Old Hickory don't want the Bill to pass," wrote a New York congressman.[17] But for its auspices the measure might have been acceptable to the Nullifiers. The importance of this issue was magnified when South Carolina chose Calhoun to manage its cause in Washington. Personal enmity would make it all but impossible for him to grasp an olive branch held out by Van Buren. Of course, friends of the American System in the northern states opposed the Verplanck Bill. They were stunned by its broad sweep as well as by the swiftness of its tariff cuts. Protection would be withdrawn in just two years, subjecting many businesses to certain ruin. The rejection of gradualism, a feature of some earlier plans to end the system, reflected the administration's anxiety to get rid of the surplus. But whether their ruin was sudden or gradual, the interests locked into the American System felt little inclination to sacrifice themselves to appease South Carolina.[18]

In view of these obstacles to the administration's plan, the opportunity to mediate the crisis reverted to Henry Clay. He had slammed the door on the South only months before. Would he a second time? Rumors that he was readying his own plan of reform appeared in the press before the Verplanck Bill was reported. In a speech on the Virginia hustings, John Randolph, no friend of Clay's, interrupted a tirade against the Proclamation, raised a finger, and emphatically declared, "There is one man, and one man only who can save the Union—that man is Henry Clay."[19] But Clay was silent. His crushing defeat at the polls had left him despondent. "Whether we shall ever see light, and law and liberty again, is very questionable," he wrote glumly.[20] Toward the end of the campaign he had been deserted by politicians who owed their careers to the American System; in defeat he found no consolation, for himself, his party, or his country. For several weeks he trifled with thoughts of retirement, but on December 1 he was again on the road to Washington, this time with hopes of reviving his political fortunes.

What direction that revival might take was still obscure to him. He was a shrewd politician, however, and it must have occurred to him that the devious southerly course he had shunned in the presidential campaign remained open, indeed seductively open in the aftermath of Jackson's Proclamation. Except for Kentucky, Clay had lost every state south and west of the Potomac. At the same time he had lost two leading protectionist states in the North, Pennsylvania and New Jersey. Perhaps he could devise a strategy of conciliation that would win political favor in the South without further eroding his base of support in the North. He agreed with the National Republicans in condemning Jackson's "double face" game at the opening of Congress. "One short week produced the message and the proclamation—the former *ultra* on the side of state-rights—the latter *ultra* on the side of nationalism." But unlike doctrinaire nationalists, Webster for instance, Clay could also say that for all the good the Proclamation intended it was "entirely too ultra" for him. He left his calling card in the Senate, then hurried off to Philadelphia for an extended visit, praying "this unfortunate affair" between the president and "his brother nullifiers" might be settled without him.[21]

Just what happened in Philadelphia to revive Clay's optimism and good humor is not entirely clear. At this time his political situation was hardly enviable. With the Verplanck Bill the Jacksonians forced him into a corner where he must either acquiesce in the destruction of the American System or incur the responsibility for disunion. How could he defeat nullification and at the same time save the system? Only by resolving a contradiction greater than that presented in Jackson's two papers. How could he yield on the tariff after the stand he had taken in the previous session? Only, it seemed, at the risk of becoming a political chameleon. And how could he deny the administration its meditated triumph, transferring the accolades of "Savior of the Union" to himself? Only at the risk of dealing with Calhoun and going into the market for southern votes. Without at once seeing his way through these difficulties, Clay decided to challenge the administration at its own game. Talks with political friends in Philadelphia convinced him that Jackson was fundamentally opposed to the tariff system, and once this hump of nullification was overcome, would seek to destroy it. His strength would be greater in the succeeding Congress, elected under his banner, than in the retiring one. The danger from the other side, from South Carolina, which he had earlier discounted, Clay now took seriously. The American System could be saved, he realized, only by surrendering it in some part; and such a negotiated surrender might save the Union as well.

Some such course of reflection during the leisure of the visit to his rich and ailing brother-in-law, James Brown, a former Louisiana senator and minister to France, now retired in Philadelphia, led Clay to form a compromise plan. Brown was a conciliatory influence; so was Josiah Johnston, his successor in the Senate and manager of Clay's recent campaign, who was also in Philadelphia. It would be mistaken to say that Louisiana sugar interests initiated the compromise; but it was from Brown, Johnston, and their friends—sugar planters and their spokesmen—that Clay learned to what lengths some protectionists would go to save the Union.[22] The true initiators, by his own account, were a committee of local manufacturers who called on him and asked anxiously what could be done to save them from ruin. In response, Clay worked up a plan to give the tariff of 1832 a long lease of seven years, to March 3, 1840, after which date only equal *ad valorem* duties could be levied, " 'solely for the purpose and with the intent of providing such revenue as may be necessary to an economical expenditure of Government without regard to the protection or encouragement of any branch of domestic industry whatever.' "[23] Whether or not this was Clay's exact language—a matter later in dispute—the project plainly offered the surrender of protection after seven years of stability and security. The formula traded *time*, of first importance to manufacturers, for *principle*, of first importance to the South. While the Verplanck Bill would preserve the principle but annihilate the manufacturers, Clay's plan presumably would save the manufacturers but surrender the principle. When he reported it to the local committee, they seemed well satisfied, buoying his hopes for a workable compromise.[24]

The plan met with a different reception in Washington, whither Clay returned at the beginning of the new year. He unfolded it at once to leading protectionists in the House who were girding for battle against the Verplanck Bill. "We had repeated interviews," Nathan Appleton later recalled. "The result was, *from first to last we refused to become parties to the measure*."[25] Appleton, the Boston representative, was himself a manufacturer and a recognized spokesman for the New England textile industry. Webster, hearing of the plan upon his arrival in the capital, was aghast. It was a flat proposition to abandon protection, in his opinion. "From that day," it was later said, "Daniel Webster set up for himself." He determined no longer to submit blindly to Clay's leadership. He became a favorite at the White House, where his zeal for the Proclamation was appreciated and where, some observers suspected, he aimed to displace Van Buren in the president's political affections.[26] Clay insisted that his plan abandoned protection only in principle, not in fact. It was secured immediately; and nothing could bind Congress seven years hence. The argument might have been expected to appeal to supposedly pragmatic politicians, but, though some manufacturers concurred, Clay found little support in Congress. So he shelved the compromise plan with renewed threats to let the opposing parties "fight it out" for themselves, and fell back into gloomy forebodings. "As to politics," he wrote to Brooke, "we have no past or future. After forty-four years of existence under the present Constitution, what single principle is fixed? The bank? No. Internal Improvements? No. The tariff? No. Who is to interpret the Constitution? We are as much afloat at sea as the day when the Constitution went into operation. There is nothing certain but that the will of Andrew Jackson is to govern, and that will fluctuates with the change of every plan which gives expression to it."[27] Meanwhile, the House began debate on the Verplanck Bill. Even if it passed that body, nobody supposed it could prevail in the Senate.

This uncertainty raised fears of outright conflict between the United States and South Carolina, between Jackson and Calhoun and all they represented. In the president's eyes Calhoun had added treason to his other crimes. Throughout the country he became the personification of nullification and disunion. (Yankee farmers, it was reported, turned the senator's somber effigy into scarecrows called "Calhouns.")[28] During the past year nullification had become a personal obsession, "an idée fixe," in the phrase of a Charleston Unionist who supposed it would snuff out an unrivaled capacity for the management of men and affairs. At every stop on the journey northward in December Calhoun had lectured to all who would listen. At Raleigh, where North Carolina legislation was in session, he talked all afternoon and evening—no matter that it was Sunday—to a changing crowd in a hotel parlor. With cavernous eyes blazing under a furrowed brow and lips quivering with scarcely suppressed emotion, he expounded tirelessly on the wonders of nullification. At Richmond he abruptly announced that South Carolina would pay no heed to Virginia's dramatic bid to mediate the dispute. The next day, as he attended the assembly and talked to the delegates, he was more cordial.[29] Arriving in Washington, he felt encouraged by the prospect. For the present, the scheme of coercion had been abandoned, though Jackson would gladly revive it if given the opportunity. "Let our people go on," the senator wrote home, "be firm and prudent, give no pretext for force, and I feel confident of a peaceable and glorious triumph for our cause and the State."[30]

The prospect changed January 16. With the concurrence of the Carolina Unionists, Jackson sent a special message to Congress calling an end to the truce. Seeing no evidence that the refractory state would yield before the effective date of the nullification ordinance, February 1, observing the army raised by the Nullifiers, responding, too, to Unionists' fears of their inability to defend the customs houses, Jackson requested additional authority in two areas: first, to facilitate the collection of customs, protect the collectors, and evade state courts—all with a view to avoiding force—and, second, to provide for more effective use of army, navy, and militia should force become necessary. Calhoun was visibly excited as the clerk read the message. When it was finished he rose and in a trembling voice denounced the president for proposing to impose military despotism in South Carolina. In his manner he reminded a Unionist observer of Milton's description of another vice regent and notable nullifier: "Vaunting aloud, but racked by deep despair."[31] To his friends at home Calhoun claimed to be pleased. Jackson's call for force would unite the South and ensure the victory of nullification. Again he urged the state to stand by its arms and give no pretext for coercion. The Nullifiers, as if in response, suspended the ordinance, meanwhile continuing their voluntary resistance; some time later they decided to reconvene the sovereign convention after the adjournment of Congress.[32] Nullification was beginning to look like "a paper tiger." It was losing even the scare value of which Calhoun had made so much. Having driven the state to the precipice, he jarringly applied the brakes. His pleas for peace, his warnings against secession, seemed to leave the state no option should Congress fail to enact meaningful tariff reform. And in January Calhoun had no reason to believe it would.

On the other hand, the president's request for additional powers—the

Force Bill, as it came to be known—would surely become law. Not many congressmen, regardless of constitutional scruples, could contemplate a state's defiance of the United States law with impunity. Throughout the crisis Jackson's position was more complicated than it appeared. He wanted, it appeared, to put down protectionism and nullification at the same time. Yet he was silent about the Verplanck Bill. After the January message, certainly, he wanted nothing to divert attention from his plan to overawe South Carolina with a show of force. The message, in fact, was generally understood to have blasted the hope of tariff reform; some even suspected this was its real purpose.[33] A Virginian who talked to the president early in February said he preferred to postpone the tariff to the new Congress, after he had triumphed over nullification and humbled his adversaries. Webster took a similar view of the president's motives. Wanting the whole credit of victory, he was not inclined to share it with those who would resolve the crisis by removing the ground of complaint.[34] Jackson talked a hard line on South Carolina. The state dared not lift a hand against the United States, he told a Unionist mission in Washington. "Within three weeks, sir, after the first blow is struck, I will place 50,000 troops in your state."[35] And the fury of the "military chieftain," with his threats to the state and its leaders, undoubtedly aided in the final settlement.

There were opposite pressures for prudence and forbearance within the administration, however. Every time he raised his voice the president widened the split in the Democratic party caused by the nationalist doctrines of the Proclamation. The administration organ, the *Globe*, obviously embarrassed by the Proclamation, tried to explain away its supposed errors. They were conveniently blamed on Secretary of State Livingston, who had drafted the state paper. The Force Bill message proceeded from the same errors, of course. When the redoubtable editor of the Richmond *Enquirer* learned of it, he bluntly told Senator William C. Rives it would prostrate both president and party in Virginia. "Even his best friends would condemn it. . . . The Jackson party in this quarter would in all probability be shriveled to pieces."[36] The Virginians, trying to save state rights from the opposite heresies of consolidation and nullification, found support in Albany. The party faithful in the New York legislature rejected resolutions endorsing the principles of the Proclamation and, instead, adopted a substitute growing out of Van Buren's report vindicating state rights—the Jeffersonian "doctrines of '98"—from the nullification heresy. Van Buren opposed the January message; even after the Force Bill was reported, it remained a matter of mortification and regret, if not of opposition, among his followers in Congress. As one of them wrote to him, "We are in the awkward predicament of having the leading measure of the administration ardently supported by the bitterest enemies of the President—ultra federalists and ultra tariffites who would delight to see the North and South arrayed against each other, while it is now probable that the whole South . . . will go against it."[37]

The Force Bill was an administration measure, but to the chagrin of party leaders like Van Buren and Ritchie its foremost champion in the Senate was

Daniel Webster. Nullification proved a fortunate event for the Massachusetts senator. It tested the mettle of his nationalist doctrine. The Proclamation, followed by the special message, opened intriguing possibilities of *rapprochement* with Jackson and party realignment on the patriotic issue of the Union and the Constitution. Checked by Clay's dominance of the opposition, Webster was not averse to changing political affiliations. When the Judiciary Committee was laboring painfully over the message, Jackson sent Livingston to Webster's lodgings, where he was confined by illness, to plead for assistance. The senator roused himself and helped the committee frame an acceptable bill. Reported by its chairman, William Wilkins, it was promptly dubbed "Wilkins' alias Webster's bill." He volunteered to act the part of the administration's Cicero in the ensuing debate. As it went forward, however, he held back, seemingly reluctant to risk himself in the forensic encounter with Calhoun that the entire nation breathlessly awaited. Webster had already won his laurels in defense of the Union; he could scarcely hope to embellish them.[38] Calhoun, too, played a waiting game. Considering the so-called Revenue Collection Bill as, in fact, "a bill to make war on a sovereign state," he introduced a series of resolutions designed to bring it to the test of principle. Calhoun's whole tendency, in keeping with his reputation as a "metaphysical" statesman, was to approach issues theoretically rather than practically and to seek resolution the hard way, on principle, rather than by the balancing of interests and accommodation to circumstances. But the Senate would not indulge him and proceeded to debate the case of the United States versus South Carolina without clearly determining the principle at issue.

On February 15, Calhoun delivered his major speech against the measure. It was, in fact, his first speech in sixteen years, which added to the drama of the occasion. Despite a snowstorm, carriages lined the streets before the Capitol, discharging eager auditors who filled the gallery and the lobbies of the Senate. The fifty-year-old Calhoun was a gaunt figure with a pale face, hollow jaws, deep sunken eyes, and dark hair that stood straight up from his head. Angular in phrase as in figure, he was seldom a pleasing speaker but almost always a penetrating one. On this day he was consumed by his feelings. He paced back and forth like a caged lion, spoke with dizzy rapidity, gradually sank under the weight of his subject, and after exhausting his voice in shrill denunciation finally became inaudible. This was the Calhoun that Clay later caricatured: "tall, careworn, with furrowed brow, haggard, and intensely gazing, . . . muttering to himself in half-uttered tones, 'This is indeed a real crisis!' "[39] The senator defended his consistency on the tariff since the act of 1816, sometimes called the "South Carolina tariff," which he insisted was for revenue only. He said much about duty and principle. The road to the presidency lay clearly before him in 1828, but seeing that it led through the valley of tyranny and corruption he declined to follow it and instead "chose to tread the rugged path of duty." He defended South Carolina's course. The Force Bill exhibited "the impious spectacle of this Government, the creature of the States, making war against the power to which it owes its existence." It was unconstitutional, of course, being founded on the radical

error of the Proclamation that sovereignty resided in an aggregate "one people" rather than in twenty-four separate peoples. It was also tyrannical. "It
has been said that the bill declares war against South Carolina. No," said Calhoun. "It declares a massacre of her citizens! It authorizes the President . . .
to kill without mercy or discrimination!" In this overwrought jeremiad Calhoun seemed actually to invite passage of "the Bloody Bill" in order to purge
the republic of vice and sin. "The country has sunk into avarice and political
corruption, from which nothing can arouse it but some measure . . . of folly
and madness, such as that now under consideration," he philosophized. Coercion, if attempted, would arouse "the dormant spirit of the people" and lead
to a rebirth of liberty.[40]

Webster was on his feet as soon as Calhoun finished. Thinking with most
observers that the senator had failed badly, Webster treated his argument
with contempt. The notes for his reply show careful preparation as well as
fresh research into the making of the Constitution. "I think I *begin* to understand the Constitution," he wrote to a lawyer friend.[41] In this he was further
indebted to Justice Story, the "loose sheets" of whose forthcoming *Commentaries on the Constitution* were circulating in the capital early in the new
year. Webster read them, of course. The debt was not all his, however.
"There is a question . . . ," it was said, "whether Justice Story wrote Mr.
Webster's Speech, or Mr. Webster wrote Judge Story's book."[42] With his
massive head, dark and solemn face, "the dull black eyes under their precipice of brows, like dull anthracite furnaces needing only to be blown," in
Thomas Carlyle's remarkable description, Webster was a majestic figure be-
fitting his oratorical fame as "The Godlike."[43] He and Calhoun, both supposed to be intellectual giants, were often compared: one empirical, the
other dialectical in method; one rhetorically spacious, the other austere; one
more luminous, the other more penetrating. Webster had the ability which
belonged to the greatest orators of sweeping away the fog from the most bewildering subject and placing it in a blaze of sunlight. "He seizes the subject,
turns it to the light, and however difficult, soon makes it familiar; however intricate, plain; and with a sort of supernatural power, he possesses his hearers, and controls their opinions."[44] Now, in reply to Calhoun, Webster said
nothing new, though some thought he expressed his nationalist doctrine with
greater force and clarity than before. Dropping the residue of legalistic contract theory, he treated the Constitution as a law of paramount obligation and
as a perpetual union of one people. The existence, not the origins, of the Constitution, was the question. The Founding Fathers had created a national government based on the will of the people and commanding assent to its laws.
For Webster this was a profoundly patriotic matter, involving not only questions of constitutional power and majority rule but the legacy of liberty and
union received as a sacred trust from the fathers. The speech was a thrilling
performance. "He ground the whole argument of Calhoun to powder," a visitor wrote from the gallery.[45] Few cared to dispute this judgment.

Calhoun, who grimly took notes throughout the two and one quarter hours
of Webster's speech, did not reply until ten days later. By then the Senate had

passed the Force Bill, with a handful of absentees but only a single dissenting vote. Calhoun, nevertheless, called his resolutions from the table and made them the basis of reply. In an offhand way Webster had conceded that if the Constitution could be shown to be a *compact*, legally and historically, the ultimate right of the states, as the contracting parties, to interpret it, would necessarily follow. Grant Calhoun the rock—more accurately his metaphysical premise—and he could build his church. "He spoke absolutely in axioms," it was said. Webster made only a hurried, faltering response. "Aye, he's dead! he's dead, sir!" John Randolph, on his last visit to the capital, muttered. "He has been dead an hour ago. I saw him dying muscle by muscle."[46] Webster's northern friends were dismayed that their Hercules had permitted his Antaeus to recover from prostration, rise up, and avenge himself. "Instead of raising him high in the air with a fatal grasp," Adams wrote, "Hercules suffered him to march off with the shout of *Io Paen*."[47]

While passage of the Force Bill was never in doubt, the prospect of tariff reform had become desperate by February. The opposition of manufacturing interests was intense. Resolutions in the Massachusetts legislature instructed the state's senators to vote against the Verplanck Bill and declared further that, if adopted, it would be such a gross abuse of power "as would justify the States and citizens aggrieved by it, in any measure which they might think proper to adopt for the purpose of obtaining redress."[48] (The same legislature, by a similarly overwhelming vote, reelected Webster to the Senate.) Obviously, the danger to the Union was not all on one side. In the House, where there was perhaps a majority for the bill, the opponents were slowly talking it to death. One after another, day after day, they occupied the floor, while the bill's friends, with only an occasional interruption, remained silent in the delusory hope of facilitating passage. "Nothing but a miracle can save us," wrote one of Van Buren's followers; another traced the mischief to the rule-or-ruin domination of Congress by the "triumvirate" of Webster, Clay, and Calhoun.[49]

At this impasse Clay astounded Congress and the nation by introducing a plan of compromise on the tariff issue. Two or three weeks earlier he had quietly resumed the effort to arrange a settlement. Rumors of bargain and coalition between Clay and Calhoun were unceasing, but they became more creditable as the session advanced. McLane detected signs of an understanding near the end of January; the fact of an understanding, growing out of supposed conversations between the two senators, was prominently reported in Philadelphia on the twenty-fifth. More significant, and creditable, were the hints dropped in the House debate of a compromise still to come from "a proper source." Silas Wright, the astute New York senator, spoke of a "complex game" in which the triumvirs united against the Verplanck Bill and kept the country on the brink of civil war until Henry Clay, in a blaze of patriotism, stepped forth to save the Union.[50] Wright's scenario was not far off the mark.

Why did Clay offer the olive branch? He had been burned once by the charge of corrupt bargain and still carried the scar. Why should he expose himself a second time? Pondering this question, some men gave him the benefit of lofty motives, while others, like Wright, suspected him of indulging a natural aptitude for self-aggrandizing games of bargain and intrigue. He did not need to do anything, of course, and might have remained in the neutral corner to which he had retired after the rebuff of his first plan to lower the tariff. Any conciliatory move, clearly, would disgust many of his friends. And what could he hope to gain from enemies as implacable as Calhoun and the whole crew of Nullifiers? Clay could not, however, overcome his fears for the fate of the American System at the hands of its greater enemy, the administration. "Jackson has decreed its subversion, and his partizans follow him wherever he goes," Clay wrote. "He has marked out two victims, South Carolina, and the Tariff, and the only question with him is which shall be first immolated."[51] To salvage what he could of the American System, to keep the policy in friendly hands even in dissolution, became an important object. He was also concerned to deny the administration the glory of peacemaking, on one side, or of Bloody Bill triumph on the other. The vision of Andrew Jackson marching into South Carolina at the head of a Union column filled him with horror. Webster never took this danger seriously; he expected the state would retreat before the Force Bill; and if conflict occurred, if the Union *was* brought to the test of force, he would be more elated than dismayed. But Clay feared Jackson's violence, even more than the desperation of the Nullifiers if they returned home empty-handed. He saw, too, that the Carolinians "were extremely unwilling that Jackson should have any credit in the adjustment of the controversy, and to prevent it were disposed to agree to much better terms for the manufacturers, if the measure originated with any other."[52] Clay smartly availed himself of this disposition.

Early in February Clay matured his second, or revised, compromise plan. Like the first, it called for the reduction of duties to the revenue level, targeted at 20 percent *ad valorem*, but instead of a grace period of seven years, the new plan proposed to effect the change gradually over nine and a half years. The idea of a gradual withdrawal of protection, in the interest of manufacturers, had been talked about for several years. Coming from southerners like Tazewell, Hayne, and Tyler, who held the protective tariff unconstitutional, it was meant as a concession. Now Clay accepted it as such, as the basis of compromise, though a decade-long concession of protection was more than the southerners had bargained for. Clay first worked through the details of his plan with protectionist friends in the Senate. Eleven or twelve of them were summoned to an evening meeting at his lodgings, and this was quickly followed by another. Webster attended the first but, significantly, not the second. "It is understood Mr. Clay will agree to almost anything, in order to settle the question, save the Nullifiers, and obtain the credit of pacification," he wrote in disgust.[53] After obtaining pledges of support from the senatorial group, Clay consulted on the proposed plan with prominent manufacturers, such as E. I. DuPont (a member of the earlier Philadelphia committee), with John Sergeant of Pennsylvania (his running mate in the recent election), and leading protectionists in the House.[54]

Proceeding in this way Clay soon found enough encouragement among his friends to warrant negotiation with his enemies. Employing the affable Kentuckian Robert Letcher as intermediary, Clay communicated the plan to Calhoun. By this time the South Carolina leader was anxiously seeking an apology for retreat and seems only to have been waiting for "The Pacificator" to make his move. Letcher apparently arranged a meeting between the senators at Clay's boardinghouse. Neither left an account of it. Benton later characterized the meeting as "cold, distant and civil," ending "without result."[55] Calhoun, though amenable to the gradual withdrawal of protection, wanted a shorter term of four or five years with sharper reductions. And that might have been the end of it but for the perseverance of Letcher and Johnston. The Louisiana senator attested to "the great trouble and labor" of the compromise. "The consultations and conferences and the difficulties and disagreements were enough to have discouraged those who were animated by less zeal," he wrote after it was over.[56] According to Benton, Johnston relayed to Letcher the latest report of the president's rage against South Carolina, including the threat to hang the chief of the Nullifiers as a traitor, and Letcher, in the middle of the night, went to Calhoun's lodgings and startled him out of bed with this horror, thereby securing his consent to the compromise as the price of escaping the gallows.[57] The story is too good to be true. At any rate, the conversations were resumed, apparently on Calhoun's initiative. High principles hung rather loosely in Clay's politics. A political relativist and pragmatist, he believed in the positive value of compromise. With him compromise, far from a subversion of principle, might be its fulfillment. Calhoun, on the other hand, professing to stand on absolute truths, could compromise only at peril. "Expediency, concession, compromise! Away with such weakness and folly!"[58] This was the image he sought to maintain. He was never enslaved by it, however. In the present crisis he realized that compromise offered the only way out and, further, that if he did not strike a bargain with Clay he would be unable to bargain at all.

Despite the interviews, the consultations, the rumors in the press, Clay's introduction of his compromise bill on February 12 marked such an abrupt change of direction that it took nearly everyone by surprise. The bill would continue the tariff of 1832 with some major modifications.[59] From January 1, 1834 (October 1, 1833 when first proposed) all duties over 20 percent would be reduced in biennial installments of one-tenth, with one-half the residue— six-tenths of the whole—taken off on January 1, 1842, the other half on July 1 of the same year. After that duties would be laid "for the purpose of raising such revenue as may be necessary to an economical administration of the Government." Clay was careful to explain that Congress could raise, or lower, the rate of duties from the 20-percent level if "the exigencies of the country" required. Without disavowing protection the bill seemed to envision a uniform 20-percent *ad valorem* rate, omitting discriminatory or specific duties, as the norm of a revenue tariff.

Presenting the bill, Clay did not dwell on his purposes. Of course, he sought to save the Union and the American System at the same time. He anticipated the objection that he was yielding to the threat of nullification, and argued that nullification was already dead, victim of the almighty sovereign, public opinion. The danger to the Union no longer came from South Carolina but from the Jackson administration. Anticipating also the objection that his bill would overthrow protection, Clay vigorously denied it. "What is the principle which has always been contended for . . . ?" he asked. "After the accumulation of capital and skill, the manufacturer will stand alone, unaided by the government, in competition with the imported article from any quarter. Now give us time; cease all fluctuations and agitations, for nine years to come, we can safely leave to posterity to provide for the rest." He conceded that no statute could permanently bind Congress, yet thought the circumstances giving rise to the proposed act would elevate it above ordinary legislation to the status of "a treaty of peace and amity." The act would be a true compromise, a mutual accommodation between the long-contending interests of manufacturers and planters, in which the former received the security of intermediate protection, the latter the promise of ultimate reduction of duties to the revenue standard. Each side surrendered a little of its particular interest for the transcendent interest of both in the Union. "The distribution," Clay concluded on a philosophical note, "is founded on the great principle of compromise and concession which lies at the bottom of our institutions."[60]

Several administration senators promptly denounced Clay's move, outraged that the man whose system of politics was responsible for the crisis, in their view, suddenly threw his solution into Congress when only eighteen days remained of the session. They were quieted by Calhoun, however, who rose to declare his approval of the principles of the bill. "Such was the clapping and thundering applause when Calhoun sat down that the Chair ordered the galleries to be cleared," wrote an observer. "The sensation was indescribable."[61] In the House, meanwhile, the bargain between Clay and Calhoun was sealed by the election of Gales and Seaton, publishers of the opposition *National Intelligencer*, printers to the House. A week later Calhoun's journalistic advocate, Duff Green, would be elected printer to the Senate. These were lucrative positions, more importantly they were positions of political influence; and the division of the spoils between Clay and Calhoun in these elections showed the strength of "the new partnership," not only positively but negatively by the humiliating exclusion of Blair and Rives, publishers of the *Globe*.[62]

Clay's bill was referred to a select committee under his chairmanship. Among protectionists in and out of Congress the plan found more critics than defenders. "It came like a crash of thunder in the winter season," said *Niles' Weekly Register*, long a powerful voice of the American System.[63] It was scarcely creditable that the author of the system proposed to save it by abandoning the very principles of protection and discrimination on which it was built. The bill was offered as a compromise, yet all the sacrifice—the doom of northern prosperity—was on one side, said the Boston *Courier*. As to saving the Union, supposing it was in danger, which Clay himself doubted, the *Courier* asked: "But is the Union to be forever a matter of compromise? Is there nothing certain, stable or efficient in the original compromise, which is em-

bodied in the Constitution? . . . And must the terms of the Union be forever
the subject of litigation, temporizing and compromise?"[64] It was easy, of
course, to read sinister motives into Clay's conduct: to say that he had
crossed the Potomac and offered to rescue the Nullifiers in exchange for the
votes of the South for president. But most protectionists, though they disagreed with Clay, did not question the honor of his motives. Most Jacksonians did little else. The compromise bill was a clever maneuver by Clay to
avoid political annihilation, they said. "Will you gentlemen of the Senate allow him this new *feather* in his cap! Will you let the vanquished dictate to
the victors?" an astonished Virginian asked. What was worse, the price Clay
exacted for the revival of his political fortunes also revived Calhoun's. "It is
all got up by the black hearted revenge of Clay and Calhoun towards Jackson."[65] To which Jackson inclined to agree.

The select committee consisted of Clay, the Jacksonians Grundy, Dallas,
and Rives, Webster, Calhoun, and John M. Clayton of Delaware. They met
more or less daily while the Force Bill was before the Senate. Webster and
Dallas were unremittingly opposed to the compromise plan. The former said
he favored gradual tariff reduction to the revenue level but thought it should
be done selectively rather than uniformly, so as to preserve the principle of
protection. Dallas epitomized the dilemma of the Pennsylvania Democrat,
but regarding Clay's bill as "a mere political maneuver" rejected it on that
ground. Grundy and Rives favored the plan. And so did Clayton, an adoring
protégé of Prince Hal, though he wanted protectionist amendments. There
were, then, more than enough votes in committee to report a bill. Whether
there were enough to pass it in the Senate and the House was far from certain, however.[66] Clayton complicated Clay's task by demanding a home valuation amendment as the price of support by a protectionist bloc centered in
his Capitol Hill mess.[67] The amendment, such as Clay himself had proposed
at the previous session, would add the equivalent of five to ten points to the
tariff duties, thereby compensating for the loss of protection. The demand
was defeated. The committee then voted four to three (Webster, Dallas,
Clayton) to report Clay's bill to the Senate with only one minor amendment.

Surprisingly, when Clay opened the Senate debate on February 21, he offered the home valuation amendment as his own. By throwing his weight behind this artifice he hoped to regain the affections of the alienated protectionists, even as he risked jeopardizing his arrangement with Calhoun, who at
once declared he would oppose the bill if the amendment was adopted. To this
decree Clayton coolly responded with his own, making his vote for the bill contingent on the amendment. It became a symbol, positively of the survival of
protection, negatively of the surrender of nullification. If Calhoun and his
friends wanted to save their necks from the halter, Clayton said, they must accept the amendment. Before the roll was called, Calhoun rose to say he would
vote for home valuation, despite his strong objections to it, because the fate of
the bill had come to depend on it. The amendment passed, 26–16.[68]

The subsequent debate in the Senate featured a dramatic encounter between Clay and Webster. The Bay Stater seized the opportunity to challenge

Clay's leadership of the manufacturing interest. He remembered the shock of Clay's original draft in January, for it not only contemplated equal duties and a revenue standard but, Webster always insisted, expressly disavowed protection or encouragement of domestic industry. He believed this was still Clay's purpose, though he equivocated to gull the protectionists. "The gentleman from Kentucky supports the bill from one motive, others from another motive. One, because it secures protection; another because it destroys protection." While this condemned the measure to absurdity in Webster's eyes, it constituted the bill's chief merit—the genius of the compromise—in Clay's.[69] Webster was troubled by other ambiguities and equivocations. Some advocates lauded the bill for its immediate benefits, among them pacifying the country, and made light of clauses that undertook to control Congress in the future. "They do not halloo till they are out of the wood," Webster remarked. But once the bill became law, he predicted, they would insist that Congress was *pledged* to the attainment of a uniform *ad valorem* tariff for revenue only. "For a poor lease of eight years, we surrender the inheritance." And why? Not to avert civil war, the danger of which had passed, if it ever existed, but "a law suit . . . a war of processes."[70]

Tempers flared when Clay charged that Webster, backed by the administration, stood in the way of "this measure of pacification," yet hurled the thunder of the Force Bill at South Carolina. "Would the Senator from Massachusetts send forth his bill without this measure of conciliation?" Clay asked. Webster denied, as he had repeatedly, that it was *his* bill. Some observers thought they heard him throw back the gauntlet, charging that Clay dodged the vote on the Force Bill three days before. In fact, he did not make this charge—one the Kentuckian would have spiritedly repulsed as an attack on his character—though he may have thought it justified. Clay had been absent the night the Force Bill came to a vote. He apologized the next day, saying he could not endure the atmosphere of the chamber after the lamps were lighted and, with a number of absentees, had not expected a vote that evening. He freely avowed then and later that, had he been present, he would have voted for the bill, reluctantly, not from any question of its propriety but from distrust of the administration. There is no reason to doubt him. Still the circumstances had been wonderfully convenient for him. His extraordinary silence throughout the Force Bill debate testified more eloquently than words or votes that he considered support of the measure incompatible with his role as peacemaker and conciliator of the South.[71]

Without concert or arrangement, but in the nature of the process, it was coming to be recognized on both sides, by Clay and Calhoun, in the administration and in Congress, that the Compromise Bill and the Force Bill would pass into law together. For men who objected to one or the other bill by itself, the compromise consisted in the marriage of these opposites. To Webster and others like him, however, it was not an acceptable marriage. One bill canceled the other by yielding the very principle of the laws it was intended to enforce. The Compromise Bill took the starch out of the Force Bill and its vaunted vindication of the Union. It was, Webster always held, "an attempt to make a new Constitution."[72] In the speech Clay delivered to close the Senate debate on February 25 he elaborated on his conception of the relationship between the two measures. Of the Force Bill he said, "I could not vote against the measure; I would not speak in its behalf." Unlike some—and he glanced across the chamber to Webster's seat—he had discovered in this crisis "no new born zeal" for the Jackson administration. The Proclamation was not only "ultra" in its doctrine, he said, it was inflammatory in its effects—more likely to provoke than to prevent civil war. The tendency of the Force Bill, even conceding its necessity, was the same. But the Compromise Bill would restore the balance between law and order and peace and concord:

> The difference between the friends and foes of the compromise . . . is that they would, in the enforcement act, send forth alone a flaming sword. We would send out that also, but along with it the olive branch, as a messenger of peace. They cry out, the Law! the law! the law! Power! power! power! We, too, reverence the law, and bow to the supremacy of its obligation; but we are in favor of the law executed in mildness, and of power tempered with mercy. . . . They would hazard a civil commotion, beginning in South Carolina and extending, God only knows where. While we would vindicate the federal government, we are for peace, if possible, union, and liberty. We want no war, above all, no civil war, no family strife. We want no sacked cities, no desolated fields, no smoking ruins, no streams of American blood shed by American arms![73]

The speech throughout was a lively expression of Clay's genius for accommodation, of his sensitivity to opposing political pressures, and his ingenuity in adapting old policies to new conditions. Webster, of course, charged him with surrendering the protective tariff in the face of intimidation and to no useful public purpose. Clay was not deterred. He honestly believed it was necessary, not to surrender, but to contract the tariff in order to save it. While Webster was apprehensive of the future, Clay willingly took his chances with it, believing the arts and industries of the country would grow stronger under the compromise:

> If they can have what they have never yet enjoyed, some years of repose and tranquility, they will make, silently, more converts to the policy, than would be made during a long period of anxious struggle and boisterous contention. Above all, I count upon the good effects resulting from the restoration of the harmony of this divided people, upon their good sense and their love of justice. . . . And how much more estimable will be the system of protection, based on common conviction and common consent, and planted in the bosoms of all, than one wrenched by power from reluctant and protesting weakness?[74]

This was the spirit of Calhoun's search for union and concurrence in federal legislation, but Clay sought to show that the goal could be reached through the give and take of the political process, without the awkward and ruinous contrivance of nullification.

Even as he was speaking, Clay had decided to suspend further action in the Senate by sending the bill to the House of Representatives. Thus it was that on the same evening, February 25, suddenly and without warning, just as congressmen were putting on their wraps to go home, Letcher rose and moved to refer the Compromise Bill directly to the committee of the whole house as a substitute for the Verplanck Bill. Received as an act of deliverance, the motion was quickly approved; and over feeble cries of protest against legislating with a gun at their heads, the congressmen, before retiring, passed the bill to third reading. The next day, after two or three hours of debate, appropriately closed by McDuffie's avowal of support, the House adopted the Compromise Bill, 119–85. As it returned to the Force Bill, McDuffie wondered at the justice or policy of fettering "the olive branch of peace" with "the sword of blood."[75] But in the eyes of most congressmen one had become essential to the other. On March 1 the House adopted the Force Bill, 149–48. The same day the Senate passed the Compromise Bill without further ado, 29–16.

Clay called March 1 "perhaps the most important congressional day that ever occurred." It was a personal triumph, of course, "the most proud and triumphant day of my life," he told Matt Davis.[76] The House sent the Force Bill, the Senate both the Compromise Bill and the Land Bill, to the president for signature. The latter was the almost forgotten child of the session. In December Clay had introduced the same measure the Senate had approved and the House had postponed in the previous session. Again the Public Lands Committee reported its own bill; again, the Senate adopted Clay's plan for distributing the proceeds of the sale of public lands to the states. After years of discussion the question was well understood. If the income of the Land Office was excluded from the revenue to support the government, government would be solely dependent on the tariff, which would tend to perpetuate the American System. Logically, then, distribution was part of the compromise, another compensatory device, like home valuation, to keep up the tariff. Clayton, one of its warmest advocates, considered distribution an integral part of the compromise. And if not passed now, he said, hopes for distribution would vanish because of the influx of new western members into the next Congress.[77] Wright, too, although he considered it "the most mischievous bill . . . that ever originated in Congress," supposed distribution passed into law as part of "a common understanding." "The Land Bill," another New Yorker wrote, "is to *reward* Kentucky for sacrificing the *System*."[78] These views testify to the coupling of distribution with the tariff in the minds of both friends and foes.

Actually, the Senate acted on the Land Bill before either the enforcement or tariff bill came to the floor, even before Clay had any conversations with Calhoun. Distribution did not enter into the negotiations; it was the object of no pledge or promise, and in that sense was no part of the compromise. Calhoun opposed distribution; like most southern and western senators he voted against the bill. Clay, as the author of both measures, acknowledged their relationship, but said they were not so far joined as to stand or fall together. Congress finally sent the Land Bill to the president on the last day of the session. It was not returned; neither was it signed. Jackson again resorted to the pocket veto. When this became known he was charged in some quarters with deliberately upsetting the compromise.[79] Clay, although angered by the veto, never took this view. Jackson had reluctantly come around to supporting Clay's tariff bill, as had McLane and even Van Buren and a portion of the New York delegation. But Jackson now opposed distribution in any form. Clay's bill was a ruse for federal support of local internal improvements; it would turn the states into mendicants of the government in Washington. "A more direct road to consolidation cannot be devised," Jackson declared. "Money is power, and in that Government which pays . . . will all political power be consolidated."[80]

Who voted to extend the olive branch and who the sword? Usually they were *not* the same persons. Of 188 representatives whose votes were recorded on both the tariff and enforcement bills, 114 voted in opposite ways: 43 for the former but against the latter, 71 against the former but for the latter. Paradoxically, compromise prevailed because of mutual antagonism to compromise. It prevailed though there was no majority for it, only for its separate measures. Clay had counted on this result; Webster had deplored it; Calhoun had acquiesced in it. The preponderant sectional vote was more or less as expected. The Northeast favored the Force Bill and generally opposed the Compromise Tariff. The South presented much the same division in reverse. The West favored both measures. Party affiliation had comparatively little bearing on the vote anywhere.[81]

The fame of the Compromise of 1833 inured primarily to Henry Clay. He became "The Great Compromiser." In the years to come the Compromise Act would generally be celebrated as an act of deliverance, a sacred compact, and a vindication of American institutions. It was often the subject of panegyric. In 1837 Ohio congressman Tom Corwin remembered the act as a political miracle:

> What, sir, were the happy, the glorious effects of that compromise? The day before that law received the President's approval was overcast with the gathering clouds of civil war, deepening, spreading, and blackening every hour. The ground on which we stood seemed to heave and quake with the first throes of a convulsion, that was to rend in fragments the last republic on earth; at this fearful moment an overruling Providence revealed the instrument of its will in the person of one man, whose virtues would have illustrated the brightest annals of recorded time. He produced the great measure of concord, and the succeeding morning dawned upon the American horizon without a spot; the sun of that day looked down, and beheld us a tranquil and united people.[82]

Of course, not everyone shared this glowing opinion of the act or its author. Webster, having opposed the act at its passage, was still denouncing it at its termination almost a decade later. "The principle was bad, the measure was bad, and the consequences were bad."[83] When Congress adjourned there were suggestions that Webster would place himself at the head of protectionist hostility in Pennsylvania and New England, where the act was perceived as a betrayal of manufacturing interests. Doubts and fears on this score were rapidly overcome, however, in the midst of rising prosperity. The great gain of the Compromise Tariff in ensuring stability offset the loss of protection, which occurred so gradually that it was hardly noticed; and it soon became popular even among eastern manufacturers. The rumored breach between Webster and Clay never materialized. But while it was difficult to argue with prosperity, Webster retained his political and constitutional objections to the act. By the fatal precedent of surrendering to the threat of nullification it created "a new Constitution," in his opinion. Doubtless he agreed with Adams who thought Clay's measure should be entitled, "An Act for the protection of John C. Calhoun and his fellow nullifiers."[84]

Nullification had been defeated, yet the Nullifiers proclaimed a victory. Calhoun left Washington on March 4, traveling day and night over snow-covered and rain-soaked roads, sometimes in open mail carts, in order to reach Columbia for the meeting of the state convention on the eleventh. He was anxious to calm the hotheads and put an end to the crisis. The convention promptly repealed the nullification ordinance, 155–4, then passed another ordinance declaring the Enforcement Act null and void. This was more than a face-saving gesture. It expressed the state's concern that the coercive power claimed for the general government would be used in an attack on the South's "peculiar institution." Having won the tariff battle with the cockboat of nullification, the Carolinians proclaimed "a still more imperious necessity of resistance" against the rising anti-slavery movement in the North. Press and platform celebrated the triumph of nullification. Governor Hayne presided at a great victory ball in Charleston. The Unionists, whose patron had been Andrew Jackson, were utterly bereft. In the fall, after a sweeping victory at the polls, the State Rights and Free Trade party ceremoniously laid the cornerstone of a monument in Charleston to the deceased prophet, Robert Turnbull, then rallied at the Circus in a tribute to their leader, Calhoun. It was Calhoun, not Clay, not Jackson, who was responsible for peace and compromise, according to these partisans; and Calhoun vaunted himself on this illusion. Nullification had overthrown the American System, he affirmed. The guns of Charleston's fortresses were again turned out to sea. A new crisis had arisen, however. Under the encouragement of the Force Bill, abolition societies began sprouting like mushrooms in the North. The South must be aroused to the danger; and as there could be no union under the bayonet, the repeal of the tyrannical law ought to be the first order of business in the new congress. After this political *coup de théâtre*, Calhoun's leadership in South Carolina was virtually unassailable. No wonder that he could later say he wanted but one word engraved on his tombstone, *Nullification*.[85]

* *Five* *

THE EMBATTLED SENATORS

For eight years, from 1832 to 1841, Webster, Clay, and Calhoun were the master spirits of the United States Senate. As long as Andrew Jackson was president they were united in opposition, though in little else. They were the ornaments of American statesmanship in the era between the founding and the Civil War. At home and abroad, making exception for their common enemy, they were the most celebrated Americans of the time. Men and women flocked to the Capitol to hear them; all across the country their speeches were read as if the fate of the nation hung on them; and whether in Washington, at home, or on the road they could never escape the noisy pomp of fame.

It was the golden age of the Senate. Beginning in comparative seclusion, with a vaguely patrician character, like the senate in ancient Rome, priding itself on its unique role as privy council to the president, its debates at first secret, then for many years barely reported, the Senate had emerged from the shadow of the House of Representatives as the first place of legislative deliberation and leadership. Alexis de Tocqueville was not alone among foreign observers in contrasting the dignity of the Senate with the vulgarity of the House.[1] Whatever the cause of its rising prestige—the triumvirs who graced it, its smallness (only forty-eight members until 1836), its indirect election (which some thought ensured superior wisdom and made the Senate what it ought to be, a congress of ambassadors from sovereign states), perhaps even its superb acoustics under a low-vaulted dome (in contrast to the cavernous echo chamber at the other end of the Capitol)—the Senate fulfilled the Whig

ideal of a great deliberative body, at once solid and briliant, dedicated to preserving liberty and self-government from tyrannical executive power.

Jackson was accused of gross abuse of power almost from the moment he
became president. It was programmed into the rhetoric of the opposition.
Only after his veto of the bill to recharter the Bank of the United States, however, was he accused of tyranny—of ruling like a European monarch rather
than an American president—and denounced as King Andrew. Each succeeding act of the so-called Bank War, from the removal of the government deposits through the issuance of the Specie Circular at the end of Jackson's administration, was executive altogether. The House of Representatives, with a
Democratic majority, bowed to the president. The Supreme Court was of no
account. But the opposition held sway in the Senate for several years. It became a republican tribunate against the despotic executive. "The Senate has
been the sole, if not the last refuge of the constitution and of public liberty,"
Clay declared in 1835. Jackson had already annointed his successor, Martin
Van Buren; and who could doubt, the senator observed, that had his bed
been fertile instead of barren he would have elevated his own son.[2] Recoiling
from the shock of King Andrew, the scattered fragments of the opposition,
which included Nullifiers and Anti-Masons as well as National Republicans,
gradually fused into a new political aggregate, the Whig party. The name had
venerable associations, of course, not only with the American Revolution but
with the seventeenth-century English struggle against Stuart kings.

The party was formed primarily to contest the presidency. Clay and Webster were instantly its foremost figures. Calhoun boasted of his independence, saying he was simply "an honest Nullifier," but the Democrats treated
him as one of the triumvirate, and he cooperated with the Whigs in most legislative matters. Because of the Compromise Tariff he and Clay were believed
to have logrolled their political interests, leaving Webster the odd man in the
combination. But as the stakes in the political game were constantly shifting,
so were the relationships of the players. Each of the triumvirs was acutely
aware of the interrelations among them and seldom made a move without calculating its effects on the others. In the conventional political rhetoric known
to every politician *men* were not supposed to matter: principles, laws, measures alone mattered. But before the example of these men, and before their
antagonist Jackson, one was tempted to echo the cry of George Canning in
the British parliament several decades earlier: "Away with the cant of 'Measures, not Men!'—the idle supposition that it is the harness and not the horse
that draws the chariot along. No, sir, if the comparison must be made, if the
distinction must be taken, men are everything, measures are comparably
nothing."[3] Measures, principles, and issues were embodied in men; and it often seemed that policies were determined, laws were made, finally, by little
more than personal political whim or passion or ambition. The men, certainly, were more necessary to the history than the impersonal forces and systems that surrounded them.

Harriet Martineau, the English popularizer of political economy, and a fascinating talker, came to Washington for a long visit in January 1835. In this

"bare and forlorn city"—like most English visitors she thought Washington "a great mistake"—she found a society like no other: "foreign ambassadors . . . , members of Congress, from Clay and Webster down to Davy Crockett . . . , grave judges, saucy travellers, pert newspaper reporters, melancholy Indian chiefs, and timid New England ladies, trembling on the vortex"—all mixed up together with nothing but the business of government to amuse them. The Senate chamber was her favorite resort during the day, and her pleasantest evenings were spent in the company of the Senate's great men.

> Mr. Clay, sitting upright on the sofa, with his snuffbox ever in his hand, would discourse for many an hour in his even, soft, deliberate tone, on any one of the great subjects of American policy which we might happen to start, always amazing us with the moderation of estimate and speech which so impetuous a nature has been able to attain. Mr. Webster, leaning back at his ease, telling stories, cracking jokes, shaking the sofa with burst after burst of laughter, or smoothly discoursing to the perfect felicity of the logical part of one's constitution, would illuminate an evening now and then. Mr. Calhoun, the cast-iron man, who looks as if he had never been born and never could be extinguished, would come in sometimes to keep our understanding upon a painful stretch for a short while, and leave us to take to pieces his close, rapid, theoretical, illustrated talk, and see what we could make of it.[4]

Between these men there were striking contrasts—Calhoun narrowly, morosely intellectual; Webster witty, easy, and pleasure-loving; Clay who had attained "truly noble mastery" over an impetuous character—but all were victims of their own unchastened ambition. "Ambition is the malady of every extensive genius," Edmund Burke had remarked.[5] And in the generation of Webster, Clay, and Calhoun the presidency seemed to be the only office in the land that could satisfy the passion for power and greatness. Each man was diminished by his pursuit of it.

1. The Bank War

In an undated memorandum headed "Objects," assigned by the editor of his writings to "about June 1, 1833," Daniel Webster sketched a kind of platform for his quest of the presidency.[1] First and foremost was the defense of the Union and the Constitution against all attacks. This meant support of the president against nullification and cooperation with southern Unionists. Next he listed, "To sustain the cause of American Capital, American Industry, and most of all *American Labor* against destructive foreign competition by reasonable, moderate but permanent protective duties." Webster thus stood by protectionism and continued his opposition to the compact between Clay and Calhoun. Like Jackson, he believed that many of the Nullifiers secretly aimed at a southern confederacy and, having triumphed over the

American System, would attempt "to blow up a storm on the slave question."
"A systematic and bold attack, now just begun," Webster wrote to a Carolina
Unionist, "will be carried on . . . against the just and constitutional power of
the government, and against whatsoever strengthens the Union of the
States."[2] In May, as abolitionists stepped up their agitation, he wrote a celebrated letter to a Georgia Unionist disavowing any power of Congress, or any
intention of northern politicians like himself, to interfere with slavery in the
states.[3] He remained optimistic about his *rapprochement* with the administration commenced in the nullification crisis and hoped to bring about a political realignment on the great issue of the preservation of the Union against
all combinations, personal, partisan, or sectional. If successful in this he
would supplant Clay on one side and Van Buren on the other. Jackson appeared cordial. In the spring he would pay a visit to New England. Whether
or not the senator was responsible for the president's tour, as some historians
have contended, he certainly welcomed it as a contribution to their entente.[4]

The main obstacle in the way of the entente was the Bank. Through his
cabinet friend Edward Livingston, about to become minister to France, Webster tried to cool Jackson's feelings toward the Bank. Although the House of
Representatives, before adjourning, had declared that the government deposits amounting to some $8 million were perfectly safe in the Bank, there
were rumors they would be furtively removed during the recess of Congress,
sending the Bank into a tailspin and ending all possibility of an amicable political solution. "The whole question of peace or war lies in the matter of the
deposits," Nicholas Biddle wrote in April. "If they are withdrawn, it is a declaration of war." So he encouraged Webster in his *rapprochement* with the administration. The senator's political object was compatible with the banker's
narrower one, for he saw clearly that removal of the deposits would create a
revulsion against the administration and drive those men who were coming
to him back into the arms of "C & C."[5]

Although he would have liked to welcome the president to Boston, Webster was unwilling to postpone again the western tour he had planned for so
long. The time was favorable. Clay gave the tour his blessing and promised
Webster a rousing reception in Lexington. The press teemed with rumors of
a breach between them. A more or less authoritative denial, apparently from
Webster's quarter, appeared in April.[6] Clay, though he supposed Webster indulged the hope he would immolate himself on the altar of compromise, was
satisfied there was no estrangement despite the sharp passes between them
in the Senate.[7] Going home in March Webster had intended to "write off"
his last, and undelivered, speech against the Compromise Bill; but stopping
in Philadelphia, he was dissuaded by Biddle, who intervened at Clay's request. "I wish you would do all you can to soothe him . . . ," Clay wrote.
"You have a large flask of oil and know how to pour it out." The banker artfully applied the oil and sent Webster off in a friendly frame of mind.[8] He buried the notes of his speech for six years.

Setting forth in May, Webster, with his wife and daughter, went first to
Buffalo, thence to Ohio. Everywhere he was hailed as the Defender of the

Constitution. Jackson's friends, more than Clay's, paid him court. In his speeches he was full of praise for the president, had scarcely a word to say about the Bank, and put himself forward as the champion of protectionism. His speeches at Buffalo and Pittsburgh, in which he espoused the new doctrine of the protection of American labor instead of the old doctrine of infant industries, were read in some quarters as manifestoes for the restoration of the American System.[9] At Cincinnati, Postmaster General William T. Barry noted, "Mr. Clay's friends, and especially his bank friends, were cold, and are dissatisfied with the speech of Mr. Webster at the dinner."[10] There his journey was cut short by a cholera epidemic in the Ohio Valley. Back in New York in July, Webster briefly resumed negotiations with Livingston that, if successful, would have put him in the Democratic party or, as he hoped, some grand party of the Union. Nothing materialized, but Webster's friends continued to puff him as the votary of the Union and the Constitution above all narrow partisanship. One of them, Rufus Choate, in a Fourth of July oration, had the temerity to describe Clay as "the setting sun" of his party.[11] Gallant Harry, after the cholera subsided, took his first swing through the eastern cities in fifteen years, catching up with Webster in Boston. There the compromise was already finding favor, and Clay pleaded eloquently for it. He was not, as reported, snubbed by Webster; but the report reflected the coolness of their political relations.[12] Webster believed Clay had sold the tariff, with the Constitution, to the South. If he had gained political ground there, he had lost it everywhere else, and if he again ran for the presidency, as Webster supposed he would, he could not possibly be elected. "You might as well move Monadnock," the New Englander said.[13]

Congress met in December amid the uproar over the president's highhanded action in removing the federal deposits from the Bank of the United States. Proceeding on his own responsibility, over the opposition of a majority of his own cabinet, including the secretary of treasury, William J. Duane, to whom the law gave custody of the deposits, Jackson had fired the secretary and appointed in his place Attorney General Roger B. Taney, a chief lieutenant throughout the Bank War. It was not pretended that the deposits were unsafe in the Bank, and therefore subject to withdrawal under provision of the charter, or that the action could not wait until Congress met. In a paper presented to the cabinet, Jackson held that immediate action was necessary "to preserve the morals of the people, the freedom of the press, and the purity of the elective franchise."[14] This was the old, tired slang of corruption, given some semblance of plausibility by the Monster's support of Clay in the recent election. Since the alternative to the B. U. S. was the deposit of the federal funds in numerous state chartered banks, the new policy fell in with the broad program of denationalization. The economic consequences were little considered, as the country would learn at its peril. Jackson acted politically. He feared that the bastard coalition of Clay and Calhoun, consummated in the nullification crisis, would merge the sinister influence of the Bank to the corrupt influence of the treasury surplus and thus doom the country to iniquity.[15] By cutting off the lifeblood of the Monster he hoped to destroy its capacity for further injury and squelch opposition hopes for its recharter. As always, Jackson's motives were complex. And the spirit of pugnacity, which kept him alive, cannot be omitted from the equation. As Felix Grundy remarked, "The general is a sportsman and must always have a cock in the pit."[16]

On his way to the capital Clay stopped at Philadelphia to confer with Biddle on the strategy to pursue in this new crisis. The Philadelphian, who was a man of wit and learning as well as of business, had become the personification of the Bank. He cared for nothing else. His country home on the Delaware, Andalusia, was an architectural copy of the Doric-porticoed Greek Revival building on Chestnut Street. He buttressed the Bank's great financial power with his own pride and arrogance, which he now opposed to Jackson's iron will. Under cover of protecting the Bank, not only deprived of the federal deposits but compelled to wind up its affairs, Biddle slashed discounts, called in loans, and as a consequence forced the hundreds of state banks suddenly to contract their business. "My own course is decided," he declared, "all the other banks and all the merchants may break, but the Bank of the United States shall not break."[17] By a contraction more severe and economically damaging than the safety of the institution required, Biddle furnished devastating proof of the Bank's power. Clay had no overweening attachment to Biddle or the Bank. But he quickly determined to force a political showdown with Jackson on the issue of removal of the deposits. Any further congressional submission to the will of the executive was unthinkable. Normally, a contest involving the power of the purse would be centered in the House of Representatives. In the Twenty-Third Congress, however, the House was in Democratic hands, while the opposition, fragmented though it was, controlled the Senate. Biddle agreed that the senator from Kentucky should be the leader of the Bank's cause in Congress. They further agreed that the question of the future of the Bank, indeed all other questions tending to divide the opposition, should be subordinated to the political and constitutional question of executive usurpation of power. Nothing was more important, in Biddle's view, than the unity of the triumvirate against Jackson.[18]

Biddle enforced this line on Webster when he stopped for an interview several days later. It did not sit easily with the Massachusetts senator. He, after all, had been the Bank's champion in 1832. But Biddle could not ignore Webster's private and professional ties to the Bank. They damaged his credibility in the cause. Webster lacked Clay's authority in the Senate. Even more to the point, a senator who had for months been singing the praises of Caesar could not be trusted to dethrone him. Webster went on to Washington in a sulk. From there he wrote to Biddle saying he had declined a proposition to appear professionally against the Bank even though "my retainer has not been renewed, or refreshed, as usual." "If it is wished that my relation to the Bank should be continued," the senator warned, "it may be well to send the usual retainer."[19]

Webster still sought the path of conciliation with the administration. The Senate, at the outset, took the power of appointing committees from the president *pro tem,* the gray-haired Jacksonian Hugh Lawson White, and returned it to the membership. Without actually opposing the change, Webster at once moved to delay election of the committees. What he hoped to accomplish was unclear. Intrigue with the administration was suspected. In the end, of course, Clay controlled composition of the committees, including the Finance Committee with Webster at its head. But the senator had given himself "a fatal stab," according to one of his colleagues, and was destined to "play the character of the bat in the fable" for the remainder of the session.[20] The sparring between Clay and Webster was prominently reported in the press. "At every available opportunity, they shiver a lance with each other," it was said.[21] Many Democrats thought "that Webster must, sooner or later, quit the Coalition," while his Boston admirers worried that the enormity of Jackson's crimes would drive him willy-nilly into the unhallowed opposition.[22] The latter turned out to be Webster's only choice. Van Buren blocked the path of conciliation with Jackson, and Webster fell into line, kicking and screaming, behind Clay's leadership in Congress. Politicians took notice of who was master and who was servant.* "If the two [men] should go duck shooting together," a Kentuckian quipped, "Mr. Clay would expect Mr. Webster to assume the office of spaniel, to bring out the birds, and the latter would not perceive that there was any degradation in the assumption of such an office."[23] In fact, Webster knew and felt the degradation. Calhoun, who had great respect for Webster and scant respect for Clay, shrewdly perceived the disparity between them on the point of leadership. "Mr. Webster will never be President," Calhoun observed. "He lacks the qualifications of a leader; he has no faith in his own convictions; he can never be at the head of a party. Though very superior in intellect to Mr. Clay, he lacks his moral courage and strong convictions. Hence Mr. Clay will always be the head of the party, and Mr. Webster will naturally follow his lead. If either of them reaches the Presidency, it will be Clay, not Webster."[24]

On December 26 Clay introduced two resolutions censuring both the secretary of treasury and the president, the latter in particular for assuming "in relation to the public revenue . . . authority and power not conferred by the

---

*A particular instance in this Congress, when the Senate was in executive session, was later described by the reporter T. N. Parmelee. Andrew Stevenson of Virginia, Speaker of the House, wished to be named minister to Great Britain. The Whigs were agreeable since it might permit them to elect one of their own speaker. Jackson, too, wanted it, but feared that Stevenson, like so many of his prominent nominees, would be rejected by the Senate. Webster's help was sought. He said if Stevenson would first resign as Speaker a majority of senators, including himself, would concur in the nomination. Stevenson resigned and John Bell, a Tennessee Whig, was elected Speaker. The Senate Foreign Relations Committee reported in Stevenson's favor. Just before the question of confirmation was put to the senators, Clay rose and denounced Stevenson, who had been especially obnoxious to him for many years. Webster, beside himself, strolled to and fro between the great columns at the front of the chamber while Clay exhausted his vocabulary of vituperation on Stevenson, concluding finally, "And now, Mr. President, where is the Whig who will dare to vote for him?" Stevenson was rejected. Even Webster violated his pledge and voted against confirmation. Some months later Clay relented and let it be known that if the Virginian were renominated he would absent himself so he could be confirmed. And so it was done.

constitution and laws, but in derogation of both."[25] "We are in the midst of a revolution, hitherto bloodless," Clay began gravely, "but rapidly tending towards a total change of the pure and republican character of the government, and to the concentration of all power in the hands of one man." He then surveyed the extraordinary acts of the president in relation to the patronage, Indian affairs, internal improvements, the currency, and so forth that threatened in another three years to obliterate the government that prevailed until March 4, 1829. "In a term of eight years, a little more than equal to that which was required to establish our liberties, the government will have been transformed into an elective monarchy—the worst of all forms of government." The present danger lay in the union of purse and sword. Like Caesar, Jackson invaded the treasury sword in hand, crying, "With money I will get men, and with men money." Clay scoffed at the reasons offered for the removal of the deposits and argued that in this matter the secretary of treasury was responsible to Congress under the 1789 law creating the office as well as under the Bank charter. And where was the federal treasury now? Scattered to the four winds, in a bank here, a bank there, about which nothing was known but their ties to the Jackson party, and over which there was no control. "The premonitory symptoms of despotism are upon us," Clay concluded, "and if Congress do not apply an instantaneous and effective remedy, the fatal collapse will soon come on, and we shall die—ignobly die! Base, mean, and abject slaves—the scorn and contempt of mankind—unpitied, unwept, unmourned!" The gallery burst into applause and cheering. After it was cleared and order restored, Thomas Hart Benton replied for the administration in his usual manner, "infinitely laborious," as Webster put it.[26] He defended the removal of the deposits, blasted the B.U.S. for manufacturing a financial crisis, and, in addition, argued that since Clay's resolutions contained impeachable matter they should be handled in the manner prescribed by the Constitution.

The debate went on for three months. Calhoun waded in on January 13.[27] Biddle had counted on the Nullifier's support—was he not, after all, the legislative father of the Bank?—and Clay had spoken confidently of receiving it. They were not wholly disappointed. Portraying himself as independent of party, hence capable of statesmanlike views, Calhoun matched Clay's zeal in attacking the administration. The issue was not "Bank or no Bank" as Democratic senators would have it. It was, as defined in Clay's resolutions, an issue of legislative versus executive power. Having said this, however, Calhoun departed from his co-adjutor. The country was, indeed, in the midst of a revolution, but it had commenced years earlier with the American System, and the present "executive consolidation" was but the second stage of the process of national consolidation. It was only because of nullification and the resolution of the tariff question, which had for so long wasted the energies of patriotic citizens in both North and South, that the Senate was capable of mounting resistance to executive tyranny. From this perspective, so different from Clay's or Webster's, Calhoun went on to intimate a radical change of outlook on currency and banking policy. If the question were one of "Bank or no Bank," he would not be found under the Bank banner, Calhoun said. A national bank was unconstitutional, Biddle's bank was pernicious, and a banking system founded on four hundred state banks—the apparent Jacksonian solution—was absurd. The only solution to the problem was to *"divorce the government entirely from the banking system,"* he declared. "You must refuse all connexion with banks. You must neither receive, nor pay away bank-notes; you must go back to the old system of the strong box, and of gold and silver."[28] Should this, rather than executive tyranny, become the issue, Calhoun would stand with hard-money Democrats along with his proverbial enemy, "Old Bullion" Benton, rather than with Clay and Webster.

Congress was deluged with petitions and memorials, some bearing the signatures of six thousand or more citizens, pleading for relief from the consequences of executive usurpation and folly. At numerous "distress meetings," the hardships brought on by bank pressures—high interest rates, unemployment, bankruptcy—were greatly magnified until the country imagined it was in the grip of economic depression. The first hour of each business day in both houses of congress for several months was devoted to the "panic memorials." Nothing in the history of public opinion had ever equaled it, senators remarked. New tactics of pressure group politics were introduced. Deputations carried their petitions to the capital, invaded the halls of Congress, and demanded an audience with the president. "Relief, sir!" Jackson screamed to one such group. "Come not to me for relief; go to the *monster*."[29] The Albany Regency senators, Silas Wright and Nathaniel Tallmadge, gave the same reply. There would be no relief from the government; the deposits would remain in the favored state banks—"pet banks" as they came to be called. In response to one of these memorials, Clay delivered a remarkable extempore appeal to the vice president, entreating him to tell his chief of the "bleeding condition" of the country: "Tell him it is nearly ruined and undone. . . . Tell him that, in a single city, more than sixty bankruptcies, involving a loss of upwards to fifteen millions of dollars, has occurred. Tell him of the alarming decline in the value of property. . . . Tell him of the tears of helpless widows. . . . Tell him how much more true glory is to be won by retracing false steps, than by blindly rushing on until his country is overwhelmed in bankruptcy and ruin. . . ."[30] An entranced reporter compared the speech to Mirabeau's celebrated apostrophe in the National Assembly in 1789, with Jackson taking the place of Louis XVI. But Van Buren showed what he thought of it when, at its conclusion, he stepped down from the chair, strolled up to Clay, and asked him for a pinch of snuff.[31] The debate was full of ominous overtones. Entering the Senate one day, Webster was told that either Wright or Tallmadge had been heard to say that the Democrats would prevail because of "the natural hatred of the poor for the rich." Webster rose at the first opportunity to denounce this appeal to class hatred. Who more than the laboring man had an interest in a sound currency and the wherewithal, in the form of bank credit, to rise in the world? The appeal was a double fraud on the country, Webster said, "a fraud which is to cheat men out of their property and out of the earnings of their labor, by first cheating them out of their understandings." Opposition senators could not find words adequate to describe the "noble passion" of Webster's rebuke. It was "a thunderbolt," and raised him and everyone off their feet.[32]

"Why cannot something be done to bring the leaders of the Senate to cooperate in manner and form as well as in substance?" Horace Binney, one of Biddle's agents, asked with an air of desperation after a month of debate. "There is something wrong there, and who is to put it right?"[33] Clay adhered to the original strategy. "The Bank ought to be kept in the rear; the usurpation in front," he reiterated to Biddle. The Bank was an unpopular and divisive issue. "If we take up the Bank, we play into the adversary's hands. We realize his assertions that the only question is a renewal of the Charter. It is the usurpation which has convinced the Country."[34] Webster, on the other hand, wished to use the distress to enforce on the country the necessity of a national bank. He hoped finally to bring Jackson to the bargaining table on a new charter. And so he hung back on the subject of usurpation and urged Biddle to ease the contraction in order to create a favorable climate for negotiation. In some circles the Bank was thought to favor this approach. Webster was perceived, in Senator Mangum's words, as "the real representative of the great manufacturing and capitalist interests of New England and the North generally." And in that capacity he sought a practical solution to restore order and confidence.[35]

In March Webster asked the Senate for leave to introduce a bill to extend the B.U.S. charter for six years, making several amendments to overcome Jacksonian objections. Biddle had approved the bill; Webster, it was understood, acted for the Bank.[36] Of course, Clay opposed it because it tore the mask from the campaign against executive tyranny and because he saw no possibility of uniting on any practical measure in the present session.[37] Clay's opposition was expected. Calhoun's was not. He had his own plan but had given no hint of introducing it until Webster made his "injudicious" move. Although the two senators were "scarcely on speaking terms," Calhoun went to Webster and pleaded with him, unsuccessfully, to drop his bill. Calhoun's own plan also called for an extension of the Bank's charter, for a term of twelve years. However, the end result to be brought about by the gradual expulsion of bank notes would be a metallic currency and the divorce of bank and state.[38] Calhoun aimed to duplicate, for banking, Clay's feat of gradually undoing the tariff. Despite obvious objections, the Bank's friends did not reject the plan out of hand; generally, it appealed to hardmoney Jacksonians. The two bills offset each other and, unfortunately for the opposition, put the senators in collision again.[39] Biddle's agents quickly cooled to Webster's bill; and when Clay threatened to table it, the senator himself made the best of a bad situation and withdrew the measure. "Our friends want *tone, decision,* and *courage,*" he complained lamely to Biddle.[40] Calhoun, too, acquiesced. Debate returned to the censure resolutions. They were adopted on March 28.

After the vote, Webster made a quick trip to Boston. On the way he stopped in New York City to aid the maiden Whig campaign against Tammany

Hall, earning the gratitude of the city's leading merchants, bankers, and lawyers. On his return he landed in New York during celebration of the Whig victory, the first anywhere under the new opposition banner. Invoking Thomas Jefferson's warning against "elective despotism," Webster exhorted the celebrants to persevere against the new Caesar-Tiberius-Cromwell-Napoleon.[41] Arrving in Baltimore on Sunday, he and several returning congressmen were met by a huge crowd lining the shore. Webster addressed them from the upper deck of the steamboat, and thereby brought upon himself the charge of desecrating the Sabbath. He had, it was later said, told the crowd "there are no Sabbaths in revolutionary times" and exhorted them to seek redress of grievances "peaceably if they could, forcibly if they must."[42] Webster, of course, denied ever saying such things. It was "a vile falsehood and slander."[43]

Webster found the Senate launched on a new wave of censure in response to the president's formal protest against Clay's resolutions. The Senate had no right to censure him except by way of impeachment, Jackson said. And in justification of his actions he asserted that the president was the direct representative of the people and their rightful protector. The Whigs denounced the first doctrine as an attack on the honor and independence of the Senate, the second as proof of monarchical pretensions. What was it, Webster asked in a speech that ended, decisively, his *rapprochement* with the administration, but a proclamation of " 'I am the state' "? Contrary to the president, the question was not whether the Senate had the right to pass its resolutions; it was whether the president had a right to protest the decision. "Infatuated man!" Calhoun exclaimed. "Blinded by ambition—intoxicated by flattery and vanity! What, that is the least acquainted with the human heart; who, that is conversant with the pages of history, does not see, under all this, the workings of a dark, lawless, and insatiable ambition. . . . He claims to be, not only the representative, but the *immediate* representative of the American people! What effrontery! What boldness of assertion. The *immediate* representative! Why, he never received a vote from the American people. He was elected by electors."[44] The upshot was another set of resolutions, again mainly of Clay's devising, in which the Senate rejected the authority of the protest and denied it a place in its journal.[45] Neither set represented more than the majority opinion of the Senate. But Clay, making the mistake of believing his own propaganda, supposed the mass of the people were rallying to the Whig banner and called the protest action "the last stroke upon the last nail driven into the coffin of Jacksonism."[46]

These hopes were dashed in the fall elections. Nothing more was heard of panic and distress after Congress adjourned. The Biddle contraction ended, and the state banks fueled expansion more rapidly than the B.U.S. ever had. The country gave three cheers for Old Hickory and booming prosperity. Here and there the new Whig coalition prevailed, but generally the elections ratified Jackson's victory in the Bank War. The "dictated succession" of Van Buren, once inconceivable, began to look inevitable. Clay had expected to oppose him. His plan, apparently, was to win enough votes in the South, supposedly in his debt, to throw the election into the House of Representatives, where he would take his chances. But he received no aid from his quondam ally Calhoun, and that "arrant knave" Duff Green conducted a journalistic campaign portraying him as a closet abolitionist and enemy of the South. Nor was there encouragement from the East. A caucus of his friends meeting in New York concluded he could not succeed and sent a messenger to Washington with the bad tidings.[47] Clay's interest in the contest waned even before the fall elections.

Webster, meanwhile, moved deliberately to become the Whig candidate. He and his Boston friends acquired a local newspaper and made it into a powerful Whig voice, the Boston *Atlas*. Among the Whig merchants, bankers, and manufacturers in Boston and New York, Webster hoped to raise $100,000 for the presidential campaign.[48] Being associated with big money was a liability as well as an asset. The Washington *Globe* kept up a drumbeat of charges and suspicions of venality. One of the rare pro-administration petitions received during the panic session, from York County, Pennsylvania, contained the assertion that Webster had been paid exorbitant fees, totaling $50,000, by his "good fat client," the B.U.S.[49] The petition was rejected, in part, on grounds it was a "gross libel." No evidence would ever be produced to prove the charge, asserted or implied, that Webster had been bribed, although he had, with other congressmen, been favored by the Bank with fees and generous loans. He grew anxious now to get clear of the Monster. More than his presidential candidacy moved him. His own Finance Committee had been instructed to make still another investigation of the Bank with a view to countering a damaging House report, and this could prove embarrassing to Webster. Most of his business was with the Boston branch, yet two notes amounting to $10,000 reposed at Chestnut Street. Since he was unable to redeem them when they came due in July, he pleaded for their renewal under some other auspices. "It is of great importance to get these matters out of the Bank of the United States," he wrote to Samuel Jaudon, Biddle's chief aide, in July. "I feel very anxious on this matter."[50] The notes were, *mirabile dictu*, picked up by a friend. Webster aimed, too, to erase his name from the books of the Boston branch. "These things being done," he told Jaudon, "I can take an early occasion next session to say, that I neither owe the Bank a dollar, nor owe on any paper discounted by the Bank, for any body, the amount of a dollar. In these times of the prevalence of slander and falsehood, it seems important to be able to make this declaration."[51] Alas, the occasion did not soon arise.

In the short session the Bank War was forgotten, and the nation witnessed the spectacle of the president indulging his "bump of combativeness," to employ the phrenological lingo then in vogue, against France. Under a treaty signed in 1831 France agreed to pay the United States $5 million in settlement of a host of spoliation claims by American citizens arising out of the Napoleonic wars. When the United States subsequently presented a draft for the first installment, the government refused payment because the Chamber of Deputies had declined to appropriate the money; and diplomatic efforts over the next year failed to break the impasse. In his December message, therefore, Jackson urged Congress to proceed on the assumption that the Orleanist government had no intention of executing the treaty and to "take redress into their own hands." He recommended, in particular, a law authorizing reprisals on French property. These threats angered the French government, which recalled its minister from Washington. Michael Chevalier, the journalist in whose American dispatches the government placed implicit faith, drew a parallel between Jackson's bullying tactics with the Bank and with France. "The General seems, in fact, to be possessed by the demon of war; for no sooner had he put his foot on the throat of the Bank than he required a new enemy, and finding in America none but vanquished adversaries, or objects unworthy of anger, he thus flings down the glove to France."[52]

Doubtless Clay concurred. War would make Jackson's tyranny complete. Clay took the chairmanship of the Committee on Foreign Affairs, to which the president's request was referred, and promptly reported against it.[53] On a straight party vote, twenty thousand copies of the report—four times the usual number—were ordered to be printed. The triumvirate stood as one against the president. Clay's resolution, embodying the conclusion of his report, passed the Senate without dissent. Again, though in a different field, he appeared as a peacemaker. Fears of war subsided, and the French government, believing that Clay's report exhibited "the sense of the country," moved toward an amicable settlement of the dispute. Clay, with his colleagues, was showered with praise. "To his masterly report . . . ," said the Baltimore *Patriot,* "may justly be ascribed this peaceful settlement. . . . Luckily for America, she has a Senate! And luckily for her also, she has in that Senate, a Clay, a Webster, and a Calhoun!"[54]

It was, in fact, the Kentuckian's only victory over his great rival. Unfortunately its luster was dimmed by the action of House Democrats who condemned him for "false reptile prudence." In the last days of the session House leaders sought under cover of the French crisis to sneak through a whopping $3 million appropriation for military and naval preparations as part of the usual fortifications bill. The senators promptly rejected this special appropriation "sprung upon us in the cover of night." In conference the House refused to recede while the Senate "adhered," causing the whole fortifications bill to be lost. Webster was prominently blamed for the loss. In a speech near the midnight hour, unreported but described as "grand and soul-stirring," Webster denounced the gigantic appropriation as a bid for dictatorial power. The threat to the liberty of the country came from within. Pleading with the Senate before the final vote, he recalled the words of a Roman orator, "Let every man's opinion be written on his forehead."[55] Recriminations spilled over into the next Congress. The Democratic leadership, regardless of foreign crisis, seemed determined to pass a huge pork barrel of military projects as its contribution to the reduction of the surplus. How far the president supported this was unclear. Most Whigs opposed it. Some believed the war crisis had been created to rally popular opinion behind Jackson for a third term. All agreed with Webster that the crisis and the Three Million Bill were expressions of Democratic "man-worship." "Sir," Webster asked in January 1836, "if on the 3rd of March last, it had been the purpose of both houses of Congress to create a military dictator, what form would have been better suited . . . ? Rome had no better models."[56]

As it happened, Webster's chief antagonist in this matter was his Massachusetts colleague in the House, John Quincy Adams. He supported the president, backed preparations for war, and accused the Senate of "dodging the question." While this issue was pending in Washington, Adams was a candidate before the Bay State legislature, in Boston, for the Senate seat vacated by Nathaniel Silsbee. He had widespread support, and he was the choice of the Anti-Masonic party in particular. His rival, who had the old National Republican following, was "Honest John" Davis who, only a year before, had bested "Johnny Q" in the race for governor. Webster favored Davis. He made this known in January simultaneously with the legislature's nomination of him for the presidency.[57] Adams was thus the underdog from the start. When the election came in February 1835, the two houses of the General Court divided, the senate choosing Adams, the house choosing Davis. The stalemate lasted for two weeks, until Adams's militant speech in Washington on the French question. "The whole mercantile community took alarm," his son wrote from Boston.[58] The senate yielded on the fourth ballot, and Davis was elected. Adams took the defeat very hard. He blamed it on the Massachusetts triumvirate of Webster, Davis, and Edward Everett, the last of whom in this "triple play" to shut him out was rewarded with the Whig nomination for governor. "[Daniel Webster] is the Mark Anthony of the trio," Adams wrote. "Edward Everett is the Octavius, and John Davis the Lepidus."[59] The disgruntlement extended to Webster's presidential candidacy, which Adams called the most profligate imaginable. His son Charles Francis published a retaliatory pamphlet in September.[60]

Never enamored of Adams, Webster was reminded of his bolt to the Republicans in 1808 and wondered if he contemplated repeating that political apostasy under cover of the French crisis. Webster the candidate was eager for Anti-Masonic votes, however, so he sought no quarrel with Adams. The following January, as the Gallo-American dispute was in the track of peaceful settlement, Webster defended his opposition to the Fortifications Bill. Contrasting his "idolatry" of the Constitution with the popular idolatry of the president, he declared that "if the proposition were now before us, and the guns of the enemy were pointed against the walls of the Capitol, I would not agree to it."[61] Although representatives were not supposed to reply to senators, Adams made this unfortunate remark the occasion for a bitter rebuke of Webster in the house. "Sir, only one step more was necessary, and an easy one it was, for men who would refuse an appropriation . . . if the enemy were at the gates of the Capitol—I say, there was only one step more, and that a natural and easy one—to join the enemy in battering down these walls." Calls of "order! order!" were unheeded. Democrats cheered him on, clapping and applauding as in in a theater.[62] It was an amazing spectacle: the congressman, and former chief executive, assailing the senior senator and presidential nominee of his state. Webster, who was present, taking his whipping in public, remarked of Adams, "He has the instinct of those animals, which, when enraged, turn upon their keepers, and mangle those who have shown them most kindness."[63] The senator prepared a reply but was persuaded to leave the task to others. In the House, George Evans of Maine not only defended Webster but scornfully dismissed Adams as a man who had become " 'the derision of his enemies—the melancholy pity of his friends.' " John M. Clayton, in the Senate, recalled the fate of the Greek who proposed to surrender the constitution in order to save the capitol: the people stoned him to death. Clayton seemed to think Adams deserved the same fate. "Such a man should never be suffered by honorable men, to stand in any party again; for this unprovoked denunciation proves that its author will be false to all parties, and true to no friend."[64] Adams injured Webster. But he injured himself much more. The Whig press pummeled him; scarcely a word was said in his defense. He became a political vagrant, with only the career of a gadfly before him. Webster said he felt sorry for him, though his pity struggled hard against his contempt. Not for several years would the two men have any intercourse with each other.[65]

The Massachusetts nomination of Webster followed the favorite-son nominations of two other Whig legislatures, Justice McLean in Ohio and Hugh Lawson White in Tennessee. Webster was commended to the nation not only as the Defender of the Constitution but also as a "MAN OF THE PEOPLE, the son of a farmer and soldier of the Revolution, [who] has risen, by the mere force of talent, and integrity, and untiring ardor in the public service."[66] Whigs in Rhode Island and Maine quickly seconded the nomination. With three sectional candidates in the field the new party might, at the least, hope to divert enough votes from Van Buren to throw the election into the House of Representatives. But Webster did not see himself as a sectional candidate. He was indignant at White, most of whose supporters were, like White himself, really state rights Republicans alienated from Jackson on the issue of executive tyranny. Between Webster's mouthpiece, the Boston *Atlas,* and southern Whig newspapers such as the Richmond *Whig* there was a wide gulf. Webster saw no way to bridge it. The new party was in danger of breaking up within a year of its birth. The rally to White in the South had so deeply disgusted northern Whigs, Webster warned, that many would be driven to Van Buren in spite of themselves.[67] An omen appeared in the spring elections, when the Whigs suffered defeat in Rhode Island and Connecticut. Webster's weakness was disclosed where he was supposed to be strongest. He had fairer hopes in the West than in the South, of course. McLean's candidacy quickly faded. It would be succeeded in the summer, however, by that of William Henry Harrison, a western military hero of the Jackson vintage.

Lacking enthusiastic support in New England, Webster could not generate popular following elsewhere. He was admired, flattered, even worshiped by the political and commercial elites of the northern cities, and because they all spoke the same language, in a clear voice, their electoral influence appeared greater than it was. These little coteries caucused with each other, talked to each other, wrote to each other, and thereby imagined they were leading the people. But Webster and his friends had not yet learned the rules of democratic politics; they talked down to ordinary people, as far as they talked to them at all, and had a positive aversion to the machinery of campaigns and elections. Webster remained an austere figure in the public eye, grand in intellect, but emotionally cold. His other liabilities included the *odium politicum* of Federalism, his ties to the Bank, and, among Whigs, his flirtation with the Jackson administration. Hailed as a "man of the people," he lacked the common touch. Hailed as a man of granite integrity ("Rocks may be rent, or moved, but nothing in the tide of time, or the tempests of party, can shake or touch his integrity"), there was too much evidence that he had submitted his politics to the interests of northern merchants, bankers, and manufacturers. Hailed as a nationalist ("North, East, West, and South have . . . been to him but one point on the compass") it was becoming evident that no two sections could unite in him.[68] Even northern friends, after measuring him on the standard of "availability," backed away. "It is the height of madness to run Webster," William H. Seward, a rising Whig star, advised in New York.[69] Henry Clay came to the same conclusion. White's candidacy had dispelled any lingering hopes he may have had for himself; and although at first professing neutrality toward the others, he obviously preferred Webster or Harrison to White. Just what it would have taken to turn Clay into a Webster supporter it is difficult to say, for Harrison's ascendancy in the West enabled the Kentucky senator to choose on unassailable political grounds. He said nothing publicly, but in August the Lexington *Observer*, generally supposed to speak for him, announced for Harrison.[70] Webster could never forgive him.

The New Englander's political hulk was dead in the water several months before it sank in Pennsylvania at the end of the year. The Anti-Masons were the main opposition force in the Keystone State. They were attracted to Harrison, but he failed to satisfy the party leaders on the strength of his commitment to Anti-Masonry. Webster sought to do so, using Everett as a go-between. Everett's nomination for governor, of course, had been part of the bargain that sent Davis to the Senate; with it Webster had hoped to win over the Massachusetts Anti-Masons. Although the coalition went on to elect Everett, the fight for the senatorial seat on top of other irritants split it apart, causing the Anti-Masonic leader, Benjamin Hallett, to decamp with the party newspaper to Van Buren and the Democrats. This did not shake Whig control in Massachusetts, but it proved embarrassing to Webster's courtship of the Pennsylvania Anti-Masons.[71] In the fall he kissed the Anti-Masonic rod. He denounced Freemasonry with all other secret orders and gave his blessing to the Anti-Masonic party. On only one point of the required pledge, the appointment of the faithful to office, did he hedge; and when questioned further, although still equivocating, Webster said, "I am altogether incapable of disappointing in that respect."[72] Harrison, meanwhile, already the popular choice of the Whigs, moved closer to the Pennsylvania Anti-Masons. He satisfied the majority faction, the "Coalitionists," who favored alliance with the Whigs, as against the "Exclusives," who wanted Webster as their candidate. When the state convention met at Harrisburg in December, Harrison walked away with the nomination. "What a farce!" exclaimed one of Webster's backers. "All agree, 'Mr. Webster is my first choice,' but we cannot carry him. Why? It seems strange that he who is the *first* choice of every one should be *less* popular than the man who is only the *second* choice, and confessedly his inferior. Ah, but he was a Federalist? Damning sin! Never to be forgiven."[73] Such was the logic of "availability."

Webster was bitterly disappointed. There were rumors, apparently unfounded, that he again sought to make terms with the administration. Earlier demands from the South that he withdraw in order to aid White's candidacy were now joined by northern and western demands in Harrison's behalf. But neither man had a proven following in New England, and so Webster's managers (Caleb Cushing, Robert Winthrop, and Everett) urged him to stay in the race, not with any expectations of success nationally but as a rallying point for the Whig party in Yankeeland. In February Webster asked the advice of the Massachusetts congressional delegation. They met (Adams absented himself) and reported that, while they still considered him the Massachusetts candidate, he should consult his own judgment. A month later he went home to talk to the Whig members of the legislature. They pleaded with him not to withdraw. The integrity of the commonwealth hung on his candidacy. "To quote parable," Winthrop said, "Massachusetts can hold her own while Mr. Webster is a candidate. They will both *decline* together. And every day that an uncertainty exists upon that point is . . . a day's advantage gained to the enemy."[74] Webster complied, and he won the Bay State's electoral vote in 1836. He won no other. The rest of New England went for Harrison. The Hero of Tippecanoe proved to be popular, but the Whigs had neither the strength nor the issues to elect him president in 1836. Webster's failed candidacy had no bearing on the result nationally, though it helped to consolidate the party in Massachusetts.

Mortified by the collapse of his candidacy, Webster talked of retirement from the Senate. Marshfield was much on his mind, as were his entangled financial affairs and the western land speculations he had embarked upon. Living alone in Washington during the fierce winter of 1836, he read his way through a small library and grew more and more despondent about the national condition. He had only one case before the Supreme Court. Formerly the rock of salvation in his eyes, the court added to his despondency. It now had a Jacksonian majority. The president had appointed Roger B. Taney to succeed Chief Justice Marshall upon his death; and the Senate had changed so much that his confirmation, earlier denied as secretary of treasury, was assured. "Story thinks the Supreme Court is *gone*," Webster wrote to Caroline in New York, "and I think so, too; and almost everything is gone, or seems rapidly going."[75] At its next term the court finally decided the celebrated Charles River Bridge case, which had engaged Webster for eight years. At issue fundamentally, as in the Dartmouth College case, was the protection of a corporate charter against legislative violation, specifically the exclusive charter of a fifty-year-old toll bridge against a newly chartered free bridge, the Warren Bridge, across the same river at the same place. Arguing for vested property rights, Webster was resigned to losing. "The court is revolutionized." Part of the revolution was the favor shown the new anti-charter doctrine fulminated during the Bank War. "Taney is smooth and plausible," Webster conceded, "but cunning and Jesuitical and as thorough going a party judge as ever got on to a bench of justice."[76] Taney's decision attacked Webster's theory of law as well as his theory of economic growth, which was founded on the sanctity of contract; and although it did not, in fact, wreck the damage Webster feared, he was never reconciled to it. The Charles River Bridge case, he said eight years later, "terminated in a manner more unfortunate, more disappointing to my professional expectations, more—I may say—confounding to my professional judgment, than any in which I have been concerned in a practice of forty years at the bar."[77]

There was gloom enough in Washington to gratify the appetites of Clay and Calhoun as well. Clay's term would expire with Jackson's, and he, too, talked of retirement. He was in mourning—the death of still another daughter—during the long session of 1836. He was tired, sad, and disgusted. "I confine myself almost exclusively to my room, except when I go to the Capitol," he wrote to Lucretia, who no longer left Ashland. "I see no body, except my messmates and the few who call on me, and I desire to see no one."[78] To such a state had the heartiest member of the Senate been reduced. "The Senate is no longer a place for any decent man," he lamented. "It is rapidly filling up with blackguards."[79] This was not entirely a pose, but if Clay thus sought to provoke a call for his reelection to the Senate, he succeeded. " 'Rome demands him,' " proclaimed the Louisville Journal. "Much as he covets domestic life and the quiet of . . . home, he must still listen to the voice of his state when she calls him to the rescue."[80] He accepted reelection in the darkest hour in the history of the Senate: the passage on January 16, 1837, of Benton's Expunging Resolution.

For three successive sessions the Whigs had beaten back the Missouri senator who had vowed to expunge the censure of Jackson from the journal. But what began as a one-man crusade became a party cause, and by means of "instruction" of senators by Democratic state legislatures, a pro-resolution majority was obtained before Jackson's term expired. The triumvirate again stood together, condemning the reckless, unprecedented, and unconstitutional proposition to deface the journal of the Senate, yet well knowing it would pass. To all of them it was the basest sort of "man-worship." For eight years Jackson had swept over the government "like a tropical tornado," Clay remarked. "What more does he want? Must we blot, deface, and mutilate the records of the country to punish the presumptuousness of expressing an opinion contrary to his own?" In a peroration that drew praise even from Benton, Clay challenged the perpetrators of the deed to explain it to the people. "Tell them that you have extinguished one of the brightest and purest lights that ever burned at the altar of civil liberty. Tell them that you have silenced one of the noblest batteries that ever thundered in defense of the constitu-

tion. . . . Tell them that, henceforward, no matter what daring or outrageous
act any president may perform, you have for ever hermetically sealed the
mouth of the senate. . . . Tell them, finally, that you have restored the glorious doctrine of passive obedience and non-resistance, and, if the people do
not pour out their indignation and imprecations, I have yet to learn the character of American freemen."[81] It was already dark when Calhoun rose to
speak. "This act originates in pure, unmixed, personal idolatry . . . ," he declared. "The former act [removal of the deposits] was such a one as might
have been perpetrated in the days of Pompey or Caesar; but an act like this
could never have been consummated by a Roman senate until the times of
Caligula and Nero."[82] Near midnight the vote was taken, twenty-four for,
nineteen against. The Whigs walked out, and as the secretary took up the
journal of 1834, drew black lines around Clay's censure resolution, and
stamped it "Expunged," the gallery broke into riot and tumult never before
witnessed in the Senate.[83]

Calhoun had taken no part in the presidential election. Some of his followers, including Duff Green and his *Telegraph*, had campaigned for White; but
Calhoun continued to "stand alone in my glory," and the state's electors oblig-
ingly threw away their votes. The Carolinian's hatred of Jackson and Van
Buren was unabated. And he had become so obsessed with the dangers
threatening slavery and the South that some of his colleagues feared he was
in the grip of hallucination. Yet he regarded the coming of Van Buren with
more equanimity than either of his fellow triumvirs. Practicing the wisdom
that things must get worse before they can get better, he only awaited the cli-
mactic disaster before rising again. He calculated, too, that Van Buren would
be vulnerable to southern influence. Unlike Jackson, he was "not of the race
of the lion or the tiger; he belonged to a lower order—the fox; and it would
be vain to expect that he could command the respect or acquire the confidence of those who had so little admiration for the qualities by which he was
distinguished."[84]

2. Calhoun and Abolitionism

For four years Calhoun acted *with* but was never *of* the Whig party. The
state rights branch of the party was a poor relation of national republicanism.
He had no hope of changing this, of turning the party into a vehicle of southern principles and interests, hence his aversion to White's candidacy and his
vaunted independence. Whiggery was useful only as a temporary expedient
in the war on Jacksonism. During these years Calhoun evolved a theory of
the degeneracy of the republic which, although founded in nullification,
went well beyond it. The first error lay in the creation of a national government. And no sooner was the Constitution established than it was corrupted
by the Hamiltonian policy of using fiscal favors and privileges, including the
"unholy alliance" with banks, to bind "the great and powerful classes of soci-

ety" to the government. Hamilton was opposed by Jefferson, who left a mighty legacy—the creed of state rights in the Virginia and Kentucky Resolutions. But while the Virginian had more genius, Hamilton had more ability; and he fixed the course of the government. Jefferson, said Calhoun, was unable to slow or alter it during eight years at the helm. The nationalism of the war created a dominant interest in the Union. Out of this came the American System. It was the Hamiltonian system enlarged, more inequitable, more oppressive, and with the tariff revenue it created a veritable cornucopia of spoils and corruption. Nullification commenced the work of reform by placing the tariff on the road to extinction. It promised to stem the fiscal bounty and, in time, to restore the confederative character of the government. The overthrow of the Bank of the United States, the heart and soul of the money power, was another important reform. Unfortunately, as it was carried out by a tyrannical president and a spoils party, the reform compounded the evils of a vicious policy. The natural end of Jacksonism, as the French crisis disclosed, was "military despotism." The only effective remedy for all these evils—executive tyranny, corrupt patronage, treasury surplus, and so on— was the severe contraction of the government. "My aim is fixed," Calhoun declared. "It is no less than to turn back the Government to where it commenced its operations in 1789 . . . , to take a fresh start, a new departure, on the State Rights Republican tack."[1] The task was made more urgent, Calhoun believed, because of the new danger that northern abolitionists, heedless of moral and legal restraints, would seize the government and impose the ultimate corruption: emancipation of the slaves.

Whatever one may think of this outlook, it provided Calhoun with a clear and steady angle of vision on the problems that came before him. It was a markedly different angle from Webster's or Clay's, of course, and also much more acute. It resulted in a legislative program first formulated in the senator's Report on the Extent of Executive Patronage in February 1835. Abuse of the patronage power had been the first public outcry against the administration. Patronage was a partisan issue, but it assumed theoretical significance when Jackson himself extended the old idea of "rotation in office," applicable to elected officials, to appointive officials, placed public service on strictly egalitarian grounds, and, reasoning that because office is not "a species of property," therefore removals for political cause were perfectly appropriate. Clay had fixed on this issue and moved to curtail the president's patronage power. Now Calhoun, calling attention to increasing executive patronage and evidence of corruption in certain departments, especially the post office, exceeding anything in "the rottenest ages of the Roman empire," moved the appointment of a committee of inquiry. He was accused of seeking a party question, and although he denied this, he certainly aimed in cooperation with the Whigs to stigmatize Jackson and the administration. Yet Calhoun gave a different turn to the discussion by linking spoils to money and grounding the abuses of the patronage in the fiscal action of the government. In this he went beyond Whig doctrine. He got his committee, with a three-to-two majority against the administration; and very soon—too soon for any but the most perfunctory investigation—it presented a report that was entirely his own work.[2]

After demonstrating the growth of federal expenditures and offices, the report made three main recommendations. First, the repeal of certain sections of the Four-Year Law of 1820 and adoption of a requirement that in all cases of executive removal the reasons for the action be submitted to Congress. The law of 1820 was a well-intentioned effort to enforce accountability on all officers handling federal funds; it had been converted by Jackson, however, into a system for vacating offices every four years regardless of performance. The same recommendation had been made, as Calhoun was careful to point out, by Senator Benton in his report on executive patronage during the Adams administration.[3] Ironically, the Missourian was now the leading defender of the administration. He sputtered and fumed at Calhoun for tracing the recommendation to him; when he labeled it a lie he was called to order and pandemonium descended. The Senate had come to expect trouble whenever Calhoun and Benton tangled. The sustained hatred between them was one of the marvels of the age. They fought each other relentlessly for twenty years, and when Calhoun died, Benton rioted in his ashes. Clay was dissatisfied with the report's proposal, also derived from Benton's report, to require the president to give reasons for removal, and called instead for what amounted to senatorial consent to removal as the corollary of senatorial consent to appointment.[4] This would repudiate the first silent amendment of the Constitution—the president's removal power—made by Congress in 1789 after James Madison's powerful argument for executive responsibility. Clay had earlier found little support for his position; now, however, most Whigs seemed to concur at least in principle.

Calhoun's other recommendations had little to do with patronage as usually understood. One concerned the regulation of the government deposits, some $10 million, in the pet banks. Executive fiat had created the pets; they were supple instruments of executive power—indeed, in Calhoun's view, they were the cause of the alarming increase of that power. The Whigs supported Calhoun's Deposit Bill, as it came to be known. In doing so they acknowledged, as Webster did, that the question of a national bank was "entirely settled" for the time being. No more than Calhoun did they approve the system, but they sought to regulate what they could not control. The final recommendation was a constitutional amendment authorizing distribution of the surplus revenue to the states until 1843, when the reduction of revenue under the Compromise Act would take full effect. With the discharge of the debt in the current year, together with a healthy retrenchment of federal expenditures, Calhoun estimated a treasury surplus of approximately $9 million annually for the next seven years. Because the Compromise Act was inviolable, the revenue could not be reduced. Nor were there any objects of utility, within the purview of the Constitution, to which the surplus could be applied. It could only feed the spoilsmen. The administration proposed huge military expenditures, as in Benton's plan of fortifications. But this was a rotten sink of corruption, Calhoun said. Money was the true source of executive patronage and power. Reduce the flow and it would decline. Government *should* decline, in degrees, as the country grew. The opposite assumption of an ever-enlarging government must prove fatal. Calhoun had opposed distribution when Jackson was its advocate; and he continued to oppose Clay's plan for the distribution of the proceeds of the public lands, which would have much the same effect. Earlier he had said that distribution would corrupt and subvert the state governments; now he argued that by giving them a stake in the federal treasury distribution would strengthen the states and turn them into "sentinels of economy" over the general government. There was no constitutional sanction for distribution, of course; Calhoun called for the impossible, an amendment, and in the end justified the policy as a temporary expedient. How far an expedient in South Carolina, the state's grand project for a western railroad, in which Calhoun was deeply interested, may have influenced his call for distribution in 1835 is an interesting question.[5] It was, in any event, another instance of Calhoun's aptitude for political flip-flop. The distribution proposal never came to a vote. And although the Senate passed both the Deposit Bill and the restriction on the removal power, the measures died in the House.

Regardless of changing objects, Calhoun aimed always to force the government onto state rights principles. Executive tyranny was but a by-product of congressional encroachment on the rights of states through the tariff and related measures. Jackson, for all his wickedness, only harvested what Congress sowed.[6] The attack on spoils, pets, and surplus revenue was part of a larger campaign to shrink the federal government and separate it from the money power of the country—a campaign more compatible, in other circumstances, with Democratic than Whig principles. Returning to Washington for the Twenty-Fourth Congress, Calhoun lamented the rise of Van Burenism in the South and worried about the president's warmongering against France. In war the spoils party would become the military party, and plunder by force would succeed the subtler arts of plunder by fraud; even if war were averted the crisis would afford spoilsmen with fresh opportunities to extend their rapacious career.[7] The crisis passed, but the problem that, in part, produced it, the surplus revenue, remained, and Calhoun feared the country would be debauched before the surplus could be eliminated. The surplus continued to grow; last year's estimates proved much too conservative; new estimates placed it at $40 or $50 million within a year's time. Deposited in some forty banks, it fueled an already dangerously overheated economy. Early in the session Calhoun reintroduced the distribution amendment of the Constitution—a futile gesture, as he knew.

Aside from the administration's defense program, the principal proposal for the surplus was Henry Clay's Land Bill. It had been a crucial measure of his political platform since 1832, when his famous report had turned a previously sectional issue into an issue between the parties. Under the bill reintroduced in December, the accumulated proceeds from the spiraling land sales of the last three years, amounting to $21 million—almost the same amount as the surplus—would be immediately distributed to the states, as would all but

10 percent of the proceeds during the next two years. The Land Bill would have the same fiscal effect as distribution of the surplus revenue. For Clay, however, it had two larger purposes: first, securing the national domain from the ravages of speculators, squatters, and politicians; second, funding under state auspices works of internal improvement the Jackson administration had rejected under the federal head. Still angry at the president for his pocket veto of the bill passed in 1833, Clay spoke lyrically of the good it would have done: "What immense benefits might not have been diffused throughout the land! . . . What new channels of commerce and communities might not have been opened! What industry stimulated, what labor rewarded!"[8] The Land Bill would eventually pass the Senate, but it was never given much chance of approval in the House. Recognizing this obstacle, and the hopelessness of a constitutional amendment, Calhoun came forward with an ingenious solution: the *deposit* of the surplus in the treasuries of the states for use as they pleased until the general government required its return. In February he had again introduced his Deposit Bill for the regulation of the pet banks. Now, three months later, he added the new feature to the old bill. He had been led to it, oddly, by the suggestion of the Democratic leader, Silas Wright, that the surplus might be invested in state securities. This was as close as the administration came to offering a constructive solution. But Wright soon backed off, then opposed Calhoun's plan. Both Clay and Webster supported it. Seeing that his own bill was bottled up in a House committee, Clay endorsed Calhoun's as embodying substantially the same purpose. Under it the existing surplus in excess of $5 million would be deposited in the state treasuries in proportion to the federal population ratio. Calhoun denied that this was distribution under another name. Although the states would have unrestricted use of the deposits, they could be recalled in a national emergency, and so had the character of interest-free loans. To this Benton snapped, "Names cannot alter things; and it is as idle to call a gift a deposit, as it would be to call a stab of the dagger a kiss of the lips."[9] The Senate, nevertheless, voted 40–6 for the Deposit Bill, the House 155–38; and Jackson, bowing to these overwhelming majorities, signed the bill into law on June 23, 1836.

Calhoun had thus been led during a period of six years from staunch opposition to distribution, through advocacy of a constitutional amendment authorizing it, to legislative enactment under the fiction of the Deposit Bill. His goal was unvarying, but he repeatedly altered the means, so drastically, in fact, that a new dialectic was required to sustain the old principles. He took delight in the political effects of his legislative coup. It confounded the Democratic leadership and proved that the party was still susceptible to his influence. That summer, in a speech at Pendleton and in public letters, Calhoun extolled the act as "the commencement of a new political era . . . marking the termination of that long vibration of our system towards consolidation . . . and its return to its true confederative character, as it came from the hands of the framers." It was, he declared, "the consummation of the Carolina doctrines," since it placed the nation's treasury in the custody of the state governments.[10] Benton agreed that the act was revolutionary. But whether the revolution was in the direction of state rights or consolidation remained problematic. The Deposit Act initially distributed $28 million to the states in three installments. They used it for a range of purposes, mostly of the internal improvements variety. In New York every dollar of the $4.5 million paid to the state went into education. None of the money would ever be returned or even requested. The fourth installment was deferred indefinitely in 1837, when financial panic struck, and the act was not renewed.[11] The revolution was thus short-lived. What the effects of distribution would have been had it become a permanent part of the federal system it is impossible to say.

One of the reasons Calhoun sought to rid the government of the surplus was to bar any support of slavery emancipation and colonization. Colonization, in particular, remained an object of Clay's distribution program; and in the wake of the Nat Turner Insurrection, the Virginia legislature, in 1832, had gone to the brink of gradual emancipation on a plan that had been advocated by Thomas Jefferson and that entailed large federal funding. Calhoun had, in fact, traced the anti-slavery movement in Virginia to the fatal temptress, the federal surplus.[12] In his public thought about slavery and abolition, as earlier about free trade and tariff, Calhoun had lagged behind advanced southern opinion. With many enlightened southerners he had not attempted to justify slavery other than as a necessary evil. Edward Everett recalled a conversation with him in 1823, when he seemed impervious to all narrow or sectional views. Questioned about slavery in the southern scheme of things, Calhoun replied it was "scaffolding, scaffolding, Sir—it will come away when the building is finished."[13] But the scaffolding, instead of coming down, became a part of the building itself. Some years later another northern congressman, Horace Binney, talked to Calhoun about slavery. Slavery, in some form, was a universal condition, he said. In the North the "wage slaves," poor, violent, and uneducated but endowed with the franchise, would one day overthrow property and liberty. This could not happen in the South, where labor and capital were united and the black slaves had no political rights. "Slavery is indispensable to a republican government," he maintained. "There cannot be a durable republican government without slavery."[14] As slavery became part of his utopia, Calhoun identified his politics and ambitions ever more closely with that grandiose "nowhere," the South. On the floor of the Senate in 1837, some years after the pro-slavery vanguard had laid the foundations, Calhoun not only proclaimed the superiority of southern society but also pronounced chattel slavery "a good—a great good."[15]

Northern politicians agreed with their southern counterparts that slavery was a local matter, beyond the reach of federal law; but two issues strenuously agitated by abolitionists forced the matter on the attention of Congress. One of these was the flood of abolitionist literature in the southern mails, the other the petition campaign for the abolition of slavery in the District of Columbia. In Calhoun's village, Pendleton, on September 9, 1835, a citizens' meeting adopted resolutions condemning the abolitionists and appointed a committee of vigilance drawn from local militia units to stop the circulation of "incendiary" publications. Similar meetings were held throughout the state. In Charleston the offending publications were impounded pending instructions from the postmaster general, Amos Kendall. Whether or not Calhoun attended the Pendleton meeting, he realized that the problem would come before Congress and prepared to act on it. Stopping at Columbia on his return to Washington, he discussed measures with the newly elected governor, George McDuffie, and legislative leaders.[16] The legislature proceeded at the governor's request to appeal to the non-slaveholding states to suppress seditious machinations against the peace and safety of the South. The formation of abolition societies and the agitation led by William Lloyd Garrison were held to be in direct violation of the federal compact. Suppression at the source might alone preserve it. Only three of the northern state legislatures noticed the South Carolina resolutions; and none acted to suppress the agitation.[17]

President Jackson, meanwhile, laid the matter before Congress. He proposed enactment of a federal law authorizing the post office to suppress the transmission of inflammatory literature in the slave states. In the normal course of things this part of the annual message would have been referred to the Post Office Committee; but noticing that only the chairman of the committee, Felix Grundy, was a southerner, Calhoun successfully moved the appointment of a select committee that reflected the dominant interest of the South in the subject. Calhoun, of course, was named chairman of the five-man committee, only one of whose members, John Davis, was a northern senator. On February 4, 1836, Calhoun submitted his report with an accompanying bill. Both were peculiarly his own. A majority of the committee refused to concur in the report; two preferred another kind of bill and one, Davis, opposed any legislation. Respect for state rights principles would not permit Calhoun to join Jackson in calling for repressive federal legislation. He referred to the example of the Sedition Act, denounced by Jeffersonian Republicans as a violation of First Amendment rights of freedom of speech and press as well as of the reserved rights of the states, and said that a federal law punishing the circulation of ideas through the mails would be equally unconstitutional with one punishing publication. To admit the authority, moreover, "would be virtually to clothe Congress with the power to abolish slavery, by giving it the means of breaking down all the barriers which the slaveholding States have erected for the protection of their lives and property."[18] While thus recognizing that federal action was a two-edged sword, likely to prove more destructive than protective of the South, Calhoun nevertheless went on to incur the same risks at another level by proposing that the federal government do indirectly what it could not do directly. It could and should cooperate in the enforcement of such laws as a state might enact for the safety of its own citizens. Looking for precedents, he cited federal assistance in the enforcement of state quarantine regulations and statutes prohibiting the foreign slave trade, neglecting to observe that these pertained to foreign commerce where the general government had exclusive jurisdiction. His bill would punish any postmaster for receiving, forwarding, or delivering any mail which the laws of the state prohibited. Slavery was as much menaced by discussion as by federal intervention, Calhoun thought. And caught between the imperative of state rights, on the one hand, and suppression of inflammatory discussion on the other, he resolved his dilemma by inventing the doctrine of "federal reinforcement" of state laws.[19]

When Calhoun's bill came to the floor it was attacked on several grounds. First, although intended to suppress agitation of slavery, it would have the opposite effect. In America's "martyr age," as Harriet Martineau labeled it, repressive legislation only played into the abolitionists' hands. Some slave state senators, friendly to Calhoun, feared this must be the result. Second, the bill violated the First Amendment guarantee of freedom of the press. Calhoun's assertion to the contrary, directed against the administration proposal, was hollow. Indeed, said Webster, his bill was worse than the Sedition Act, since it would impose prior restraint upon the dissemination of anti-slavery opinion. Third, the bill in effect made the laws of the states laws of Congress by adoption, opening up a boundless field of power and fundamentally changing the character of the government. If Congress could "reinforce" laws enacted under the police power of the states, where, Clay wondered, were the constitutional limits? Fourth, it arrayed the United States on the side of slavery, subverting the principle that slavery was a local institution with which Congress had nothing to do. Every free state citizen, Davis warned, would be forced to participate in the evils of slavery by deprivation of his right to speak against it. Calhoun acknowledged the conflict between the two authorities in the federal system, but thought that the superior claim belonged to the states—the twelve states—whose survival was at stake. "Will any rational being," he asked rhetorically, "say that the laws of the States of the Union, which are necessary to their peace, security, and very existence, ought to yield to the laws of the general Government regulating the Post Office, which at best is a mere accommodation and convenience, and this when this Government was formed *by the States* mainly with a view to secure more perfectly this peace and safety?" It was manifest, Calhoun said in April, that the northern legislatures lacked the political courage to act in the matter. Action was therefore incumbent on Congress. Failing to adopt the bill, Congress would aid and abet the abolitionists. "Should such be your decision . . . ," the senator declared, "I shall say to the people of the South, look to yourselves—you have nothing to hope from others."[20] Undeterred, the Senate voted down Calhoun's bill, even after its punitive provisions were softened to lure wavering Democrats. Meanwhile, administrative action by the post office quietly put a stop to the delivery of abolitionist propaganda where it was not wanted; and although southern congressmen continued to protest, they made no further effort to secure legislation against so-called incendiary publications.

The campaign for the abolition of slavery in the District of Columbia went on for several years. Congress had been receiving and quietly disposing of abolitionist petitions that prayed for abolition where Congress itself was held to be sovereign. The Senate routinely received and referred the petitions to the District Committee, where they died, until Calhoun waved a red flag in January. Upon two petitions being presented by Ohio Senator Thomas Morris, Calhoun moved the question of receiving them. They were, he said, "foul slanders" on fully half the states of the Union and could not be tolerated. Moreover, as Congress had no power to abolish slavery in the District, no more than in South Carolina, he argued, the petitions should be rejected. Finally, the time had come to put a stop to the agitation that endangered the Union.[21] Perhaps half a dozen senators favored abolition of slavery in the District, where it was a particularly grating comment on American liberty, but no one seriously entertained the proposition. This was not the issue. The issue basically, omitting petty political considerations, was whether this annoying problem should be resolved on the level of principle or of expediency. The two extremes, defined by Calhoun and the abolitionists, met in favoring the former course. Most senators and representatives—the issue was also before the House—regardless of party or section favored the latter. Because of congressional jurisdiction over the District, the constitutional bar Calhoun raised against the petitions was specious at best. To abolish slavery in the District might be impolitic; it was probably not unconstitutional; and it was surely not unconstitutional to consider it. The senator's contention that the guarantee of the right of petition extended no further than presentation was equally specious. If practitioners could only knock at the door but never be heard or received, the right was empty, as Clay and others had pointed out. Moreover, denial of "the sacred right" of petition would inflame rather than dampen the agitation. The abolitionists, still only a small sect in the North, would appear in a new guise, no longer simply the enemies of slavery but the friends of civil liberty. The attention paid to them would increase as their cause was dignified by association with the cause of constitutional liberty. This was not only the northern view. "Sir," said Georgia's senator John R. King of Calhoun's motion, "if Southern senators were actually in the pay of the directory of Nassau Street,* they could not more effectively cooperate in the views and administer to the wishes of these enemies to the peace and quiet of our country."[22]

Calhoun's purposes were complex. He wished to preserve the Union, supposedly endangered by northern fanatics. While claiming to act on the defensive, he became fanatical in opposing them, impervious to appeals to reason and forbearance. He wished also to use the external threat of the abolitionists to unite the South behind his leadership. When King questioned his motives, Calhoun denounced him for sowing seeds of discord in the South. "It is the duty of every member from the South, on this great and vital question, where union is so important to those whom we represent, to avoid everything calculated to divide or distract our ranks."[23] The question, he de-

---

*The New York City headquarters of Arthur and Lewis Tappan, philanthropists and leaders of the American Anti-Slavery Society.

claimed, was "our Thermopolae." For to admit by the reception of petitions the authority of Congress to abolish slavery in the District would be to abandon one of the "outworks" of the South to the enemy. Who could doubt that assault on the citadel would follow? "Here the subject of abolition would be agitated session after session, and from hence the assaults on the property and institutions of the people of the slaveholding States would be disseminated . . . over the whole Union."[24] Only by defense of the outworks was their hope for the South within the Union; if in the process the number and ardor of the abolitionists increased it could not be helped. The South had great resources. It could stand alone, defending its life, character, and institutions, and would do so rather than perish. "It is not we, but the Union, which is in danger," Calhoun declared in his concluding speech on the question. "It is that which demands our care—demands that the agitation of the question shall cease here—that you shall refuse to receive these petitions, and decline all jurisdiction over the subject of abolition, in every form and shape. It is only on these terms that the Union can be safe. We cannot remain here in an endless struggle in defense of our character, our property, and institutions."[25]

It was March, and on a different abolitionist petition, before the Senate voted down Calhoun's motion 36–10. It then approved 36–6 James Buchanan's motion to receive the petitions but immediately to reject the prayer of the petitioners. This solution to the problem had the support of Van Buren and the administration. It looked like "juggling" to Calhoun, for it left the door open to the petitioners. He denounced the motion as "a fatal stab" to the rights of the people of the slaveholding States, and when the roll was called he marched out of the chamber. No one followed him, not even his junior colleague William C. Preston, which some thought a mark of Calhoun's isolation on the issue.[26] Clay voted with the majority, of course. He thought that Congress had full authority over slavery in the District, yet had no wish to exercise it; and he marveled at the hallucination that could produce a mountain from this molehill. Webster voted with the minority. The petitions should be respectfully received, printed, referred to committee, discussed, and reported upon. To suppress discussion, directly or indirectly, was foolhardy, he warned. In the end none of these modes—Calhoun's, Buchanan's, Webster's—prevailed. The Senate stumbled on a subtle refinement of procedure: when a petition was presented, someone moved not to receive it, and another quickly moved to table this motion, which was done. Without meeting Calhoun's principle, the procedure achieved the same effect.

Calhoun's defeat in the Senate had been preceded and, to an extent, brought on by a similar defeat in the House. His young friend James H. Hammond, a freshman congressman in the South Carolina delegation, had been given charge of the campaign in the House to close the doors to the abolitionists. But another member of the delegation, Henry Laurens Pinckney, bolted, and as chairman of the House committee to which the subject was referred introduced resolutions in February that conformed to the administration position rather than to Hammond's and Calhoun's. Under the "Pinckney Gag," as it came to be known, abolition petitions would be received and tabled without further ado. This was, said Calhoun, "the first blow against us."[27] Of course, it weakened his position in the Senate. Hammond's angry but futile opposition to the resolutions in the House was backed up by Duff Green's editorial blast in the *Telegraph*. Pinckney had surrendered the constitutional right over slavery in the District and opened Congress to the abolitionist assault on the South. Pinckney's betrayal was especially grating because he was considered one of Carolina's best and brightest. Son of Charles Pinckney, a framer of the Constitution and early leader of Jeffersonian Republicanism in South Carolina, he had graduated from the college, studied law with his brother-in-law, Robert Y. Hayne, built the Charleston *Mercury* into the state's most influential newspaper, served in the legislature, as mayor of Charleston, and since 1833 as the city's representative in Congress. He was a Nullifier and follower of Calhoun. No one knew why he bolted (some suspected "religious fanaticism," while others said he was "in the market" for political favor), but he was denounced as a traitor from one end of the state to the other. "Carolina has disowned him," said the Edgefield *Advertiser*. "She has blotted his proud name from the escutcheon of her patriots and statesmen."[28]

The attack on Pinckney was brutal. Calhoun did not participate in it directly, but it was led by his political friends in behalf of his authority in South Carolina. Pinckney spiritedly defended himself. The administration press in the North, beginning with the Washington *Globe*, lauded his political courage for sponsoring a sensible resolution of the controversy that Calhoun tried to turn into a medium of disunionism. Nor was Pinckney without support in Charleston. Although he was read out of the State Rights party, he announced his candidacy for reelection in August. His accompanying address was not only a defense of his conduct as in the best interest of the South but also an attack on the malice and tyranny of Calhoun, though the senator was not named, and other members of the South Carolina delegation.[29] It was feared for a time that the "Pinckney party" would coalesce with the Unionist remnant and revive the conflict that had torn the state apart at the height of nullification. This was averted for two reasons. First, many Unionists hated Pinckney for his leadership of the Nullifiers in Charleston and would not support him merely for the pleasure of injuring Calhoun. Second, the State Rights party, probably at Calhoun's direction, invited the Charleston Unionists to name one of their own to oppose Pinckney. They chose the scholarly Hugh Swinton Legaré. Endorsed by the *Mercury*, he went on to defeat Pinckney in the fall election.[30] Thus was the rebel chastised and thus was Calhoun's leadership in South Carolina politics consolidated. Henceforth, with rare exceptions, former Unionists rallied to Calhoun's standard in defense of slavery.

During the summer Calhoun turned his attention to a railroad project that had been gestating for several years. The idea of a great western railroad, connecting Charleston with the Ohio and Mississippi rivers, was born in 1833. It was part of the movement to revive Charleston's sagging economy—the positive counterpart of nullification—and it would provide as well the commercial underpinning of the still elusive South-West political alliance. The Louisville, Cincinnati, and Charleston Railroad Company, under Hayne's leadership, was chartered at Columbia in December 1835. A convention to mobilize interstate support met at Knoxville, Tennessee, the following summer. On the basis of engineering surveys the company adopted a northwesterly route, from Charleston through Columbia to Asheville, North Carolina, thence by way of the French Broad River and Cumberland Gap through the mountains into Kentucky. From the beginning Calhoun favored a more southerly route; and in September, accompanied by Colonel James Gadsden, he explored on horseback an alternate pathway through the Carolina Gap, some distance west of Fort Hill, which would connect with the headwaters of the Tennessee. Upon his return he championed this route, maintaining it was more practical than the well-known passage of the French Broad. He stated the case at length in a letter to the editor of the Pendleton *Messenger*, which was widely reprinted. With his neighbors he arranged public meetings in Pendleton and in other towns expected to benefit from the Carolina Gap route. And he urged friends to purchase enough stock in the company to gain control of the board of directors, which would finally choose the route.[31]

This conflict was at its height in the fall of 1836, coinciding with the election, when the Louisville, Cincinnati, and Charleston Railroad Company offered its stock for sale. It was, of course, another source of discord in the state. More than that, as it pitted "Calhounites" against "Haynites," and upcountry against lowcountry, the conflict threatened to split the State Rights party. By challenging Hayne and making a big issue of the route, Calhoun, some thought, actually aimed to become president of the railroad. Indeed, his good friend and congressional ally, Francis W. Pickens, predicted he would be elected and would quit the Senate to accept the presidency.[32] While it is interesting to contemplate Calhoun in the position of a captain of industry, and to imagine what might have been the course of American history in that circumstance, he never seriously entertained the idea. Before returning to Washington in December, he told Pickens, "I am no candidate and regret that my name has been placed before the public."[33] He deplored the menacing political schism on this issue, for nothing was more important than the unity and harmony of the state; and he hoped that the proposed routes would be carefully studied to enable the company to make the best choice. At the organization meeting of the railroad in Knoxville, in January 1837, Hayne was elected president, Calhoun a director, and decision was made for the French Broad route. Deeply disappointed, Calhoun refused to accept the decision as final and at every opportunity pressed for a southerly route, though not necessarily the Carolina Gap, which the railroad engineers considered impractical.

The failure of the other sta'es concerned in the railroad—North Carolina, Ohio, Kentucky, Tennessee—to meet their financial obligations to it was a severe setback. Alone of the five states, South Carolina invested her share of the federal surplus under the Deposit Act, amounting to $1 million, in the stock of the western railroad. The project that rose on the high tide of prosperity floundered when the country began a long descent into depression in 1837. It became, what it had been at its inception, simply a South Carolina project. The sensible thing, Calhoun now argued, was to abandon the grand design of a railroad to the Ohio Valley and to combine South Carolina's railroad interest with Georgia's by running the line from the Savannah River through Athens and around the mountains to the head of steam navigation on the Tennessee. Such a railroad would be primarily a carrier of cotton.[34] Hayne and the board would not budge. And in October 1838, although detailed surveys had yet to be completed, they renewed their commitment to the original design. Angry at this, sure that it must end in failure, Calhoun resigned from the board and sold his stock. He still believed, as he explained to Hayne, that a western railroad was of vital importance commercially and politically, but it should link up with the Tennessee and the southwest. Hayne, in reply, expressed regret over Calhoun's resignation, which was bound to shake public confidence in the project, and forcefully defended the board's position.[35] Less than a year later, Hayne was dead, and the company sank under the depression. Calhoun's prophecy of disaster was fulfilled. Would the result have been different had the company followed Calhoun's advice? Probably not. But the only trunk line from South Carolina westward completed before the Civil War followed, more or less, the southerly route he had advocated.

The railroad was the supreme agent—and the age's supreme symbol—of industrial capitalism, yet it obviously had an important place in Calhoun's conception of a united South organized around plantation agriculture. Back in the Senate he resumed the fight against the abolitionists. The flood of petitions rose. To his opponents this was the result of his intransigence; to Calhoun it simply verified his prediction. "The only way to resist was to close the doors; to open them was virtually to surrender the question." Concession was fatal to the South. He recalled his warning four years earlier in reply to Webster on the Force Bill: the doctrine that the general government could determine the extent of its own powers and enforce them at the point of a bayonet would be joined to the conscience of northern abolitionists whose influence would grow until the two great sections of the Union were arrayed in deadly conflict. Already the abolitionists controlled the pulpit, the schools, a part of the press in the North; soon by the power of their voices and their votes they would dictate to parties and command governments. "It is easy to see the end," Calhoun said. "By the necessary course of events, if left to themselves, we must become, finally, two people. . . . Abolition and the Union cannot coexist."[36] Curiously, in the light of this Cassandra-like utterance, there had just issued from Duff Green's press a futuristic novel, *The Partisan Leader*, whose anonymous author was the Virginian Nathaniel Beverley Tucker. Looking ahead a dozen or more years, Tucker imagined Van Buren in his fourth term, a virtual dictator, and portrayed the events leading to the establishment of a southern confederacy under a brilliant leader called, mysteriously, "Mr. B——." As Green observed in recommending the novel, although the characters wore visors, they were among those presently on the public stage. "Mr. B——," of course, was Tucker's idol, John C. Calhoun.[37]

3. War of the Giants

The first shock waves of financial panic and distress were reverberating through the land when Martin Van Buren was inaugurated President on March 4, 1837. Cotton prices fell precipitously, leading to the collapse of several great mercantile houses in New Orleans; bank credit, previously so plentiful, grew tight everywhere, and unemployment rose in eastern cities. Democrats inclined to blame the panic on money stringency, which had its source in the Bank of England, and on overtrading and speculation in the United States. Whigs, on the other hand, blamed the Jackson administration. Webster, Clay, and Calhoun, however much they might differ on the remedy for the disease, were united in tracing it to the madcap financial course that began with the destruction of the Bank of the United States. Jackson had hoped to stem the forces of expansion, speculation, and inflation; instead, having removed the only effective check on them, he released the very evils he deplored. The removal of the deposits, the use of deposit banks, the multiplication of uncontrolled state banks, the soaring treasury surplus—these policies stimulated the boom. At last, in July 1836, Jackson moved to break it; but his action was as clumsy, the results as disastrous, as before. His Specie Circular, requiring the payment of public lands in gold and silver, broke the speculative bubble in the West; at the same time, however, it drained the specie reserves of eastern banks, which were already feeling the pressure of withdrawals under the Deposit Act, and signaled the turn to hard-money policy, jolting the confidence of the business and financial community.[1]

As he was about to leave the capital for home after the inauguration, Calhoun was asked by Virginia newspaper editor Richard Crallé what could be done about the country's financial condition. "There is no remedy, sir," he snapped. "It is too late. You cannot prevent the catastrophe." Four years of bungling exacted a heavy toll. "The system became like a man delirious with fever, and the Government administered incessant doses of the strongest stimulants." Revulsion was inevitable. Where it would lead he did not know. "The times are as unsound as the currency," he concluded, "and the excitements of party are little calculated to qualify us for the emergency."[2] The emergency arrived in May when the eastern banks, including most of the pets, suspended specie payments. The new administration was thus crippled from the start. Calhoun still associated himself with the Whig opposition. The "national portion" of the party was wearing out, he remarked, while the portion that looked to him was gaining strength. On most questions, omitting abolitionism, he had been able to cooperate with Clay. Together they had beaten off Jacksonian sniping at the Compromise Act. Calhoun even spoke of a plan to establish a new opposition press, succeeding the *Telegraph* (Duff Green was going into more lucrative business), to be edited jointly by his friend Crallé and Clayite George Prentice of the Louisville *Journal*.[3] During the long summer at Fort Hill, however, Calhoun began to sing a different tune.

Webster was apprehensive of "the *Southern* opposition" led by Calhoun, and he was tired of laboring in Clay's shadow. He felt dull, heavy, lethargic; it showed in his lackluster performance in the Senate. In January he wrote to Robert Winthrop, speaker of the Massachusetts house, of his desire to resign four years into his term. It would not be a permanent retirement but a leave of absence, perhaps of two years, during which he would attend to his disordered financial affairs and find the leisure to travel at home and abroad. Meanwhile, political characters and events would sort themselves out and, if prospects warranted, he could make another run for the presidency. When the word leaked out there was great consternation. "The State will not allow you to retire. The Whigs will forbid it. The country will not assent to it."[4] Such was, in essence, the report of the committee Winthrop appointed to consider the senator's request. He was urged to withdraw it. And hearing the same plea from friends in New York and elsewhere, he did so.[5] He had arranged to make a speech in New York after Congress adjourned to quiet fears that he intended to abandon public life permanently. Now he decided to use the occasion to chart directions for the Whig opposition at the outset of the Van Buren administration.

The brilliant reception Webster was accorded in New York—a procession in an open barouche up Broadway through cheering throngs—followed by the speech before thirty-five hundred people jammed into Niblo's Saloon was, as George T. Curtis said, "one of the chief landmarks in his political career."[6] He restated his position on all the old issues, and on the new one of the annexation of Texas, the republic that had recently won its freedom from Mexico, expressed firm opposition. Reviewing the history of the Jacksonian assault on the banking and currency system of the country, he concluded with a gloomy forecast: "I greatly fear, even, that the worse is not yet. I look for severer distress; for extreme difficulties in exchange; for greater inconveniences in remittances, and for a sudden fall in prices." Democratic leaders considered this virtually an invitation to New York bankers and merchants to close their doors. "It was," Benton wrote in retrospect, "the first formal public step . . . to inaugurate the new distress, and organize the proceedings for shutting up the banks, and with them, the federal treasury, with a view to coercing the government into submission to the Bank of the United States and its confederate politicians."[7] Two months hence the New York banks suspended specie payments. Banks in other commercial cities, headed by the Philadelphia successor to the Bank of the United States, followed suit. Webster gloated upon the fulfillment of his prophecy. To Benton and the Democrats, of course, it was the prophecy that induced the panic.

Democratic suspicions failed to take account of the fact that Webster himself had become a prince of speculators who, regardless of politics, could have felt no interest in bursting his own bubble. During the past year he had bought heavily in western lands. "In the hope of realizing such advances as would enable me to live without carrying the Green Bag [practicing law] any longer," as he later explained the plan to Nicholas Biddle, "I put every chip I could rake and scrape, cash and credit, in lands."[8] Sometimes on his own, sometimes in partnership with astute capitalists, like his Boston friend Thomas H. Perkins, or with on-the-spot experts like General George W. Jones, the Wisconsin territorial delegate to Congress, Webster bought tens of thousands of acres of western lands—how much, he himself never really knew—prime agricultural lands, mineral lands, canal lands, prairie boom town lands in Michigan, Ohio, Illinois, and Wisconsin. Hoping to make money, he was, in this respect, no different from the mass of eastern speculators. But on one tract in northern Illinois he envisioned a great western farm, which he named Salisbury after his New Hampshire homestead, where he could indulge his fondness for agriculture and perhaps one day retire. This, with some of his other ventures, was meant, too, to demonstrate his confidence in the West. Increasingly, he identified his politics with the interests of that section, well knowing, of course, that without a western following he could never be elected president.[9] He had planned a grand tour of the West during the spring and summer both to look over his investments and to court popularity. But he was broke, and because of the financial crisis had difficulty raising the several thousand dollars required for the trip. Finally, he managed to tap one of his political friends, Caleb Cushing. In May he headed for Pittsburgh. Webster's party included his wife, his nineteen-year-old daughter Julia, and young William Pitt Fessenden, a godson from Maine, who doubled as aide and press agent.

Webster's tour took him down the Ohio, as far west as St. Louis, northward to Chicago, and home by way of Detroit, where his son Fletcher had settled, near the end of July. Everywhere he stopped it was a holiday. Farmers and their families came from long distances to hear Godlike Daniel. There were bands and processions, balls and barbecues, and speech after speech before audiences repeatedly described as the largest in the short memory of western cities. At Lexington the Websters were the guests of Henry Clay for a week. The spring races were at full tilt, and Webster entered into the frolic. Clay accompanied the party to St. Louis. Before a noisy concourse on the riverbank Webster, as usual, presented himself as the friend of the West, but for the first time he broke through his Yankee stiffness and reserve and sought to appear as western in speech, character, and manners as he was in politics. It was a rip-roaring stump speech—the first in his career. "What I am, my fellow countrymen, you all know: I am a plain man," the orator said. "I never set up for anything. . . . I am a farmer, and on the yellow sands of the east, many a time have I tilled my father's field, and followed my father's plough. . . . Give me acres; I care not whether upon the rich rolling prairie of Missouri, or among the stormbeaten sands of old Plymouth county: there is warmth and hospitality for both, and each is dear to my heart." Reaching out, he clasped one hand on the shoulder of a hardy farmer. "This honest man, God bless him! is as truly my friend as though I clasped his hand as the descendant of John Hancock in Faneuil Hall!"[10] The gesture, like the speech, was not entirely convincing. Fessenden remarked that for all the enthusiasm of Webster's reception—a succession of civic triumphs—he seemed to repel strangers and gained little popularity by personal intercourse.[11] But the gesture uniting the son of John Hancock to the Missouri farmer, Faneuil Hall to the Mississippi shore, was a remarkable instance of Webster's effort to overcome old prejudices, level the Allegheny barrier, and marry East and West in his politics.

The tour was conducted against the background of bank stoppages, business failures, and government fiscal crisis. Van Buren called a special session of Congress to meet in September. Before he reached Chicago, Webster cut short his itinerary, omitted Wisconsin altogether, and journeyed home in July. Meanwhile, whatever he gained politically in the West was canceled by the error of eastern friends who impulsively thrust him forward as a presidential candidate. Winthrop, Cushing, and the Massachusetts crowd were eager to capitalize on the western trip. But the nomination should not again come from the Bay State. New York should lead. A powerful cadre existed in the sponsors of the March address. Hiram Ketchum, Webster's confidential friend in the metropolis, was at its head; the New York *American*, under Charles King's editorship, was its voice. Six weeks after Webster went West, the *American* hoisted his banner. In an article, "The Next Presidency," it argued that the recent election had exploded the doctrine of "availability" and that the Whigs should turn to their true leaders, of whom the greatest was Webster. This was followed by a mass meeting on June 28. Ketchum delivered the main speech; a formal nominating address and resolutions were then adopted.[12] Several weeks earlier Webster had seemed anxious to defer a decision on the presidency. Nothing he had said since then, as far as the record shows, pointed to the New York nomination. It was thus a surprise, though perhaps not a complete surprise, to him. Clay's managers in New York remonstrated against the nomination. Whigs throughout the country condemned it as premature. It turned Whig against Whig on the presidential question when they ought to be uniting in a common front against the administration. Southern Whigs, in particular, were mortified by the nomination, since Webster was dead weight below the Potomac. Had he been left alone, said Thurlow Weed, the magician of New York Whiggery, the senator would have come out of the West a strong candidate; but the June nomination "utterly extinguished Mr. Webster." His loss became the party's gain, for the importunate nomination impressed Whigs with "the stern necessity" of a national convention to ensure union on a single candidate.[13]

Henry Clay again had his political sights trained on the presidency. Learning from Webster's error, he pleaded with his New York friends (Willis Hall, Matthew L. Davis, William A. Lawrence, James Watson Webb, and others) to avoid the same mistake. "If, in the paroxysm of the sufferings of the Country . . . in the first six months of a new administration, we initiate measures to determine the next Presidential election, do we not expose our patriotism to the charge of selfishness and insincerity?" he asked. While casting no stones at Webster, Clay could not refrain from disparaging comment. "Truth compels me to add," he said, "that the cordial and distinguished reception of Mr. Webster at the West (with which I have greatly rejoiced) ought to be viewed as homage to his acknowledged ability rather than as indicating any general disposition to support him as a candidate for the Presidency."[14] His plea was heeded; even so, Clay's friends in the city formed a complete skeletal organization. Officially, Clay was not a candidate; in fact, much to the distress of Thurlow Weed, whose power was upstate, Clayites as well as Websterites were racing for the nomination. Near the end of the year, after the Whig victory in the November election, the five-months' correspondence between Clay and the New York committee was released to the press. It created a sensation, being regarded as the equivalent of candidacy. On January 12, following a wave of public meetings in the West, the Kentucky legislature formally placed the state's favorite son in nomination.[15]

In the early months of the Van Buren administration Clay had every expectation of strong support in the South, the Calhoun faction included. The signs of cooperation between the senators in the last congress had not gone unnoticed. When Jackson called Calhoun to account for a statement in debate that implicated him in the furious land speculation he professed to deplore—that appeared to accuse the president himself of being a land speculator—it was Clay who came to the Carolinian's defense, condemning Jackson for still another "monarchical" invasion of the privileges of the Senate, while Democratic senators, even those from the South, sat in silence.[16] The best evidence of the vitality of the coalition, however, was the senators' defense of the act that gave it birth, the Compromise Tariff. Struggling against a soaring surplus, unhappy with the Deposit Act, Jackson had requested Congress to reduce the tariff immediately to the revenue standard. Compromise-busting measures were introduced in both houses. Clay and Calhoun—Webster, too—resolutely defended the compromise. Clay, with obvious pride, viewed the 1833 act as a sacred compact, like the Constitution and the Missouri Compromise. Calhoun detected in these moves to violate it a devious political game to foment discord on the tariff. He recalled the infamous Tariff of Abominations, by which Van Buren, Silas Wright (sponsor of the present Senate bill), and other northern Jacksonians had tricked southern congressmen into voting for outrageously high duties in the belief they would cause the bill to be defeated by New England votes. But the bill passed, as intended. Now the South was offered small favors at northern expense. Why? In order to reopen the entire system, Calhoun answered, revive the politics of "tariff juggling," and renew exploitation of the South. "Let me tell my Southern friends," he lectured, "that I know the men with whom we have to deal. Abandon the compromise, and they will be among the first to resist all future reduction. We see the bait, but we do not perceive the hook that lies under it. . . . But I can tell these fishers, they shall not catch me. I was caught once following the same lead. I am not to be caught a second time."[17] The legislative attack on the Compromise Act failed. Speaking at Charleston on his return home, Calhoun blasted it as "the work of politicians alone, with the purpose of re-embroiling the North and South."[18]

There were, then, reasonable grounds for the confidence of southern Whigs that the coalition would continue and, indeed, finally triumph over the enemy. Both the great Whig divisions, state rightists and nationals, could support Clay, it was believed.[19] The repugnance of the former to Webster brought the issue into focus in June. The Charleston *Mercury*, with the southern Whig press generally, viewed the proceedings in New York with dismay. Webster could not carry a single state south of the Potomac. He was, the newspaper conceded, "a great orator and profound thinker," but he was chained to the far northern corner of the Union by "the narrow and puritanical bigotry of heart" that had once made him a Hartford Convention Federalist and now made him the favorite of murderous abolitionists. "Mr. Webster will not *do*," the *Mercury* declared. "The Northern Whigs may kick as they please, and talk high of not submitting to Southern dictation, &c, &c., but we tell them plainly they cannot and shall not impose a candidate upon the Opposition of the South. . . . If we cannot have a Southern State Rights man—if John C. Calhoun, by going upon the forlorn hope of truth, *is* (politically) dead upon the ramparts. . . . If for the disinterestedness *above* and a political sagacity *beyond* the age, he is to be sacrificed as a martyr to principle, at least call upon us to support someone worthy of our enthusiastic trust. Give us a man of some noble traits, a bold, brave, gallant, high-minded man of genius, who, though we see his political errors, we can yet assure ourselves will do nothing *mean*. Give us such a man for instance as HENRY CLAY."[20] Clay was heroic, Clay was chivalrous, Clay was southern. The *Mercury*, published by Calhoun's lowcountry friends, therefore endorsed him. Yet within two or three months, as true as the needle of a compass, it followed Calhoun's change of course and denounced Clay.

That change was in process two or three months before the special session of Congress. The panic threw the banking system into chaos. When the suspension of specie payments reached most of the deposit banks, the government was placed in the predicament of having no safe or lawful depositories for its money. In this situation Calhoun saw an opportunity to divorce bank and state, a move he had advocated in principle in 1834, drastically reducing the fiscal action of the government and forcing it back into the narrow channels of the Constitution. Suddenly the government was so poor and crippled it could be reformed. This must lead as well, Calhoun thought, to a "reorganization of parties" along the old lines of state rights and consolidation. And so while the *Mercury* exalted Henry Clay, while Duff Green advocated merger into the Whig party, Calhoun contemplated withdrawing from the unnatural alliance of the last five years and offering himself as a rallying point for the original Jackson party.[21] He believed, of course, that Van Buren was weak, that he possessed none of Jackson's "despotic popularity," that he was a fox succeeding the lion, and that the mass of Democrats "would gladly leave him, if they saw where to go." As his colleague Preston observed, "He considers

Mr. Van Buren as actually defunct—altogether past resuscitation—and that his party is without a head, and under the necessity of having one."²² He remained obsessed with the security of the South, and came to feel it was safer with the Democrats than with the Whigs. Van Buren's inaugural pledge to resist any federal interference with slavery, including slavery in the District of Columbia, was a good omen. Oddly, Calhoun had come by a circuitous route to accept Van Buren's fundamental proposition that the Democrats of the North were the natural allies of the slaveholders of the South; and like Van Buren he imagined he was treading in the footsteps of Thomas Jefferson.

Calhoun was hardly prepared for the program the president calmly outlined to Congress on September 5, however. "Van Buren has been forced by his situation and the terror of Jackson to play directly into our hands," he wrote home gleefully, "and I am determined, that he shall not escape us."²³ The crucial recommendation that the government separate itself from all banks and operate its own system—an independent treasury—for receiving, disbursing, and transferring funds might be made the cornerstone of Calhoun's program as well as Van Buren's. Quick to signal his support, he was also quickly attacked for deserting his friends and joining the Jacksonian war on banks. Clay, Webster, Preston—all the Whig senators—were dumbfounded by Calhoun's demarche. So were the Democrats, starting with the president himself. And they wondered whether to sing or to cry over the acquisition.

On September 18, Calhoun made his first attempt to explain his position.²⁴ By an extraordinary course of events the government had been brought to the threshold of a new era, he said. The collapse of the deposit bank system broke the government's connection with banks. Some advocated restoring the system. Such was the position of a mainly Democratic faction, the Conservatives, led by Senators William C. Rives and Nathaniel Tallmadge. Given the correlation between state banks and state rights, well established in Jacksonian rhetoric, this approach might have been expected to appeal to Calhoun. But he thought the system beyond repair and opted for independence from all banks. Three years before he had proposed to extend the B.U.S. charter as an interim measure on the way to divorce. He had, he insisted before incredulous auditors, yielded to the establishment of the Bank in the first place, in 1816, solely as a measure of necessity. He had always opposed a national bank in principle. Now, for the first time, he felt free to choose the true course. "The Government stands in a position disentangled from the past, and freer to choose its future course than it ever has been since its commencement. We are about to take a fresh start. I move off under the State rights banner. . . . I seize the opportunity to reform the Government; to bring it back to its original principles; . . . to give an ascendancy to the great conservative principle of State sovereignty, over the dangerous and despotic doctrine of consolidation." Before concluding, Calhoun notified the Senate he would offer an amendment to the administration's divorce bill, providing for the gradual exclusion of state bank notes in payment of government dues. This "specie clause" would place the government on the hard money standard. It would repeal the congressional joint resolution of

1816, of which Calhoun had been the principal author, authorizing the treasury to receive the notes of specie paying banks in lieu of gold and silver. This had, in fact, been the government's practice since the days of Alexander Hamilton. The amendment was potentially more revolutionary than the bill; and it created consternation among Democrats at the White House and in Congress who had hoped to avoid this explosive issue.[25]

The independent treasury would be debated up, down, and sideways during the next three years until all the arguments were stereotyped in the public discourse. Should the revenue—some $30 million—be used as the basis for mounting bank credit? No, said the advocates of divorce, because it involved the government in the fluctuations and hazards of business and vice versa. Yes, said the Whigs, for credit was the life of enterprise; it was narrow, selfish policy to lock up the revenue from the people. The independent treasury looked to the relief of government, not of the people; and while it would secure the federal treasury in a strongbox, the system would do nothing to secure or regulate the currency of fifteen million Americans. "A hard money government, and a paper money people!" Clay exploded.[26] Behind this issue, of course, was the old one of positive or negative government. Van Buren condensed the Democratic creed into an axiom: it is the duty of the people to support the government, but the government should not support the people. To this Webster opposed, "Government must do for individuals [that] which individuals cannot do for themselves."[27] This included the full measure of the government's constitutional responsibility for the currency founded in the coinage and commerce clauses. A stable and uniform currency was a necessity of commerce and a duty of government; it had been largely achieved under a national bank and the government's receipt of bank notes convertible into gold and silver, which stamped "the broad seal of the Union" upon them.[28] Calhoun rejected Webster's sweeping interpretation of the commerce power and held, contrary to his position in 1816, that the coinage power was limited to the regulation of gold and silver coins. Constitutional opinions so changeable were discounted, like cheap bank paper, by everyone.

The core of the senator's case was the argument that the union of bank and state created a privileged interest which, like a giant parasite, lived on the growth of governmental power. Banks and a tax consuming government were natural allies. "It is to this mischievous and unholy alliance," as Calhoun later phrased the argument, "that may be traced almost all the disasters to have befallen us, and the great political degeneracy of the country. Hence the protective system; hence the associated and monstrous system of disbursements; hence the collection of more money from the people than the Government required; hence the vast and corrupting surpluses; hence legislative and executive usurpations; and finally, hence the prostration of the currency and the disasters which give rise to our present deliberations."[29] Opponents of the administration bill could not decide whether it was likely to terminate in a great government bank with its own fiat money or in no bank and hard money. Either way the experiment would be fatal. If hard money policy prevailed, the progress of a young, growing, and enterprising people would be brought to a halt. A government bank system, on the other hand, raised the specter of union of purse and sword with the accompanying dangers of corruption and tyranny.

It was Calhoun's position, in a sense his apology, that the war on executive tyranny was over. "That terminated, we part with our allies in peace; and move forward . . . under the old republican flag of 1798."[30] When his red-headed, ruddy-faced colleague, Preston, dared to suggest he had become "an administration man," Calhoun heatedly denied it. "I am not an administration man, nor any other man's man, but I am my own man. I belong to the smallest party of the country. I am simply an honest nullifier." As the laughter subsided, Calhoun went on to say that while the danger of executive usurpation had ended, the greater danger of congressional usurpation remained. "I know well my latitude and my longitude: I keep a log-book and a good reckoning. I know the position of the parties on all sides. . . . I know where the administration party is: its reckoning has run out; and it has *only one alternative*, namely to go back to the old republican principles. . . . Could I, a member of the State Rights party," he asked, "hesitate [about] what course to pursue in so remarkable a juncture? It was as clear as the noonday sun."[31] Nonsense, said Preston. The Democratic party, which Calhoun imagined was merely "a personal party" of Andrew Jackson doomed to dissolution under his successor, had not changed, despite Van Buren's placidity, nor could it be controlled by the senator. The bitter clash between Calhoun and Preston was as astonishing as the events that produced it. Preston was a protégé, Calhoun's handpicked choice for the Senate. Now he quit his place near Calhoun and took a seat at the opposite side of the chamber within whispering range of Webster and Clay. The Columbia *Telescope*, owned by Preston and the newspaper voice of the "Columbia Regency," as it was called, immediately came out against Calhoun.[32] As to the senator's claim that the administration had joined him rather than the reverse, the Whigs were incredulous. "We Have Met the Enemy and We are Theirs" was the title of one editorial, widely reprinted.[33] John J. Crittenden, Clay's Kentucky colleague, was mystified by Calhoun's conduct; but whatever his motives—and he forbade from judging him unkindly—his betrayal "produced more surprise than *effect*."[34] The independent treasury bill, with Calhoun's amendment intact, finally passed the Senate by a single vote, only to be tabled by the Whig-Conservative majority in the House. Of nine South Carolina representatives only Francis Pickens voted with the administration.

Calhoun, nevertheless, returned home in October vaunting his accomplishment. "My situation was extraordinary," he wrote to his daughter Anna. "I held the fate of the country . . . in my hand, and had to determine in what direction I should turn events hereafter." Having made up his own mind, he was determined to change the mind of the state. "Never did I see the future more clearly and what our interest, honor, and safety demanded. I would be grieved to think, that the State Rights party should falter at such a moment."

If it did, the South would fall irretrievably under northern domination.[35] George McDuffie, from his upcountry plantation Cherry Hill, beseeched Calhoun to pause and reconsider his course. "We must be content to regulate and restrain the banks as far as we can," he said, "but I cannot believe either in the wisdom or practicality of any measure which looks to their destruction."[36] Most of the former leaders of the State Rights party—James Hamilton, Hayne, Preston of course—disapproved. So did Waddy Thompson, the representative of Calhoun's own district, and Governor Pierce Butler. No one, however, wished a trial of strength with Calhoun; and the party leaders, ever mindful of the imperative of unity, moved to contain the contest. In November Calhoun explained his position in a public letter to the Edgefield *Advertiser*. The Panic of 1837, coinciding with Van Buren's accession, had completely altered the political landscape, he wrote. The administration was placed on the defensive. "It was clear that, with our joint forces [Whig nationals and nullifiers], we could utterly overthrow and demolish them. But it was not less clear that the victory would enure not to us, but exclusively to our allies and their cause." By supporting the administration effort to divorce bank and state, on the other hand, political parties would be forced back on "the old and natural division of state rights and national," which was most advantageous to the South.[37]

Until the Edgefield Letter, Hamilton later remarked, the independent treasury had not ten advocates in South Carolina; suddenly it had many, and the conversion Calhoun worked in the legislature at Columbia on his return to Washington in December was compared to that of the apostle on the road to Damascus.[38] The governor's message was pro-banking. The planter interest of the state had always been closely identified with the B.U.S. and the Bank of South Carolina. But the legislators blamed Butler, along with Preston, for "all the supposed *Treason* against Calhoun." By an overwhelming vote they adopted resolutions declaring a national bank unconstitutional and endorsing the independent treasury.[39] It was a stunning victory for Calhoun. The hopes of many, the fears of some, that he had mutilated himself politically were laid to rest. Although he failed to rally a large following in the South, he attracted powerful allies in Virginia and elsewhere.

When Congress resumed, Calhoun seized upon the slavery issue to test and solidify his new political position. The mob murder of the abolitionist editor, Elijah Lovejoy, at Alton, Illinois, in November, combined with fears over the annexation of Texas, inflamed abolitionist feelings. In the House, before the "gag rule" could be adopted, Vermont congressman William Slade presented several abolitionist petitions. In the Senate, at the same time, Clay and Calhoun clashed over the mode of handling petitions. Clay reiterated his opinion that the matter of slavery in the District of Columbia should be made the subject of inquiry and report. It might thus be separated from the libertarian issue of the right of petition, which threatened to make abolitionism popular in the North. A carefully drawn report, Clay believed, would quiet the country. Calhoun emphatically disagreed: slavery in the District was not a matter for inquiry, deliberation, or argument. The next day

Benjamin Swift, of Vermont, introduced resolutions of the state legislature against the annexation of Texas and for abolition in the District. The resolutions also instructed the Vermont senators on these issues. This action of a sovereign state was a shocking escalation of the controversy, Calhoun declared. "Vermont has struck a deep and dangerous blow into the vitals of our confederacy."[40] The House quickly achieved an uneasy truce by adoption of another gag; but Calhoun demanded "a holy pledge" by the Senate to oppose further aggression against slavery. This took the form of a series of six resolutions which aimed to throw an impregnable constitutional barrier around slavery wherever it existed—in the states, in the District, in the territories (Florida then being the only territory)—and which declared, alluding to Texas, that refusal to annex territory lest it extend slavery was a violation of the compact among equal sovereign states.[41] These highly abstract resolutions naturally provoked argument about the very question Calhoun insisted could not be argued and cast suspicion on his motives. In his defense he said, first, that the only security for the South was constitutional, and second, that he sought to rally the Democratic party to its old state rights creed.

The first four of Calhoun's resolutions concerning slavery in the states were adopted, after minor amendment, by wide margins. Webster dissented, but Clay, with most Whigs and the solid phalanx of Democrats, indulged Calhoun's penchant for metaphysical declarations. When the Senate took up the fifth resolution securing slavery in the District and the territories, Clay introduced a series of counter-resolutions. The most important of these recognized the right of petition and the constitutional authority of Congress over slavery in the District, but said that interference with it would have "a direct and inevitable tendency to disturb and endanger the Union." Others confined the declaration on the territories to the case of Florida, where slavery already existed and should not be disturbed by Congress, and deferred the question of Texas. Clay viewed Calhoun's resolutions as an attempt, on the one hand, to blackmail the Democrats, and on the other to set a trap for him. If he conceded too much to Calhoun's principles, he jeopardized his following among anti-slavery Whigs; if he conceded too little, he jeopardized his support in the South.

In the end the debate became a personal duel between them. It was a fascinating exhibition of contrasting political styles: one thrusting, the other parrying; one metaphysical, the other pragmatic; one inflammatory, the other conciliatory. Clay sensed that the difference between himself and Calhoun was less one of ends than of tactics or means: "He goes for strong language, menacing tones, and irritating measures; I for temperate, but firm, language. . . . We ought not to be perpetually exclaiming, wolf, wolf, wolf. We are too much in the habit of speaking of divorces, separation, disunion." Clay offered the homely metaphor of a scolding wife, threatening her husband with divorce over every petty argument, to which the husband prudently responds, not with idle menace, but with "those natural and more agreeable remedies that never fail to restore domestic harmony." And to this Calhoun retorted: "Expediency, concession, compromise! Away with such weakness and folly. Right, justice, plighted faith, and the Constitution: these, and these only, can be relied on to avert conflict."[42]

Yet even Calhoun finally, reluctantly, voted for Clay's substitute resolutions. Altered to make them more palatable to him, the resolutions nevertheless acknowledged the authority of Congress over slavery in the District and in the territories. Clay believed he had "outfoxed" his rival. "I have borne myself in such manner as to lose nothing neither at the South nor at the North."[43] Calhoun demurred. He had forced Clay to "straddle." At the same time he had drawn the administration to his position. Webster, who voted against Clay's substitute resolutions, condemned the whole proceeding for forcing the Constitution into a pro-slavery straitjacket. "Mr. Clay and Mr. Calhoun, in my judgment," Webster said, "have attempted in 1838, what they attempted in 1833, *to make a new Constitution*."[44]

This conflict was only a prelude to the "day of settlement" between Clay and Calhoun—one of the memorable parliamentary encounters in American history—in February. Debate had shifted to the independent treasury bill. Calhoun, its foremost advocate, said it was "one of the greatest civil contests in modern times."[45] But after the administration, hard-pressed for votes to pass the bill, eliminated the specie clause, Calhoun turned against it. Clay cried "mad dog" against the independent treasury in any form; in the end, when his national bank kite wouldn't fly, he supported Rives's state bank plan as "a good half-way house." Clay had held his tongue about Calhoun's defection during the special session, thinking he would return to the fold when he discovered no one was following him; but the Edgefield Letter was a declaration of apostasy and, when followed by the demonstration at Columbia, it angered Clay. Suddenly, in the course of a major speech against the independent treasury on February 19, he turned from reasoned argument to personal vituperation of his former ally. The arduous campaign they had waged together was about to end in victory, he said, when the senator from South Carolina went "horse, foot, and dragoon" to the enemy. There had been nothing like it since Achilles abruptly and without notice withdrew his army from the siege of Troy. But Achilles had been wronged; the Whigs had done no wrong to Calhoun, rather they had given scope to his genius and relied upon his fidelity. Still he left. "He left us, as he tells us in the Edgefield letter, because the victory which our common arms were about to achieve, was not to enure to him and his party, but exclusively to the benefit of his allies and their cause." This, said Clay, was the first time he had heard that personal and party gain was the basis of their alliance or a just cause for ending it.[46]

Calhoun let three weeks pass before he replied. His carefully composed speech "smelt of the lamp," as Benton observed, and was delivered before a packed house with the senator's characteristically clipped eloquence. Clay had, some said, violated the decorum of the Senate, descending to "a vulgar gasconading sort of sarcasm" in abuse of an honorable colleague. Calhoun sought to turn these feelings to his advantage by appearing on the defensive and pretending that he, not Clay, was the injured party. "He stood like Demosthenes," Crallé wrote, "on a very similar occasion, in the Areopagus—

pouring forth the precepts of an elevated patriotism, and hurling the shafts of indignant innocence against Easchines, *his* accuser."[47] Calhoun defended his political character and consistency. Although he censured Clay for argument *ad hominem*, he returned the shot with twice the force. As to the imputation of base motives, founded on the Edgefield Letter, he insisted his only purpose was to save the cause of state rights and the South from being swallowed up. "I stamp it, with scorn in the dust. I pick up the shaft, which fell harmless at my feet. I hurl it back. What the Senator charges on me unjustly," he declared, having first stamped his foot, then hurled defiance across the chamber with scornful eyes, "*he has actually done*. He went over on a memorable occasion, and did not leave it to time to disclose his motive."[48] Calhoun thus revived after several years' slumber the old canard of "corrupt bargain" between Clay and John Quincy Adams in 1825.

Replying at once—it was said that Clay could fire without rest while Calhoun required time to load—the Kentuckian reflected disparagingly on the quick turns and reversals that had marked Calhoun's career, and marveled at the delusion that now led him back into the arms of Van Buren and the Democrats. He poured ridicule on the boast of the Edgefield Letter that nullification had destroyed the American System. The Compromise Act, far from being extorted by nullification, had been a compassionate concession to its weakness and folly, Clay declared. Touching on the history of the compromise, he recalled that Senator Clayton had come to him pleading for Calhoun and his beleagured band: " 'They are clever fellows, and it will never do to let old Jackson hang them.' " It was in this spirit, he continued, that he had offered the compromise. The idea that it abandoned protection was another delusion. Calhoun had, in fact, been compelled to sanction protection constitutionally, and at every step in the making of the compromise it was the Nullifiers who yielded. A rejoinder, then another reply and rejoinder concluded the affair, with each side claiming the victory.

Now Webster took up the cudgels. In a powerful speech punctuated by droll wit and ridicule, the Massachusetts senator cut up and scattered Calhoun's vaunted consistency. "Where am I?" he asked, rubbing his eyes like Rip Van Winkle. "In the Senate of the United States? Am I Daniel Webster? Is that [pointing] John C. Calhoun of South Carolina, the same gentleman that figured so largely in the House of Representatives in 1816, at the time the Bill creating a National Bank passed that body. What have I heard today? The Senator attempting to maintain his consistency . . . in my presence?"[49] Webster recalled the man he had once known and admired, "a generous character, a liberal and comprehensive mind engrossed by great objects," and regretted that, separated by so vast a political void, they seemed destined never to meet again. With a sense of the government's tendency toward disintegration almost as desperate as Calhoun's sense of the opposite, Webster took more seriously than Clay the senator's aim of rearing a nullification party in the house of Jackson and Van Buren. "He is in the engine car! The rest [the administration], all passengers." No speech of Webster's in the last five years was so much admired. It was "masterly." Indeed, the *National*

Intelligencer called it "the greatest of all his speeches," a judgment with which Clay agreed.[50] Replying a week later, Calhoun, humorless as always, again struggled to vindicate himself. He confessed that in the aftermath of the war he had deviated from the true republican faith—"the old Virginia school of politics." Let this be a lesson to the young: "Avoid, as you would the greatest evil, the least departure from principle, however harmless it may at the time appear to be."[51] Calhoun then launched into an attack on Webster. He proclaimed himself a patriot, but his patriotism was confined to New England; he made a fetish of the Union, but had never cast a vote favorable to the South; he professed to act for the people, but his allegiance was to the moneyed class. "What a contrast between profession and performance! What strange and extraordinary self-delusion!"[52]

A dramatic reprise of "the conflict of giants" occurred on January 3, 1840. Webster was not yet in his seat; Clay and Calhoun were the gladiators, and the issue was the same as before. At the opening of the new Congress the administration supported Calhoun's good friend, Francis Pickens, for the speakership. He was not elected, but Calhoun's followers, in turn, voted with the administration in a crucial party contest over the New Jersey delegation, thereby ensuring a Democratic majority and eventual passage of the Independent Treasury Bill. Just before the new year Calhoun arranged through a mutual friend to be taken to the White House and presented to Van Buren, a man with whom he had not spoken for almost a decade and whom he had bitterly denounced as a Judas, a Janus, and a Catiline. Although the senator had cooperated with the administration in financial affairs during the last two years, he had steered an independent course in other areas and kept a personal distance from the president. The embrace at the White House completed the *demarche* begun by Calhoun at the special session. What were the secret articles of this alliance? There had been nothing like it since the infamous coalition of Lord North and Charles James Fox in 1783.[53] And Henry Clay might hope that the public outrage, which in that instance had opened the way for William Pitt, would work in the same fashion for him.

Addressing himself to a bill introduced by Calhoun to cede public lands to the states in which they lay, Clay wondered if this could be one of the articles of the new accord. (As Clay knew, Calhoun had introduced the same bill in 1837.) Inasmuch as the senator had "made his bow in court, kissed the hand of the monarch . . . and agreed henceforth to support his edicts," the public had a right to know what pledges had been made, what compromises entered into."[54] Calhoun waxed indignant at the suggestion that his personal relations had anything to do with his politics. He had made no pledges or compromises—Clay was the expert on that subject. After chiding Calhoun for again resurrecting an ancient, and exploded, political canard, Clay repeated his little speech on the virtues of compromise and said that but for a particular compromise the senator from South Carolina would not now be orating in the Capitol. Calhoun jumped to his feet to repel the insinuation that he, South Carolina, or the Union was under any debt of gratitude to

Clay for the Compromise Act. "The senator was then compelled to compromise to save himself. Events had placed him flat on his back, and he had no way to recover himself but by compromise." He recalled how Jackson, by his Proclamation and subsequent message, had rallied the northern friends of Clay's system, including his Massachusetts rival, who would have reaped the honors had the contest come to blows. "Compromise was the only means of extrication. He [Clay] was thus forced by the action of the State, which I in part represent, against his system, by my counsel to compromise, in order to save himself. I had the mastery over him on that occasion." The Whigs laughed. Clay, who had come to believe Calhoun would "die a traitor or a madman," was more astounded than amused by this fanciful history.[55] "The senator says, I was flat on my back, and that he was my master. Sir, I would not own him as a slave." A roar went through the gallery. Clay paused, surveyed the chamber, elevated his body, and declared scornfully, "He MY master! and I compelled by him! . . . Why, sir, I gloried in my strength." And he went on to recall the circumstances of the Compromise Act. No greater sensation, a veteran correspondent wrote, had ever been produced in the Senate.[56] Calhoun made only a feeble reply.

But to return to the previous Congress: when it adjourned in July 1838 Calhoun undertook to purge the South Carolina delegation of those who actively opposed him on the divorce of bank and state. They had, he said, done "incalculable" harm to him, to the state, to the South.[57] The chief culprit was Preston. Not only had he impudently opposed Calhoun on the independent treasury, he had also taken Clay's side in the debate on the slavery resolutions. In the spring Whigs were mentioning Preston as a vice presidential candidate. This combination of abolitionism, bankism, and Clayism, on top of brazen ingratitude to Calhoun, could not be tolerated. Preston, for his part, thought his colleague had "bamboozled himself" with the idea that hard money and no-bank was a state rights project for the benefit of the South.[58] Preston's term had four years to run. Calhoun could only snipe at him. When the junior senator tried to rally support at a great barbecue in Columbia, Calhoun pointedly declined the invitation, then gloated over the failure of the festivities.[59] Three congressmen who had opposed the independent treasury, John Campbell, Hugh Legaré, and Waddy Thompson, were targeted for defeat. Legaré, of course, had been Calhoun's candidate against Pinckney in the Charleston district. Now he had sinned and must be immolated in turn. Thompson, in Calhoun's own district—the most Whiggish in the state—was a Conservative who advocated a modified deposit bank system. He was very popular, but a candidate was finally found to run against him; and for the first time in his career Calhoun took to the stump, canvassing the district to defeat Thompson. At neighborly barbecues in shady groves during the late summer, Calhoun addressed crowds of a thousand or more in his excited manner on the "constitutional treasury system," always followed by Thompson who, lacing his logic with jest, was more than a match for the senator.[60] Thompson was easily reelected. So was Campbell. Legaré was beaten, however, with the help of Van Buren's friends in Charleston.

Calhoun thus suffered a partial defeat made worse by the final rejection of his railroad plan; but it was the last defeat he would suffer in South Carolina. Henceforth the legislature danced to his tune; it named governors and senators only after he approved them. The congressional delegation under his deputy, Pickens, answered to Calhoun's leadership. Preston became a political cripple. He and Thompson were the only charter members of the State Rights party who, having followed Calhoun into the Whig coalition, remained Whigs after he left it. Preston's newspaper, the Columbia *Telescope*, folded the next year. He was tagged the "non-accredited senator from South Carolina" until he retired from politics at the expiration of his term.

Calhoun's power rested not on charisma or organization but on a political ideology that postulated unity in the state and eventually in the section as the only means of securing slavery and the South from an encroaching northern majority. In pursuit of unity Calhoun made a bold bid in 1840 to erase the lingering legacy of discord from nullification by bringing Unionists and others still outside the State Rights fold into one great party. Reconciliation had been going forward for several years. The cooperation between Calhoun and Joel R. Poinsett, now Van Buren's secretary of war, showed it. The ultimate vehicle of reconciliation, however, was John P. Richardson, a former Unionist, like Poinsett, and congressman whom Calhoun backed for governor in 1840. Brought forward by the Charleston *Mercury* in January, Richardson was viewed at once as the candidate of the lowcountry faction led by Robert and Albert Rhett and the latter's brother-in-law, Franklin H. Elmore. Since the senator had reportedly "pushed Richardson" at Charleston on his return to Washington in December, his nomination was seen as a signal not only of reconciliation but of the ascendancy of the Rhett-Elmore interest over the mind of Calhoun. The other main interest centered upon Pickens and his friends. They were still smarting from defeat in the recent speakership contest, which they blamed on the "vile intrigue" of Robert Rhett to split the southern vote by the nomination of Dixon H. Lewis of Alabama. "I am for fight," Pickens wrote when he learned of Richardson's nomination, and he urged Hammond, the former congressman, to enter the race. Hammond was champing at the bit. He agreed with Pickens on the disgrace and folly of reconciliation. But, he said, "*a voice must come from Washington.*" It never came. Calhoun, although he professed neutrality, supported Richardson. Pickens wrote apologetically to Hammond: "He has come down upon me as to harmony, reconciliation, etc, etc, so that I have almost offended him by refusing to acquiesce in his advice."[61] Richardson was "a mere man of straw stuffed by Calhoun," as Preston remarked.[62] Yet his election as governor had high symbolic importance. It ended the old division. It marked the metamorphosis of the State Rights party into the Democratic party in South Carolina. This development paralleled Calhoun's political movement in Washington and, of course, was meant to support it. In his inaugural address the new governor could proclaim, "We are all nullifiers, we are all Union men."[63] Henceforth Calhoun's authority was rarely challenged and never successfully. As political wiseacres quipped, when Calhoun took snuff South Carolina sneezed.[64]

4. Webster, Clay, and the Whig Triumph

One of Daniel Webster's friends at the bar, Horace Binney of Philadelphia, once said to him, "You can be the king of this country if you will simply let it be known that you are unalterably resolved never to be a candidate for the Presidency. You will always be Senator from Massachusetts, and such will be your hold on the people everywhere, by reason of your extraordinary ability, that you will have the power of selection. . . . You will be the Warwick, the kingmaker."[1] But in Webster's day nothing but the presidency could satisfy the passion for greatness. Webster could no more abjure it, wrapping himself in the senatorial mantle, than could Clay or Calhoun. Now, in the presidential sweepstakes of 1840, the two Whig chieftains threatened to cancel each other out, opening the way for William Henry Harrison, the old warrior who had carried off one-quarter of the electoral votes in 1836.

Clay and Webster, united in opposing the leading measure of the Van Buren administration, the independent treasury, constantly tilted with each other in the Senate. They were pointedly at odds on Calhoun's slavery resolutions, for instance. Even when they agreed, as on a measure forcing repeal of the Specie Circular, they quarreled like children over the merits of authorship. The bitterest quarrel, at least on Clay's side, concerned public land policy. Democratic senators, led by Thomas Hart Benton, pressed for renewal of the preemption system, recently expired, and for enactment of the Missourian's Graduation Bill. Under the former, which had been law more or less regularly since 1830, squatters on the public domain were forgiven their illegal trespass and when the land came up for auction permitted to purchase as many as 160 acres at the minimum price of $1.25 per acre. Clay, who had always opposed the system, unleashed a violent tirade against the bill. Preemption was a colossal fraud. The "hardy pioneers" so much eulogized as the worthy beneficiaries were, in fact, "lawless rabble" employed by greedy speculators to gobble up the best lands in the West. What the West wanted, he maintained, were solid middle-class people with modest capital who would pay a fair price for land and promote concentrated rather than scattered settlement. Preemption was still another Jacksonian "experiment" in dismantling a wise and equitable national system supposedly for the good of the many but in fact for the enrichment of a few.[2] There was considerable truth in the indictment. Calhoun agreed with it, on the whole; but the solution to the public land problem, he thought, was dismantlement in another form. Cession of the lands to the new states, he argued, was the only policy that would purge the general government of their corrupt influence and the only one compatible with state rights.

To the astonishment of everyone, Webster spoke in favor of preemption. He had been gravitating toward a pro-settler land policy even before his western tour. Preemption, he said, was fair and equitable, generally benefiting the actual settlers; moreover, since squatters could not be kept off the public domain, it was the only policy consistent with the realities of the frontier.[3] Clay was surprised to hear these opinions and angry at Webster for bucking his leadership and going with the administration on an issue of such importance.[4] He assumed Webster was pandering for western votes. Harry of the West could not be accused of that. But neither could he defeat preemption. The bill passed both houses with a combination of Democratic and western votes—Clay's was the only western vote against it in the Senate. The Graduation Bill, which Webster also favored, failed in the House. As long as Clay lived it would never become law.

Webster felt neglected and unappreciated by the Whigs in Congress, most of whom backed Clay for the presidential nomination; and although his followers successfully blocked legislative endorsements of his rival in several northern state legislatures, it became evident in 1838 that he could not turn these defensive actions to his advantage. Before Congress adjourned, Clay appealed to him to withdraw. Webster declined, yet he heard the same appeal from his own friends, who worried that his candidacy was becoming a stalking-horse for Harrison.[5] Upon his return to Boston he wallowed in the acclaim of another of those great festive dinners in his honor, this one got up in the name of the mechanics and tradesmen of the city and held in Faneuil Hall, where tables were laid for 1,660 patrons. (The $3 tickets were reportedly hawked for $15 and more.) Draped across the gallery was a large banner bearing an inscription from Webster's March speech against the subtreasury: "I am, where I have ever been, and ever mean to be: HERE, standing on the platform of the general Constitution—a platform broad enough and firm enough to uphold every interest of the whole country—I SHALL STILL BE FOUND." Edward Everett, who presided, spoke on the vital link between money and liberty. Addressing Webster in a strain of unsurpassed eloquence, exalting the "sublime spectacle" of his triumph over the administration, Everett brought tears to the senator's eyes. He responded briefly. Several hours of speech making, punctuated by the popping of champagne corks, filled the evening.[6]

But homage to Webster was more an expression of civic pride than of political confidence. Abbott Lawrence, always a main pillar of support, told Webster he was throwing his money and influence behind Clay. On September 14 the Boston *Atlas*, for several years Webster's acknowledged journalistic voice in New England, dropped him as a candidate, simultaneously dismissed Clay's claims, and came out for Harrison. In an editorial series, "The Next Presidency," provoked by the Whig defeat some weeks earlier in the Maine election, the *Atlas* called upon the party to become as overtly democratic in its principles, rhetoric, and tactics as its adversary, and in this connection urged the necessity of taking up a popular presidential candidate whose chief qualification was his appeal to the passions and prejudices of the masses of men.

"What avail all other qualifications under Heaven," the editor asked, "if the candidate be not popular?"[7] The distinguished Whig statesmen lacked democratic character and talents. They were *aristocratic Whigs*." The Hero of Tippecanoe, on the other hand, was "the *people's* candidate"—the perfect Whig answer to General Jackson. Webster was as silent as the grave about this bombshell. A Boston journalist later said in his reminiscences that the *Atlas's* editor, Richard Haughton, showed a preliminary copy of the editorial (actually written by Richard Hildreth) to Webster, who was so enraged that he ordered Haughton out of the house, but then, agreeing to hear the explanation, swallowed his pride and held his tongue on the subject.[8] Whatever the literal truth of the story, it was consistent with the senator's response. Robert Winthrop, who had been briefed by the editor, wrote to Everett on the day of the first article, "I am inclined to think that it will excite no murmurs at Marshfield."[9] The Boston *Daily Advertiser*, under Everett's influence, acquiesced; the *Courier*, which was devoted to Webster and projected the "aristocratic" image the *Atlas* disliked, said the democratic manifesto was "suicidal" and thought it important to establish the senator's "innocence" of any part in it.[10] It was, in fact, later reported that Webster disavowed any prior knowledge of the *Atlas* editorial. Innocent or not, enraged or not, he and his friends quickly realized that the brunt of the manifesto fell upon Clay. He it was whom the *Atlas* held responsible for the humiliating defeat in Maine. He it was, and not Webster, about whom there was a real issue of availability and popularity. "Our Clay champions in the West will writhe under it," Winthrop observed of the new course. "But to them a reply is easy—'You have been eager to give up Webster . . . you insisted on Clay's availability. We now meet you on your own ground. We go for availability also, and believing Harrison to be *most available*, we skip Clay as well, and go for the General.' "[11]

As predicted, Clay took the *Atlas* manifesto as an attack on him. "I am mortified—shocked—disgusted . . . ," he wrote to Harrison Gray Otis, one of the knot of Bostonians—"aristocratic Whigs" in *Atlas* parlance—who favored him mainly because he was believed to have the popularity Webster lacked.[12] For several months Clay had suspected Webster of fronting for Harrison. While still reluctant to draw that conclusion, he found it hard to avoid after the "treachery" of the *Atlas*. His own press in Lexington might credit Webster's reported disavowal, but Clay, in the privacy of his heart, could not.[13] The fact that Webster remained a candidate, not only stalking for Harrison but checking the flight of his own followers to Clay, was especially infuriating. Until now Clay had been conducting a passive campaign in accordance with the Whig consensus on a convention nomination a year hence. But the movement against him in Massachusetts, together with hostile maneuvers in other northern states, led Clay to take off the wraps and go after the nomination. Surveying the political scene after the disappointing fall elections, he concluded that he was being forced on the defensive in the North by the rising influence of abolitionism among Whigs.[14] In the West, where he had forfeited old claims of support, he trailed Harrison badly. Only in the South was Clay the banner candidate of the Whigs. Even a dedicated southern state rightist like Nathaniel Beverley Tucker, baffled by the gyrations of his hero Calhoun, declared for Clay.[15] He returned to Washington for the final session of the Twenty-fifth Congress determined to strike a blow at abolitionism and, simultaneously, enhance his claim on the political affections of the South.

On February 7, 1839, presenting a petition of citizens of the District of Columbia remonstrating against congressional interference with slavery, Clay expounded his views of slavery and abolition at length. He had been concerned with the question since his political debut in Kentucky forty years ago. For most of these years it had never been a political problem for him. He had championed liberty, or the Union, or one policy or another with scarcely a thought of its bearings on an institution that held over two million black men, women, and children in bondage, some of them his own chattels. But in the changing political climate of the last several years the question of slavery and abolition was everywhere; it could not be evaded, it penetrated every issue, it figured in every political calculation; and Clay found himself assailed by ultraists in both the North and the South. Clay's opinions on slavery stemmed from his Virginia Jeffersonian heritage. He deplored the institution, searched for ways to ameliorate it, and hoped for its eventual extinction. Meanwhile, however, he defended slavery, and slave property, as lawful and as necessary to the white man's rule in the South.

Clay expressed his anti-slavery feelings through the American Colonization Society. He had presided over the organization meeting of the society in 1816, when he was elected a vice president, and upon the death of James Madison in 1836 Clay became its president.[16] In the speeches he delivered before the annual meetings of the society in Washington and before the Kentucky auxiliary, Clay argued fundamentally that the black race could not be integrated into American society. Because of unconquerable prejudice, the blacks could be tolerated only in the status of slaves. Yet slavery was an unmitigated evil, for the masters as well as the slaves. The ultimate solution for both races, therefore, was the return of the blacks to "the land of their fathers." There was "moral fitness" in this, Clay said, for it would redeem a hideous wrong with the gift of civilization. "Every emigrant to Africa is a missionary carrying with him credentials in the holy cause of civilization, religion, and free institutions."[17] Some leaders of the society viewed colonization as a step toward general emancipation, but Clay insisted that the movement looked solely to the removal of the free blacks, the most degraded, vicious, and dangerous members of the race, in his opinion. (The official name was the American Society for Colonizing the Free People of Color in the United States.) Its mission was truly national, for free blacks inhabited both North and South, and it posed no threat to slavery. In fact, as Clay acknowledged, colonization would strengthen slavery by removing its most troublesome element—the *tertium quid* of the institution—the free blacks.

Nevertheless, while this was the sole purpose, colonization, fairly supported, would eventually make possible the extinction of slavery. Clay assumed, optimistically, an essentially stable black population. He figured the annual increase of free blacks at 6,000. The annual removal of an equivalent number to Liberia, which the society founded on the west coast of Africa in 1821, would gradually reduce the stock to insignificance. More importantly, the success of this experiment ought, in Clay's opinion, to embolden the slave states to adopt plans of gradual emancipation tied to the colonization of the freedmen. Estimating the annual increase of the slave population at 46,000, Clay maintained that by the regular removal of approximately that number over a period of thirty-three years, during which the white population would grow at a prodigious rate, the proportion of blacks in the American population would fall from 20 to 10 percent. Free white labor would drive out slave labor, robbing it of the value it earlier possessed, marginalizing it to the society, until the nation could at last rid itself of this "foul blot." In his enthusiasm for great projects, Clay never doubted that the United States was capable of this colonization enterprise. It would cost $1 million a year and employ one-ninth of the shipping of the country. Clay advocated, as had Jefferson and Madison, federal grants to the states in aid of emancipation and colonization. Such aid was provided in his original distribution bill; it was later eliminated, but he continued to hope that part of the federal surplus would be devoted to this purpose. It was not, of course; and the American Colonization Society, which in its best year, 1832, sent 645 colonists to Liberia, dwindled to insignificance. By 1839, although he continued to head the society, Clay realized that slavery, instead of gradually receding before a combination of moral, demographic, and economic forces, was a stronger institution than ever before.

It was as the country's foremost advocate of colonization that Clay discovered the political risks of walking a tightrope on slavery. The society had strong southern backing in the early years, but beginning with the Nullifiers many in the South came to see it as a thinly veiled conspiracy to abolish slavery. Clay himself was careful to hold the society within the bounds of its mission, even as he linked its work to gradual emancipation. His early advocacy of emancipation in Kentucky was well remembered. He now thought a constitutional convention to abolish slavery in the state was more likely to set back the cause than advance it; yet he endorsed the convention plan for Missouri, where he thought emancipation had a sporting chance.[18] Denouncing slavery from the platform, Clay sometimes spoke with the fervor of an abolitionist. Of the new school of southern apologists who, with Calhoun, thought slavery a blessing, he declared at Lexington in 1836, "*I am not one. . . . I consider slavery as a curse*—a curse to the master, a wrong, a grievous wrong to the slave. In the abstract it is ALL WRONG; and no possible contingency can make it right." Only painful necessity could excuse the wrong.[19] Clay's means might be different, rejecting the immediatism of the northern fanatics, for instance, but, said southern ultraists, his goal was the same as the abolitionists'. Indeed, he was more dangerous to the South than they because he came in the guise of a friend.[20]

Abolitionists made the same objection from their side. Not Calhoun, not McDuffie, nor any other advocate of slavery was as dangerous as the senator from Kentucky draped in the shining mantle of philanthropy. In 1832 William Lloyd Garrison, leader of the new breed of radical abolitionists, published a blistering attack on the American Colonization Society as an agency of "the slave power." Clay, of course, suffered from the charges of inhumanity, hypocrisy, and malignity directed against the society. Other abolitionists, reluctant to alienate Clay, sought to convert him. One of these was James G. Birney, formerly a colonizationist, who moved from Alabama to Kentucky in 1833 and attempted to publish an abolitionist newspaper. He liked and admired Clay, but concluded after a long interview in 1834 that he had "no conscience" about slavery. He would act against slavery only as far as it suited his political convenience. "Friend as I have been with him," Birney wrote sadly after migrating across the Ohio River, "I am more the friend of liberty and righteousness."[21] The poet John Greenleaf Whittier was another. He had, with his Yankee friend George Prentice, worshiped Clay. Several poems, widely published but later disavowed as "my boyish folly," were hymns of praise to the Star of the West.[22] When the issue of Texas annexation reared its head in 1837, Whittier begged Clay to cast off political shackles and embrace the abolitionist cause. He replied with his usual candor, saying that in his opinion the northern agitators were "highly injurious to the slave himself, to the master, and to the harmony of the Union"; moreover, "that, instead of accelerating, they will retard abolition, and, in the mean time, will check other measures of benevolence and amelioration." Whittier was still unwilling to give him up, not even the next year when Clay made what the poet thought a bad compromise with Calhoun's slavery resolutions.[23] Lewis Tappan, the New York philanthropist, opened a dialogue with Clay aimed at converting him to immediate emancipation. The senator's generosity of spirit had always led him to the side of freedom and equal rights, Tappan wrote, and but for narrow political restraints would surely prevail on this issue. "How much you could effect for the millions in involuntary servitude by taking a noble stand in their behalf. What a close to a brilliant career should you assist the cause of human rights in behalf of the oppressed, downtrodden, and dumb in your land."[24] But Clay was as loath to become a born-again politician as he was to become a born-again Christian; and when Tappan, in 1838, began to threaten him with political defeat at the hands of abolitionists, Clay ended the correspondence.[25] The differences seemed irreconcilable. What could he do to satisfy the abolitionists? Resign from the American Colonization Society? Free his own slaves, up to sixty at the time? Enlist in the moral crusade? Impossible! But Clay could not ignore the threats of abolitionist leaders and their newspapers. They presaged the entrance of abolitionism into politics. Its influence was first felt in the Whig party of key northern states. Clay believed it helped turn Massachusetts Whigs toward Harrison, for instance. Since he could not appease the abolitionists, Clay decided to go on the attack, blacken them in the public eye, and cripple them at their entrance on the political stage.

Such was the purpose of Clay's remarkable speech on February 7, 1839.[26] He was careful to separate the *ultras* from the *humanitarian* abolitionists,

the Quakers for instance, and from *apparent* abolitionists whose real purpose was to vindicate the rights of speech, press, and petition. The ultras
had but a single cause. By advancing it from the moral to the political forum
they had created a new situation, for they rejected the ordinary political
means of persuasion, bargain, and accommodation, leaving only resolution
by force and violence. Clay defended his position on slavery in the District,
slavery in the Florida territory, and on the power of Congress to regulate
but not prohibit the interstate slave trade. The ultimate goal of the abolitionists, of course, was to end slavery everywhere. But here they were met by insuperable obstacles. The Constitution left the power over slavery to the
states, and Clay endorsed Van Buren's inaugural pledge to keep it there.
The massive reality of slavery could not be dealt with on standards of abstract right and justice. As long as the Africans remained in large numbers in
the southern states, even if the chains of bondage were lifted, Clay said,
they must be ruled by white men. The alternatives were a war of the races,
leading to the extermination of one or the other, or racial amalgamation con-
taminating both. A final obstacle was the enormous capital investment in
slaves. Clay estimated it at $1,200,000,000. There could be no immediate
emancipation without compensation for this property. Abolitionists evaded
the problem by appealing to the speculative idea that man cannot hold property in man. To this Clay opposed the amoral axiom: "That *is* property which
the law declares *to be* property."

If these considerations were insufficient to dissuade the abolitionists, Clay
went on, a genuine interest in the cause they espoused should dissuade
them. For their agitation had already set the cause back half a century. He
cited Kentucky, where gradual emancipation had once been within reach; he
cited the reaction in southern law and opinion, which had increased the rigors of slavery. Clay, once so sanguine, no longer hoped for change in his lifetime. The Founding Fathers had confidently left the problem to Clay's generation; and he left it, not to the next generation, but to distant posterity. His
justification was fundamentally the same as theirs: the preservation of the
Union. If abolitionism conquered the opinion of the free states, Clay warned,
disunion and civil war must be the result. "I am, Mr. President, no friend of
slavery," he solemnly concluded. "The searcher of all hearts knows that every pulsation of mine beats high and strong in the cause of civil liberty. . . .
But I prefer the liberty of my own country to that of any other people; and
the liberty of my own race to that of any other race. The liberty of the descendants of Africa in the United States is incompatible with the safety and liberty of the European descendants. Their slavery forms an exception—an exception resulting from stern and inexorable necessity—to the general liberty
of the United States. We did not originate, nor are we responsible for this necessity. Their liberty, if it were possible, could only be established by violating the incontestable powers of the states, and subverting the Union. And beneath the ruins of the Union would be buried, sooner or later, the liberty of
both races."

Calhoun rose immediately and pronounced the speech "the finishing stroke" to abolitionism. While still far from sound on all points, Clay had been driven from the middle ground to the defense of slavery and the South. "This is," Calhoun crowed, "a great epoch in our political history." It augured the ending of the abolitionist penetration of American politics, against which he had fought for several years.[27] The Ohio Democrat Thomas Morris, observing the "billing and cooing" between the senators, detected a new political alliance uniting Whig money power and southern slave power. "The cotton bale and the bank note have formed an alliance; the credit system with slave labor."[28] The sensation produced by Clay's speech was magnified by Calhoun's jubilation over it. A newspaper caricature represented Clay with his foot on a black man receiving the congratulations of Calhoun with his foot on another, the eyes of both appealing to heaven.[29] Edward Everett, in Boston, who also suspected a new understanding between Clay and Calhoun, urged Webster to take the floor and purge the Whig party of Clay's noxious doctrine. But Webster had not even heard Clay's speech (he was in the Supreme Court arguing the Alabama cases on the rights of corporations in interstate business) and, wrapped in silence most of the session, he lacked the spirit to reply.[30] There was no alliance or understanding. Calhoun hailed Clay's attack on the abolitionists but did not confuse motive with effect. The motive, he believed, was political: to rally the southern Whigs. Southern Democrats, who lauded Van Buren as "a Northern man with Southern feelings," made light of Clay's conversion, saying it would have come with better grace two or three years earlier or, at least, before the North began to drop him as a presidential candidate.[31]

Clay's speech immediately became infamous in the North. It jolted most Whigs and saddened more than it angered abolitionists. "Verily," wrote William Jay, "slavery has achieved a triumph that attests its withering power over exalted genius and high and generous aspirations—a triumph for which humanity must weep and patriotism blush."[32] For Whittier the speech was the last straw. The great disappointment, he wrote in the *Pennsylvania Freeman*, was not in the southern slant of the speech, for that was anticipated, "but in the weakness and absolute imbecility of its arguments—in the maudlin pathos—the overstrained affectation of patriotism, and shallow sophistries with which it abounds." It was the crashing of an idol: the idol of Clay as noble genius. Calhoun's manly consistency, even in criminal error, was preferable to "the cant and hypocrisy" of Clay, said Whittier.[33] Joshua Giddings, the first of the abolitionist congressmen, had also idolized the Kentucky senator. By endorsing his presidential candidacy, Giddings had placed himself in jeopardy with his Ohio constituents. Learning of the speech after it was delivered (unlike most of the senator's major speeches this one was not publicized in advance), he requested an interview with Clay to clarify certain points. When the meeting occurred, Clay told Giddings coldly that the speech, which had been published, required no explanation and he would give none. Twenty-five years later, in his *History of the Rebellion*, Giddings called the speech the most unfortunate of Clay's life.[34] The most celebrated reply came from the pen of William Ellery Channing, the eminent Boston divine. A year and a half earlier he had addressed a public letter to the senator urging him to oppose Texas annexation. Now he filed a gentle but devastating rebuttal. The idea that slavery concerned the South alone was patently false. Emancipation would be difficult but not impossible. If property was anything the law declared to be property, then, Channing said, he and the honorable senator might become chattels. Finally, to say that there was no hope for ending of slavery but in the extinction or the expulsion of the Negro was both weak and inhumane, especially in the mouth of a man blessed with the genius of compromise.[35]

It was in connection with this speech that Clay delivered the immortal line, "I had rather be right than be president." Speaking to a meeting of Clay Whigs in Philadelphia the next month, William C. Preston explained the circumstances of the senator's offhand remark. Preston had entered the Senate with deep prejudices against Clay but became intimate with him after the break with Calhoun in 1837. The two senators, it was said, were "like Siamese twins," constantly chirping, exchanging snuff, walking arm in arm. Yet Preston's former Carolina friends remembered him as the source of the damning assertion attributed to Clay at the Virginia Springs in 1830 that a leading object of protectionism was "to reduce the value of slave labor so low that it would compel the owner . . . to emancipate."[36] All his old prejudices had vanished, Preston explained at Philadelphia. He had been won over, not by Clay's eloquence, not by his great services, but by his fearless and noble character. "No man ever looked danger in the eye with a more determined, unblinking countenance, when in the pursuit of truth, or the sustainment of right, than Henry Clay." On one occasion, he continued, Clay had done him the honor of consulting him on a bold step; and when Preston pointed out the injury it would surely do to his presidential prospects, Clay replied, "I did not send for you to ask what might be the effect of the proposed movement on my *prospects*, but whether it was right; I HAD RATHER BE RIGHT THAN BE PRESIDENT."[37] Only sometime later, in elaboration, did Preston trace the avowal to the slavery speech. He added, further, that Clay had actually written out the speech and read it in advance of delivery to several friends from different sections. Clay was miffed by Preston's divulgence of the remark and the circumstances, but he never denied making it.[38] Few Whigs, or Democrats, disputed the boldness or even the nobility of Clay's character. But the declaration that he would rather be right than president was a pleasantry no hardened politician took seriously.

Clay returned to Kentucky in March fully expecting to become the nominee of the Whig national convention that was to meet at the end of the year. In contrast to Harrison, whose public service had ended a decade earlier, his principles and policies were well known. He stood for adherence to the Compromise Act, distribution combined with a revenue producing public lands policy, a national bank as soon as it became politically feasible, resistance to abolitionist pressures yet, at the same time, opposition to Texas annexation, and a constitutional amendment limiting the chief magistrate to a single six-year term. To a mass electorate, however, a relatively unambiguous record like Clay's could prove more of a liability than an asset. Even those who professed to be his friends worried about all the enemies he had made, as was suggested by a Whig circular in the months before the convention. Clay, it premised, could not be elected because:

> The old JACKSON MEN will oppose him.
> The ABOLITIONISTS generally, will oppose him.
> The violent anti-masons will oppose him.
> The Irishmen, who have already denounced him for the attack on O'Connell, will oppose him.
> The enemies of the United States Bank will oppose him.
> The WESTERN SQUATTERS will oppose him.
> The Southern State Rights men will oppose him.
> Now, in the name of Heaven, shall we run the risk of this opposition, or even the show of it?[39]

The bad-mouthing of Clay was reduced to a system in New York. There Webster Whigs and political opportunists seeking an alternative to both Clay and Harrison started a boom behind another military hero, General Winfield Scott. Clay was the object of a "triangular correspondence" said to have been started by Scott's backers. A wrote to B lamenting Clay's weakness in his district and urging B to do all he could in his; B delivered the same message to C, and so on. Scott was the cat's-paw in this game to create the opinion that Clay could not win.[40]

In the summer Clay made a swing through New York, from Buffalo to Saratoga Springs to Manhattan. Everywhere his reception was brilliant. Great cavalcades, up to two miles long, followed him from town to town; artillery saluted him; huge crowds gaped at him and roared approval when he spoke. It was the height of the season at Saratoga. "All the world is here," Philip Hone wrote, "politicians and dandies; cabinet ministers and ministers of the gospel; officeholders and officeseekers; humbuggers and humbugged; fortune-hunters and hunters of woodcock; anxious mothers and lovely daughters. . . ."[41] Clay delivered the mandatory speech before an audience estimated at six thousand—the largest he had ever faced—attended a fashionable ball in his honor, and talked politics with Whig leaders. Scott was at Saratoga—so was Van Buren—pumping his own candidacy. By this time, in August, he had overtaken Harrison in New York and threatened to overtake Clay. According to Scott, the tumultuous tribute to Clay was a facade. There were no votes behind it, yet the Whigs still adored Clay and gave him the benefit of a brilliant reception. Thurlow Weed, in fact, told Clay the awful truth and begged him to withdraw.[42] The triumphal procession—the greatest since Lafayette's—continued, to Albany and New York City, Philadelphia, Baltimore, and White Sulphur Springs in September.

Webster, meanwhile, basked in triumph of another kind in England. For fifteen years he had wanted to visit England, the land of his ancestors, of Shakespeare and Milton, of Blackstone, Pitt, and Burke, of almost everything he held dear. A flare-up on the disputed northeastern boundary be-

tween Maine and New Brunswick before Congress adjourned raised the prospect of Webster's going to England as a special envoy, but this passed. As
usual, he had no money and was head over heels in debt. Despondency
about his private affairs contributed to his despondency about the country's
affairs. His reelection to the Senate by overwhelming majorities in the Massachusetts legislature made no impression. Chancellor Kent, who saw him at
the Astor House, the elegant new hostelry on Broadway, described him as
spiritless and care-worn. "He talked a great deal about the two Adamses, and
told anecdotes of them and of General Stark, and Indian stories of the war of
1756, and he eulogized Washington and Hamilton."[43] In the same nostalgic
vein Webster described the planned journey abroad as "one of liberal curiosity alone"—a visit long overdue to "the elder branch of the family . . . my
kith and kin of the old Saxon race."[44] In fact, Webster had another object in
view. He hoped to unload many of his western landholdings and also to broker several state bond issues entrusted to his care.[45] The prospects in this regard were not encouraging in 1839, as the nation slid into deep depression
and foreign investors lost confidence in the United States. The immediate
problem of money for the English journey was solved, as in the past, when
his rich Boston and New York friends came to the rescue. A purse and a loan
totaling some $30,000 were raised.[46] That Webster received generous assis-
tance was acknowledged by the Whig press, although the amount was not disclosed. Figures as high as $75,000 were reported in Democratic newspapers,
which also linked the senator to an alleged conspiracy of international bankers and abolitionists.[47] Before he embarked Webster prepared a statement to
be released when he reached London announcing his withdrawal from the
presidential race.[48] He indicated no preference among the candidates and
took no further part in the Whig nomination.

The convention met at Harrisburg on December 4. Clay had a plurality of
delegates, but control of the convention was in the hands of eastern politicians who had decided he could not be elected. A rule was adopted whereby
the majority of a delegation cast the state's entire vote. The rule worked
against Clay. It canceled out his substantial plurality support in several northern delegations, Pennsylvania and New York for instance, and ensured that
states less likely to vote Whig in the general election—the southern states in
particular—did not dictate the nominee. Clay's friends tried to overturn the
rule but without success. On the first ballot he had 103 votes to 94 for Harrison and 57 for Scott. As the balloting continued Scott gained, Clay slipped,
and Harrison held steady. On the fourth ballot Weed and the New York
Whigs, who had been backing Scott to hold off Clay, threw their votes to Harrison. The result was reported 148 for Harrison, 90 for Clay, 16 for Scott.
Among the free states only Rhode Island stuck with Clay, while Harrison was
shut out in the South.[49] Hearing the news at his hotel room in Washington,
Clay could not conceal his disappointment. "My friends are not worth the
powder and shot it would take to kill them," he reportedly said. "I am the
most unfortunate man in the history of parties: always run by my friends

when sure to be defeated, and now betrayed for a nomination when I, or any one, would be sure of election."[50] In this latter judgment he was undoubtedly correct. Regardless of his political liabilities, the Democratic depression combined with the appeal of the Whig economic program would have ensured Clay's election in 1840.

Clay put on the face of magnanimity. A letter he had furnished to the Kentucky delegation in the event of defeat was read amid a chorus of eulogy. In it Clay expressed "cordial support" for the nominee.[51] The convention went on, in what would turn out to be the cream of the jest, to nominate John Tyler for vice president. This, it was later said, was the result of a bargain between Clay and Tyler and their respective friends. Eager for the support of the Conservatives in Virginia, where they might tip the balance to the Whigs in the presidential election, Clay had earlier backed William C. Rives, the insurgent leader, against Tyler, the Whig candidate, in a critical senatorial contest. He had even propositioned Tyler to withdraw, it was alleged, thereby permitting Rives's reelection, in return for becoming Clay's running mate in 1840. If such a proposition was made, which is unlikely, Tyler must have rejected it, for he did not withdraw and the senatorial contest ended in stalemate; moreover, at the convention Clay could not deliver his part of the bargain.[52] In fact, Tyler was nominated for the sensible reason that he added balance to the Whig ticket headed by a "national" and a northerner who was also suspected of abolitionism. Bargain or not, Clay would accomplish his immediate object in Virginia, for Tyler withdrew from the senate race and Rives won reelection. A longer time, a later chapter, would disclose the deeper ironies of this affair with Tyler for Clay, for the Whigs, and for the country.

Clay still considered himself the head of the Whig party, and if he had any doubts about it, or about working for Harrison, they were submerged in the love feast staged for his benefit in Washington after the Harrisburg convention. The returning delegates poured out unmerciful compliment on the great man. It was not, they said by way of apology, that they loved Caesar less but that they loved Rome more. And they hailed Clay for the noble sacrifice of himself "to the great principle of our political faith, which prohibits man worship."[53] Clay made a dozen speeches during the ensuing campaign, and harped constantly on this theme. In June, returning to his Virginia birthplace, he delivered a major address in which he traced all the evils of the government, all the distresses of the country, to the career of executive usurpation commenced by Andrew Jackson. He laid down his own platform for the party, expressing regret that the convention had not offered a platform or issued an address. When the Democrats did so at their convention in May, Clay drafted a proposed statement of Whig principles. But it was greeted with stony silence, and Clay acquiesced in the nonsense and nothingness upon which the Whig campaign, like the Harrison nomination, was based.[54]

In March a Democratic newspaper reported that a Clay partisan, hearing of the Whig nomination, observed derisively "that upon condition of receiving a pension of $2,000 dollars and a barrel of cider, General Harrison would no doubt consent to withdraw his pretensions, and spend his days in a log cabin on the banks of the Ohio."[55] What was said in derision the Whigs promptly turned into a winning theme. The Hero of Tippecanoe became the Log Cabin and Hard Cider candidate: the humble personification of the republican virtues of industry, frugality, simplicity, and common sense. So it was "Huzzah for Harrison!" "Go it, Tip! come it, Ty!" in festival, song, and slogan. Jacksonian Democrats denounced the campaign as a mockery of democracy. For the Whigs, of course, it marked their embrace of democracy; in a sense, they simply reenacted on a larger stage the Jacksonian campaign of 1828, with poor little Van Buren, who allegedly supped from gold spoons in the White House, substituted for the aristocratic Adams.

> Old Tip he wears a homespun suit,
> He has no ruffled shir-wir-wirt!
> But Van he has the golden plate,
> And he's a little squir-wir-wirt![56]

After Congress adjourned Clay stumped for Harrison in Indiana, Ohio, and Tennessee. At Nashville he bearded the old lion in his den, not only vindicating himself against the hoary charge of "corrupt bargain" but recklessly accusing Jackson of appointing defaulters—he named Edward Livingston, among others—to high office. Clay was in good form. On arrival in Tennessee he had asked about his old friend Felix Grundy; told that he was away making speeches for the administration, Clay remarked, to the delight of his audience, "Ah! At his old occupation, defending criminals!"[57] Unfortunately, the good humor of the Nashville speech was spoiled by Clay's asperity toward Jackson, who promptly returned "the gross epithets" of the senator.[58]

Godlike Daniel was the star performer of the Whig campaign. His English journey had been only a modest success financially; by dint of great effort he returned at the end of the year no poorer than when he left. But it had been a stunning literary and social success. Despite rumors of default and repudiation by the states, English opinion of American institutions was rising in 1839, and Webster was introduced in the press as their most illustrious exemplar. While not as popular as Henry Clay, he was without peer as a constitutional jurist and statesman and, it was said, the rival of Lord Brougham in powers of mind. "America never sent to Europe a man of whose endowments she is so proud."[59] Promptly dubbed "The Great Western," after the celebrated Transatlantic steamship, Webster made an indelible impression on the English. Benjamin Disraeli called him "a complete Brother Jonathan"; Henry Hallam, the historian, described him as "the beau ideal of a republican senator"; Sydney Smith, the literary wit, said he struck him "much like a steam engine in trousers"; and Thomas Carlyle wrote for his American friend Emerson a brilliant description—"crag-like face," "dull black eyes . . . like dull anthracite furnaces," "mastiff mouth"—that captured his physical presence.[60] Webster met most of England's great men, attended the Queen's Ball, went regularly to the House of Commons (and sat on the Tory bench next to Robert Peel), scratched his name on the whitewashed wall of Shakespeare's birthplace at Stratford-on-Avon, observed agricultural practices, went fox-hunting at Belvoir Castle in Scotland, and in the fall made a hurried trip to Paris. The financial collapse in the United States caused a panic among English bankers and investors in American stocks. Webster did what he could to cushion the shock. At the request of the House of Baring, he offered his opinion that the state securities filling the portfolios of English creditors were a legal as well as a moral obligation since the states were sovereign political communities. The opinion, for which Webster was reportedly paid £1 thousand, was reassuring to the creditors. (Read closely it also offered some reassurance to proponents of state rights.) In the United States, however, Democrats accused Webster of plotting with the bankers to force the assumption of state debts by the general government.[61] This would become an issue in the election year. Of course, Webster and the Whigs denied entertaining any idea of assumption.

Financial gloom was dissipated by the shining political prospect Webster discovered upon his return. The unity of the Whigs around Harrison was amazing to behold. There was no friendship between the respective friends of Clay and Webster, however. The former blamed Webster for the defeat at Harrisburg, while the latter clung to old grudges against Clay. But the senators themselves called a truce. At the first opportunity, the Whig Young Men's Convention in May, they appeared in the same parade, spoke from the same platform, delivered the same message, and retired together amid thunderous applause.[62] The exhilaration of the Log Cabin and Hard Cider campaign revived Webster's political spirits. He knew it was humbug but it was humbug in a good cause, and he took Machiavellian delight in beating the Democrats at their own game. About Harrison he had supposedly said in 1835 that he could have no part in elevating a man "who is justly the scorn and ridicule of his foes, and the pity and contempt of his friends."[63] Webster denied saying it—there is no corroborating evidence that he had—but regardless of his opinion then, he seemed satisfied with the candidate in 1840. The general was honest and amiable, likely to surround himself with good men, and he showed none of the ignorance and recklessness of Jackson and Van Buren in financial affairs.[64] By spring Webster, with most of the Whig leaders, smelled victory. The election acquired a new dimension. At issue was not only the choice of a president but the determination of the succession. Harrison was pledged to a single term; the man who became his prime minister, or in the course of the campaign scored impressively with the Whig faithful, would be in a commanding position. Obviously, Webster and Clay were the leading contenders. Abiding by the voluntary truce, they nevertheless recognized the stakes in the game. Clay, who had long been on friendly terms with Harrison, was content to play a modest role in the campaign; Webster, on the other hand, transformed his public character and appeared in a dramatic new light.

The senator made over two dozen speeches and was heard by well over a hundred thousand people. Some three thousand trudged up Stratton Mountain in Vermont to hear him. The largest throng ever assembled in the

United States, variously estimated from twenty-five to fifty thousand, heard him deliver a declaration of Whig principles, drafted by himself, at Bunker Hill. Ten thousand heard him speak in Wall Street; and the same number reportedly crowded into Capitol Square, Richmond, for his first major address south of the Potomac. Webster's message was not new. He denounced the boom and bust financial policies of the past eight years; he blasted the subtreasury system, which Congress had finally enacted into law, with its directive toward hard money, saying that it must increase deflationary pressures and lead to a low-wage economy; he called for restoration of a national system of commerce and currency, including a national bank; and, of course, he assailed the growth of executive power. What was new was Webster's rhetorical style. Taking what he had learned on the western stump, blending it with the homespun motif of the campaign, Webster spoke the language of the common people and behaved as one of them. Gone was the solemn manner, the swollen eloquence, the lofty Corinthian flourishes and figures—gone was "the oratorical windmill." In its place was a style that was direct, light, and witty, popular without condescension, and Doric in its simplicity.[65]

This new Webster was first disclosed in a speech at Saratoga on a hot August afternoon. Farmers and their families from miles around and many hundreds of people who came by train from Troy, Schenectady, and other places filled a pine grove to hear Webster. He mounted the flatbed of a wagon (after a hastily erected platform collapsed) and spoke for three hours. To his standard appeal on behalf of Whig measures, he added several affecting touches. He offered his Marshfield fishing companion, Seth Peterson, as a model of American character and striving. And recalling his own humble beginnings in the New Hampshire hills, he said, "Gentlemen, it did not happen to me to be born in a log cabin, but my elder brothers and sisters were born in a log cabin." He went on to speak of the annual pilgrimage he made with his children to the natural font of republican virtue, the ancestral log cabin in the wilderness. This was, some thought, the gem of the speech that in its entirety was "the *chef d'oeuvre*" of American political discourse.[66] Several weeks later under a huge tent pitched on the village green of Patchogue, on Long Island, Webster declared at the outset, "I come to make no flourishes or figures, but to make a plain speech to the intelligence of this country." His character, he said, was as plain and democratic as his speech. "The man that says I am an aristocrat—is a liar!" Professions of democracy by the so-called Democratic party were false. Names must not be taken for things, Webster warned. In the adage of farmers, "fine words butter no parsnips." The Whigs were the true democrats. Harrison's election would restore the government to "the true democratic principles of Mr. Jefferson."[67] A verbatim report of the speech appeared in the New York *Herald* within twenty-four hours—a journalistic milestone. The editor, James Gordon Bennett, took pride in this and also in the accurate reporting which, he insisted, communicated Webster's "Shakespearean" wit and manner for the first time. The pamphlet edition of the speech went like "wildfire"—sixty-five thousand copies in three days.[68] Democrats were not amused. Silas Wright, who had years of experience rebutting Webster, picked up his trail on Long Island; William Cullen Bryant, Bennett's rival on the *Evening Post*, was apoplectic over the senator's professions of democracy; and Benjamin F. Butler, Van Buren's attorney general, undertook in a speech at Tammany Hall to prove that Webster was indeed an aristocrat in his politics. All his favorite measures, Butler said, "are calculated to give advantages and benefits of a pecuniary kind, to particular classes, to the exclusion of the rest of the people—to increase the inequality of wealth in our community—to make the rich richer and the poor poorer—and to give, in many cases, to the few, a command over the labor and the minds of the many."[69]

From New York Webster went to Richmond. There he renewed the pledge first made in Alexandria in June, that Massachusetts and Virginia, North and South, were bound by "a sacred compact" barring interference with slavery in the states, and not one "jot or tittle" of it would be violated with his consent.[70] Again, he pursued the theme of restoration, calling for a "civil revolution," like Jefferson's in 1800, that would return the government to its republican foundations; and he baited his speech with praise of the gods of Virginia Republicanism. Thomas Ritchie exploded: "In the whole course of this campaign, we have seen no humbug so audacious, no trick so absurd, as this attempt of the head of the [Federalist] Essex Junto to pass himself off as a Jeffersonian Democrat."[71]

Returning to New Hampshire for the close of the campaign, Webster took sick and withdrew to Marshfield at the end of October. A great Whig victory was foreshadowed by the state elections that began in August. Two and a half million votes were cast in the presidential election, which represented an increase of one-third over the popular turnout four years earlier and was an estimated 80 percent of the electorate. Harrison and Tyler carried every state except New Hampshire (where last-minute efforts by Webster would not have altered the outcome), Virginia (where Rives blamed the narrow Whig defeat on Webster's visit), South Carolina (where there was no popular election and Calhoun controlled the electoral vote), Missouri, Arkansas, and Illinois. The election marked the maturation of "the second party system," as historians have named it, in which two balanced parties, Whigs and Democrats, each with a national constituency, and basically identical in structure, style, and techniques, contested for control of the government. (A third party, the Liberty party, with James G. Birney as its candidate, emerged in 1840, marking the entry of abolitionists into presidential politics; but it had no bearing on the outcome.) In defeat some Democrats claimed the Whig victory was a mockery of free government. "Had we been beaten, in a fair field, by such men as Webster or Clay, by manly argument, we should feel but half the mortification we do at being beaten by such a man as Harrison. And in such a fashion! We have been sung down, lied down, drunk down."[72] Henceforth in American politics both parties would be parties of the people, parties of democracy, regardless of name or slogan or bogus ancestry. What else the election meant, aside from repudiation of the Van Buren administration, it was difficult to say. But the Whigs were free to make of it what they could, and in that process Webster and Clay were sure to have a crucial role.

* *Six* *

THE WHIG DEBACLE

William Henry Harrison may have been elected president, but Henry Clay was still the leader of the Whig party. Harrison himself was little inclined to dispute the point. Like Clay, who was five years his junior, he was a native Virginian who had made his career in the West and risen to fame in the War of 1812, though in a military rather than a civilian capacity. As an Ohio congressman after the war, and sometime later as a senator, he had followed the Star of the West; and it was Clay to whom he owed his appointment as United States Minister to Columbia in 1828. Not long before the Whig nomination in 1839 Harrison confessed to Clay how "distressing and embarrassing" he felt his position toward him to be. "How little can we judge of our future destinies. A few years ago I could not have believed in the possibility of my being placed in a position of apparent rivalry to you. Particularly in relation to the Presidency. An office which I never dreamed of attaining and which I had ardently desired to see you occupy."[1] The silver-haired general had neither friends nor enemies; he owed his nomination in part to that and in part to the belief that, unlike Clay, he would be a weak leader, easily bent to the will of local party potentates. It was not true that he stood for nothing: he stood for the Whig principles and policies advocated by Henry Clay. He believed in legislative supremacy and repeatedly pledged himself to a single presidential term. Obviously he would look to the Whig giants, Clay and Webster, for leadership of his administration. The only question was which of these rivals would be chief.

Soon after the election Harrison paid a visit to Kentucky, ostensibly on family business, and Clay hastened to Frankfort to meet him. There was some wariness on both sides. Harrison did not wish to add to the impression that he was under the senator's thumb, while Clay feared the influence of Charles Wickliffe and his family with the president-elect. It was rumored that the Old Duke, an anti-Clay and anti-bank Whig, would be named postmaster general in the new cabinet and from this patronage post mount a challenge to Clay in the Bluegrass State. But the senator's position had seldom been stronger. He had won plaudits for magnanimously campaigning for Harrison, and he came out of the contest, it was said, "with the whole of Kentucky at his back." The state gave Harrison his largest popular majority. It also elected a Clay stalwart, Robert Letcher, governor. Under the circumstances Harrison could scarcely begrudge Clay's counsel. The Wickliffe challenge, such as it was, collapsed when Harrison, on the senator's recommendation, subsequently named another Kentuckian, John J. Crittenden, to his cabinet as attorney general.[2]

At Frankfort Clay persuaded Harrison to visit him at Ashland. There he had ample opportunity to fill the general's head with his own ideas. In the opinion of the Democratic press, Clay virtually dictated the design of the new administration. Clay would be Harrison's Warwick. The opinion tended to be confirmed when the Kentucky newspapers reported, not quite accurately, that Harrison toasted Clay at a public dinner as "the fittest man in the nation for the presidency." From the first, although Harrison offered him the choice of position, Clay insisted he wished to stay in the Senate.[3] The way was thus opened for Webster to become the dominant figure in the cabinet. Acknowledging his political differences with Webster, frankly admitting that his confidence in him had been badly shaken during the last eight years, Clay nevertheless felt that the New Englander should hold a high place in the administration. He recommended other Whigs, in addition to Crittenden, who enjoyed his confidence, for instance John M. Clayton, his candidate for secretary of treasury. He also pressed upon Harrison his favorite measure, a special session of Congress to be called immediately upon the inauguration of the new regime.[4]

While it suited Clay's political style and ambition to remain in the Senate, it suited Webster's to go into the cabinet. He was tired of the Senate, and had thought of resigning in any event; he had not been tested in high executive office; above all, he needed executive power and influence to compensate for his weakness in the party. With Clay out of the picture, Harrison gave Webster the choice of the two top cabinet positions, state and treasury, hinting toward the latter. Webster, having just arrived in Washington for the session of Congress, replied within twenty-four hours, expressing his preference for the State Department and accepting the office should it finally be offered. The emotional plea of his daughter Julia that he retire—"Do come back to us, dear Father"—went unheeded, and Webster was positively ecstatic over the administration's prospects.[5] Before he could become secretary of state he must settle his huge debt, about $114,000, to Nicholas Biddle's bank in Philadelphia. A hurry-up settlement was achieved in March, wherein Webster turned over to the bank most of his western landholdings—farm lands, mineral lands, town lands—some twenty thousand acres all told.[6] Fortunately the problem caused Webster no public embarrassment. He did not escape from the Senate without incident, however. When his letter of resignation was read, red-faced Alfred Cuthbert of Georgia, with the spirit of a gamecock, rose and charged that the senator, who was absent, had changed his opinion to the injury of the South on the power of Congress to interfere with the interstate slave trade. Clay rebuked Cuthbert for his impudence and paid generous tribute to Webster for his services in the Senate. As to the interstate slave trade, he would attest that Webster had not changed his opinion. Clay was entitled: several days earlier he had been associated with Webster before the Supreme Court in a challenge of Mississippi's constitutional bar to the purchase of slaves in other states for resale within its borders. The court reached no definite conclusion in the case, *Groves* v. *Slaughter;* but some of Webster's reasoning was curious. Although Congress had exclusive jurisdiction over interstate commerce, in his opinion, slaves were a species of property upon which Congress could not act. The South seemed unlikely to quarrel with this. The case attracted little interest, yet may have precipitated Cuthbert's attack. He did not confine himself to the slavery issue. Conceding Webster's intellectual power, he deprecated his moral character. "Intellect! . . . What is it without sympathy with mankind, without magnanimity, without a deep sense of what is due to the people?" Webster had failed in every crisis: the war, the tariff (he opposed the Compromise of 1833), and the struggle against abolitionism.[7]

Clay was the foremost advocate of a special session of the Twenty-Seventh Congress, when the Whigs would come into possession of both houses. In his eyes "a great civil revolution" had occurred and, impetuous as always, he could hardly wait to get on with it. Harrison's cabinet, once completed, was satisfactory to Clay. John Bell of Tennessee, the secretary of war, was a friend, and he had no objection to George Badger of North Carolina at the Navy Department, though he could not have been happy with Francis Granger, the ally of Thurlow Weed, as postmaster general. Treasury offered the principal disappointment, however. Not that Clay opposed Thomas Ewing, a warm admirer from Ohio, whom Harrison named. But he had championed Clayton's appointment so tenaciously, in fact, that Harrison reportedly ended their last interview on the subject with the rebuke, "Mr. Clay, you forget that I am President."[8] Clay saw Webster's hand in the rejection of Clayton. Webster ingratiated himself with Harrison from the moment he arrived in the capital and quickly gained influence over him. Everyone understood that the success or failure of the first Whig administration depended upon the ability of Clay and Webster to work together. Washington observers noted every sign of cordiality or hostility between them. Democratic newspapers showed them in conflict; Whig newspapers accented harmony. But whether one or the other the fate of the administration hung upon it. Harrison even joked about it. At a White House dinner, he told Thomas Hart Benton, "If you don't like anything in my administration, put it to Clay and Webster, but don't harpoon me." Benton agreed to separate the throne from the powers behind it.[9]

The political struggle between Webster and Clay had already begun. The bone of contention was the appointment of the Collector of the Port of New York. Webster's candidate was Edward Curtis, sometimes known as the senator's jackal in New York, who was also part of Weed's political family. Clay had adopted a rule of non-interference in the patronage scramble, but he made an exception of this case. First, because the collector controlled five hundred jobs in New York and with this army could command the vote of the city or even the state. Second, because Curtis had engineered the Scott boom in 1839 and so had been the principal agent of Clay's defeat in the Harrisburg convention. No one could doubt where Curtis's allegiance would lie in 1844. "Ned" Curtis, said Clay, was "a base scoundrel." Yet his hostility was directed less to him than to his patron, Webster. Clay supported R. C. Wetmore, a New York merchant, for the collectorship. Gadsby's Hotel was filled with the candidates' respective friends, two-thirds of them candidates for the subordinate offices in the customs house, according to James Gordon Bennett, the redoubtable editor of the New York *Herald,* who was getting up the first true press corps in the capital.[10] After the inauguration Harrison nominated Curtis, and he would be confirmed. Webster won this crucial test. Six weeks into the new administration, it was said, not a single friend of Henry Clay had been awarded office in New York City.[11]

Harrison had carried a draft of his inaugural address across the mountains. It was discussed in council and Webster, who was appalled by its turgidity, prevailed upon the old hero to allow him to revise it. William W. Seaton liked to tell the story of how Webster came late to dinner at his house and, much agitated, confessed he had just killed two Roman emperors and seventeen proconsuls as dead as smelts.[12] Even so, a host of Roman worthies, straight out of Plutarch—Camillus, Scipio, Brutus—survived in the ninety-minute address Harrison delivered before an immense throng at the east front of the Capitol on March 4. Clay had no responsibility for the address, but it offered a perfect prescription for legislative ascendancy in the government. That government is a democracy, Harrison said. The primary power rests with the immediate representatives of the people in Congress. The great danger, from which the country had suffered long enough, lay in the accumulation and abuse of power by the executive branch. Harrison renewed his pledge not to seek reelection and called for a constitutional amendment to secure the single-term limitation permanently. He disclaimed all control over the treasury and expressed opposition to use of the veto power except on constitutional grounds.[13]

Perhaps because of these principles, Harrison was all the more apprehensive of Clay's imperious tendencies. The senator carried his campaign for a special session into Congress. "It has sown dissension and alarm in our ranks and strengthened the confidence of our enemies," wrote one Whig congressman. Whig newspapers divided on the issue. Webster was opposed, and, according to Bennett, so was Harrison lest he surrender his administration at the outset to Clay. When the question was laid before the cabinet at the time of the inauguration, there were three for and three against a special session, Harrison breaking the tie with his negative vote.[14] Nothing was definitely decided, however, and Clay grew impatient. On Saturday, March 13, he dispatched a letter to Harrison warning him of the danger of vacillation and saying he would dine with him that evening, when he hoped to hear a decision. For the general's convenience he enclosed a draft of the proclamation of the special session. Harrison shot back: "You use the privilege of a friend to lecture me and I will take the same liberty with you—you are too impetuous." He promised a decision on Monday and told Clay that henceforth he should not expect personal interviews with the president. Clay was crushed. He replied as he was preparing to leave for home on Monday. Ever since their meetings in Kentucky, he said, his enemies had been poisoning Harrison's mind against him. He denied the charge of "dictating" to the president and went on to defend himself against another charge, which had not been made, of interference in appointments, that of Curtis in particular. Harrison should not trouble himself with an answer.[15] And he did not. But on Wednesday he called a special session of Congress to convene on May 31. Financial exigencies, including the collapse of the United States Bank in Philadelphia, impending bankruptcy of several western states, and a depleted treasury, had made the session unavoidable. Even Webster championed it in the press.[16]

Clay never saw Harrison again. He died suddenly of pneumonia one month to the day after his inauguration. With this astonishing event all the political dice must be recast. For the first time in the nation's history the chief magistracy fell to the vice president, John Tyler.

1. *Tyler Too*

The courtly fifty-one-year-old Tyler had known and admired Clay for twenty-five years. Like Clay he had been reared in the Virginia Republican school; unlike him he had changed neither his state nor his constitutional principles. One of his first important votes in Congress had been against the Bonus Bill, and he had consistently opposed all the measures of the American System. Tyler drifted into the Jackson party, yet kept his independence and risked political suicide when he defended Clay against "bargain and corruption." He always took pride in the part he had played in framing the Compromise Act, by which, he said, Clay "rescued his country from civil war."[1] Although he had supported Jackson's Bank veto, Tyler backed Clay's resolutions against the president on the removal of the deposits; and rather than comply with the instructions of the Virginia General Assembly to vote for the Expunging Resolution, Tyler resigned his Senate seat in 1836. Virginia Whigs made him their vice presidential candidate that year. Three years later he was the Whig senatorial candidate against the incumbent, William C. Rives. Clay, it may be recalled, threw his support to Rives, the Conservative Democrat. The Tylerites felt betrayed, and one of their leaders, Henry A. Wise, later insisted that in reparation Clay agreed to make Tyler the party's vice presidential candidate in 1840. While there may be poetic justice in making Clay responsible for Tyler, the story flies in the face of logic and events. If he had been "bribed" with the offer of the vice presidency, Tyler would presumably have withdrawn from the senatorial race. But he did not, and it ended in a stalemate, although Rives would be elected a year later. And why would Clay, who was expecting to head the Whig ticket, and who was, in fact, the candidate of the Virginia Whigs, want Tyler as his running mate? Tyler's presence on the ticket with Harrison made sense. He was a southern Whig, a state rights Whig. He provided "balance." But nobody could have imagined him on a ticket with Clay in 1840. Tyler, as it turned out, couldn't even carry Virginia for the Whigs. When Clay afterward met Wise in Washington, he remarked coldly, "I congratulate myself that Virginia has gone for Mr. Van Buren; we will no longer be embarrassed by her peculiar opinions."[2]

However much Tyler liked and admired Clay, he was philosophically more attuned to John C. Calhoun. His opposition to executive power was fundamentally opposition to consolidation, and like the Carolinian he could profess high principles to the point of absurdity. Calhoun was discouraged by the election. The country had sunk under a "moneyed oligarchy." "We are a changed people," he wrote, "and no more like what we were even thirty years ago, than if we were a different people." He had been returned to the Senate with the unanimous vote of the state legislature, backed up by resolutions declaring that South Carolina, after the healing of old divisions, "now presents to the enemies of her policy an undivided front and is prepared, as she is resolved, to repel . . . every aggression upon her rights, as a sovereign republic."[3] In the winter session Calhoun was in a constant frenzy, denouncing the entire Whig program and pushing his favorite measure, long since proven impracticable, for the cession of western lands to the states. He expected that Harrison, whose election as president was only "an affair of personal gratification and vanity," would be little felt, and Clay would control the Whig administration, although there would be discord brought on by the scramble for the succession. Webster, in a gloating editorial penned for the *National Intelligencer*, called Calhoun's position "absolutely ludicrous." Never in political annals, he said, referring to Calhoun's desertion of the Whigs in 1837, "was there an instance in which political crookedness met with a more sudden and awful retribution." But Calhoun liked his position. He saw an opportunity for ascendancy in the Democratic party and election to the presidency in 1844.[4] In the spring he journeyed to Alabama to visit his son Andrew and the cotton plantation in which he had a heavy stake. While he declined to make speeches, he made public appearances at Selma, Montgomery, Marion, and other towns, talked freely with planters and politicians, and was, said one, "more gazed at than the devil would be in the midst of a Methodist revival."[5] Tyler's accession upset Calhoun's calculations, of course. Not only was the president an old-fashioned Virginia Republican but intimates of his political circle—Littleton Tazewell, Abel Upshur, Thomas Walker Gilmer, Beverley Tucker—were also Calhoun's friends in the Old Dominion. It was too early to speculate, however, what bearing Tyler's presidency might have on Calhoun's future.

Of more immediate concern was its bearing for Webster. Suddenly his fortunes were tied to a president whose constitutional principles he abhorred. Clay, at least, began from the basis of personal amity with Tyler, and if that would not support political collaboration he could, as was his want, go his own way in Congress. Quickly caught up in the work of the State Department, besieged by job seekers, and busy establishing himself in Washington, Webster gave little thought to the problem, however. Personal affairs took him to Boston, to Philadelphia, and to New York, where he buried his father-in-law. "My head is nearly turned," he wrote on April 11. "In five weeks, we have had three Presidents, besides which I have been hurried from one death bed to another, under very harrowing circumstances."[6] About Tyler he was guardedly optimistic. The great question was whether he could rise above past principles and positions. "My hope is that he will consider himself *instructed*, not by one single State, but by the *Country*," Webster remarked, alluding to the Virginian's opposite course in 1836.[7] Webster never considered resigning. He could scarcely afford to do so. Still over his head in debt, without a clear dollar to his name, the patience of his friends exhausted, he nevertheless purchased a magnificent house on President's Square (later named Lafayette Square) reportedly for $24,000 including furnishings, and before long he was entertaining lavishly.[8] Nor did Tyler seek Webster's, or anyone's, resignation. Politically, he had no choice but to retain Harrison's cabinet. His Virginia friends were mortified, of course, that an old Federalist and mercenary should be at the head of the cabinet.[9] Anomalous as this was, Webster's presence was the only thing, Tyler realized, that lent credibility to his administration in the eastern states. Webster's enemies in Whig ranks, seeing he was vulnerable, undertook to drive him from the cabinet. Centered in New York City, the movement was led by the same politicians and newspapers that kept up a running battle against Ned Curtis. In the West it was sparked by George Prentice and the Louisville *Journal*.[10]

On April 19 the new president issued an address to the people couched in Whig rhetoric and intended to reassure the faithful of his commitment to the principles and policies on which "Tippecanoe and Tyler Too" had been elected. Without taking the single-term pledge, he showed appropriate deference to Congress, promised to sanction "any constitutional measure" looking to the restoration of a sound currency, and in all matters said he would "resort to the fathers of the great Republican school for advice and instruction." The terms were broad enough to cover incorporation of a national bank as well as a protective tariff. Reading the address at Ashland, Clay was pleased, yet not without misgivings. He wrote to Tyler seeking clarification. Guardedly, in reply, Tyler indicated support for additional revenues and for distribution of the proceeds from sale of the public lands. He supposed repeal of the independent treasury was inevitable, but hoped the matter of a national bank would remain dormant in the special session. The public mind was not prepared for it; the economy was so depressed he doubted capitalists would invest in it; and to those considerations he added his usual constitutional objections. Could Clay frame a measure to obviate these? Tyler asked. He, in any event, would propose nothing and reserve decision on any measure Congress might enact. While this put the ball in Clay's court, it in no way committed Tyler to play.[11] For reasons that had more to do with Whig ideology than with the needs of the government and the economy, Clay had his mind set on a national bank. He had earlier discussed a plan with Ewing in the capital. The secretary understood that it could not be postponed and promised to forward a finished plan when requested by Congress. "No man can be better disposed than the President." Should a bank bill finally be presented to him by Congress, he would sign it, Ewing confidently predicted. "His former opinions, some of them unfortunately of record, will trouble *him* but not, I think, the *country*. He speaks of you," the secretary told Clay, "with the utmost kindness, and you may rely upon it his friendship is strong and unabated."[12]

On this cheering note, Clay set out for Washington. Tyler's message at the opening of Congress shed no further light on his course; with regard to a bank he was, indeed, more inscrutable than before. A "fiscal agent" to facilitate collection and disbursement of the revenue, and supportive of a sound currency, was highly desirable. The American people had condemned all the systems heretofore tried, but he would concur in the adoption of any system agreed upon by Congress, provided it was constitutional.[13] What Tyler wanted mattered little. Clay was in command of Congress, and there was nothing obscure or equivocal about his agenda.

Within a week, after discussion in the Whig caucus, Clay presented his agenda. First, repeal of the independent treasury law. Second, incorporation of a national bank. Third, provision for an adequate revenue by tariff duties and a temporary loan to cover the projected deficit. Fourth, distribution. Fifth, passage of necessary appropriation bills. Sixth, certain improvements in the banking system of the District of Columbia.[14] The program was ambitious but surprised no one; the key measures were identified with Clay and the Whig party. Whig majorities in both houses of Congress—up to fifty in the House and seven in the Senate—supported by a Whig president, offered an unparalleled opportunity for party government. Having been on the defensive politically for so long, Clay was eager for positive legislative accomplishment. One of his Kentucky lieutenants, John White, was elected Speaker of the House. An old associate, Samuel Southard of New Jersey, became president *pro tem* of the Senate and, in the absence of a vice president, its presiding officer. On Clay's motion, committee chairmen—twenty-two of them—were elected, other members being appointed by the president *pro tem*. Clay had himself placed at the head of the Finance Committee and, more importantly, arranged for the appointment of a select committee under him to deal with the crucial business of currency and fiscal management.

From the beginning of the session Clay was attacked for playing the part of a "dictator." Of course, such adjectives as "arrogant," "imperious," and "over-bearing" were part of the standard vocabulary used to describe his political persona, and enemies vied with each other to break him down. But now he had the power to support his domineering passion. "Mr. Clay is carrying every thing by storm—his will is the law of Congress," a Tennessee representative complained. His followers, including several known abolitionists, were at the head of all the House committees.[15] Clay usually turned aside criticism with a jest. Was he a tyrant? "Ask Charles [his black servant] if I am not a kind master." But as the mid-summer heat descended on the capital and the Senate fell behind Clay's timetable, he grew irritable and threatened unprecedented changes in the rules to expedite business. His aim from the first had been to finish the session in sixty days; and by dividing responsibility for major legislation between the two houses, by taking decision on important issues in caucus before they reached the floor, and by moving the hour of daily business back to 10:00 A.M., this had seemed reasonable. Now, as the session limped into August, Clay accused the opposition of deliberate obstructionism. Calhoun was a principal culprit. The senators clashed repeatedly on procedural questions. Pointing to the House as a model of legislative efficiency, Clay threatened to introduce two of its rules: the one-hour limitation on speeches, and admission of the "previous question" motion, cutting off debate, in committee of the whole. Calhoun, though he never seemed to mind gagging abolitionists, denounced Clay for seeking to impose "a gag system" on the Senate; and Clay sensibly dropped the matter.[16] Whether or not he was despotic, everyone agreed on the Kentuckian's extraordinary power. Except for at most three Whigs in the Senate and perhaps twenty in the House, his word was law, according to the correspondent of the New York *Herald*. "His is the ascendancy of a powerful intellect and a bold determined spirit over lesser minds and fainter hearts. It is the preponderance which can only be acquired by the loftiest talent, and unfailing resources of mind, united to a courage equal to any emergency, and perseverance that no difficulties can thwart or discourage. Never," said this veteran capital reporter, T. N. Parmelee, "was there more cheerful submission—more unhesitating devotion. If he was to intimate a wish that the majority of the Senate should go to [Hell] . . . , they would immediately raise a committee to ascertain the most direct and eligible route."[17] No other Whig, certainly, had the same system of policy and the personal boldness to fight for it, or understood as well as Clay what was necessary to sustain the party before the country.

Clay's first measure, repeal of the independent treasury, moved through Congress quickly. He reported the bill from the Finance Committee on June 4 and it passed the Senate five days later. Argument had been exhausted during the three years leading up to adoption of the measure in 1840. Although Democratic retreat from hard money had removed some objections to the system in the Whig view, it still injuriously affected the currency and credit of the country and failed to provide sufficient national regulation and control. Nothing was more clearly mandated by the election than repeal of the independent treasury. The night Tyler signed the bill into law, Whig celebrants conducted a mock funeral, marching in procession behind the sub-treasury's coffin from the Capitol to the White House and back to Clay's boardinghouse at Seventh and D Street.[18]

Treasury Secretary Ewing, as promised, forwarded his plan for establishing a bank as the fiscal agent of the government. Capitalized at $30 million, it would be incorporated in the District of Columbia and authorized to establish branches only with the assent of the states concerned. These two features were obviously intended to accommodate Tyler's constitutional views. The cabinet went along in the interest of consensus and also to counteract the alarming influence of the "Virginia Cabal" on the president. Webster, in a series of unsigned editorials in the Intelligencer, pleaded with the Whigs to support this moderate plan rather than "beat the field of constitutional argument all over again, in the vain hope of coming to a perfect unity of opinion." He conceded that the veto of the states on branches was a departure from prior principle and practice, which held that the branching power was national and that the general government achieved its purposes without the aid or assent of the states; but, Webster remarked lamely, forbearance in the exercise of power is not surrender of it.[19] The argument made little impression on the vast majority of Whig legislators, editors, and merchants. They considered the branching power vital to a strong banking system and a uniform currency. Two New York newspapers, Charles King's American and James Watson Webb's Courier and Enquirer, which reportedly spoke for Wall Street— and in the past for Daniel Webster—promptly denounced the treasury plan. Meanwhile, the plan was referred to Clay's select committee. In the senatorial caucus, where it was thoroughly discussed, Clay scarcely spoke lest he add to his reputation for dictatorship. On every point the senators instructed the committee to report a bill for a national bank similar to the charter of 1816.[20]

Clay reported the committee bill on June 21. Aside from small details, for instance raising the permissible annual dividend from 6 to 7 percent, it differed from the administration plan principally in its granting of unrestricted branching power. This was considered necessary to the national character of the institution. Without it, said Clay, the bank would exist only at the sufferance of the states; it would operate unequally and erratically, and therefore fail in its mission.[21] As Senate debate began, Webster, switching roles with Clay, who was inflexible, became the conciliator. No principle was at stake, in the secretary's opinion. The Fiscal Bank was desperately needed to revive the nation's economy. Because this was generally recognized, every state, with one or two short-run exceptions, was expected to assent to it; and without the branching restriction the Supreme Court, as presently composed, would probably find the act unconstitutional at the first opportunity. To his friends in Congress and in the press, Webster insisted the Ewing plan was the best obtainable.[22] On July 1, Virginia's Senator Rives, acting for the administration, moved to amend Clay's bill by the requirement of state assent to branches. Tyler would compromise no further. Clay stood his ground. When Rufus Choate, who was Webster's successor, urged that without the amendment the bill could not become law, and he *knew* this, Clay demanded to hear how he knew it. Choate replied, in effect, that this was none of the gentleman's business. When Clay persisted, badgering the senator to admit that he was speaking for Webster, Choate refused to oblige, and the chair finally ordered both senators to take their seats. On July 6 the Rives amendment was defeated, 38–10. The Democrats, disapproving of the plan, voted against the amendment. Only seven Whigs joined Rives, four of them New Englanders. Webster continued his efforts. Through the offices of his friend Hiram Ketchum in New York, his arguments for the "half a loaf" treasury bill were carried in the *Commerical Advertiser*, the only respectable city daily still open to him. Whig newspapers throughout the country were dismayed by Webster's betrayal of high constitutional principle and lifelong preachings of national responsibility for a sound and uniform currency. "We are almost constrained to weep for the fallibility of human greatness," wrote Prentice.[23]

Clay could easily defeat the treasury plan and turn back dilatory Democratic amendments, but after the defection caused by the Rives amendment he did not have the votes to carry his own bill in the Senate. He decided to let it sleep while catching up with business forwarded from the House. For the fourth year in the last five the government was running a large deficit. The Whigs blamed this on bad financial management incident to the separation of the government from the banking and currency of the country. Moving to take up the $12-million-loan bill passed by the House, Clay was denounced by Calhoun both for the precipitousness of the measure—this was one of the occasions for charges of "gag rule"—and for attempting to resuscitate the Hamiltonian system. Similar bills during Van Buren's administration, for which Calhoun had voted, were intended only to meet treasury exigencies, but this bill, the senator thundered, was part of a diabolical plot to create a funded debt for the enrichment of the moneyed class. All the other elements were in Clay's program: bank stock, increased revenues, and conversion of the public lands into a fund for corruption of the people and the states. He concluded with an appeal to the southern states, always victimized by this system of public plunder. "Well," Clay replied blandly, "this unequal disbursement of the public money was in the nature of things, and if the Creator had made the tides to rise higher in Boston and New York than on the Gulf, it was no fault of this Government."[24] The bill quickly passed on a straight party vote and became law.

After a sleep of almost two weeks, the Fiscal Bank Bill was no nearer to passage than before. Acknowledging this, Clay offered a compromise. A state's assent to the establishment of a branch of the Fiscal Bank would be assumed unless the legislature voted to prohibit it in the first session after enactment of the statute, provided further that if a branch thereafter became *necessary* in any state the bank could establish it. Opponents scorned the amendment. It was "childish," "a shallow trick," "a pretended compromise." Apparently meant as a concession to southern Whigs, it made a mockery of state rights. Who was responsible for this so-called compromise? The obvious answer was

Clay. "Again," said the Richmond *Whig*, "he has stepped forward to save the nation!" But Massachusetts congressman Robert Winthrop, who was close to Webster, wrote some days later: "The *Compromise* which the Great Compromiser takes the credit of was a *Cabinet concoction*, at which Clay kicked tremendously at the outset, but of which he now seems willing to wear the wreath." Nearer the truth, perhaps, was the *Herald* correspondent who said that the compromise was put together by Clay's old friend, Peter B. Porter, of New York. Visiting in Washington, Porter held conversations with William C. Preston, who had not yet committed his vote, and together they proposed a conciliatory amendment to Clay. At the same time, as it happened, Clay learned that a similar amendment had been carried to the president by Richmond congressman John Minor Botts, who said it received Tyler's approval.[25] In offering the compromise, Clay hoped a formula had been found that, however shallow it appeared, would secure passage of his bill and, just possibly, Tyler's approval, thereby averting an explosion in the Whig party. The compromise amendment passed with one vote to spare—Preston's vote made the difference—and the following day, July 28, the Senate approved Clay's bill, 26–23.[26]

After moving swiftly through the House without further amendment, the Fiscal Bank Bill reached Tyler's desk on August 7. Ten days of suspenseful waiting followed. Some observers saw in Rives's vote against the bill a sure sign of Tyler's disapproval; and the *Herald*, which had a pipeline into the White House, freely predicted a veto. Calhoun, on the other hand, expected the president to sign the bill, for although his principles were against it he lacked the resolve to assert them.[27] Clay, along with Webster, hoped Tyler would draw a distinction between his legislative and executive character and approve as president, acting for the whole country, what he would not approve as a Virginia congressman. But Tyler returned the bill with his veto on the sixteenth. He objected not only to the branching power, which had been the subject of compromise, but, surprisingly, to the bank's authority to discount notes and engage in local business in addition to foreign exchange. Although he disagreed with the policy of the bill, this was not the basis of the veto. Tyler emphasized that, bound by his oath of office and consistent with his own character, he could not sanction legislation he deemed unconstitutional. He thus fell back upon his old opinion that incorporation of a national bank was "the original sin against the Constitution."[28]

Whig reaction across the country ranged from sighs of regret to cries of perfidy. In Kentucky Tyler was burned in effigy.[29] The men in Washington had braced themselves for the shock of the veto and rebounded quickly. Webster was disheartened but declined to quarrel with the president's motives; and to keep the Whigs in good humor he held a bachelors' party the evening of the veto. In caucus that same day the Whig congressmen had agreed on the course to pursue on remaining legislation, including a new bank project that would reconcile the president, unite the party, and save the administration. Marvelously, all that had been lost by the veto was regained within twenty-four hours. Work on the second bill began at once. After the House adjourned on the sixteenth, Virginia congressman Alexander H. H. Stuart called on the president to explore grounds of agreement. Tyler voiced approval for a bank that would act as a fiscal agent of the government, employ agencies in the states, and deal in bills of exchange, but not in local promissory notes. For such a bank he would not require state assent. "Now if you will send me this bill I will sign it in twenty-four hours," he told Stuart.[30] And he instructed him to go to Webster and have the bill prepared. Stuart did not find Webster, but Tyler agreed that John Sergeant and John M. Berrien, of the House and Senate respectively, should frame the bill in consultation with the president and cabinet. The new bill was thoroughly discussed; every provision, including the agency's name, Fiscal Corporation of the United States, which was free of the opprobrium attached to the word "bank," met the president's wishes. After approval of Ewing's draft on the eighteenth, Tyler directed Webster to inform Sergeant so he could introduce the bill in the House.[31]

But first the old bill had to be decently buried. For two days, August 17 and 18, the order of the day in the Senate had been for Clay to speak at noon in reply to the veto message; and he had twice postponed his speech lest it disturb the negotiations in progress. The delay had a cooling effect. For Clay's answer to Tyler on the nineteenth was respectful and temperate. Men who had known him for years remarked upon his restraint.[32] He spoke of his long friendship with the president, his high hopes of the session, and his willingness to compromise his own convictions to secure adoption of the bank bill. The president seemed to think he would dishonor himself as well as the Constitution by signing a bill his conscience disapproved. But to found political virtue and reputation on so small a stock was a losing game. "Can any man be disgraced and dishonored who yields his private opinion to the judgment of the nation?" Clay asked. "Does any man, who at one period of his life shall have expressed a particular opinion, and at a subsequent period shall act upon the opposite opinion, expose himself" to what Tyler called "the ridicule and scorn of all virtuous men"? If so, James Madison, the Father of the Constitution, was dishonored and disgraced, as must have been countless statesmen, including Clay himself who had changed his opinion on a national bank. And if the president could not sign the bill, a veto was not his only option. He might have allowed it to become law without his signature. Or he might have resigned. Clay was being ironical. After all, Tyler's boasted reputation for political honor and conscience rested upon his resignation as senator in obedience to the instructions of his state. Why should he not consider himself similarly instructed by the nation in this instance?

Rives replied, actually less to the speech Clay made than to the one the senator had anticipated. He called it an "open and violent attack" on the president, impassioned and bitter and filled with charges of betrayal and usurpation. Having thus, as Ewing recalled the confrontation, "brought *himself* within the lion's bound, [Clay] sprang upon him with unrestrained . . . impetuosity and poured forth . . . the whole torrent of his feelings in the most high toned and powerful invective."[33] Rives had introduced the question of motives; very well, Clay would discuss motives. It was being said that he had deliberately picked a quarrel with the president in order to discredit and displace him. But this was absurd. There was also a rumor abroad "that a cabal exists—a new sort of kitchen cabinet—whose object is the dissolution of the Whig party—the dispersion of Congress, without accomplishing any of the great purposes of the extra session—and a total change, in fact, in the whole face of our political affairs." He did not charge Rives with being one of the cabal, and on the whole thought the materials for the meditated third party "insufficient to compose a decent corporal's guard," but it had succeeded in poisoning his relations with the president. Clay concluded with a stirring peroration, much admired at the time, on that *courage* that soars above personal pride, vanity, and conceit and is "absorbed by one soul-transporting thought of the good and the glory of one's country." Charge and counter-charge reverberated in the House of Representatives when gaunt Henry A. Wise, one of the "corporal's guard," defended the Tyler faction of the party, and Thomas Marshall, the brilliant inebriate Kentuckian, vindicated Clay.

The Fiscal Corporation Bill passed the House after two days debate on Monday, the twenty-third. On the same day it was referred to a special committee in the Senate. This was not Clay's committee, since his support could not be relied upon. Nor, it was beginning to appear, could Tyler's. He was annoyed by Clay's imputation of selfish and scheming motives. His blood boiled when he read a private letter, copied and forwarded to him surreptitiously, written by Congressman Botts to a friend at a Richmond coffeehouse. Once a trusted ally, Botts felt betrayed by Tyler. In this "coffee-house letter," penned on the sixteenth, the day of the veto, he accused Tyler of double-dealing and conspiracy with his state rights friends to form a third party in association with sympathetic Democrats; but the Whigs, he declared scoffingly, would "head Captain Tyler, or die." Now Tyler drew back from his own bill. Meeting with the cabinet on the twenty-fifth, gloomy and depressed, he said he would not sign the bill, and he begged the secretaries to get it postponed. Facing a second veto, followed inevitably by the dissolution of the cabinet, Webster communicated at once with the Massachusetts senators. Postponement had been Tyler's wish from the moment of the veto, though he was not disposed to bar a second trial; but Botts's extraordinary letter bared a design to "entrap the President," and to remove any suspicion of this design, Webster said, the Whigs in Congress should give up the second bill. When Clay and his legislative lieutenants were approached, they refused; they refused to cooperate with the president in abandoning his own bill. As to a design to embarrass and head Captain Tyler, the judgment of Senator Benton, no friend of Clay or of a bank, on this political farce is worth pondering: "Mr. Clay had no such design. . . . He had no design or object in embarrassing him. . . . The only object was to get him to sign his own bill— the fiscal corporation bill—which he had fixed up himself title and all—and sent out his cabinet to press upon Congress—and desired to have it back in three days, that he might sign it in twenty-four hours."[34]

The Senate on Clay's
Retirement. Mezzotint and
etching by Thomas Doney,
after painting by James A.
Whitehorne. *Courtesy of
the National Portrait
Gallery, Smithsonian
Institution*

Clay as Father of the
American System. Painting
by John Neagle. *Courtesy
of the Art Collection of the
Union League of
Philadelphia*

The Hone Club Portrait of
Webster. Painting by G. P.
A. Healy. *Courtesy of the
National Portrait Gallery,
Smithsonian Institution*

Harry of the West after the
Defeat of 1844. Painting by
G. P. A. Healy. *Courtesy
of the National Portrait
Gallery, Smithsonian
Institution*

Farmer of Ashland.
Engraving by H. S. Sadd,
after painting by James W.
Dodge. *Courtesy of the
University of Kentucky
Photo Archives*

Squire of Marshfield.
Lithograph after sketch by
G. P. A. Healy.

Marshfield. Engraving after daguerreotype by H. B. Hall. *Courtesy of Dartmouth College*

Ashland. Engraving by F. Hegan, after painting by James Hamilton after daguerreotype by J. M. Hewitt. *Courtesy of the Henry Clay Memorial Foundation*

While the second bill was in committee, the Senate proceeded to enact the remaining measures of Clay's program. The most important of these was distribution, the Land Bill, as it was called. Aside from its other merits, it was much wanted as a measure of relief by debtor states; and since the bill incorporated a provision for prospective preemption, to which Clay closed his eyes, it was especially popular in the West. Tyler was an advocate. With Clay he viewed the proceeds of public land sales as a trust, rather than as revenue, and so distribution was safe from constitutional objections. But Tyler also considered that distribution was tied to the revenue ceiling of the Compromise Act, and if this was broken through it must be surrendered. That act would expire on June 30, 1842. Clay, nonetheless, had chosen to defer debate on the tariff until the regular session. Meanwhile, the revenue bill he advocated would raise several million dollars by taxing articles currently admitted duty free. This did not, he thought, violate the Compromise Act. Calhoun was the leading opponent of distribution in the Senate. It was unconstitutional; it was "rank agrarianism"; it was a scheme to revive protectionism and, in effect, to assume the state debts; and it would lead, not to further consolidation, as he had formerly held, but to the dissolution of the Union—the inevitable result of dividing and dispersing the revenue.[35] The bill passed, but only after it was logrolled with a bankruptcy bill. The latter had not been on Clay's agenda. It was demanded by broken businessmen and their creditors in eastern cities where there were loud cries for relief. A national law of bankruptcy, overriding the chaos of state insolvency laws, had always been a favorite but unsuccessful measure of Daniel Webster's. Now it was enacted in the twinkling of an eye because eastern Whigs voted for distribution in exchange for western and southern votes for bankruptcy.[36] Congress finally enacted the Land Bill with the proviso to suspend distribution of funds to the states should the tariff break through the mandated ceiling. Despite this, despite the impoverished treasury, and disappointing land sales, the act was hailed in Whig quarters as "the most important law ever enacted by an American Congress."[37]

When the Fiscal Corporation Bill was reported to the Senate floor on schedule, September 1, Clay for the first time said he would vote for it. "Though but half the loaf, it is still better than no bread," he remarked; and he was perhaps more inclined to take the bill after Tyler had abandoned it. The bill's passage was thus assured. On the second day of debate, in a situation that cried out for comic relief, Clay referred to a resolution earlier offered by a colleague to inquire into certain rowdy disorders in the vicinity of the White House on the night of the veto message, and suggested that those disorders had actually grown out of an irruption in the mansion itself when a host of Democratic celebrants descended upon it. What a spectacle:

> I think that I can now see the principal *dramatis personae*. . . . There stood the distinguished Senator from South Carolina . . . tall, careworn, with furrowed brow, haggard, and intensely gazing, looking as if he were dissecting the last and newest abstraction which sprang from the metaphysician's brain, and muttering to himself, in half-uttered sounds, "This is indeed a

real crisis!" Then there was the senator from Alabama [King], standing upright and gracefully, as if he were ready to settle in the most authoritative
manner any question of order or etiquette, that might possibly arise between the high assembled parties on that new and unprecedented occasion.
Not far off stood the honorable senators from Arkansas and Missouri [Sevier
and Benton], the latter looking at the senator from South Carolina, with an
indignant curl on his lip and scorn in his eye, and pointing his finger with
contempt towards the senator, whilst he said . . . "He call himself a statesman! Why, he has never even produced a decent humbug!"

Benton protested he was not present, to which Clay unblinkingly rejoined,
"I was only imagining what you would have said if you had been present." He
continued the parody: Cuthbert "conning over in his mind on what point he
should make his next attack upon the senator from Kentucky"; Linn, of Missouri, "in pleasing meditations on the rise, growth, and future of his new colony of Oregon"; and concluding with an impersonation of James Buchanan's
somnolent eloquence that sent waves of laughter over the chamber.[38]

This time Tyler returned the bill with his veto in five days. The exchange
provisions, he feared, would not prohibit local business, and he objected to
omission of provision for state assent to local agencies of the corporation, although the bill in this respect, as in every other, was drafted to his own
specifications. Again he declared his sacred and solemn duty, lest he "commit an act of gross moral turpitude," to veto acts of Congress he deemed unconstitutional. He praised the veto power as "the great conservative principle of our system" and identified his will in exercising it with the duty to
"guard the fundamental will of the people themselves" from violation by a
majority in Congress. This doctrine, sometimes named "the doctrine of
presidential guardianship," was close to Jacksonian ideas of executive prerogative Tyler himself had condemned.[39] With the second veto message he
forfeited all claim to Whig leadership. A president whose opinions on financial policy and executive power flew in the face of his party; who, if not actually deceitful, was weak-minded, muddled, and vacillating; who confused
personal courage with political courage—such a president forfeited a good
deal. But most Whigs, trying to account for Tyler's behavior, gave little
weight to such factors of character and opinion or to the veto messages,
which merely disguised Tyler's basic political purpose. This was deliberately, designedly, to force a break with Clay and the mass of Whigs and,
with his Virginia friends, go into business for himself. Clay had been apprehensive of some such purpose from the beginning and, of course, his own
willfulness contributed to the result. After the first veto he had vowed to
live a hundred years, if necessary, to wreak revenge on Captain Tyler and
company. And on the last night of the session, after the second veto, he did
not hesitate to compare Tyler to Benedict Arnold: "Tyler is on his way to
the Democratic camp. They will give him lodgings in some outhouse, but
they will never trust him. He will stand here, like Arnold in England, a
monument of his own perfidy and disgrace."[40]

Four members of the cabinet—Ewing, Bell, Badger, and Crittenden—

resigned forty-eight hours after the veto; and Granger soon followed. Webster did not. He immediately called a meeting of the Massachusetts delegation and, after saying he saw no sufficient cause to resign, asked their advice. They gave him the advice he wanted. Presumably Webster went through the reasons he would soon give to the public: his cordial relations with Tyler, the unfinished business of a bank or fiscal agency, the work of his own department in foreign affairs, and the importance of maintaining a strong Whig presence in the administration. There were other reasons unstated: his personal finances, his liking for executive power and patronage, and, never to be overlooked, his hostility to Clay. While most Whigs acquiesced in Webster's decision to stay in the cabinet, or even gave him credit for patriotism, on grounds the national interest required it, some of his best friends worried about the consequences for his political future. Winthrop, for instance, told him frankly that he was safe only as long as it was understood that he served at the president's request because of the condition of foreign affairs. "But the idea, which is beginning to prevail, that you intend to commit yourself personally with his fortunes . . . will subject you to remarks of the most painful character." All who adhere to Tyler, the congressman warned, will sink with him.[41] Webster had no ears for the counsel, however. He went to Tyler after the other officers had turned in their resignations. "Where am I to go, Mr. President?" he asked. "You must decide that for yourself, Mr. Webster," Tyler returned. "If you leave it to me, Mr. President, I will stay where I am." Whereupon Tyler rose and extended his hand: "Give me your hand on that, and now I am willing to say that Henry Clay is a doomed man from this hour."[42]

On the same day, Saturday, September 11, while Tyler was frantically assembling a new cabinet, the Whig congressional caucus met to denounce him and to chart a course for the party. On Monday, the last day of the session, an address drafted by John P. Kennedy, of Maryland, with the weekend assistance of Clay, was adopted by the fifty or more Whigs who remained in the capital. It bemoaned the catastrophe that had befallen the party. It placed all blame on the president. Nevertheless, the manifesto boasted of the accomplishments of the extra session. Except for the bank, every measure of Clay's program had been enacted. An appropriate bank or fiscal agency remained a Whig goal, and the congressmen pledged themselves as well to seek sweeping reduction of presidential power.[43] The address proved awkward for New England Whigs loyal to Webster. Although several of them attended the caucus, only one finally signed the address. Webster's Bay State friend Caleb Cushing, who had joined the Corporal's Guard in the House, issued a counter-address charging that "caucus dictatorship," not executive usurpation, was the problem.[44] Cushing would never be forgiven by the mass of Whigs.

The Whig manifesto was the signal for Clay's followers across the country to hoist his banner for the presidency in 1844.[45] In the eyes of his enemies, of course, that was the object in view from the start. Going home he met with an enthusiastic reception all along the route. Breaking with Tyler, Clay was stripped of patronage and influence, indeed saw executive power turned against him immediately by Wickliffe's appointment as postmaster general. Clay said nothing publicly about Webster's decision to stay with the administration. His private advice, in a conversation just before his departure for Kentucky, was similar to Winthrop's. Webster was justified only as long as the national interest required his services at the State Department.[46] But Clay must have felt that Webster was painting himself into a corner from which it would be difficult to escape. What did he expect? That Tyler and the Whigs would kiss and make up? That Tyler would raise a third party in which he might find a home? That Tyler, in due time, would appoint him minister to Great Britain? For the present, Webster was exceedingly bitter at Clay and pleased to be in any office from which he might annoy him.

From this political imbroglio Calhoun appeared to emerge as the only winner. There was speculation during the cabinet crisis that Calhoun would be offered a position in the administration. It was to become, after all, a Virginia Republican administration, and the Corporal's Guard, which some thought Calhoun's Guard, was eager for his appointment. But Webster's decision to remain secretary of state apparently closed the gate on Calhoun's joining the administration. It was unlikely in any event. At the session's close Calhoun sought to dispel the notion, popular with Whigs, that Tyler had gone over to the Democrats, or that the Democrats would have him, and counseled his followers to keep their distance from the administration. While he saw the absurdity of Tyler's ambition to win the presidency in his own right, the senator also recognized that any force Tyler brought into the field would eventually redound to his benefit. At home in October he started up his own presidential candidacy. Picking up the enthusiasm of his friends, Calhoun began to think he would be the Democratic standard-bearer in 1844 in the ultimate contest with Henry Clay.[47]

Clay returned to the regular session determined to retire as soon as the proprieties and the circumstances allowed. Not to return at all, although that was his personal preference, would have opened him to the charge of abandoning a sinking ship. Clay acted a retiring part during the session. He served on no committees. Suffering from ill health, he was often indisposed, and he participated hardly at all in the social life of the capital. He described himself as "a looker on at Verona," while his friend Crittenden, preferring Plutarch to Shakespeare, said that he sat calmly, defiantly "amidst the wreck like Marius on the ruins of Carthage."[48] In his annual message to Congress, Tyler recommended creation of a public institution, called the Exchequer, to take care of the government's money and also to engage in exchange and issue notes backed by specie. Webster contributed substantially to the development of this ingenious plan and begged the Whigs to bury the hatchet and support the president. There was movement in this direction, but when Willie Magnum delivered a speech in opposition it was taken as a signal from Clay for continued war on the administration. Extremes met—Clayites and Bentonites—in opposition to incorporating an institution that was neither a bank nor a sub-treasury but had characteristics of both. The bill was lost before it could be brought to a vote.[49] The Whigs generally gave up the issue in disgust.

Congress's agenda, at least in domestic affairs, varied little from the special session. The deluge of petitioners under the Bankruptcy Law, even before it took effect, aroused fears that debtor relief would undermine property and contract and led to widespread demands for its repeal. The Kentucky legislature instructed its senators to vote for repeal. Clay refused, and his vote in the Senate saved the law, although it would be repealed in the subsequent session. Again Congress authorized a loan to keep the government in operation during a depressed time. In compliance with the September manifesto, Clay introduced resolutions for several constitutional amendments to curb executive power. The most important of these would permit majority override of a veto and do away with the pocket veto. The Founding Fathers, believing that the executive should be strengthened to check encroachments by the legislative power, had been proved wrong, Clay argued, as he reviewed the history of expanding executive power under the Constitution. The veto contradicted the principle of majority rule and drew after it a host of powers undreamed of by the framers, for instance the power of initiating legislation. Dictation in the special session, he said, had come from the president who undertook to impose his views of bank policy on Congress.[50]

Calhoun delivered the main speech in opposition. It reflected his effort, only recently begun, to give "scientific development" to his opinions on government. He attacked Clay's fundamental assumption that the people of the United States constitute a nation and the numerical majority is its voice. "Instead of a nation," said the Carolinian, "we are in reality an assemblage of nations, or peoples." The voice of the people is not to be found in any one organ, such as Congress, but in the harmonious blending of many. The veto power is part of a comprehensive system of checks and balances, the purpose of which is to prevent majority rule. Clay was right about one thing: there had been an alarming increase of presidential power. But the cause of this was Congress. "He [the president] has grown great and powerful, not because he used his veto, but because he *abstained* from using it." The danger of executive tyranny, Calhoun insisted, was nothing compared to the tyranny of the majority, which Clay's amendment would hasten.[51] As political science, certainly, Calhoun's speech was much superior to Clay's. The gentleman from Kentucky, who had alluded to the "weakness and imbecility" into which the general government had fallen since the Jacksonian revolution, never seemed to understand that the growth of executive power went along with the growth of democracy and national power. The only cure for this condition, apparently, was for Clay to be elected president. In the paroxysm of reaction against Jackson, Clay acquired an almost morbid fixation on "monarchical tyranny." For most Whigs it was a convenient slogan, useful in generating emotion for other issues, but not to be taken seriously as an issue itself; and in 1842, unmoved by their leader, the Whigs let the anti-veto resolutions die—another monument of Whig defeat.

The great debate of the session was on the tariff and distribution. Clay hung back, but finally, in February, introduced resolutions calling for higher duties on the principle of a tariff for revenue with incidental protection and also for repeal of the proviso of the Distribution Act suspending it in the event the tariff exceeded the ultimate 20-percent-level of the Compromise Act. Obviously, additional revenue was essential. Tyler, backed by Webster, endorsed higher tariffs but demanded sacrifice of distribution. The final drastic reductions under the Compromise Act occurred in 1842 when, as it happened, the economy was deeply depressed. Manufacturing interests demanded a return to protectionism. The cause of collapsing prices, bankruptcies, unemployment, and general business stagnation, said Abbott Lawrence, the Massachusetts Whig industrialist, was very simple: "We import too much and manufacture too little." It was one of the unfortunate legacies of the Compromise Act. Pennsylvania ironmakers joined New England textile manufacturers in the renewed agitation; and they were supported as well by Louisiana sugar planters and the Kentucky hemp industry, in which Clay was interested.[52] In 1833 the senator had justified the gradual withdrawal of protection on the theory that after another decade's growth America's infant industries would be strong enough to compete in a free market. Clay never acknowledged that the theory had failed—and he must have thought that it had not received a fair trial—but he added his voice to the rising chorus of protectionism. "Free trade is a beautiful vision, existing in the imagination of philosophers and theorists, and practically repudiated by all nations." In this reply to a New York Whig address, he reasserted all the old arguments for tariff protection, concluding that, fortunately for the harmony of the Union, the treasury required higher tariffs for revenue. These might be arranged to furnish incidental protection within the spirit of the Compromise Act; and the friends of protectionism, looking to substance rather than names, ought to be satisfied with that.[53]

Clay and Calhoun again exchanged recriminations over the Compromise Act. While the former insisted that nothing now proposed violated the spirit of the letter of the act, the latter cried betrayal. Had black become white? "Were the people of this country blind? Were they deaf? Were they fools?" Calhoun asked. If Clay prevailed, the South would have traveled full circle back to 1832, with a tariff level of 30 percent or higher, and oppressed as before.[54] But Clay's resolutions were approved, after which the House proceeded with a tariff bill. Long before it could be debated, Clay had retired. Seeing that the new tariff could not be ready by July 1, Congress first passed the "little tariff," extending the current rate of duties of the Compromise Act one month and providing further that this should not suspend distribution. Tyler, invoking the sanctity of the compromise, vetoed the bill. Angry Whigs, led by Botts, started a movement to impeach him. Clay, from Ashland, opposed this but urged firmness on distribution. "I think you cannot give up distribution without a disgraceful sacrifice of independence," he advised. Don't imagine the people side with the president. "The more vetoes the better now!—assuming that the measures vetoed are right."[55] In August Tyler vetoed the tariff bill—his fifth veto—solely because it provided for continuing distribution. The Whigs were outraged. For most of them, tariff and distribution were reciprocal, part and parcel of the great compromise of 1833. Tyler held that they were incompatible and forced the Whigs to choose between them. Clay advised his friends, "Go home!" But sensibly, sullenly, they yielded distribution to the tariff. He had no direct responsibility for the new tariff, which furnished more protection than he had called for or expected. He soon made it his own, however, and in apology for any violence it may have done to the historic compromise cited the sacrifice not only of distribution but of home valuation.[56]

Clay's "valedictory" on March 31 was an epoch in the history of the republic. Crittenden, his successor, said it was "something like the soul's quitting the body."[57] The timing of his resignation had been fixed by the approaching Whig convention in North Carolina, where he would be nominated for the presidency. A hush came over the Senate, as crowded as it had ever been, when Clay rose at the appointed hour to deliver his farewell. Silas Wright thought he looked suddenly old, sad, and, although a consummate actor, powerless to exploit the histrionic possibilities of the occasion: "It was tame, very tame."[58] Clay recalled his orphaned boyhood, his immigration to Kentucky, and the unfailing support of the people of his adopted state since he first entered Congress in 1806. He passed an encomium on the Senate, apologized to any members he may have hurt or offended from a temper too ardent, and consigned to oblivion all personal and political animosities. When he finished there was scarcely a dry eye in the chamber. Preston rose and, though it was only three o'clock, called for adjournment. As Clay broke free of the crowd, he noticed Calhoun at a distance, walked over, and the two men embraced in silence.[59]

To the stated reasons for retirement, health and personal affairs, both in poor condition, Clay might have added his intention to run for president. At a deeper level there was still another reason, disgust—disgust at being cheated out of the Whig nomination in 1839, disgust at Harrison's untimely death, disgust at Captain Tyler and his crew, at Webster, at the collapse of the bright promise of the Whig victory of 1840, carrying with it renewed dangers of national disintegration. The tameness of the valedictory was a polite overlay on the bitterness, which broke out in his letter to the North Carolina Whigs. Instead of harmony, cooperation, and high purposes, Tyler had created discord, distrust, and defeat. "A president without a party, and parties without a president!" Clay exclaimed. "A president denouncing his friends and courting his political opponents, who, in their turn, without entertaining for him the least respect or confidence, give him flattery and praise enough just to deceive and delude him! A president who, affecting to soar in an atmosphere above that of all parties, and to place himself upon the broad and patriotic foundation of the whole nation, is vainly seeking, by a culpable administration of the patronage of the government, to create a third party!"[60] Tyler and Webster unblushingly used the patronage against Clay. Newspapers devoted to him were cut off from the business of printing the laws. And he was slandered by Tyler's confidant, Wise, who all but accused him of murder in the notorious congressional duel four years earlier that took the life of Jonathan Cilley of Maine.[61] Wise was forced to retract, but the slander could never be obliterated.

In the quiet of Ashland, where he returned on April 21, nine days after his sixty-fourth birthday, Clay hoped to find relief from disappointment and renewed hope for the future.

2. *Webster at State*

Amid the crash of Whig expectations in Congress, the secretary of state labored to redeem the administration by accomplishments in a field somewhat removed from congressional control—foreign affairs. Anglo-American relations were in a perilous state when Webster came into office, and his diplomacy immediately focused there. For several years the Canadian frontier from the St. Johns River to the Straits of Mackinac seethed with unrest. Under William Mackenzie, Canadian rebels seeking independence from Great Britain conducted looting forays across the border and, appealing to the Spirit of 1776, recruited thousands of Americans into their secret patriotic society, the Hunters' Lodges. A "liberated" island just above Niagara Falls served as the rebels' headquarters in 1837. It was regularly supplied from the American shore by the steamboat *Caroline*. On the night of December 29, a party of loyalists crossed the border, captured the steamer, took it into the Niagara River, and burned and sank it. In the turmoil an American was killed. The incident provoked outrage. President Van Buren dispatched General Winfield Scott to calm tempers on the Niagara frontier; and the *Caroline* Affair was put on the track of diplomacy. From the beginning the British government took responsibility for the act, which it justified as a legitimate pursuit of "pirates" into American territory. In 1839 the so-called Aroostook War broke out in the Maine wilderness. When news of the conflict, so far bloodless, reached Washington in February, Webster, in a speech widely interpreted as warlike, berated the administration for failing to get a settlement of the northeastern boundary, still undetermined after fifty-six years, and declared that if the British would not settle the matter by the Fourth of July the Americans should settle it themselves.[1] Congress voted funds for Maine's defense, authorized the president to expel the British from the disputed territory, and called for a special mission to London. In the end, Van Buren was content to send General Scott to negotiate a truce with authorities in New Brunswick.

Both affairs, the boundary and the *Caroline,* were deposited on Webster's desk on March 4, 1841. The latter, after a sleep of three years, had been suddenly revived by the arrest near Buffalo, and subsequent indictment for murder and arson, of a Canadian deputy sheriff, Alexander McLeod. The British minister, Henry Fox, at once claimed the protection of His Majesty's Government for the prisoner, since the destruction of the *Caroline* was an act of public force; but Webster's predecessor, John Forsyth, declined to interfere with judicial proceedings in the sovereign state of New York. On the twelfth Fox demanded McLeod's release. The issue was between two nations; the courts of New York had nothing to do with it, and persistence in the Forsyth doctrine would strain Anglo-American relations to the breaking point. This put Webster on the spot. In reply, he defended the American position that the attack on the *Caroline* was not a legitimate act of self-defense and reiterated the demand for an apology and satisfaction. Webster conceded, nevertheless, that the McLeod case belonged to the law of nations and indicated it would be removed from ordinary courts of justice. Meanwhile, with Harrison's approval, he sent Attorney General Crittenden on a mission to New York to confer with the governor and attend to McLeod's defense. The governor was William H. Seward, a fellow Whig, from whom he expected cooperation in the administration's effort to secure dismissal or removal of the McLeod case without the appearance of interference in the internal affairs of New York. Having earlier talked to a Seward emissary in Washington, Webster assumed the governor would direct a *nolle prosequi* in the case, just as the president would do if it were in a federal court. Seward quickly disabused the secretary of this assumption. Webster might have a problem with Britain, but he, the governor, had no less delicate a problem with the people of New York. They demanded that McLeod be prosecuted; politically he could not support Webster even if he agreed with him, which he did not. Seward objected to Webster's interference and told Crittenden, in Albany, that if Washington would back off and let the case run its course all would be well because McLeod had an ironclad alibi (he could not be placed at the scene of the crime) and was sure to be acquitted. This plea evaded the issue, in Webster's opinion; even if it finally led to McLeod's release, it would not fulfill the duty of the government.[2]

Between Webster and the ambitious forty-year-old governor there was no very friendly feeling at the outset, and nerves grew jagged during several months of jousting over McLeod. The more Webster learned about the Hunters' Lodges, the more fearful of war he became. Perhaps ten thousand men south of the border were leagued with the Canadian malcontents, he told Tyler. In July a raiding party sacked the state arsenal near Buffalo. So powerful had the Hunters' Lodges become in New York, Webster wrote hysterically, that even Governor Seward felt compelled to contribute to the patriot fund. "He is a contemptible fellow, and that is the end of it." A mutual friend tried to soften his feelings. But to no avail. "Webster is as savage as a meat axe against you," Seward was told; and he vowed to do whatever was necessary to free McLeod from the clutches of New York.[3]

The most direct way to accomplish that was by writ of habeas corpus. In May, after finding a reputable defense counsel, Webster helped prepare the case asking the New York Supreme Court to discharge the prisoner because the act in question was a public one, which placed him under the jurisdiction of the United States. Two months later Judge Esek Cowen delivered the verdict of a unanimous court against McLeod. In the absence of a declared war, as in this instance, the court said, the precedents in international law were sufficiently ambiguous as to authorize the prisoner's prosecution in state court for crimes possibly committed on his own responsibility. Webster was contemptuous of the opinion. He wished to appeal to the United States Supreme Court, but McLeod, more confident in his alibi than in the court, opted for an early trial on the criminal charges. Fox lodged another protest, but he dropped his threatening tone and seemed reassured by both governments' precautionary measures to protect the prisoner and preserve peace on the frontier. The New York court had agreed to a change of venue, so the trial took place in the comparative quiet of Utica in October. Webster had urged the defense counsel, Joshua Spencer, to present the international law plea; the judge barred it, however, and after a parade of witnesses the case went to the jury on McLeod's impregnable alibi. Within thirty minutes the jury returned a verdict of acquittal.[4]

The outcome would probably have been the same, and might have been reached sooner, had Webster followed the hands-off policy of his predecessor. His fight with "little Seward" damaged him politically in New York and caused Democrats in Congress to charge him with improper interference in the administration of justice in New York and also for "peculiar solicitude" toward Great Britain in his correspondence with Fox. Benton rashly compared the secretary's law book approach in the McLeod Case to Andrew Jackson's "law of the heart" execution of Arbuthnot and Ambrister: "Better far to throw away the books, and go by the heart. Then, at least, they [public officials] would always have the consolation of being on their country's side."[5] Fortunately, the critics were well answered, for it must be said that Webster's conduct in this matter was both correct and constructive. He felt vindicated when Daniel Tallmadge, a New York judge, published a scorching rebuttal of Judge Cowen's opinion. While Tallmadge lacked the prestige of Story, whom Webster had asked to write the rebuttal, it was an effective pamphlet and, being dedicated to him, appealed to his vanity. He saw that it received wide circulation. After the case was settled, Webster drafted a bill authorizing federal courts to grant writ of habeas corpus to a prisoner who was a foreign subject held for acts committed on order of his government. The succeeding January he entrusted the bill to Senator Berrien, and it was enacted into law.[6]

Another incident, on another front, further inflamed Anglo-American relations only a month after the McLeod trial. An American brig, the *Creole*, sailing from Hampton Roads to New Orleans with a cargo of 135 slaves, was violently seized by 19 of them. With knives and head spikes the mutineers took possession of the vessel in the middle of the night, killed a passenger, injured officers and crewmen, and demanded that the captain steer the *Creole* to a British port. At Nassau, in the Bahamas, British authorities turned down the pleas of the captain and the American consul that the vessel and cargo be returned to the United States. They detained the 19 mutineers pending instructions from London and immediately freed the other slaves in accordance with precedents set since the British Emancipation Act of 1833 ending slavery in the islands. Northern abolitionists cheered the British action, while it was denounced in the South. Calhoun, in the Senate, called it "a gross outrage" and urged the president to demand indemnity for the freed slaves and surrender of the mutineers. Calhoun had established his position in resolutions concerning the brig *Enterprise* in 1840. The *Enterprise* was also engaged in the interstate slave trade, but stress of weather rather than mutiny had driven her into a Bermuda port. The slaves were seized and then liberated. Calhoun's resolutions, which the Senate adopted unanimously, declared that a vessel on the high seas engaged in a lawful trade is, according to the law of nations, under the jurisdiction of its own flag; that when forced into a friendly port the vessel with its persons and property are governed by the laws of the state to which they belong; and, therefore, that the seizure of slaves on board the *Enterprise* was illegal.[7]

Now, in taking the same grounds on the *Creole*, Calhoun was acting against the background of prolonged, acrimonious controversy between the former United States Minister to Great Britain, Andrew Stevenson, and successive British foreign ministers, Lord Palmerston and Lord Aberdeen, over the employment of "visit and search" on the high seas in the effort to suppress the African slave trade. The United States had outlawed the trade in 1808; it was pledged by the Treaty of Ghent to cooperate in suppressing it; in 1824 it entered into a convention with Britain in which the mutual right of search was ceded to that end, but a crippling congressional amendment excluding American coastal waters from search doomed the convention. Since then the United States had done virtually nothing to suppress this damnable traffic. American vessels continued to engage in it, and slavers of other countries sought protection by fraudulently sailing under the American flag. Britain, especially after 1833, stepped up her efforts. Palmerston's favorite project, the Quintuple Treaty, containing the mutual right of search, was signed in London in December. The five powers (Britain, Russia, Prussia, Austria, and France) hoped the United States might become a signatory. But old feelings against Britain in the matter of maritime rights died hard. Stevenson accused the British of rank hypocrisy: under the guise of philanthropy she sought to consolidate her power further as Mistress of the Seas. President Tyler, in his annual message to Congress in December, backed Stevenson, denounced the Quintuple Treaty, and said that American carriers would not suffer vexatious stoppages or searches by British patrols.[8] In the early months of 1842, when the attack on the *Caroline* was still not redressed, when Anglo-American issues of maritime rights were revived in association with old feelings of national honor and hostility to Britain, when the South's grievance over slavery reinforced the North's grievance on the Canadian frontier, offering a seemingly unparalleled opportunity for combined action and mutual gain, it was not hard to imagine still a third war against Britain. And who should be the secretary of state but Daniel Webster, the young Federalist foe of the second war thirty years earlier.

At the end of January Webser dispatched instructions on the *Creole* to the newly appointed American Minister to Great Britain, Edward Everett, his Bay State friend and colleague of many years. After a straightforward statement of the facts, Webster based the claim for return and redress on the proposition that the slaves are "recognized as property by the Constitution of the United States, in those states in which slavery exists." The *Creole* was engaged on a lawful voyage; forced into a foreign port where slavery was illegal, it violated no British law and never came properly under British jurisdiction; its deck was an extension of American soil, and its persons and property, including the felons, remained under American law. The authorities at Nassau, therefore, should have promptly restored the vessel to its master and crew, enabling them to resume their voyage, and released the felons for transport to their own country for trial. Nothing less was required by "the comity of Nations," Webster declared. In the absence of an extradition treaty, he did not actually expect return of the felons but was building a case for indemnification. Compensation for the mass of slaves freed by British authorities, an act which, he said, "cannot but cause deep feeling in the United States," similarly depended upon international law. The instructions closed with a plea for nonintervention in domestic affairs as the foundation of peace among nations.[9]

Everett would have little opportunity to act on this dispatch since, as Webster knew when he wrote it, the case of the *Creole* was included on the agenda of a special diplomatic mission the newly installed Tory government of Sir Robert Peel and Lord Aberdeen had decided to send to the United States at year's end. At home, publication of the *Creole* letter caused a strong reaction. In the Senate, Calhoun said he read it "with great pleasure," not alone because of its eminent ability but also because of the quarter from which it came.[10] No southern statesman chose to quarrel with Webster. Northern abolitionists, on the other hand, condemned the letter. Samuel J. May said that it "out Calhouns Calhoun himself," and he furnished Webster with the condemnatory resolutions adopted at Plymouth where he had decried the slave trade twenty-two years before.[11] Among abolitionists generally Webster was still considered a friend, though they had grown wary since his speech at Richmond in 1840, and they were alarmed by the doctrine of the *Creole* letter. For several years the political branch of northern abolitionism had been elaborating the doctrine of "freedom national, slavery local." That the Constitution did not recognize slavery was, of course, a basic premise of the campaign for abolition in the District of Columbia. But now Godlike Daniel had apparently nationalized the institution abolitionists sought to denationalize.

The leader of this movement in Congress was Joshua Giddings, the Ohio Whig. In March he introduced resolutions repudiating Webster's assertion that the Constitution recognized slaves as property in states where the institution existed, and holding further that, even if that were true, slave status ended beyond the borders of the state wherein slavery existed in positive law. The law of the state could not extend to the high seas. Since freedom was the national as well as the natural condition, the *Creole* slaves and mutineers were rightfully free men. The House, still operating under a gag on slavery, officially censured Giddings for his resolutions and would not allow him to speak. (As he left the floor Henry Clay, who had observed the vote, extended his hand and thanked the congressman for defending the right to speak.) Giddings resigned and immediately won reelection on the censure issue.[12] The most searching analysis of the *Creole* Letter, at least from a moral standpoint, was William Ellery Channing's pamphlet, *The Duty of the Free States*. The Boston minister, while scrupulously avoiding personal asperities, attacked the doctrine extending the bonds of servitude beyond the states in which slavery existed. The idea that the character impressed upon a man at birth or at home followed him everywhere was monstrous. Moreover, it implicated the free states in support of the monstrosity.[13] Webster had little patience for divines who reasoned on principles of right and wrong rather than of law; but he must have been troubled by Justice Story's dissent to his demand for the return of the slaves under international law. Story, who in the previous year had delivered the majority opinion of the Supreme Court freeing the mutinous slaves in the famous *Amistad* case, told Webster that the status of slaves internationally was entirely a matter of discretion with sovereign states.[14]

During the winter Webster settled into the State Department and patiently awaited the arrival of Britain's special envoy, Alexander Baring, Lord Ashburton. The new government's decision for a special mission both surprised and pleased Washington. After the stormy Palmerston regime, the Peel and Aberdeen ministry sought to calm the waters in Anglo-American relations and to reduce tensions with France. It had often been observed that Tory administrations in Britain tended to be more generous toward the United States than the Whigs, who still imbibed jealous fears toward a rival. (Clay had offered a toast at a White House dinner when Van Buren was president: "Tory Ministers in England and France, and a Whig Ministry in the United States!")[15] The Tories, like the American Whigs, were an organized opposition party elevated to power in an open election—the first in British history—and between the two parties there were conservative sympathies that augured well for diplomacy. Webster, delighted by the mission, was even more delighted by the envoy. In part, this was because of his poor opinion of Henry Fox, the resident minister. The nephew of Charles James Fox—his only claim to fame—he had come to Washington by way of Brazil and promptly made himself as inaccessible as possible. A withered, gray, little old man, addicted to opium, overwhelmed with debts, he never entertained and his only amusement was at cards where but a few men, like Clay, became well enough acquainted to appreciate his wit and accomplishments. Webster said that since Fox seldom rose before 4:00 P.M., the department must make an appointment in advance, for which he would agree to rise at 2; and he remarked jokingly, there was little danger of the peace being broken while Clay kept watch over him by day and Fox by night.[16] On the positive side, Ashburton was a perfect choice. He had distinguished himself as a friend of the United States as early as 1808, when he championed the neutral trade against the British orders in council; even before that the Barings' banking house had financed the Louisiana Purchase, and ever after remained a dominant force in American economic development. In both private and pub-

lic finance, Webster and Ashburton were well acquainted. The Baron had retired from leadership of the firm several years earlier, but he retained large
personal and financial interests in the United States. His wife was a Pennsylvania native. He was, in Palmerston's sneering opinion, "a half Yankee" himself. This was Ashburton's first and probably, at sixty-seven years of age, his
last venture in diplomacy. Writing to Webster upon his appointment, he said
that during the thirty-five years he had held a seat in one or the other houses
of Parliament he had always aimed to promote peace and harmony between
the two countries, and he expressed fond hopes for the negotiations.[17]

The State Department, on Pennsylvania Avenue, was only a stone's throw
from the White House and Webster's residence on the square. The small office staff was ably managed by his son Fletcher, who eagerly accepted the
chief clerkship after everything collapsed in the West. The business of the
department still included items of "home" affairs, some years later to be transferred to the new Interior Department; but foreign affairs took most of Webster's time. The menu was varied: complex negotiations of commercial claims
against Mexico and Latin American countries; the protection of American
merchants and missionaries in the Near East; Danish sound duties and trade
with the German Zollverein; and the making of a commercial treaty with
China. Webster was generally well served by his choice of ministers. The appointment of the scholarly Everett to the Court of St. James and of the country's leading man of letters, Washington Irving, as minister to Spain were especially notable. Matters of foreign policy were the very stuff of domestic
politics, of course. Anglo-American relations offered proof of that, and the
range of problems from Texas to California and to Oregon, involving Mexico
as well as Britain, were like sticks of dynamite waiting to explode. The president and the secretary, in defense against Clay and the Whigs, formed a mutual admiration society. Webster respected Tyler's integrity and, for a time,
returned to the old delusion of a middle party, or no-party, which would triumph in Tyler's reelection. Visitors at Tyler's Virginia home, Sherwood Forest, on the eve of the Civil War, were touched by his homage to the memory
of his Yankee secretary of state, whose portrait hung prominently in the dining room.[18] But the Tyler-Webster alliance began to fall apart before it could
be put together. Politically, as it soon became evident, Webster could bring
Tyler no support, and so he could expect nothing from him. And in the conduct of diplomacy Tyler's aggressive defense of slavery and southern interests, particularly the annexation of Texas, which he pressed upon the secretary as early as October 1841, opened a chasm that could not be bridged.
Nonetheless, the duties of office settled most agreeably on Webster. "They
fall in with the general course of my studies and attainments, so far as I have
any attainments," he remarked, "are of a large and comprehensive nature,
and lead every day to new acquisitions of knowledge."[19] He liked being secretary of state. He liked the dignity of the office; he liked the power to shape
events; he liked the salary; he liked his boss; he liked his living arrangements
and the social life of the capital.

The social scene was gayer than it had been for fifteen years. The first lady

being an invalid, the duties of mistress of the White House devolved upon
the president's daughter-in-law, Priscilla Tyler, who was coached by the
doyenne of Washington society, Dolley Madison. For the first time the
grounds of the mansion, only recently landscaped, were opened to the public; on some evenings the Navy Band played and cabinet officers, senators,
and foreign ministers were observed promenading with ordinary citizens.[20]
In November, after a long absence, Mrs. Webster returned to the capital to
preside over the refinished and richly furnished "Swann House" on the
square. There was gossip of a breach between Webster and his wife brought
on after Herman Le Roy's death. "Her father left her something handsome,"
Louisa Catherine Adams reported to her husband, "but he has tied it up so
fast, that her husband cannot touch it; and he has threatened to break the
will." Others said he might break the marriage as well.[21] The gossip subsided
during the winter social season. "Mrs. Webster looked like a queen," a guest
wrote after a lavish entertainment, "her stately form rising preminently
above all the other ladies. . . . She had some 10 or 12 rooms thrown open
and her splendid mansion is one of the most magnificently furnished
houses . . . I have ever seen." A Massachusetts congressman remarked that
a dinner at the Websters' was "the most beautiful thing" in the world; unfortunately he could not enjoy it for wondering whose money supplied the table.[22]
The height of felicity for Webster were the visits of distinguished English
guests. Lord Morpeth, the Earl of Carlisle, arrived on tour in January. He
liked Washington well enough, but laughed at the moniker "City of Magnificent Distances." It had the look, rather, of "half a dozen indifferent villages
scattered over a goose common." Of the eminent public men his lordship
met, Webster, he supposed, the most cordial to Great Britain, but he found
Clay "much the most attractive." Dining at the Websters was a little like dining at a London town house. In the vestibule one was confronted with portraits of the Queen, the Duke of Wellington, Lord Melbourne, and other
worthies. Webster was a grand host, "very gracious, but never I think light in
hand," Morpeth observed.[23] On Morpeth's heels came Charles Dickens. He
called Washington "the City of Magnificent Intentions": "Spacious avenues,
that begin in nothing and lead nowhere; streets, mile long, that only want
houses, roads, and inhabitants; public buildings that need but a public to
complete . . . " It was dull, straggly, and rude, almost as bad as the rest of
the country which Dickens "pickwicked" in his American Notes.[24]

Ashburton arrived on the HMS Warspite, at Annapolis, on April 4, and he
and Webster quickly got down to business. The minister was empowered to
treat on every issue in controversy between the two countries, the northeastern boundary at the head of the list. The Treaty of 1783 had described a
boundary that upon subsequent investigation proved to be a geographical impossibility. Jay's Treaty had provided for a joint commission to find and survey the line, but to no avail. The problem was passed over at Ghent, but in
1827 the two governments referred the boundary for arbitration to the King
of the Netherlands. Between the claimants to the disputed territory he
awarded about two-thirds to the United States and one-third to Britain.

Whitehall accepted, but the United States, because of Maine's intransigence, rejected the award. In 1839 Palmerston sent a new team of surveyors into the wilderness, and they came out with a report that, although nonsense as cartography, the foreign minister hailed as a complete vindication of the British claim. Upon this shaky foundation he proposed a new joint commission on the boundary. Project and counter-project passed between London and Washington, but nothing had been settled when Van Buren left office. A dead halt after fifty-seven years. Webster, with Tyler's consent, refused to be a partner in Palmerston's plan. Fortunately Aberdeen's arrival at the foreign office opened the way to a new and conciliatory approach. "Survey and exploration! As if there had not already been enough of both!" Webster exclaimed. He hoped to live long enough to see the boundary settled. As lumbering advanced and settlers moved into the Aroostook valley, where British and American soldiers already faced each other, the situation became more and more dangerous. But there was faint hope of settlement unless the question could be rescued from "the labyrinth of projects and counter-projects, explorations and arbitrations, in which it was involved."[25] Discarding the question of right, discarding the pursuit of the 1783 boundary, Webster proposed a compromise settlement on a *conventional* line. Aberdeen was agreeable. His instructions to Ashburton were to obtain some improvement over the Dutch king's award. But Aberdeen soon found that this was impossible; besides, the lands in question were "as worthless . . . as probably any tract on the habitable globe."[26] He cheerfully entered into Webster's plan for a compromise settlement.

Webster had already implemented a political strategy designed to break down Maine's resistance. During the summer a Downeast politician and entrepreneur, F. O. J. Smith, had offered his services as an unofficial agent to educate or propagandize Maine leaders and citizens on the virtue of compromise. For a small fee plus expenses Smith would orchestrate a campaign consisting of articles planted in newspapers, the circulation of petitions, and lobbying at Augusta. A few thousand dollars, he observed, would accomplish more than armies. Webster got Tyler's authorization to use secret service funds at his disposal for this purpose. The line taken was one of no official retreat from the American claim but willingness to make adjustments in the interest of peaceful settlement. In Webster's mind such a settlement must involve, on the American side, some sacrifice of territory, for which the state might be compensated, mainly to enable the British to effect communication between Halifax and Quebec; and the British must concede the navigation of the St. Johns through New Brunswick to the sea.[27] After Smith began his campaign in the fall, Webster wrote to the governor, senators and congressmen, and judges, Whig and Democrat, to enlist aid and assistance. He painted a bleak prospect, either open warfare or more years and treasure wasted in the search for an elusive dividing line, unless the people of Maine were willing to make concessions. In February he threw out the idea of state-appointed commissioners who would come to Washington and join unofficially in the negotiations with Ashburton. By thus drawing Maine into the proceedings he aimed to overcome distrust and to commit the state to the result. Senator Ruel Williams carried the unusual proposal to the newly elected governor, John Fairfield, a Democrat. There was movement among Democrats, who were the dominant party, toward conciliation, Webster learned, but the governor was timid and afraid to take the next step, which was to convene a special session of the legislature to appoint commissioners. In April, one week after Ashburton's arrival, Webster formally laid the proposal before the governor; and he called the legislature into session on May 18. Webster similarly involved Massachusetts in the negotiations by virtue of the parent state's large landholdings in Maine.[28] The calling in of commissioners proved to be a "grand stroke," as Webster himself felt entitled to boast.

In May, while the Maine legislature met, the secretary went to Marshfield for rest and relaxation. Before leaving he wrote reassuringly to Everett about the prospect for agreement on all issues, yet confessed "my fears stick deep in the boundary business," not because of Ashburton but because of jealousy and distrust in Maine.[29] Stopping in Boston, he asked the Harvard historian, Jared Sparks, to meet with him. While conducting research in the French archives three months earlier, Sparks had found a map of North America marked with "a strong red line" which, from other evidence, he inferred was the boundary line decided upon by the peace commissioners in December 1782. To Sparks's amazement the line ran wholly south of the St. Johns, indeed well below the Aroostook. "In short," as he informed Webster of the discovery, "it is exactly the line now contended for by Great Britain, except that it concedes more than is claimed."[30] Webster was not surprised. Four years ago he had seen a similar old map with marks in an unknown hand corresponding to the British claim. He knew, and Sparks knew, that such documents, however interesting, were unauthoritative and proved nothing. His object was to abandon spurious claims based upon spurious maps and surveys. When Everett alerted him to the possibility of finding in London the actual map of the British peace commissioners with the "Oswald line" corresponding to the American claim, Webster shot back, "forbear to press the search after maps in England or elsewhere!"[31] But there is no diplomacy without guile, and so however worthless Sparks's "red-line map" would be in the bargaining of diplomats, it might be just the thing to wring concessions from Maine. He asked the historian to go to Augusta and very discreetly show a copy of the "red-line map" to the governor. At this time Webster was confident commissioners would be appointed; his worry was that they would be hampered by instructions. Sparks's mission was to avert this. Webster breathed a sigh of relief when the professor reported from Augusta that the governor was well disposed and, upon his recommendation, the legislature voted no instructions to the appointed commissioners.[32]

The commissioners (four from Maine, three from Massachusetts) arrived in Washington as the summer began. Ashburton fretted under the heat of the capital, the quarrels among the commissioners, and the turbulent state of the parties, which posed a threat to any Anglo-American accord. In the process Webster had brought about, he negotiated face to face with Ashburton, conveyed his proposals to the commissioners, then reported back and resumed discussions with the minister. Finally, on July 22, an agreement was struck. Under it the disputed Madawaska territory below the St. Johns was divided, more or less as under the Dutch award. In exchange the United States received navigation of the river and a small strip of land on the eastern border; and it would pay each of the states, Maine and Massachusetts, $150,000 in compensation. It was very much the settlement Webster had envisioned from the start. After running the boundary in the northeast, he and Ashburton continued to draw it in detail from Lake Champlain, where the United States recovered Rouse's Point commanding the entrance—a great gain in Webster's view—through the St. Lawrence and the Great Lakes to the Lake of the Woods and due west on the 49th parallel to the Rocky Mountains. Webster celebrated the event with a dinner at his home on the twenty-third. The president, cabinet officers, Fox and Ashburton and suites, commissioners, and a few senators and congressmen toasted the boundary settlement as the harbinger of peace and concord.[33]

Webster and Ashburton now turned in earnest to other problems. Border disturbances and the *Creole* mutiny had shown the need for an extradition agreement. Story, ever responsive to Webster's requests, furnished a draft. It was the basis of Article XI of the treaty, overriding Tyler's objection that it failed to provide for cases of mutiny or return of fugitive slaves.[34] On several issues beyond immediate resolution—destruction of the *Caroline*, the *Creole* Affair, and impressment—the two diplomats exchanged notes explaining their positions. While not part of the treaty, these notes proved valuable; and Webster's, in particular, upon their publication, won for him the éclat of having elevated the diplomatic note and dispatch to a branch of literature.[35] In the case of the *Caroline*, his careful limitation of the right of pursuit or invasion in the name of self-defense to cases of overwhelming necessity, where there is "no choice of means, and no moment of deliberation," was a permanent contribution to international law.[36] The two nations were directly at odds on the *Creole*. Webster's note reasserted the claim of protection of persons and property on American vessels under international law, which seemed to satisfy the southern Whig lawyers he consulted, though it did not satisfy abolitionists. Ashburton's hands were tied but, for his part, he pledged a policy of restraint by British officials dealing with American ships driven into their ports. On impressment Webster enjoyed the luxury of appealing to American patriotism. The special significance of his memoir on this subject lay on the negative side, as a rejection of subtle applications of visit and search to stamp out the slave trade. Something must be done against the barbarous traffic, however. Webster proposed that the United States and Britain maintain independent naval squadrons (a minimum of eighty guns) on the coast of Africa, each engaged in patrol and authorized to board vessels suspected of slaving. Ashburton accepted. The "joint cruising" plan became Article VIII of the treaty. It was no more than the long-deferred fulfillment of an obligation descending from Ghent, and as each nation was to confine its searches to vessels under its own flag, the agreement in no way compromised the historic American position.[37]

Tyler forwarded the treaty to the Senate on August 9. Rives, who managed the debate in executive session, let out the secret of the "red-line map." While potentially embarrassing, it worked in the treaty's favor and undoubtedly added to Webster's reputation as a diplomatist. Benton and Buchanan led the opposition to ratification. They thought Webster a hopeless Anglophile who had been badly outmaneuvered by Ashburton. But they found few followers; and Calhoun's speech for the treaty, it was said, "settled the question."[38] The Senate's consenting vote, 39–9, was the largest majority ever recorded for a treaty. The negotiators had already said their farewells and exchanged their portraits; and the Englishman had departed for northern points, where he was toasted in a manner usually reserved for native statesmen. In an editorial penned for the Washington press, Webster—an avid editorialist—lauded Ashburton: "He came not to make difficulties, but to make a Treaty." The secretary did not neglect to praise himself as well.[39] The treaty came back with the Queen's signature via the *Great Western* on November 4. Webster, in New York at the time, heard the one-hundred-gun salute from the Battery and the noisy cacophony of the harbor. At city hall, where the chamber of commerce waited upon him, he joined in the honors for the treaty.

He had reason for pride. The Webster-Ashburton Treaty was a resounding success in the United States. In Britain it had yet to run the gauntlet of debate in Parliament. Palmerston flayed at it mercilessly as "The Ashburton Capitulation." He thought the joint-cruising accord worthless and predicted, correctly, that the United States would not fulfill its duty. Yet, for this, Ashburton had yielded the British position on visit and search. Palmerston denounced the retreat on the northeast boundary. While he did not agree with those who charged Webster with "deceitful trickery" in withholding the evidence of the "red-line map," this was, in Palmerston's opinion, another instance of the American's superiority in the arts of diplomacy.[40] The "battle of the maps" crossed the Atlantic. In the succeeding April Webster defended his conduct at a meeting of the New York Historical Society. "I see no reason," he remarked drolly, "why I should have felt myself bound to go to Lord Aberdeen and tell him that there was, or there might be, a map or other document at Paris which, if found, would strengthen the British claim."[41] The British prime minister agreed with him. Indeed, Peel confessed in Parliament that Ashburton had in his possession a map purporting to show "the Oswald line," and it supported the American claim, yet he said nothing of it to Webster.[42] Palmerston's flaying of Ashburton was matched by his flattery of Webster, a man of "gigantic intellect and noble patriotism" who added the Yankee knack for sharp bargaining. When poor Ashburton received an address from a rare American critic of the treaty who thought it, rather, the Webster capitulation, he replied wittily "that your views of my sagacity and of Mr. Webster's neglect suit my purposes here admirably."[43] In a moment of reflection on their joint work, Ashburton said to Webster there must be something right about a treaty that was not entirely pleasing to either side. The idea that one or the other negotiator failed to strike "a sharp bargain" was mistaken. "The real merit of the settlement is that it will not stand that description on either side."[44]

Repercussions from the treaty were felt over several years. When a copy reached the desk of the American minister in Paris, Lewis Cass, he angrily demanded to be recalled. Article VIII was a personal affront. Not only did it abandon cherished American principles; it knocked the props from under the campaign Cass had been waging against French ratification of the Quintuple Treaty. This was curious, for the self-same article was read in London as abandonment of the British position. Cass, the Michigan Democrat, whom Webster had viewed as a rival since their school days in New Hampshire, was an Anglophobe. The "holy alliance" against the slave trade was another step in the British scheme to command the oceans of the world. Such was the burden of Cass's pamphlet on the question published in Paris in February. Webster despised the minister's argument along with his meddling in this matter. Tyler heartily approved of it, however, and the secretary was compelled to communicate that approval to Cass. When the Chamber of Deputies subsequently refused to ratify the Quintuple Treaty, Cass took credit himself, though, in fact, it was simply Premier Guizot's "tit for tat" against Palmerston.[45] An acrimonious correspondence ensued between Cass and Webster, in which both preened themselves before their American audience. Webster was justified in claiming, as he did in an editorial written for the *Intelligencer* the following March, that the joint-cruising accord had determined French policy toward suppression of the slave trade and delivered the death blow to the Quintuple Treaty.[46]

The political showdown on the treaty did not come until 1846, after Webster returned to the Senate. Charles Jared Ingersoll, a combative Philadelphia lawyer who had entered Congress at the same time as Webster, as forthright an advocate of the war as Webster was an opponent, and who had never forgiven him for his Federalism, delivered a blast against the treaty in the House of Representatives. Ingersoll also revived old charges that Webster yielded on the *Caroline* and interfered with the course of justice in the McLeod case.[47] What triggered the attack was the question of the Oregon boundary. Webster had committed the "gross absurdity" in 1842 of separating the northeast boundary from the northwest boundary: "They should have been kept indivisible. The giving up of one would render more difficult the settlement of the other." Oregon had been discussed, but Ashburton, begging the want of instructions, preferred to leave it to another time, and Webster acquiesced. He had a low opinion of the Oregon country and thought that the motives and objects of those who hankered for it arose "this side of the Rocky Mountains," in short, in political stratagems rather than in concern for the rational interest.[48] When New York Senator Daniel Dickinson associated himself with Ingersoll's criticisms, Webster found opportunity to reply. And what a reply it was. Winthrop said he had never seen Webster so angry. Vice President George M. Dallas, who was in the chair, was stunned by Webster's ferocity. "He grit his teeth, scowled, stamped, and roared forth the very worst and most abusive language I have ever heard uttered in the Senate," Dallas said. This was a different Webster. He was not known for invective, but here, it was reported, the invective exceeded that of Cicero, Burke, and Sheridan, to say nothing of Randolph, Clay, and Benton.[49] Where there was so much wrath, Ingersoll supposed, there must be much guilt, so he now pursued his investigation into the State Department. There he discovered the expenditures from the secret service fund. Returning to the House, he charged Webster with misappropriation of funds and corruption of the press, and demanded an investigation. The refusal of President James K. Polk to break the seal of secrecy on the contingency fund, combined with Tyler's testimony defending Webster and assuming full responsibility for the expenditures, doomed the project. The charges recoiled against Ingersoll. Webster accused him of defalcation as a district attorney in Philadelphia some years before. "Sir," said Webster contemptuously at the conclusion of this affair, "I leave him in the worst company I know in the world—I leave him with himself." Apparently Ingersoll, utterly devastated, offered an apology to the senator, who declined to receive it.[50]

In the fall of 1842, when Webster basked in the sunshine of the treaty, he was perfectly positioned to quit the Tyler administration. To the Manifesto Whigs, of course, the only possible defense for his remaining in the cabinet was the overriding national interest in an Anglo-American settlement. Now that it had been achieved, vindicating his own judgment, Webster was expected to resign and rejoin the Whig brethren. Many had continued unsparing in their harsh feelings toward him. In January 1842 George Prentice had published in the Louisville *Daily Journal* an editorial, "Anecdote of Daniel Webster," that gave a lurid account of the Godlike's seduction of the wife of a poor clerk in his department. She had come to him asking employment as a secretary. After sending her to an adjoining room to provide a specimen of her handwriting, Webster came in, closed the door, and pounced upon her declaring, "This, my dear, is one of the pregoratives of my office." She screamed and clerks rushed in, thus forestalling "the old debauchee." Affidavits from Washington, one of them filed by Webster himself with a local magistrate, forced Prentice to retract the story, with the apology, however, that Webster's lusty escapades were about as notorious as his dishonesty in business matters. The Washington *Independent,* Clay's voice in the capital, took the same line.[51] Having to make oath to his chastity was deeply mortifying to Webster. "All English annals show nothing so humiliating," George Bancroft remarked gloatingly. Webster blamed Clay for this ugly attack and supposed its aim was to drive him from the cabinet. When he did not budge and public opinion reacted against it, "a sort of truce," as Webster said, was declared in the hostilities.[52] No one really believed the wretched story. Yet its appearance suggested something amiss in Webster's character. Calhoun, a moral purist, thought that Webster had rendered himself "universally odious."[53]

Webster returned to Boston in September in a state of uncertainty about retirement. Accepting the invitation of a public reception at Faneuil Hall, he was offered the ideal forum to discourse upon the treaty and to announce his own plans. He remained at Marshfield during the meeting of the Massachusetts Whig Convention on the fourteenth. His advice, offered to a friendly member of the party's central committee, was unreservedly against the nomination of a presidential candidate, that is, Henry Clay. Even if Clay were electable, which Webster doubted, his early nomination would hurt the Whigs in the coming state elections.[54] But he did not expect his advice to be heeded. The Bay State party had fallen under the control of Abbott Lawrence, who had treacherously dropped Webster in 1838 and whose personal feelings had been poisoned by the patronage and policy disputes of the Tyler administration. The convention condemned the administration, called for "a full and final separation" of the Whig party from John Tyler, and, as expected, nominated Clay for the presidency. Praise for Webster's "masterly" conduct of the Ashburton negotiations in no way mitigated his feelings toward the convention. Because of it he dreaded the Faneuil Hall date two weeks hence and wished he had never agreed to it.[55]

All Boston was on tiptoe to hear Webster. The hall was filled to suffocation. One observer said Webster "looked like Coriolanus," the proud leader who, having been cast out of Rome, now meditated whether to save or destroy it. Another spoke of the "sublime sadness" that sat upon his countenance. After disposing of Anglo-American affairs, Webster launched into a tirade against the Whig leadership. He denounced the separation from Tyler; he called a national bank, the pursuit of which had led to the separation, "an obsolete idea"; and gave vent to his long repressed hostility to the Compromise Tariff. It was an extraordinary speech, Quincy Adams wrote in his diary, "bitter as wormwood to nearly the whole of the Whig party . . . boastful, cunning, jesuitical, fawning, and insolent; ambiguous in its givings out, avowing his determination not to let them know whether he intends to resign his office or not . . . and dealing open blows at the late Whig Convention."[56] Some marveled at his courage, others at his folly. "He was at every moment upon the brink of all his audience hatred," George Ticknor said, "and it is still a wonder how he got through without being mobbed." The convention had declared a divorce from the Tyler administration. To this Webster said, "Generally, when a divorce takes place, the parents divide the children. I shall be glad to know where I am to go." With this plaintive query, he threw a glance at Lawrence, who sat on the platform, and declared, "I am a Whig, a Massachusetts Whig, a Boston Whig, a Faneuil Hall Whig . . ."[57]

The speech created a sensation. A few Whigs applauded it, but the overwhelming number thought it a great blunder, damaging to the party in the short run and permanently alienating Webster from Whig affections. Why had he done this? Because of sordid ambition for office, patronage, and money, some said. Others speculated that Webster aimed to break up the Whig party and rear a Webster-Tyler party in its place. Everyone detected the cloven hoof of jealousy of Clay. "Our modern Anthony, it seems, means no longer to succumb," Frank Blair wrote in the *Globe*. "Here . . . for the first time, Mr. Webster displays the courage of a man."[58] Whatever the reason, the Faneuil Hall speech revealed a fatal want of judgment in the Godlike Man. "If he had resigned his office of Secretary of State the day after the Ashburton treaty was ratified, and come back into the Whig ranks openly and heartily," as B. W. Leigh reflected sometime later, "he would have stood instantly upon such high ground as he never before attained to. How he should have wanted the judgment to see the vantage ground . . . the vast and brilliant prospects which seemed so obvious to everybody else, seems to me quite unaccountable." Webster ' "missed the figure' " and Leigh, too, could offer no better explanation for this blindness than hatred of Henry Clay.[59]

"Where am I to go?" Webster had asked the Massachusetts Whigs. His problem, in part, was to find a suitable exit, which is to say one that was an entrance as well. The door to the Senate was open, since Choate would happily resign, but Webster said he had no desire to return to the Senate. The embassy in Paris was available, but ignorance of the language was a bar. "I could go nowhere but to England," he hinted to Everett, "and you are yet hardly warm in your place." Besides, he was too poor.[60] A British mission, nevertheless, either as resident minister in place of Everett or as a special envoy figured in Webster's calculations for the next several months. It was even suggested that he had deliberately held off negotiation of the Oregon boundary in order to use it as the means of effecting his resignation from the cabinet. He had developed an ingenious plan—"the tripartite plan"—for settling the diverse problems of Mexico, California, and Oregon all at once. Responding to the suggestion of Waddy Thompson, United States Minister to Mexico, Webster had authorized him to sound out Santa Anna, the president, on the acquisition of the port of San Francisco in exchange for the assumption of Mexican debts to American citizens. San Francisco, with whatever portion of California that came with it, was essential to the growth of American commerce in the Pacific, in Webster's opinion. He had subsequently hinted to Ashburton that if Britain would use its influence with Mexico in behalf of this acquisition, the United States might be willing to accept the Columbia River boundary in the northwest, provided it retained an "enclave" giving commercial access to the Straits of Juan de Fuca. Neither Mexico nor Britain showed interest in the tripartite plan, but the political pressure for an Oregon settlement, ending the joint occupancy that had existed for twenty-four years, kept it on Webster's agenda. In February Tyler, who liked the plan and seemed eager to facilitate Webster's departure, tried out the project of a special mission on the House Foreign Affairs Committee. Although the Bay State members, Adams and Cushing, supported it, the committee disapproved, and the project was dropped.[61]

An alternate route had been surveyed to reach the same goal, however. With the Treaty of Nanking ending the Opium War, Britain obtained European-style trading privileges with five Chinese ports. American trade was still confined to Canton and was limited, moreover, to the exchange of specie for tea and other exports. In a special message drafted by Webster, the president asked Congress to authorize an extraordinary mission to the Celestial Empire seeking American trade on the same terms as the British. And who did the secretary propose for this mission? Edward Everett. Both mission and nominee were approved on the last day of the Twenty-Seventh Congress in the face of Benton's angry charge that it had been cooked up for no higher purpose than to furnish a graceful exit for the secretary of state. The Boston *Daily Advertiser*, whose publisher, Nathan Hale, was Everett's brother-in-law, made the same charge. The minister himself, who would normally make any personal sacrifice for Webster, was already seething over rumors that he was to be supplanted or overshadowed when he learned dismayingly of his appointment as commissioner to China. Webster hastened to assure him, contrary to what he read in the *Daily*, that he had not the slightest wish to go abroad; indeed, if Everett were to vacate the London mission there wasn't one chance in a thousand he would fill it.[62] But he protested too much. Not even Everett believed him. And without apology he declined the China mission.

Webster never found the graceful exit he sought. Resigning on May 8, 1843, the same day he penned instructions to Caleb Cushing, who was named commissioner to China, he returned to private life. Had the conduct of foreign relations been the primary concern, Webster might have stayed in office. A new project for a commercial treaty with Britain had taken his fancy. Greeted with a storm of protest when Webster outlined the plan just after leaving office, some observers saw evidence in it that he was tacking toward Calhoun. The basic problem, as always, was Tyler. He had plunged headlong into a quest for the Democratic nomination, thus severing his last link to the Whigs and giving to the administration a political turn that was downright offensive to Webster. Moreover, Tyler had set his sights on the annexation of Texas. In the end, Webster said, he yielded to the judgment of his friends and "the importunity of my wife, who has imbibed a mortal aversion to my remaining in the cabinet." Sixty-one years old when he retired to Marshfield as a private citizen, Webster had no expectations of returning soon, if ever, to public life.[63]

3. *Calhoun, the Presidency, and Texas*

In 1843, for the first time in thirty-two years, none of the triumvirate held public office. Calhoun resigned his Senate seat in March to run for the presidency. He had given notice to the legislature four months earlier. His colleague, William C. Preston, had already resigned rather than obey legislative instructions. The lawmakers at Columbia, obliged to elect a new governor as well, were thus presented in December with an extraordinary opportunity to declare the political heart and mind of the state. In every other state of the Union elections to these great offices were party contests. In South Carolina they were contests within a governing elite conscious of the importance of subordinating personal and factional rivalries to harmony and unity in the state; and although his hand might be invisible, Calhoun was the major personal force in this process. James H. Hammond was elected governor, which repaired the humiliation of his defeat by John P. Richardson, the old Unionist, two years before and co-opted a brilliant but irascible man who, left to himself, might become a loose cannon on the deck of the ship of state. George McDuffie was enticed out of retirement to fill the seat vacated by Preston. This went smoothly. The election of a successor to Calhoun proved difficult, however. Lowcountry politicians claimed the seat to balance McDuffie. Calhoun apparently backed Robert Barnwell Rhett, the three-term congressman from the Colleton district. "It was said," Preston reported, "that Rhett was consecrated to the office by the imposition of Calhoun's own hands."[1] But Rhett was unpopular, and the legislators balked at the appearance of dictation. On the third ballot they elected Daniel E. Huger, a respected Charleston lawyer and reformed Unionist.

The same legislature nominated Calhoun for the presidency. Georgia, by prior arrangement, quickly seconded the nomination. Calhoun was the first declared Democratic candidate, though everyone understood that Martin Van Buren expected to be the party's standard-bearer again in 1844. The New Yorker held no public office, hence was shielded from potentially damaging controversy. Calhoun's managers sought the same protection for him. The next Congress, one of them wrote, "will be full of moves to entrap you."[2] Benton, the Van Buren leader in the Senate, was particularly adept at laying political traps, and one was readily at hand in Oregon, where southern and western interests were in conflict. Yet many of Calhoun's friends, even if they approved his presidential candidacy, were bewildered by his resignation. He deprived himself of his most effective forum and left his great enemy, Benton, in command of the Senate. Besides, what would he do with himself? For Henry Clay running for the presidency was an occupation, but Calhoun only intended to withdraw into the quiet of Fort Hill. Perhaps that is what he most wanted, the pleasure of managing his farm and the leisure to write "the book" he talked about and which a Virginian described as "John Taylor of Carolina with metaphysical variations."[3]

It was essential to Calhoun's image that the public perceive him as only a spectator to his candidacy. The idea of disinterested devotion to high principle had become so deeply enmeshed in his own ambition as to be indistinguishable from it. Advocates turned the unblemished purity of his personal life, which no one disputed, into an emblem of his political character. Nobly elevated above the evils of the time, Calhoun was neither a wire-puller, like Van Buren, nor a "table-orator." Clay traversed the country in quest of the presidency—he was the original table-orator. Webster had toured the West and taken to the stump; Van Buren had recently toured the southwest. But Calhoun, reticent, averse to self-dramatization, refused to travel or, with rare exceptions, to appear in public. His standard response to invitations from around the country was that the presidency was too high an office to be sought by personal canvass. To one of his advisers, who tried to overcome this old-fashioned attitude, Calhoun replied that there was still an influential portion of the people who regarded the office as a reward for merit and service, rather than an object of electioneering, and he expected to earn their trust.⁴ In the act of shunning his public Calhoun thus paid it the compliment of sharing his noble view of politics. This was presumptuous; and the aspirant for the presidency who had never crossed the Appalachians or, for many years, the Mason and Dixon Line, and seemed indifferent to doing so, suffered serious handicaps.

The record of Calhoun's services was well known, and it would be made accessible to all through the publication of his *Life and Speeches* in 1843. The Charleston *Mercury* ran the Calhoun banner with the motto, "Free Trade; Low Duties; No Debt; Separation from Banks; Economy, Retrenchment; And a Strict Adherence to the Constitution." Nothing novel here. A veil was thrown over issues of slavery and abolitionism as Calhoun appealed for northern Democratic votes. Among the old issues of public policy, the tariff was given first place. It remained the paramount example of the fiscal action of the general government despoiling the South and, as Calhoun hoped to show, "the producing classes" of the North as well. He and his Carolina friends considered the tariff of 1842 an outrageous betrayal of the Compromise of 1833. The state had accepted the Compromise Tariff only on the condition that any act thereafter violating it would be nullified; and the state might have nullified the recent act, Hammond thought, but for Calhoun's presidential ambitions. The tariff was an issue not alone with the Whigs but more importantly in 1843 with Van Buren and the Albany Regency. The former president's friends in Congress, Silas Wright at the head, had voted for the infamous tariff of 1842. Calhoun could never forget that they were the authors of the Tariff of Abominations, "the real cause of all the calamity which has since befallen the country and the party," he said. Six years before he had hoped that the lash of economic depression would reform them. He and his little band had come to their aid. But, Calhoun lamented, "As soon as they believed that the Whigs were beaten through our exertions, and we trammelled by the machinery of party, they turned round and courted the Tariff and Abolition parties at our expense. It is the game they have always played at our expense, till we are nearly ruined in property and character."⁵ Old feelings against Van Buren, revived by the new tariff, thus drove Calhoun's campaign.

The conduct of the campaign was left to an inner circle of advisers. Nearest home, and nearest in Calhoun's affections, was Francis Pickens, representative of the Edgefield district in Congress until he accompanied Calhoun into retirement. A wealthy planter and third-generation leader of a distinguished upcountry family, Pickens counted Calhoun among his cousins and, according to Hammond, "is supposed to control him in all practical matters."⁶ At the head of the Charleston Central Committee stood Franklin H. Elmore, who also headed the powerful and politically embroiled Bank of the State of South Carolina. Elmore was a moderate; he had supported Calhoun's policy of reconciliation with Unionists over the advice of Pickens and also of Hammond. The latter was unkind but not entirely unjust when, in his diary, he dismissed Elmore as "a good fellow, without talents, information, or energy."⁷ Robert Barnwell Rhett was the most prominent of a trio of brothers who in the eyes of rivals constituted, with Elmore, "the Regency" devoted to Calhoun in the lowcountry. Albert Rhett was supposed to have control of the Charleston *Mercury*, while Barnwell conducted the Calhoun newspaper, *The Spectator*, in Washington. Dixon H. Lewis, the prodigious Alabama congressman—he weighed over four hundred pounds—had important South Carolina connections, having graduated from the College and, like Albert Rhett, having married one of Elmore's sisters; but he was also the ablest politician among Calhoun's advisers. Another out-of-stater, Virgil Maxcy, had known Calhoun since they were law students together. A Maryland lawyer and politician, he had only recently returned to the United States after five years service as *chargé d'affaires* at Brussels. An eager young Virginia congressman, Robert M. T. Hunter, headed the Calhoun Central Committee in Washington. Although he had entered Congress in 1837 as a state rights Whig, Hunter soon fell under Calhoun's influence and became a state rights Democrat. All these men, with marginal figures like McDuffie and Duff Green, were rivals for Calhoun's favor. They were frequently at odds on the management of the campaign, and in such matters rarely received help from their leader, who remained passive and aloof at Fort Hill.

Just as in 1823, Calhoun had delusory ideas of his political strength outside South Carolina. In the Deep South his hopes for Georgia, Alabama, and possibly Mississippi were not unrealistic. Although he promised protection for sugar within the limits of a revenue tariff, the tariff of 1842 had placed Louisiana safely in Whig hands.[8] North Carolina was intransigently Whig. Virginia was the principal battleground of the campaign for the Democratic nomination. The historic alliance of New York and Virginia, upon which Van Buren had reared the Jacksonian Democratic party, had to be broken if Calhoun was to prevail. The alliance subverted the unity of the South by holding Virginia, the section's natural leader, in thrall. For Calhoun it represented all the evils of spoilsmanship and party management that were ruining the country. In 1843, as the Calhoun campaign began, Virginia seemed winnable. His old enemy, Thomas Ritchie, head of the legendary Richmond Junto, was heard to speak kindly of him; and a host of young Virginians, starting with Hunter, were zealots for Calhoun. The political destination of the Tyler Whigs remained uncertain, but their best men, Thomas Walker Gilmer and Abel P. Upshur—the latter would become Webster's successor in the State Department—were friendly to Calhoun. Tyler himself had thrown some bones of patronage to Calhoun's followers in hopes of quieting his candidacy, but he had been "most egregiously bamboozled," it was said, and of course withdrew his favors when Calhoun opened his campaign.[9] The spoils had been particularly useful in New York City, where Calhoun sought to mount a challenge to the Albany Regency.

Nothing was more astounding in the campaign than the flirtation between Calhounites and Locofocos. The latter were the dregs of the egalitarian Locofoco party that had briefly won control of the regular Democratic organization in New York City in 1837. Most of the party had been absorbed into Tammany Hall by 1843, but some of them, never reconciled to Tammany or to Van Buren, tried to keep up the agitation. Calhoun's presidential candidacy was a convenient vehicle for waging their local battle. That was not the whole of it, however. The Locofocos were radical free-traders, haters of every kind of privilege, and chanters of the Jeffersonian axiom, "That government is best which governs least." So they felt an ideological affinity with Calhoun and even imagined the slaveholding South was the natural ally of equal rights and *laissez-faire* in the North. But this was a shallow basis for cooperation. The Locofocos were "rank agrarians," demagogic in manner and majoritarian in principle—altogether strange political bedfellows with Calhoun. And as Charles Sellers has written, "The prim wantonness with which Calhoun and his gentlemanly managers yielded to the seductions of democratic politics was matched by the virginal ineptitude with which they played the game."[10]

The Dorr Rebellion occurring at this time focused national attention on the question whether or not a majority of the people may rightfully frame a new government regardless of the provisions of the constituted government. Leaders of the disfranchised populace in Rhode Island had met and framed a "People's Constitution" and proceeded to elect a government independent of the incumbent regime. The problem was forced on Tyler, who backed law and order, and spilled over into Congress in 1842. Calhoun drafted a series of resolutions that expressed sympathy with the Dorrite Suffrage party but denounced the pretension of making a new constitution by the naked will of the popular majority. The resolutions lay dormant because nothing in the course of Senate business called for them in 1842. Lewis thought that much of the agitation of the Rhode Island Question, in and out of Congress, was intended "to head Calhoun." It was, in fact, one of the traps his advisers hoped to avoid by his resignation. But he could not, and would not, avoid it during the campaign, even at the risk of injuring his candidacy with the northern Locofocos. Calhoun finally offered his views in a public letter. Again, he sympathized with the Dorrite aims but said that to admit the Dorrite principle would be to deliver the death-blow to constitutional government: "It would be to admit, that [the numerical majority] had the right to set aside, at pleasure, that which was intended to restrain it. . . . It would be, in short, to attribute to it the same divine right to govern, which Sir Robert Filmer claimed for kings." Calhoun went on to say that if he were president he would, in a case like Rhode Island, invoke the United States Constitution's *guarantee clause*—the guarantee of republican government—in behalf of the legitimate government. His letter, unaccountably, was not published, much to Calhoun's disappointment, but to the relief of Hunter, who was already nervous about the damage done by the Rhode Island Question.[11] When that question took the form of a law case, *Luther v. Borden,* finally argued before the Supreme Court in 1848, the counsel on the Dorrite side was Benjamin F. Hallett, leader of the dissident Massachusetts Democrats who had championed Calhoun in 1843, while the counsel on the law-and-order side, agreeing fundamentally with Calhoun, was Daniel Webster.

Calhoun hated the very word *democracy*. The government of the United

States, like the government of South Carolina, was not a democracy, it was a *republic*, and Calhoun called himself a Republican. The name Democrat was of northern coinage, he said, and "as usually understood means those who are in favour of the government of the absolute numerical majority to which I am utterly opposed and the prevalence of which would destroy our system and destroy the South."[12] Yet he unhesitatingly associated himself with *democracy* in his quest for the presidency. The address of the South Carolina nominating convention in May identified Calhoun with "the democratic creed." "He is the true representative of *the great essential principles of democracy—freedom of human pursuits*, in the exemption of industry from unnecessary burdens and exactions."[13] Perhaps Calhoun was attempting to lift the odium from *democracy* by identifying it with his own creed. He may have been encouraged in this by Orestes Brownson, the Boston radical, with whom he corresponded. Brownson's famous tract, *The Laboring Classes*, in 1840, had appealed to workingmen to vote for Van Buren and the democracy. Whigs seized upon it as a disclosure of the true "class war" doctrine of the Democratic party, and Van Buren allegedly blamed the Brownson pamphlet for his defeat. The defeat proved traumatic for Brownson. It shattered his faith in *vox populi vox Dei* and landed him four years later in the arms of the Roman Catholic Church. In the interim he turned to Calhoun as the savior of the republic. Brownson promoted the southerner's candidacy through his writings in *The Democratic Review*, the party's literary journal, until deepening conservatism forced his departure and led him to launch a journal under his own name in 1844. Brownson no longer believed the rule of the popular majority was liberating. On the contrary, the more democratic the suffrage, he wrote, reflecting the disillusionment brought on by the Whig victory in 1840, "the greater will be the influence and the more certain the triumph of wealth, or rather of the business classes."[14] The true interest of the laboring classes lay neither in democracy nor in consolidation but in constitutional checks and balances on the exploitative uses of government by the business classes. Thus along an entirely different route, and in a different vocabulary, Brownson had reached the same conclusion as Calhoun. He endorsed the state rights platform, including the theory of "concurring majorities." Calhoun was delighted with this convert. "There is scarcely a view taken or a sentiment expressed," he declared of a Brownson article, "in which I do not fully concur."[15] He approved of Brownson's radical criticism of northern industrial society, since it could be read as an implicit endorsement of slave labor; and he rejoiced, of course, that a northern intellectual embraced southern political principles.

The campaign *Life* of Calhoun was published by Harper & Brothers in February, 1843, just in time for distribution in Congress before adjournment. This compacted seventy-four-page tract was supposed to be accompanied by a volume of speeches, to which it was a kind of preface, but the *Speeches* did not appear until several months later. The *Life*, written in the third person, was published without ascription of authorship. Whether it was essentially an autobiography or a biography is an issue that has never been settled. It may have been a little of both. The evidence suggests that Calhoun wrote the bulk of it, drawing on previous biographical sketches, such as Maxcy's of 1831, during the fall of 1842, and delivered the manuscript to Hunter for completion when he returned to Washington. Joseph A. Scoville, a leader of the New York group, looked after arrangements with Harper, read the proof sheets, and signed the contract.[16] Consistent with the public image he culti-vated, Calhoun could not possibly have appeared as the author of a eulogistic life of himself. So he wished to have the authorship imputed to others, like Hunter, however minor their contribution.

The *Life* is a dry, stiff, and stilted narrative of Calhoun's political career seen through his own self-adulatory eyes. Throughout he is trumpeted as "the master statesman of his age." Among his many virtues none is more ex-tolled than "stern obedience to his principles," heedless of ambition, fear, en-mity, friendship, or popularity.[17] Without apology for any errors he may have committed early in his public life, Calhoun "nobly redeemed" himself, it is said, from the time of his election as vice president, when he recovered the old Republican political creed and made it the foundation of his politics. No speeches from the early period, except Calhoun's maiden effort in the House, were included in the volume of speeches. This provoked the charge of "suppressed speeches" and deliberate misrepresentation. Like Saturn of old, said Gales and Seaton in the *Intelligencer*, the statesman swallowed his own progeny. Calhoun promptly apologized for a title that falsely repre-sented the ground surveyed by the *Speeches*. He had himself selected them, thirty-eight in number, and did not mean to deceive anyone. That he would consign to oblivion his early speeches on the bank, the tariff, and internal im-provements was scarcely surprising; it was more interesting, certainly, that he omitted his speech of May 6, 1834, in reply to Jackson's protest against the censure resolutions, along with all the subsequent speeches against the Expunging Resolution. Both *Life* and *Speeches* seemed designed to placate the gray eminence at the Hermitage, who had yet to declare himself on the Democratic nomination. Harper added the caveat, "subsequent to his elec-tion as vice-president," to the title of the *Speeches*. Embarrassed by this con-troversy, the publisher was also disappointed by the sales of the work. It had hoped for a repetition of the firm's success with Harrison's campaign life and had planned accordingly. But many congressmen and others who had prom-ised large subscriptions had trimmed them substantially. By June, only eigh-teen thousand copies had been sold.[18]

Calhoun staked his challenge to Van Buren for the nomination on the mode of constituting the national convention of the party. Everywhere, since the adoption of the convention system, delegates had been elected in prelimi-nary state conventions under a measure of central control. This corre-sponded to the system of presidential election in which electors everywhere were chosen on a statewide "general ticket," with the notable exception of South Carolina, where they were chosen by the legislature. Calhoun at-tacked the existing nominating system and called instead for the election of delegates in congressional districts. The challenge was issued in *An Appeal to the Democratic Party,* which Rhett drafted, in January 1843. "The voice of the people," this pamphlet maintained, "must be taken in parts to obtain the whole."[19] Local election was acclaimed as more democratic. It broke the despotism of majority rule and gave minorities a voice. The proposed reform blended neatly into Calhoun's political theory. He had other, more practical reasons for advocating it, however. Without the proposed reform he could not dent Van Buren's strength in the North and West. Calhoun's following outside the South was in small pockets, like the sect in New York City, which might be productive of delegates in local contests but not in state conventions. Moreover, by standing for local election the Calhounites were well positioned to attack Van Buren as a party boss, "hackneyed in the by-paths of mercenary politics," whose despotic power lay in caucus management and dictation. This played into the familiar image of the Fox of Kinderhook. In his first campaign for the presidency, Calhoun had employed much the same rhetoric against William H. Crawford, when the evil was embodied in the congressional caucus. Now, twenty years later, Van Buren was Calhoun's Crawford.

But the present system of delegate selection by conventions packed with the corrupt functionaries of centralized party machines, Calhoun argued, was "a hundred times more objectionable" than King Caucus of old. The caucus had been dethroned in order to admit the people directly into the nomination and election of the president. Instead, control passed to party machines. In the *Life* Calhoun expressed his profound disappointment with this outcome even as he recognized the organizational imperatives that led to it: "The chance is between discord with all its consequences, and the dictation of party leaders with all its effects."[20] The problem was perfectly obvious in the Empire State. With local elections in thirty-six districts, how was a party to achieve consensus, much less control? Van Buren hinted that while he might be willing to gratify Calhoun, his associates, Silas Wright and others, had insuperable objections. They did not fear the loss of a single district from the introduction of Calhoun's plan, and they doubted Van Buren would lose anything nationally; but they did fear "spurious representation," stemming from spurious notions of democracy, and consequent confusion, discredit, and disorder.[21] Whatever the merits of the proposed reform, Democratic leaders in other states did not take kindly to instruction on democracy from South Carolina. And in South Carolina, no one was more opposed than Calhoun to any innovation, including statewide elections, that would fracture the political unity he and his friends imposed on the state. Of course, the reform appealed to politicans who were out of power or out of favor and who saw in the "district ticket" the means to unseat the party leaders.[22] But such support availed little. The Calhoun campaign was more successful with another demand: deferral of the national convention from December 1843, which conformed to precedent, to May 1844. This would give Calhoun's followers more time to organize and would also allow more time for political events to unfold—events like the annexation of Texas—that might favor his candidacy. The Van Buren Democrats finally agreed to the demand—and lived to regret it.

The first critical test for Calhoun came in the Virginia Convention on March 2, 1843. Father Ritchie, as it turned out, may have changed his tune on Calhoun, but not his colors; and the Richmond Junto, "the tail of the Albany Regency" in Calhounite opinion, held firm control of the convention. Ritchie was eager for his friend, Andrew Stevenson, to become vice president, which furnished an additional inducement to support the northern presidential candidate. The Calhoun forces were outnumbered and outmaneuvered. Losing Virginia was a hard blow to Calhoun's candidacy. The *Mercury* cried fraud, but there was nothing to be done. A month later, in the congressional elections, Hunter and two other incumbents associated with Calhoun were defeated. Again his managers cried fraud, in this instance the fraud of gerrymandering the districts to shut out Calhoun's adherents.[23]

The troubles of the campaign produced jealousies and irritations among Calhoun's advisers. McDuffie charged that Rhett, with his arrogant manner, brought more odium than honor to the candidate. "I know of no man who is injuring you so much," the senator wrote. Pickens had no confidence in Elmore and, in fact, disapproved of the whole forward strategy of the campaign. "Your position in the old Democratic or Jackson party was peculiar and had been for years," Pickens wrote in July. "There was deep jealousy and ill feeling towards you in it. Your great talents and services were just beginning to increase your popularity. . . . Your policy was to stand still, and let Van Buren draw the secret opposition of all the other aspirants until he was run down and by that time your strength would be such as to secure an easy triumph. But if you attempted to move upon and make issues in advance in that old party they would become alarmed and all would move against you." Precisely that had occurred on the convention issue, where the old party leaders adroitly played up the idea of South Carolina dictation to draw the fire toward Calhoun and away from Van Buren.[24] Other problems centered on the Washington newspaper, *The Spectator*. Circulation was poor, and it was starved for funds. Maxcy complained of the piddling support provided by Calhoun's Carolina friends. "Can't you rouse them?" he pleaded in August. Calhoun made a gesture or two in that direction; but in South Carolina, where there was no experience in national two-party politics, the energies and talents for waging elections were feeble at best. Joseph Scoville had been brought to Washington to conduct *The Spectator*. But he was overzealous; his bustling, aggressive style offended the southern gentlemen in charge of the campaign. Scoville appropriated the title "Secretary of the Calhoun General Committee," and issued a circular naming Levi Woodbury of New Hampshire to the second place on the ticket. Neither Calhoun nor the Charleston committee had been consulted. No one disapproved of Woodbury, but the naming of a running mate was premature and could only injure Calhoun. In this instance, the candidate himself intervened, and Scoville was removed.[25]

The knockout blow to the campaign was administered by the New York Democratic Convention, at Syracuse, on September 5. Maxcy had written an address and resolutions, adopted by a Calhoun meeting in New York City, to serve as instructions for the election of delegates to the national convention at Baltimore. But they were peremptorily rejected by the Syracuse convention, which went on to elect a slate of delegates on a general ticket pledged to Van Buren. Calhoun, unwilling to admit defeat, declared the outcome of the Syracuse convention fortunate for his candidacy, since it clearly drew the issue between the people and the "juggling politicians."[26] The Charleston committee immediately issued a broadside accepting the challenge thrown down at Syracuse and, in defiant tones, risking the rupture of the party on the principle of district election. This reaction ruffled the feathers of many Democrats, including some who had heretofore been supportive of Calhoun's candidacy. As one of them wrote in the *Democratic Review* in October, Calhoun had already tried the good feelings of fellow Democrats by attempting to dictate nominating procedures, and to follow that with an implied threat to walk out of the Baltimore convention unless he could have his way was more than the party could tolerate.[27] Defeat in New York was followed by a series of defeats in New England. Although Calhoun had shown strength there, Van Buren prevailed handily in all the fall elections. In the South, Alabama was lost, and Georgia alone adhered to Calhoun. Yet Georgia was an embarrassment. The Calhoun delegates had been appointed by the legislative caucus and confirmed in the state convention, the people having had no voice in the proceedings. Georgia seemed to show the hypocrisy of Calhoun's democratic professions.[28] The death blow to the campaign came in December when the House of Representaties convened under Democratic control and proceeded to elect Van Burenites to all the offices from speaker to doorkeeper.

Calhoun took up his pen to draft an address announcing his withdrawal from the Baltimore convention. The grounds offered for this action were two: the tariff and the mode of constituting the convention. Hunter and Rhett deemed the former important because of the virtual certainty that the major presidential candidates would be protectionists of one degree or another. "A run between Mr. Clay and Mr. Van Buren . . . will utterly demoralize the South, to be followed by the loss of the good old State rights doctrines . . . ," Hunter wrote. "The object now is, not victory, but to preserve our position and principles; the only way, under [the] circumstances, by which we can preserve our influence and the safety of the South."[29] At the urging of Maxcy, Elmore, and Lewis, however, Calhoun scratched the tariff as a consideration in his decision and also softened the recriminatory tone of the address. Arguing that he could not permit his name to go before a convention constituted on false principles, Calhoun forcefully restated his position on the election of delegates in districts "straight from the people." The present system was not only despotic but "destructive of the foundation on which the whole structure of the State rights doctrine is reared."[30] The address was finally published at the end of January, just in time for the Virginia convention, where it was expected to produce an explosion. But the Calhoun delegates were conciliatory, even submissive. Pledging their support to "the Democratic candidate," the delegates turned the convention into "a love feast." "The palmetto has cottoned to the cabbage at last," George Prentice commented on these Democratic nuptials.[31] The *Mercury* immediately struck the Calhoun banner. This caused consternation in the ranks, since the address was obviously framed as a withdrawal from the Baltimore convention, not as a withdrawal of candidacy. Some Calhounites talked of an independent candidacy, perhaps in combination with Tyler; and they accused the Charleston Regency of unseemly haste in striking Calhoun's colors. "He has been deceived and ruined by [his] supposed friends." But Calhoun uttered no complaint. Abstention was now the true policy, he said, adding that he was relieved to be free of "the wretched scramble" and looked forward to returning to the work on government commenced over a year before.[32]

Calhoun spoke of his retirement as permanent. Politics had been taken over by spoilsmen and demagogues. "The school of Burr has triumphed over that of Jefferson." It was no longer a fit vocation for a man of principle. Approached about returning to the Senate in the place Huger would make for him, Calhoun declined, saying he could do no good there.[33] How long he might have held out in the normal course of things cannot be known, for there occurred on February 28, 1844, one of those random events which in its consequences makes a mockery of every attempt to impose some grand law on the history of nations. On that day the USS *Princeton*, a new steam-powered battleship, played host to a large presidential party in an excursion on the Potomac. Upon the last firing of one of the cannon, as many of the guests loked on, the gun itself exploded, killing instantly five of them and several seamen. Virgil Maxcy was one of the dead, as were Abel B. Upshur, secretary of state, and Thomas Walker Gilmer, secretary of the navy. The loss of the two cabinet officers was devastating to the Tyler admininstration, of course; and, with the addition of Maxcy, it was politically devastating to Calhoun. The next day Henry A. Wise called on McDuffie to propose that Calhoun be invited to become secretary of state. The senator concurred and without further ado wrote to Calhoun asking if he would accept the office. Wise, meanwhile, carried the proposal to Tyler. The congressman later said that Tyler broke into a rage over what had been done and declared that Calhoun was the worst possible choice for the office, since he would stamp "slavery" on the administration's great project, the annexation of Texas. But, so the story goes, the president yielded rather than repudiate the offer that had already been made. In sober truth, Tyler seems to have recognized at once, as did almost everyone else, that Calhoun was the obvious man for the crisis.[34] The more interesting question is why Calhoun chose to join an odious, bankrupt, and expiring administration. He accepted at once—the Senate had already consented—and was on duty in the State Department on April 1.

Calhoun accepted with such alacrity because he saw an opportunity to serve the South and the Union by the consummation of Texas annexation and settlement of the Oregon boundary. And who can doubt that he also saw an opportunity, as James G. Blaine later suggested, to exact "an historic revenge which the noblest minds might indulge" on Martin Van Buren?[35] The project for annexation of the Republic of Texas was well advanced in the spring of 1844. A treaty was secretly in negotiation. Calhoun had had nothing officially to do with this, although unofficially he had been kept informed and offered his advice during the silent progress of annexation. Gilmer, while still a Virginia congressman, had given the first hint of the project in a letter published in the newspapers in January 1843. Alleging that Great Britain had designs on Texas, Gilmer artfully appealed for annexation as a matter of national interest and national benefit. The letter was, said Benton, like "a clap of thunder in a clear sky."[36] He detected Calhoun's hand in it. But this was an hallucination, like the senator's elaborately composed theory of a Calhoun conspiracy for the annexation of Texas either to destroy Van Buren or to force southern secession or both. Gilmer had pressed the Texas question on Calhoun during his last months in Congress, but there is no indication that he actively pursued it. He was sometimes urged to make it an issue in his campaign for the Democratic nomination. He never did, not even after every hope of northern support had vanished. He had already contracted ideas of the interconnections between British capitalism and British abolitionism that made him receptive to charges of imperial designs on Texas. Duff Green, while abroad, had harped constantly on the thesis that British philanthropy simply masked a drive for world industrial and commerical hegemony. Having made the discovery that the free labor of her colonies—the cotton producers in the East Indies, the sugar producers in the West Indies—could not compete with the same products of slave labor, Britain set out to "abolitionize the competition." Thus the argument that traced the British campaign against the slave trade to mercenary motives was extended to British foreign policy generally. Modern economic historians, with more sophistication but somewhat less cynicism, have described a theory of free-trade imperialism to explain the complexity of British motives.[37]

A British plot engineered by Lord Aberdeen to abolitionize Texas, potentially a major cotton producer, fit right in with the thesis. In July, Upshur received a report from Green that Aberdeen had talked to an American abolitionist and agreed on behalf of the government to make a large interest-free loan to Texas as an indemnity for the abolition of slavery. Upshur used this information to reopen currently stalled annexation negotiations with the Texas government. At the same time he wrote a long letter to Calhoun outlining a frightful scenario should the British plot succeed. The slaves in the Southwest will flee to Texas; the slaveholders will seek to reclaim their chattels by force; this will cause war between the United States and Britain; the northern states will refuse assistance, leading, in turn, to disunion; and Britain will flood the country with her manufactures, causing depression, disorder, and revolution. The only escape, Upshur concluded, was to annex Texas as a slave state. He begged Calhoun for his views and asked him to broach the subject in the South. In reply, Calhoun encouraged Upshur to pursue diplomacy with Britain and to educate the American people on the necessity of annexation.[38] The secretary's subsequent actions conformed to this advice, though it is misleading to say he was guided or inspired to Calhoun. The *Madisonian*, the administration newspaper in the capital, started a propaganda campaign, which culminated in Robert Walker's sensational *Letter Relative to the Annexation of Texas* early in the new year. Edward Everett, in London, was instructed to protest the British government's intervention in Texas and to obtain the incriminating evidence that would support the extraordinary measure of a treaty of annexation. Aberdeen emphatically and repeatedly denied the report of a plot to abolish slavery in Texas or any other unfriendly designs in that quarter.

Undaunted, Tyler and Upshur went ahead with the still secret treaty project. At the opening of "the president-making session" of Congress, Tyler mentioned annexation but withheld commitment, and the question was not discussed. In Washington for the term of the Supreme Court, Webster picked up the scent of annexation. Upshur was discreet, but hearing him allude to "a particular project" he hoped to accomplish, Webster "felt Texas go through me," as he reported to a Boston friend.[39] Annexation would mean war with Mexico, which had never recognized Texas independence, and as it involved the expansion of slavery it threatened the Union. Webster had publicly opposed the project when it first arose in 1837. Now the time had come, he decided, to arouse the country against it. He persuaded Winthrop to introduce anti-annexation resolutions in the House. He alerted Gales and Seaton to the danger. "It is high time to alarm the country," he wrote to Charles Allen, a Whig leader in the Bay State, on March 13. And he asked Allen to see to the publication of a letter he had addressed to a group of citizens of Worcester in January. The letter reiterated the dangers he had pointed out in 1837, reiterated his opinion that annexation was unconstitutional, and concluded with the ancient wisdom, "We have a Sparta. Let us embellish it." Webster's letter, the first salvo against annexation, was circulating in the nation's press when the *Intelligencer* disclosed that a secret treaty of annexation had been concluded with Texas.[40] The news sent shock waves through the North. Stock prices on Wall Street plunged. In the South annexation revived flagging Democratic spirits and worried the Whigs.

Entering the State Department, Calhoun stepped precisely into Upshur's shoes. On April 18, after the treaty was signed but before it was submitted to the Senate, he seized upon an obsolete dispatch from Aberdeen, which Upshur had left on his desk, and made it the occasion for joining the defense of annexation to the defense of slavery. Calhoun's letter to Sir Richard Pakenham, the British minister, took the official British avowal of seeking "the general abolition of slavery throughout the world" as a direct threat to the United States, regardless of the disavowal of designs on Texas. British economic and diplomatic pressure must inevitably place Texas under her control, lead to abolition there, and endanger slavery in the United States. The British government could think what it pleased about the African race, Calhoun went on, but she could not force her policy on the United States or alter the evidence of at least half a century that the Africans fared better under conditions of servitude than of freedom. Calhoun cited data from the recent census purporting to show that within the Negro population the ratio of deaf and dumb, blind, idiotic, and insane in the free states was 1:96, compared to 1:172 in the slave states. Everything went to prove that the race had attained its highest elevation of morals, intelligence, and civilization in the slave-holding South. It was an unusual diplomatic dispatch. Pakenham answered briefly, repeating British assurances of peace and tranquillity in Texas; Calhoun rejoined, and the British minister, realizing he was being used in a propaganda campaign that looked more to domestic than to foreign politics, let the correspondence die.[41]

Politicians then and historians since have debated Calhoun's motives for writing the Pakenham Letter.[42] The administration line on annexation was that it was strictly a question of national interest unconnected with slavery. Calhoun's letter, which went to the Senate along with the treaty and became public knowledge on April 27, placed annexation on pro-slavery grounds. Could he have been oblivious to the effect of this? Some said that he was and had simply committed a blunder. But this was unconvincing. On the contrary, Blair contended in the *Globe*, "He knew that it [the Pakenham Letter] would array the whole North against the treaty, and prove fatal to it. His aim, then, was to make it an exclusively southern sectional question, to make himself the champion of the southern rights involved, and take the chances for advancement held out by a project which involved in its consummation the dissolution of the confederacy." For the *Globe*, as for Benton, the letter was the final act in Calhoun's Texas conspiracy, even though, ironically, it looked to the defeat of annexation. "Disunion is at the bottom of the long-concealed Texas machination . . . ," Benton declared in the Senate. "Under the pretext of getting Texas into the Union, the scheme is to get the South out of it."[43] But this imputed to Calhoun a capacity for cunning, intrigue, and double-dealing he did not possess, and falsely ascribed to him disunionist aims in 1844. To some degree, certainly, Calhoun was actuated by political considerations. By linking Texas annexation to the defense of slavery, he divided political parties at the Mason and Dixon Line, terrifying Clay and the Whigs and undercutting Van Buren in the South. A no less important consideration, however, was Calhoun's desire to use the diplomatic exchange with Pakenham, as he explained, "to bring out our cause . . . fully and favorably before the world."[44] Racism was part of that cause, and Calhoun, with his penchant for theory, sought to found it on allegedly scientific principles. In recent years he had given more and more open expression to his racial feelings. In the previous Congress he had attempted, unsuccessfully, to exclude free Negroes and mulattoes from enlistment in the Navy except as cooks and stewards. "It was wrong," he maintained, "to bring those who have to sustain the honor and glory of the country down to the footing of the negro race—to be degraded by being mingled and mixed up with that inferior race."[45] He took a distinct interest in the work of the early American ethnologists—Josiah Nott, George R. Glidden, and others—who furnished a bogus science to corroborate the data of a bogus census. This thinking was reflected in the instructions Calhoun penned to the United States Minister to France in August. Here, more than in the Pakenham Letter, he dwelled on the debility of the African race, except in bondage, as well as on Britain's desire to abolish slavery in order to cripple and destroy her rivals.[46] The cause of slavery, which was the cause of the South, of white supremacy, of civilization, was also a national cause demanding national protection and commitment, in Calhoun's view. The defense of slavery in Texas and its admission as a slave state had become necessary to secure slavery in the Union. Annexation was thus another link—a vital link—in the chain of nationalization of the institution.

On the day the Pakenham Letter was published, the press also carried the separate letters of Clay and Van Buren opposing the immediate annexation of Texas. These letters, more than Calhoun's, doomed the annexation treaty in the Senate. And the damage Calhoun wrought against Van Buren was nothing compared to the damage the New Yorker did to himself. Ritchie and the Junto withdrew their support, dissolving the old alliance, and Van Buren's candidacy faded everywhere in the South. As a result, Van Buren was unable to muster the two-thirds vote required by the rules of the Democratic Convention in Baltimore for the nomination. On the ninth ballot the delegates nominated the "dark horse" candidate, James K. Polk of Tennessee. Calhoun rejoiced in this outcome. Polk was an annexationist, like his political father, Andrew Jackson; his nomination would tend to unite the South, break up the Whig party, and eliminate Clay, for so long a distracting power in southern politics. Given this flattering prospect, Calhoun told his friends, the best course for South Carolina was to "do nothing."[47]

Barnwell Rhett disagreed. The defeat of a bill—the McKay Bill—to adjust the tariff downward, together with the rejection of the Texas treaty, both by Democratic votes, proved once again that ordinary politics offered no hope of saving the South. Before Congress adjourned Rhett tried to get up an address of the South Carolina delegation proposing that the state be placed in a position to act on its sovereignty the succeeding spring. McDuffie backed Rhett in this move. Even Governor Hammond suddenly found himself in Rhett's corner. "[But] at the eleventh hour," Hammond reported, "Calhoun came in and broke it up, chanting praises to the Union and to peace."[48] Rhett was not finished. On his return home, addressing a public dinner of his constituents at Bluffton, he assailed the Democratic party, acknowledged his divergence from Calhoun, and called on the state to redeem the pledge of 1833 unless Congress, in the next session, acted justly toward the South. Several of the Bluffton toasts became notorious because they betrayed defiance of Calhoun even as they saluted him: "We will follow him as long as he is true to us"; "If South Carolina acts without him, I am with her—if he leads, we will follow."[49] All through the lowcountry parishes ardent young spirits, who had grown up under Calhoun's tutelage, became restless and threatened to rebel. The *Mercury* joined the Bluffton Movement, as it was now called, and Calhoun suddenly turned into a hero of the rival Charleston *Courier*. Langdon Cheves, an old secessionist, interrupted his retirement to reiterate his opposition to nullification by a single state, although he advocated resistance in cooperation with other southern states. "You sleep on a volcano," Cheves warned. "But as often as the tongue lisps resistance, you are met by the eternal cry of the Union! the Union! the danger of the Union! and you are subdued by it. Until you can throw off this thralldom . . . you are unprepared for resistance."[50]

This thralldom to the Union was Calhoun's work, of course. No man, he had boasted to dissident southern congressmen, prized the Union more than he. In August he intervened to crush the Bluffton Movement. It was the worst possible time to raise the specter of disunion, he insisted. The South had to contend not only against the tariff but against abolitionism; and to defeat that, and to annex Texas, the South must remain in the Union and elect Polk. He had not, as had been reported, abandoned nullification. The survival of the Union itself depended upon the power of nullification, he maintained, but it should not be employed where it was self-defeating. The recipient of this epistle, Armistead Burt, quickly dropped his support of Bluffton and, according to Rhett, helped squelch the movement. Elmore, at Calhoun's prompting, called a mass meeting of the party at Charleston, which pledged its support to Polk and backed Calhoun's leadership. The Bluffton Movement wilted. Returning to Washington in the fall, the secretary stopped at Charleston and brought John A. Stuart, the *Mercury*'s errant editor, back into the fold.[51] Calhoun's was still the solitary star shining in the southern firmament.

It had been only nine months since Calhoun and Rhett were in perfect accord on the treachery of party and the curse of president making. Calhoun, of course, strenuously denied that his "do nothing" course, his opposition to "the action party," was dictated by aspirations for the presidency in 1848. But skeptical politicians refused to believe him. He was sacrificing South Carolina and the South "on the altar of his ambition," Hammond opined. The hope of the presidency was absurd, yet it continued to bewitch Calhoun just as his star continued to bewitch, and paralyze, the South.[52]

4. Clay and the Election of 1844

The gloom that had enveloped Henry Clay in Washington thickened upon his return to Kentucky in the spring of 1842. Everywhere he found greater economic "embarrassment and distress" than he had imagined. Clay had himself suddenly fallen into heavy debt. He resumed a desultory law practice in partnership with his son James, took out a mortgage on Ashland, and explored various business ventures to repair the family fortune. Writing to John Quincy Adams of the sad condition of the country, Clay observed, "The contemplation of what we are, what we were, and what we might have been is enough to sicken the heart. But it is our duty not to despair."[1] In May Lord Morpeth stopped for a visit of several days. He marveled at the luxuriance of the Bluegrass country and found Clay his usual affable self. Morpeth was followed by Martin Van Buren, together with his traveling companion, James K. Paulding. For all their political wars, Van Buren and Clay remained good friends. Many people expected, of course, that they would become the presidential candidates of their respective parties in 1844; and in that year they would be charged with having earlier negotiated the "Treaty of Ashland," wherein they agreed to cooperate in shutting out challengers and in opposing the annexation of Texas, thereby keeping both parties in their traces.² But such an agreement probably never crossed the minds of these old warriors who pleasantly traversed a large field of political reminiscence at Ashland.

The Old Prince feigned indifference to the presidential election. On June 9 the citizens of Lexington staged a great festival in his honor. Toasted as "Farmer of Ashland, Patriot and Philanthropist—the American statesman and unrivaled orator of the age,"* Clay responded with a two-hour speech that, like his conversation with Van Buren, also dwelled on the past. He reviewed his early political career and thanked the people of Kentucky for their unfailing loyalty and support. He recalled, in particular, the gross libel of "corruption and bargain" in 1824 and, for the first time, publicly admitted, not the crime charged against him, but the error of judgment in accepting the appointment as secretary of state. He painted an appalling picture of national decline in the decade since 1832 and laid the responsibility on the head of Andrew Jackson. Without foreclosing the possibility he would become a presidential candidate, Clay denied he already was one, describing himself as a passive spectator of the movements in his behalf. He concluded with an exhortation to the Whigs in his audience: "Arouse! Awake! Shake off the dew-drops that glitter on your garments, and once more march to battle and to victory!"³ "No speech ever came in better time and more admirably," wrote Willie Mangum. ". . . It has fallen with electrical effect," all the more so because it coincided with another insolent veto by Captain Tyler. As if by prearranged signal, Whig state conventions in Georgia and Maine nominated Clay; mass meetings in New York, Philadelphia, and elsewhere did the same. William G. "Parson" Brownlow captured the prevailing sentiment in the banner he spread upon the Jonesboro *Whig:* "Henry Clay vs. THE WORLD." The only flicker of opposition, that of General Scott, died by July.⁴

In the fall Clay traveled to Indianapolis in order to fulfill what he described as "an old engagement" to speak there. Inevitably the journey took on the trappings of a campaign swing. Harry of the West had lost some of his popularity north of the Ohio by backing policies considered hostile to common settlers and the interest of new states. He may have hoped that the trip would

---

*It would be a shame to omit the rest of the sentiment: "—illustrious abroad, beloved at home: in a long career of eminent public service, often, like *Aristides*, he breasted the raging storm of passion and delusion, and by offering himself a sacrifice, saved the republic; and now, like *Cincinnatus* and *Washington*, having voluntarily retired to the tranquil walks of private life, the grateful hearts of his countrymen will do him ample justice; but come what may, *Kentucky will stand by him*, and still continue to cherish and defend, as her own, the fame of a son who has emblazoned her escutcheon with immortal renown."

put a shine on his western image. He spoke first before the Ohio Whig Convention in Dayton. It was a boisterous throng.

> To Dayton we have come my boys,
> All in a great array
> And we will sing and shout aloud,
> Hurrah for Henry Clay!
> In eighteen hundred forty-four
> The people all will say,
> That for our President we'll have
> The *Patriot Henry Clay!*
> Hurrah, hurrah, hurrah for Henry Clay
> Hurrah, hurrah, hurrah for Henry Clay.

Clay spoke often—more than he wanted. Arriving in one small town at the end of an exhausting day of travel, he was determined only to show himself to the crowd that had gathered, but hearing someone shout, "Hurrah for General Jackson!" Clay fired back, "Hurrah for General Jackson, that's your cry, is it? And where's your country?" then launched into a thirty-minute lecture comparing the fate of the country under Jackson to that of Rome under Caesar and Pompey, who were also hurrahed by the people.[5]

Prior to his arrival at Richmond, Indiana, on Saturday, October 1, Clay had learned that a deputation of the Indiana Anti-Slavery Society wished to present a petition got up at its annual meeting, just concluded, calling on him to emancipate his slaves. Arrangements were made for the presentation at the hotel on Sunday morning. But at the welcoming ceremonies on Saturday afternoon, attended by up to ten thousand people (the crowd was swelled by the Yearly Meeting of the Indiana Society of Friends at Richmond), the Whig congressman who presided announced that if the abolitionists had anything to present to Clay they should do it openly and publicly. Whereupon Hiram Mendenhall, amid great commotion, made his way to the platform and handed the petition to the congressman. It was read. Clay then replied at length in a speech that, while not wholly spontaneous, was a remarkable instance of his oratorical readiness. Slavery was an enormous evil, Clay said, but it was part of the fabric of American life and institutions and should be dealt with on its own terms rather than on the terms of abstract morality. As in the past, he condemned notions of immediate emancipation and the political agitation of slavery issues. Against the "monomaniacs," he commended the quiet but resolute example of the Quakers, who opposed the abolitionist petition. The petitioners knew nothing of his slaves, Clay said, yet they presumed to tell him what was best for them. "Here is Charles," he continued, turning to the familiar figure of his personal servant grinning broadly at the side of the platform. "He is in a free state and entirely at liberty to leave me if he desires to do so, and if you who present the petition will prepare a place for my slaves at home where they can be provided for, and enabled to make a living, I will gladly release them all; but as it is, it would be an act of cruelty." Standing directly over Mendenhall, Clay closed with a devastating rebuke: "Go home, Mr. Mendenhall, and attend to your own business, and I will endeavor to see to mine."[6]

"Go home, Mr. Mendenhall!" would resound through the coming campaign. Most Americans considered it a merited rebuke of meddlesome agitators of various causes, including abolitionism. Seventy-nine years later it would be permanently memoralized at Richmond by a bronze tablet affixed to a huge granite boulder. The abolitionists would never forgive Clay for the reprimand or permit him to forget it. He had committed "the unpardonable sin." For James G. Birney, head of the Liberty party, the speech confirmed what he and his friends had known since 1839. Henry Clay, "of all our public men, [is] the most dangerous, because the boldest or the most insidious, according to the exigency, and always the most plausible in his attacks on the cause of human freedom."[7] Clay reached his destination, Indianapolis, on October 5. There he spoke to a huge throng gathered at the governor's farm east of the city. Nothing he said at Indianapolis overcame the fears of antislavery Whigs that he could not carry the states of the Old Northwest.

In November the Kentucky Whig Convention, at Frankfort, added its endorsement of Clay, and the candidate appeared to address the assemblage. (The reporter noted a sign of changing times: the barbecue following the convention omitted alcoholic beverages.)[8] Despite the swelling unanimity on its choice of a candidate, the Whig party was badly defeated in the fall elections. Webster, unable to resist the temptation to crow, released to the press a letter he had written to a Massachusetts Whig in August predicting that Clay's nomination in the Bay State and elsewhere would bring defeat at the polls. Among the Kentuckian's friends the publication was seen as further evidence of the animosity that consumed Webster "and changed the bold statesman and generous rival into the envious and designing foe, who watched the opportunity to stab and would 'smile yet murder while he smiled.' "[9] Clay had not known whether to laugh or cry over Webster's Faneuil Hall speech. "Was ever a man so fallen as Mr. Webster?" he asked. It was "a most vulnerable production" and he was tempted to reply. He checked himself, however, and left the reply to others, like John M. Clayton, who delivered a powerful defense of Clay and the Compromise Act in a speech at Philadelphia.[10]

As winter came on Clay took passage down the river to New Orleans. For three months he suspended political correspondence and kept to his resolution against public appearances and speeches. Although he had business in the courts at New Orleans, Clay went there mainly for reasons of health and pleasure. His older brother John lived in New Orleans, as did a son-in-law and grandchildren. His claim on the political affections of Louisianans antedated the War of 1812, indeed antedated statehood; and he counted among his friends many of the great sugar planters, like Alexander Porter of Oak Lawn, who were again growing rich because of the tariff of 1842. He was constantly assured that the state was "thoroughly Whig," yet, he remarked ruefully, it had never voted for him. And as events unfolded it would not in 1844.[11] Clay was a hero in New Orleans. Even his attendance at the St. Charles Theater was announced in the playbills; he, more than William Macready or Edwin Forrest, was the star attraction. The unique chemistry between Clay and New Orleans was captured in the Dutch-accented verses that appeared in the New Orleans *Tropic* after his arrival for the winter season.

> Vell, Henry you're in town at last,
>   Ve're wery glad to see you,
> Ve'll breakfast and ve'll dine you,
>   And ve'll sup you and ve'll tea you;
> Ve'll have some very cozy chats
>   And that old hand ve'll shake,
> Vich, ven the country said the vord,
>   Vas never known to quake.
>
> It's wery fortunate for us
>   That yu veren't born a Turk,
> You might, among the ladies here,
>   Do so much orrid work.
> They think of you the blessed day,
>   At night ven in their beds;
> Its vell their *politics* to turn
>   But not to turn *their heads*.
>
> They soon vill be a beggin you
>   To give em locks of hair,
> Take my advice, don't do it Hal,
>   You haven't much to spare.
> Vat though you easy can command
>   The *Vigs* of all the State
> You von't be werry anxious for—
>   A vig upon your pate.[12]

Clay returned to Lexington in March persuaded there was a rising Whig tide in the South. He delivered a blistering oratorical attack against the Tyler administration. He huddled with his Kentucky associates, whose optimism was scarcely less repressible than his own. The inner political circle included Crittenden, who had succeeded Clay in the Senate; Robert Letcher, the governor; Garrett Davis, congressman from the Ashland district (as it was now called); an old friend and neighbor, Leslie Combs; and his cousin and antislavery conscience, Cassius Marcellus Clay. All admonished Clay to stop making speeches. Let him keep cool, stay home, and hold his jaw, was Letcher's advice. "In fact, he must be *caged*—that's the point, *cage him!*"[13] For a man whose life had been a grand procession, who was a master of political dramaturgy, and who thrived on public applause, caging would prove difficult. Yet Clay easily rejected the importunities of Clayton and others to tour the East during the summer. "If you were here and saw my lawns, trees, flocks and herds—this paradise of a Country . . . ," he wrote in May, "you would not be so unreasonable as to propose that I should be sweated to death in the Atlantic cities this summer."[14]

A newspaper in Lexington, the *Observer and Reporter,* and another in

Washington, were directly devoted to Clay's cause, while 95 percent of the Whig press nationally sang his praises. Every crossroads, it seemed, soon had its Clay Club. Tokens of affection and esteem—bolts of cloth, barrels of salt— poured into Ashland.¹⁵ Artists came to take his likeness. The grandest of these works was John Neagle's six-by-ten full-length portrait commissioned by the National Clay Club of Philadelphia. Clay stands in a portico, the pillar of Constitutional Liberty on his left, as he gazes with a beaming countenance upon the emblems of American freedom and prosperity: the flag; a globe on which Latin America is seen; a plow, anvil, and shuttle; and a ship under sail in the distance. A fine mezzotint engraving by John Sartain, in 1843, made Neagle's perhaps the best known likeness of Clay. Its closest rival was an engraving, after J. W. Dodge's painting, of "The Farmer of Ashland," in which Clay appears seated amid the rural scenery of his estate. Musicians sang Clay's praises in literal fact. The most famous of the ballads, published in New York with a lithograph likeness and an autograph letter on the cover, was John H. Hewitt's "The Kentucky Gentleman":

> The fine Kentucky gentleman,
> Whose heart is in his hand;
> The rare Kentucky gentleman,
> The noblest in the land.¹⁶

Writers assayed his biography and edited his speeches. Two editions of the speeches, one of them complete, the other nearly so, appeared in 1843. Both were prefaced with typically florid memoirs. *The Life and Public Services of Henry Clay*, by Epes Sargent, was the first substantial biography since Prentice's a decade earlier. A forty-year-old Massachusetts native, Sargent had become well acquainted with his subject while employed as the Washington correspondent of the Boston *Atlas*. He wrote with Clay's blessing and even managed to extract from him an occasional reminiscence. Published in a cheap pamphlet edition during the ensuing presidential campaign, Sargent's *Life of Clay* reached tens of thousands of readers.¹⁷ A stream of cheap books and pamphlets—*The Clay Minstrel, The Clay Almanac, The Ashland Textbook*—began to come off the presses eighteen months before the candidate's nomination.

One of the problems that worried Clay during the restful summer at Ashland was what to do about Daniel Webster. Instead of reingratiating himself with Whig leaders upon leaving the Tyler cabinet, Webster made a speech at Baltimore that infuriated many of them. Tying up with the British movement toward repeal of the Corn Laws, he advocated an attempt to regulate commerce between the two countries by a treaty in which the United States would trade off high protective duties on manufactures for low British duties on American agricultural exports. Webster acknowledged the difficulties of this course, including the constitutional objection (the power to regulate foreign commerce in a legislative power), but argued that the greater permanence of treaties as well as the mutality of benefits recommended it. At the same time, curiously, he firmly opposed reciprocity treaties in the carrying trade and commended the old British navigation law as the appropriate model for the United States.[18] The speech was an enigma. Penetrating the veil of motives, some observers supposed it represented another answer to Webster's question, "Where am I to go?" He would go to London to negotiate a treaty of commerce or, as the Boston group that inspired the speech seemed to imagine, he would be named by the president head of a high commission, rather like a British royal commission, to develop in concert with other nations a liberal commercial code. Others believed that Webster, having been alienated from his old following among Whig manufacturers like Lawrence, was attempting to cultivate wealthy merchants in foreign trade, like David Sears, the head of the Boston group who had corresponded with him. Still others saw in the speech a bold *demarche* toward conciliation and union with Calhoun. Webster had "lent himself to Southern folly," said Lawrence, and sealed his doom. Perhaps his veiled aim was to break up the tariff party in the North and draw western farmers into an alliance with southern planters. Clayton took this view in a scorching answer to the Baltimore speech. Such a motive was consonant with opposition to Clay, and if Webster persisted in it must eventually drive him into the arms of Calhoun. Whatever Webster's motive or aim, his speech fell wide of the mark. There was the usual reception when he returned to Boston at the end of May, but newspapers reported that Faneuil Hall was "barely respectably filled." So devastating was the response to the scheme of commercial treaties that it was soon as dead as last year's almanac.[19]

Webster appeared to better advantage in his old role as the Yankee Demosthenes, dedicating the Bunker Hill Monument on June 17, 1843. "A duty has been performed," he declared, recalling the commencement of the lofty monument eighteen years before. The spectacle was sublime—a vast multitude crowded the ampitheater rising from the platform at the base of the monument. Webster dedicated it not to the battle whose name it bore, nor to the men who died there nor even to the principles of the Revolution, but to the grand sentiment of American nationality. "This column stands on Union." Again recalling Americans to "the sacred trust . . . received from our fathers," the orator acknowledged that his threadbare eloquence was unequal to the occasion. "[The monument] is itself the orator. . . . The powerful speaker stands motionless before us." Waldo Emerson underscored the point in his assessment of the oration, which he thought feeble compared to earlier efforts. "It was evident that there was the monument, and here was Webster, and he knew well that a little more or less of rhetoric signified nothing. . . . He was there as the representative of the American Continent; there in his Adamitic capacity; and that is the basis of the satisfaction that people have in hearing him, that he alone of all men does not disappoint the eye and ear, but is a fit figure in the landscape."[20]

The patriotic occasion was marred for many Whigs by the jarring presence of John Tyler. Indeed, in Quincy Adams's opinion, it had been desecrated into a vehicle for Tyler and Webster to regain popularity, and he refused to attend.[21] Although he had left the cabinet, Webster had not abandoned the

Tyler administration or the hope of effecting some *modus vivendi* between the president and his followers and the mass of the Whig party. Hope faded fast in the fall, however, and Webster scrambled to get aboard the Clay bandwagon. Clay himself extended no helping hand. He remained profoundly distrustful of Webster and his "Custom House clique" in New York, whom he suspected of playing the same game as in 1839, publicly praising him to the skies but privately circulating doubts of his electability. The Bunker Hill celebration was "a cover for concocting their machinations."[22] In September Webster used the occasion of a speech at the state fair in Rochester, New York, to take back what he had advanced at Baltimore only four months before and return to conventional Whig doctrine on the tariff.

Just at this time, Webster's New York friends made the proposition for the reunion of the New Englander with Clay and the Whigs, to be sealed by the offer of the vice presidential nomination. William H. Seward, now practicing law in Rochester, communicated the proposition in a "strictly confidential" letter to Clay's old friend, Peter B. Porter. "There must be a reconciliation between Mr. Clay and Mr. Webster; between Clay's friends and Webster's friends," Seward wrote. "Clay for President and Webster for Vice President. We could then sweep the field as we did in 1840." It was further understood that, with Clay and the party committed to the one-term principle, Webster would have "a clear field" for the succession in 1848. Clay, or his prominent associates, should make the appropriate overture to Webster who, Seward insisted, knew nothing of this. Porter referred the proposition to Clay, saying he had already dismissed the idea of an overture coming from him.[23] Clay approved. He would strike no bargain for the vice presidency, most certainly not with a renegade Whig. He suspected, moreover, that Webster's continued enmity was less injurious to the cause than any strength he could bring by reconciliation.[24] Webster's friends generally acquiesced in this rebuff, but James Watson Webb, editor of the New York *Courier and Enquirer*, bolted and nominated Webster. Promptly squelched, finding almost no support, the editor also received a lecture from Clay on Webster's infidelities. Many Whigs shared the view that Webster had lost his usefulness to the party. He wished to reunite, they said, to serve not the party but his own ambition. "Let the prodigal son be welcomed to his father's house," wrote Senator Berrien. "But can the Whig party consistently with their own self-respect invite his return by the tender of the second office in their gift? . . . Shall his name be emblazoned on the same standard with that of Henry Clay?"[25] Obviously not. Webster, the consensus was, must show himself a good Whig before the party could touch him.

He attempted to make amends during the November election in Massachusetts. Several weeks earlier he had patched up relations with Abbott Lawrence. The choice of a gubernatorial candidate, George N. Briggs, who was acceptable to Webster, facilitated his reentry into the party. At a great Whig rally in Andover four days before the election, he reiterated long-held opinions on the tariff, the currency, and other issues; and he was subsequently given a share of the credit for the turn of political fortune that elected Briggs.[26]

In Washington that winter, appearing before the Supreme Court and trying to sell his house, Webster continued to describe himself as a private citizen and outwardly showed little interest in the political wars. He was reportedly engaged in writing a history of the Constitution and the Washington administration. Actually, Webster panted for Whig recognition and place. The vice presidency still loomed in his sight. Hostility to Clay was not easily forgiven among Whigs, however. Some undoubtedly saw political advantage for themselves in the exclusion of Webster, so they kept up the attack. Others professed to be alarmed by the rising volume of rumor and innuendo about Webster's venality, intemperance, and similar offenses. Nevertheless, Webster observed "a returning feeling of kindness" toward him in the capital. Dining on a saddle of lamb at Senator Mangum's, he managed to "bury the hatchet" with several southern Whigs who had gone into opposition with Clay. Unfortunately, all his efforts at reconciliation seemed hesitant and begrudging. "He ought to have returned like Achilles from his tent, blazing in armour," one wrote. "But Webster is not an Achilles."[27]

Although the candidate himself would be the most important issue, Clay intended to wage the campaign on the old Whig economic issues with which his name was so closely identified. The country managed to survive without a national bank; it was no longer a live issue, and Clay only mumbled the old homilies on that subject. The state of the treasury rendered distribution dormant. The tariff, therefore, occupied the foreground of attention. Clay bore no direct responsibility for the tariff of 1842, and it did more violence to the principles of the Compromise Act than he would have wished; but he acquiesced in the act, indeed before long engraved it on his banner. It was a subject, as already observed, on which Clayton made the speeches for him. The iconography of Neagle's portrait reinforced the image of the Father of the American System. Clay, in one of his public letters, said that the government was instituted to promote general prosperity, and that all the great economic interests in all parts of the Union should receive its "parental care and attention." John P. Kennedy's sprightly Defense of the Whigs, in 1843, traced Whig economic nationalism to the Madisonian Platform of 1815 and charted a genealogy of parties approved by Clay.[28] In reply to an inquiry from S. F. Bronson, a Georgia newspaper editor, in September, Clay said that the true policy with respect to the tariff was found in the principles of the Compromise Act: "That whatever revenue is necessary to an economical and honest administration of the general government, ought to be derived from duties imposed on foreign imports. And . . . that, in establishing a tariff of these duties, such a discrimination ought to be made, as will incidentally afford reasonable protection to our national interests." In the main, the principles were embodied in the existing tariff; and because of the remarkable progress of American manufactures, he did not think higher protection would be required in the future.[29]

The letter was designed to appeal to moderate protectionist sentiment in the South. The crucial battleground of the election, Clay believed, was the southern states. Van Buren, whom he expected to oppose, was most vulnerable there. The former state rights faction of the Whig party had disappeared in the wake of the Tyler catastrophe. The growth of protectionism in the South, signaled by southern Whig support of the Tariff of 1842, led Clay to believe that the country might at last be united on his platform. The tariff, once an issue between sections, was increasingly an issue between parties. Southern planters and businessmen were no longer enchanted with the boasted benefits of free trade. Despite lower tariff duties in the United States, the depression of cotton prices continued. Planters worried about the competition of cheap India cotton in British markets; and they looked more appreciatively on the prosperity of New England textile mills. In the process of stealing the world market in coarse cottons from the British, the northern producers consumed more and more of the southern staple. The rise of southern manufactures was another part of the economic picture that was changing southern minds on protection and the home market. As the young Georgia Whig, Robert Toombs, observed, recalling Webster's remark about a national bank, "this theory of free trade at the South is being very generally considered 'an obsolete idea.' "[30]

In order to exploit what a recent historian has called "a fundamental ideological transformation among southern Whigs," Clay laid plans for a great campaign swing through the region. Yielding to the pleas of North Carolina Whigs to visit the state, he filled up an itinerary that would start from New Orleans about February 1, 1844, and terminate in Washington at the end of April, just before the national convention in Baltimore. Ohio Whigs had arranged for a colorful stump speaker, John W. Bear, known as the "Ohio Blacksmith," to precede the candidate. In November he started down the river in company with a man named Mosely, who was styled the "Kentucky pumpborer." Like two pilot fish before the shark, Bear and the Borer, harangued for Clay at country crossroads, on street corners, and in taverns, usually three or four weeks in advance of Great Hal himself.[31] The Whig party rebounded in the fall elections, regaining control of the state houses in Massachusetts and Georgia, although it was still a loser in New York. Clay was supremely confident as he left Kentucky. During the winter he visited the parishes and towns around New Orleans. His tour of the Deep South took him to Mobile, Montgomery, Milledgeville, Savannah, Augusta, Columbia, and Charleston. A Georgia humorist, Joseph Jones, captured the thrill of these visits for the "lokeyfokys" in his account of the farmer who, in this year when the Millerites were predicting the end of the world, went to Augusta that he might not die without shaking the hand of Henry Clay: "It seemed like the whole country was movin to one pint—all gwine to see Mr. Clay. Men and wimmin, galls and boys, niggers and all, was dressed up within an inch of their lives, and runnin through the streets lookin out for Mr. Clay." Cannons were fired to announce his arrival. From the front steps of city hall, before which the crowd gathered, Whig gentlemen showered him with praise. Clay then spoke for an hour and a half. "I reckon you mought have heard a grasshopper sneeze in any part of the yard—the people was so quiet." It was useless to describe the speech; everybody knew that the sun did not shine brighter than Clay's oratory. The next day, at the masonic hall, the farmer got his wish to shake Clay's hand. That evening he attended the ball, where he felt "monstrous awkward" and marveled at Clay "promenadin . . . and shakin hands and talkin to the galls." The ball was followed by a supper that "banged everything" the farmer had ever seen.*

Presumably at Augusta, as elsewhere, Clay talked mostly about the Tyler debacle and the tariff. He trumpeted the virtues of the Compromise Act for the South and held that if it had been violated by the tariff of 1842, the violation was on both sides.[33] Clay declined to discuss Texas. When Crittenden tried to force the issue upon his attention in December, Clay said it was an unnecessary distraction and ought to be passed over in silence by Whigs in Congress and before the public. He did not need to be reminded that a quarter century before he had denounced the Monroe administration for abandoning the American title to Texas in Adams's Transcontinental Treaty with Spain. The euphemism "reannexation," employed by Texas partisans, was a compliment to Clay. But the United States was large enough, he now thought. Tylerite claims of British designs on Texas were mistaken; even if true, Britain had the benefit of acting under the color of freedom, while the United States would be advancing slavery. Because Mexico still claimed Texas, annexation would lead to war. Annexation was irresponsible; it was also impractical. A two-thirds majority could not be obtained in the Senate to ratify a treaty of annexation. "Why then present the question?" Clay asked. "It is manifest that it is for no other than the wicked purpose of producing discord and distraction in the nation."[34] This view was echoed by the Whig leaders Clay met in the South. Annexation, said Alexander H. Stephens, "is a miserable political humbug got up as a ruse to divide and distract the Whig party at the South." He advised Clay, in Georgia, to maintain his public silence. Nothing he heard or saw in the South led Clay to a different conclusion. Everywhere, he said, "I have found a degree of indifference or opposition to . . . annexation which quite surprised me." Nevertheless, recognizing that forbearance might be interpreted as timidity, Clay decided about the time he crossed the Savannah River to offer a public statement on annexation timed to his arrival in Washington.[35]

Reaching Charleston on Saturday, April 6, ten days after Calhoun's departure for Washington with the city's blessing, Clay was marched through crowded streets—King, Broad, and Meeting—under triumphal arches, garlanded with spring flowers, hung with wreathes of evergreen, to a reception at the theater. Not many years had passed, a Democrat observed, since every Charleston son would have hanged him in effigy. But now there was ac-

---

*Jones went on to describe the "old coon": "There's somethin about him that draws one to him and that makes one feel perfectly familiar although we feel that we are in the presence of a great man. He's monstrous ugly, if you go to sifferin out his features like you would common people's—but for all that, he's the best looking man I ever saw. His mouth is like an overseer's wages, extendin from one year's end to the other, but when he speaks you wouldn't have it any smaller if you could. It seems like nature made it so a purpose to give free vent to the patriotic emotions of his noble heart. His eye sparkles with the fire of genius—his broad forehead looks like the front view of the Temple of Wisdom, and all his features bespeak him the noblest work of God—*an honest man!*"[32]

tually a Clay Club in Charleston, a Whig party in the state; and so insidious were Clay's charms that some Democrats, disappointed by Calhoun's withdrawal, were lured to his candidacy. On Monday he received visitors, and in the evening both parties joined to honor him at a grand ball and supper at the Charleston Hotel.[36] Resuming his peregrinations, Clay at last arrived in the North Carolina capital, where he was the guest of Governor John Morehead. Before the statehouse, under a bright sun, he addressed a cheering throng estimated at ten thousand. "His mind seemed to *pervade* the assembly, to *control* their sentiments, passions, hopes, and fears," a reporter said of the orator.[37] Several days later, April 17, Clay put his signature to a public letter, soon to be known as the Raleigh Letter, on the Texas Question. In it he reviewed his connection with the question, alluded to the alienation of the American claim in 1819, and expressed astonishment that the government had secretly negotiated an annexation treaty about to be sent to the Senate. If Texas could be obtained without loss of national character, without risk of war, without jeopardizing the Union, and with the approbation of the American people, he would favor annexation. But there was no public opinion for it, it was decidedly opposed in one part of the Union, and it would almost certainly embroil the United States with Mexico. "Annexation and war with Mexico are identical," he declared.[38]

Clay read a draft of the letter to Morehead and two other Whigs at Raleigh before dispatching it to Crittenden for publication upon his arrival in Washington. Crittenden reportedly blanched. But he saw to the letter's publication in the *Intelligencer* on the morning of April 27, within hours of Clay's arrival. Whatever apprehensions he may have felt over the publication were relieved by the knowledge that Van Buren, too, opposed annexation. "The public mind is too fixed on the Presidential question," he said, "the current is running too strong and impetuously to be now affected by Texas."[39] Some months later the statement would seem laughable. But in April, remarkably, Van Buren converged with Clay, and the overwhelming sentiment was against annexation. The *Globe*, an afternoon newspaper, published Van Buren's Texas letter on the same day as Clay's. The New Yorker, too, wished to fight the battle on the old issues. When the Raleigh Letter reached General Jackson at the Hermitage, he chuckled. "Clay [is] a dead political Duck." No man opposed to annexation could be elected president, in his opinion. Van Buren's epistle then came to hand. "It's a forgery," the General said unbelievingly. "Mr. Van Buren never wrote such a letter."[40] Many southern Democrats were equally incredulous. Van Buren, after all, was the prototype of the "northern man with southern principles." But as the truth sank in, they fell away from Van Buren, and Calhoun had his revenge. Clay's letter, on the other hand, was received with almost universal satisfaction among Whigs.

The convention on May 1 was a jubilant Clay pageant: "Clay portraits, Clay banners, Clay ribands, Clay songs, Clay quick-steps, Clay marches, Clay caricatures, meet the eye in all directions." The coon had been adopted as the Whig mascot; Clay, in fact, *was* the coon, "the same old coon," primed to outwit the Fox of Kinderhook. "Coons perched on balls of public opinion, rallying over foxes, and other foxes 'raising the old Harry,' garnish the emporiums." A delegation of live coons came from Missouri! Huge Clay banners pictured him as the Mill Boy of the Slashes, the Father of the American System, and the Farmer of Ashland. There were Clay cigars, Clay hats, Ashland coats, Ashland canes, Clay shaving mugs and razor straps.[41] The convention made quick work of the presidential nomination, then proceeded to nominate, on the third ballot, Theodore Frelinghuysen of New Jersey for the vice presidency. Known as "The Christian Statesman" for his leadership on moral and religious causes, Frelinghuysen was a surprising choice, even to Clay, though observing the "balance of morality" it gave the ticket, he thought the nomination astute, as did others. "Clay, being by the admission of his friends a good deal of a runner, will run none the worse for having a deacon to ride him."[42] The convention, for the first time, adopted a platform, summing up the principles and policies of the party as Clay had expounded them. It made no mention of Texas.[43] As was customary the candidate himself did not appear. He accepted the nomination in Washington on May 2. On the same day, Webster addressed the so-called "ratification convention" at Baltimore. Acknowledging old differences with Clay, Webster said he knew of none that survived, and he rejoiced in the nomination. At that Parson Brownlow walked out, but most Whigs applauded the speech as the welcome bond of reconciliation between the Whig giants. Webster presumably approved of the Raleigh Letter, although it stole his thunder with anti-slavery men in the North. He remained "utterly astonished" by the course of Tyler and Calhoun on Texas.[44]

Clay took another vow of silence and retired to Ashland. Three weeks later he learned that the Democratic convention had nominated James K. Polk of Tennessee. While sorry to lose such a worthy and agreeable foe as Van Buren, Clay supposed the nomination must work to his advantage. He could ask with everyone else, "Who is James K. Polk?" He knew him, of course, from his fourteen years of congressional service as a faithful toiler in the Jacksonian vineyard. In 1839 "Young Hickory" had been elected governor of Tennessee. But two successive defeats at Whig hands had reduced him to an aspirant for the vice presidency. Magically, Texas lifted him to the presidential nomination. Clay had no kind feelings toward him. Nor did he fully grasp the transforming effects of Polk's nomination on the presidential election. Polk was an annexationist. Suddenly Texas, which Clay and Van Buren had agreed to eliminate as an issue, became an issue. Clay found himself on the defensive, timid rather than bold, *against* rather than *for* national pride, power, and expansion. Not only was it an unnatural posture for him; it seemed likely to injure him in the West where he had hoped to win seventy-two electoral votes. The Polk nomination was most damaging in the South, however. At one stroke it rendered Clay's southern strategy obsolete.

On the Whig side, the presidential campaign revolved around three issues: the tariff, Texas and slavery, and the character of Henry Clay. One reason for Clay's unfriendliness toward Polk was his cynical revival of the "bargain and corruption" canard—the foundation of all attacks on Clay's character—during the Tennessee gubernatorial election in 1843. At that time Clay called Polk to account but was ignored. He found some consolation in the resolution subsequently adopted by the legislature rescinding its promulgation of the charge almost twenty years ago. After Polk's nomination, Clay queried Gales and Seaton, "Was that [revival of the old libel] the cause of his selection? Or Jackson's motive in desiring it?"[45] In Congress, on the stump, and in the press politicians raked over this ancient affair. Yet Carter Beverley, one of the principal accusers, had retracted the notorious charge and apologized to Clay. And old John Quincy Adams, in an address at Maysville during his western tour in 1843, again denounced the great lie, adding that "as I expect shortly to appear before my God, to answer for the conduct of my whole life, should these charges have found their way to the Throne of Eternal Justice, I will, in the presence of the Omnipotent, pronounce them false."[46] Clay contemplated publishing a full vindication which would "carry the war to Africa" by showing that the Jacksonians were the true intriguers in 1825. Discretion prevailed, however, in part because James Buchanan, the chief witness (he had told Letcher that if Clay would announce for Jackson he would, upon Jackson's election, be named secretary of state), refused to lift the ban of confidentiality on his testimony. All Clay did, in the end, was to authorize publication of his letters to Frank Blair. They revealed nothing prejudicial, though some flippant remarks about Adams required a note of apology from the author.[47]

Clay complained that he was accused of "every crime in the Decalogue," and this was quite literally true, as one Democratic tract showed. A handbill called "The Embodiment" formed a text collecting all the slanders into a visual image of the man surmounted by a crest featuring a pistol, a cigar, a pack of cards, and a brandy bottle—Clay's armorial bearings. None of the charges was new; as in the past, most of them were put in circulation by the little knot of enemy politicians in Lexington, the most prominent of whom were General John M. McCalla, James Guthrie, and Robert Wickliffe.[48] There were some new wrinkles in 1844, however. Joshua Leavitt, editor of *the Emancipator*, the newspaper of the Liberty party and its presidential candidate, James G. Birney, published an influential pamphlet, *The Great Duelist*, the point of which was less to arraign Clay for the crime than to show that dueling was a system of intimidation, violence, and false chivalry inseparable from the system of slavery. Perforce the great duelist was the great patron of slavery as well.[49] The assault on Clay's character showed him to be ill-tempered, dissolute, violent, and morally unfit for the presidency. His friends were kept so busy answering these attacks that they had little time for anything else. Many witnesses testified to the morality of Clay's private life. "Mr. Clay and His Revilers," a publication got up in Lexington, was widely circulated in the press. So, too, was the statement of the Reverend Henry B. Bascom, a prominent Methodist minister and Clay's friend and neighbor for many years. While acknowledging that Clay was not a professed Christian, Bascom vouched for his good character; and when Democrats, in reply, accused Bascom of perjury, other Lexington ministers and elders came to his defense.[50]

Nothing afforded Clay greater satisfaction at the outset of the campaign than the unanimity among Whigs—North, South, and West—on the tariff. Southern opposition, he believed, had in the past been the root cause of the anti-slavery agitation and of other bad feelings toward the section in the North. He had gone to great lengths to encourage southern liberality, tacking the modifier "incidental" on his protectionism, in the belief it would harmonize the Union and promote general prosperity.[51] As the campaign progressed, however, Clay found himself attacked in the South for continued adherence to protectionism and in the North for abandoning it. Democratic doggerel portrayed him talking out of both sides of his mouth on the tariff.

> Orator Clay had *two tones* in his voice;
> The one squeaking *thus*, and the other down *so*;
> And *mighty* convenient he found them both—
> The squeak at the *top* and the guttural *below*.
>
> Orator Clay looked up to the North;
> "I'm for the tariff PROTECTIVE," said he;
> But he turned to the South with *his other tone!*
> "A tariff for revenue only 't will be!"[52]

Clay invited criticism, of course, by striking these different tones in the two sections; yet this was nothing compared to the outrageous fraud perpetrated by Polk's "Kane Letter" upon the electorate of the northern states. Seeing that his chances were desperate in Pennsylvania, particularly, unless he could satisfy coal and iron interests, Polk advertised himself as a greater protectionist than the Father of the American System. He had never cast a protectionist vote; no informed politican expected that, if elected president, he would deviate from lifelong anti-tariff principles. Wishing to make sure of this, Calhoun sent Pickens on a mission to Nashville to confer with Polk. Pickens returned persuaded of the candidate's fidelity, despite the Kane Letter, and this knowledge proved useful to Calhoun in quelling the Bluffton revolt.[53] In the North, Webster was an unwilling witness against Clay's protectionist credentials. During the tariff debate of 1842, when he was embittered against Clay, Webster had stated to Henry A. Wise that the original draft of the Compromise Act provided for duties to be laid, after the nine-year period, "without reference to the protection of any domestic articles whatever." Without naming his informant, Wise had inserted this pernicious statement in a letter to his constituents, and in August 1844 Webster was revealed as the author.[54] Of course, it supported the idea diligently circulated by northern Democrats that Clay was soft on the tariff. Whether or not it hurt Clay, it proved embarrassing to Webster, who was still laboring to erase the stigma of hostility to him. Speaking to mammoth Whig rallies thorughout the Northeast, Webster took Clay's line that the tariff was "the great question" and extolled its benefits to ordinary workers and farmers.

The Raleigh Letter had placed Clay firmly in opposition to Texas annexation. Polk was just as firmly for it. From the beginning of the campaign, some of Clay's counselors worried that by a slip of the tongue or the pen he might weaken or compromise his position on one or another issue. But he rebuffed every move to "cage" or control him. "I intend to conduct the campaign myself," he said. "It shall never be charged upon me that I am in the hands of a committee. I will not surrender my independence, or submit to be guided by anybody."[55] Pro-slavery annexationists tied the Raleigh Letter into the conception of Clay as an abolitionist. Opposition to annexation was opposition to slavery. Such was the view set forth in Robert Walker's *The South in Danger*, published in September, although the pamphlet was so violent it recoiled on the Democrats and probably cost Clay few votes. The pro-slavery conception of Clay, on the other hand, cost him dearly. The Liberty party kept up a constant barrage on the twofold theory that it could divert no votes from Polk and that a specious friend is the worst of enemies. His opposition to annexation was merely expediential, abolitionists said; they denounced him as "rotten as a stagnant fish pond" on slavery; and they portrayed him in cartoons whipping slaves. Especially obnoxious to the candidate was "the 'white slave' slander." In the first debate on the restriction of slavery in Missouri, Clay had allegedly said, "If gentlemen will not allow us to have black slaves, they must let us have white ones; for we cannot cut our firewood, and black our shoes, and have our wives and daughters work in the kitchen." No such words were recorded anywhere in 1819, but sixteen months later a Vermont congressman ascribed them to Clay in a note appended to a speech recently delivered in the House. Neither Clay nor anyone else took notice of the quoted passage in 1820; but in 1844—not for the first time—it was dredged up and used to besmirch his image in the North. Clay, of course, denied the allegation.[56]

Most anti-slavery Whigs were loyal to Clay, though their patience was sorely tried as the campaign progressed. For the Ohioan Giddings, whom dedicated abolitionists cursed for "selling out" to Clay, the test was whether or not the candidate remained faithful to the doctrine "slavery local, freedom national." In the long run the proscription of Texas depended on the theory that slavery was a denationalized institution. Giddings worried over suggestions of Clay's backsliding, but was satisfied by his reaffirmation of support for this doctrine in September.[57] Yet it was at this very time that Clay suffered a loss of nerve on Texas and inflicted two critical wounds on his campaign. One was the publication of Clay's second "Alabama Letter," as it was named from the address, in which he separated the slavery issue from the annexation issue in an apparent effort to conciliate southern opinion. What many in the North perceived as a moral question, annexation, he tended to treat as a matter of tactics and timing. "Go home, Mr. Mendenhall!" was bad enough, but this "horrid letter," said Seward, suddenly jeopardized the election in New York. At the Astor House, resting between campaign appearances, Webster was dumbfounded. "I feel pretty tolerably angry," he wrote. He met with Weed and Greeley, the former especially despondent, to discuss how to deal with what they saw as vacillation and retreat on Texas. In clarifying letters, Clay denied any change of position; indeed the Alabama Letters were meant to sustain the Raleigh Letter.[58] Although the letters might, in truth, be read that way, they were certain to be read otherwise in the heat of the campaign. The second Alabama Letter, in particular, seemed designed to shore up Clay's following in the South after Texas emerged as the dominant issue. Polk coolly wrote the Kane Letter without injury to himself in the South, but Clay could not avoid serious repercussions from the Alabama Letter because it played into his reputation for trickery and political gamesmanship. The pathetic part of this was that it was needless. Nothing compelled Clay to issue a further statement on Texas. Having done so, the mistake was irreparable.

The flap over the Alabama Letter was made worse by what succeeded it: Clay's repudiation of his Cousin Cash. During the last four years this high-spirited Kentuckian had fought a duel with Robert Wickliffe, Jr., and fought with a bowie knife against Sam Brown in defense of his own and Cousin Henry's political honor. The latter successfully defended him against the charge of mayhem against Brown. Cassius Clay manumitted his slaves and became Kentucky's most celebrated abolitionist. Believing that the "Liberty men" could be persuaded to vote for Clay, he toured the North during the summer with the candidate's blessing. In New York, after publication of the Alabama Letter, he wrote to Clay to make sure he was not misrepresenting him on Texas. Clay replied frankly that he was, that because they were cousins (many people actually supposed thirty-four-year-old Cassius was the candidate's son) everything he said was charged to him, that the courtship of abolitionists was endangering the cause in the South, and that Cassius was wrong to think they would ever vote for Henry Clay. Unfortunately, Clay's letter was intercepted by Democrats in New York and spread across the newspapers. Again, he appeared nervous, irresolute, and incapable of controlling his own campaign.[59]

As the campaign drew to a close, Clay fretted over the rising importance of an issue—nativism and the immigrant vote—barely observable on the political horizon in the spring. The Whig party was generally unpopular with immigrants, whether the Germans in Ohio or the Irish in New York City, largely because local Whig elites looked down on them and backed legislation, such as temperance laws, which they disapproved. Clay himself was not associated with the nativist currents in his party, but Frelinghuysen most emphatically was, and his support of Protestant moral uplift proved a mixed blessing to Clay's candidacy. "No Popery" banners waved over the Whig cause in the country and in the city. Clay repeatedly turned aside pleas that he take a stand favorable to nativist restrictions on immigration and naturalization, mainly on the apology these were local rather than national questions. But the danger for Clay, as he finally recognized, was on the other side. At the eleventh hour, when he apprehended the loss of the election in New York, Clay joined with Seward and others in a special appeal to the Roman Catholic Bishop, John Hughes, who, it was believed, with the wave of his crozier could decide the city's vote.[60]

By early November, when voters trooped to the polls in most states, Clay's optimism had dimmed, and he could contemplate his defeat. The popular vote totaled 2,698,609, and Clay trailed Polk by 38,180. The electoral vote margin was wider, 170 to 105. Clay won eleven states, eight fewer then Harrison in 1840. He won four of the six New England states, plus New Jersey, Delaware, Maryland, North Carolina, Ohio, Kentucky, and Tennessee. New York, with 36 electoral votes, was the critical loss. Polk carried the state by approximately 5,000 votes. If Clay had received a fraction of the 15,000 ballots cast for Birney, he would have won New York; and with the addition of Michigan, where the Liberty party vote was also decisive, he would have won the election as well, 146 to 129. The Texas issue almost surely cost Clay Georgia. All commentators agree that the Democrats captured Louisiana by fraud at the polls.[61]

Coming at the hands of "Young Hickory," it was a humiliating defeat—the ultimate kick in the pants after a life of distinguished public service. Clay bore himself stoically. "I see him daily," Combs wrote, "and my heart bleeds when I look upon his noble countenance—serene and calm as a summer day—no mock-heroic disdain of popular approbation and yet a high consciousness of unrewarded public services and unappreciated merit. . . . He utters no complaint, although he considers himself forever off the public stage."[62] Clay, like most Whig analysts, blamed the defeat on a combination of fraud (not only in Louisiana but by illegally naturalized immigrant voters in New York), humbug (the Kane Letter), slander, and abolitionism. In these circumstances, John P. Kennedy said, the true patriot would rather fall with Clay than rise with Polk. "Glorious defeat, honorable disaster!"[63] The Richmond *Whig* consoled Clay with Alexander Pope's lines:

> One self-approving hour whole years outweighs
> Of stupid starers and of loud huzzas:
> And more true joy Marcellus exil'd feels
> Than Caesar with the senate at his heels.

Prentice and Greeley, who loved Clay beyond all other public men, reprinted in their respective newspapers "He Is Not Fallen," the verses Whittier had written a dozen years ago and for the last several years had tried to forget.

> Not Fallen! No! As well the tall
> And pillar'd Alleghany fall—
> As well Ohio's giant tide
>   Roll backward on its mighty track,
> As he, Columbia's hope and pride,
> The slandered and the sorely tried,
>   In his triumphant course turn back.[64]

* $\mathcal{Seven}$ *

PRIVATE LIVES, PUBLIC IMAGES

As James K. Polk laid plans for his administration, John C. Calhoun felt confident he would be invited to remain secretary of state. And if invited, he would almost certainly accept. With Francis Pickens as intermediary, he had worked out a political understanding with Polk. In addition to offering assurances on the tariff, Polk had apparently agreed to dump Frank Blair and the *Globe*, long a thorn in Calhoun's side, as the newspaper voice of the Democratic administration. The support that Calhoun and his friends brought to the Democratic ticket had been, in their view, responsible for its success in at least three southern states—Virginia, South Carolina, and Georgia. Calhoun's remaining in the cabinet, he was assured by a leader of the Richmond Junto, was essential to the ascendancy of the party in Virginia. Polk and his friends must understand this. "They dare not touch a hair on your head."[1] The State Department had political advantages for Calhoun as well. It was, for the present, a good station from which to contemplate a presidential race in 1848. Moreover, there was important unfinished business, such as negotiation of the Oregon boundary, which he was loath to leave to other hands. The business of Texas annexation would be completed by the Tyler administration. Considering the election a popular mandate for annexation, the president recommended that it be accomplished quickly by a joint resolution of Congress. In other circumstances Calhoun undoubtedly would have denounced the procedure, which required only a majority vote in both houses, as unconstitutional. But in this case he rose above principle. As finally adopted, the resolution contained some face-saving amendments that permitted even Thomas Hart Benton to vote for it.

Meanwhile, in South Carolina, the radical challenge to Calhoun's leadership came to a head in the state legislature. In his final message, the retiring governor, James H. Hammond, firmly aligned himself with Barnwell Rhett and the Blufftonites against Calhoun. Betrayed by the tariff of 1842, the South had also been attacked at its heart's core, the institution of slavery, by rejection of the Texas treaty. Northern abolitionist fanaticism must be confronted, Hammond insisted. This meant the adjournment of politics as usual, the end of homilies to the Union, and the adoption of measures that would place the destiny of the state or the section in its own hands. Pickens, who occupied the Edgefield seat in the senate, at once responded to this "firebrand" with resolutions of confidence in the incoming administration in Washington. Pickens was assumed to speak for his master, though he acted on the spot, without instruction, lest hasty action by the ultras impair Calhoun's standing in Washington as well as in South Carolina. The question to be decided, Pickens was told by John A. Stuart, the *Mercury's* editor and a Charleston representative, was "whether the State was to lick [Calhoun's] toes forever." The senate promptly and unanimously approved Pickens's resolutions. After intermittent and often bitter debate, they were finally adopted on a divided vote in the lower house near the end of the session. At the same time the legislature elected the moderate, William Aiken, over the radical Whitemarsh Seabrook, the next governor. Hammond, with ample justification, felt "repudiated." He also felt that this worst suspicions of Calhoun had been confirmed. He had "crushed" South Carolina under the heel of wicked personal ambition. "God send him a safe deliverance, tho' I see no way for it."[2]

But South Carolina's vote of confidence in Polk and the Democratic party did not secure a seat for Calhoun in the cabinet. Polk felt no obligation to Calhoun and quickly saw the problem as how to drop him gracefully. His free trade doctrines were unacceptable to the Pennsylvania Democrats who had rallied to Polk. He was despised by leaders in the Van Buren following. Benton would shake the pillars of the Senate rather than support Calhoun. As secretary of state he had shown himself capable of diplomatic blunders, such as the Pakenham Letter. But at the head of his liabilities was the fact, acknowledged by all, that he aspired to the presidency in succession to Polk, who had committed himself to a single term. Calhoun, in sum, was too heavy a burden. Polk offered the State Department to James Buchanan, a Pennsylvanian and a Van Burenite, with a record of service almost as long, though not nearly so distinguished, as Calhoun's. The Carolinian learned of this near the end of February when Polk offered him the London ministry. But, as Polk knew, he was totally averse to going abroad; he declined immediately and in decided terms. The Charleston *Mercury* reported on March 3 that Calhoun was dumped in a deal for the votes of New York's senators on Texas annexation—a not implausible but unsubstantiated story.[3] Calhoun never learned exactly why he was forced out, and he quarreled more with the manner in which it was done than with the decision it-self. He went home convinced that the new administration would be a con-tinuation, both in men and in measures, of "the Jackson Dynasty." He kept silent and, for the present, treasured the peace of retirement at Fort Hill. His friends, meanwhile, began to map strategy for another campaign.[4]

As Calhoun went out of office, Webster came back in. On January 16 the Bay State legislature elected him to the Senate in place of Rufus Choate, "the nosegay orator," who resigned with the excuse of weariness and ill health. Such an event had been expected for several months, ever since Webster's return to the Whig party of Massachusetts. His tastes, unlike Choate's, ran more to the Senate than to the bar. Clay's defeat came as a shock even to Webster, who had never had any confidence in his candidacy: "This free country, this model republic, disturbing its own peace, and perhaps the peace of the world, by its greediness for more slave territory, and for a greater increase of slavery!"[5] In his campaign speeches Webster had downplayed the Texas issue, doubtless out of deference to southern Whigs; nevertheless, he did not shrink from declaring his belief that "it is a scheme for the extension of the slavery of the African race" and that it risked, at bot-tom, the perpetuity of the Union.[6] All Massachusetts Whiggery opposed Texas annexation. The conservative leadership under Abbott Lawrence was morally soft on the issue, however. As Emerson remarked, "Cotton thread holds the Union together—unites John C. Calhoun and Abbott Lawrence." Webster ingratiated himself with the young anti-slavery Whigs led by Charles Allen, Stephen Phillips, and Charles Francis Adams; and, as already observed, he used the Texas issue as a means of regaining favor with the Bay State party.

Webster was arguing a railroad case in Boston when the legislature con-vened in January eager at this late hour to voice anew the state's opposition to Texas annexation. The young Whigs proposed a convention, non-partisan but under Whig auspices. Webster approved and may have had a hand in writing the call of the convention, believing it would meet the public de-mand for action and also keep the play from the abolitionists who, in south-ern eyes, appeared to run the state. When the call was circulated for signa-tures, Lawrence, Nathan Appleton, and other conservative leaders declined. Annexation was a foregone conclusion, they felt. The time for agitation had passed; continuing it would only further alienate the southern Whigs. With Lawrence the issue had a personal aspect as well. "No sir," he reportedly said. "We will not help Daniel Webster to right himself by this Texas move-ment."[7] Webster, too, under pressure from New York Whigs, it was said, fi-nally withheld his own signature, but Allen signed the call for him, saying he could repudiate it if he dared. As the day of the convention, January 29, ap-proached, Webster grew more remote. At last, three days before, on a Sun-day, he met with Allen and Phillips in his Boston law office to draw up an ad-dress for the convention. Pacing back and forth, he dictated the opening part, the constitutional argument, while his auditors took it down. What was unconstitutional under the treaty power was doubly so under a mere joint resolution of Congress. Finishing the argument, Webster took out his watch, remarked he didn't know what to say under the slavery heading, and adjourned for dinner, intending to conclude on Monday. But Monday came, and Webster, as his young friends finally learned, had taken the train for New York. Allen and Phillips finished the address—the bulk of it—and Allen read it to the convention on Wednesday.[8] The address, generally attributed to Webster, was well received by the six hundred delegates from throughout the state, although abolitionists thought it timid. The convention established an Anti-Slavery Committee of Correspondence consisting of Adams, Allen, and Phillips. Its continuing protest against annexation, right down to the admission of Texas to statehood in December 1846, was futile; but this same group, by starting the Boston *Whig*, gave increasing definition as well as voice to "conscience" Whiggery and enforced its separation from the "cotton" Whigs of whom Webster, alas, was indubitably one.

Unfriendly observers later noted the coincidence between Webster's running off prior to the Texas Convention and the raising of a fund among the Whig magnificoes to support his return to the Senate.[9] There was certainly no causal relationship between these events. The subscription fund was begun without Webster's knowledge or sanction just after his reelection to the Senate. The plan was to raise $100,000, one-half in New York and one-half in Boston, which would be invested and the income paid to Webster as an annuity during his lifetime. The Boston part was two-thirds subscribed when Webster learned of it fifteen months later. Lawrence, interestingly, was not among the forty subscribers. The senator accepted the annuity in the spirit in which it was given, as an expression of gratitude for his services and as a response to the problem of keeping the best men in politics. He took the money, as Henry Adams quipped, "not as pay, but as honorarium." And in view of the anticipated loss of income from the law, he could see it as nothing more than his just dessert.[10] The investors did not expect to control Webster's opinion; rather, it was because of the correspondence between his opinions and their interests that they considered him a good investment. As Thomas Wren Ward, the American agent of Baring Brothers, and probably the man behind the scheme, explained it to his boss, "I consider him [Webster] as a sort of public property. He uses his great powers on the side of the public faith, peace, and good government and must be sustained, with all his failings."[11]

In the weeks following Clay's defeat, letters of condolence and a stream of gifts—silver plate, plow, quilts, books, boots, hat, snuff box, jewelry, and a thoroughbred filly—poured into Ashland. For Clay, as for most of his friends, defeat bore all the earmarks of finality. Next April 12 he would be sixty-eight. His political career, except for a little of this and that, was over. Calhoun had predicted it, and he rejoiced in it: "It will be the last of Clay; and when he disappears from the public stage, the Whig party will disperse. . . . Mr. Clay has been a great disturbing power in the harmonious and regular movements of our Government. . . . He has done much to distract the South, and to keep the West out of its true position."[12] Calhoun, of course, would modify his political strategy in light of Clay's removal from the stage. Whigs mourned the loss of their leader and at once laid plans to memoralize him. In New York City they commissioned Thomas Crawford, an American in Rome, to erect a marble statue, and the Henry Clay Festival Association was formed for the annual celebration of his birthday. Philadelphia Whigs planned to raise $20,000 for a statue by Hiram Powers. A group of Virginia ladies formed the Henry Clay Statue Society for the erection of a monument in the state capital. The Clay Testimonial Society of Kentucky proposed to raise a great stone column on an eminence above the Kentucky River near Frankfort.[13] Clay must have wondered if he hadn't died and gone to Heaven. Most of these projects eventually materialized, but they were several years premature, as were the announcements of Clay's political death.

In the winter Calvin Colton, the Whig publicist, arrived at Ashland to commence what would become the statesman's authorized biography. Consciously withdrawing from the public eye, Clay declined all invitations to speak or tour, even gave up the winter gaiety of New Orleans, and reduced his diet of newspapers to the *Intelligencer* and one or two west of the mountains. In January it was learned that he had emancipated his servant Charles Dupuy, famous for his travels with his master and as a figure in many of his speeches. Charles's loyalty to Clay had infuriated abolitionists. Now he was free by Clay's own hand, although Democrats jeered that he had, in fact, won his freedom in a bet with Clay on the election.[14] He kept up correspondence with a number of Whig leaders, and while he offered little advice, he was not averse to expressing his opinion. Texas annexation, which had come like a thief in the night to rob him of the presidency, was completed in a "fatal act" of Congress, he said. "It will, I fear, totally change the peaceful character of the Republic, converting us in the end into a warlike, conquering Nation, until we raise up some Military Chieftain who will conquer us all."[15] Thus he brought into his own perspective the downward tendency of the republic since Andrew Jackson trooped onto the stage a quarter century before.

Clay, too, was the beneficiary of private philanthropy, although in circumstances widely different from Webster's. In 1843 his son Thomas failed in business, and Clay was in jeopardy as the endorser on his notes in the amount of $25,000. Ashland was the security for this debt. Financial problems lay heavily on Clay's mind all through the presidential campaign. He sold some properties and managed some reduction of the debt before his friends learned of his plight and, quietly, without his knowledge, took measures for his relief. The movement began in New Orleans with his great friend, Dr. William Newton Mercer, and the Whig merchants of the city. By January 1845, $5,000 had been raised. The trustees of the fund thus started sought equal amounts from well-to-do Whigs in Boston, New York, Philadelphia, and Baltimore. As the money was raised the debt was discharged. Believing Clay would never accept a donation, his friends acted in secrecy. Clay first learned of the business when he received a canceled note from the Lexington bank. "Nothing could exceed the delicacy and respect to my feelings . . . ," he wrote after it was over. "The names even of my generous benefactors have not been communicated to me, and I am left to conjecture."[16] Several of Clay's creditors, prompted by this movement, canceled his personal debts as well. Within a few months he was virtually free of debt, and Ashland, his most valuable property, was unencumbered. This, too, was a monument to the Whig statesman.

Webster, Clay, and Calhoun were all three "a sort of public property." Their private lives, their homes and families, were in the public domain. All three lived on country estates—Marshfield, Ashland, Fort Hill—which were imitative in idea, if not in fact, of the famous estates—Mount Vernon, Monticello, Montpelier—of the founding generation. The perception of the private character of each man helped shape the public persona, and that, individually and collectively, was among the major dramatic creations of the age.

1. *Clay at Ashland*

Clay took pride in the title "Farmer of Ashland." The estate that had been his home for forty years was the finished creation of his own heart and mind. It answered to no model and owed nothing to anybody but himself; like his life, it was "self-made." The beauty of the place was in the land—the cover of luxuriant grass with clusters of trees of great variety laid out in the manner of a park. The house itself was modest almost to the point of being plain. A two-and-one-half-story brick with single-story wings, it was sometimes called Federal in style but was actually quite eclectic. (The exterior of the present house dates from 1857, when it was remodeled in a faintly Italianate manner.) Clay's office, library, and bedroom were on the first floor. The semi-oval drawing room, where Clay received visitors, was comfortably furnished; the walls were covered with paintings and engravings, some of Clay, some family portraits, and his bust reposed on a pedestal in one corner. On one wall hung the huge canvas *Washington and His Family*, a fine copy of the original by Edward Savage, which had been intended to accompany Clay to the White House. Throughout the house were other articles similarly diverted to Ashland from their original destination. As James Parton observed, the house had become "a museum of curious gifts" to the famous statesman.[1] It retains the character of a museum today in the custody of the Henry Clay Memorial Foundation.

Although quiet and secluded, Ashland lay only a mile or so east of Lexington and was easily accessible to the numerous admirers who flocked there and gave it a celebrity inseparable from its master's. Lexington, with a population of eight thousand, had grown very little in recent years. It was a pretty town, looking "as if some of Miss Austen's people lived in it," according to Lord Morpeth; and despite economic stagnation, it maintained a prosperous appearance. On some days as many as four or five parties of visitors, often total strangers, often without prior notice, drove out from Lexington and wound their way up the resplendent tree-lined carriage road to Clay's door.

He had sought adulation, and perhaps he should have been gratified by this display of it, but it was sometimes, as he told a friend, "excessively oppressive." If the hour was right, tea was served to the guests in the drawing room. "I am obliged to supply, when these strangers come, all the capital of conversation . . . ," he said. "They come to look and to listen, and a monosyllable is all that I can sometimes get from them. I am occasionally tempted to wish that I could find some obscure and inaccessible hole, in which I could put myself, and enjoy quiet and solitude during the remnant of my days."[2] Lucretia Clay was conspicuous chiefly by her absence. Almost a recluse, she was, said Morpeth, "a good lady on household cares intent."

In size Ashland was about six hundred acres in 1845. Two-thirds were in cultivation—corn, wheat, rye, hemp—and one-third were in park, which doubled as pasture for Clay's fine horses and cattle. The slave population fluctuated; numbering almost sixty, it was probably larger at this time than ever before. Fewer than half of them labored in the fields, and they lived in narrow whitewashed quarters some distance from the main house. Ashland was a large farm by Kentucky standards, yet not among the largest. In Fayette and adjacent Bourban County, the heart of the Bluegrass, there were a dozen farms in excess of a thousand acres.[3] But Ashland was generally considered an exceptional farm under the care of an exceptional farmer. Just as he had, many years earlier, drawn upon the example of Kentuckian Isaac Shelby's farm in formulating the idea of the American System, Clay imagined that Ashland, under his improving hands, was the American System in epitome.[4]

Actually, Clay's most important accomplishment as an agriculturist lay behind him. This was in the importation and breeding of pure-blooded livestock. He kept up a pure stock of Merino sheep, up to a hundred or more, at considerable expense, and experimented with other breeds. He bred English Hereford, Durham, Devon, and Ayershire cattle. He bred thoroughbred race horses. In 1832 he joined with three other Kentuckians in purchasing the stallion "Stamboul," only one of four genuine Arabians in the United States; placed at stud near Lexington, the horse was expected to sire as great a race in the United States as "Godolphin" had in England. During his lifetime Clay was interested in a number of the thoroughbreds celebrated by the American turf. The Maltese jackasses which he imported at high risk from the Mediterranean proved to be a good investment; one of these later sold for $5,000, and it was not unusual for offspring to command prices of $1,000 and $2,000. With Spanish sheep, English cattle, Arabian horses, and Maltese asses, to say nothing of Chinese fowl and Portuguese pigs, Ashland was a veritable international conclave of livestocks. "The progress of these animals from their infancy to maturity," Clay wrote with delight, "presents a constantly varying subject of interest, and I never go out of my house, without meeting with some of them to engage agreeably my attention."[5] But Clay disposed of much of his livestock in a great sale at Ashland on October 16, 1841, and thereafter reduced sharply the scale of activity. "Blooded stock has become a great drag," he observed.[6]

The decision to cut back on the livestock operation was prompted, in part, by the decision to invest heavily in hemp making and manufacture. Clay's money, as already noted, helped start his son Thomas in the manufacture of rope and cotton bagging in Lexington. His interest in hemp went back many years. A natural product for the rich limestone lands of central Kentucky, it seemed to offer better prospects as an income-producing staple crop than tobacco or cotton. Because of the huge market for the principal manufactured products, rope and bagging, they had long been objects of tariff protection. Now, thanks largely to his own efforts, government policy was especially helpful. In 1841 Congress directed the Navy to purchase American hemp products wherever possible, and two years later the department set up hemp-buying agencies. The new tariff offered further encouragement. "I am going to rig the Navy with cordage made of American Hemp—Kentucky Hemp—Ashland Hemp," Clay exulted to Clayton.[7] But prices remained depressed. Actively seeking contracts during his journey down the Mississippi in December 1842, Clay met with little success. The Navy continued to purchase Russian cordage in preference to American; and when Clay experimented with the water-rotted method of treating the raw hemp, which supposedly accounted for the superiority of the Russian product, failure was the result. The collapse of his son's company was a crushing blow. Two years later a fire consumed the factory and all its contents, only partially covered by insurance.[8] In addition to mortgaging Ashland, Clay was compelled to sell most of his "outland" property—a nearby farm, a house in Lexington, land in Missouri—at sacrifice prices. His estate was substantially reduced. Yet the heart of it, Ashland, was preserved and made secure, thanks to the generosity of his friends.[9]

Clay had returned to law practice chiefly with a view to helping another son, James, establish himself at the bar in Lexington; but straitened financial circumstances caused him to view it with some earnestness. The practice was not large, however, and only rarely did it produce a handsome fee. Arguing his last criminal case in 1846, the Old Prince preserved his perfect record in this field. He had been retained as the chief defense attorney for Lafayette Shelby, the grandson of old Isaac Shelby, accused of drunkenly murdering a man in the middle of Lexington. So great was the crowd that came to see and hear Clay that the trial, sufficiently sensational in itself, was finally moved from the county courthouse to Morrison Chapel at Transylvania University. Clay pleaded self-defense for his client, a wayward son, not unlike some of Clay's own, and asked that he be acquitted because of the eminent services of his family over three generations. The jury could not agree on a verdict; Shelby was released on bond to be tried again. The community was outraged. Clay's influence on the side of the rich and powerful, as in the Wickliffe murder case seventeen years before, was again manifest, and many people blamed him for what amounted to acquittal. Shelby, presumably without any prompting from Clay, skipped bail and headed for Texas.[10]

Clay's disappointments as a statesman, while great, were exceeded by the disappointments, the losses and the sufferings, he felt in his family. Instead of solace, his fireside offered desolation. Lucretia bore him eleven children—six daughters and five sons. Of the former, three died in infancy. The death of ten-year-old Eliza en route to Washington in 1825 was followed a month later by the loss of Susan, the wife of Martin Duralde of Louisiana and the mother of two children. The surviving daughter Ann, who had married James Erwin and with a family of five children lived at a place called Woodlands adjoining Ashland, died in December 1835. "Alas! my dear wife, the great Destroyer has come," Clay wrote from the Senate, "and taken away from us our dear, dear, only daughter!" Ann had been a special favorite. "Never was a father blessed with one more filial, more affectionate or . . . more beloved by all." Her loss was a wrenching blow and Lucretia felt that he never recovered from it.[11]

All but one of the five sons survived the father, so with that grievous exception the problem lay elsewhere than with "the great Destroyer." Theodore, the eldest, was the brain-damaged child; he was mentally deranged (the great tragedian Edwin Forrest said he based his conception of *Lear* on his youthful observation of poor Theodore) and had been institutionalized for many years. Thomas, whose business failure caused Clay so much trouble, had been a constant trial. Calhoun, when secretary of war, had given him a cadet's appointment to West Point, but Thomas flunked the qualifying examination. Thereafter he attended Transylvania and slipped into bad habits. "I despair of him," Clay wrote in 1830. He transferred his hopes to Henry, eight years younger, and let him know it: "Oh! my dear son no language can describe to you the pain that I have suffered on account of these two boys, [Theo and Tom]. My hopes rest upon you and your two younger brothers."[12] The burden was almost too much for young Henry. He, too, had been appointed to West Point. And he performed well, but under the added pressure of his father's anxiety for his success resigned after a year. He subsequently took to the law, married and raised a family, and began to fulfill his father's hopes. James, the fourth son, was his father's law partner. John, the last, loved the sporting life and finally settled into farming.

Disaster struck in 1847. At the outbreak of the Mexican War, Henry Clay, Jr., joined a Kentucky volunteer regiment and was elected a lieutenant colonel. He was badly wounded, shot through the thigh, during close combat with the enemy in the Battle of Buena Vista. Clay ordered his men to withdraw, surrendering to one of them his pistols, which had been a gift from his father. "Tell him," he said, "that I used them to the last." As the enemy approached in overwhelming numbers, the troop withdrew, and looking back they beheld their gallant commander wielding his sword as the enemy set upon him with bayonets.[13] Henry Clay, Jr., died a hero's death in a war his father deplored and despised, in the battle, moreover, that made a national hero of General Zachary Taylor. Clay did not bear his grief alone in this instance; it was scarcely less supportable for that, however. "What are all other adversities to this?" the nation asked. "What are public honors to the head of Mr. Clay when domestic griefs crowd around his hearthstone—his children and his children's children filling every private avenue with sorrow, shame, and adversity," Rebecca Gratz wrote movingly several years later. "I know no spectacle more sad than to see such a man, honored, beloved, and labouring for the good of all—and above all for his country—with such a desolate home for his affections."[14]

The last affliction, the death of the hero son, drove Clay into the arms of the church. He had never been touched by anything he recognized as religious experience or felt any call to Christian faith. Although he attended church services with more and more frequency as the years passed, especially after his retirement to Lexington, where Lucretia was a member of the Episcopal Church, religion lay lightly upon him. His relations with God, while cordial, were anything but intimate. In 1844 his running mate Theodore Frelinghuysen, along with other ministers of the gospel, took a personal interest in Clay's salvation to his considerable annoyance. He said he did not doubt the importance of faith in Christ but that its blessings had yet to be bestowed upon him. With the death of his son, the public interest in Clay's spiritual well-being swelled.[15] And on June 22, 1847, in the presence of members of the family and several special friends, the Reverend Edward F. Berkley, Rector of Christ Church, in Lexington, baptized Henry Clay with water from a huge cut-glass punch bowl in the drawing room at Ashland. "Baptized at seventy in a punch bowl!" an irreverent biographer exclaimed merrily in 1929. "Could there be a more delightful epitome of Kentucky life a century ago."[16]

An affliction of another kind, slavery, was beyond the solace of religion. Clay had been on intimate terms with slavery all his life. Being a slaveholder, more particularly a border-state slaveholder, was an important part of his public image. In the South he was denounced and distrusted for his anti-slavery sentiments, while in the North he was a special object of abolitionist hatred. Clay's name figured in the work songs of Kentucky slaves:

> Heave away! Heave away!
> I'd rather co't a yaller gal,
> Dan work for Henry Clay
> Heave away, yaller gal, I want to go.[17]

Incidents connected with his own slaves were reported in the press. If he advertised for runaways, as he did on occasion, it was noted. Years earlier, in 1829, he had been forced to defend himself in a suit brought in the Circuit Court of the District of Columbia by a slave, Charlotte, or "Black Lotty" as she became known, for her freedom and her children's freedom. Clay prevailed in the suit, which he believed had been got up to injure him politically; a decade later, he freed Charlotte and a daughter. The records of Fayette County show that Clay manumitted a number of slaves, of whom the faithful Charles was the most famous. Charles had nobly resisted the blandishments of abolitionists. His successor, Levi, at Newport in 1849, agreed to leave his master for the price of $300. Levi became a fugitive on Saturday, pocketed the money, and returned to his master on Monday.[18]

In 1846 the abolitionist press circulated a horrific address by Lewis Richardson, a fugitive from Ashland who had escaped to Canada. Richardson had been a slave at Ashland for nine unhappy years, he said. Contrary to general report, Clay was a cruel and heartless master. His slaves never had enough to eat. He had never given Richardson a cap or any bedclothes, except a small, coarse blanket. His overseer was a specialist in flogging. Last December, for a trifling offense, Richardson said, "Clay had me stripped and tied up, and one hundred and fifty lashes given me on my naked back." It was then that Richardson determined to flee, regrettably leaving his wife behind; but he would rather be buried in the Detroit River than go back to Ashland. "I now feel as independent as even Henry Clay felt . . . running for the White House," Richardson concluded cheerfully. "In fact I feel better. He has been defeated four or five times, and I but once. But he was running for Slavery, and I for Liberty. I think I have beat him out of sight."[19] When the story reached Lexington, the overseer at Ashland, Ambrose Barnett, and four knowledgeable white men testified that Richardson was a hard-drinking, insolent, unmanageable, and violent slave. There was "never a worse negro," according to Barnett. Nor was there ever a more indulgent master than Clay. Knowing it was against his wishes to whip a slave, Barnett had nevertheless once and only once been sufficiently provoked to lay sixteen lashes on Richardson. When he took off, Clay's response was good riddance, and he forbade any pursuit of the fugitive.[20]

Except among dedicated abolitionists ready to believe the worst of him, it seems unlikely that Richardson's story sullied Clay's reputation as a kind master. Much more controversial were his opinions on issues of policy involving slavery. Although it was mainly an honorific post, Clay remained president of the American Colonization Society to the end of his life. In 1845 the Kentucky members bought from the parent society a forty-square-mile tract in Liberia for the colonization of the state's free blacks and named the capital "Clay Ashland." Had a plan of gradual emancipation been adopted, with support for colonization, something might have come of "Kentucky in Liberia." But by 1851 only 297 Kentucky free blacks had been transported to the African country.[21] All Clay's earlier hopes for the doom of slavery founded on economic and demographic forces had been blasted. The force of public opinion had gone backward in Kentucky. Several years earlier he had actually opposed a movement for a constitutional convention to initiate gradual emancipation on a plan such as he had advocated lest the backlash caused by the abolitionist agitation jeopardize the good contained in the present constitution and laws, for instance the ban on interstate slave traffic. There was simply no sufficiently formed opinion for forward movement against slavery in the state. The legislature, in 1838, rejected the call for a convention by a four-to-one margin. For his part in this, and his Senate speech the following year, Clay was never forgiven by the abolitionists.[22]

In an effort to revive the faltering anti-slavery movement in Kentucky, Cassius Clay started a newspaper, *The True American*, in Lexington, which promised to be as spirited as its editor. Even before the appearance of the first issue in the spring of 1845, Clay and his press were threatened with violence by pro-slavery Democrats of whom Charles Wickliffe was the most prominent. Although not a party to Cassius Clay's enterprise, Henry Clay had held out the promise, at least so Cousin Cash thought, to protect him and his press from mob violence. But when the showdown came in August, Clay took off for the Virginia springs. A mob gathered; among its leaders was Clay's son James, a lawyer, and it claimed to act under the sanction of his name. Cassius Clay escaped assassination, with which he said he was threatened, but his press was removed and *The True American* silenced. Afterward he angrily accused Henry Clay of treachery and cowardice. "Speak not of Henry Clay!" he wrote to a friend. "That this man for whom I have laboured all my life, and risked my life and fortune—standing up for his adherents when the Wickliffe power overawed the Davis party and turned the current in favor of the Whigs—I fear that Mr. Clay *put the storm in motion* and then hurriedly left me here to die!"[23] He called upon Clay for an explanation. It is not clear that he received one. Henceforth his feelings toward Clay fluctuated wildly. But in 1848, just as Henry announced his availability for the Whig presidential nomination, Cassius shocked the nation by publicly accusing him of complicity in the alleged assassination attempt of 1845. This was madness. Cassius Clay remained convinced, however, that his old idol had no true heart against slavery, that he "wanted the glory of free principles, without the self-sacrifice," that he was, in fact, by his insidious persuasiveness the great enemy of human freedom.[24]

In 1849 Clay made one final effort—typically halfhearted, in Cousin Cash's view—to put slavery on the road to extinction in Kentucky. At this time there was support in both parties for a convention to revise the 1799 constitution. Slavery, of course, would be on the reform agenda. On February 17 Clay set forth his views in an impressive letter addressed to Richard Pindell but intended for the people of Kentucky. Regardless of the odium it would bring on him, he insisted on the letter's publication. "I owe that to the cause and myself, and to posterity," he said.[25] In a manner any abolitionist might approve, Clay attacked arguments current in the South to justify slavery. If the institution was a blessing to the black race, why could not the same doctrine be employed in other circumstances to justify subjugation of the white race or some portion of it? If it were just for one race to enslave another, what was to stop a nation advanced in civilization from reducing a backward nation to bondage? "Nay, further, if the principle be applicable to races and nations, what is to prevent its being applied to individuals?" Clay asked. "And then the wisest man in the world would have the right to make slaves of all the rest of mankind." He went on to describe his plan of gradual emancipation, adapted from the original Jeffersonian model, wherein slaves born after a certain date would be freed at adulthood, employed under the authority of the state for three years, and with the capital thus accumulated, transported to Liberia and supported there for the first six months. A few southern Whigs spoke up for the plan, but generally Clay was arraigned as a traitor to the South for advancing it. "Henry Clay's true character now stands revealed," the Richmond *Enquirer* editorialized. "The man is an abolitionist. He takes his position with Giddings and Hale."[26] Even so, abolitionists were not quick to own him. His plan of gradual emancipation was inhuman and impractical; and behind the facade of anti-slavery sentiment, they decried "the same old coon" come to rob the northern conscience. Clay wrote an address for a mass meeting of emancipationists in Lexington. He presided over the statewide assembly of emancipationists in the capital in April; unfortunately, it could not agree on the terms of a plan of emancipation. Nearly all emancipationists were Whigs, of course, but not all Whigs were emancipationists. Indeed, the division in the party on this question helped bring about the decline of the Whigs in Kentucky. The emancipationists canvassed the state for delegates to the constitutional convention. Well before the August election, Clay departed for Saratoga, Newport, and other eastern points. Again he appeared to be a "springtime patriot" at best. By seeming to give up the cause, he ensured its defeat, although it was probably lost in any event. Not a single emancipationist was elected. "No movement was ever more completely negatived," George Prentice wrote in the Louisville *Journal*. "It is abundantly demonstrated that emancipation never can be carried in Kentucky at the ballot box."[27] Yet five-sixths of the white people were nonslaveholders. The retrograde tendency Clay had detected in 1838 had amply fulfilled itself. The apprehended backlash came at once. The legislature repealed the law restricting importation of slaves to ownership and labor in the state.

Clay was in excellent health during these years. "He looks well, and talks, as usual, 'like a book,' " one visitor remarked.[28] He appeared younger than his years, and except that his hair was grayer and thinner had changed very little. Tall and slender, with a lithe, swinging gait, lambent eyes, and a bright, playful, grinning countenance, he was a uniquely arresting figure. Everything about him was long: long body, long legs, long face, long mouth. Phrenologists offered Clay as proof of their science: his warm, active, liberal, and sanguine temperament had its source in the size and shape of his head— unusually long in proportion to breadth. No one ever called him handsome or fashionable, indeed he was thought as plain and homely as an ordinary western farmer; and garbed in black with a wide collar and cravat, nothing in his dress enhanced his features. Yet the charm of Clay's personality was irresistible. Women, in particular, felt it. The secret of that attraction was one of the minor mysteries of the age. In courtrooms and legislative chambers, at balls and public festivals women gathered around Clay like bees around a flower. The white gloves kissed by Clay became treasured mementoes. If only women had the franchise, it was said, he would have been elected president again and again. In his declining years, when he traveled to New Orleans or Newport or White Sulphur Springs, Clay invited the attentions of fashionable women without even the hint of impropriety. Octavia Walton Le Vert, the most prominent of these friends, was a very piquant young lady, the granddaughter of a Georgia signer of the Declaration of Independence, the wife of a Mobile physician, one of "the scribbling females" about whom Nathaniel Hawthorne grumbled, and a fashionable southern belle with a large circle of admirers. She made Clay's acquaintance in New Orleans, induced him to sit for a portrait, and saw him often during the last eight years of his life. For Octavia Le Vert, at least, Clay was like the hero of a romantic novel. "With all those lofty and commanding qualities which sway senates, and guide the course of empires," she said after his death, "he had a heroism of heart, a chivalry of deportment, a deference of demeanor, which . . . [are] irresistible talismans over the mind of the gentler sex."[29]

With his unusual features and animated countenance, Clay was a difficult subject for protrait artists. He had sat "more than one hundred times"—a pardonable exaggeration—he complained in 1845, yet no artist had produced "a correct likeness," and he had grown weary of the operation. Many observers echoed Clay's judgment. Cousin Cash dismissed all the portraits as caricatures; Thomas C. Johnston, himself an artist, said they captured "only the body without the soul."[30] Clay generously acknowledged that the fault lay with him rather than the artists, "for my face never retains long the same expression, and especially when I am under excitement, it changes every moment."[31] Clay in repose was not Clay at all. John Neagle tried to catch him in the speaking mode; and although he made a grand picture, he did not succeed in the likeness. Clay thought better of the likeness produced by G. P. A. Healy, who came to Ashland in 1845 on a commission from Louis Philippe, the French king. Clay's repugnance to sitting was matched by Healy's irritation at the constant interruptions of callers and his subject's fidgetings, at one moment taking snuff, at another chewing on striped peppermint candy. Even so, Healy was captivated by Clay and his conversation; and he got on the canvas the warmth of his subject and the subtle mingling of geneality and astuteness in his countenance. "You are a capital portrait painter . . . ," Healy reported him as saying. "You are the first to do justice to my mouth, and it is very pleased to express its gratitude."[32]

If it was difficult to capture Clay on canvas or in stone, it was not much easier to define and delineate his character in words. He was a "self-made man," like Benjamin Franklin and a long line of celebrated Americans; moreover, he it was who, in extolling the virtues of enterprising manufacturers in 1832, introduced the phrase "self-made man" into the language.[33] Clay was *sui generis*. "He is independent alike of history or the schools; he knows little of either and despises both," Tom Marshall wrote. "His ambition, his spirit, and his eloquenece are all great and entirely his own. If he is like anybody, he does not know it. He has never studied models, and, if he had, his pride would have rescued him from the fault of imitation. He stands among men in towering and barbaric grandeur, in all the hardihood and rudeness of perfect originality, independent of the polish and beyond the reach of art."[34] Yet men made comparisons. Cassius Clay was not alone in thinking that Henry Clay and Andrew Jackson, so opposed in politics, were alike in character. Englishmen, and some Americans, repeatedly compared Clay and Lord Brougham. As parliamentary leaders they shared traits of impassioned eloquence and cool effrontery, though Clay boasted none of Brougham's literary attainments.[35] In the thought and writing about Clay, several recurring, often contradictory, images may be discerned; and each of them—the Prince, the Gamester, the Dictator, the Actor—reflects facets of an extraordinary personage.

Although presumably suggested by Shakespeare's "nimble-footed madcap," the image of Prince Hal came to encompass much more. Clay was one of nature's noblemen. He had a genius for talk, for wit and repartee, for the sparkling *bon mot* and the satiric jest. He was liberal, manly, and open in his views. He commanded the affection of even his political enemies. He had remarkable self-possession. His sense of the dignity of his own person was such that he could not tolerate any slur upon it. He was great, not so much in intellect—though strong, it was undeveloped—but in moral courage, as he had shown repeatedly in his public life. He had that boldness which, however foolish, as Bacon said, "doth fascinate." Prince Hal was a natural leader of men. So ambitious was he to lead, in fact, that he could not and would not follow. Webster, by contrast, while his superior in isolated power, lacked both the ambition and the talent to lead. "Mr. Clay," a Washington reporter wrote, "is not great in himself alone. He combines and directs the greatness of others, and thus, with whatever direction he takes, he moves with a resistless might. The secret of all this . . . is to be found in that most potent of all human influences, a true and ready *sympathy*. . . . There are no barriers between his heart and the heart of others."[36]

The image of the gamester had its source in Clay's youthful proclivity to gambling. John Quincy Adams, drawing upon his memories of Ghent, was among the first to see the Kentuckian in this light. "In politics, as in private life, Clay is essentially a Gamester," he wrote in 1819, "and, with a vigorous intellect, an ardent spirit . . . , and a very undigested system of ethics, he has all the qualities which belong to that class of human character."[37] Long after he gave up high-stake games like brag, confined himself to the whist table, and grew quite sedate in his conduct, Clay could not rid himself of the gamester image. It was the repository of whatever remained of his western swagger and intrepidity. It encompassed as well his reputation for political cunning and shrewdness, his talents as a legislative broker of powerful economic interests, and his genius for bargain and compromise. The gamester, by definition, was without principles. While Clay had often scored impressively in this role, he had also often outsmarted himself, most egregiously so in 1825. "Mr. Clay is a gamester in politics," the Charleston *Mercury* editorialized in 1839, "but not a cool one. His temper, unrestrained, exhibits frequent ebullitions from the excitement of the game. He stakes on every likely popular card that turns up, whether red or black; and though he often wins a shrewd trick, and dips deeply into the bank, he loses in the long run."[38] Clay was adept, yet there was such a thing as too much management, and he disclosed the fault.

The image of Clay the Dictator took form in the famous Extra Session of 1841. Both Webster and Calhoun, as well as devoted Tylerites, contributed to it. But Clay's domineering nature had been recognized for a long time. Over it, Harriet Martineau had observed, he had obtained "truly noble mastery," and she wondered what it must have cost him.[39] Strong emotions broke through the princely calm in angry outbursts, stinging rebukes, and haughty self-assertion. This was quite another image. It emphasized Clay's obduracy, arrogance, and headstrong determination, all characteristics which, in the view of some observers, he shared with the pertinacious Jackson. In the Dictator, Clay's very virtues, pursued to excess, turned into vices: the capacity to lead became domination, boldness became precipitancy, wit became invective, firmness became obstinacy. Webster remarked on Clay's excesses during the Tyler imbroglio: "His irritable temper brooks no contradiction, and [as he is] by far fonder of invective and retort, than the influence of soft persuasion, neither friend nor foe . . . can expect quarter." Clay was so fond of admiration, of pleasing the gallery, Webster said, that he could not pass up an opportunity to score at another's expense even if it planted a dagger in the heart. "While no man, in his speeches, gains more general applause, no man inflicts so much private pain, or creates so deep-seated a dislike in the bosom of his adversaries." And yet, like a petulant child, Clay could quickly turn as cool and soothing as a summer shower. The Dictator reverted to Prince Hal. "He is in fact," said Phillip Hone, "the spoiled child of society; everybody loves him, subscribes to his opinions, and finds excuses for his foibles."[40]

Like Webster, but unlike Calhoun, Clay was a great performer as well as a great presence. Thus the image of the Actor. "What an actor he would have made!" Healy exclaimed. Everyone recognized Clay's histrionic abilities. They contributed to that excess of which Webster complained. Forrest, conversing with Clay during the great debate of 1850, remarked favorably on a statesmanlike speech by Louisiana Senator Pierre Soulé, only to be met by vehement criticism that finally dismissed the senator with the line, "He is nothing but an actor, sir—a mere actor." Then, suddenly remembering to whom he was speaking, Clay softened his tone, waved his hand, and said to Forrest, "I mean, my dear sir, a mere French actor!" Departing, Forrest remarked to his companion, "Mr. Clay has proved, by the skill with which he can change his manner, and the grace with which he can make an apology, that he is a better actor than Soulé!"[41] With a magnificent voice, an expressive countenance, and extravagant gestures, Clay commanded the feelings of his audience in a theatrical manner. The question naturally arises of whether *he* was "a mere actor." No one, not even his worst enemies, ventured to suggest this. Whatever his faults, Clay was acknowledged to be a true statesman; and if he was also habitually an actor, the role he enacted, as Parton suggested, was Henry Clay writ large. Having created his own public character, he made showy gestures—"Go home, Mr. Mendenhall!"—to dramatize himself to the nation. "Characters in public life," it has been said, "were indeed one of the great creations of the time; and they often seemed to gain their emphasis less from a closely packed individuality than from bold and conscious self-picturization."[42] Such was certainly the case with Clay, to a lesser extent with Webster, while Calhoun exemplified "closely packed individuality."

Clay was an orator, of course, and oratory was a mode of public perfor-

mance as well as of public discourse. The legend of Clay as a natural genius—
"the artificer of his own destiny"—who owed nothing to art or education
came into existence to explain Clay the orator. Natural force and earnestness
filled the vacuum of education. No false glitter or literary embellishments or
Ciceronian periods got into his speech, unless by a misguided attempt to
cover up the deficiencies of education. The idea that Clay was nature-taught,
that his oratory was "as free and wild as the elk of the forest," went along with
his western character. Because of it hundreds of western youths, it was said,
gave up their Greek and Latin and decried college. Oratory was the supremely republican art, for republican government was government by advocacy, discussion, and persuasion. The aim of the orator was not to convince
but to persuade, not to find the truth but to motivate action in behalf of men
and measures. The highest faculties of the mind were wasted in this work.
The orator in deliberative bodies, William Hazlitt wrote, "has no occasion to
dive into the depths of science, or to soar aloft on angels' wings. He keeps to
the surface. . . . Refinement, depth, elevation, delicacy, originality, ingenuity, invention, are not wanted: he must appeal to the sympathies of human nature, and whatever is not found there, is foreign to his purpose."[43] Clay embodied this conception, however overdrawn, beyond any other eminent man
of his time. He was generally considered the most Demosthenic of American
orators, since he spoke only for practical effect and employed eloquence as a
tool of statesmanship. Action was his aim: oratory to impel the will. Even
Clay's physical action, which was unstudied, graceless, and inordinate, was
seen as the outer expression of inner force and conviction. "He moved from
his desk," one observer wrote. "He walked up and down between the rows of
seats. He took snuff. He used his hands freely. He varied his voice; was sometimes rapid, sometimes slow, sometimes solemn, sometimes playful. . . . He
had the air of an accomplished actor playing a part with great skill but with an
eye always on the audience and their applause."[44] Unfortunately, none of the
action of his speeches could be transmitted to the printed page. The reported
speeches were but skeletons of the originals. *

Clay was commonly credited with great political skill. And certainly in the
field of legislative leadership he scaled heights rarely equaled in America.
Even when he failed, as he usually did, for he was usually in opposition, he
was applauded for the strength of his views, his resourcefulness, his courage
and tenacity. From 1832 onward, or even from 1824, his life was a series of
magnificent hopes and disastrous defeats, punctuated here and there—the
Compromise of 1833 stands out—by a triumph. He became, in Martineau's
phrase, "a disappointed statesman." Repeatedly denied in his quest for the
presidency, Clay could explain every defeat without ever blaming himself,

---

*On occasion political enemies, in this instance Frank Blair, in the Washington *Globe*, took a
dim view of orator Clay: "His whole system of argumentation may be defined in a single phrase,
the *argumentum ad ignorantian*—the lowest appeals to the coarsest ignorance. . . . Masterbook
gesticulations, self-complacent airs, slang phrases, hackneyed anecdotes, crocodile tears, whee-
dling cajoleries, fustian fanfaronade, alternate imprecations and supplications—all these together, or in succession, make up the *eloquence* of this spurious patriot and vulgar hero."[45]

hence without ever defeating himself. Yet these defeats laid bare his political deficiencies. Always in the high ropes of policy, Clay had neither the talent nor the patience for the hard work of organization and mobilization that occurred on and below the decks of partisan political craft. He possessed none of the skill of his Democrat friend Van Buren in coalition building, in the use of local party machinery in national politics, and in the management of elections. He had no Lexington Regency to match the Albany Regency. Immensely popular, Clay was apt to equate popularity with political strength. He carried into presidential politics the same personal style that distinguished his legislative leadership and he seemed to believe it would produce the same effect. But operating as his own political manager, Clay made mistake after mistake. He pushed when he should have pulled; he talked when he should have kept silent; he was precipitate when he should have been cautious; he conciliated when he should have been resolute; he made a virtue of consistency when consistency had become absurd; and he was slow to exploit new issues when the old ones had lost their punch with the electorate.

In the legislative arena, where he excelled, Clay was identified with three matters of high policy: the American System, legislative supremacy, and the preservation of the Union. The first of these envisioned dynamic economic growth under the fostering hand of the general government. It rejected the emerging "classical" economics model of the free market with its political counterpart in negative government, and instead proposed to employ governmental powers, the revenue system in particular, for national purposes. During the National Republican years, the American System platform was substantially enacted into law. Thereafter, it found a home—not altogether hospitable—in the Whig party. But the national character of the American System was undermined. Assailed and then dismantled by the regnant Jacksonian Democracy, it became increasingly associated with privileged propertied interests and the local political elites that served them. The American System, although it remained the system of improvement and progress, was perforce transformed into the *conservative* platform. Clay himself grew more conservative—in his opinions, political fears, social connections, finally in his religion. He had himself struck a critical blow, as Webster had argued, at the integrity of the American System in 1833. For in compromising the protective tariff he gave priority to other objectives— the Union, anti-Jacksonism, the presidency—and by adopting the ultimate goal of "a tariff for revenue only," Clay not only muddled the terms of debate between Whigs and Democrats but participated willy-nilly in the movement that terminated in the Democratic Walker Tariff of 1846, supposedly founded on that principle. The other leading measures of the American System were diverted or defeated. Democratic individualism was the spirit of the age. The Whigs gradually accommodated themselves to it, and in doing so, although they reaped the political rewards, yielded the large and comprehensive vision of public policy received from the National Republicans. From the perspective of the Polk administration, Clay's political career presented a scene of exploded policies and debauched principles.

He was not given to looking back, but had he done so he would have been amazed by how little of what he had labored and fought for survived. Much the same may be said of the long campaign Clay waged against executive tyranny. He believed that Jackson dangerously upset the balance of the Constitution, aggrandizing the powers of the president at the expense of Congress and also the Supreme Court. Jackson's was the first "imperial presidency." The history of liberty was the history of the restraint of executive power, which was, as Webster said, "the lion that must be caged." Legislative supremacy was the accepted republican doctrine. Clay imbibed it with his original Jeffersonianism. The Jacksonian redefinition of republican government in terms of executive power—in the distribution of patronage, in the veto of legislation, in challenging the ultimate authority of the judiciary on the Constitution, above all in making the president into the popular organ of government—shocked and dismayed Clay and his party. Their opposition was justified. But in the hysteria that accompanied it, Clay failed to recognize that the growing power of political parties made strong executive leadership essential to effective government, indeed all the more so in a government charged with positive responsibility for the national welfare. When he attempted in 1841 to found a regime on legislative leadership, the result was a political disaster. Clay's final resolutions on legislative versus executive power in 1842 were set aside and soon forgotten, except in the vestiges of Whig ideology. Yet if he did not win, Clay did not really lose this battle. For in the paroxysm of reaction against King Andrew, Clay and his party formed the political sentiment that practically ensured, with a partial exception for Young Hickory, the succession of weak presidents down to the Civil War.

The preservation of the Union had been a dominant motif in Clay's career since the Missouri Compromise. It was not less so, of course, in Calhoun's and Webster's. The political dramaturgy of these great men revolved more and more around the Union. The last act of the drama had yet to be played.

2. Webster at Marshfield

"Oh, Marshfield! Marshfield!" Webster would cry out longingly as he labored over affairs of state in Washington. Marshfield was always in his affections, and never far from his thoughts. It was to Marshfield that he retired in 1843; and the next three years, for all their political torment, offered to him a feast of rural delights. "There, at Marshfield," George T. Curtis wrote, "was gathered all that could gratify the strong, healthy tastes of his nature—the fields, the streams, the ocean, in which he often spent whole days from the early dawn to the hours of darkness."[1]

Webster acquired this property in Marshfield, South Parish, in 1832, having earlier spent several summers there with his family. Only ten miles from Plymouth Rock, it was pleasantly associated with the lore and legend of the Pilgrim Fathers. The mansion had been built before the American Revolution. Webster purchased the place from the builder's son, Captain John Thomas, who continued to live there until his death in 1837. His two sons, Ray and Henry, were taken into Webster's employ. At that time the estate consisted of 160 acres, the mansion and several outbuildings. The large square two-story frame house, with a piazza all around, made no claims to elegance but was roomy and comfortable. The real charm of the place belonged to its situation. From the gently undulating lawn before the house, one looked south to the sea a mile off and in every direction to marsh and meadow, ponds and woods. It was a landscape—one imagines an atmosphere—such as Martin Heade might have painted.

Webster rapidly acquired adjoining properties until Marshfield (or Green Harbour, as he sometimes called his place) grew to some 1,200 acres dotted with small houses, barns, and other buildings. He was constantly making improvements, some of a practical agricultural nature, drainage for instance, others for appearance and amusement. Seeing tasteful improvements—a summer house, a fish pond—at places he visited, Webster wanted to duplicate them at Marshfield. The size of the mansion was doubled, mainly by the addition of a sprawling west wing in 1843. Built on his daughter Julia's plan, this was in the vaguely Gothic style, featuring high-pitched roofs and dormers, of rural architecture of the time. It provided a great room for a personal library of over one thousand volumes, which had been homeless since Webster sold his Boston house in 1839. His law library remained in his Tremont Street office; and Webster kept still another collection of books, this one devoted to agriculture and natural history, in a small detached study at the corner of the garden sloping down from the house. He laid out landscaped walks around the property, built causeways through the marshes, and planted trees—orchards, avenues, copses, groves—in great profusion. One can only imagine what the place looked like when he had finished with it. For it is all gone. The mansion burned in 1878. Of it Nathaniel P. Willis, who visited Marshfield in its prime, wrote, "though the picture of English refinement and rural comfort, [the house] is still an unpresuming exponent of the fifteen hundred acres which surround, as well as the distinction which inhabits it."[2]

Marshfield was a saltwater farm. When he settled there, Webster said to the neighbors who called, "I have come to reside among you as a farmer, and here I talk neither politics nor law."[3] He was already a farmer, of course, the proprietor of the family homestead, Elms Farm, between the hills and the Merrimack River in New Hampshire; but farming at the edge of the sea was another matter altogether, and Webster set out to master it. When he acquired the place, it yielded annually a few tons of hay and little else. With expanded acreage and improvements, Marshfield came to yield six hundred tons of hay, eight hundred or a thousand bushels of corn, one thousand bushels of potatoes, five hundred of oats, five hundred of turnips, and four hundred of beets. Or so Webster claimed. When he arrived his neighbors knew almost nothing of the value of kelp harvested from the sea as a fertilizer. Webster demonstrated this to them. Thereafter, when mighty storms deposited this "ocean manure" on the beaches, as many as one hundred and fifty teams of oxen were employed to transport it to the area farms.[4] On the farm were seventy to a hundred head of cattle and approximately the same number of sheep. Webster was an enthusiast about sheep, favoring the heavy South-downs and Leicesters, specimens of which he had brought back from England in 1839. His big flock of sheep—five hundred or more—grazed the New Hampshire hills; but these English varieties, he said, liked the seaside pastures, and he kept them more for mutton than for wool.[5] Webster sold sheep and cattle, chickens, even oxen, at market, together with crops of potatoes. Turning a profit was out of the question, however. He lavished money on Marshfield. None of his improvements could be justified in terms of return on investment. Even if they could be, he would never know it, since he kept no accounts and never balanced income against expenditures. If he was, as he said, "naturally a farmer," he was also naturally as careless in farm management as he was in all his financial dealings. He employed a small army of laborers at Marshfield, along with an overseer, a boatman, and five or six house servants. Such an establishment, such prodigality, could only be justified in terms of personal gratification. And who paid for that? Henry Thoreau, reflecting on Webster's boast that he was the best farmer in Marshfield, wrote that, if that was so, the rest must be a sorry lot, for he farmed with other people's money, and indeed it would be cheaper to keep him in the county poorhouse.[6]

Webster loved to be outdoors at Marshfield. "There is nothing in this world, or at least for me," he wrote, "like the air of the sea, united to a kind of lazy exercise, and an absolute forgetfulness of business and cares."[7] As always, he rose on "the wings of the morning" at four to five o'olock. The cocks in the barnyard, it was said, mistook his candle for the break of day. Often he was out fishing before the sun splashed upon the waters of Massachusetts Bay. His constant companion, the "Commodore" of the sailboat, was Seth Peterson, "a droll, red-faced old salt" who came to Webster with the house. They fished for mackerel, halibut, and cod, and did some lobstering too. Once, returning home, not long after the "Sea Serpent" had been reported in the bay, Webster told the helmsman, who was facing the other way, that he saw the fabulous creature dart in and out of the water, then added imploringly, "For God's sake never say a word about this to any one, for if it should be known that I have seen the sea serpent, I should never hear the last of it." In the nearby streams Webster fished for trout. "I never saw anybody so smart at taking a trout from his hole," said Peterson.[8] Mornings when he was not fishing, Webster might be hunting for duck, woodcock, and marsh birds. The Farmer of Marshfield was an avid sportsman. After breakfast, Webster made his rounds, visiting with the animals, observing the laborers, and inspecting improvements. There was always correspondence to attend to, of course. "I sometimes try to read here," he remarked, "but can never get on, from a desire to be out of doors." He gave himself up to company in the late afternoon and evening. Dinner was usually at four—the work of his fine Negro cook Monica McCarty, whose freedom he had purchased from Judge William Cranch in Washington and who was highly prized for her Maryland delicacies.[9]

While never the tourist attraction Ashland became, Marshfield did not want for visitors. Webster was "the very perfection of a host." The "great man" was forgotten, the air of gloomy abstraction that so often enveloped him was lifted, and politics were adjourned at Marshfield. "At one moment, instructive, then, as full of life and glee as a boy escaped from school," Philip Hone wrote in 1845, "he sings snatches of songs, tells entertaining stories, and makes bad puns, in which his guests are not far behind him." Guests at Marshfield were privileged to see him undressed, as it were—in the farmer's rustic attire or in the fisherman's loose coat and long boots and a slouched hat that, Hone imagined, a Mexican bandit might have coveted. Webster dressed for dinner in the costume for which he was famous—blue coat with brass buttons, white cravat, buff vest—though Hone thought it "as incongruous for Daniel Webster as ostrich feathers for a sister of charity." At dinner Webster "talked like a book," his conversation rich in anecdote and reminiscence, while Mrs. Webster made up for any loss of dignity occasioned by her husband's volubility. "The Table is capital; everything is given at the top of the heart; and while there is no empressement, every wish is anticipated."[10] After the enlargement and remodeling in 1843, the house was "very prettily fitted up." "Pictures, pieces of statuary, choice engravings, and curiosities of every description are displayed in the greatest profusion." One guest remarked that the bedroom to which he retired was liberally decorated with prints of English country estates and castles.[11]

Webster enjoyed good health except for diarrheic illness and an especially aggravating malady. From his fiftieth year on he was a chronic sufferer of pollinosis, commonly known today as hay fever, and known to Webster as "the summer catarrh." It struck every August, on or about the twenty-third of the month, and lasted four to six weeks. Eyes and nose grew irritated, followed by sniveling and sneezing that Webster described as "truly transcendental," until he seemed to melt away in nasal and lachrymal effluence. Inflammation of the eyes often kept him from reading or writing for days at a time. Once asked what he took for it, Webster replied, "eight handkerchiefs a day." And, one supposes, more than a little whiskey and brandy. Neither cause nor cure was known. A Philadelphia physician Webster consulted treated it as "a nervous affection." Seeking relief, Webster vacillated between the hope of finding it in the mountain air of New Hampshire or in the sea air of Marshfield, and, of course, found it at neither place.[12]

Whether because of the hay fever or in spite of it, Webster usually gravitated to Elms Farm in late summer or early fall of each year. Here, too, he had added to the property, until it grew to a thousand acres and supported a hundred head of cattle and many hundreds of sheep. Webster's affection for the place was inseparable from memories of family and childhood. A native son—the most eminent of those "Sons of New Hampshire" who had gone off to Boston and elsewhere to become rich and famous—he was known to everybody, old and young, in and around Franklin. In 1843 he threw a big "chowder party" for some three hundred guests in an oak grove on Andover Pond (now named Webster Lake) where he owned a boat house and a beach. The scene he observed from the family homestead—the meadow and pasture and surrounding hills, the white stones marking the graves of his mother and father, brother and sisters—made this to him "the sweetest spot on earth" and called to mind the verses of Watts's hymn:

> A little spot, enclosed by Grace
> From out the world's wide wilderness.

Unfortunately, the railroad invaded this peaceable kingdom in 1845. The line of the Northern Railroad—from Boston up the Merrimack Valley, reaching toward the Connecticut River—passed within fourteen feet of the house and rattled its rafters three or four times a day. Never one to stand in the way of progress, Webster chose to live with the intruder. Two years later he spoke in celebration of the opening of the railroad from Franklin to Grafton. The railroad had defaced his meadow and brought noise and ugliness to Elms Farm, he said. "But I have observed . . . ," he continued philosophically, "that railroad directors and railroad projectors are no enthusiastic lovers of landscape beauty. . . . Their business is to cut and slash, to level or deface a firmly rounded field, and fill up beautifully winding valleys. . . . Their business is to make a good road." And no invention, more than the railroad, promised greater benefits to mankind.[13]

Three of Webster's children, all by his first wife, grew to adulthood. One of the pleasures of retirement at Marshfield was the opportunity to be close to Julia. Often visiting from Boston, where she lived with her husband, Samuel Appleton, and their children, Julia shared her father's love of the place. Before he left office Webster saw to it that both his sons were publicly employed. Fletcher, the dutiful older son of fair talents, was appointed secretary to Caleb Cushing's commission to China. Edward, the wayward son, who gave his father considerable pain and grief before he finally graduated from Dartmouth and began to read law, was named secretary to the Northeast Boundary Commission and spent the next several years in the Maine wilderness. When the Mexican War came both the young Websters were volunteers. Colonel Fletcher Webster commanded the 12th Infantry Regiment, often called "the Webster Regiment." He returned, eventually inherited Marshfield, and died in a war his father would have approved. Major Edward Webster was less fortunate. He died of typhoid fever in Mexico in February 1848. The father had only begun to recover from this blow when Julia expired after a long illness, probably tuberculosis, in April. Webster's affections ran deep, and the death of these children, although he was outwardly stoical, broke his heart and sapped his strength. Suddenly he appeared old. In May he planted two weeping elms in front of Marshfield, naming them "The Brother and the Sister," as a memorial to Edward and Julia. "I hope the *trees* will live," he remarked. Later he arranged for the removal of his children's remains from Boston graves to the family plot at Marshfield.[14]

These were peak years of Webster portraiture. With the possible exception of John Quincy Adams, who actually liked sitting, Webster sat for more artists than any other American of his time, although he was scarcely less approachable in this regard than Henry Clay and, according to Healy, "looked upon us as so many horseflies."[15] Artists clamored to paint and sculpt Webster not just because he was famous but because atop his undistinguished frame reposed one of the most extraordinary heads known to creation. Chester Harding, the Boston artist, who claimed that Webster sat for him twenty times, thought him "the greatest man" he ever saw, and never greater than when he threw off the mantle of the great man. Mathew Brady, among the last to portray him, said that Webster's head and face were the grandest he ever photographed. The black hair, the majestic brow, the saturnine complexion, "the crag-like face" with its "dull black eyes," and "mastiff mouth, appropriately closed," in Carlyle's often-quoted description—all this begged to be painted. Phrenologists, as they had with Clay, found their science exhibited in the correspondence between Webster's head and his intellect. "A larger mass of brain perhaps never was, and never will be, found in the upper and latter portion of any man's forehead than that contained in his," one of them wrote.[16] Hiram Powers, who made a plaster model at Marshfield in 1836, later finishing the bust in marble in Florence, was awed by Webster: "He always made me think of Michel Angelo's gigantic statutes," Powers wrote, "natural, but one of nature's exaggerations; out of her common way of working, but still her own work."[17] Fascinated by the marvelous features of the godlike man, artists usually failed to do justice to the mere mortal. This was certainly Caroline Webster's opinion. "They are all caricatures," she said. "It seemed to be thought that a high forehead, large eyes, and dark eyebrows made a likeness; but those who thought so quite mistook the true character of the man." They omitted, most unfortunately, his warmth and geniality.[18] Webster understood the importance of the visual image to the character a statesman transmitted to posterity. He took his own idea of Washington, he said, from Gilbert Stuart's portraits. A friend and admirer had commissioned Stuart in his old age to paint Webster. But it was not a good portrait. At first, dazzled by Stuart's reputation, Webster said he was willing to "go down to posterity" with the likeness; later, however, when it hung at Marshfield, he remarked to Caroline one evening he would just as soon see "the other side of the canvas."[19]

The most important artist to work at Marshfield during these years was G. P. A. Healy; and with the exception of Harding, the fashionable Boston portraitist, he was finally the most prolific limner of Webster. Healy first painted him in Washington on the commission from Louis Philippe. The king was much taken with the portrait when it was placed on view in Paris. At Healy's suggestion he now commissioned a gigantic historical canvas depicting Webster's Reply to Hayne, which he thought a promising companion to "Benjamin Franklin at Court," already in hand. Upon returning to the United States, and after working at the Hermitage and Ashland, Healy was invited by the Hone Club to make a picture of Webster for the princely sum of $550. Organized by Philip Hone in 1838, the club consisted of fifteen New

Yorkers, all of whom considered Webster a divinity. So Healy went to Marshfield in the fall with two commissions. He completed the simpler one first. His seated Webster, garbed in dignified black, as Hone preferred him, and surrounded with the properties of a statesman—globe, quill pen, sheaf of paper—made a tremendous hit when it was hung in Hone's dining room the following spring. To celebrate the occasion the club members uncorked their best wine, read portions of a speech Webster had recently delivered, and with glasses raised, eyes turned upon the portrait, drank the statesman's health "three times three."[20] Healy returned to Marshfield in 1848 to complete the full-length likeness for the historical canvas. It was at that time, perhaps for Mrs. Webster's amusement, that he painted the "Squire of Marshfield" in hunting garb under the elms. "Webster Replying to Hayne," to give it the final title, was a complex work, involving over a hundred individual portraits, most of them painted from life, in an elaborate composition that measured sixteen-by-thirty. Healy returned to his Paris studio to finish it. Louis Philippe, meanwhile, was overthrown. Looking now to Boston for a purchaser, Healy took his picture there in 1851. Placed on public view, it created a sensation. The city bought it and hung it in Faneuil Hall, the scene of so many Webster triumphs, at the time of his death.[21]

Ever since the debate with Hayne, Webster was perceived above all as the Defender of the Constitution. He was, indeed, a living monument of the Constitution and the Union—a figure of bronze, stern-visaged, from whose lips issued the words, "Liberty and Union, now and forever, one and inseparable." Many of the paintings and statues were but dead versions of the living monument. That, in turn, represented the Olympian Webster, Godlike Daniel, whose majestic powers of mind and speech were dedicated to preserving the sacred trust passed on by the fathers. But much about Webster's character was less than godlike. A counter-image took form to explain it. In 1846, following Charles Jared Ingersoll's congressional attack on Webster, William L. Yancey of Alabama aired the rumors of the senator's being "pensioned" by his wealthy Massachusetts friends and concluded that he had "two characters, which, Proteus-like, he can assume, as his interests or necessities demand—the 'God-like' and the 'Hell-like'—the 'God-like Daniel' and 'Black Dan.' "[22] Webster had picked up the appellative Black Dan in his youth, when it was suggested by his dark complexion. But it had been forgotten until Yancey chose the same name to describe the dark side of Webster's character.

The contrast between Godlike Daniel and Black Dan was a contrast between intellectual power and moral weakness, between patriotism and ambition, virtue and venality, the genius of statesmanship and the artifice of politics. Webster the mythic statesman, Defender of the Constitution, "natural Emperor of men," in Emerson's words, and Adamitic spokesman of the nation, was constantly jeopardized by Black Dan; and this was more than a personal problem because of the nation's stake in the symbol of Godlike Daniel. The tension and the contradictions between the two characters ran throughout Webster's career. His weak moral sense was illustrated most obviously by his financial dependency, on Biddle's bank or on Boston's rich men, his apparent blindness to the public implications of that, and his nortorious failure to pay his debts. He was selfish in using the services of others without acknowledgement. A case in point was Justice Joseph Story. When his son began to assemble letters for a memoir of his father, who died in 1845, Webster refused to supply important letters in his possession or to permit publication of any of his own letters, thereby—the son surmised—keeping the world in ignorance of his intellectual debt to Story. Although Webster gave a eulogy following the justice's death, he never did deliver a promised discourse on his life and services, as William Wetmore Story complained.[23] No man was more devoted to Webster for as many years as Edward Everett. Webster himself described him as "a sort of 'Alter Ego' " and exploited him shamelessly. After Everett's return from England, Webster set him to work on his *Diplomatic Papers*, published in 1848, then on editing his speeches and writings. When Everett was inaugurated president of Harvard in 1846, Webster made a showy late entrance, taking his seat on the stage after the opening prayer and hymn, just as Everett rose to speak. "Of course," as Emerson wrote, "the whole genial current of feeling flowing toward him was arrested, and the old Titanic Earth-Son was alone seen." The house shook with applause, and the gallery was a sea of waving handkerchiefs for five minutes. Fortunately for Webster, Everett seemed willing to suffer almost any indignity for him.[24]

Big of brain, Webster was not known for bigness of heart. Alexis de Tocqueville, during his travels, attempted to interest Webster in humanitarian prison reform only to be brushed off with the observation it was useless to attempt to reform criminals. "Webster . . . ," the Frenchman concluded, "cares only for power."[25] He had a cold Yankee character, at least in the eyes of non-Yankees; and it defeated every effort to make himself popular. No current of sympathy passed from his heart to the heart of the American people. Politicians who idolized Webster, and who came to Washington to meet him and offer their services to his presidential aspirations, were sometimes chilled and turned off by the manner of their reception. Yet this Yankee had a marvelous talent for friendship. Certainly he had more true friends— friends of the heart rather than of politics—than Clay or Calhoun, and he held them longer. "He required to be loved, before he could be known," G. S. Hillard observed. "He, indeed, grappled his friends with hooks of steel."[26] Webster's temperament was as variable as the Marshfield skies, often sunny but at other times as black as a thunder cloud. In the latter mood, self-absorbed and gloomy, he was likely to be as saturnine as his complexion and as unapproachable as a porcupine. A little-known artist, Francis Alexander, captured this Webster in the remarkable portrait painted for Dartmouth in 1835. Here, in marked contrast to the dignified statesman-hero, was a wild, dark, brooding, almost Byronic figure—the very image of Black Dan.

Webster had displayed impressive qualities of leadership as secretary of state, but in Congress, where talents of another order were required, he was seldom a leader, usually a follower. He was reserved and unsociable; he seemed more at home with the conversation of scholars, clergymen, lawyers, and captains of industry than with that of congressmen; he commanded admiration, even awe, but not affection. He had neither taste nor talent for political in-fighting, for the intricacies of legislation and parliamentary maneuver. During all his years in Congress, he gave his name to no great creative work of legislation. In debate, when sufficiently aroused, everyone recognized that he was capable of gigantic efforts productive of extraordinary results; but as was observed in comparison with Clay, Webster was a man of isolated power. "He has no ambition to lead. . . . He seldom rouses his energies, except in crisis; and even then it is only after he has made every possible calculation on the fate of the day."[27] He was ambitious for the presidency, of course, yet remained under the delusion it was a prize awarded on merit.[28] In Webster power of intellect and power of will were altogether out of balance; and this was the explanation generally offered for his deficiencies as a leader. Another theory, preferred by some biographers, maintained that he was "naturally indolent." Harriet Martineau, who observed him closely in the 1830s, took this view. "The chief interest to me in Webster's pleading [before the Supreme Court] and also in speaking in the Senate," she wrote, "was from seeing one so dreamy and *nonchalant* roused into strong excitement. . . . Webster is a lover of ease and pleasure, and has an air of the most unaffected indolence and careless self-sufficiency. It is something to see him moved with anxiety and the toil of intellectual conflict; to see his lips tremble, his nostrils expand, the perspiration start from his brow; to hear his voice vary with emotion, and to watch the expression of laborious thought while he pauses, for minutes together, to consider his notes and decide upon the arrangement of his argument. These are moments when it becomes clear that this pleasure-loving man works for his honours and his gains."[29] Habits of pleasure and indolence increased with age, James Parton thought. The image of the rustic Squire of Marshfield sustained this view. Yet it flew in the face of ample evidence of industry and vigor in all Webster's pursuits.

In his declining years, Webster gained an unenviable reputation for drunken and licentious behavior. For the most part it was confined to narrow political circles; occasionally, as in the instance of the reported sexual assault in 1842, anecdote and gossip reached the general public, threatening irreparable damage to the Godlike. A frame and temperament such as Webster's required "a little swing and margin," a Boston friend observed, and he may not have been strictly faithful to his marriage vows; yet there is no solid evidence of clandestine affairs or sexual indiscretions. After his death Webster's authorized biographer, George T. Curtis, investigated several reports of that nature and concluded they were all political calumnies. The only one that was even plausible concerned Mrs. John Agg, in whose Washington home Webster boarded after the death of his first wife. But neither the letters between them nor those between Webster and her husband, a newspaperman, nor the testimony of mutual friends supported the idea that she was Webster's mistress.[30] Regardless of the purport of the Black Dan image, Webster was certainly no libertine in his relations with women.

Much more substantial were the reports of excessive drinking. Chancellor Kent described the senator at a dinner party in 1840: "He is 57 years old, and looks worn and furrowed; his belly becomes protuberant, and his eyes deep in his head. . . . He has been too free a liver. He ate but little, and drank wine freely."[31] That Webster drank freely in his later years—wine at dinner, brandy frequently, whiskey on occasion—is well established. Dr. George Ellis, pastor of the Unitarian Church in Charlestown, recalled that Webster stopped at his house before going to the platform to dedicate the Bunker Hill Monument and, asking for the brandy decanter, filled a tumbler to the brim and drank it off. After the ceremony, he returned, repeated the operation, chatted for a while, and left perfectly composed. It was not unusual, of course, for a public speaker to take a drink as a stimulant. But in this matter, as in others, Webster was extravagant. At the Rochester Fair several months later, he pleaded illness upon arrival, and William H. Seward substituted for him in his first scheduled speech. If he was not already drunk, he became so at dinner that evening when, it was said, he fell into the arms of the mayor, who was presiding, after offering a toast. Denying these reports, Webster's friends pointed out that he spoke superbly for two hours, and they blamed any apparent tipsiness on the water and the fatigue of travel.[32] Reports of Webster's drunkenness crested after his return to the Senate. Abolitionists, rapidly losing faith in his character, thought it a symptom of his debauchery. Horace Mann, the Bay State congressman and then senator, said that Webster was often "so drunk on the floor of the Senate that he could not articulate his mother tongue." Yet Alexander H. Stephens, the Georgia congressman who lived next door to him, insisted that he never saw Webster intoxicated. This accorded with the testimony gathered by Curtis and other friendly investigators after the great man's death.[33]

The truth of the matter seems to be, first, that like many, perhaps most, public men of his time, Webster drank a good deal, though less than some of his prominent contemporaries; second, that his drinking together with his Lucullan appetite injured his health and undoubtedly contributed to the liver disease that eventually killed him; third, that his drinking habits did not significantly impair his mental powers or his functioning in public office. As Gamaliel Bradford observed, "Webster's love of the sunrise and habit of five o'clock in the morning are quite incompatible with serious dissipation."[34] Finally, Webster's capacity for drink entered into his capacity for grandeur, which was part of his reputation. Two examples may be offered from the rich vein of anecdote and legend. The present-day sojourner in Boston, in the vicinity of Faneuil Hall, who happens into the Union Oyster House, established in 1826, and sits at the bar may read the plaque above him: "The Original U-Shaped Mahogany Oyster Bar where Daniel Webster was a constant customer. He drank a tall tumbler of brandy with each half dozen oysters and seldom had less than six plates." In the fall of 1850, Jenny Lind, "The Swedish Nightingale," beginning her triumphant tour under the management of P. T. Barnum, performed at the National Theater in the capital. All of official Washington was there. Coming from a party at the Russian Minister's, Web-

ster was exhilarated and responded vociferously, especially to the diva's rendition of Scandinavian national songs. Near the close of the concert, he called
upon her to sing "The Star-spangled Banner." She complied; Webster joined
in the chorus; and when she finished to thunderous applause, he rose and
bowed majestically as if in behalf of the nation. The grandiose gesture, as
Constance Rourke has suggested, was worthy of the man whom Americans,
with their extravagant bent, called the Godlike.[35]

Religion was a small element in Webster's character. The feebleness of his
religious devotion, some thought, was the source of his moral infirmity. He
had been brought up, it may be recalled, a strict Congregationalist on the
Calvinistic and Trinitarian side; but upon his removal to Boston, he joined
the Brattle Street Church, not because he had changed his views but because Joseph Buckminster was the pastor and because it was the fashionable
thing to do. The overreaching worldliness of Boston Unitarianism had troubled Grace Webster. He seemed indifferent, however; and religion sat as
lightly on Caroline, an Episcopalian, as it did on her husband. Webster was
quite ecumenical in his religious habits and affiliations. He owned a pew in
the old Village Church in Franklin, attended the Brattle Street Church when
in Boston, and the Congregational Church in Marshfield. Upon his return to
the Senate he attended the Episcopal Church near the Capitol which, according to its minister, the Reverend C. M. Butler, he especially admired for its
liturgy and conservatism. Webster never doubted the truths of Christian
revelation. In the celebrated Girard Will Case he made clear his belief that
religion, particularly Protestant Christianity, was the foundation of virtuous
life. He was a lifelong student of the Bible, which he considered the word of
God, and a life member of the American Bible Society. He had in mind writing a book on the evidences of Christianity but, as with other literary projects, nothing came of it.[36]

Webster's proposed three-volume "History of the Constitution and Washington's Administration," had it been written, might have provided a fuller,
clearer exposition of the political ideas that ran through his numerous orations and speeches. The dominant motif was conservatism. And what was to
be conserved, fundamentally, was the heritage of the Founding Fathers, the
Constitution, the Union, and Anglo-American law. The true glory of American statesmanship was to preserve and perpetuate the work of the Fathers.
"We can win no laurels in a war for independence," he had declared. "Earlier
and worthier hands have gathered them all. Nor are their places for us by the
side of Solon, and Alfred, and other founders of states. Our fathers have filled
them. But there remains to us the great duty of defense and preservation."
The sons, it seemed, had only "sentinel duty" to perform—an inferior but
nonetheless essential service.[37] Webster's faculty of veneration, as the phrenologists would say, was very large. The purpose of his patriotic oratory was
to inculcate sentiments of veneration, to breathe an aura of filial awe into
American institutions, and mingle them with what Abraham Lincoln would
call the "mystic chords of memory." Yet at the same time, Webster exalted
the progress of knowledge and invention, commerce and improvement. It

was the great mission of the American people to preserve institutions of "ordered liberty" in an Age of Progress. "We are bound to show to the whole world . . . ," Webster declared in the aftermath of the European revolutions of 1848, "that a regular, steady, conservative government, founded on broad, popular, representative systems, is a practicable thing." The European revolutionaries imagined that freedom was simply a matter of willing it. They were wrong; it required experience, prudence, balance, restraint to keep freedom from running into license and anarchy.[38]

The different facets of Webster's conservatism may be examined through some of his later law cases. He had first addressed the issue raised by the Dorr Rebellion when he was secretary of state, and he finally had an opportunity to defend the established "charter government" of Rhode Island in a case before the Supreme Court in 1848.[39] He thought, and the court would agree, that because the issue was political it could not be settled judicially; nevertheless, it was fortunate that the case came before the court since it involved the greater question of "the true principles of government in our American system of public liberty." Against the claim of the Dorr rebels on behalf of the "People's Constitution," Webster argued, as had Calhoun, that the people, even if a majority, may not raise a new government except under the sanction of the established government. The American system, far from contemplating permanent revolution, premised from the start that the will of the people may be realized without destruction of traditional institutions. "Through the whole proceeding, from 1776 to the latest period, the whole course of American public acts, the whole progress of this American system, was marked by a peculiar conservatism. The object was to do what was necessary and no more and to do that with the utmost temperance and prudence." Webster often expounded this Burkian idea. The American system, with its English pedigree, was the work of time and experience, he said in 1847. "When our Revolution made us independent, we had not to frame government for ourselves, to hew it out of the original block of marble; our history and experience presented it ready made and well proportioned to our hands."[40] With these sentiments, it was no wonder that tears came to Webster's eyes when he entered Westminster Abbey for the first time.

The religious face of Webster's conservatism was disclosed in the Girard Will Case. The will of Stephen Girard, the Philadelphia merchant prince, left several million dollars to erect a college in the city for poor white male orphans, with the specific condition that no ecclesiastic, minister, or missionary of any sect be admitted to the premises, thereby protecting the tender minds of the boys until they were of an age to decide their religion for themselves. Girard's heirs contested the will. It was upheld in Pennsylvania courts and carried on appeal to the Supreme Court. Webster was the chief counsel for the appellants. The case attracted unusual interest. The tomblike chamber of the court in the Capitol was filled to overflowing. The spectacle of Godlike Daniel arguing against a will that, at least in the eyes of the Protestant clergy, was inspired by Satan himself was sure to be as dramatic as it was important. Argument lasted ten days; Webster spoke, or rather preached, for three of them. On the "technical" side, he maintained that the Pennsylvania courts could not administer this charitable trust, in part because of the clause excluding clergymen. Opposing counsel made short work of this argument. The longer and impassioned argument on the religious side was, as Justice Story remarked, "an address altogether to the prejudices of the clergy."[41] The proposed school did not qualify as a charity because it was derogatory to the Christian religion. "No, Sir! No, Sir!" Webster pounded. "If charity denies its birth and parentage, if it turns unbeliever, it is no longer charity."[42] The aim, he said, was not only the exclusion of clergymen, although that was intolerable enough, but the propagation of infidelity. Girard was a copyist of Paine, Volney, and other notorious infidels. The United States was a Christian nation, Webster insisted. Christianity was the foundation of the civil order. He went on to cite a string of cases in England and the United States holding that Christianity was part of the common law. The common law was part of the law of Pennsylvania. Ergo a charitable bequest inimical to Christianity violated the law of the commonwealth. Story, who presided in Chief Justice Taney's absence, returned the unanimous judgment of the court against the appellants. In his famous *Commentaries,* Story had pointedly rejected the liberal secularism of Thomas Jefferson and maintained that Christianity was indeed part of the law of the land. He did not now back away from that position, but he agreed with counsel for Girard's executors that the exclusion of Christian ministers was not an exclusion of Christianity. Story could scarcely conceal his contempt for Webster's argument—an argument of clergymen, not of lawyers, and one that, if upheld, would reduce American religious freedom to a narrow range—and this cast a pall over their friendship in the months before the justice's death.[43]

Webster continued to uphold the doctrine of vested property rights propounded in the Charles River Bridge case. The doctrine of the Taney Court in that case, it may be recalled, was that corporate charters should be construed in ways that did not obstruct economic progress. The doctrine was wrong, in Webster's opinion. Progress depended on the protection of the property committed to large-scale corporate enterprise. In 1845 he represented the Boston and Lowell Railroad Company before the Railroad Committee of the Massachusetts legislature. The committee had before it a petition for the charter of another railroad between Boston and Lowell. Although a clause of the charter of the existing company protected it from competition, the legislature had reserved the right to alter or repeal the charter. Webster pointed to the enormous capital invested in Massachusetts corporations, including twenty-one railroad corporations. All this enterprise depended on the confidence of investors that their property was secure from injurious competition and speculative adventurism. The cry against vested rights, Webster declared, was "un-American." And in this case he prevailed.[44] In 1848, arguing the same question of policy but a new point of law before the Supreme Court, he lost. Here the franchise of a Vermont bridge company, which Webster represented, was negated by the state's exercise of the power of eminent domain for the purpose of building a highway. The use of eminent domain in this way was still young, although it had been sanctioned by Webster's good friend Lemuel Shaw, Chief Justice of the Supreme Judicial Court of Massachusetts. Webster appealed to the nation's highest tribunal to turn back this new invasion of the rights of contract. "[If] the legislature, or their agents, are to be the sole judges of what [property] is to be taken, and to what public use it is to be appropriated, the most levelling ultraisms of Anti-rentism or agrarianism or Abolitionism may be successfully advanced." But the court declined to interfere.[45]

Webster's nationalism was conservative in that it aimed to check the centrifugal tendencies of the Union. He spoke eloquently of the uniqueness of American federalism which, for the first time in the history of the world, combined the freedom of local institutions with the authority of a central government in a harmonious system. He quoted Pope's lines, "All nature's discord/Keeps all nature's peace," to describe the American political universe. Yet his fears were all on the side of discord and disintegration, so he sought to strengthen the national authority. The most direct means to accomplish this was by the exercise of the commerce power. The needs of an expanding commerce, of an open field free of interstate barriers, had given rise to the Constitution, Webster always believed. The road of commerce was the quickest road to nationalization. Commerce belonged to the whole Union. "There is . . . ," Webster declared in 1843, "nothing more cementing, nothing that makes us more cohesive, nothing that more repels all tendencies to separation and dismemberment, than this great, this common, I may say this overwhelming interest in one commerce, one general system of trade and navigation, one everywhere and with every nation of the globe."[46] Since his early argument in *Gibbons v. Ogden*, Webster had advocated exclusive congressional jurisdiction over interstate commerce. The Supreme Court, to his regret, persisted in recognizing concurrent power in the states. In the 1840s he found himself repeatedly employed in opposition to his own state on this issue. Massachusetts, like two other New England states, had enacted a temperance statute prohibiting the sale of liquor in small quantities without a license. When the *License Cases* reached the Supreme Court, Webster asked the justices to strike down the statutes under the commerce power. They declined either on grounds of the state's police power or on grounds of concurrent power over commerce.[47] In the *Passenger Cases*, which finally involved a New York as well as a Massachusetts statute, the issue was whether the state could levy a tax, paid by shipmasters, on immigrants in their ports. The case was immensely important in Webster's opinion, and never did he have a more laborious one. He argued it in the district court, the circuit court, and during four terms of the Supreme Court. "In the days of Marshall and Story it [the Massachusetts law] would not have stood for one moment." Now, in 1847, the bench was filled with justices—a majority of them southerners—whose very appointment Webster had opposed. In this instance he prevailed narrowly, and he again lamented the failure of the majority to establish the plentitude of the national commerce power. "I am tired of these Constitutional questions," he remarked. "There is no court for them."[48]

Central to Webster's conservatism was an ideological commitment to democratic capitalism. The development of such an ideology was a common concern of Whig publicists in the 1840s; and the ideas adumbrated in Webster's speeches were more fully developed by Calvin Colton, Daniel Barnard, and other contributors to the *American Whig Review*, founded in the aftermath of the party's defeat in 1844. Webster had always held that popular government rested upon laws that secured the wide distribution and the free alienation of property. Democratic government, at the same time, undergirded private property because all the people had a stake in it. With the growth of industrial capitalism, however, the number of propertyless workers increased, as did the pace of democratization, and the danger arose that, to employ the conventional terminology, either property would take power or power would take property. It was to this dilemma that the ideology of democratic capitalism was addressed.[49]

Webster maintained, first of all, that in America there were no classes of propertied and propertyless, capitalists and workers, rich and poor. It was "the genius of our Constitution to distribute property generally, and generally to preserve equality in the condition of men."[50] In contrast to Europe, America was a middle-class country. Years earlier, in the debate on removal of the deposits, Webster had stunned the Senate by accusing the Jackson party of arraying the poor against the rich. Yet six months later he found himself accused in the Jacksonian press of having said, "Let Congress take care of the Rich, and the Rich will take care of the poor." Such a theory might today be called "the trickle-down theory." Webster firmly denied he had ever uttered the words, and since the charge kept popping up, he denied it repeatedly. He had always held, he said, "that the Laws should favor the distribution of property to the end that the number of the very rich and the number of the poor may both be diminished as far as practicable consistently with the rights of industry and property; and that all legislation in this country is especially bound to pay particular respect to the *earnings of labor;* labor being the source of comfort and independence to far the greatest portion of our people."[51] The wages of labor were secured and improved by policies promoting industry and a sound currency.

Webster glorified American labor. In this country, where there was no broad distinction between labor and capital, every working man was an incipient capitalist. The maxims of the European political economists did not apply. "In Europe the question is, how men can live. With us the question is, how well can they live." Americans were concerned not with subsistence, and therefore the cheapness of bread, but with purchasing power; and with that went rising expectations unknown to Europe. Where labor created a capital, as in the United States, it is not miserable drudgery, Webster maintained: "It is cheerful, contented, spirited, because it is respectable, and because it is certain of its reward. Labor everywhere mixes itself with capital.

The fields around us, how many of them are tilled by their owners! The shops in our towns, how many are occupied by their proprietors, for the convenient pursuit of their callings!"⁵² The greater the profits of capital, the greater the profits of labor was a doctrine that upset Ricardo. But it was sound Whig doctrine.

Democratic capitalism was furthered, in Webster's view, by liberal laws of incorporation and the support of popular education. Demagogues denounced chartered corporations as instruments of privilege; in fact, they were great equalizers. By aggregating wealth, corporations made possible large industrial enterprise which, in turn, raised the demand for labor and its rewards. "You may go through the whole civilized world and see what has been done to place those who are less rich on an equality with those born rich," said Webster, "and you will find nothing equal to our system of granting charters for manufacturing corporations to all the people." The same might be said in another sense of public service corporations, which had a monopolistic character. The railroad, for instance, was not only a great technological innovation but a breakthrough in elevating the condition of mankind. The railroad lessened isolation, made everyone mobile, and jostled the rich and the poor. "[In] the history of human inventions there is hardly one so well calculated as that of railroads to equalize the condition of men."⁵³ It was an age of improvement, of course, and Webster hailed the advance of "popular knowledge" as another instrument of democratic capitalism. In this he generalized about the United States in terms of New England, where there was a heritage of common schools and where Horace Mann had launched his school reforms. Nowhere else in the world, Webster declared, was the laboring community educated; nowhere else could the laboring man, by the pursuit of education, backed by his own industry, become a capitalist.⁵⁴

Of Webster as an orator much was written during his lifetime and much has been written since, yet his power remains elusive. Some traced that power to superior learning and intellect. Far more than Clay or Calhoun, he was steeped in a tradition of literary culture, which included the ancients but was primarily English; and this nurtured a prose style sometimes compared to Burke's. Webster was a reader to the end of his days. A record of the books he borrowed from the Library of Congress after his return to the Senate included Audubon's *Ornithology*, Elliot's *Debates*, Bacon's *Works*, Macaulay's *Essays*, Dryden's *Virgil*, McGugar's *History of the Sikhs*, Moore's *Epicurus*, Burton's *Anatomy of Melancholy*, Campbell's *Lives of the Lord Chancellors*, and a variety of poetry, drama, and fiction. He was fascinated by the "noble certainty" of the natural sciences, read extensively in geology—Humboldt's *Cosmos* was a favorite book—and remarked near the end of his life that he would gladly have exchanged the "bad company of lawyers and politicians for the society of scientific and literary man." Distinguished men of letters considered Webster one of them. His patriotic oratory, in particular, was admitted into the canon of American literature. When the literary circle in New York planned a tribute to James Fenimore Cooper after his death in 1851, Webster was invited to preside, for, he was told, "in the literature of this country you hold, among the living, the foremost place."[55] (In the end, he did not attend.) Yet Webster was neither a philosopher nor a litterateur but an advocate. Sometimes, as in the Girard Will Case, when he borrowed from doctors of divinity, he received more credit for learning than he deserved. In one of his last addresses, at the New-York Historical Society, he chose a classical subject and, in the judgment of scholars, fell flat on his face.[56]

Others attributed much of Webster's power to sheer physical presence. "He owes half his fame to it," said James Russell Lowell. While not a giant in size—5'10" and 200 pounds—he appeared a giant, majestic, cast in the heroic mold, mainly because of his great head. He must be an imposter, so the story went, for no man could be as great as Webster looked. Henry Cabot Lodge, a later biographer, echoed the observation of Webster's contemporaries in saying that the example of his physical presence was altogether without parallel in modern times.[57] His costume, his gravity, his elevated language undoubtedly contributed to the effect. Some observers assigned first importance to the artistry of Webster's rhetoric. To the modern ear, it may seem ponderous, but in the nineteenth century it was considered chaste, clears, and direct. He spoke in "golden sentences," sentences that fell like "the strokes of a trip hammer," sentences that were luminous not only by themselves but in the masterly flow of the discourse. His rhetorical sytle was uniquely his own—it was "Websterian." Clay had more enthusiasm, Calhoun stronger logic, but neither possessed Webster's artistry. He adapted his rhetoric to the different purposes of the courtroom, the legislative chamber, and the ceremonial platform, alternately speaking powerfully to the heart or to the head as the occasion called for. Always he spoke virtually without movement or gesture. His voice was resonant but had no melody, indeed was "as monotonous as thunder" in one description. Rarely did he indulge in brilliant allusions or in purple passages.[58] Yet he was capable of bold flights of imagination. The apostrope to Lafayette—"Fortunate man!"—at Bunker Hill, for instance, and the celebrated "drumbeat" passage in his speech against Jackson's Protest.*

Webster could be insufferably dull and dry and, as earlier remarked, he tended to become diffuse and long-winded in his declining years. In December 1846, at Philadelphia, he spoke to an audience of some 1,200 people— the ladies had been admitted after dinner—for five hours. A five-hour after-dinner speech was deemed egregious even in that day of long speeches. "Its column length suggests the sea serpent," said the London *Times*. Indeed it

---

*"On this question of principle, while actual suffering was yet afar off, they [the American colonies] raised their flag against a power to which, for purposes of foreign conquest and subjugation, Rome in the height of her glory is not to be compared—a power which has dotted over the surface of the whole globe with her possessions and military posts, whose morning drum-beat, following the sun, and keeping company with the hours, circles the earth with one continuous and unbroken strain of the martial airs of England."

When someone asked Webster if this was "an impromptu," he retorted: "An impromptu! Why the idea first occurred to me twenty years before, while I was standing on the Heights of Abraham, and I have been trying to work it into shape ever since. But I never succeeded to my satisfaction until now."[59]

merited the riposte Henry Clay once made to a congressman who exclaimed in a long-winded reply that while Clay spoke to the present he spoke to posterity, upon which Clay remarked, "Yes, and you seem resolved to speak until the arrival of *your* audience."[60]

3. *Calhoun at Fort Hill*

Fort Hill, Calhoun's home for the last twenty-five years of his life, still stands graciously on a knoll amid tall cedars and oaks and rows of boxwood, above the Seneca River in western South Carolina. Two trees, an arborvitae and a hemlock, said to have been the gift of Clay and Webster respectively, grow near the house. Today Fort Hill is engulfed in the maze of Clemson University, which in cooperation with the United Daughters of the Confederacy has restored the mansion as a shrine to the statesman. In Calhoun's time it was a quiet and somewhat remote situation, two hundred and fifty miles from Charleston, four miles from the nearest village, Pendleton, and not easily accessible from any direction. Few strangers undertook pilgrimages to Fort Hill.

A simple two-story white frame house, enlarged into the shape of a *T*, it has no architectural distinction but boasts a Greek pediment and portico in front, at the top of the *T*, and long high-columned piazzas on either side, at the leg of the *T*. The long drawing room, or parlor, behind the piazzas, is spacious and brightly lighted, furnished with family heirlooms, and hung with family portraits. Across the hall is the dining room, with a beautiful Duncan Phyfe banquet table; at one end over a high mantle hangs a full-length portrait of Calhoun painted by a Belgian artist after a Brady daguerreotype taken in Washington in 1849; and at the other end, of particular interest, is "the historic Constitution Sideboard." Made of mahogany paneling removed from the USS *Constitution* ("Old Ironsides") after the frigate was condemned in the 1820s, it was, according to a not very creditable tradition, given to Calhoun by Clay in gratitude for a speech on the Constitution. The house has eight bedrooms—scarcely enough to accommodate Calhoun's family at its fullest. An outside kitchen adjoins the house by a covered passageway on the west side; and at the rear stands the master's office, a one-room structure also fronted by a columned portico.[1]

Fort Hill was a working farm, and Calhoun depended on it for his livelihood. It was probably in better condition, under better management, in 1843, when he left the Senate, than ever before. Having recently acquired an adjacent property, he owned approximately 1,000 acres, of which 450 were in cultivation. The land rolled southward over hill and dale to the river. There Calhoun had a grist mill, and he kept a boat for pleasure cruises. In the bottom lands he grew corn, on the high ground cotton—120 acres of cotton—and he had fields of oats, wheat, corn, potatoes, and rice as well. The remaining acreage was in orchards, pasture, and woodlands. Fort Hill was worked by seventy to eighty slaves. The house servants were quartered near the mansion, while the field hands occupied units of a long barracks-like stone structure in the valley below. The slave families were allowed to cultivate a patch of cotton or a garden of their own.[2]

By all accounts Calhoun was a considerate master and a superb farmer. He brought to farming the same resolute self-confidence, the same analytical skills, the same passion for system, even the same obsession that he brought to public affairs, all infused, however, with much more practical good sense. "His whole heart and soul seemed to be absorbed in the farm," an observer wrote. His habits were regular. Except for an hour or two in his office, which doubled as his library, Calhoun was out of the house, riding over the plantation, from early morning to early afternoon. After dinner he surrendered himself to his family and the society of neighbors and visitors. Evening conversations on the piazza were his delight. On Fridays, and on the Sabbath, he usually went to Pendleton.[3] Calhoun meant for his farm to be an example to his neighbors, nearly all of them smaller and poorer farmers than he. He introduced hillside ditching, which proved a boon in an area where leaching of the soil and runoff from the fields caused severe erosion. He introduced Bermuda grass for grazing, imported blooded cattle from England, experimented with new crops, rice for instance, and worked to increase his cotton yield. He was "a perfect Napoleon" in system and management.[4]

Floride Calhoun had given birth to ten children. Three had died in infancy; all the others, who ranged in age from sixteen to thirty-four in 1845, grew to maturity and outlived their father. Floride, earlier a fine lady of Washington society, had become a toilsome and high-strung housewife. What her problem was it is impossible to say, but she combined enormous nervous energy, which vented itself in storms of industry, with a complaining and domineering temperament. Calhoun referred to her "suspicious and fault-finding temper" and her "apoplectic tendency," which had been the cause of much vexation in the family. "It has been the only cross of my life," he wrote mournfully.[5] Pretty well emptied of affection, the marriage had come to rest on little more than a sense of duty. Floride had no interest in Calhoun's public career and seldom accompanied him to Washington. But he was the soul of kindness, showing great patience and consideration toward her and demanding nothing less from his children.

Andrew, the oldest child, had followed his father's footsteps and gone to Yale, but after a year he was expelled for misconduct and never returned. Sometime later he married Margaret Green, Duff Green's daughter, and went off with his father's backing to carve out a cotton plantation in the Alabama "Black Belt." Anna, the elder daughter, was the pride and glory of the family. Alone of the children, she seemed to have inherited her father's mental endowments. He adored her and took her to Washington as his aide, amanuensis, and companion in 1834, when she was only seventeen years old. Four years later she married Thomas Green Clemson, a mining engineer from Philadelphia. Their life during the next dozen years was peripatetic, but the Clemsons and their two children were not infrequently at or near

Fort Hill; and in some respects the Yankee engineer proved more of a son to Calhoun than his own offspring. Patrick, the second son, graduated from West Point in 1841, and thereafter had a thoroughly undistinguished career in the United States Army. John was in and out of college and, in spite of ill health, earned an M.D. degree in Philadelphia in 1848, to the delight of his father. Cornelia had been permanently crippled by her fall from a swing in childhood. She never left the family nest. James had entered the University of Virginia in 1843 only to be expelled after a year for refusing to testify against a fellow student charged with some offense. Along with "Willie" (for William Lowndes), three years younger, he later attended South Carolina College in Columbia. The youngest sons and Cornelia were the only children frequently at home during Calhoun's years in retirement at Fort Hill.[6]

Of all the decisions Calhoun made on behalf of his children, backing Andrew in his Alabama venture proved most fateful for the family's fortune. Cane Brake, as the virgin plantation was called, cost $20,000. It was a joint venture in which the partners were not only Andrew and his father but also the new son-in-law, Clemson, who arranged the loan to finance it in Philadelphia.[7] Within four years most of the 1,200 acres had been cleared and a third of them were in cotton. Unfortunately, after this promising start, cotton prices collapsed and did not soon recover. Cane Brake turned into a bad investment. Moreover, Clemson quarreled with Andrew over plantation operations and opted out. Calhoun, deeply grieved by the family quarrel, mollified Clemson—without much success—and was compelled to assume his share in 1843. Long the envy of his neighbors for never being in debt, Calhoun was now saddled with a large debt for the rest of his life. In 1845, on behalf of Cane Brake he sought a long-term loan of $30,000 from Abbott Lawrence and his Boston friends. They put together a package, but Calhoun evidently balked at the terms, for he declined the loan and continued short-term financing with the Bank of the State. Franklin Elmore, in Charleston, was his banker as well as his political manager, and neither gentleman was careful to keep these roles separate. In exchange for ready financial accommodation at the bank, Calhoun offered advice on current public events and trends of special interest to bankers. At the same time, he pointedly refused to aid the anti-bank party in South Carolina politics. Calhoun took the debt to his grave. In 1850 friends in Charleston raised a purse of $27,000 for the dual purpose of relieving Calhoun's estate and sending him to Europe for his health. He died before he could be asked to accept the money; later presented to the statesman's family, it saved Fort Hill.[8]

Although Calhoun always claimed to be in good health, he suffered an attack of congestive fever in February 1845 from which his lungs never fully recovered. His voice became weak and scratchy, and he took on the emaciated appearance characteristic of his final years. Tall and gaunt, with a complexion "bronzed by the southern sun," a full and deeply furrowed forehead, bushy eyebrows below which were sunk a pair of "dazzling, black, and piercing eyes"—variously described as hazel, gray, or yellow-brown—prominent nose, hollow jaws, a thin mouth slightly turned down at the corners, firm square chin, and over all a thick crop of iron-gray hair that fell from his head like a lion's mane—the perfect likeness of Milton's Satan, according to one observer, while others were struck by the resemblance to Andrew Jackson at the same age.[9] Brady's camera best captured this figure with its intense, gazing expression. It was very real, yet seemed to bear no resemblance to the kind and amiable man nearly everyone acknowledged Calhoun to have been.

Calhoun's aversion to sitting for artists exceeded that of either Webster or Clay. He was induced to go to a daguerreotypist in Washington for a portrait to be used as a frontispiece in his *Life* in 1843. But he hated all the plates; they made him look "pale and ghastly," he said, and he would not permit use of any one of them. Joseph Scoville then chose the bland engraving of Washington Blanchard's miniature of a younger Calhoun for the frontispiece.[10] There are fewer likenesses of Calhoun than of his fellow triumvirs partly because of this aversion but partly, too, because he was out of the way of artists at Fort Hill. They came there, but with rare exceptions his sittings were in Washington. There, in 1835, he befriended Hiram Powers, the young sculptor from Ohio who had set up his workshop in the basement of the Capitol and who was staked to study in Italy by John S. Preston, the senator's brother. Visitors to Powers's studio in Florence in later years saw plaster busts of all the triumvirs lined up in a row. Preston, meanwhile, raised a subscription in Charleston for a life-size marble of Calhoun. This great statue, in which Powers draped the statesman in a toga under the same head he had carved in 1835, survived a shipwreck off the coast of Long Island and was finally unveiled in Charleston eight months after Calhoun's death, only then to be destroyed during the Civil War.[11] Another sculptor befriended by Calhoun was Clark Mills, who later gained international fame for his equestrian statue of Andrew Jackson in Washington. A common plasterer working in Charleston, Mills perfected a method of taking a cast for a bust from the living face. Calhoun was among his first subjects and patrons. The plaster product was much applauded, and Mills was encouraged to carve it in marble. He came to Fort Hill in 1845 to take another "bust impression." The finished marble bust was purchased by the Charleston City Council, which also voted Mills a gold medal. Many people thought it the best likeness of the mature statesman.[12]

In 1845 Calhoun was still the hero, primarily, of a single state. It was the Charlestonians, and the students at South Carolina College, who sought portraits of Calhoun. A decade earlier Harriet Martineau had described the senator's return from Congress as "like that of a chief returned to the bosom of his clan."[13] Of course, everyone had heard that when Calhoun took snuff South Carolina sneezed. There had been periodic revolts against Calhoun's domination, most recently the Bluffton Movement; but all had failed, leaving only vague memories of the victims—William Smith, Henry Laurens Pinckney, William C. Preston. But many Palmetto State patriots remained restive under his leadership. "His shadow falls heavily upon our young men, and darkens all their pathways," William Gilmore Simms, the novelist, wrote discouragingly in 1847. Simms talked of organizing a "Young Carolina" party, which would include Hammond and others of like mind, against the Calhounite "Hunkers"; but nothing came of it.[14]

In due time, Calhoun would come to stand for the South. He would attain on a symbolic level the sectional ascendancy he could never attain politically. Among anti-slavery men in the North he already appeared as the evil genius of the Slave Power. "Calhoun is the high-priest of Moloch—the embodied spirit of slavery," old John Quincy Adams believed. The image was sufficiently pervasive in 1849 to enter into literature. In Herman Melville's satiric romance, *Mardi*, Nulli, "a cadeverous, ghost-like man with . . . wondrous eyes—bright, nimble, as the twin corposant balls [St. Elmo's fire], playing about the ends of ships' royal-yards in gales," is the chief of the southern tribe of Vivinza. He is also a slave-driver drawing blood and tears from his victims with every crack of the whip, and a raving disunionist.[15] Calhoun as a person, apart from his ideas and politics, was virtually unknown in the North. If not Satan or Moloch, he appeared as the personification of southern chivalry. People in the North, Dixon Lewis told him, "think you are proud and haughty, even aristocratic in your manners and bearing, and austere to a degree which would make you personally offensive to all but your friends."[16] Clay was known everywhere, and everywhere the people felt him a friend; in 1847 the South would see Webster in the flesh; but Calhoun, because of his social and sectional exclusiveness, was a scarecrow outside the south Atlantic states.

In the eyes of nearly everyone who knew him, Calhoun was a man of saintly or, as chivalry would have it, Roman character. His private life was unblemished; he was plain, kind, and unassuming; he was wholly without guile; and he indulged in none of the ordinary vices. "He was undoubtedly the chastest public man America has yet produced . . . ," it would later be said, "the very incarnation of pure reason and pure morals."[17] Webster declaimed on the New England founders, and Marshfield was washed by the waves that brought the Pilgrims ashore; but in his habits he was the Cavalier, Calhoun the Puritan. Seeing life as a struggle against evil, Calhoun took delight in doing his duty. "I hold the duties of life to be greater than life itself," he confessed to Anna, "and that in performing them manfully, even against hope, our labour is not lost, but will be productive of good in after times. Indeed, I regard this life very much as a struggle against evil, and that to him who acts on proper principle, the reward is in the struggle, more than in the victory itself, although that generally enhances it."[18] This rectitude and moral earnestness was Calhoun's religion, if it may be called religion. Despite his Presbyterian upbringing, he never belonged to any church. In Washington he was a consistent friend of the Unitarian church and, like Thomas Jefferson, thought Unitarianism "the true faith" which "must ultimately prevail over the world." At home Calhoun usually attended the local Episcopal church, to which Floride belonged. While perhaps not indifferent to religion, this moral Calvinist never made a personal profession of faith.[19]

The most famous characterization of Calhoun's was Harriet Martineau's "cast-iron man, who looks as if he had never been born and never could be extinguished."[20] She, of course, was speaking of the Calhoun of 1835, but her observations of a man in the grip of ideological possession were just as true, even truer, a decade later. Her metaphor of "an intellectual machine" was striking, and soon repeated by others. The story was told of a senator who when asked why he resigned from his mess replied, "To escape thought and Mr. Calhoun." Even political associates sometimes melted under the strain of working with him. "Calhoun . . . ," Lewis complained, "is too intellectual, too industrious, too intent in the struggle of politics. . . . There is no relaxation with him."[21] This conception of his mind went along with the conception of his austere character, conjuring up the image of a cold, severe, overwrought, and humorless man. But it was untrue, or certainly far from the whole truth, others observed. Brady, who had this preconception of Calhoun, found in him, on the contrary, "great personal magnetism." In social intercourse, he showed uncommon address and tact. Although less drawn to society than in his earlier years, Calhoun was still an amazing conversationalist. "He was the most charming man in conversation I ever heard," wrote John Wentworth who met Calhoun as a freshman congressman from Illinois in 1844.[22] Many said the same thing, some adding the qualification, however, that there was neither wit nor fancy nor amusement in his conversation. It was "always a disquisition." He conversed in the same imposing manner he brought to the Senate floor. "In his rapid and dazzling dissertations," wrote a Washington journalist, "he so hurried you on from one novel and yet philosophic-looking generalization to another that you were always on the stretch to keep up . . . and you could do little but to resign yourself helplessly to what appeared the irresistible strength and subtlety of his intellect."[23]

Calhoun's intellect, it was generally agreed, was "metaphysical," which is to say inclined toward nebulous abstractions and oversubtle reasoning that, however logical, bore little relation to the real world. His persistent tendency was to assume dogmatically certain first principles and run them out to the remotest consequences, arbitrarily excluding everything in conflict with the train of reasoning. While the ingenuity and power of that reasoning commanded respect, it also invited contemptuous dismissal. Men of affairs usually agreed with Burke that that was metaphysically true was likely to be politically false or impractical. Calhoun appeared as the Calvin of American politics—a deductive reasoner to wrong conclusions. Like Butler's *Hudibras*

> He could distinguish and divide
> A hair twixt South and Southwest side.[24]

Calhoun's friends insisted he was practical as well as speculative, and they could point to his record as a cabinet minister and a farmer. The self-reliance of Calhoun's intellect was astonishing. As Charles C. Pinckney later wrote, "His mind always seemed to work from within, by spontaneous impulse, not by external influences, either educational, social, or political."[25] Beyond a fair knowledge of the classics of political theory, Calhoun's letters, speeches, and writings give little evidence of learning or taste or reading. Indeed he once boasted of not having read a book in twenty years. Yet he gleaned much from what he did read—newspapers and the quarterlies mostly. Besides, his friends said, "his mind was so active, that he thought more in a year than other men, even of equal talents, would in ten."[26] He was truly Emerson's "transparent eyeball," knowing nothing but seeing all, "head bathed by the blithe air and uplifted into infinite space" by the exhilaration of his own truth.

The question of personal ambition loomed large in the reckonings of the South Carolinian's character. "Mr. Calhoun was pure of all vice but the vice of ambition," William J. Grayson shrewdly observed, "which grew stronger by the virtues that restrained him from other indulgences." Thus while Clay's ambition was tempered by his sociability and Webster's by his flaccidity, Calhoun's knew no restraint.[27] The great object of that ambition was the presidency. The Charleston *Courier*, after the 1844 debacle, accused him of "a prurient desire for the presidency," and in the North some felt, as Rufus Choate did, that Calhoun was so "disappointed to death" by the long frustration of his ambition that, while it might not be wicked, it was no longer honorable either. He was portrayed by his friends, and he portrayed himself, as a disinterested statesman whose only obligation was of the lofty kind that prefers duty, principle, and glory to office and power.[28] Yet the sudden shifts and turnings in his politics, however he might rationalize them, disclosed a preternatural opportunism. For the problem was not that Calhoun, in the manner of democratic politicians, veered around in his politics to be before the wind, but that he acted perversely toward his own interests, arousing the disgust even of ardent followers. "With the most upright intentions," Beverley Tucker, the Virginian, wrote, "he cannot preserve his perpendicular for six months together: eager for public favour, he always finds out the most unpopular side of every question; and devoted to consistency shows it by always setting his face *against* the wind, let it blow from what quarter it may." As a political leader he ruined all he touched. Never, Tucker thought, was there a man who so often surprised his friends, his enemies, and even himself by ever-recurring aberrations.[29] What the disturbing cause of this malady might be, Tucker did not know. Obviously, it was associated with Calhoun's effort to maintain all his primary loyalties—the Union, the South presidential aspirations—in the face of increasing contradiction. But however majestic in intellect, he was, said Tucker, "the most unskilled leader of a party that ever wielded a truncheon."[30]

Calhoun's oratorical style was the nearly perfect expression of his character and intellect. It combined "clear analysis, suppressed passion, and lofty earnestness." His only eloquence inhered in his argument. "He spoke as Euclid would have spoken," said Choate, who was himself Ciceronian, believing that the inert argument required the momentum of eloquence to reach its mark.[31] Calhoun spoke with precision, without tropes, figures, analogies, or allusions. He spoke almost always without notes, and excelled in impromptu debate. "His voice was harsh, his gestures stiff, like the motions of a pump-handle," a keen observer wrote. "There was no ease, flexibility, grace, or charm in his manner; yet there was something . . . that riveted your attention as with hooks of steel."[32] For all his machine-like rhetoric, Calhoun was, according to a Washington journalist, the most difficult man to report in the Congress: "He spoke with extraordinary fluency and rapidity, at times uttering short, piquant sentences that had the force of a round shot, and then running into a prolonged and involved sentence that required a sharp man to follow and comprehend."[33] Since there was so little winning in the manner of Calhoun's oratory, one had to be taken, if taken at all, by the matter.

Calhoun began to write a systematic treatise on government after he left the Senate; and he returned to it in 1845. There were reports then it would soon appear, but the work was unfinished when Calhoun returned to the Senate and would not be published in his lifetime. It finally appeared in two parts, A Disquisition on Government and A Discourse on the Constitution, in the year after his death. In these works Calhoun distilled most of the ideas formed in response to the movement of events since the 1820s. They offered few surprises to anyone who had followed Calhoun's career; but the Disquisition, in particular, established Calhoun as an original thinker and philosophical statesman of universal interest.[34]

"I am a conservative in its broadest and fullest sense," Calhoun had declared, "and such I shall ever remain, unless, indeed, the Government shall become so corrupt and disordered, that nothing short of revolution can reform it."[35] The republic would survive only by adherence to its original principles. The South, for complicated historical reasons, had become the primary conservative force in the Union; and Calhoun, its foremost leader, was engaged in a purely defensive struggle against three great enemy forces: democracy, centralism, and abolitionism. In their political outlook all three men, Webster, Clay, and Calhoun, offered different versions of conservatism. All were, in a sense, defensive; but while the other two rose above their fears and held out the promise of achievement and progress, Calhoun was profoundly pessimistic. With his foreboding vision, he looked for only enough justice to prevent disaster.

First among the elements of Calhoun's political theory was state-rights constitutionalism. In the American system, state rights afforded the chief restraint on the power of the general government and, after the suffrage, the primary means of protecting southern rights and interests against "consolidation." The idea that the states, or the people of the states, had a direct and final voice in determining the limits of the Constitution was hardly original with Calhoun, although he gave it finished form in the theory of nullification. While he no longer advocated the process of nullification, he continued to espouse the theory behind it. The conception of the United States as one nation was a fundamental error, he maintained: "Instead of a nation, we are in reality an assemblage of nations, or peoples . . . , united in their sovereign character immediately and directly by their own act, but without losing their separate and independent existence."[36] As the exponent of state rights, Calhoun appeared to some men the rightful heir of Thomas Jefferson. But in Jefferson's creed state rights were in the service of the fundamental human rights of freedom and self-government. Calhoun converted the doctrine into a defensive weapon against democracy and consolidation. In this he was the heir of reactionary Jeffersonians—Randolph of Roanoke, John Taylor of Caroline, and other Old Republicans—disappointed and dismayed by the nationalizing course of government under the Virginia Dynasty. Repeatedly in his later years, finally in the *Discourse,* Calhoun traced the degeneration of state rights constitutionalism to the aberrations, deviations, and surrenders of Jefferson and his successors.[37]

Calhoun rejected the liberal philosophy of natural rights that inspired and infused the Declaration of Independence and in its place reared a conservative philosophy that emphasized human inequality and selfishness and the dangers of popular misrule. The philosophy owed more to Hobbes than to Locke, and more to John Adams than to Jefferson. Man is by nature a self-regarding creature, driven by passions of arrogance, jealousy, and revenge, which are destructive of the social state; and government is instituted as a controlling power necessary to the existence of society. There are no natural or inalienable rights; all rights are acquired or conventional, existing only in the sight of positive law. Liberty itself is a reward, "a reward reserved for the intelligent, the patriotic, the virtuous and deserving," which each community bestows or withholds in the light of imperatives of security and authority. The liberty of some inevitably rests upon the slavery of others.[38] Thus in Calhoun's theory liberty occurs only in the thick context of institutional balances, adjustments, and discriminations. He borrowed from Aristotle and a long line of political philosophers ending with Adams the idea of a balance of orders or classes, which is the basis of republican government; but he superimposed geographical divisions upon the older social ones. A sectional balance, therefore, overlaid the balance between the few and the many. The radical error in Jacksonian America was the notion that the people, counted as so may individuals, are the state. This was reflected in the tendency to describe the government as a democracy instead of a republic and to assume, as in the Dorr Rebellion, that a majority of the people may make and unmake government. Calhoun doubtless approved of the distinction drawn by his scholarly friend Francis Lieber, Professor of History and Political Economy at South Carolina College, between Anglican and Gallican liberty, the former resting on organic laws and guarantees, the latter simply on universal suffrage and majority rule.[39]

Calhoun upheld the system of patriarchal slavery in the South as superior economically, politically, morally, to the system of capitalism based on white wage labor in the North. Yet in the curious symbiotic relationship between them, the survival of the latter depended on the survival of the former. It is the law of civilization that one class or race lives off the labor of the other, he said. The system of African slavery is but one expression of that law. It is a necessary system in the South, for without it there must be a war of extermination between the races, ending in a return to savagery. Although exploitative of the Africans, slavery sustains white freedom and self-government in the South. For all the whites, rich and poor, belong to the master class and share the same rights and esteem. In some respects it is a superior system even for those who labor under it than the "wage slavery" of the North; and it has the inestimable advantage of exempting southern society from the disorders and violence of the conflict between capital and labor.

In 1842 Albert Brisbane, a brash young social reformer just returned to America from study in Europe, called on Calhoun in Washington and, after striking a conversational spark in the initial meeting, entered into an exhausting discussion of society and government during six successive evenings. To Brisbane's optimism about the future, Calhoun opposed his pessimism. "I am not an advocate of slavery . . . ," Calhoun protested. "I care nothing about slavery, it is entirely a secondary question with me. In three hundred years' time there will not be a negro on the face of the globe. As the Indian is now retreating before our civilization, so the negro will gradually be eliminated and his place taken by a higher and more intelligent race; it is only a question of time. I advocate slavery in the South because it is a guarantee of stability." He went on to explain that because the planters owned the laborers, there was no conflict between them. "In the North," on the other hand, "the capitalist owns the instruments of labor, and he seeks to draw out of labor all the profits, leaving the laborer to shift for himself in age and disease. This can only engender antagonism; the result will be hostility and conflict, ending in civil war, and the North may fall into a state of social dissolution. Our system of the South is the counterpoise to this, and for that reason I wish to maintain it so as to bridge over the dangerous period, and enable the nation to arrive quietly . . . at a higher social state."[40] Similar ideas resounded in Calhoun's senatorial speeches. "In this tendency to conflict in the North, between labor and capital, which is constantly on the increase, the weight of the South has [been] and will ever be found on the conservative side. . . . This is our natural position, the salutary influence of which has thus far preserved," he said in 1837, "and will ere long continue to preserve our free institutions, if we should be left undisturbed."[41] In this manner Calhoun appealed to the conservatism of the North to join forces with the conservatism of the South in a united rejectionist front. Some recent students have contended that his political strategy was to forge an alliance between the planters of the South and the capitalists of the North.[42] However logical that might have been, given his proto-Marxist assumptions, Calhoun never seriously proposed or pursued anything of the sort. To do so he would have had to become a Whig. Instead of cultivating northern capitalists, Calhoun perversely cultivated Locofoco Democrats. In truth, the idea of a union of the master classes was an exotic turned up by Calhoun's speculative mind. It ran counter to the other currents of his thought and politics and, of course, found no echo in northern conservatism, which was optimistic, nationalistic, and democratic. Webster's democratic capitalism may have been spurious, but it was much closer to northern aspirations than Calhoun's utopia bottomed on slavery.

In Calhoun's philosophy democratic government, at least at the national level, is inevitably accompanied by spoils and corruption—"the cohesive power of public plunder"—and degenerates into despostism. Although power has passed from the rulers to the ruled, in a large state the citizens are divided by conflicting interests and these interests combine to form parties which compete for the control of the government. The great prize—the apple that is the source of all corruption—is control of the fiscal action—taxation and spending—of government. But it is not simply that the majority party furthers its own economic interests at the expense of the minority; the parties, with the honors, patronage, and favor they may bestow, become interests in themselves, and so democratic politics deteriorates into a struggle for power over party machinery. It is here, as William Freehling has shown, that Calhoun's interest-group theory of political behavior encounters rather awkwardly the theory of spoilsmen controlling politics.[43] The system of nationally organized parties, Calhoun believed, broke down one of the principal constitutional checks on the power of the general government: the jealousy and resistance of the state governments. "Instead of a contest for power between the government of the United States, on the one side, and the separate governments of the several states on the other, the real struggle was to obtain the control of the former—a struggle in which both States and people have united."[44] Calhoun's anti-partyism in South Carolina, including his opposition to the popular choice of presidential electors, was part of a rear-guard action to preserve the states as jealous guardians against the centralizing force of political parties. It was too late, of course. Decay had set in with the Jacksonians. "When it comes to be once understood that politics is a game," Calhoun warned, "that those who are engaged in it but act a part; that they make this or that profession, not from honest conviction . . . but as the means of deluding the people, and through that delusion to acquire power . . . the people will lose all confidence in public men . . . [and] become indifferent and passive to the government abuses of power, on the ground that those whom they may elevate under whatever pledges, instead of reforming, will but imitate the example of those whom they have expelled."[45] This time was near at hand, Calhoun thought, when he wrote the *Disquisition*. Principle and policy were rapidly losing all influence in elections, being succeeded by cunning, deception, fraud, and demagoguery. Calhoun foresaw a succession of increasingly violent vibrations between corrupt parties, leading to confusion, anarchy, and finally revolution.

The problem attacked in the *Disquisition*, however, is that of the tyranny of an interest-based majority, and Calhoun expounded the theory of the concurrent majority to counter it. In every society there is an incessant struggle between a major and a minor party for control of the government. In a democracy control is established through a popular or numerical majority. It is always tyrannical. The minority may use the suffrage to defeat it, perhaps even become a new majority; and it may appeal to the legal restraints of the constitution. But these protections are insufficent, Calhoun argued. Solution to the problem begins with the recognition that there is a majority of interests as well as of number. The conflicting interests must be armed with the power of arresting the popular majority in order to secure the common good. This concurrent majority prevents oppression and, as it requires the consent of each interest to put the government in action, it fosters conciliation, compromise, and consensus. The checks and balances of the United States Constitution were designed to secure such a government, Calhoun thought. Thus he had deduced nullification from the principles of the Constitution. The concurring majority in that theory was three-fourths of the states in their constitution-making authority. But he was no longer advocating nullification. Nullification was an anachronism. The restraints of the Constitution had collapsed, becoming almost meaningless, under the sway of majoritarian democracy. In the Madisonian theory of American government, the multiplicity of conflicting factions or interests naturally worked to protect minorities and to render impossible a tyranny of the majority, whether of class or section or interest. But this theory, too, had broken down. Like interests had combined in the North to form a sectional majority hostile to the South and slavery.

A new *organism*, unknown to the Constitution, never contemplated in the theories of Madison and Jefferson, was necessary to effect the concurrent majority. Calhoun offered a number of doubtful historical examples of such an organism: the Roman tribunate, the *liberum veto* of the old Polish constitution, the balance of King, Lords, and Commons in Great Britain, and the Iroquois Confederacy. (Interestingly he did not, in the *Disquisition*, cite the South Carolina constitution, although he always said it made the state government the joint or concurrent organ of the two great sections of the state.) In the United States, the critical division was sectional, and so the problem must have a sectional solution. Calhoun reserved this for the *Discourse*. The new constitutional organism took the form of a dual executive, one elected from each section and both armed with the negative power.[46] It is difficult to conceive of anything more unrealistic and impractical. Asked his opinion of the plan, the newspaper humorist Jack Downing remarked, "Well, I guess, if the country depended upon laws to live on, it would starve to death as sure as an ass between two bundles of hay."[47] The alleged realism of Calhoun's political theory was limited to its Hobbesian premises. His conception of American politics in bipolar terms, with a massive, uniform, static majority tyrannizing over a less massive but no less uniform, static minority, bore no resemblance to reality and justified the politician's reproach, "metaphysical." Nor was it any more realistic to suppose that the peculiar institution of the South could be saved by inventing a new constitution, although that offered further evidence of Calhoun's fidelity to the Union.[48]

In September 1845 Calhoun decided to return to the Senate. Upon his retirement he had concurred in the prevailing opinion that he should keep his private station, thereby staying out of harm's way, and position himself for the presidency in 1848. The prospect of his candidacy, even if it failed to materialize, provided leverage with the Polk administration.[49] It was not long, however, before other voices were urging Calhoun to return to the Senate. "Your retirement is ruin and annihilation to us," a Virginia follower wrote imploringly. While friends of the Polk administration longed for his leadership in the Senate, its enemies were no less eager for his presence as a check on obliquities. Whig merchants in New York City told South Carolina congress-man Isaac Holmes that Calhoun was the only man who could save the coun-try from war with Britain over Oregon.[50] The "besotted folly" of Polk's de-mand for the whole of Oregon—"54° 40' or Fight"—weighed on Calhoun's mind, too; and this, together with what he called "the incompetency of our two Senators"—McDuffie was ill and Huger inexperienced—persuaded Cal-houn to accept Huger's standing offer to step aside.[51]

At the same time Calhoun agreed to attend the Memphis Commercial Con-vention as a South Carolina delegate. Apparently James Gadsden, president of the old western railroad which had been reincorporated as the South Caro-lina Railroad Company, persuaded Calhoun to go. Gadsden clung to the dream of rail connection that would make the West tributary to the South. Calhoun shared this dream, despite repeated disappointments and frustra-tions; and no one, in Clay's opinion, had made a bolder move for western suf-frages than the South Carolina senator some years earlier with his bill for the cession of the public lands. Now as the nation's economy revived there were fresh stirrings in the West—projects for railroads and other improvements, tariff reform, and the conquest of foreign markets for the disposal of a bur-geoning agricultural surplus. In this development Calhoun saw the opportu-nity of consummating, at last, the long meditated political alliance of South and West. He traveled first to the Alabama plantation, then, with Andrew and Patrick in tow, proceeded to the Mississippi by way of Mobile and New Orleans, thence up the river to Memphis. The convention was attended by al-most six hundred delegates from fifteen states interested in the commercial development of the Mississippi valley. Calhoun was elected president and delivered the opening address. After the usual discourse on the sanctity of the Constitution, reiterating the principles of state rights and strict construc-tion, Calhoun declared that the Mississippi River was "an inland sea" and therefore as eligible as the bays and harbors of the Atlantic coast or the Great Lakes for federal funding of improvements under the commerce clause. Nothing in Calhoun's philosophy anticipated the proposition that South Carolinians might be taxed for the removal of snags in the Mississippi River. It required on the part of his followers another rapid readjustment of political sights.[52]

On the return trip Calhoun visited Vicksburg, where he was honored by a grand ball at the home of the wealthy Whig lawyer, Sargent Prentiss. The statesman heard a welcoming address from the district's newly elected con-gressman, Jefferson Davis, whom he had appointed to West Point twenty-one years before. Calhoun seemed more interested that evening, however, in the congressman's young bride, an accomplished local belle, Varina How-ell Davis, who concluded after three hours of conversation that Calhoun was more a moral and mental abstraction than a politician.[53] Coincident with his return home at the end of November, the South Carolina legislature elected him United States Senator by a unanimous vote, excepting four blank ballots cast to protest the Memphis address.[54]

* *Eight* *

ORDEAL OF THE UNION

Webster and Calhoun found many familiar faces in the Senate to which they returned in December 1845. Among the Whigs were John M. Clayton, Willie P. Mangum, John M. Berrien, John J. Crittenden, George Evans—all seasoned veterans of the political wars and proven legislative leaders. Among the Democrats were Dixon H. Lewis and George McDuffie, who were part of Calhoun's cohort, and his ancient enemy "Old Bullion" Benton. The scholarly and ponderous Lewis Cass was at the head of a squadron of western expansionists—eagle-screamers of Manifest Destiny—that included William Allen, the inebriate chairman of the Foreign Relations Committee, David R. Atchison, Benton's Missouri rival, as well as a freshman member, Jesse Bright of Indiana. The Democrats, although they had a clear majority, suffered from deepening divisions, from Calhoun's independence, and ineffective leadership. Two former Democratic leaders, James Buchanan and Robert J. Walker, had been lost to James K. Polk's cabinet, while a third, Silas Wright, had been elected governor of New York. In that state the rift between "Barnburners" and "Hunkers," which had commenced on local issues, rapidly spread to national politics and pitted Van Buren's increasingly antislavery Albany Regency against Democrats eager to maintain the old intersectional alliance with the South. Polk declared his position in this conflict when he appointed William L. Marcy, a Hunker leader, secretary of war, and shut off patronage from the Barnburners. The two newly elected senators, John A. Dix and Daniel S. Dickinson, represented the opposite sides, Barnburner and Hunker respectively. Among other new faces was Si-

mon Cameron, a protectionist but otherwise malleable Whig, who succeeded to Buchanan's seat in Pennsylvania; Reverdy Johnson, of Maryland,
with whom Webster had dueled at the bar; Thomas Corwin, a past governor
of Ohio reputed for his campaign oratory; and "Honest John" Davis, the Bay
State Whig from whom Webster had been alienated for several years. The
seating of the Texas senators raised the membership to fifty-six. One of the
Texans, Thomas Rusk, was a native of South Carolina and in his youth a protégé of Calhoun. He was an accession for the senator. His colorful colleague,
Sam Houston, the hero of Texas independence, who leaned back in his chair,
put his feet on the desk, and contentedly whittled on a stick, proved a devoted follower of the president.

The Twenty-Ninth Congress was a watershed. It was the last congress until the Civil War to enact major domestic legislation that did not concern
slavery. Beginning with Texas annexation, the old issues of political economy between the parties were eclipsed by issues of slavery, expansion, and
the Union. These issues tended to polarize the parties sectionally, threatening to turn them into agencies of disunion rather than of union. Before that
could happen, however, the major parties in most of the states were torn
apart by these new issues, together with others like nativism, in which
some politicians found an alternate route to survival as they tried to rede-
fine their programs and compete for the suffrages of the electorate. The process was already manifest in the New York Democracy. New York Whigs of
a conservative stripe struggled against the "abolitionizing" of the party; the
breach between "cotton" and "conscience" Whigs deepened in the Bay
State; and in Georgia the Whig leadership fought the "southernization" of
the party. A generational change accompanied the change in the substance
of politics. The oldest of the old leaders, Andrew Jackson, died six months
before Congress convened. Although the second generation of American
statesmen was still in control, young men—the third generation—were
knocking at the doors of power. Some of them, with birthdates twenty-five
or thirty years later than those of Webster, Clay, and Calhoun—Stephen A.
Douglas, Andrew Johnson, Alexander H. Stephens, John Wentworth, Jefferson Davis—still labored in the House of Representatives in 1845. Democrats controlled the House, of course; but it was an unruly body, which the
Polk administration could never take for granted.

The cries of Manifest Destiny ushered the administration into power, and
Manifest Destiny became its theme. The theme was as old as America itself:
"Westward the course of empire takes its way." In the summer issue of the
Democratic Review, its editor, John L. O'Sullivan, tied Texas annexation to
"the fulfillment of our manifest destiny to overspread the continent," thereby
launching the glossy phrase on the seas of expansionist rhetoric.[1] Manifest
Destiny united the idea of an American mission to extend free institutions to
the idea of geographical predestination to occupy the entire continent. Polk
asserted the substance of the idea, with a hint of the phrase, in his annual
message to Congress on December 2. "The people of *this continent* alone
have the right to decide their own destiny," he declared, then went on to reaf-

firm the Monroe Doctrine's ban on European interference and colonization. In this connection he reasserted the American claim to the whole of Oregon, with the northern boundary at 54° 40' latitude, and recommended to Congress abrogation of the joint occupancy accord between Great Britain and the United States.[2] For many years the United States had sought to settle the boundary at the 49th parallel. Britain had refused primarily because the commercial interests of the Hudson Bay Company extended as far south as the Columbia River, which it offered as the boundary. Webster and Ashburton, it may be recalled, had made no attempt to break the stalemate on this issue. Since then American pioneers had crossed the Rocky Mountains and poured into Oregon; before long they set up the claim to 54° 40', and this became a Democratic shibboleth in the election of 1844.

From the first, Calhoun opposed this pretension. The American claim was good only as far as the 49th parallel, he argued in a Senate speech prior to his retirement in 1843; and until Britain was willing to compromise on that line, joint occupancy was in the nation's interest, since Oregon was being colonized by our own people. He defended his friendliness to the West. It was he, after all, who, as secretary of war, had planted the American flag at the far reaches of the Missouri River. But in the present instance conquest was to be achieved by "a wise and masterly inactivity."[3] (The authorship of this axiom was variously attributed to John Randolph, Lord Chatham, and Sir James McIntosh. The latter has the superior claim, but whether his *Vindicae Gallicae* was Calhoun's source is not known, and his use of the axiom antedated the Oregon question.) Later he took pains to differentiate such a policy from inaction. "He who does not understand the difference between such inactivity and mere inaction—the doing of nothing—is still in the horn-book of politics, without a glimpse of those higher elements of statesmanship by which a country is elevated to greatness and prosperity. Time is operating in our favor with a power never before excited in the favor of any other people."[4] Calhoun believed he had left Oregon in the train of settlement when he retired from the State Department. All that was necessary was for the new administration to stand still. But Polk and Buchanan acted precipitously, running the risk of war with Britain as well as the loss of a fair settlement of the Oregon boundary.[5]

With these views Calhoun was likely to find more support among Whigs than Democrats. Before leaving Boston in November, Webster denounced Polk's warmongering over Oregon. The man who shall plunge two great nations into war on this question, he declaimed, "must expect himself to be consumed in a burning conflagration of general reproach." However it was resolved, the people on the far Pacific shore, imbued with Anglo-Saxon ideas of self-government, would not long consent to remain under either nation: "They will raise a standard for themselves, and they ought to do it." Far from advocating a continent-filling destiny for the United State, Webster envisioned the rise of "a great *Pacific republic*." He was not alone in this. Thomas Jefferson and Senator Benton had expressed similar views on the limits of American expansion.[6] Such views were not popular in 1845, however, least of all with James K. Polk. After the British minister spurned an initial conciliatory overture, the dogged president decided, as he told a congressman, "that the only way to treat John Bull was to look him straight in the eye" with a demand for all of Oregon.[7]

Polk was no less bellicose toward Mexico. The joint resolution annexing Texas caused the Mexican government to break off diplomatic relations with the United States and to assume a hostile tone on issues concerning the Texas boundary, payment of the damage claims of American citizens, and American immigration to New Mexico and California. Polk ordered General Zachary Taylor into Texas, and by the fall a force of 3,500 men—about half the United States Army—was stationed on the Nueces River, some one-hundred-fifty miles above the Rio Grande, which the Americans claimed. Meanwhile, the administration learned that Mexico might be ready for comprehensive negotiations, including the possible sale of New Mexico and California. In November, Polk dispatched John Slidell, a Louisiana congressman, on a special mission to Mexico City. Making this known in his annual message, Polk left no doubt that peace or war with Mexico rode on the outcome of the mission.

In that message Polk also recommended two principal measures of domestic legislation: revision of the tariff on the revenue standard and restoration of the independent treasury. Congress would enact both in 1846. In foreign affairs, Polk would win his high-stake gamble for Oregon and, after a war, his goals in Texas, New Mexico, and California. A narrow, secretive, lumpish, and colorless man, Polk was also a man of clear views and gritty determination. Measured by its results, no four-year presidency in American history so fully realized its goals. Nevertheless, in the eyes of Calhoun and Webster, and also of Henry Clay, the Polk administration was an unmitigated disaster for the country.

1. "The Forbidden Fruit"

Not long after Congress assembled Calhoun called on Polk to express his opposition to the demand for the whole of Oregon and for giving the requisite notice to revoke the joint occupancy convention with Britain. Polk, who kept a diary, said that Calhoun was in fine humor but was as obstinate in his pacific policy as he, Polk, was in the belief that only the threat of war would extract a compromise settlement from Britain; and the senator left him after giving his own notice of opposition to the administration. Calhoun made other visits to the White House but could not shake the president's resolve. Reluctantly, Polk concluded that the senator was not only a troublemaker but something less than a patriot.[1] While the House debated a notice resolution such as the president wanted, the Senate had its own debate on the claim to the whole of Oregon. Hoosier senator Edward A. Hannegan accused Calhoun of betraying the West in the sectional bargain that linked the "reannexation" of Texas to the "re-occupation" of Oregon: "Texas and Oregon were born the same instant, nursed and cradled in the same cradle—the Baltimore Convention [of 1844]—and they were at the same instant adopted by the democracy throughout the land. There was not a moment's hesitation, until Texas was admitted; but the moment she was admitted, the peculiar friends of Texas turned and were doing all they could to strangle Oregon!"[2] Calhoun had been party to no bargain, however, and he tried to calm western anger by showing that the same precipitousness that won Texas would lose Oregon.

Calhoun was the leader of the "peace coalition" in Congress, which included the little band of southern Democrats devoted to him, some in the Van Buren following, surprisingly even Benton himself, and most of the Whigs outside the West. Several of Calhoun's political intimates, like Francis Pickens, disapproved of his break with the administration over Oregon, believing that the southern interest in tariff reform or in a western political alliance was of overriding importance. Others, like Duff Green, warmly approved the senator's stand. In February the House passed the notice resolution. Day after day, week after week, it was the special order of the day in the Senate and debated inside and out. Calhoun delivered his major speech on March 16. Observing that the new British ministry under Lord John Russell showed every disposition to compromise, Calhoun now said he favored notice, provided it looked to an amicable settlement. He dwelt at length on the costs of war, not only in money and lives, but in the shock it must give to the political system, to improvement, and to the hope for free trade. He again attempted to reconcile his course on Oregon with his course on Texas, pointing out that in both cases he sought to obtain American objectives without war. And he maintained that Mexico, with whom the country had many problems, would never be brought to the peace table as long as Anglo-American war loomed over Oregon. Congratulations poured in on Calhoun for his speech. Green called it "the crowning effort" of his life; Edward Everett thanked him for rendering an "inestimable service"; and in England, whence Everett had returned, the speech was said to have dissipated all talk of war.[3]

From the outset Webster, with most Whigs, had been content to let Calhoun lead on this issue. Webster was, moreover, preoccupied in the spring with his defense of the Ashburton Treaty against the charges initiated by Charles Jared Ingersoll. And so, although he entered into the debate, Webster never made a speech on the Oregon question. But the ambiguity of Polk's purpose increasingly troubled him. He could not believe that Polk expected or wanted a war with Britain. Why, then, when negotiation was far from exhausted, had he tied the notice decision to an ultimation for all of Oregon? For that left nothing to negotiate about. In the end, Polk must either back down, and suffer the embarrassment, or go to war to back his bluff, which would be folly. The tactics were all wrong, Webster felt, and he opposed the notice resolution unless it was freed from the ultimatum.[4] Finally it was, in effect, by the addition of language declaring the object in view to be a peaceful settlement; and in this form the Senate adopted the notice resolution by a large majority, which included Calhoun and Webster, over a minority of fourteen headed by its original proponents. By the time Polk acted on the resolution in May, the British ministry had already decided to propose extending the boundary along the 49th parallel to the Pacific. Polk took the unusual course of asking the advice of the Senate before accepting the British proposal. With approximately the same fourteen in opposition, the Senate advised acceptance, and the matter was settled on June 15. Calhoun considered the Oregon treaty a personal triumph as well as a triumph of the Senate over a bullheaded president and his party.

The Oregon question reverberated in Calhoun's domestic politics. He sought legislation to implement the new policy on internal improvements announced at Memphis and tariff reform more or less along the lines of Secretary of Treasury Walker's elaborate report to Congress. On Calhoun's motion in February the Memphis Memorial, from the pen of James Gadsden, was referred to a special committee, and he returned a report five months later. The delay probably reflected his waning enthusiasm for the project. The Memphis address threatened to give him the reputation of a trimmer among his own followers. In the pages of the *Southern Quarterly Review* the conception of the Mississippi River as an "inland sea" was held up to ridicule.[5] The improvement of the Mississippi was another source of friction with the Polk administration. But having embarked on this plan to strengthen ties with the West, Calhoun was reluctant to drop it, especially in the face of charges of abandoning the West on Oregon. His report expanded on the earlier address. As if to demonstrate the purity of his constitutional principles, he rejected all the grounds previously offered for federal internal improvements power, then proceeded to derive the power to improve navigable waterways through three or more states from the same commerce power that had always justified the establishment of lighthouses, buoys, breakwaters, and so on along the seacoast. The term *commerce*, as used in the Constitution, he said, referred only to transit by water. It referred primarily, though not exclusively, to foreign commerce. Roads and canals, as well as railroads, indeed most rivers, did not qualify for aid under Calhoun's construction. It was thus closely guarded. No construction was more latitudinarian, however, than that which postulated "ports of entry" in the great valley of the Mississippi. Calhoun's report concluded with authorization for a board of engineers to survey the Mississippi and its tributaries and make recommendations to Congress.[6] Tacked onto another bill, the authorization passed the Senate but was sidetracked in the House, which had in hand a huge "pork barrel" rivers-and-harbors bill. When it came to the Senate, Calhoun opposed it. But the bill passed, only to be met by Polk's veto. His construction was narrower than Calhoun's, for he saw no difference between rivers and roads and canals. *All* internal improvements were under state authority, in his opinion.[7] The veto undermined Calhoun's strategy of *rapproachement* with the West. As more urgent matters claimed his attention, one idea thrown up by the Memphis address assumed unexpected importance. He justified the policy of federal land grants to railroads, such as he had previously voted for, on the ground the government was a *proprietor* and in that capacity—not as a *sovereign*—it could spend money to enhance the value of the public domain. That the direct beneficiaries were the railroads seemed not to concern him. The doctrine was broad enough to cover support for the National Road and other internal improvements Calhoun had earlier opposed.[8] More importantly, however, this doctrine of proprietorship entered into Calhoun's thinking about the federal government's power over slavery in the territories.

The tariff of 1846, sometimes called the Walker Tariff, was enacted several weeks after Parliament repealed the Corn Laws, thereby opening the British market to American foodstuffs. Keen observers then, and historians since, thought the tariff act was given in exchange for the repeal, with the settlement of the Oregon boundary thrown into the bargain.[9] The fact that all three matters came to a head in June suggests the dynamic interrelationship among them. As passed by the House on a distinct party-line vote on July 3, the tariff bill provided an exclusively *ad valorem* system (minimums and specific duties were eliminated) with seven classes of duties ranging from 5 to 100 percent, plus a duty-free class, for the enumerated articles, and a 20 percent duty for everything else. No one could say what the average was, but it was nearer to 30 percent than to the supposed revenue standard of 20 percent. Advocates acclaimed the bill as the legitimate outcome of the Compromise Act of 1833. Henry Clay disagreed, voicing his opposition in an editorial penned for the Lexington *Observer*.[10] Calhoun applauded the bill, yet took no part in the debate when it came to the Senate. Manufacturers lobbied against it, as if their very survival was at stake. They set up exhibits near the Capitol designed to show the superiority of American manufacturers and the truth of the axiom, "high duties make low goods"; spokesmen like Abbott Lawrence forcefully restated the case for protection.[11] Webster thought the bill "infamous," yet he waited until the eleventh hour to move against it. The leading Whig senators who had taken their cue from Clay—Clayton, Crittenden, Magnum, Evans—determined to kill the bill. This was not impossible. Four Democratic senators—both the Pennsylvanians, one from Connecticut and one from the North Carolina—were opposed. The fate of the bill would probably depend on the casting vote of the vice president, George M. Dallas, who could hardly please Polk and Pennsylvania at the same time.

In this situation Webster decided to seek a compromise. Huddled with his friend and adviser Edward Curtis, he worked up a substitute providing for immediate reduction of the current duties, under the tariff of 1842, by 25 percent (subsequently revised to 20 percent) and after five years by a further 8 percent. Dispatched posthaste to Boston, the plan was coolly received by the industrial leaders, who preferred to kill the House bill; but as the chances for its passage rose, they fell in behind Webster's substitute as the second-best solution.[12] On July 25, as Congress was racing toward adjournment, Webster made his major speech on the tariff bill. Most of his argument was familiar. Especially interesting, however, was his appeal on behalf of northern labor: "Labor, as an earning principle, or as an element of society working for itself, with its own hopes of gain, enjoyment, and competence, is a different thing from that labor, which, in the other parts of the country, attaches to capital."[13] And in Europe, he observed, free trade was only another name for cheap bread. But no one worried about the price of bread in America. The mass of free laborers worried about getting ahead, and in this the protective tariff was their ally. The House bill, Webster said in a final flurry, pitted "the luxurious classes" against "the industrious masses." At the conclusion of his speech, the senator offered his substitute. Everything had come to hang, as he well understood, on the vote of Spencer Jarnegin of Tennessee, who, although a Whig, felt bound by his instructions to vote for the House bill unless some compromise offered him a way out. Webster worked on Jarnegin and believed he had his vote for the substitute. But Clayton surprisingly intervened with a motion to commit the bill to the Finance Committee with instructions to amend, which superseded Webster's motion. The next day the committee asked to be released from its instructions, which was done, and the bill returned to the floor. It passed, 28–27, with Jarnegin's vote making the majority. Webster was disgusted, less with Jarnegin than with Clayton, Crittenden, and the other devotees of Henry Clay. They wanted to keep the tariff alive as a political issue, Webster believed, and if they could not defeat the bill they preferred to rally the troops at the next election rather than take his substitute.[14] No such rally would occur, however. The Walker Tariff succeeded as a revenue measure, and although it did little for American agriculture, despite repeal of the Corn Laws, only the woolens industry was seriously injured by it. The tariff endured for eleven years, longer than the Whig party, as the country rode a wave of prosperity.

More important for the future was the congressional declaration of war against Mexico on May 13. Several months earlier, after the Mexican government refused to receive Slidell, Polk's special envoy, he ordered General Taylor to advance to the Rio Grande, opposite the Mexican army at Matamoros. Simultaneous with Slidell's return and recommendation for action, the president received Taylor's report of a skirmish in which eleven Americans were killed, several wounded, and others captured. American blood had been shed on American soil, Polk said, and with cabinet approval he asked Congress for a declaration of war. Congress promptly complied, voting a $10-million-appropriation and a call for volunteers. Yet from the beginning, the expediency and the justice of the Mexican War were at issue. Calhoun was one of four senators who abstained on the declaration of war (two Whigs voted against it; Webster was absent, attending Everett's inauguration at Harvard). Calhoun objected to the preamble, which said that "a state of war exists." Under the Constitution war could not exist until it was declared by Congress. He distinguished between the act of repelling an invasion and the act of going to war, and thought that the former described the present situation. The president's action, forcing a declaration of war on Congress without deliberation or reflection, effectively divested that body of the war-making power.[15]

Writing to Andrew of this appalling turn of events, Calhoun said he smelled danger some six weeks earlier when he was told by a colleague, Clayton, that Polk had ordered Taylor to the Rio Grande. "It cannot be so! It is impossible!" Calhoun then replied. Assured of the truth of the report, Calhoun said that Taylor must be stopped, and he urged the Whig leaders to intercede with the president, explaining he dared not do so himself lest he lose weight on Oregon, which was still pending. First an Oregon settlement, removing the threat of Anglo-American war, then settlement with Mexico: this was Calhoun's scenario. But Polk rewrote it. The Whig party, fearful of tempting the fate of the Federalists a generation earlier, acquiesced in the war.[16] The war, Calhoun said to his friends at home, "has dropt the curtain on the future." He could not penetrate it and was almost afraid to try.[17]

The problem magnified in August when an obscure Pennsylvania congressman, David Wilmot, introduced an amendment to an appropriation bill looking to the acquisition of territory, which laid down the "express and fundamental condition" that "neither slavery nor involuntary servitude shall ever exist in any part of said territory." The Wilmot Proviso was quickly adopted in the House, but neither bill nor proviso could be acted on in the Senate before adjournment. Calhoun gave it little thought as he started for home. But as events unfolded, the Wilmot Proviso dramatized the sad truth of the war for Calhoun: "Mexico is to us the forbidden fruit; the penalty of eating it [is] to subject our institutions to political death."[18]

Calhoun took the western route home, following the track of his father some ninety years before, through the Shenandoah valley, stopping at White Sulphur Springs, and seeing for the first time places that were part of the family's history.[19] He had already come under criticism at home for his opposition to the Mexican War. He was not surprised by this. The country had the military ardor of raw youth. But he was angered and dismayed by the quarter from which the boldest attack came, his old and trusted friend, Francis Pickens. In June, at a meeting to raise volunteers in Edgefield, Pickens had offered pro-war resolutions and, in this connection, reportedly made "sneering remarks" on Calhoun's course.[20] He had taken advantage of the popularity of the war, Calhoun wrote to his daughter Anna, to spill all his bad feelings toward him, and he undoubtedly hoped to mount his own political ambition on Calhoun's ruin. Warmly committed to the Polk administration, Pickens had been cooling toward Calhoun for some time, as the senator recognized. He believed Pickens was responsible for the article in the *Southern Quarterly Review* harshly critical of the Memphis address.[21] For his part, Pickens denied any intention of assailing or displacing Calhoun. He hurried to Washington to defend himself. Calhoun declined to see him until he explained himself. Pickens did so through McDuffie and others, and Calhoun returned his call. Civility was restored but, heartbreakingly, nothing more.[22] Pickens might deny much, he might swear his loyalty; but he could not deny "The Edgefield Proceedings." He believed, apparently, that Calhoun wounded himself politically by refusing to vote for the war and, being a blunt man, Pickens hoped to correct his course by saying so. But he succeeded only in wounding himself. Indeed, he committed political suicide. Was he not Brutus? The people of South Carolina could never forgive him. They raised the Palmetto Regiment, which embarked for Texas at the year's end, but they also kept faith with Calhoun, the South's leading spokesman against the war. In December he was unanimously reelected to the Senate for a full term.

Calhoun returned to Congress determined to bring the war to a rapid close. Making war was inevitably centralizing; the revenue to finance it must upset the finances of the country and, after the struggle to reform the tariff, force it upward again; above all, by raising the specter of new slave territory, the war inflamed abolitionist feelings in the North and turned all parties against the South. "They are willing that our blood and treasury shall be expended freely in the war to acquire territory, not for the common good, but as the means of assailing and ruining us. We are made to dig our own grave," Calhoun wrote gloomily.[23] Not long after the session opened, he called at the White House at the president's invitation. Matter-of-factly explaining his predicament over conducting the war with two generals, Taylor and Winfield Scott, the senior American army officer, who were jealous of each other and both out of sympathy with the administration, Polk requested the senator's help on the appointment of Benton as a lieutenant general serving as a kind of chief of staff in Washington. Apparently the Missouri senator was not content to bask in the military renown of his son-in-law, Captain John Charles Frémont, who had just raised the American flag in California, and he sought high command from the president. It was fatuous, of course, for Polk to expect Calhoun's aid in such a project. Instead, he vigorously advised against it. The two men talked freely about the war. Calhoun said he approved of appropriations provided they were made with a view to negotiations that would end the war, but under no circumstances could he vote for an appropriation with the Wilmot Proviso. Polk remarked that slavery could probably never exist in the lands won from Mexico. Calhoun readily agreed, adding that he had no wish to extend slavery, but that the issue of principle and honor was more important then any acquisition of territory. As the session proceeded, Polk blamed Calhoun for defeat of the bill authorizing the appointment of a lieutenant general and accused him and his three or four ardent followers of defecting to the Whigs, thereby giving them effective control of the Senate. He was, said Polk, "the most mischievous man in the Senate."[24]

Publicly and privately, Calhoun urged the administration to adopt a defensive posture, holding the country already in possession—Taylor had captured Monterey—and using it as a bargaining chip in the negotiation of peace. Again he seemed to be calling for "masterly inactivity," while Polk, pursuing an offensive strategy, whipped his generals to greater enterprise and exertion. With regard to the conduct and the aims of the war, Calhoun occupied a middle position. On one side were those who advocated conquest. Cass spoke for them—the trumpeters of Manifest Destiny—when he declared, "We want almost unlimited power of expansion. That is our safety valve."[25] Within a few months, after the Battle of Buena Vista and the capture of Vera Cruz, they would be calling for the conquest of all of Mexico. On the other side were those who, although willing to vote money and arms to carry the war to conclusion, opposed any territorial acquisition. Webster held this position. Berrien embodied it in an amendment to the war appropriation bill. But it was most forcefully articulated by Tom Corwin in answer to Cass. With twenty million people and one billion acres of land, the Senator from Michigan still professed to want room. "This," said Corwin, "has been the plea of every robber chief from Nimrod to the present hour. I dare say that Tamerlane descended from his throne built of several thousand human skulls and marched his ferocious battalions to further slaughter, I dare say he said, 'I want room'. . . . Alexander, too, the mighty 'Macedonian madman', when he wandered with his Greeks to the plains of India. . . . Many a Monterey had he to storm to get room.' "[26] Calhoun did not oppose the acquisition of territory. Public opinion, backed by American arms, had already decided that California and New Mexico must be added to the Union, and he approved of "forbidden fruit" in that quantity; but he firmly disapproved of the acquisition of Mexican provinces inhabited by "the colored race" and therefore unfit for self-government.[27]

Calhoun's motives for opposing the administration's conduct of the war were first pointedly attacked by Hopkins L. Turney of Tennessee during debate on the Three Million Bill in February. Was not the Senator from South Carolina the author of Texas annexation? Had not annexation led to the war? Was not the war of his own making? What, then, could account for his opposition but ambition for the presidency? Calhoun leapt to reply: "I am no aspirant—never have been—I would not turn on my heel for the Presidency—and he has uttered a libel upon me. . . ." The chamber quaked, the presiding officer gaveled for order, as Calhoun continued, "if he supposes that I am capable of voting upon any question with reference to the Presidency, or any other consideration but a regard to truth, justice, and my country! No, sir. The whole volume of my life shows me to be above that. . . . No, sir, I want no Presidency; I want to do my duty."[28] Calming down, he went on to assert that the cause of the war was Polk's marching order to Taylor, and he offered the apology of the pending Oregon treaty for his silence. But Calhoun would never be allowed to forget Clay's prophecy: "Annexation and war with Mexico are identical." The Washington *Union,* the administration newspaper under Thomas Ritchie's editorship, joined in the attack on Calhoun. Throughout the country the Democratic press charged "moral treason" against opponents of the war, just as Ritchie had done against Federalist opponents of "Mr. Madison's War"; and Calhoun would not emerge unscathed. An offensive article in the *Union,* entitled "Another Mexican Victory," alluded to Calhoun's temporary stoppage of the Three Million Bill. The senator's friends struck back, calling for the expulsion of Ritchie and the *Union* from the floor for issuing "a public libel" of the Senate. The Whigs rejoiced at the opportunity for revenge on their long-time enemy, Thomas Ritchie. Calhoun demanded a vote on the expulsion resolution. And Ritchie was expelled, twenty-seven yea to twenty-one nay.[29] This "disgraceful deed," said the editor, came only a year after Calhoun had cooperated in setting up the new party press in the capital and Ritchie had indulged the hope that they might undo the past. Obviously he was mistaken. "Mr. Calhoun cannot disabuse his mind of the ruling passion of his life. . . . His fiery and restless spirit seeks its gratification in the possession of power. He must rule in our public councils. He must sweep on to the great object of his political life."[30]

Calhoun enjoyed his power over Polk, his revenge on Ritchie, his frustration of Benton's fantasy; but if he expected in this way to advance his presidential ambition, he was more deluded than even the most skeptical Calhoun-watchers suspected. The news of every American victory on the battlefield, as it was said, proved "quite as fatal to Mr. Calhoun as to the Mexicans."[31] Meanwhile he took alarm at the mounting popularity of the Wilmot Proviso; and that danger, together with the failure of his anti-war effort, turned Calhoun in a new political direction, one that he would pursue relentlessly to his death. In the House of Representatives, the cause of slavery exclusion had been embraced by the New York Barnburners. The Wilmot Proviso could no longer be dismissed as the work of some desperate political gamester. It was inscribed upon a political standard long considered friendly to the South. As bluff Robert Toombs, himself a Georgia Whig, remarked, "The South had once relied on these New York 'natural allies,' on northern men with southern principles; but he [Toombs] now perceived that . . . they had been actuated only by a desire for power and spoils."[32] Although denounced as a direct attack on the South, the no-slavery proviso was added to the Three Million Bill. The House also passed a bill for the organization of the Oregon Territory. Its provisional laws excluded slavery, and no one ever imagined slaves in Oregon. The bill called for extending the no-slavery proviso of the Northwest Ordinance to Oregon. Calhoun disapproved, and at his direction Armistead Burt, congressman from the Edgefield district, offered an amendment that instead excluded slavery in Oregon "inasmuch as the whole . . . lies north of 36° 30'." So at this time Calhoun was prepared to support extension of the Missouri Compromise line to the Pacific as a solution to the problem of slavery in the territories. But Burt's amendment was rejected by an overwhelming northern vote.[33] The Oregon Bill was subsequently tabled in the Senate. On February 15 the Senate received the Three Million Bill with the Wilmot Proviso attached. And four days later Calhoun introduced his pivotal Resolutions on the Slave Question.

The time had come, Calhoun said, for the South to consider its position in the Union should slavery be excluded from the new western territories. Already the South was a minority everywhere but in the Senate. "Sir, the day that the balance between the two sections of the country—the slaveholding states and the non-slaveholding States—is destroyed, is a day that will not be far removed from revolution, anarchy, civil war, and widespread disaster. The balance of the system is in the slaveholding States. They are the conservative portion."[34] Calhoun went on to say that, although he had been willing to acquiesce in the expediency of the Missouri Compromise line, its very principle was false and subversive of the Union. The resolutions he then offered held that the territories are "the joint and common property" of the several states, that Congress cannot deprive any state of equal rights in the territories, that Congress may not bar citizens with slave property from migrating to the territories, and that in forming a constitution the people of a territory are entirely free to decide matters for themselves except for the constitutional requirement of a republican government. Nothing in Calhoun's thought anticipated the idea that citizens have property rights in the territories, that slaveholders may, in effect, carry the laws of their respective states into the territories. Barnwell Rhett had made this claim in the House a month before; apparently Calhoun took the basic idea from him.[35] The doctrine of the resolutions was generally compatible with a conception of the Union as the creation of the states and of the federal government as an agency of the states; nevertheless, it came somewhat strangely from a man who professed not to care about the expansion of slavery, who conceded it could not exist in the new territories, and who had so recently proposed to settle the question on the principle of exclusion of slavery above a geographical line. After the resolutions were read, Benton rose and labeled them the "firebrand" of disunion. Four days later, in an eagerly awaited speech, with Ritchie and the entire cabinet seated in the gallery, Benton undertook to "skin Calhoun." The old Roman called it "my first Calhouniac," and it was, in fact, the first of a series of tirades against the senator and "the Calhoun Proviso" during the next three years.[36] Calhoun replied, defending his consistency and devotion to the Union. The resolutions were not brought to a vote, nor was that Calhoun's purpose. His purpose, rather, was to lay the foundation for a new "Platform of the South."

Congress adjourned having enacted the Three Million Bill, with Calhoun's vote, and he hurried home via the Wilmington steamer persuaded that the South was in grave danger. The Virginia legislature, then in session, promptly adopted the doctrine of Calhoun's resolutions more or less in his own words; the Virginia resolutions, in turn, were adopted by the meeting the senator addressed as the guest of the City of Charleston on March 9. The great cause of the conflict between North and South, he said, was not divergent labor systems or interests, or jealousies on one side or the other, or even divergent views of the Constitution, but the system of national politics wherein the rival parties courted the votes of a noisy minority of abolitionists in order to win "the rich and glittering prize of the Presidency." The South, too, was implicated in this system. Party loyalties divided the people. The party press observed "a profound silence" on the vital question of slavery and what was required for its protection. "Henceforward," Calhoun preached, "let all party distinctions among us cease." And he called for a new party founded on the unity of the South and dedicated to the protection of slavery as paramount to the preservation of the Union.[37]

The Charleston speech evoked cheers in South Carolina, but few echoes were heard from other southern states. Everywhere the speech was read as the call for a sectional party. Calhoun's motives were puzzling. Although he denounced presidential politics, he was still suspected of playing a desperate game for the presidency by partisans of the Polk administration. He would break up the Democratic party on the slavery issue, place himself at the head of the South, and try to throw the next election into the House of Representatives, where he hoped to prevail. Some observers said he was "absolutely insane" on the subject of slavery; but if he really cared about slavery, as others observed, he must have been blind not to see that the national character of the political parties tended to sustain the institution, and if it had been smothered in silence, which was untrue, it was because the parties sought to avoid sectional discord. Benton, of course, thought he aimed at disunion.[38] But Calhoun was not ready to abandon the Union; as to the presidency, it had, in fact, ceased to be an object of interest; and as to slavery, it had become more a matter of southern honor and principle than of interest. What Calhoun sought in 1847 was to shock the North into recognition of a crisis on slavery and to drive politicians, regardless of party, from the ground of compromise. "It is a true maxim," he wrote to an Alabama sympathizer, "to meet danger on the frontier, in politics as well as war. Thus thinking, I am of the impression, that if the South act as it ought, the Wilmot Proviso, instead of proving to be the means of successfully assailing us and our peculiar institution, may be made the occasion of successfully asserting our equality and rights, by enabling us to *force* the issue on the North. Something of the kind was indispensable to rouse and unite the South."[39]

During the spring, summer, and fall at Fort Hill, Calhoun carried on a more extensive correspondence than usual with a view to rousing and uniting the South. He urged the completion of the Nashville Railroad, which would be an iron band of union through the center of the slaveholding states. He encouraged the formation of southern rights associations. He wrote his defense of the electoral law in South Carolina, which he held up as an example to the other southern states.[40] The Charleston Regency acquired the *Southern Quarterly Review* and placed it under the editorship of J. Milton Clapp, who had been editing the *Mercury*. There was talk—nothing more—of commercial retaliation against the northern states and also of a southern convention. More importantly, Calhoun worked with Henry W. Conner, chairman of the corresponding committee in Charleston, to raise money for a newspaper in Washington devoted to the southern cause. The fight with Ritchie, and the *Union*'s ongoing attack on Calhoun, had pointed up the need for "a faithful sentinel" in the national capital. Calhoun had discussed the matter with Duff Green before Congress adjourned. Green put a price tag of $25,000 on the project and offered himself as editor. But Conner, Elmore, Calhoun, and others, for all their efforts, failed to raise the money. In June, Elmore wrote that Hammond was standoffish, Pickens had not been heard from, and Burt seemed uncertain. So dim were the prospects in the sister states that Calhoun, upon returning to Washington, was ready to drop the project.[41]

While Calhoun was thus attempting to dissolve old party allegiances, Webster toured the South in order to cultivate the Whig faithful. The senator again had his eye on the presidency. Unfortunately, the issues raised by the war shook the ground beneath him in Massachusetts. At the previous fall convention of the Whig party in Boston, the Conscience Whigs had appealed to

Webster to join them in the adoption of sweeping anti-slavery resolutions. Let the Defender of the Constitution dedicate his golden years to ridding the nation of slavery, fulfilling the promise of the Plymouth oration over a quarter of a century before, young Charles Sumner implored: "Do not shirk the task. . . . The aged shall bear witness to you; the young shall kindle with rapture, as they repeat the name of Webster; and the large company of the ransomed shall teach their children, and their children's children, to the latest generation, to call you blessed; while all shall award to you yet another title, which shall never be forgotten on earth or in heaven—*Defender of Humanity*—by the side of which that earlier title shall fade into insignificance, as the Constitution, which is the work of mortal hands, dwindles by the side of Man, who is created in the image of God." But Webster neither heard nor responded to the plea. Later, in a demonstration of unity, he walked into the convention arm in arm with Abbott Lawrence, and the cheering delegates tabled the radical resolutions.[42] In Congress, Webster did not disguise his opinion that the Mexican War was illegal and unjust, that it offered grounds for impeachment of the president, yet he took no action. He was pleased with Calhoun's "defensive line" speech, saying it had "dug the channel into which the opinion of the country is to flow."[43] He was impatient with the resolutions of the Massachusetts legislature against the war and for the Wilmot Proviso. However unjust *we* may think the war to be, he wrote to Fletcher, the minority must yield to the majority and see it through. "And snarling and grumbling, and all attempts to sever one's self from what the country has decided upon, are but the effusions of narrow feelings."[44] He endorsed the Berrien amendment to the Three Million Bill, which premised support on making peace. In principle, Webster was for the Wilmot Proviso, indeed declared it had been his own proviso since 1838, yet believed it was impolitic and misdirected. Southern Whig objections to the proviso were insurmountable; the only way to deal with them, Webster thought, was to acquire no more territory. However, after defeat of the Berrien amendment Webster had no alternative but to vote for the proviso, and he did so with apprehensions that it would needlessly complicate the problem of slavery in the territories.

The southern tour Webster had planned would take him to the major cities of the South Atlantic states, thence to New Orleans, returning north by way of Louisville, Nashville, and Cincinnati, all in about seven weeks. Delayed by business in Washington, the Websters and their traveling companion, Josephine Seaton, the daughter of his old friend, only got off near the end of April, as the warm season began, and they arrived in Charleston about the time of the year when denizens of the lowcountry thought it foolhardy for strangers to visit there. In the course of satisfying his intellectual curiosity about the Lower South, Webster sought to enhance his presidential prospects as well. He made it a condition that he would not deliver any set speeches or address contentious political questions. But at elaborate receptions, dinners, and ceremonial occasions, he could not avoid speaking or, however indirectly, touching on current issues and events. At Charleston he was honored by all the grandees as "a monument of American mind," one who stood in the same relation to New England as Calhoun to the South and Clay to the West, and one in whom the whole nation, without regard to party or section, took pride.[45] Some of his Bay State compatriots were concerned lest things be turned around and Webster be seen as honoring Charleston so soon after the official emissary of the commonwealth, Samuel Hoar, who had been sent to protest the routine imprisonment of colored seamen on Massachusetts vessels calling at the port, had been run out of South Carolina.[46]

An excursion on the Cooper River, in the steamer *Calhoun*, gave Webster a glimpse of rice cultivation; and after the mandatory ball, he set out for Columbia, where he was the guest of William C. Preston, president of South Carolina College. The students illuminated their houses, built bonfires, and after a torchlight procession serenaded Webster. His response was so curt and cold it bordered on insult. "I am afraid he is wanting in heart," Preston remarked apologetically. Throughout the visit, Professor Francis Lieber said, "he remained cold, torpid, like an alligator, and was in his intercourse absent to a degree of discourtesy which many considered rudeness." Following the governor's reception, where the guest of honor was again as somber as a thundercloud, he visited Wade Hampton's plantation, Millwood, where, it was said, all the slaves were cleanly dressed and happily at work in the fields to receive him. Impressed by this view of the plantation system, Webster was heard to say that "no change could be made which would benefit the slave."[47] In Savannah he was received at Monument Square, which honored two of Georgia's Revolutionary heroes, Count Pulaski and Nathaniel Greene, the latter a native son of New England. Supreme Court Justice James M. Wayne, introducing the senator, lauded him for his commitment to the compromises of the Constitution. As Wayne surely knew, the Bay State legislature had enacted resolutions to abolish the Constitution's three-fifths clause, and Webster himself had at one time advocated this. Yet in his response he seemed to accept the embrace of the compliment, saying he stood by the Constitution *as it is*, then delivering a paean to the Union. The Union was more than a legal arrangement, more than a compromise of interests, or a deduction of political economy, or a result of philosophical reasoning; it was a *sentiment* that made "brethren in feeling" of citizens from one extremity of the confederacy to the other.[48]

Webster fell ill in Savannah, abruptly ended his tour there, and hurried back to Boston, where he arrived on June 6 looking thin and several shades blacker than usual.[49] From a political standpoint, the southern tour had been disappointing. Everywhere he went the presidential talk among Whigs was of General Taylor, the Hero of Buena Vista. This undoubtedly contributed to Webster's torpor, and but for illness he might have been happy for another excuse to return home. At the end of September, just as the catarrh left him, he attended the Whig convention in Springfield. The state party was split two ways: between the Cotton and Conscience Whigs and between the Massachusetts Whigs under Lawrence and the Webster Whigs. The latter wished their leader nominated for the presidency and also opposed Davis's renomination for the Senate. The Lords of the Loom under Lawrence backed Davis and, although favoring Taylor, sought to block any endorsement for the presidency. The Conscience Whigs found themselves in the enviable position of being courted by both sides. Lawrence, although opposed to their aggressive anti-slavery platform, acquiesced in the election of many Conscience delegates with a view to using them as a cat's-paw against Webster. Soon after the convention opened Stephen Phillips, one of the original Conscience Whigs, moved that it was inexpedient to make a nomination for president. A long pause ensued. The chairman, George Ashmun, Webster's good friend, was taken by surprise, but after some confusion was saved by George T. Curtis's motion to table. That motion was adopted, 242–232. It was a narrow escape. Fewer than a majority of the delegates could be mustered to defeat a move to kill Webster's nomination. And in the presence of Godlike Daniel himself, it was, as Sumner said, humiliating.[50]

Although the convention went ahead to nominate Webster without opposition, the earlier vote rendered the prize almost worthless. Content with this, Lawrence rallied his troops to defeat a resolution pledging all Whig candidates to support the Wilmot Proviso. The Conscience Whigs felt betrayed. They would never attend another Whig convention. In a ninety-minute address, Webster tried to soothe injured feelings on both sides but appealed particularly to the Conscience wing of the party. Again he denounced the Mexican War as vicious and wrong, yet deprecated resistance outside constitutional channels. Again he opposed the acquisition of territory even if free and spoke somewhat defensively of the Wilmot Proviso, toward which he might have felt friendlier had not all the merit of the doctrine gone to its recent discoverers. "I deny the priority of their invention," he said. "Allow me to say, sir, it is not their thunder." Finally, he declared that the time for congressional action against the war was fast approaching. Unless the president showed at the convening of the new Congress that the war was prosecuted for the sake of the Union and the people, "then Congress ought to pass resolutions against the prosecution of the war, and grant no further supplies."[51] The language and doctrine were reminiscent of 1814. Webster returned to Congress still convinced that the best way to handle the slavery issue was to acquire no territory from Mexico, but also, in accordance with Massachusetts opinion, more resolutely opposed to continuation of the war.

2. Three Statesmen and a "Frontier Colonel"

Until an impressive string of Whig victories in the midterm elections of 1846, Henry Clay showed no interest in making another race for the presidency. He had not ruled it out, but was perfectly passive to all inquiries and deplored premature agitation of the question. Leading Whigs in the Senate counted as friendly to him—Clayton, Crittenden, Mangum—declared Clay *hors de combat*. Early presidential speculation centered on General Scott. Many names were mentioned, however, some new, like Tom Corwin of Ohio, others hardy perennials of faint bloom, like John McLean, associate justice of the Supreme Court, and, of course, Webster. Whig success at the polls perked Clay's interest. Before going to New Orleans for the winter, he told Horace Greeley, whose New York *Tribune* was perhaps the foremost newspaper in the country, that his decision for or against candidacy would be controlled by events, above all by the manifest voice of his countrymen. He had a horror of becoming the "forlorn hope" of the party, but he would respond to popular demand. James T. Morehead's impending retirement opened a vacancy in the Senate. Some counsellors urged Clay to make himself available, but he could not think of returning to the body from which he had taken an historic valedictory. In February, when the legislature was stalemated on the major candidates after twenty-four ballots, Clay's name was dramatically placed in nomination, without his consent, then quickly withdrawn as a breakthrough occurred.[1] In the Whig party, however one felt about Clay's running for the presidency, it was understood by all concerned that until he made up his mind nobody could move with confidence.

In the spring, after returning to Lexington, Clay was taken "completely by surprise" by the movement for General Taylor. The Battle of Buena Vista made him a national hero and a presidential contender at the same time. Because of disagreement on the conduct of the war, Taylor was at odds with Polk and before the year was out asked to be relieved of his command. He returned to his Louisiana home. Whether a Whig or a Democrat no one knew, but Whig politicians all over the country began to claim "Old Rough and Ready" one of their own and to see in him the man-on-horseback who could lead them back into power. On April 1, 1847, James Watson Webb, the veteran editor of the New York *Courier & Enquirer,* came out boldly for Taylor. Nomination by the Pennsylvania Whig convention followed. Prominent Whig leaders and newspapers jumped on the bandwagon. The Louisville *Journal* led the way in Kentucky. George Prentice, its editor, simply assumed that Clay was not a candidate. Crittenden, Clay's devoted ally for many years, making the same convenient assumption, placed himself at the head of the Taylorites. Although born in Virginia, Taylor had grown to manhood in Kentucky, and he and Crittenden were lifelong friends with family connections. Crittenden turned to Taylor for the best of political reasons: he looked like a winner.[2] Clay, still grieving over his son's death on the battlefield, was exasperated by the Taylor boom. Of the general's politics nothing was known. A Louisiana cotton planter, he had spent most of his life on frontier outposts and had never as much as cast a vote for president. The general himself at first labeled the idea of his candidacy "visionary." Clay again warned against warrior chieftains. The republic seemed fated to terminate in military despotism. Yet all the previous chieftains elevated to the presidency, including the Whigs' Harrison, had at least proven eminence in civilian capacities. Taylor did not. Still, Clay preferred the gruff, honest, and straightforward Taylor to Scott, a man of disgusting vanity; and if finally faced with the dilemma of choosing between him on a Whig ticket and any Democratic candidate, he would run the risk with Taylor.[3]

Near the end of July, Clay set out on an eastern tour that took him to the Virginia springs and finally to the seaside resort of Cape May. Politics, as he repeatedly said, were no part of his object. He was fleeing the grief and anguish that invested Ashland: "Finding myself in the theater of sadness, I thought to fly to the mountain's top, and descend to the ocean's wave, and, by meeting the sympathy of friends, obtain some relief from the sadness which surrounded me."[4] But as much as he might try, Prince Hal could not avoid the adulation of crowds and the excitements of politics. At Cape May boatloads came from New York and elsewhere to see him. The *Tribune* reporter said he did not seem perceptibly older than when last seen in the East eight years ago: "His hair is just gracefully streaked with silver, while his face is unwrinkled and his step has the elasticity and vigor of youth." Beseeched by Whig committees from Boston, New York, and other cities to visit them, Clay refused all the invitations.[5] Some of the party potentates, like Abbott Lawrence, who might have preferred Clay, decided he was not a candidate and climbed aboard the Taylor bandwagon. In New York, Weed and Seward were already aboard, while their old ally, Greeley, clung to Clay. In an editorial, "The Presidency in 1848—Mr. Clay," published as the sojourner retraced his steps for home, Greeley maintained that Clay had not been fairly beaten in 1844, that despite his well-publicized resolution to abstain from another campaign, he had not barred candidacy in response to broad popular demand, and that in view of the collapse of the Polk administration he was the only leader upon whom the great majority of the people, including many Democrats, could unite. The editorial was interpreted as a trial balloon for Clay's candidacy. Whether he had any responsibility for it, nobody knew; but its source, Greeley's *Tribune*, an anti-war, anti-slavery, and anti-southern newspaper, was extraordinary.[6]

When he got home Clay was amazed by the Taylor ground swell in Kentucky. The state had been swept by Taylor meetings during the summer. With a touch of paranoia Clay wondered if these movements were aimed not only at nominating Taylor but also at destroying him. "They wear the aspect of impatience under the ties which have so long bound me to the State and to the Whig party, and an eager desire to break loose from them," he wrote Crittenden. Crittenden owed Clay an explanation, and he demanded one from him.[7] Unfortunately the senator could offer no explanation that spared Clay's feelings. Their long political friendship was broken. The most he could do was shield Taylor from the damage. Since the general had yet to declare himself a Whig, the movements in his behalf had a superficially non-partisan character, which irritated Clay all the more. Immediately after the August election, in which the Whigs again prevailed, the Taylorites in Lexington advertised a citizens' meeting at the courthouse to consider the propriety of a nomination for the presidency. The *Observer* denounced the move, saying it was premature and would only antagonize the Whigs of the Union. When the meeting occurred on September 13, with about 220 in attendance, Leslie Combs, George Robertson, and other Clay stalwarts managed to defeat resolutions nominating Taylor, though after their departure a residue of 97

Taylorites adopted the resolutions. Later a packed meeting in neighboring Bourbon County overrode Garrett Davis's plea and adopted similar resolutions.[8] Frantically, in October, Clay's friends got up a "secret circular," communicated only to party activists, saying that the number and size of the Taylor meetings had been exaggerated in the press and that the great body of Kentucky Whigs remained loyal to their old leader who, under "a concurrence of weighty circumstances," would not refuse the party nomination. Inevitably the circular became public, further embarrassing the Clay party.[9]

If Taylor was to be stopped, Clay himself must take the offensive. Thus far his only published utterance on the Mexican War had been the silly remark in New Orleans that he would like to go and "slay a Mexican." The time had come, if he expected the nation to turn to him, for Clay to assume a leadership position on the war. "Is there no proper way to get Clay to come before the public with his opinions . . .?" Tom Corwin asked a Cincinnati journalist close to the Kentuckian in October. To be sure, he held no public office and was not a candidate for one. But such a man should not withhold his opinions from the people. Had he forgotten his immortal words to Judge Brooke in 1825: "What is a public man worth if he cannot sacrifice himself to the public good?" Webster had just declared at Springfield the power and the duty of Congress to withhold supplies if necessary to end the war. "If [Clay] would come out as Webster has done on both the war and slavery," Corwin said, "it would make our cause impregnable as Gibralter and the Whigs in the coming Congress would act like Whigs. And he (if he lives) can be what he pleases, and if he dies, it will send his monument up to the heavens." Whether or not Corwin's message reached Clay, others of a similar purport certainly did. An editorial in the Philadelphia North American, a newspaper under Clayton's influence and now devoted to Taylor, openly challenged "The Sage of Ashland" to counsel the nation.[10]

The capital of Mexico had fallen to American arms when, on a rainy Saturday, November 13, Clay delivered his first speech in several years before a suspense-filled audience in Lexington. (In the audience was a freshman congressman from Illinois, Abraham Lincoln, who was visiting Lexington, his wife's former home, on his way to Washington, and who, of course, took the opportunity to see and hear his "beau ideal of a statesman.")[11] The state of the Union was as dark and gloomy as the Lexington weather, Clay began. He came before the public simply as a private citizen eager to aid in delivering the country from the perils that surrounded it. He spoke of the evils and the injustice of the war. He blamed it on Texas annexation and Polk's belligerency; and without questioning the patriotic motives of the congressmen who voted for a war bill that was "a palpable falsehood," said that "no earthly consideration" could have moved him to vote for it. After a mournful tale of conquering nations and conquerors, Clay compared the prospective dismemberment of Mexico to that "most nefarious and detestable deed," the dismemberment of Poland. He said nothing of the Wilmot Proviso, but spoke clearly against the expansion of slavery. At the conclusion of the address, Clay offered eight resolutions. The first impeached Polk for starting the war; others called upon Congress to declare the war's purposes and objects and, should the president deviate from them, directed that it be brought to a halt; still others denounced conquest and slavery expansion; the last called for the citizens to speak out in public meetings.[12] Whatever the public was to make of it, the speech was a milestone in the history of newspaper reporting. When Clay finished at 2:00 P.M. a courier on horseback carried an abstract of the speech through the rainstorm eighty-five miles to Cincinnati; there, by the wonders of the telegraph, it was transmitted to Pittsburgh, thence relayed to Philadelphia, and finally to New York for publication in the *Herald* on Sunday afternoon. Clay's words traveled one thousand miles in twenty-four hours. And in forty-eight hours the verbatim text of the resolutions was on New York's streets.[13]

The "Lexington Platform" was enthusiastically adopted in Whig meetings across the country. "Rejoice with us, friends of Peace!" Greeley wrote in the *Tribune*. "Henry Clay has spoken and the war has received its death blow!"[14] In the Democratic press, the speech and the resolutions were branded "treasonous." Anti-slavery newspapers, while applauding Clay's opinions against war and conquest and slavery expansion, complained of his silence on the Proviso. Whigs like Corwin and Webster, similarly opposed to territorial acquisition, had added that if territory was taken it must be free; but Clay avoided the question of slavery in the territories altogether. Nor did the Lexington speech escape censure in conservative Whig quarters. Webb, in the *Courier & Enquirer*, recalled his support for Clay in every campaign from 1832 through 1844, but warned that his unpatriotic resolutions, if adopted as a platform, would be "suicidal" for the Whig party. Southern Whigs, with whom Taylor was most popular, gave the speech a mixed reception.[15] They saw that it was angled toward the North and that if it was, in effect, a declaration of candidacy, Clay would appeal primarily to the northern electorate— "a Southern man with Northern feelings." Taylor was like a gift of Heaven to the southern Whigs: a slaveholder, a cotton planter, a popular hero, unencumbered by the old politics, uncommitted on new issues but receptive to guidance. It did not follow from Taylor's popularity in the South that Clay could therefore count on the North to sustain him. William H. Seward, exactly the kind of northern Whig leader to whom the Lexington speech was angled, said it was "surpassingly beautiful" and made a deep impression. "But it is too late. This is just such a speech as Mr. Clay ought to have made four years ago." It was too late, the New Yorker felt, for him to regain credibility among anti-slavery Whigs.[16]

In Kentucky, meanwhile, the respective leaders of the Clay and Taylor forces reached an understanding designed to limit the damage from an open contest between them. The Taylorites, who had hoped that the general might be chosen by acclamation, agreed to nomination in a national convention; further, the delegates chosen to the convention would be uninstructed, except that they were to cast their ballots for the candidate ascertained to be the choice of the nation; finally, all would abide by the choice of the convention. Prentice, who presided over this accord, which Clay himself approved, announced it in the *Journal* on November 30.[17]

Hopes for peace with Mexico were dispelled by the president in his message to the opening session of the Thirtieth Congress. American arms were triumphant, but Polk was compelled to report the collapse of the negotiations commenced by the administration's peace commissioner, Nicholas P. Trist, who had been ordered to return home. The prospect was thus for protracted war and prolonged occupation of Mexico. Firmly adhering to his course, Polk rejected the advice of expansionists who called for the conquest and absorption of "All Mexico," as well as Calhoun's idea of holding a defensive line, believing it could only operate to the enemy's advantage. Calhoun, nevertheless, returned to this idea. He acted against the background of resolutions promptly introduced by Dickinson, and backed by Cass, providing that the status of slavery in the lands acquired from Mexico would be decided by the territorial legislatures established in them. If adopted, the doctrine—soon to become known as "popular sovereignty"—would as effectively exclude slavery as the Wilmot Proviso, Calhoun thought. Immediately, he called upon the *Mercury* to oppose it. Calhoun also believed, erroneously, that the resolutions originated with the administration as a panacea for ridding Congress of the problem of slavery in the territories and for reuniting the Democratic party.[18] Thus believing, Calhoun's vexation with "Mr. Polk's War" reached a fever pitch.

On December 14 the South Carolina senator introduced two resolutions condemning any policy that looked to the conquest or absorption of Mexico. In his opinion, this must be the result of Polk's policy. Vindicating the defensive strategy he had advocated, Calhoun said that all the American victories had sapped the strength of the Mexican government to make peace. He sought precedence for his resolutions over the administration's Ten Regiment Bill but was outmaneuvered by Cass. The resolutions never came to a vote, though Calhoun was given time to speak on them on January 14. He had earlier called Mexico "forbidden fruit." Now he described the horrors of ingesting it—racial amalgamation, unsettlement of slavery, destruction of liberty, an imperial Union and an imperial president. Since he had no objection to a "territorial indemnity" from Mexico or, indeed, to the purchase of whole provinces (California and New Mexico), just how far his aims diverged from Polk's was unclear. Nevertheless, he was exceedingly vehement in his denunciation of the administration and the war. The speech created a sensation. Calhoun's colleague A. P. Butler wrote excitedly to Elmore: "Some think it was the highest effort of his life."[19] Afterward, John Greenleaf Whittier, fascinated by the irony of the Texas expansionist repelled by an expansionist war, penned a verse missive "To John C. Calhoun":

> Sore baffled statesman! when thy eager hand,
>   With game afoot, unslipped the hungry pack,
> To hunt down Freedom in her chosen land,

Hads't thou no fear, that ere long doubling back,
Those dogs of thine might snuff on Slavery's track?[20]

Webster, of course, agreed with most of what Clay and Calhoun said against the war. If he was angry at Clay, as were some of his Boston friends, for "stealing the thunder" he had cracked at Springfield, he never said so. Besides, he left the thunder behind him in Massachusetts. Only near the closing hour, on March 17, did Webster speak against the Ten Regiment Bill. It could be said in extenuation that he had a heavier than usual load at the Supreme Court and that in February he learned of Edward's death and Julia's illness. No wonder he "labored under deep depression," in the words of the Senate reporter, whan he spoke at last. Regardless, it came distressingly "out of season," as Gamalial Bailey editorialized in the National Era, the anti-slavery newspaper in the capital.[21] The Treaty of Guadalupe Hidalgo had been received and already ratified by the Senate. Trist had disobeyed orders and negotiated an unauthorized treaty, yet a treaty that was too good for Polk to refuse. And so Webster denounced the war after peace had been made and denounced the acquisition of territory after it had been acquired. Under the treaty Mexico accepted the Rio Grande as the southern boundary of Texas and ceded New Mexico and California to the United States for $15 million along with the assumption of the claims of American citizens amounting to over $3 million. Opposition to the treaty came from Democrats who wanted all of Mexico and from Whigs who wanted none. Webster was among the latter. Calhoun voted for the treaty, and Clay, who was in the capital when it arrived, advised the president to accept it.

Clay had arrived in Washington on January 10 to argue a case before the Supreme Court and to preside over the annual meeting of the American Colonization Society. No one doubted, however, that his chief purpose was to reconnoiter the Whig presidential sweepstakes. When he left home his inclination, as far as he had any, was against running, and he expected to say so publicly before his return. In the capital he was smothered with adulation and affection. Several hundred people greeted him upon his arrival at the railroad station and escorted him to the United States Hotel, where he came out to address the crowd from the balcony. "He cannot move without having a throng at his heels. He lives in an atmosphere of hurras."[22] Everybody remarked on how fit and vigorous he looked. He renewed old acquaintances in Congress; he dined at the White House, where Webster and Calhoun were among the guests; and held a levee. The House chamber was packed to hear his address to the Colonization Society. His unwavering devotion to the Society's cause during thirty years was a remarkable instance of Clay's pertinacity. On this occasion he could not help but regret that the same energy that had gone into abolitionism had not been put into colonization.[23] When he appeared before the Supreme Court in a celebrated New Orleans bank case, the chamber was packed to suffocation, "chiefly by females," an associate justice complained, "scarcely one of whom could comprehend the mere legal questions to be discussed," but who came to see, hear, and possibly touch Henry Clay. Clay, who himself sat next to seventy-nine-year-old Dolley Madison, did not disappoint them. And he won his case, earning the magnificent fee of $7,000, nearly all of which he promptly applied to a debt.[24]

But Clay's magnetism, while as great as ever, was no longer as daunting. Going to his old followers, begging them not to desert him, he awakened the interest of some in his candidacy, yet could not shake the committment of the prominent Whig leaders to Taylor. Webster, himself a candidate and never an unbiased witness where the Kentuckian was concerned, said he did not think there were five men in Congress who gave Clay a chance for the nomination, and for the first time his personal friends had the courage to tell him the truth. Some of the men who urged him to make the race, it was felt, had other objects in view. They wished to stop Taylor or they secretly supported Scott or found Clay's candidacy useful in state contests. "The great trouble with the Whigs," one Washington reporter wrote cuttingly, "is to manage and get rid of Clay."[25] Southern Whigs, especially, felt this way. The "Clay storm" was in the North. "Bah!" Toombs exclaimed. "He can deceive nobody here. The truth is he has sold himself body and soul to the Northern Anti-slavery Whigs." But while the South fell away from Clay, he did not rise to the opportunity in the North. All he had to do was endorse the Wilmot Proviso. "*He* knows my position," Joshua Giddings wrote. Obviously Whigs of Giddings's stripe could not vote for Taylor. If Clay, or someone, was not nominated on an anti-slavery platform, they would have to go elsewhere; and so they were reluctant to give him up utterly.[26]

Greeley was the torchbearer of a Clay candidacy free-soilers could support. The irrepressible editor came to Washington and persuaded Clay, who was about to return home via Philadelphia, to change his plans and go to New York. In advance of his arrival Greeley staged a mass meeting at Castle Garden, where Clay's nomination was loudly acclaimed. His tumultuous reception followed, spreading over several days and coinciding with the obsequies for John Quincy Adams, who had collapsed in the House and died some days later.

While Clay was in the East, the Kentucky Whigs met in convention at Frankfort. The Taylorites wanted to nominate Old Zack, as they had earlier attempted to do in the legislature; but old guard Whigs held them to the pact negotiated the previous November. Again, Clay's friends did not regard him as a candidate and predicted he would withdraw from the field before the national convention. But to preempt his decision was unthinkable. Prentice agreed, writing in the *Journal*, "it would look most ungracious in the Whigs of the State of Kentucky . . . , which is indebted to him for an immortality of glory and fame, to move against him so long as a strong desire is manifested in other quarters to run him . . . and so long as his own decision is doubtful."[27] A Kentucky Whig nomination of either Taylor or Clay would tear the party to pieces and cause the defeat of its gubernatorial candidate. "I am satisfied that Clay won't think of running the race out," observed Robert Letcher, who loved Clay but backed Taylor. "But great God, if he could have foreseen

The Cast-Iron Man in 1849.
Daguerreotype attributed to Mathew
Brady. *Courtesy of The Beinecke Rare
Book and Manuscript Library, Yale
University*

Statesmen of Compromise and Union. (*Left*) Daguerreotype of Webster attributed
to Meade Brothers. *Courtesy of Dartmouth College* (*Right*) Daguerreotype of Clay
attributed to Martin B. Lawrence and also to Mathew Brady. *Courtesy of The
New-York Historical Society, New York*

Webster in Oratorical Attire. Daguerreotype by Southworth and Hawes. *Courtesy of the Museum of Fine Arts, Boston*

The Fort Hill Portrait of Calhoun. Painting by De Bloch. *Courtesy of Clemson University*

Photograph of Fort Hill Today. *Courtesy of Clemson University*

Last Days of Webster. Painting by Joseph A. Ames. *Courtesy of The Bostonian Society/Old State House* .

the predicament in which he had placed his friends and his party . . . he would not have hesitated a moment about declining."[28] The state convention made no nomination. However, eleven of the twelve delegates elected to the national convention were Taylorites.[29]

Buoyed by the New York demonstration, which was backed by the resolution of the Whig legislative caucus in Albany favoring his nomination, Clay put the best light he could on the Frankfort proceedings and returned home confident he was still the true leader of the Whig party. On April 10 he ended speculation on his candidacy by releasing a letter "To the Public" saying that, although he had no desire to run, he felt it his duty to do so for the sake of the Whig ticket in the free states and because of the excellent prospects of his ultimate election. Torn between desire and duty, he would allow the national convention to determine his fate and, whatever the decision, cheerfully acquiesce in it.[30] It was a puzzling statement from the man who "would rather be right than president." It suggested either that he did not know his own heart and mind or that he must, indeed, rule or ruin the Whig party. The letter was read with disappointment and regret by many of Clay's warm friends. Crittenden, in a sad last letter to Clay, restated his honest conviction that he could not be elected, while Taylor's prospects improved daily. At least the period of coy dalliance was over and Clay's candidacy was out in the open. Taylor Whigs could abandon specious neutrality and political gamesters could no longer employ Clay as a stalking-horse to defeat Taylor. Southern Whigs were incensed by Clay's letter. Offering a free-state apology for running, Clay forfeited the vote of the South.[31] Taylor's managers moved quickly to counter Clay's announcement. At Baton Rouge, where the general was again engaged in sedentary employment, they got him to sign a letter addressed to his brother-in-law, Captain John S. Allison, which was intended to remove lingering doubts about his Whig credentials. Declaring himself "a Whig but not an ultra Whig," Taylor went on to express an appropriately deferential attitude toward Congress and pledged not to abuse the veto power, which pleased Whigs everywhere but especially in the South. The Allison letter was purposely vague on the issues between the parties and the sections. This vagueness was one of the candidate's appeals. As James Russell Lowell humorously put it in *The Biglow Papers:*

> Another pint that influences the minds o' sober judges
> Is that the Gin'ral hezn' gut tied hand and foot with pledges;
> He hezn' told ye wut he is, an' so there aint no knowin'
> But wut he may turn out to be the best there is again.[32]

Another candidate, Daniel Webster, was virtually forgotten in the spring of 1848. Morose, despondent, laboring under the torments of Job, he seemed unable to arouse himself. An address of the Whig members of the legislature reiterated the nomination of the Springfield convention. Two Boston newspapers, the *Courier* and the *Atlas,* supported Webster, as did the *Commercial Advertiser* in New York. The latter ran a series of articles championing Webster over the signature of "A Whig from the Start," which were widely reprinted and issued as a pamphlet. The principal author was Hiram Ketchum, the New Yorker who had been a Webster spokesman for several years, though Everett, Charles March, possibly others, contributed to the series.[33] Webster was offered to the people as the quintessential Whig: a leader of the party of progress and improvement, one who believed that the high aim of the national government was to develop the resources of the country and give employment to its labor, one who believed in the supremacy of law and the Constitution. The revolutions of 1848 in Europe underscored the importance of the United States setting a dignified example of republican government. Webster embodied dignity and principle as against the tawdry party standard of "availability." But neither Webster nor his advocates had confidence in his candidacy. Southern Whigs would not support a northern man, even one who had so recently courted them and who swore to uphold southern rights; and he had done little to earn the trust of anti-slavery Whigs in the free states. Many of his former backers in New York and New England had gone over to Taylor. Given the formidable obstacles, knowing politicians speculated that Webster's real aim was the vice presidential nomination on a ticket headed by Taylor. Webb, who still considered himself Webster's friend, pleaded with him to adopt just such a course. His road to the presidency, the editor importuned, was through the vice presidency.[34] But Webster could not tie himself to "General Availability." Indeed, as he told his Whig friends in Boston, he could never support "a swearing, fighting frontier colonel."[35]

The Democrats had already nominated Lewis Cass, the Michigan senator, for the presidency when the Whig national convention met in Philadelphia on June 7. Cass was the leading proponent of the "popular sovereignty" solution to the problem of slavery in the territories. The platform was silent on this question, however. The convention turned down a southern resolution embodying Calhoun's doctrine on the equal rights of slaveholders in the territories. Both Democratic nominee and platform worked to the advantage of the southern Whig choice, Taylor. Greeley was apprehensive for Clay as the convention opened. The Clay Whigs had been outmaneuvered in several state conventions; some of his delegates were shifting to Scott; and the Whig congressmen who were delegates favored Taylor. But New York appeared safe, and Greeley looked for a close contest.[36] On the first ballot, 279 delegates from thirty states cast 111 votes for Taylor, 97 for Clay, 43 for Scott, 22 for Webster, and 6 for two others. Clay's vote was concentrated in the East, Taylor's in the South. New York fell away when Weed came out openly for Taylor. On the third ballot, after Clay's managers forced an adjournment, the New England vote, including a portion of Webster's, went to Taylor. Truman Smith of Connecticut was the Judas held responsible for this loss. Clay's vote, declining on each ballot, collapsed on the fourth, and Taylor was nominated. Millard Fillmore of New York was named for the vice presidency. In the end, as Leslie Combs wrote to Clay the next morning, his own friends nominated Taylor. The Kentucky delegation was rotten. Only one of its members stood with Clay. And the Ohio delegation, whose twenty-two votes Clay had been led to expect, betrayed him for Scott. "They would not take a true *ultra* Whig and a constitutional conservative slaveholder," Combs wrote angrily, "and they have gotten an *ultra* Slaveholder and no particular Whig."[37] The convention adopted no platform, as if in acknowledgment that the nomination had been made by "spontaneous combustion" or "gunpowder popularity." Greeley called the Philadelphia convention "a slaughterhouse of Whig principles."[38]

Clay readily agreed with Greeley. "I fear the Whig party is dissolved," he sulked. With the nomination of Old Zack it had been transformed into "a mere personal party," like the Jackson party twenty years earlier. He would have nothing more to do with it. "My race is run."[39] But for many Whigs, the problem of the party had been Clay's personal domination. They exulted in his defeat as a liberation. "Thank God, we have got rid of the old tyrant at last!" the Virginian William S. Archer exclaimed.[40] More common were feelings of sadness and regret. The ratification meeting, which followed the convention became a "lugubrious political festivity," as speaker after speaker endeavored to account for the repudiation of their political father. If they had committed parricide, it was because they loved him so much. An Alabama delegate, Joseph G. Baldwin, wrote home: "I grieve to think that the last hope of elevating this great man to the presidency—no—of elevating the presidency to that great man, is extinguished, and extinguished by his friends. I grieve to think that the news of his rejection may have lacerated and will lacerate his noble heart." But nothing could add to Clay's fame; and to save him from another infamous defeat was, said Baldwin, "the last homage we could pay him."[41] Greeley could not accept the rejection. Returning to New York, he orchestrated a mass meeting of Clay's followers, started a campaign sheet named *That Same Old Coon*, and worked for an independent Whig nomination. Clay never countenanced this movement and finally acted to squelch it. Six weeks before the election, Greeley hoisted the Taylor banner in the *Tribune*.[42]

Clay focused his recriminations on Crittenden. The fact that Crittenden was the Whig candidate for governor in 1848 kept the issue between them as hot as a firecracker. Had Crittenden betrayed his political mentor and friend? And if so, should he be elected governor of Kentucky? A confidential letter circulating in the newspapers quoted Crittenden as saying that Clay had been "a deadweight on the party for the last twenty years." No one who knew Crittenden believed that. And he promptly stamped it a fabrication. The letter issued from the same local Democratic factory that had libeled Clay for twenty years. In this instance, of course, Crittenden, more than Clay, was the intended victim. He was stigmatized as a political turncoat when in fact, as long as Clay was in the field for the nomination, he had dutifully supported him.[43] Despite Clay's hard feelings toward Crittenden, he never made any public accusation against him. As the Taylor campaign accelerated in the fall, Clay was criticized for failing to endorse him. Among the critics, he understood, was Crittenden, who had been elected governor. But Achilles kept to his tent. He was, he said, "determined to preserve untarnished my humble fame."[44]

It was a pity Webster could not rejoice in the overthrow of Clay. But he, too, was mortified by the nomination of the frontier colonel. Lawrence and the Cotton Whigs might be for him, but the nomination produced, as Webster had predicted, a revolt in Bay State Whiggery. On June 28 some seven thousand anti-Taylor Whigs, for the most part Conscience Whigs, assembled at Worcester to decide their course. Led by Charles Francis Adams, Charles Allen, and Charles Sumner, among others, the gathering adopted the principles of the Barnburner-led meeting at Utica, New York, a week before, which principles were conveyed by the slogan, "free soil, free labor, and free men." The free-soil movement opened still another door of opportunity to Webster. On the sixteenth, just returned from Philadelphia, he sat dumbly on the platform of the Whig ratification meeting in Faneuil Hall listening to Lawrence, Choate, and a parade of speakers endorse Taylor. Why did he not go off and join the free-soilers? They had, after all, supported him for the Whig nomination. Now they were in the market for a presidential candidate of their own. They threw out hints to him. They challenged him to fulfill his genius in some great work of humanity. "Of what profit are the hands of a giant in the picking up of pins?" they importuned. Webster did not attend the Worcester meeting; he sent his son as an observer, however, and was thought to be in sympathy with it. One of the convention's resolutions, which Fletcher Webster approved in advance, called upon the senator to speak out for free-soil principles. Many of those in attendance considered him the natural leader of the movement.[45] Significantly, the convention declined to endorse the Barnburners' nomination of their leader, Martin Van Buren, at Utica. Might it have taken up Webster? The answer will never be known, for he quickly slammed the door on the free-soilers. "The men are all low, in their objects," he wrote disdainfully to Fletcher. Besides, even if they would have him the free-soil movement was too feeble to merit his support. He had been stung once for abandoning the Whigs; he would not risk being stung again. "I see no way but to *fall in,* and acquiesce," he told Fletcher. "The run is all that way. We can do no good by holding out. We shall only isolate ourselves. Northern opposition is too small and narrow to rely on."[46] The leading newspapers devoted to him, the *Commercial Advertiser,* the *Atlas,* and—after the resignation of its veteran editor, Joseph T. Buckingham—the *Courier* all announced for Taylor. Webster's caution and conservatism, assisted no doubt by his "perpetual thralldom to State Street," in the words of a Conscience Whig, left him no alternative.[47]

Finally, on September 1, after Congress adjourned, Webster made a little speech at Marshfield endorsing Taylor. Appearing in blue and buff before a mixed audience of reporters, farmers, and politicians, the senator dwelled on the dangers represented by Cass, the Democratic standard-bearer, and upon the absurdity of the Free Soil ticket headed by Van Buren, who had been nominated at the Buffalo convention of the new party. Yet he could find nothing good to say for Taylor. Indeed the Whig nomination, he declared in a cutting phrase, was "the nomination not fit to be made." Taylor might wonder at the worth of such an endorsement. "Was ever anything so cold as Webster's Marshfield pronunciamento?" Whigs asked. Yet it may have slowed the defection of northern Whigs to the Free Soil ticket. The speech had worth of another kind to Webster. For it he was reportedly paid $2,000. Asked before his death by Millard Fillmore, the president of the United States, if there was any one thing he really regretted in his political life, Webster replied, "I regret that I ever voted for a soldier President."⁴⁸ Clay would never have to make the apology. Not only did he withstand the pressures to endorse Taylor, but being ill on election day, he never even fulfilled the promise to vote for him.⁴⁹ There was much handwringing among the Whigs as they trooped to the polls to elect the frontier colonel president. They had cast off their eminent statesmen and taken up a military hero in order to regain power. But when had it been otherwise? Seward asked plaintively. "Was Aristedes, was Cato, was Cicero more fortunate? Is it not by popular injustice that greatness is burnished?"⁵⁰

Such was Taylor's popularity in South Carolina that Calhoun was tempted to endorse him. The enthusiasm for the general, at least before the Philadelphia convention, transcended party lines and tended to work toward that breakup of parties which Calhoun considered the essential first step in the reformation of government. Further, as a southerner and slaveholder Taylor offered a potential rallying point for the South. Even after the Whig nomination, Calhoun looked benignly upon a prospective Taylor administration. It would not be free-soil, nor would there be any incentive for northern Whigs, once ensconced in power, to move in that direction. All the recent blows against the South had come from Democrats: from Wilmot, from Van Buren and the Barnburners, from Benton and Cass. The Democracy of South Carolina sent but one delegate to the Baltimore convention that nominated Cass, and then repudiated it for rejecting the southern resolution on slavery in the territories. "In my opinion, the best result, that can take place," Calhoun wrote from Washington in July, "is the defeat of General Cass, without our being responsible for it." Many of Calhoun's friends actively supported Taylor in the belief he would be a southern president on a southern platform. But Calhoun counseled neutrality between the "two miserable factions" whose electioneering debased the state. And neutrality was the position advocated by the *Mercury*.⁵¹

In July Congress stumbled into a crisis over the bill to organize the Oregon territory. Tabled in the previous Congress, when neither the Wilmot Proviso formula nor the Missouri Compromise formula could be approved, this bill which was of no practical significance whatever put a deadlock on Congress. The Senate refused to accept the no-slavery proviso of the House bill. After the party conventions were out of the way, Polk pushed for a settlement on the 36° 30' formula, thinking it might settle the question for California and New Mexico as well as for Oregon. On June 27 Calhoun made the first of several important speeches on the question. For the most part, it was an extended commentary on his resolutions of the previous year. Calhoun began with the proposition that Congress had no constitutional authority to legislate for the territories. The provision of Article IV, Section 2, giving Congress power "to dispose of and make all needful rules and regulations respecting the territory or other property belonging to the United States," simply enabled the government to function as a holder and manager of property. The reference to "territory" meant the public lands and nothing else. Calhoun invented this idea of proprietorship, as earlier noted, to rationalize his support of federal aid to internal improvements in the territories. In applying it to the problem of slavery in the territories, he was following in the track already blazed by Cass in his celebrated Nicholson Letter setting forth the doctrine of popular sovereignty.[52]

The idea was so airy that even Calhoun could not sustain it very long. He conceded that by virtue of the right to acquire territory Congress had some legitimate power to govern it. The territories and the lands within them were the common property of the states; and Congress, acting as the agent of the joint owners and partners, must administer the territories fairly and justly, without discrimination against any of the partners. In other words, slaveholders were entitled to equal access to, and equal rights in, the territories. There were, to be sure, some bad precedents against this position, notably the Northwest Ordinance and the Missouri Compromise. The latter, Calhoun said, had been forced upon the South and had never been sanctioned there. This was patently untrue. The Missouri Compromise had been a southern measure, basically; and as New York senator John A. Dix undertook to show, Calhoun had approved of it as a member of James Monroe's cabinet. Furthermore, he had only recently advocated extending the key principle of that compromise to Oregon and the conquered territories. Yet here he was, on the Oregon Bill, maintaining that if the Union perished, the future historian would devote the first chapter to the Northwest Ordinance, the second to the Missouri Compromise, and the third to the present agitation. If possessed of a philosophical mind, the historian would trace the problem to its root cause, the proposition in the Declaration of Independence that "all men are born free and equal." Calhoun went on to expound his anti-Jeffersonian views of man and nature, society, and government. From that "most dangerous of political errors," embodied in the nation's birthright, emanated abolitionism, Dorrism, and the current European revolutions. From the same error came the no-slavery proviso of Jefferson's Ordinance of 1784, the precursor of the Northwest Ordinance, and through it "the deep and dangerous agitation which now threatens to engulf, and will certainly engulf, if not speedily settled, our political institutions."[53] The senator did not stop with closing the front door—the congressional door—to the exclusion of slavery; he closed the back door as well by denying any power—any popular sovereignty—in the people of the territories to exclude slavery prior to passage into statehood. Here he left the 1847 resolutions behind him and set up a new dogma of "the instantaneous transmigration," in Benton's phrase, of the Constitution to the territories. As if in contradiction to himself, Calhoun now insisted on the omnipotence of the Constitution in the territories. Slavery, once conceived as a local institution protected by state sovereignty, was now as nationalized and protected in the territories as if it were under the American flag on the high seas.

The Senate adopted the administration-backed amendment to the Oregon Bill and, predictably, it was rejected in the House. Seeking a way out of the impasse, Senator Clayton, on July 12, moved to refer the problem to a select committee of eight senators divided equally between North and South. Calhoun was a member. At first he voted for the Missouri Compromise formula despite his conviction that it was unconstitutional and unjust. When it was defeated, finally by a five-to-three vote, the committee put together a compromise that had the merit of providing for all three territories and at the same time booting the problem out of Congress. The Oregon territorial law excluding slavery would be accepted as a *fait accompli;* New Mexico and California would be forbidden to legislate on slavery, and provision would be made for its status to be determined expeditiously in the federal courts. On July 19, after Calhoun withdrew his objection to this last crucial provision, the committee approved the Clayton Compromise, as it was called, and reported it to the Senate. The committee had agreed, Clayton said, that the compromise "should speak for itself"—another way of saying it spoke in different tongues. Several days' debate culminated in a twenty-one-hour session, during which senators dozed in their seats or slept on sofas in the lobbies, finally arousing themselves to vote on the Clayton Compromise at 7:53 A.M. on the twenty-seventh. It passed, 33–22. Dispatched to the House, it was treated with what senators could only describe as contempt. On the motion of Georgia's pale, stoop-shouldered, brilliant little Whig, Alexander H. Stephens, the bill was tabled before a word could be uttered by either side.[54]

Returning to the House bill for organizing Oregon with the slavery restriction, the Senate again substituted the Missouri Compromise formula. Calhoun's speech for this amendment was, in part, an elegy on the South— the despised, abused, and degraded South—in part a trumpet call for southern unity and, if need be, independence. The amendment would achieve nothing in Oregon, of course, but it might just possibly open New Mexico and California to slavery. Again, no sooner was it enacted in the Senate than it was rejected in the House. At the last gasp, on August 13, after another exhausting all-night session, the Senate narrowly adopted Benton's motion to recede from its amendment, then approved the House bill, 33–22. Webster, whose prolonged absence had been the subject of comment, spoke and voted for the bill. Calhoun not only voted against it but had the last word on its passage. "The great strife between the North and South is ended . . . ," he declared gravely. "The effect of this determination in the North is to convert all the southern population into slaves; and I will never consent to entail that disgrace on my posterity. . . . The separation of the North and the South is completed."[55] The senator's dismay was only increased when the president signed the bill into law.

Calhoun delivered the same message on a hot August night before a packed house at the Theater in Charleston. Since issuing his call for southern unity from the same platform nearly eighteen months before, the country had plunged into deeper crisis, he said. The passage of the Oregon Bill was a wanton assertion of power by the North. It was wholly insensitive to southern rights and interests. If it had nothing to do with Oregon, as Webster remarked, it had everything to do with the exclusion of slavery in New Mexico and California and everywhere else within the reach of federal law. Two southern senators, Benton and Houston, had betrayed their section and voted for the Oregon Bill. Had they been true, it might have been defeated. Regrettably, the South was divided and distracted by the presidential election. Calhoun's advice, in which he believed all but possibly one member of the state's congressional delegation concurred, was to stand aloof from the election. "Remember that the Carolinian who is farthest from you in opinion is nearer to you than any Northern man of either party." If only the South would unite, rallying a militant party devoted to southern rights, the Union might yet be saved. But if it should fail, and disunion come, Calhoun was confident the South would prevail.[56]

Oddly enough, on the same day the *Mercury* reported Calhoun's speech, it came out for the Democratic ticket of Cass and Butler. Calhoun's injunction of neutrality was forgotten as the election approached. The state's Taylor Democrats had supposed that Calhoun was secretly with them. But no encouragement came from Fort Hill, and the Taylor movement faded rapidly in the fall. James H. Hammond, an early Taylor backer, was again disappointed in his idol: "He was *afraid* to come out for Taylor lest he should *lose all his own chances* with the Democrats." Others were even less charitable, suggesting Calhoun could not bear to see any southern man in the presidency but himself.[57] As for growing support of the Democratic ticket in the state, it was said that Calhoun was "out-generalled" by Rhett, Elmore, and company.[58] This may have been the case. Yet his easy acquiescence in the movement to keep the state in the Democratic column suggested that he favored this outcome despite his public commitment to neutrality. During the fall Calhoun took the time to "write off" his last speech on the Oregon Bill. It was unusual for him to rewrite a speech for publication, and in this instance he seems to have interpolated into the text remarks from various speeches. Published in the Pendleton *Messenger* on October 20, Calhoun considered it the manifesto of the movement for sectional unity that would terminate in a convention of the southern states at the close of the Thirtieth Congress next March.[59]

Taylor would then be president. After a campaign that was apathetic to the point of dullness in most places, his election came as no surprise. In view of population growth and the addition of four states (Florida, Texas, Wisconsin, and Iowa), the popular vote for Taylor did not actually improve on Clay's in 1844; but Old Zack carried New York and Pennsylvania, along with six southern states (compared to Clay's three), which more than made up for his loss of all the western states to Cass. The division proved, Clay thought, that he could have been elected with the same ease as Taylor, gathering the same votes, Georgia excepted, and adding Ohio. The 10 percent of the popular vote recorded for Van Buren did not affect the outcome of the election.

Stopping at Columbia in December, Calhoun prevailed upon the legislature to back his position. By unanimous vote the lawmakers declared "that the time for discussion has passed, and that the General Assembly is prepared to cooperate with her sister states in resisting the application of the principle of the Wilmot Proviso to such territory [California and New Mexico] at any and all hazards." Alabama, Virginia, Florida, and Missouri soon took the same position.[60] In Washington, Polk, in his last message to Congress, pleaded for extension of the Missouri Compromise line to the Pacific. But this was impractical; and it soon became apparent that Calhoun opposed any settlement in the current session. The theater of action for the senator shifted from the chamber to the corridors. Just before Christmas he was part of the effort to convene a caucus of the southern members of Congress—the first since 1838—with a view to uniting on a sectional platform. Of the full complement of 121 senators and representatives for the fifteen slaveholding states, about 70 attended the caucus. Prominent Democrats, like Benton and Houston, were among the absentees, though most were Whigs. With Taylor's election, the southern Whigs were riding high. But if Calhoun's sectional politics succeeded, as one historian has observed "southern Whiggery would become merely a tail to the Calhoun . . . kite." Leading Whigs who went into the caucus, like the Georgia duo of Stephens and Toombs, did so "in order to control and crush it."[61] Calhoun pleaded with the congressmen to agree on a forthright address to their constituents. Never, a long-time observer said, was he more vehement: "He rose to the heights of Demosthenian ardor; his gestures were bold, and for the first time I ever observed it in him, he stomped the floor with his foot."[62] Named to a committee of fifteen to prepare an address, Calhoun, of course, became the draftsman.

After committee approval, the proposed address was reported to the caucus, which met in the lighted Senate chamber on the evening of January 15. Ninety members were present. A large crowd gathered outside. Houston moved that the doors be opened, but this was defeated after thirty minutes' debate. The address provoked acrimonious discussion. The Whigs, in particular, objected to its "bullying" and "threatening" tone. Successive motions to approve and to table the address were defeated. Finally, near midnight, Berrien moved that the address be recommitted with instructions to make it into an appeal to the whole Union, and this was adopted, 44–42.[63] Berrien drew up such an address. Calhoun dissented from it, and the committee referred both addresses—Calhoun's somewhat moderated—to the caucus on January 22. Many Whigs, wanting no address at all, had withdrawn; the caucus had dwindled to about sixty. The majority easily rejected Berrien's address, moved as a substitute. It then approved Calhoun's. (The discrepancy in the vote count reported in the press ranged from 42–17 to 32–19.) Passed around for signatures, the address was finally signed by forty-eight representatives and senators—just over one-third of the southern members. Only one Whig signed.[64] "We have completely foiled Calhoun in his miserable attempt to form a southern party," Toombs wrote gloatingly to Crittenden. Calhoun himself, ill and disheartened, was heard to remark to a friend, "I see I have nothing to live for."[65] Three times during the short session, according to Barnwell Rhett, the frail and tottering statesman fainted in the Capitol. During one of these spells he remarked that his course was done and the battle must now be fought by younger men. When Rhett protested that the South looked to him for salvation, Calhoun replied tearfully, "*There*, indeed, is my only regret at going—the South—the poor South!"[66]

The *Address of the Southern Delegates in Congress to their Constituents* was immediately published, and although the original aim of a manifesto of southern unity had miscarried, it carried on ominous thrust of its own. Surveying the aggressions of the North upon the South, Calhoun kept the focus on the territories issue, while also noticing the personal liberty laws of the free states, which undermined the guarantee of the fugitive slave clause of the Constitution, and the newly mounted campaign in the current session to abolish the slave trade in the District of Columbia. Everything before the Congress negated the security of the South and portended the overthrow of slavery. The address concluded with a horrendous description of the consequences of that event: the white race prostrated, the blacks, backed by an all-powerful national government, ruling with the aid of profligate whites, the country becoming "the permanent abode of disorder, anarchy, misery, and wretchedness." The disaster might yet be averted. Let the South unite, forcing the North to pause and turn back from its insane course. "If it should not, nothing would remain for you but to stand up immovably in defense of rights involving your all—your property, prosperity, equality, liberty, and safety. As the assailed, you would stand justified by all laws, human and divine, in repelling a blow so dangerous, without looking to consequences, and to resort to all means necessary for that purpose."[67]

The Thirtieth Congress sputtered to a close without resolving the great question of the territories. The House, as expected, passed a bill to organize territorial governments in California and New Mexico with the exclusion of slavery. Illinois's young senator, Stephen A. Douglas, Chairman of the Committee on Territories, tried repeatedly to get Senate action on his bill for the immediate statehood of California, but without success. Congress was faced with making arrangements for the temporary government of both territories. On February 24, Isaac P. Walker of Wisconsin offered a rider to the Civil and Diplomatic Appropriation Bill, then before the Senate, providing for the extension of the United States Constitution and laws to the territories and the establishment of temporary government by the president. Douglas supported it, although the real author of the amendment, according to Benton, was Calhoun. Whether he was or not, the Walker amendment, if adopted, would be a major victory for Calhoun. At the very least it would supersede Mexican law in the territories, and it would also provide a statutory basis for Calhoun's doctrine of the "instantaneous transmigration" of the Constitution. In the course of debate, he and Webster engaged in a fascinating colloquy, which added a new and somewhat bewildering chapter to the twenty-year dialogue between them on the nature of the Union and the Constitution. Webster, who had earlier proposed to hold the conquered territories temporarily under existing local laws, ridiculed the idea of extending the Constitution to them or even to territories organized by Congress: "Why, sir, the thing is utterly impossible. . . . What is the Constitution of the United States? Is not its very first principle that all within its influence and comprehension shall be represented in the legislature?" The Constitution extended only to the states; the territories belonged to the United States but were not *of* the United States; and the Supreme Court had so held. Calhoun rose at this. Does not the Constitution pronounce itself "the supreme law of the land"? "What land?" Webster returned. "The land; the Territories of the United States are part of the land," Calhoun answered. "It is the supreme law, not within the limits of the States of this Union merely, but wherever the flag waves." The idea that the Constitution follows the flag, moreover that the flag bears slavery in its folds, flew in the face of the whole history of the government, Webster maintained; and he confessed surprise that a senator so distinguished for strict construction should contrive to extend the Constitution to conquered provinces in the absence of provision or authority. By what authority, then, can Congress govern the territories? Calhoun asked. By explicit provision to make all needful rules and regulations for the territory of the United States, Webster replied.[68]

The Senate went on to adopt the Walker amendment on a close vote. The House instantly rejected it and substituted Webster's interim plan of governing in accordance with Mexican law. This came back to the Senate as the fifty-third amendment in the report of the conference committee on the appropriation bill. Before the Senate could act the midnight hour of March 3 struck, and the Congress had expired. Amid much disorder, some senators refusing to act further, the clock was turned back, and before adjournment at seven-thirty Sunday morning Webster got the Senate to recede from the Walker amendment.[69] Thus the general appropriation bill was passed, and the need for temporary government in California and New Mexico was met. It was, all considered, one of Webster's best legislative achievements. For Calhoun, who saw his constitutional doctrine rejected in both houses, it was among his worst defeats. And coming after the rebuff of his bid to unite the South behind his leadership, it was doubly painful.

3. *The Compromise of 1850*

While Henry Clay passed the winter in New Orleans, the General Assembly of Kentucky elected him to the United States Senate in the place of John J. Crittenden, the new governor. When first asked to become a candidate for the position, Clay had expressed his "repugnance," as before; but the more it was talked about, the more he warmed to it until, by the time he left for New Orleans, he willingly placed himself at the disposal of the legislature. Actually, Clay could scarcely suppress his desire for the Senate seat, as was made evident between the lines of his letters.[1] If he had any legislative purpose in mind, he never mentioned it. Some Whigs feared that he aimed to stir up a storm with the new administration. Clay's bitterness over Taylor's election as president had not abated. In his own mind, the results of the election vindicated his judgment that, if nominated, he would have been elected.[2] This was fantasy, of course, but it sustained Clay's delusion of supreme leadership in the Whig party, and for that reason might prove dangerous. Crittenden's "Young Indians" were unhappy about returning Clay to the Senate, but, given the dissension within the party and the threat from the Democratic side, they had no choice. In Washington there were feelings of anxiety and apprehension over "ancient Henry's" return. "Whigs speak of it with disconsolate faces, and Democrats with a rubbing of hands, and a wicked, chuckling jollity," it was reported. Almost everyone assumed he came to "play the dictator again," to wreak his stored-up feelings of disappointment, envy, and revenge upon Taylor, as he had earlier wreaked them upon John Tyler. "He comes to play his last game," Tyler himself remarked, "and I mistake him if he does not play it desperately." The Young Indians who had hoped to make a place of eminence for themselves must again confront the old Whig idols. "With Webster at one end, and Clay at the other," a New Jersey senator wrote, "we intermediates [will] have a beautiful time of it." Was there nothing to be done? A cabinet appointment was out of the question. John M. Clayton had suggested to Crittenden that Clay be named minister to France: "It is *the* place for the greatest statesman of the age, *now*."[3] But Clay would never have accepted a foreign appointment, certainly not after the Kentucky Whigs elected him senator.

Clay encountered Taylor on the boat to New Orleans early in the new year. They had a perfunctory interview. The Kentuckian's well-advertised hostility to Taylor as the Whig candidate had barred friendly intercourse; and relations between them continued cool and distant as the president-elect formed his cabinet and gave shape to his administration. He asked no counsel of Clay, and Clay volunteered none. The same was true of Webster. The Taylor Whigs shunted the old potentates aside as they reared the administration on the elements that brought the general to power. Truman Smith, who had managed the campaign, insisted that the cabinet be formed of Taylor men. "In nominating General Taylor we set aside man-worship—the bane and curse of the Whig party," he wrote to Crittenden. "The same rule should be observed in organizing the cabinet. I want *no everlasting great man* in that body."[4] A cabinet of respectable mediocrity was the result. Clayton, as secretary of state, was its ablest man. Clay could not fault that appointment, or that of another old friend, Thomas Ewing, to head the new Department of Interior. The rest were men of small consequence. "Whenever any one of them shall drop out or be 'hove over,'" Greeley remarked, "he will sink like a stone and never be heard of again."[5] Where the balance of influence would lie in the new administration remained to be seen; but it would obviously be less a Whig than a Taylor administration, which bore out Clay's foreboding that Old Zack, whatever else he might be, was no Whig.

The fact that both Clay and Webster were anxious to find places for their sons in the new administration opened promising avenues of conciliation. None of Clay's sons or close relations had been on the federal payroll. He took pride in this but also felt some resentment. Harrison had promised a diplomatic post for young Henry. Neither he nor Tyler fulfilled the promise, however, and instead of entering a career of civil service, Henry met a soldier's death in Mexico. Now Clay sought a similar post for James. Finally, in May, after hearing that Taylor's feelings toward him were more amicable than he had supposed, Clay swallowed his pride and wrote to the president on James's behalf. Within a month James B. Clay was named *chargé d'affaires* to Portugal.[6] Fletcher Webster had formerly held posts in the government. His father wished him to be appointed federal district attorney for Massachusetts. While the cabinet was being formed there were rumors that Webster himself would be named secretary of state. These were mistaken. He was averse to serving under Taylor, and he was not asked. On the whole, he expected nothing for himself or his friends. He had no acquaintance with Taylor and realized he had not ingratiated himself with his Marshfield speech. Obviously, Lawrence and the Massachusetts Whigs would be favored in the distribution of patronage. Webster felt, nonetheless, that he deserved consideration for his son. Meeting Taylor before the inauguration, he was pleasantly surprised by his open and friendly manner and supposed that he meant well, though he knew no more than his boot about public men and issues. Webster pressed Fletcher's appointment with Clayton and others, but relied mainly on William H. Seward, newly elected to the Senate from New York and rapidly gaining influence in the Taylor administration, to carry it to conclusion. On March 25 Seward learned that the president had committed the Massachusetts post to another. "Webster was amazed. . . . He went home debating with himself and me whether to adhere to the party."[7] The next morning he remonstrated with Taylor at the White House. Taylor explained that the district attorneyship had been promised to George Lunt who had helped nominate him at Philadelphia. Webster protested that Lunt, whom he thought "a coarse-grained person," was unfit, but to no avail. He was deeply wounded. "No disappointment to myself could come half so near my heart," he wrote his old crony, Ned Curtis.[8] In the end Fletcher Webster was appointed surveyor of the port of Boston; but the senator's affections had been permanently alienated.

Without influence in the Taylor administration, unable to anticipate its course in the slavery crisis, the triumvirs approached the new Congress and, as it came to pass, their acme of political glory with feelings of apprehension and dismay. After a leisurely summer at Marshfield, when he again stared at the unreceding waters of debt and vowed to get rich in the Mexican claims business, Godlike Daniel returned to the platform in the fall. His declining health was beginning to show. N. P. Willis, who sat near him at an anniversary dinner commemorating the embarkation of the Pilgrims, observed, "He was really ill—much thinner than I had ever seen him, and so debilitated that, in his least emphatic sentences, the more difficult words failed of complete utterance." His countenance, while genial and kindly, was somber, "unlighted with health or impulse," said Willis.[9]

Clay, with a chronic cough and surrounded by cholera, went east in July—the springs at Saratoga, the beaches at Newport—in search of health. Called out by the crowds, he would say drolly, "*And here I am! The same old coon! If you are disappointed in the exhibition, you know it costs you nothing, and so goodbye!*"[10] Back in Kentucky, he made an appearance at the constitutional convention. The convention, as earlier noted, was a terrible defeat for Clay personally as well as for the Whig party. So great was his loss of popularity, from advocacy of gradual emancipation, that some observers doubted he could any longer carry the state. And, indeed, citizens of Trimble County, meeting at the courthouse, adopted resolutions denouncing Clay's abolitionist opinions and asked the legislature to demand his resignation as United States Senator from Kentucky.[11]

Calhoun, that summer, nursed his illness, struggled with his financial problems, added the finishing touches to the *Disquisition on Government*, and, without stirring from Fort Hill, presided over the disunionist movement. Responding to his counsel, delegates from various local committees of safety and vigilance that had sprung up after the Southern Address assembled at Columbia and agreed to set up a state central committee to correspond with other states in planning for a southern convention in the coming year.[12] It was thought important that another state, unencumbered by the legacy of nullification and secession, appear to lead in this movement, however. An opportunity presented itself in Mississippi, where the Southern Address had fallen on fertile ground. "No State could better take the lead in this great *conservative* movement than yours," Calhoun wrote enthusiastically in July. On his advice a bipartisan convention was assembled at Jackson in October. Calhoun's role was kept secret, so secret in fact, that it was not even known to Daniel Wallace, the South Carolina congressman whom the governor sent to Jackson as an observer. "I tell you but *in confidence*, that I saw clearly that *our old statesman*, was perhaps at the bottom of this movement," Wallace wrote to Governor Whitemarsh B. Seabrook. The Jackson address called on the southern states to appoint delegates to a convention at Nashville the following June. "If the South is to be saved now is the time," Calhoun declared. At his instigation the General Assembly of South Carolina chose four at-large delegates to the projected convention and recommended the election of others in the congressional districts. Several southern states quickly followed this example.[13]

Calhoun also wrote a reply, an "Address to the People of the Southern States," in his running battle with Benton. He had accused the Missourian and Sam Houston of treachery to the South, it may be recalled, in the passage of the Oregon Bill. Houston defended himself and in an address to his constituents blasted the Carolinian for ill-concealed designs against the

Union. Calhoun deigned no reply. The sixty-seven-year-old Benton, whose term would expire in 1850, was fighting for his political life in Missouri.[14] The legislature adopted resolutions, which he called "a mere copy" of Calhoun's of 1847, and made them instructions to the Missouri senators. The intent was less to back Calhoun than it was to head Benton. He flouted the instructions, of course, branding them disunionist; and in May delivered his second "Calhouniac" at Jefferson City. Benton turned the accusation against him—that of giving over lands won by southern blood to the free states—back upon Calhoun. By virtue of the Missouri Compromise, the sacrifice of Texas to Spain, and other actions, "Calhoun did more in less time to abolish slavery, diminish its area, and increase that of free soil than any man that has ever appeared on the face of the earth." He did it, moreover, for no nobler purpose than to win northern votes for the presidency. As to California and New Mexico, neither nature nor law would ever admit slavery there. "What, then, is all the uproar about?" Benton bellowed. "Abstraction, the abstract right of doing what cannot be done! . . . All abstraction."[15] Calhoun's rebuttal was calm, pointed, and effective. He dismissed Benton's argument against him as preposterous and reasserted his doctrine of the equal rights of slaveholders to the territories. Spread across the Missouri newspapers the address ran to ten columns, and as many as ten thousand copies of the pamphlet version, it was said, were printed in St. Louis alone.[16]

Returning to Washington in December, Calhoun wanted to be as near the Capitol as possible. He took rooms at Hill's boardinghouse in the "Old Capitol," the building that had housed Congress after the War of 1812, on the site now occupied by the Supreme Court. Haggard and feeble, coughing incessantly, subject to fainting spells, Calhoun had the appearance of a dying man. During the summer he had retained Joseph Scoville, a reporter for the New York *Herald*, as his secretary. Scoville helped look after him, as did Armistead Burt and his wife, Calhoun's niece, who boarded with him. The Websters continued to reside at "Vine Cottage," below the Capitol, where D Street merges into Louisiana Avenue. There was scarcely a more familiar figure in Washington than Webster. Almost any morning, unless the weather was foul, he might be seen, casually dressed, with a basket under his arm, strolling to the market and exchanging greetings as he went. Clay took up residence in the National Hotel at the corner of Pennsylvania Avenue and Sixth Street. He hired a valet—a free black man. The British minister, Sir Henry Bulwer, was a neighbor in the hotel. Clay mingled little in society. His health had improved, but he suffered from persistent colds and a cough the doctors called bronchial. Dining at the White House soon after his arrival, Clay found the president civil, if not cordial, and reported a "very uncomfortable" state of affairs in the government and among the Whigs.[17]

Taylor, it seemed, had exhausted his popularity in the presidential election. In patronage matters, always a prolific source of bickering and complaint, he was guided primarily by the northern Whig satraps who had backed his candidacy. In New York this meant Weed and Seward. Elected to the Senate in 1849, Seward aspired to be the power behind the throne. Fillmore, the vice president and leader of New York's conservative Whigs, was virtually shut out of the patronage. But Weed and Seward not only controlled the patronage; they also gave a distinctly anti-slavery and free-soil direction to the Taylor administration. Daniel Barnard, a respected conservative voice at Albany, published a pamphlet, *Whig or Abolition? That's the Question*, in which he charged that Weed, Seward, and their minions aimed to transform the Whig party into an abolitionist party, which would destroy its national character.[18] Southern Whigs were astounded by Taylor's tilt toward free-soil. In one of his first important acts, the president dispatched Georgian Thomas B. King to California to expedite the process of statemaking. Congress had left California under a form of military government—Mexican law administered by an American general—which became intolerable as the "forty-niners" in quest of gold swelled the population to one hundred thousand before the year's end. Taylor proposed to skip the territorial stage altogether in California, and as soon as an appropriate constitution could be drawn up admit her as a state. This would conveniently skirt the issue of the Wilmot Proviso. Yet it would have exactly the same effect: the admission of a new free state without any guarantees or compensations to the South. The Whigs suffered setbacks in the fall elections in the cotton states; and they returned to Congress with varying degrees of apprehension over the Louisiana planter they had elected president.

Symptomatic of deepening sectional discord was the protracted contest to elect a speaker in the House of Representatives. The Whig caucus nominated the previous speaker, Robert C. Winthrop, a polished Bostonian and the soul of moderation; but he subscribed to the Wilmot Proviso, and mainly for this reason half a dozen southern Whigs led by the brace of Georgians, Stephens and Toombs, bolted and supported the Democratic candidate, Howell Cobb, also of Georgia. Eight or nine Free Soilers gave their votes to Wilmot. No candidate could obtain a majority through sixty-two vexatious ballots. Finally, for the first time in its history the House resorted to a plurality rule, and it elected Cobb on the sixty-third ballot. The Democrats then proceeded to organize the House, as they had already organized the Senate. Not only were the Whigs a minority in Congress, but they were split along sectional seams. No effective leadership came from the president. In his message to Congress, Taylor said he expected soon to receive California's application for statehood, which he would recommend, and not long after New Mexico's. He pleaded with Congress to abstain from exciting topics of a sectional character. As far as Taylor had a plan for settling the crisis of the Union, this was it.[19]

And it was, as historian Allan Nevins has said, "quite unrealistic." Southerners might be reconciled to California entering the Union as a free state, but they expected something in return. The rights of slaveholders in the territories had been arrogantly cast aside, many southerners of both parties believed, and their favorite compromise solution to this vexed problem, the extension of the 36° 30' line to the Pacific, would be closed forever by the admission of California as a single free state. Northern Whigs, although some clung to the Wilmot Proviso, generally supported the Taylor plan. But it offered southern Whigs no place to stand against the rising tide of disunionism. The Nashville Convention, the ultimate product thus far of Calhoun's effort to unite the South, would meet in June; and southern Whigs were desperate to find some ground between Taylorism and Calhounism.[20] The president's fixation on California, as if it were the only urgent problem, ignored a host of sectional issues that begged for resolution by Congress. Territorial governments were wanted for New Mexico and also Deseret, or Utah, with its thriving Mormon community at Salt Lake City. The organization of New Mexico depended upon settlement of the disputed boundary with Texas. One of the first measures to come before the Senate was the Fugitive Slave Bill, drafted by James M. Mason of Virginia. Intended to overcome the deficiencies of the 1793 statute, which was a dead letter in the North generally, where there were an estimated 30,000 runaways worth $15 million, Mason's bill was a litmus test for southerners of the North's readiness to meet a clear-cut constitutional obligation growing out of slavery.[21] The issue of slavery in the District of Columbia continued to fester. Not that the institution had any actual importance there. (Of the total population of 40,000, just under 8,000 were free blacks and only 2,110 slaves.) But abolition of slavery in the District would be a mortal blow to slavery in the South and, therefore, in the judgment of many southern congressmen, sufficient cause in itself for secession.[22]

Henry Clay came into Congress without any plan of his own. He soon became convinced, as in 1832, that the crisis was real, not simply a scarecrow got up by the South, and that Taylor's policy was wholly unequal to it. He had not been consulted, of course, which left him free to go his own way whenever he could see it clearly. Before Christmas he was calling on friends in Kentucky to organize Unionist meetings to counteract the southern Hotspurs; and at the beginning of the new year he was pondering "some comprehensive scheme of settling amicably the whole question, in all its bearings," though he had yet to work out the details.[23] Impulsively, on a rainy January evening, Clay bundled himself into a carriage and made an unscheduled visit at Webster's house. The two senators, although they had hardly exchanged ten words with each other during the last eight years, bore much the same relationship to the Taylor administration and shared the same devotion to the Union. The Kentuckian, frail and coughing constantly, outlined the plan he had been maturing for three weeks; and the Bay Stater, without committing himself unreservedly, consented to the plan in substance and praised Clay for his patriotism.[24] The image of the Great Pacificator was always before Clay. He hoped to repeat the triumphs of 1821 and 1833, crowning his career with still another, and greater, Union-saving compromise. And if in this he also gave way to an irrepressible passion to lead—to play the Dictator—it was in a situation that cried out for leadership.

Another thing Clay and Webster shared, in common with the great body of their countrymen, was veneration of George Washington. Not long after their interview, and just prior to the introduction of his compromise resolutions, Clay asked the Senate to authorize the purchase of the manuscript copy of Washington's Farewell Address. Having read in a Philadelphia newspaper that this precious document, which reposed with the family of the newspaper publisher to whom Washington had sent it, was about to be sold at auction, Clay argued that it should not be lost to the nation, especially not now when the "spirit of disunion" was abroad in the land. He spoke movingly of a Washington memento—a broken goblet used in camp—at Ashland, which he treasured above any other possession. Webster promptly seconded Clay's resolution. He spoke with the same sentiment of the collection of Revolutionary medals once belonging to Washington, which he had purchased after Congress declined to do so on niggardly constitutional grounds. Precisely on these grounds Jefferson Davis objected to the purchase of the Washington manuscript, pointing out that there were printed copies of the Farewell Address in abundance. This was of a piece with Calhoun's earlier opposition to congressional purchase of James Madison's records of the federal convention, to acceptance of the Smithson bequest, to an improved census (let each state take its own census, he had suggested), and so on. But Congress authorized purchase of the manuscript.[25]*

On January 29 Clay rose at his desk and upon being recognized declared, "Mr. President, I hold in my hand a series of resolutions which I desire to submit to the consideration of this body. Taken together, in combination, they propose an amicable arrangement of all questions in controversy between the free and slave states, growing out of the subject of slavery." He proceeded to enumerate each of the resolutions. First, the admission of California as a free state. Second, organization of the balance of territory acquired from Mexico, that is New Mexico and Utah, without restriction as to slavery. Third, adjustment of the boundary between Texas and New Mexico. Fourth, assumption of the pre-annexation Texas debt, which had been premised on a revenue from imports. Fifth, non-interference with slavery in the District of Columbia. Sixth, prohibition of the slave trade in the District. Seventh, a more effective fugitive slave law. Eighth, congressional disavowal of authority to interfere with the slave trade between slaveholding states. When Clay finished, a number of southern senators jumped to their feet. Rust was angry over the proposal to give part of Texas to New Mexico. Davis declared that, although presented as a compromise, the resolutions offered nothing to the South. The Whig Berrien and the Democrat Butler wanted it known at the outset that they could never acquiesce in these resolutions or legislation based on them. Clay tried without much success to shut off debate until he had an opportunity to develop his propositions at length.[27]

Clay's major speech came on the order of the day on February 5 and 6. The galleries were full from an early hour; the crowd overflowed into the lobbies, the rotunda, and the library; as in former times fashionable ladies were accommodated on the floor of the chamber. Indeed, nothing like it had been

---

*Several weeks hence Edward Coles, a Virginia-born contemporary of Clay's, sent him a copy of Madison's "Advice to My Country," a heretofore unpublished document, in the hope that in the senator's hands it might be used to good effect. Sometime later it was published in the press. A solemn last testament of some two hundred words, in it Madison said, "The advice nearest my heart and deepest in my convictions is that the Union of the states be cherished and perpetuated."[26]

seen since Clay's leave-taking eight years ago. "What a squeeze! Benches, corners, desks, avenues, doors, windows, passages, galleries, every spot, into, upon, under, behind, or before, from which man or woman could see or hear the lion of the day, were filled, used, or occupied."[28] Oddly, on this occasion, neither Calhoun nor Webster was in his seat, the former being confined to his sickroom, the latter arguing a Georgia bank case before the Supreme Court. At the appointed hour, 1:00 P.M., Clay rose at his desk on the rear row to the left of the rostrum. Although obviously laboring under physical strain, he spoke with the musical voice of old, with the same passionate intensity, and treated his audience to a complete forensic performance, including the mandatory pinch of snuff, in this instance borrowed from Senator Dawson of Georgia. Beginning gravely, he said he had never before risen to address an assemblage "so oppressed, so appalled, and so anxious." He spoke of what was necessary, generally, to a sound compromise. It should settle all the controverted questions. It should demand no sacrifice of "great principle" by either side. Yet it should require mutual concession of opinion, feeling, and interest.

Clay discussed the resolutions one by one. California was quickly disposed of. The people were even now framing their constitution. "If slavery be interdicted within the limits of California, has it been done by Congress—by this Government? No, sir. The interdiction is imposed by California herself."[29] This was meant for the South. To the North Clay said it was absurd to insist on the Wilmot Proviso, since it could have no effect after California became a state. (Eight days later the president laid before the Senate the proposed constitution of California.) With respect to New Mexico and Utah, Clay invoked two truths: first, that as the Mexican law was against slavery it now had no existence there; second, that all the circumstances of nature—climate, soil, productions—effectively barred slavery from the country. "What do you want?" Clay roared at the free-soilers. "You want that there shall be no slavery introduced into the territories acquired from Mexico. Well, have not you got it in California already, if admitted as a State? Have you not got it in New Mexico, in all human probability, also? What more do you want? You have got what is worth a thousand Wilmot provisos. You have got nature on your side."[30] Without actually barring slavery in the territories, Clay's plan was plainly calculated to exclude it. No issue was more troublesome than Texas, for it involved slavery, the boundary, the debt, and the claims of bondholders. Clay reviewed the history of the boundary, and while shedding no new light on the problem, usefully linked the boundary to the debt. Slavery in the District was a hackneyed topic. The constitutional power to abolish it was conceded but, as in the past, Clay deemed it inexpedient until three conditions were met: the consent of Maryland, the consent of the District, and compensation for slave property. The District slave trade, on the other hand, was a disgrace in the eyes of most southerners as well as northerners, and might readily be abolished without injury to the slaveholding states. The seventh resolution called for a strengthened fugitive slave law. Clay interpreted the fugitive slave clause of the constitution as an obligation upon citizens to aid in the recovery of runaways. The sense of the obligation had eroded in the North, however. Several states had enacted personal liberty laws to aid and abet the fugitives. The Supreme Court in the case of *Prigg* v. *Pennsylvania* (1842) had declared unconstitutional a state law interfering with the rendition of fugitives, yet had also removed any obligation on state officials to help enforce the federal law. Clay refused to believe the court meant what it said. If enforcement of the fugitive clause was an exclusive federal responsibility, requiring only that the states not interfere, then Draconian measures might be necessary to effect the constitutional guarantee. Without committing himself to Mason's bill, Clay said he would go with "the furthest Senator from the South to impose the heaviest sanctions on the recovery of fugitive slaves."[31] In concluding, Clay reviewed the history of the Missouri Compromise, taking the opportunity to set the record straight on its authorship, and offering it as an example of the victory of reason over passion. At the same time, he dismissed out of hand the southern proposal to extend the 36° 30' line to the Pacific. Finally, to southern disunionists he declared, "War and dissolution of the Union are identical and inevitable"; and he implored senators on both sides to pause at the edge of the abyss and save the Union that is the light of the world.

It was a measure of Clay's success that ultraists in both North and South condemned his compromise plan. Senator Chase of Ohio dismissed it as "sentiment for the North, substance for the South," while abolitionist William Jay released a torrid blast in the New York *Evening Post*. On the other hand, Senator Henry S. Foote of Mississippi—sometimes called "Hangman" Foote, after he had vowed to hang a fellow senator, John P. Hale, from a tall tree should he come to Mississippi—said there was more in the speech to mortify the South than in all the speeches of the abolitionists Garrison, Phillips, and Douglass.[32] In Congress Clay got more plaudits than votes for his efforts. "I do not find that any party, any clique, any section will adopt his plan of accommodation," a reporter wrote several days later.[33] This was correct. Yet the sweep and boldness of the compromise plan, and the drama of its advocacy by seventy-three-year-old Henry Clay, ensured it a sympathetic public hearing. "What a singlar spectacle . . . !" wrote the editor of the New York *Herald*, never friendly to Clay. "Of all the leaders of the old parties, of all the aspiring spirits of the new ones, including General Taylor and the whole of his cabinet, from head to tail, not a single soul, not a single mind, has dared to exhibit the moral courage to come out with any plan for settling the whole question, except it is Henry Clay, who, solitary and alone, faces the crisis with as much calmness and composure as General Taylor did the Mexicans at Buena Vista."[34] Of course there were objections to the plan. But its moral effect was tremendous. It rallied Unionist hopes and sank the hopes of disunionists. Downcast southern Whigs, contemplating "the disastrous opposites," Taylor's plan and the Nashville Convention, found a safe middle way in Clay's compromise.[35] Astonishingly, with his speech and resolutions,

Clay had seized the initiative from the president, centered it in the Senate under his leadership, and set the legislative agenda for the country.

In doing so he alienated himself further from the administration, from former friends like Clayton, who felt bitter toward him, and Taylor himself who was portrayed as undergoing the agonies of Lear. Clay also found some strange political bedfellows. Lewis Cass and Stephen A. Douglas, respectively the old and the young lion of the Democratic party, were supportive. Martin Van Buren asked Frank Blair to convey his congratulations, saying to Clay that he had added "a crowning grace to his public life . . . which will be more honorable and durable than his election to the Presidency could possibly have been." Blair concurred in the sentiment, but having not spoken to Clay for almost a quarter of a century, entrusted the message to his son-in-law. Not long after, when Blair appeared at the Capitol, Clay made the *amende honorable,* and one old and painfully broken friendship was restored.[36] Thomas Ritchie, whose friendship dated back to Clay's Virginia youth but who had been a political foe since 1824, commended the spirit of the compromise resolutions in the *Union*. However, he objected strenuously to the assumption that the territories remained under Mexican law, which had the same effect, as Clay himself said, as extending the Wilmot Proviso to them. Knowing what a valuable ally Ritchie could be, Clay sought an interview with him. Ritchie came with two associates to Clay's room at the National Hotel on February 10. He was the Old Prince, of course, showing "the most warming courtesy and kindness," as if they had never been separated, said Ritchie, and after a frank exchange of views he left deeply impressed with Clay's patriotic motive. "How superior did he rise above all private feuds and party considerations! With what indefatigable zeal, and with what an indomitable spirit did he pursue the great object he had in view!" the editor wrote in retrospect. Receiving some assurances from Clay on the main point at issue, Ritchie swung around and supported the compromise. He told Clay if he could settle the crisis and give up the White House, he would "plant a laurel on his tomb."[37]

Speech making on Clay's resolutions went forward, but their author, and the Senate, had yet to determine how to act on them. In his review of the legislative history of the Missouri Compromise, Clay had mentioned the part played by the "committee of thirteen" in the final settlement. Some thought he was suggesting a similar vehicle for the general scheme of compromise offered by his resolutions. This was certainly Senator Foote's impression. When Clay supported separate and prior action on the California statehood bill, Foote expressed "unbounded astonishment." He was "throwing into the hands of his adversaries all the *trump cards* in the pack." The garrulous little Mississippian read Clay a lecture on the duties he owed to the South. To this Clay returned a memorable reply:

> I know whence I came, and I know my duty; and I am ready to submit to any responsibility which belongs to me as a senator from a slaveholding State. Sir, I have heard something said on this and on a former occasion

about allegiance to the South. I know no South, no North, no East, no West, to which I owe any allegiance. . . . My allegiance is to the American Union and to my own State. But if gentlemen suppose they can exact from me an acknowledgment of allegiance to any ideal or future contemplated confederacy of the South, I here declare that I owe no allegiance to it, nor will I, for one, come under any such allegiance, if I can avoid it.[38]

As to the resolutions, he had supposed that inasmuch as they dealt with different subjects the Senate would act on them individually, and he disparaged Foote's "omnibus" approach, which "introduced all sorts of things and every sort of passenger." Clay thus introduced into legislative usage the name of a new form of urban transit. (In September a beautiful new omnibus in the capital would be named the *Henry Clay*, bearing his likeness on both side panels.) Foote persisted, however, and Clay himself gradually came to see the advantages of an omnibus approach.[39]

Calhoun resumed his seat after an absence of six weeks on February 18. In his opinion the time for compromise had passed. He rejoiced in the growing number of southern state legislatures committed to the Nashville Convention, and contemplated secession with something like equanimity. Scoville, his secretary, kept him abreast of northern opinion. An article by Henry Ward Beecher in *The Independent,* holding there could be no harmony or compromise between North and South, because their civilizations were diametrically opposed, prompted him to comment, "Mr. Clay should read that article." At the end of February, he began dictating, between spasms of coughing, his last major speech. When finished, he revised Scoville's copy. Webster visited Calhoun on March 2 and got a preview of the speech. Lacking the strength to deliver it, Calhoun had expected Butler, his junior colleague, to perform this service; but Butler, offering the excuse of poor eyesight, asked Mason to serve instead. Feeling the awesomeness of the responsibility, the Virginia senator had the speech printed and read it from the proofsheets. On a breezy fourth of March, a little after noon, Calhoun entered the Senate on the arm of James Hamilton, and after exchanging greetings proceeded to his desk near the center of the chamber. Looking like a spectral wraith, a mane of thick gray hair framing ashen, emaciated features, Calhoun slumped into his chair, wrapped his black cloak around him, and listened motionless as Mason, directly behind him, read the speech.[40]

The great question before the country, Calhoun began, is "How can the Union be preserved?" But like a physician studying a disease, one must first inquire, "How has the Union been endangered?" And to this inquiry the speech was devoted. Basically, the Union had been endangered by northern aggressions that had destroyed the sectional equilibrium. Calhoun traversed old ground and rehashed old arguments to show how the "federal republic" of 1787 had been transformed into "a great national consolidated democracy," ruled by a northern majority hostile to the South. In 1787, in 1820, in 1848 the South had been shut out of the territories. Political power had shifted to the North. Until now an equilibrium had been maintained in the

Senate. But the admission of California would end it. California was the final test of northern intentions. Rushed into statehood on the "monstrous assumption" that the Mexican law continued in force there and that the people might, without the authority of Congress, make their own constitution, the pretensions of California were utterly anarchical, and she should be remanded to a territorial condition. If she was not, the South would draw the appropriate conclusion. Some of the strongest cords of the Union had already snapped, those of the great Protestant churches, for instance, and nothing significant remained except the cords of the great political parties. Not a ray of hope showed through Calhoun's speech. It was all unrelieved gloom. Mason added to this impression, reading the speech, according to a young congressman, "in a very haughty and defiant tone, well calculated to engender the bitterest feelings." In the end, with no plan to save the Union, and only contempt for Clay's and Taylor's, Calhoun made the cryptic recommendation of a constitutional amendment "which will restore to the South in substance the power she possessed of protecting herself, before the equilibrium between the sections was destroyed." He did not disclose the form of this amendment, although he probably meant a dual executive along the lines of the proposal sketched out in the *Discourse*, as yet unpublished.[41]

Webster and Clay, who listened intently throughout, gathered around Calhoun when the speech was finished. Their interest was less in what was said, which was past hope, than in the sad spectacle of a great man going to his death with disunion on his lips.[42] Generally, the speech met with a grimly negative response. The most hardened disunionists, even as they uttered amen to Calhoun's judgments and prophecies, realized that it drove every wavering southerner from the cause. The speech came too early or too late. It was made against the current Clay had started—the current of conciliation and compromise—and increased Union feeling tenfold in reaction. It was, said one reporter, "a sort of *memento mori* for the Union." Senator Cass referred to the "sombre hue" that pervaded the speech, which seemed to betray its preparation in a sick chamber, and said it avowed as plainly as the handwriting on the wall of the King of Babylon, "God hath numbered thy kingdom and finished it."[43] The very next day Senator Foote, who had been associated with Calhoun in the movement that led to the Nashville Convention but was veering toward Clay and compromise, protested the idea that the South required a constitutional amendment as the *sine qua non* of a settlement. In this Calhoun did not speak for the South, nor had he consulted the South. The South had always placed its faith in the Constitution as it is, said Foote. At this moment, Calhoun appeared on the floor. "Did he accuse me of disunion?" he asked. In the succeeding exchange between them, the Carolinian reiterated his belief that the southern states could not safely remain in the Union without a specific guarantee of their rights and interests.[44]

Anticipation had been building in the capital for the speech of the third member of the Great Triumvirate. Spending most of his time at the Supreme Court, Webster had taken little part in the congressional proceedings. The slavery agitation constituted, in his opinion, an altogether unprecedented interference with the business of the government, which included at the top of the agenda tariff revision. "But the Union is not in danger," he wrote complacently in January. By the end of February complacency had turned to alarm. The first of the great Union meetings on behalf of Clay's resolutions had occurred in New York City, and when the commercial and industrial interests of the eastern cities spoke Webster listened. He had encouraged Clay's initiative; the senator had, Webster remarked, "sustained himself far beyond my expectations."[45] The court's adjournment during the month of March coincided with the necessity Webster felt to take a stand in the great debate. Just what that stand should be, he was not sure. "I mean to make an honest, truth-telling speech; and a Union speech," he wrote uneasily to a Boston friend, "but I have no hope of acquitting myself with more than merely tolerable ability."[46] A Union speech was certainly expected. Many northern Whigs and Free Soilers hoped for much more. They hoped Webster would position himself well north of Clay's resolutions. Taylor Whigs hoped he would come out squarely for the president's plan. Some admirers hoped he would make himself into a flaming oracle against slavery, perhaps less to save the Union than to save his soul. They wished to hear Godlike Daniel speak the law of God. Two weeks before the speech, it was said, Webster inquired of a friend at home, "how much free-soil Massachusetts would bear," for he was "going to make a speech and wanted it up to the mark."[47] The South was not without its own hopes and expectations, however. Near the end of February the New York *Herald* reported that Webster would present his own compromise plan based on the extension of the Missouri Compromise line to the Pacific, California being divided into two states, and guarantees to the South on a sectional balance. "Such a compromise . . . will astonish New England. It is a bold move; but it is perfectly safe. . . . The Union, today, is believed to be in the pocket of Daniel Webster." The South, in gratitude, would make him president.[48] Calhoun himself had promised it, Waddy Thompson told Webster. "Besides the eloquence, genius, and great public services, Mr. Webster possesses many noble qualities," Thompson reported Calhoun as saying. "I shall most probably never recover my health but if I do I would not only not allow my name used against him but would regard it as a sacred duty to support him."[49]

When the day for Webster's speech came, on March 7, no one was sure what he would say, but not since the Reply to Hayne did the fate of the nation seem to hang so fatefully on the wisdom, eloquence, and power of one man. The evening before, Winthrop had called at Webster's home. He found him with Fletcher, Ned Curtis, and also Peter Harvey, a Boston hanger-on of his later years, in the throes of preparation, but declining to discuss the speech other than to offer assurances that he would say nothing on the Wilmot Proviso. Winthrop, an administration loyalist, fully expected Webster to support the president's plan.[50] He was in for a surprise. The exordium of the speech promised much. "Mr. President," Webster began, "I wish to speak today, not as a Massachusetts man, nor as a Northern man, but as an American, and a member of the Senate of the United States. . . . I speak today for the preservation of the Union. 'Hear me for my cause.' " He spoke for over three hours. It was not among his best oratorical performances. He was slow and ponderous, with long, senseless pauses. "His speaking seemed painfully laborious. Great clumps of perspiration stood upon his forehead and face, notwithstanding the slowness of his utterance," which suggested to this auditor, an Ohio Free Soiler, the pangs of a guilty conscience.[51]

Seeking a historical perspective on the crisis, Webster spoke of the curious change in the state of opinion in the two sections on slavery. In the youth of the republic, everyone considered slavery an evil and blamed it on the mother country; the South, more than the North, took the lead against it. Everyone agreed, too, that slavery was strictly a local institution, that the foreign trade should be prohibited, as it was from 1808, and that slavery should be excluded from the Northwest Territory. Standing in the same chamber, on almost the same spot, twenty years ago, Webster had claimed the honor of the Northwest Ordinance for Massachusetts only to be denounced by Hayne, Benton, and others who claimed it for the South. How things had changed. Now the South disowned it. Yet the change was entirely natural. Cotton became king, and the whole interest of the South fastened on the extension of slavery. Texas was the last major conquest of the South, of cotton and slavery. Webster thus reached his fundamental proposition, "that there is not at this moment within the United States, or any territory of the United States, a single foot of land, the character of which, in regard to its being free territory or slave territory, is not fixed by some law, and some irrepealable law, beyond the power of the action of the government." Slavery was coextensive with the limits of Texas, whatever they were determined to be. The law of nature, of soil, climate, and geography, excluded slavery from California and New Mexico and Utah. Without backing off from his long-standing opposition to the admission of slave territory, Webster held that a legal bar was no longer necessary. It was pointless to exclude slavery where it could not go. "I would not take pains uselessly to reaffirm an ordinance of nature, nor to reenact the will of God," the senator declared. "I would put in no Wilmot Proviso for the mere purpose of a taunt or a reproach." The South would be justified in considering that a "theoretic wrong," derogatory of its character and institutions. Although the argument had been made by others, including Clay, Webster clothed it in rhetoric that made it his own.

Webster balanced the grievances of the North and the South with regard to slavery. The North hated slavery; but Webster condemned abolitionist fanaticism. Without exception his complaints against the South concerned matters of attitude and opinion that admitted no legal redress. The North was tired of hearing threats of secession, for instance. "Secession! Peaceable secession! Sir, your eyes and mine are never destined to see that miracle. The dismemberment of this vast country without convulsion!" In fact, secession was a natural as well as a political impossibility. Not even the wildest enthusiast could break the Mississippi valley in two. Calhoun interjected, "No sir! the Union can be broken." But neither man wished to shiver lances on this subject again. One of the principal southern grievances against the North, as

Webster proceeded to show, admitted a specific legal remedy. The return of fugitive slaves was an obligation on every officer bound by his oath to uphold the Constitution. He regretted the court's opinion in the Pennsylvania case; he said he would support Mason's bill on this subject. Webster's peroration, with its Burkian overtones, recurred to the ideals of Liberty and Union enshrined in the Reply to Hayne. "Never did there devolve on any generation of men higher trusts than devolve upon us, for the preservation of this Constitution and the harmony and peace of all who are destined to live under it. Let us make our generation one of the strongest and brightest links in that golden chain which is destined, I fondly believe, to grapple the people of all the States to this Constitution for ages to come." And he called up an image of the continent-wide republic, washed on its opposite shores by the two great seas of the world, that was as beautiful, mighty, and complete as the silver buckler of Achilles.[52]

All over the country Webster was hailed for a splendid exhibition of patriotism and statesmanship. The reception was unusually cordial in the South. The Charleston *Mercury* called it "emphatically a great speech." Southerners who had always acknowledged Webster's genius but thought him deficient in courage now made honorable amends. "He has this day exhibited a higher degree of moral courage than ever graced a great captain on the battle field," said the Baltimore *Sun*. "This speech is Webster's apotheosis."[53] Here was a northern man, a senator uniquely qualified to speak for the North, who treated the South fairly and stood for compromise. Southern Whigs, already given ground for hope by Clay, became convinced that the crisis could be resolved and disunionism defeated. "Webster's speech," Winthrop remarked, "has knocked the Nashville Convention into a cocked hat."[54]

Free Soilers and anti-slavery Whigs were unhappy with the speech from the first. After dinner on the seventh, an Ohio congressman approached Winthrop and said that if the speech went to the country as it was delivered it would overturn the Whig party of the state: "Ohio can't stand it. New York can't stand it. Massachusetts can't stand it—and there will be no Whig State left."[55] But the speech appeared in the press the next morning without correction or revisal. Turning his attention to the pamphlet edition, which became the authorized edition, Webster made several small changes, for instance inserting a passage critical of the exclusion of colored seamen in southern ports, and indicating that his approval of Mason's Fugitive Slave Bill depended on certain amendments. With Curtis's help in Washington, Webster sent out under his own frank over one hundred thousand copies of the speech before the end of March. Still the demand had not been met. He dedicated the speech to the people of Massachusetts, and was especially eager to spread it among them. Wanting a Latin motto for a handsome edition, he took Winthrop's suggestion, *vera pro gratis*, meaning that it became him to speak what is true rather than what is agreeable. Webster was so pleased with the sentiment that he had it engraved on his personal seal.[56]

The speech of the 7th of March struck New England like a hurricane. At first, the Boston *Atlas* doubted the accuracy of the telegraphic report. When it was confirmed, the *Daily Advertiser* and the *Courier*, the other leading Whig newspapers, came to Webster's support, while the *Atlas* spoke for the opposition. Not a single member of the Bay State delegation in Congress, except George Ashmun, it was said, endorsed the speech; like Winthrop they regretted that their leader had not raised his appeal for union and concord upon "a safe New England platform." Outside Boston, according to the *Atlas*, only six Whig newspapers in New England defended Webster. What had he done wrong? He who had given fame to the Northwest Ordinance and its no-slavery proviso had dismissed the Wilmot Proviso as shibboleth and humbug. He had given priority to the law of climate over the law of conscience. He had talked blithely of carving additional slave states from Texas. He had interpreted the fugitive slave clause of the Constitution as if it were a binding legal contract on the people of the free states. He had advocated a stronger fugitive slave law without insisting that it regard the slave as a person as well as a chattel, and in the face of the evidence that it would not weigh a feather in controlling the northern conscience. In this, above all, he had not been truthful. The speech's sins of omission, such as the abolition of slavery in the District, or even the slave trade, which Clay had proposed, were also great.

But after all the arguments had been analyzed, Waldo Emerson's simple question went to the heart of the matter: "*How came he there?*"[57] How came the Yankee Demosthenes on the side of slaveholders? How came the great advocate in opposition to the people who retained him? To this question Boston's anti-slavery preachers, philosophers, and poets returned two main answers. First, they described the defect of moral sensibility. In other parts of the country the speech raised Webster's reputation for moral courage, but it was this that he lost in New England. Among the congressmen, Horace Mann, the educator, most felt the shock of betrayal. "Webster's intellectual life has been one great epic," he wrote from Washington, "and now he has given a vile catastrophe to its closing pages. He has walked for years among the gods, to descend from the empyrean heights and mingle . . . in a masquerade full of harlots and leeches."[58] Emerson, similarly, scribled in his journal " 'Liberty! liberty!' Pho! Let Mr. Webster for decency's sake shut his lips once and forever on this word. The word *liberty* in the mouth of Mr. Webster sounds like the word *love* in the mouth of a courtezan."[59] Second, the Yankee censors pointed the finger of blame at presidential ambition. His first reaction on reading the speech, said Theodore Parker, Boston's brilliant abolitionist preacher, was that "the Southern men" must have offered Webster the presidency. It was Parker who at Faneuil Hall addressed a meeting of citizens called to protest the speech. Billed the "Anti-Webster Meeting," it adopted resolutions that denounced the 7th of March speech as "a speech 'not fit to be made.' " The senator offered the apology of statesmanship—*vera pro gratis*—but this insulted the intelligence, said Parker. The speech could only be explained as "a bid for the presidency." Nothing in American history compared to Webster's betrayal, except the treason of Benedict Ar-

nold.[60] No speech, certainly, ever excited greater moral indignation. It found
its most enduring expression in Whittier's *Ichabod:**

> So fallen! so lost! the light withdrawn
>   Which once he wore!
> The glory from his gray hairs gone
>   Forevermore!
>
>   * * *
>
> Of all we loved and honored, naught
>   Save power remains;
> A fallen angel's pride of thought,
>   Still strong in chains.
>
> All else is gone; from those great eyes
>   The soul has fled:
> When faith is lost, when honor dies,
>   The man is dead!
>
> Then, pay the reverence of old days
>   To his dead fame;
> Walk backward, with averted gaze,
>   And hide the shame![61]

Conspicuous by its absence was a Faneuil Hall rally for Webster. Edward
Everett, himself deeply troubled by the speech, had at first thought to call
such a meeting, but he gave it up as too hazardous and likely to heighten the
formidable dissent in the community. The counter-demonstration took the
form of the "Boston Testimonial," a letter of thanks and support for the 7th of
March speech signed by some eight hundred citizens of Boston and vicinity.[62] Many of the distinguished names were there—Rufus Choate, George
Ticknor, Thomas H. Perkins—though there were striking omissions, Everett's for instance. The mass of conservative Whigs, identified with the Bay
State's banking, commercial, and manufacturing interests, stood by Webster. An article in the *North American Review,* the literary voice of New England conservatism, lauded the "moral grandeur" of the statesman's position
in opposition to intolerance and fanaticism on both sides. Webster, like Clay,
suddenly found himself in the embrace of old enemies. There was none older
than Ike Hill, the Democratic leader of New Hampshire. That "a dismal dog"
like Hill should embrace Webster was hardly surprising, Emerson thought,
but that Webster should return the embrace and pronounce it one of the
most gratifying incidents of his life, and publish the correspondence, seemed
the ultimate degradation.[63] There were others who wished to believe that
Webster's moral depravity went beyond politics. A young Washington journalist, Jane Grey Swisshelm, employed by the *Tribune,* wrote a libelous
story portraying Webster as the secret father of a family of free black children
in the capital. Embarrassed, Greeley quickly retracted and apologized for
the story, which surpassed belief.[64]

---

*"And she named the child Ichabod, saying, The glory is departed from Israel, because the ark
of God was taken. . . ." I *Samuel,* 4:21.

The great debate rolled on in the Senate. Seward's speech on the eleventh was taken in the North as the antidote to Webster. It was, for many northern Whigs, the speech Godlike Daniel should have made. The studious, bespectacled New Yorker was no orator; he read his speech, so elaborately prepared—it was his maiden effort in the Senate—and the galleries emptied after the first twenty minutes. In a sense, Seward replied to all the triumvirs. Starting with Clay, he rejected the very idea of legislative compromise, calling it "essentially vicious" since such compromises undercut consideration of separate measures on their merits and because they demanded the surrender of judgment and conscience to expediency. He rejected Calhoun's call for safeguards. Nothing in the Constitution assumed or mandated an equilibrium between the sections; the guarantees Calhoun wanted were unworkable and unacceptable. All three men, Seward thought, overreacted to the crisis and endangered the Union they professed to save. This was especially true of Webster, whom he criticized on all major points. It was the business of legislators to reenact the law of God, and that was precisely what Congress should do for the territories. He invoked a "higher law than the Constitution" to ensure freedom in all the public domain. Free soil was the nursery of free men. In the end, however, Seward offered no remedy, neglecting even to endorse Taylor's policy; and the speech made more of an impact outside Congress than within it. The American Anti-Slavery Society immediately published ten thousand pamphlet copies.[65]

Calhoun died on Sunday morning, March 31. The next day several senators, beginning with Clay and Webster, delivered brief eulogies. Clay's voice rose slowly as the recollections of forty years rushed upon him, and he finished touchingly, "I was his senior, Mr. President, in years—in nothing else." Webster spoke of the personal kindness between them through all political vicissitudes. The qualities of Calhoun's mind and character, he said, were compacted in his eloquence: "It was plain, strong, terse, condensed, concise; sometimes impassioned—still always severe." Benton declined to speak. "He is not dead, sir—he is not dead. There may be no vitality in his body, but there is in his doctrines," the Missourian protested.[66] Official Washington crowded the Capitol at noon on Tuesday, a lovely spring day, for the funeral in the Senate chamber, which had been stripped of desks to make room for the mourners. The Reverend Charles M. Butler, chaplain, delivered the funeral sermon, after which a cortege bore the casket to the Congressional Cemetery where the body was temporarily interred. On April 4 the vice president appointed a committee of six senators to convey Calhoun's remains to South Carolina. Webster was one of the six, but he decided this would be carrying his "southern courtesy" too far, and he withdrew.[67]

In the Palmetto State members of Calhoun's family were at the center of a controversy over the stateman's last resting place, whether at Fort Hill, Columbia, or Charleston. Finally, Charleston won out, at least for the present, and Calhoun made his last journey there attended not only by the senators but also by a distinguished committee of Charlestonians and two of his sons. Honors were paid all along the route. At Richmond, Calhoun's body lay in state in the Virginia Capitol. When the Wilmington steamer docked at Charleston on the twenty-fifth, the casket was conveyed in a great military procession to Citadel Square. "The hearse was magnificent, and so lofty upon a large catafalco that it seemed to threaten all gateways made by human hands," a foreign observer wrote. "Many regiments paraded in splendid uniforms, and a large number of banners with symbolic figures and inscriptions were borne aloft." The entire front and battlements of the Citadel were draped in mourning. The body was then carried to City Hall, where it lay in state for a day. At last, on April 26, the body was entombed in the cemetery of St. Philip's Church.[68]

All the while South Carolinians heard sermons, discourses, and eulogies on John C. Calhoun. There was no answer to the question on everyone's mind: Who would assume the fallen robes and with what effect? He had died a disunionist, it was generally believed. In one of his last letters home, he had written of his disappointment that Webster, whose speech was so gratifying, appeared unable to sustain himself before the torrent of northern opinion. "Can anything more clearly evince the utter hopelessness of looking to the North for support, when their strongest man finds himself incapable of maintaining himself on the smallest amount possible of concession to the South . . .?"[69] In Charleston the planning of obsequies merged with the election of delegates to the Nashville Convention. One speaker at a mass meeting compared Calhoun's death to that of a Spartan chief, causing no faltering in the ranks, and serving "only to rally to the defense of the South every true Southern heart."[70] Calhoun might prove more dangerous dead than alive, as Benton feared, for now his doctrines were "hallowed by the grave" and the restraints he had exercised on the southern fire-eaters were removed. Committed disunionists like Rhett would no longer have to sit back while Calhoun shuffled the cards. From this point of view, he died at the right moment. "It was as if a ball had struck Wellington as soon as he had uttered the words, 'Up Guards, and at them,'" Beverly Tucker wrote to Hammond.[71] No one, certainly, could take his place. "Mr. Calhoun did all the thinking for the State and has died without appointing his Executor," Alfred Huger observed. "The State is at sea without a pilot," in William Gilmore Simms's metaphor, for the effect of Calhoun's eminence had been "to dwarf all the men about him."[72] Governor Seabrook muffed the opportunity to pass the torch firmly to a successor. His first choice, James Hamilton, declined, as did his second, Langdon Cheves, both for good reasons; he then named Elmore, who accepted and died within a month, to be succeeded briefly by Robert Barnwell. Finally, Rhett won election to the coveted seat in the fall.

Meanwhile, in Washington, as the speech making wound down, the Senate prepared to take the next step on Clay's resolutions. His original idea, as far as he had one, of beginning with California and proceeding measure by measure to the end was not wholly incompatible with Taylor's objectives, but when he drew back from that and embraced Foote's omnibus strategy, he placed himself directly at odds with the administration. Clay thought now, he said, after all the excitement that had been generated, that the best chance for California as well as for the other measures was to treat them in combination. Any fool could see that the foes of one measure would therefore be united against all measures, although it was equally true that the friends of one measure would acquiesce in others to achieve their object. Clay believed that in the House of Representatives, at least, a majority existed for the whole scheme of compromise but not for the parts. Moreover, separate bills might encounter the president's veto, which would upset the balance compromise required. "I go for honorable compromise whenever it can be made," Clay said. "Life itself is but a compromise. . . . All legislation, all government, all society, is formed upon the principle of mutual concession, politeness, comity, courtesy; upon them, everything is based. . . . Compromises have this recommendation, that if you concede anything, you have something conceded to you in return."[73]

Webster hedged his bets. The 7th of March speech was a call for a comprehensive settlement, virtually an endorsement of Clay's resolutions, even if Webster had failed to mention them. When it came to legislative strategy, however, Webster drew back and seemed to support the administration. His vacillation, it was said, had already cost him much of the good will he had earlier gained in the South. "What can be said of a man who deserts to the enemy, fights one battle, and deserts back again?" wrote one of his critics. "Morally he is not worth the powder and ball it would take to end him."[74] Benton led the last-ditch fight against Foote's motion to refer the whole caboodle to a committee of thirteen. Finally brought to a vote on April 18, it was adopted, 30–22. Webster was in the minority, along with Seward, Chase, Hale, Smith, and Benton. Clay was again the Napoleon of Congress. He, and Webster too, instead of sustaining Taylor, went to work, wrote a disheartened Kentucky Whig, Orlando Brown, "to weave anew the broken web of their own political fortunes"; and this, rather than saving the Union, was their true object. Yet even Brown's good friend and ally, Crittenden, had concluded that Taylor's plan had been superseded by events and that the *whole* sectional crisis over slavery must be settled.[75]

While Clay's committee—he was named chairman, of course—went to work, most congressmen fled the capital. Webster, who had been elected to the committee but did not participate, returned to Boston to face his accusers. Arriving on an afternoon train, he was driven to Bowdoin Square, before the Revere House, where some five thousand people awaited him under darkened skies. He heard a welcoming address and, as the sun appeared, replied from the open barouche. He spoke of the paralysis caused by the slavery question and of the great importance of a settlement that would enable Congress to get on with the business of the country in the old harmonious way. He defended his position on the return of fugitive slaves and thought it was time for Massachusetts to subdue its prejudices on the subject.[76] This issue, even more than apostasy from the Wilmot Proviso, was especially awkward for him. "The constitutional question is clearly with the South," Everett observed, "and this has misled Mr. Webster and some other sound lawyers. They argue the question as they would a land title before the Supreme Court." Even Webster's most conservative friends, like Ticknor and Choate, agreed that he had fumbled this issue.[77] Horace Mann was his principal accuser. In letters to the *Atlas* he had the temerity to charge Webster with bad Latin as well as bad morals. The senator, for his part, thought Mann puerile and snubbed him. In reply to a complimentary address from Newburyport, Webster took the opportunity to make a full statement of his views on the fugitives question. Beginning characteristically—Emerson remarked that Webster "lives by his memory"—with the history of the subject, he traced the principle of the return of fugitives back to the New England Confederation of 1643 and maintained that no one in 1793 regarded the Fugitive Slave Law, *sans* jury trial, "repugnant to religion, liberty, the Constitution, or humanity." Although he found no constitutional requirement for a jury trial, he was ready to provide it in order to allay excitement and remove objections. This was, he said, one of the amendments in the draft of the bill that lay in the drawer of his desk when he made the 7th of March speech. Like the Wilmot Proviso in the deserts of New Mexico and Utah, the Fugitive Slave Law was an abstraction in New England. In the six states, only two seizures had occurred in the last quarter century, Webster said. Why, then, was there so much vehemence on the subject? "I suspect," he answered, "all this to be the effect of the wandering and vagrant philanthropy which disturbs and annoys all that is present, in time and place, by heating the imagination on subjects distant, remote and uncertain." It was, in sum, "false philanthropy," "transcendental philosophy," and "abolitionist enthusiasm."[78] After returning to Washington, he introduced his own bill; even Mann could find no fault with it.

Still fighting illness, Clay wrote the report of the Committee of Thirteen as a guest of Charles Calvert, part owner of the National Hotel, at his estate, Riversdale, across the Maryland line; and he presented it to the Senate on May 8. Fundamentally, the recommendations of the report embodied Clay's resolutions. The main recommendation was the "Omnibus Bill." This provided for California statehood, territorial governments for New Mexico and Utah which barred the assemblies from legislating for or against slavery, and a settlement of the Texas debt and boundary. A fugitive slave bill allowed jury trial in the state from which the alleged fugitive fled. (To allow it in the state of capture would be to make a nullity of the guarantee, Clay explained.) A final bill abolished the slave trade in the District. Passage of the entire plan was necessary, Clay pleaded, to heal the wounds of the nation.[79] How far the committee had been divided, how far it was from a unanimous report, became evident as the members rose to express their differences. There was no majority for the plan in the Senate. Support was strongest among southern Whigs and northern Democrats. Yet there was a majority receptive to debating the measures and coming to some resolution of the crisis. On the fifteenth, as the debate began, Douglas tested the sentiment of the body by a motion to table with a view to considering California statehood by itself. It was defeated, 24–28.

Immediately, the president reaffirmed his adherence to his own plan and dismissed the editor of the administration newspaper, *The Republic*, which had been overly friendly to Clay. Under a new editor, the senator said, the administration made "open war, undisguised war," on the Committee of Thirteen plan, and all the influence of the cabinet secretaries and other partisans was brought to bear in and out of Congress. With so little support in the Senate, Clay had no tolerance for executive interference, and he rebuked the president in a capital speech, pronounced by some of the senior members the greatest ever delivered in that body. It had become his painful duty, Clay said, to contrast the president's plan and the committee's plan: "Here are five wounds—one, two three, four, five—bleeding, and threatening the well-being, if not the existence of the body politic. What is the plan of the president? Is it to treat all the wounds? No such thing. It is only to heal one of the five, and to leave the other four to bleed more profusely than ever, by the sole admission of California, even if it should produce death itself." Clay went on to describe the five wounds, ticking them off on his hand, and spoke of the president in mingled terms of scorn and anger. "After the observations which I addressed to the Senate a week ago, I did hope and trust there would have been a reciprocation from the other end of the avenue, as to the desire to heal, not one wound only—which being healed would exasperate instead of harmonizing the country—but to heal them all. . . . But instead of concurrence with the committee, on the part of the Executive, we have an authentic assurance of his adherence exclusively to his own scheme." The administration responded full-blast in the pages of *The Republic*, where Clay was portrayed as vainglorious and dictatorial.[80] "His course reminds everybody of his action when Tyler came in," Chase observed. Actually, there were important differences. Then, he had been unquestionably the leader of the party. Now he was old and defeated, the leader of no one, and in danger of becoming an outcast, like Webster in 1842. Clay was sustained by his confidence that the American people supported him against the administration. It was the administration, he wrote to Lucretia, that seemed "utterly regardless of public feeling and opinion, and blindly rushing on their own ruin, if not the ruin of the country." In the widening breach between Clay and Taylor, Whigs foresaw the dissolution of the party.[81]

"The debates have fallen into a regular humdrum monotony," Seward wrote home near the end of June. "Fashion has withdrawn her court. The weather is oppressively hot." Some senators called for a brief recess, but Clay was opposed and instead won agreement to convene an hour earlier each day. The air of the chamber improved when the red carpet was taken up and the draperies removed.[82] Other business was shunted aside. Congress was deluged with petitions praying for tariff revision. Clay dutifully presented several of these, but when his aid was solicited by a Boston committee, he snapped, "Don't talk to me about the tariff when it is doubtful whether we have any country. Go and see your Massachusetts delegation and urge them to lay aside their sectional jealousies, to cease exasperating the South, and to cultivate the spirit of peace. Save your country and then talk about your tariff."[83] Obviously, Clay, and Webster too, held tariff reform hostage to the compromise. Whether or not this produced any votes for it is unclear; but protectionists and business interests, generally, showed their support for conciliation and compromise in Unionist rallies in eastern cities.

The Nashville Convention came and went without incident. An address written by Rhett resounded with the music of southern nationalism but made no proposal more threatening than to meet again in the fall. In the Senate the opposite forces arrayed against the compromise sought to pull it apart and to amend it to death. Southern ultraists clung to the Missouri Compromise solution, including the division of California, which might provide a Pacific presence to a future southern confederacy. The Nashville address also endorsed this stale proposition. Northern free-soilers, of course, sought to introduce the Wilmot Proviso into the Omnibus Bill. On matters of less consequence, Clay was quite flexible. For instance, in regard to the vexed question of the status of slavery in the territories, he silently dropped his opinion that the Mexican law prevailed, accepted amendatory language that might be construed as offering protection to slave property, though he foresaw no practical effect from it, and finally approved, with Webster, a formula that would ensure ultimate decision by the Supreme Court. The latter, of course, was a legacy of the so-called Clayton Compromise. Clay was at his best in the cut-and-thrust of legislative debate. His titanic encounter with Benton grew so heated that the Senate abruptly adjourned to cool off. Clay's perseverance was a marvel. Every morning he was at his desk, attired as always in a black dress coat and high white collar, shaking hands, smiling to everyone, his face, slightly flushed, registering the whole gamut of emotions, and rising to speak at the slightest provocation. "When in moments of excitement . . .," Grace Greenwood observed, "he stands so firm and proud, with his eye all agleam, while his voice rings out clear and strong, it almost seems that his apparent physical debility was but a sort of Richelieu *ruse,* and that the hot blood of youth was still coursing through his veins, and the full vigor of manhood yet strong in every limb. The wonderful old man!"[84] The gallery was always with Clay, and he deliberately played to it as if he were Kean or Forrest, even if his colleagues were no longer amused. Webster, the personification of granite-like heaviness and calm, remarked that Clay, for all his spectacular talents, was not a good leader in a crisis for want of temper. "He is irritable, impatient, and occasionally overbearing; and drives people off."[85]

Prospects for passage of the compromise soared when President Taylor died suddenly on July 9. In the days just before he fell ill, the president's conflict with Clay and his followers in Congress, particularly the southern Whigs, had deteriorated because of the danger of bloodshed on the Texas–New Mexico frontier. Encouraged by Taylor, New Mexico, still under a military governor, made application for immediate statehood not only under an anti-slavery constitution but with an eastern boundary Texas refused to accept. The governor of the Lone Star State prepared to send troops to Santa Fe; other southern states promised assistance. In mock imitation of Andrew Jackson, the president vowed to defend New Mexico with force. Obviously, a bloody conflict on the Texas border or premature action for statehood in

New Mexico (not admitted to the Union until 1912) would wreck the compromise. Southern Whigs led by Stephens and Toombs were angry at Taylor, and he, reportedly, had prepared a message announcing his support of New Mexico just before his death. "Mr. Hilliard," Webster later told the Alabama congressman, "if General Taylor had lived we should have had a civil war."[86] But the message was left unfinished and undelivered. Millard Fillmore, the new president, was known as a friend of Clay and compromise; indeed, he had told Taylor that should the Omnibus Bill finally depend on his casting vote, it would have it. Clay could not disguise his elation over the change of command at the White House. "There never was such a metamorphosis," Blair observed. "Everybody remarked the joy visible in his face and manner, amidst the general consternation and ensigns of mourning. It is thought that he and Fillmore and Webster have patched up a coalition." And so they had. They were frequently seen closeted together. Webster became secretary of state in the new cabinet, at Clay's behest, it was said. The whole influence of the administration was thrown behind the compromise. "The government is in the hands of Mr. Webster, and Mr. Clay is its organ in Congress," Seward wrote glumly.[87]

Webster delivered his last speech in the Senate on July 17. It was an appeal for passage of the compromise, unaccompanied by any fanfare of valedictory. As always, the senator gave a fresh turn to hackneyed arguments. Congress had been paralyzed by slavery issues for several years, he said; vital interests, including those of Massachusetts, had been ignored. The heritage of a single nation had been assailed by ultraists on both sides, North and South, and by the tendency to impute to whole sections the extravagant ideas or actions of a few. Thus it was falsely assumed that the South was disunionist because the Nashville Address squinted that way; thus it was that abolitionists created a distorted image of the North in the southern mind. The gallery applauded every patriotic effusion. Webster concluded by reminding the senators that the eyes of the world were upon them. The question was nothing less then the survival of the republic. "No man can suffer too much, and no man can fall too soon, if he suffer or if he fall in defense of the liberties and Constitution of his country."[88]

Near the end of July, Clay dared hope that the Omnibus and the other measures would be enacted, first in the Senate, then in the House. He made a three-hour summation on the twenty-second before a packed house and to the accompaniment of an often boisterous gallery. "I never heard Clay more eloquent or saw him exhibit greater resources of mind," Blair told Van Buren.[89] He drew up the sectional balance sheet of compromise. The North gained California as a free state; it secured New Mexico detached from Texas, and both New Mexico and Utah organized as territories with the high probability they would eventually become free states; and it secured the end of the slave trade in the District of Columbia. The South escaped the assertion of a dangerous principle, the Wilmot Proviso; it secured within the limits of Texas several hundred square miles of disputed territory and benefited indirectly from the payment of a $10-million debt; it got an effective fugitive slave law and the quietus of agitation for abolition in the District. If the South received less, or even nothing, in the territories, that was not because of the laws of Congress, Clay reiterated, but because of laws of nature. He, too, like Webster, assailed the abolitionists; and he singled out Rhett for attack as a southern disunionist. Did he mean to say that Rhett was a traitor? he was asked. No, Clay replied emphatically, but if he had pronounced certain sentiments attributed to him in Charleston, about raising the standard of disunion, "he will be a traitor, and I hope he will meet with the fate of a traitor." The gallery broke into thunderous applause. To those who said that compromise never settled anything, he reminded them of the Missouri Compromise and the Compromise of 1833, of which the same had been said, yet both had healed the wounds and restored the peace of the country. "I believe from the bottom of my soul," the old gladiator concluded, "that this measure is the reunion of this Union. I believe it is the dove of peace, which, taking its aerial flight from the dome of the Capitol, carries the glad tidings of . . . harmony to all the remotest extremities of this distracted land."[90]

Just as the dawn seemed to be breaking, however, the Omnibus collapsed at its most vulnerable point, the Texas boundary. Laboriously, the Senate had agreed on an arrangement whereby a commission would finally fix the boundary, Texas continuing to exercise jurisdiction in the disputed area in the interim. But on the next day, July 31, James A. Pearce of Maryland, believing the arrangement unjust to New Mexico, wished to strike it, and knowing no other way to accomplish his object moved to strike the entire New Mexico section of the bill. Pearce, long an ally of Clay's, was friendly to the compromise. Told that his amendment would defeat the Omnibus Bill, he replied, "If it does, then I cannot help it." He was later charged with obstinately rejecting other less damaging means of achieving his object. However this may be, Pearce's amendment passed and opened the way for dismantlement of the Omnibus piece by piece. The enemies of the compromise celebrated. The scene was graphically portrayed by the reporter for a New York newspaper. "Jefferson Davis' face grinned with smiles. Old Bullion's few hairs actually bristled with delight. *He* had routed *Clay! He* had smashed the Omnibus to atoms. Seward was dancing about like a little top. . . . Barnwell's spectacles twinkled and Butler's gray hairs flourished more than ever. Chase was shaking hands with Soulé the Frenchman." On the other side, all was dejection. Clay sat "melancholy as Caius Marius over the ruins of Carthage," then silently walked out of the chamber.[91]

The next day Clay returned to survey the wreckage. Charges and countercharges passed between him and Pearce. But putting recrimination aside, Clay now pleaded for passage of the compromise measures one by one. "I was willing to take the measures unified. I am willing now to see them pass separate and distinct."[92] He had not the health nor the will to attend to this, however, and he retired to Newport for rest and recuperation. Douglas assumed the burden of guiding the various bills, several of which he had himself drafted, through the Senate. He and Pearce collaborated on a bill to fix the limits of Texas as they stand today. When Clay returned on August 27, the Senate had finished with all but the District bill and awaited action by the House on the others. In September Fillmore signed all the measures into law.

The Compromise of 1850 substantially embodied the resolutions Clay had introduced in February. Of course, they had finally been enacted under another leadership and in another form than he had proposed. Some senators believed he had erred in opting for the omnibus strategy and that as solitary measures they would have been enacted with much less travail. Benton thought the fact that in the end only sixteen or seventeen senators voted for all the bills, yet all the bills passed, proved the error of Clay's approach. Clay declined to engage in postmortems. As he had often said, the question of combining or separating the bills was "the merest question of form," and any vehicle, omnibus or whatever, was good that arrived. Foote, who was largely responsible for the legislative strategy, said that but for the bills being combined, thus forcing all the elements into the discussion, the compromise would have failed. Dickinson, the New York Democrat who supported Clay, found fault with Benton's logic that because the bills had passed separately, therefore they should never have been united. On the contrary, sectional fears and jealousies were abated by keeping the measures united, and public opinion, which forced the settlement on a reluctant Congress, was aroused precisely because all the critical issues were set before the country in one format at one time. Douglas, who had opposed the omnibus strategy from the first, declined to take undue credit for himself. The question of form was of "small moment." Clay's leadership was a mixed blessing. The Taylor administration hated him, and many old enemies, Whig and Democrat, opposed the compromise simply to defeat him. "But let it always be said of old Hal that he fought a glorious and patriotic battle," Douglas wrote. "No man was ever governed by higher or purer motives."[93]

Clay and Webster participated in the jubilant celebration of the compromise in the capital. In meetings throughout the country, it was hailed as a final settlement of the slavery question. Clay's prediction that it would become popular, like the previous sectional compromises—"the reunion of this Union"—proved valid, at least in the short run. In the long run, the Compromise of 1850 bore more the character of a truce than a final settlement. This did not diminish its value or importance. The Union was preserved by a truly monumental legislative achievement. The fatal flaw of the compromise was the Fugitive Slave Act. As finally passed, it was a Draconian "catch slave law," without jury trial or other guarantees for the blacks, and without any reckoning with the northern conscience. Webster was not responsible for the act, but in this matter he had misrepresented the North and made promises to the South that could not be kept. He would not escape the consequences, as for the next two years fugitive slave cases kept the fires of controversy burning. Meanwhile, he rejoiced in "the Providential escape" provided by the Compromise and slept soundly for the first time since the 7th of March. "We have now gone through the most important crisis . . . since the foundation of this government, and whatever party may prevail, hereafter, the

Union stands firm."[94] Clay's sentiments were the same as he went home to the peace of Ashland and the honors of Kentucky.

4. *Last of the Giants*

An air of tranquillity descended on the nation in the aftermath of the Compromise of 1850. Depleted attendance at the Nashville Convention, which had adjourned pending the outcome in Congress, reflected the calming effect of the compromise in the southern states. The Upper South, led by Virginia, declined to send delegates to the November meeting. Although it denounced the compromise and asserted the right of secession, the convention ended not with a bang but a wimper and left the little bands of southern nationalists disabled in their own states. In Georgia the election of a convention to deliberate on the state's course resulted in an overwhelming victory for the Unionists led by Stephens, Toombs, and Cobb. The convention, assembled in December, adopted resolutions pledging the state to abide by the Compromise of 1850 "as a permanent adjustment of this sectional controversy," provided, of course, that its measures were adhered to in the North.[1] Unionists throughout the South applauded this "Georgia Platform." Even in Mississippi, where the irrepressible Foote prevailed over the malcontents, a special session of the legislature decided to give the compromise a chance to work by postponing any state convention for twelve months.

The decision was closer in South Carolina. Rhett returned from Nashville as the legislature convened at Columbia. Governor Seabrook's message was disunionist in spirit, combining a eulogy of Calhoun with a denunciation of the compromise, which he called "another triumph of the fell spirit of abolitionism."[2] Rhett, whom he had appointed official orator before the assembly, portrayed the fallen statesman as the prophet of secession. The Union never had a better friend, he declared, since its survival depended on the conservative principles for which Calhoun gave his life. But the Union had been undermined by the forces of consolidation and abolition. In his last speech, Calhoun redeemed the honor and the liberties of the South. "It was the last flash of the sun, to show the ship of State her only port of safety, as darkness and the howling tempest closed around her. He died—for his work was done. If the South would not heed his warnings and counsels, why should he live? But if she regarded them . . . why should he not die?" And Rhett ventured to say that had Calhoun lived one more hour to speak in the Senate, he would have wrenched from a despairing heart the word he had refused to utter all his life, *disunion*.[3] The legislature went on to elect Rhett over Hammond, who had suddenly taken on Calhoun's role of moderation and restraint, to the vacated Senate seat. At the same time, however, the lawmakers postponed for a year any further movement toward secession. Meanwhile, a widening breach developed between immediate secessionists, who would have the state act alone if necessary, and cooperationists, who looked to concert with the sister states. The former, led by Rhett and the *Mercury*, were an embattled minority in 1851, as most of the state's trusted leaders—Butler, Hammond, Hamilton, Cheves, Burt—some of whom claimed to speak for the dead statesman, took the cooperationist line; and in the fall, with the aid of the Charleston merchants and old Unionists like Joel Poinsett and Benjamin Perry, they routed the secessionists at the polls. "The peril of disunion, always exaggerated," the New York *Times* observed, "has ceased to be even a scarecrow."[4] Seeing the defeat as a repudiation of his leadership, Rhett, with what his biographer calls "fanatical consistency," resigned from the Senate and withdrew from public life.

Over all this, Calhoun cast his shadow. The governor, in that same November message, recommended that the state build a grand monument in memory of Calhoun and also undertake the publication of his political writings. The monument should rise at the center of a four-acre public park to be laid out before the state capitol, and it should contain Calhoun's mortal remains. The political writings were an enduring legacy. "Every citizen within our limits should possess a copy of this legacy to the cause of constitutional liberty," said Seabrook.[5] No action was taken on the first recommendation, but the legislature appropriated $10,000 for the speedy editing and publication of Calhoun's political treatises, the *Disquisition on Government* and the *Discourse on the Constitution*. The work was put in the hands of Richard Crallé, the Virginia intimate of the deceased statesman, and it was published in Charleston the succeeding fall. A local newspaper commented, "The writings of Mr. Calhoun were edited in Virginia; the stereotyped plates were cast in New York; they were then sent to Columbia, where impressions were struck off; the sheets were thence transferred to Charleston in order that the books might be bound; and now they are bound, there is really no publisher in the State to see to their publication."[6] Although published under the direction of the General Assembly of South Carolina, the copyright belonged to the family, which expected to profit from the publication. In this they would be disappointed. Few copies of the volume were sold, despite frequent notices in newspapers and periodicals. It provided the first authoritative exposition of "the Calhoun constitution," including the proposal for a dual executive. But the threads were spun so fine, terminating in such airy conclusions, that for all the praise heaped upon it in the South the volume commanded little interest, while in the North it scarcely commanded respect.[7] Crallé went on to edit and publish, in New York, Calhoun's speeches, reports, and other writings, the entire series being completed in six volumes in 1855. Despite repeated moves inside and outside the General Assembly to raise a monument to the statesman, none was realized. The nearest thing to a public monument was Hiram Powers's statue of a Roman senator, in Charleston, which, it may be recalled, was recovered from a shipwreck with one of its arms missing.

Although Clay remained a senator, he retreated from public view and lapsed into virtual silence on the Compromise of 1850. Webster, on the other hand, became the voice, indeed the very personification, of the compromise before the nation. Throughout the long struggle in Congress, he had worried, with most of his friends, that he might have risked himself in a losing cause. It was only after the August victory of Samuel Eliot in the special election for Boston's congressional seat that Webster knew he was "not a dead man" in Massachusetts. The election, which came about because of Winthrop's elevation to the Senate in his place, was like a vote of confidence, for Eliot was a Webster Whig and author of the Boston Memorial got up in support of the speech of the 7th of March.[8] Then, as the bills were signed into law, Webster's joy over his deliverance added to his conviction that the compromise had saved the Union and, if faithfully executed, would become the permanent settlement so much wished for. With a vigor that belied his sixty-eight years, and in spite of all his ailments, Webster entered upon the two most strenuous years—the last years—of his life full of official business, politics, some law, and much speech making focused on the single theme, the preservation of the Union and the Constitution.

Returning to the State Department after seven years, Webster found much of the business familiar. As in the past, Mexico, Central America, and the Caribbean seemed to command disproportionate attention. Webster dealt with filibustering expeditions against Cuba. He pursued negotiation of the Tehuantepec Treaty, commenced by his predecessor, for construction of a railroad across the isthmus separating the Caribbean and the Pacific, only to see it finally rejected by Mexico; and he sought to open an alternate route in Nicaragua, which would add a crucial link to global American commerce. When foreign affairs offered opportunity to advance Webster's domestic purposes, he did not hesitate to exploit it. The most dramatic instance was the Hülsemann Letter of December 21, 1850. On behalf of his government the Austrian *chargé d'affaires*, the Chevalier Hülsemann, protested the mission earlier dispatched by President Taylor to observe and offer discretionary assurances of recognition to the Hungarian revolutionaries against the Hapsburg Empire. The revolution led by Louis Kossuth had been crushed, but Austria remained indignant over American encouragement of anarchy and insurrection. Before leaving for New England in October, Webster threw out ideas for a reply to his chief clerk, William Hunter, who prepared a draft and forwarded it to the secretary at Marshfield. He also asked Everett to draft a reply, which he did most dutifully, only to learn later that he got no credit for it. There was a fine line, as Webster recognized, between voicing American principles in the world and adhering to non-intervention in the affairs of foreign nations, as his idol, Washington, had advised. Webster was no revolutionary, of course, yet he had almost thirty years earlier delivered a brilliant speech for the independence of Greece, and he now returned to the spirit of that appeal, not because he was an enthusiast for Magyar liberty, but because, as he confided to Ticknor, he wished to write a reply "which should touch the national pride, and make a man feel *sheepish* and look *silly* who should speak of disunion."[9]

The interest the United States took in the revolutions of 1848, Webster replied to Hülsemann, arose from no disposition to intervene in foreign nations but, rather, from the fact that those revolutions had their origins in the ideas of freedom and self-government upon which the American republic was founded. In defense of those ideas, and consistent with their own character, Americans could not withhold their sympathy from struggling peoples abroad. Patriotic boast was his purpose, and so Webster informed Europe's crowned heads of the power that attended the blessings of American liberty: "The power of this republic, at the present moment, is spread over a region one of the richest and most fertile on the globe, and of an extent in comparison with which the possessions of the house of Hapsburg are but a patch on the earth's surface." He went on to speak of the rapidly multiplying population, the prosperity, and the progress of the United States. The letter was widely read and admired, but, standing apart from any burning controversy, it did not have the influence at home Webster had hoped for. After the president forwarded the Hülsemann correspondence to Congress, and a motion was made to print ten thousand extra copies to be spread across the land, Clay registered his opposition. Hungary's fate had long since been sealed, and if Webster's letter had any relationship to peace and unity at home, Clay did not see it. The motion for extra copies was defeated. Webster was offended, yet not really surprised that Clay, "a great moral tyrant," should once again attempt to put him down.[10]

Webster's most embarrassing moment as secretary of state came on February 25, 1851. Not long after entering office he had contracted with three banking houses (the Boston branch of Baring and Brothers, Howland and Aspinwall of New York, and Corcoran and Riggs of Washington) to make payment of the last installment of the $15-million indemnity to Mexico under the Treaty of Guadalupe Hidalgo. When the appropriation bill was before the House of Representatives, Charles Allen, the Worcester free-soiler, charged that Webster was under obligation to these houses, that he was "a servant and stipendiary of bankers and brokers," and that he had, in fact, agreed to become secretary of state only on the condition that his wealthy friends raise a purse to supplement his salary. Allen had tilted with Webster before. The fact that he was a lame duck, defeated in the last election and serving his last week in the House, may help to account for the boldness and folly of a Massachusetts representative performing the office of an Ingersoll by accusing Godlike Daniel of venality and corruption. No sooner had Allen finished than George Ashmun arose to denounce the attack as despicable. Allen called for an investigation, but such was the disgust of the House that it declined even to entertain a motion on the subject.[11] That a fund had, again, been raised for Webster was not denied. Allen said it came to $45,000 split between Boston and New York. This was fairly accurate at least as to the goal, though evidence suggests that some of the subscribers failed to meet their pledges and the fund fell short of the goal.[12] The main issue was whether or not Webster had made the fund a condition precedent to his becoming secretary of state. His Boston banking friend, Franklin Haven, supposedly could testify to this, but Haven flatly denied ever receiving any such instructions from Webster; and there is no hard evidence to support the allegation. The secretary's ties to bankers were notorious, but no venal purpose could be found in his choice of the three houses for the indemnity business. (The case of Corcoran and Riggs is intriguing, however. William W. Corcoran wrote off Webster's debt to him, amounting to approximately $10,000, after the 7th of March speech.)[13] Private pecuniary support for a high government official was certainly not the common practice in Webster's day—at least not in the United States—but it was accepted in his case as a necessary price for eminent service. He had been earning up to $17,000 a year in his law practice; he would have to surrender most of that income to serve as secretary of state at an annual salary of $6,000. The annuity would simply help lessen the loss. Besides, it was said, since the benefactors were unknown to him, he could not use his office to their benefit.[14]

In promoting the Compromise of 1850, appearing at Union rallies and on other patriotic platforms, Webster sometimes felt that the existing party alignments made no sense and that the system should be remodeled along the lines of a Union party, consisting of all those, Democrats as well as Whigs, who had acted together in the great crisis, and an opposition party. As opportunities arose, he used the government's patronage to further Unionist objectives. The Bay State was a special problem for him. His political base had been eroding for several years. Among the Cotton Whigs, Abbott Lawrence was the dominant power, and Taylor's appointments had gone to his followers, with Lawrence himself becoming Minister to Great Britain. The anti-slavery element blamed Webster for the Fugitive Slave Law and rejected his position on the finality of the compromise. Weakened by division and dissension, the Whigs suffered defeat in the fall election. When the legislature convened in the new year, Democrats and Free Soilers coalesced and divided the political plums between them, the former getting the governorship, the latter the senate seat held on interim appointment by Winthrop. The ultimate election, after countless ballots, of Charles Sumner, brilliant, arrogant, contemptuous of Webster and compromise, was the crowning insult.[15]

Webster fought with the Bay State over the enforcement of the Fugitive Slave Law. The law was not as he would have preferred it; but it was the law, it was constitutional, and survival of the Union depended on its enforcement. "No man is at liberty to set up, or affect to set up, his own conscience as above the law, in a matter which respects the rights of others, and the obligations, civil, social, and political due to others from him. Such a pretense saps the foundation of all government," Webster wrote in a public letter.[16] Yet the act of 1850 was peculiarly objectionable. Owners might capture escaped slaves without legal warrant, which seemed to condone kidnaping; the act provided for a new class of officers, "commissioners," to assist the federal courts in hearing cases; if their decision favored the owners, commissioners received a fee of $10, if the fugitive, $5; fugitives could not testify in their own behalf, nor could such processes as *habeas corpus* be used to block rendition; obstruction of the law was punishable by a fine of $1,000 and six months imprisonment.[17] In the eyes of abolitionists, along with other believers in a higher law than the Constitution, the statute was diabolical and should be resisted. They disagreed with Webster's premises that the Union was in danger, that agitation should be stilled on the most important question of the day, that there ever was or could be a final settlement that left over three million people in slavery. To the old catechism, "What is the chief end of man?" Webster returned, not "To glorify God and enjoy him forever," but "To save the Union."[18] Black Dan was a moral insect to these abolitionists, and they swatted him mercilessly.*

This was more than a battle of words, more than a theoretical debate; it revolved around a series of fugitive slave cases in the "Cradle of Liberty." The Vigilance Committee, led by Theodore Parker, vowed that no fugitive would be returned from Boston. The first case, that of William and Ellen Craft, fugitives from Georgia, came to a head in November when Webster was in the city. He prevailed upon a reluctant federal marshal to haul them before a commissioner, but before the marshal could act the Crafts' protectors smuggled them aboard a ship bound for England. In February 1851, William Wilkins, known as Shadrach, was arrested on a warrant issued by a commissioner, George Ticknor Curtis, who was Webster's lawyer and friend during his last years. Dana sought a writ of *habeas corpus* from Chief Justice Lemuel Shaw. Refusing the writ, Shaw thereby sustained the constitutionality of the law. The hearing went forward. When Curtis allowed a delay, and Shadrach was being escorted from the courtroom, he was forcibly seized by several black men and at once carried off to Canada. Parker called the rescue "the noblest deed done in Boston since the destruction of the tea in 1773." Webster was furious. He declared the resistance and rescue, "strictly speaking, a case of treason," for forceful resistance to law was equivalent to levying arms against the country.[20] Upon hearing the news from Boston, Clay broke silence, denounced the outrage—doubly outrageous because the rescue was accomplished by a Negro mob—and called on the president for a full report. Fillmore promptly issued a proclamation, drafted by Webster, demanding prosecution of the offenders. An unwilling district attorney finally indicted eight men, three of whom were eventually tried but none convicted.[21] The Thomas Sims case occurred in April. Again Webster was in Boston, and he kept close watch over it. Again Shaw denied the petition for *habeas corpus*, affirming the law's constitutionality in a full-dress opinion. Abolitionists rallied on the Common and plotted another rescue. On the eleventh Curtis remanded Sims to the custody of the agent and in the dark hours of the next morning he was spirited away to Georgia on the brig *Acorn*.[22]

Two or three days later the Board of Aldermen of the city denied the use of Faneuil Hall to a committee of citizens who wished to offer Webster a public reception. The board had earlier rejected an abolitionist request to use the fa-

---

*Richard Henry Dana, Jr., cleverly parodied Webster's expounding on the Fugitive Slave Law and the Constitution by imagining him at Faneuil Hall expounding on the "Law of Gravitation": "I am for Gravitation! (Applause) I have always been for Gravitation! (Renewed applause) I always shall be for Gravitation! Under the law of Gravitation was I born, under the law of Gravitation have I lived, and by Divine permission, and leave of certain of our fanatical friends, I expect to die and be buried under the law of Gravitation. (Great sensation) No small portion of my life has been devoted . . . to the expounding of this law. . . ."[19]

mous hall for an address by Wendell Phillips, and alluding to "the excited state of the public mind," treated the request for a Webster meeting in the same fashion. Webster's friends, like Rufus Choate, who had agreed to make the welcoming address, were ashamed and indignant, not only because God-like Daniel was placed on the same level with Phillips but because of the sup-pression of free debate in Boston. Webster, too, was indignant and said so publicly. The Common Council, the other branch of the city government, quickly, unanimously, and apologetically overruled the aldermen and ex-tended an invitation to Webster to meet with them in the hall. He refused with a grand gesture, declaring, "Nor shall I enter Faneuil Hall, till its gates shall be thrown open, wide open, not 'with impetuous recoil—grating harsh thunder,' but with 'harmonious sound, on golden hinges moving,' to let in freely and overflowing, you and your fellow-citizens, and all men, of all par-ties, who are true to the Union as well as to liberty."[23]* On the morning of the twenty-second, before departing for New York, a large crowd in Bow-doin Square called him out of his hotel, the Revere House. In a brief ad-dress, he declaimed his theme: "Union! Union! Union! Now and forever."[24]

In May Webster accompanied the president on a five-hundred-mile tour over the track of the newly completed Erie Railroad in the state of New York. Having just recovered from a bout with dysentery, he dreaded the journey. "I see four elements of distress in it: 1. Heat. 2. Crowds. 3. Limestone water. 4. The necessity of speech-making." The last was worst of all, for he felt he had exhausted his opinions and "all that remains in my mind is as 'dry as a re-mainder biscuit, after a voyage.' "[25] Most of the speaking occurred on the re-turn voyage, after Webster left the presidential party in Buffalo. In that city, addressing a great audience standing in a drenching rain, Webster defended his course in the prolonged controversy over slavery and blamed the ordeal through which the country had passed upon the mistakes of others—slave-holders, expansionists, abolitionists, and free-soilers. He used the metaphor of a "house divided," which Lincoln would employ with telling effect in 1858, to point up the necessity for accommodation and compromise to preserve the Union. How much easier it would have been for him, a northern man, to have stood on the Wilmot Proviso and turned his back on the South! But be-lieving that posture must lead to civil war, he had stood on the Constitution and the Union.[26] At Syracuse, "that laboratory of abolitionism, libel, and trea-son," in his private opinion, Webster spoke in defense of the Fugitive Slave Law. Political duties, such as those arising from the Constitution, are no less matters of conscience than duties arising out of domestic relations. "It is trea-son, *treason*, TREASON, and nothing else," to interfere with the enforce-ment of the law, and culprits should incur the penalties of treason.[27] At Al-bany he repeated these views, compared the "higher law" fanatics to the Fifth Monarchy men of Cromwell's time, and declared solemnly, "I yet be-

*Heaven open'd wide
Her ever-enduring gates, harmonious sound
On golden hinges moving.
(*Paradise Lost*, bk. VII, 1. 205)

lieve firmly that this Union, once broken, is utterly incapable, according to all human experience, of being reconstituted in its original character, of being re-cemented by any chemistry, or art, or effort, or skill of man."[28]

What Webster said in New York he also said in Virginia. At the end of June he went with Caroline to Capon Spring, near Winchester, for rest and relaxation. The local citizenry insisted on a reception, a dinner, and a speech, and Webster obliged. To preserve the Constitution, he said, it must be preserved in all its parts. When different parties enter into a compact, none may disregard one provision and expect the others to observe the rest. So it was with the Fugitive Slave Law. "A bargain cannot be broken on one side and still bind the other side." And to immense cheering, the Yankee Demosthenes declared, "I am as ready to fight and fall for the constitutional rights of Virginia as I am for those of Massachusetts. . . . I would no more see a feather plucked unjustly from the honor of Virginia than I would see one so plucked from the honor of Massachusetts."[29] In some quarters the speech was read as yielding to the South the theory of the Union as a compact of sovereign states with the correlative right of secession. Everett told Webster he could not say in the authorized edition of the speech what the newspapers reported him as saying. Webster concurred, and directed his secretary to make appropriate revisions; yet the speech was published in Washington as delivered with the addition of only an explanatory note. When a North Carolinian read Calhoun's theory between the lines of the speech, and wrote Webster about it, he denied any change of opinion on the Constitution or the right of secession. A constitution that was repeatedly and flagrantly violated might be dissolved, but only by revolution. There was no secession apart from revolution.[30] The letter was immediately published. In the years ahead, however, and long after Appomattox, defenders of the Confederacy maintained that at Capon Springs, Daniel Webster, the Defender of the Constitution, admitted all that the South ever claimed and conceded the right of secession.[31]

The ulterior motive of all this speech making was election to the presidency. Despite the handicaps of age and illness, Webster still hoped to realize his highest ambition. Before the New York trip he huddled with Curtis and other advisers in the city, who were joined by Haven, Harvey, and Fletcher Webster from Boston. After his return the Boston group, which included Everett and Choate, set things in motion for an independent Unionist nomination. The decision to go that route registered, on the one hand, the opinion of Webster's weakness among Bay State Whigs and, on the other hand, the confidence that the different political fragments that had coalesced on the Compromise of 1850 would continue to cohere with a presidential aspirant like Webster. In June the Webster Central Committee started a petition campaign and invited the election of delegates to a state convention for the purpose of nominating him.[32] The only declared Whig candidate was General Scott. Although one of the tiredest political horses in the stable, he was being groomed for still another race by Weed and Seward, this time as the northern anti-compromise candidate. Clay, at last, knew he was finished politically. Webster took comfort in that and expected to inherit much of

Clay's following. His anxieties centered on Fillmore. He liked the president and thought well of his performance. They occupied the same position before the country. Fillmore was silent about his intentions, but Webster supposed he was a candidate. Fillmore could not, under any circumstances, allow Weed and Seward to determine his successor; and he had gained a considerable following, especially among southern Whigs. Webster set his own course without consulting Fillmore. Friends who did consult him gave Webster reason to believe "the coast will be clear."[33] In Boston, on November 25, a convention of delegates from across the state nominated Webster for the presidency. Two weeks earlier the Whig party had scored a narrow victory in the state election; however, it was not large enough to break the bastard coalition or to elect their candidate—Winthrop—governor. The result seemed to vindicate Webster's independent course.[34]

In Kentucky that fall, Clay, after some hesitation, decided to return to Washington for the Thirty-Second Congress. He had come home the previous spring by way of Havana, hoping to be revived by the sun and the sea. The relief, such as it was, passed quickly. He had a case pending before the Supreme Court, which carried a handsome contingent fee, and he wanted to win it. He was also reluctant to force a second senatorial election on the General Assembly. Since the constitutional convention of 1849, the Whigs had been sharply divided, in part over slavery issues; and between the dominant leaders, Archibald Dixon and John J. Crittenden, there was no peace. In the August election of 1851 the party lost the governorship and got only an even split in the congressional races. Whigs lost the Ashland district for the first time in memory. Many voters seemed to think that the Democratic candidate, young John C. Breckinridge, was Prince Hal's annointed successor, and he trounced his opponent, old Leslie Combs. The Whigs retained control of the legislature; nevertheless, the two factions fought to a draw on the choice of a successor to Joseph R. Underwood and finally had to agree on a compromise candidate.[35] Clay stayed out of the fight, though his sentiments lay with Crittenden. In the fall he received a letter signed by five hundred New Yorkers inviting him to come east and speak for the Compromise, the Constitution, and the Union. He was asked to do what Webster had been doing for many months. But his health would not even permit him to entertain the idea. He replied in a long letter, which was, as Carl Schurz said, "his last appeal to the American people." Thirteen months after the passage of the Compromise, Clay expressed confidence that it might yet become the final settlement he had hoped for. But he lectured the North on violations of the Fugitive Slave Law, believing they must foment disunion; and he lectured the South at length on the absurdity and the criminality of "peaceable secession." Any attempt to practice that idea ought to be "put down at every hazard," Clay declared sternly.[36]

In December Clay again took up residence in the National Hotel. He answered the roll call of the Senate but never again appeared alive in the Capitol. Two weeks later he sent to Kentucky his resignation effective nine months hence. Horace Greeley, who called about this time, was shocked at his condition. Although his mind was "unclouded and brilliant as ever," Clay was "already emaciated, a prey to a severe and distressing cough, and [he] complained of spells of difficult breathing." No physician, the editor thought, would give him two months to live.[37] He was experiencing the last stages of consumption, though no one uttered the dread word. Everybody called on Clay. He had outlived malice and ambition, envy and calumny; and he wished to die at peace with all men.

One of his callers early in the new year was Louis Kossuth, the Hungarian patriot who came to the United States in search of support for the freedom and independence of his homeland. Webster, whose Hülsemann Letter had raised Kossuth's hopes, was now faced with containing them. "I shall make him no speeches," Webster said. But he did. When the charismatic revolutionist came to Washington a number of congressmen gave him a public dinner at which Webster spoke. He chose his words carefully, but took nothing back.[38] Two days later, on January 9, attended by Cass and several others, Kossuth called on Clay. From a man known the world over as the first North American champion of South American independence, the Magyar revolutionist might have expected more than sympathy. But Clay protested the policy of soliciting material aid in the United States and, in a voice still trumpet-toned, read Kossuth a little lecture on American principles of non-interference in European affairs. The recent *coup d'etat* of Louis Napoleon taught the American people the desperation of liberal institutions abroad and the first duty of preserving them at home, he said. "Far better is it for ourselves, for Hungary, and for the cause of Liberty, that, adhering to our wise, pacific system, and avoiding the distant wars of Europe, we should keep our lamp burning bright on this western shore as the light of all nations, than to hazard its utter extinction amid the ruins of fallen or falling republics in Europe." Kossuth demurred, and in the melancholy cadences of the stricken children of freedom pled his cause. On departing, Clay grasped the patriot's hand, saying, "God bless you and your family! God bless your country—may she yet be free!"[39] It was a stirring moment made the more memorable as the statesman's last counsel.

Visitors to Clay's sick chamber brought with them the excitements of the presidential election and, of course, tried to draw him into it. In March he put an end to speculation by endorsing Fillmore for the Whig nomination. Webster was hurt and disappointed. Even from his deathbed, it seemed, the Kentuckian could not resist the opportunity to stab at him. But Clay was beyond malice in 1852. He supported Fillmore for the same reasons Webster would have supported him had he not been a candidate, because Fillmore was a Unionist who had been faithful to the Compromise of 1850 and because he had substantial support in both the North and the South. With the approach of the nominating conventions, it became evident that the bonds of party, while fractured and bruised, were still firm and that the Unionist movement had shriveled away. Recognizing this, Webster and his friends dropped the Unionist strategy and sought the Whig nomination in conventional fashion.[40] His prospects were poor in any event. The southern Whigs, who were necessary for his nomination, were rallying to Fillmore. Despite a major effort in New York, Scott was ascendant there. In New England, Massachusetts was safe, and so probably were Connecticut, Rhode Island, and New Hampshire.

While on a visit to Marshfield in May, the carriage in which Webster was riding overturned, pitching him headlong to the ground. He escaped serious injury, or so it seemed; but the accident was a shock to his whole system and the sprains and bruises to his arms and shoulders caused him much pain. It was in this condition that he addressed the Boston citizenry at Faneuil Hall on May 25. He had been invited by the council and the aldermen, still anxious to rectify the error of the previous spring. Choate, on introducing him, exulted that the gates of the famous hall had been thrown open, as Webster had demanded. "Aye, and on golden hinges turning!" The speech was memorable for the occasion—Webster's last appearance in Faneuil Hall—rather than for its contents. Abstaining from political questions, he rambled incoherently through a variety of topics connected with Boston and liberty. One unfriendly auditor thought it "a melancholy spectacle," doubted that an eighth part of the speech was understood, and suspected that Webster, if not drunk, was "half paralyzed."[41] A new six-volume edition of Webster's *Works* had just been published in Boston. Prefaced by an elegant biography composed by Everett, who had also generously edited and supervised the work during the previous eighteen months, it was a summation of the statesman's life that he could happily leave to posterity.

The Whig convention met at Baltimore on June 16. Two weeks earlier, in the same place, the Democrats had nominated Franklin Pierce of New Hampshire for president on a platform that accepted the finality of the Compromise of 1850. The Whigs, too, adopted this so-called "southern platform," which was also the Webster and Fillmore platform, opposed by the Scott forces. On the first ballot the delegates cast 131 votes for Scott, 133 for Fillmore, and 29 for Webster. Scott's strength was in the Middle Atlantic and the West, Fillmore's in the South, Webster's in New England. Obviously, Webster's vote added to Fillmore's would have given the president more than the majority, 147, needed to nominate. Through forty-six ballots in two days, Webster's vote never rose above 32, and the Fillmore and Scott totals fluctuated little. "My friends will stand firm," Webster telegraphed the convention. "Let the South answer for the consequences. Remember the 7th of March."[42] Southern Whig leaders, who were friendly to Webster but pledged to Fillmore, made an offer to the New Englander's managers. They had ascertained that if Fillmore was given up, up to 106 of his votes would go to Webster. So if Webster could produce 41 votes on his own account—more than his best ballot—the South would undertake to nominate him. Reportedly the effort was made, but to no avail.[43] At 9:00 A.M. on Monday morning, June 21, Webster dispatched instructions to throw his votes to Fillmore. He informed the president immediately, who, in turn, told Webster he had asked that his nomination be withdrawn. As it turned out, neither the Fillmore nor the Webster managers heeded the instructions. Webster's wish that Fillmore be nominated was subverted. And Scott was victorious on the fifty-third ballot.[44] Late that night in Washington boisterous Whigs serenaded Webster at his Louisiana Avenue home. Called out in his dressing gown, he said enough to show he was heartbroken. Never alluding to General Scott, he spoke of the glittering stars and said he would rise in the morning, as always, with the song of the lark. Retiring, some of the revelers felt they had heard a funeral sermon.[45] Webster was, in truth, mortified by the Baltimore nomination, and blamed it on the infidelity of the southern Whigs and the folly of Fillmore and his supporters. Regrettably, it "wrote a false chapter in the history of the country."[46]

Henry Clay lay on his deathbed at the National Hotel. When spring came he had hoped to go home and die in the arms of his dear wife but by then he was too feeble to travel, and Lucretia herself was not well enough to go to him. When in the first week of May his case was given up as hopeless, Clay's son Thomas came to his bedside and with the servant, James, stayed with him to the end. The end came quietly, June 29, at 11:17 A.M.[47] The news was heard in Congress as soon as it assembled, and both houses adjourned. The next day was filled with eulogies by senators and representatives. Young and old, Whigs and Democrats, northerners and southerners lauded the Prince of the Senate, recalling his bold and gallant character, his oratorical genius, his services and patriotism. The best of these eulogies was Seward's. He identified Clay not with conservatism but with conservation. "Conservation was the interest of the nation, and the responsibility of its rulers, during the period in which he flourished." Clay made himself into a "tribune of the people," yet gave strength and organization to the national government. No statesman since the Revolution was more impartial between conflicting interests and sections, said Seward. As a result of his work, "The Union exists in absolute integrity, and the Republican system is in complete and triumphant development."[48] Several of the eulogists spoke of "that great triumvirate" that had magnetized the age, of whom now only one survived. The next morning the richly mounted mahogany coffin bearing Clay's remains was drawn by gray horses in a funeral procession up Pennsylvania Avenue to the Capitol. In the packed Senate chamber the Reverend C. M. Butler, who had administered holy communion to Clay before his death, delivered the funeral sermon. Among all the sad faces observed during the ceremony, Frank Blair thought the saddest was worn by Daniel Webster.[49] The ceremony concluded, the coffin was carried to the Rotunda of the Capitol, where Clay lay in state for twenty-four hours. He was the first American accorded that honor.

Clay had expressed the wish to be buried in Lexington. To take him there, the committee of senators decided, with the family's approval, to travel a roundabout twelve-hundred-mile route in what has accurately been called "the greatest display of funeral pageantry the country had ever known."[50] On July 2 the black-draped funeral train left Washington, stopped at Baltimore, and arrived at Philadelphia that evening, where Clay's body was borne in a torchlight procession to Independence Hall to lie in state until the next morning. The steamboat *Trenton* carried the coffin and the six attending senators to

New York City. The elaborately canopied coffin was drawn by eight white horses up Broadway through crowds and between buildings decórated with emblems and inscriptions—that Astor House was shrouded in black bombazine from cornice to sidewalk—to its resting place in City Hall. There twenty thousand mourners paid last respects to Clay on Sunday, July 4.[51] The cortege continued up the Hudson River to Albany, thence on the Erie Railroad to Buffalo, thence to Cleveland, Cincinnati, and Louisville, finally arriving in Lexington at dusk on July 9. In towns and cities all along the route bells tolled, guns fired, flags waved, and shops closed as the body of Prince Hal passed before crowds of silent spectators. As the bell of the mail boat that carried him down the Ohio River reverberated through the woods and villages, people hurried to the banks and waved. At Rising Sun two hundred young women dressed in white with flags in their hands lined the river bank.[52]

After the funeral in Lexington on July 10, Clay was laid to rest in a cemetery plot he had chosen. Sometime later John J. Crittenden, at Louisville, delivered one of the more memorable eulogies. The two old friends had been fully reconciled before Clay's death; indeed, it was publicly reported, although denied by Thomas, that from his deathbed Clay had acknowledged his injustice to Crittenden in 1848.[53] The orator reviewed Clay's long career, lauded him as Kentucky's favorite son, and said the great object of his life was the Union and the Constitution. Of more interest was Abraham Lincoln's eulogy at the Illinois State House in Springfield. Throughout a public life of fifty years, Lincoln said, Clay had been "the most loved, and the most implicitly followed by friends, and the most dreaded by opponents, of all living American politicians"; there had never been a moment from 1824 to 1848 when "a very large portion of the American people did not cling to him with an enthusiastic hope and purpose of still elevating him to the Presidency." "With other men, to be defeated, was to be forgotten; but to him, defeat was but a trifling incident . . . ," Lincoln continued. "The spell—the long-enduring spell—with which the souls of men were bound to him is a miracle." While Crittenden, like most eulogists, placed the Union highest in Clay's political affections, Lincoln gave first place to human liberty. And so he was led to discuss Clay's position on slavery, which damned him to hell in the opinion of abolitionists. Clay did not perceive, nor had any man yet had the wisdom to perceive, how slavery could be at once eradicated without producing a greater evil, the dissolution of the Union, even to the cause of liberty itself. So he opposed both extremes, abolitionism and pro-slavery disunionism. The program of the American Colonization Society, Clay believed, made possible the ultimate redemption not only of the African race but of the African continent. Lincoln agreed with him. In concluding, he prayed that Clay's glorious dream of "restoring a captive people to their long lost father-land" might be realized. It would be the capstone of his works for human liberty.[54]

Clay's will provided for the gradual emancipation and colonization of the children born to his slaves, who numbered thirty-five, after January 1, 1850, basically on the same plan he had proposed to Kentucky. The post-nati would be liberated, males at eighteen, females at twenty-five, and after the earnings of three years' labor, colonized in Liberia. The plan was a testament of faith not only in the colonization scheme but in the survival of the Union. It would, of course, be superseded by the Thirteenth Amendment of the Constitution. Clay left an estate of about $100,000 unencumbered and in good order, according to his executor. Ashland remained in the family, the home of James B. Clay, while Lucretia lived with her youngest son, John, on an adjacent farm until her death in 1864. Friends at once began a campaign to raise a colossal monument to Clay in Lexington. The Clay Monument Association was formed. After reviewing a number of designs, it chose that of a 120-foot column with a Corinthian capital surmounted by a 12½-foot statue of the statesman. It would be completed in 1861. Several years later Clay's remains were transferred to the sarcophagus at the foot of the monument. Tom Marshall, who may have understood the Kentucky statesman as well as anyone, thought the monument honorable but quite useless to his fame: "They may lay their pedestals of granite—they may rear their polished columns till they pierce and flaunt the skies—they may cover their marble pillars all over with the blazoning of his deeds, the trophies of his triumphant genius, and surmount them with images of his form wrought by the cunningest hands—it matters not—he is not there. The pinion'd eagle has burst the bars. . . . He is not dead—he lives. . . . He needs no statue—he desired none. . . . He carved his own statue, he built his own monument."[55]

While Clay was on his last journey to the Bluegrass State, a living but sick and despondent Webster returned to Boston. Before leaving he came to the point of resigning; the president, anxious to please him, offered him the British ministry. Webster later told Everett he declined, first, because the post was beneath his station, and second, because of the probability of an early recall, since he supposed Pierce would be elected president. Other evidence suggests that Webster wanted the appointment and passed it up because of Caroline's opposition.[56] Boston still loved Webster and gave him a great parade and festive party on the Common on a hot Friday afternoon. Webster's speech was a paean to the history of Massachusetts.[57] He went off to Franklin for what proved to be his last gaze upon the peaceful meadows of Elms Farm. He got a hearty welcome from his Marshfield neighbors near the end of July and turned his mind to literary projects, but was unexpectedly called back to Washington on official business. Early in September, suffering from diarrhea as well as the summer catarrh, he went home to Marshfield to die.

During these months Webster firmly refused to endorse Scott. Whigs throughout Massachusetts held "rejection meetings"—rejection of the Baltimore nomination—and a movement was started to nominate Webster on a "Union Whig" ticket. In the close circle of friends and advisers, only George Curtis encouraged and endorsed this movement. It made no headway outside the Bay State. Curtis hoped to arouse the southern Whigs, many of whom would not vote for Scott. But Curtis had no following—his reputation had been shaded by association with the Fugitive Slave Law—and from all sides Webster heard that the movement was unworthy of his fame. He offered it no support. Yet he turned back urgent requests to issue a statement discountenancing the movement. Dictating a letter to Moses Grinnell and other New York friends, he said that no earthly consideration could induce him to do anything that might even remotely suggest concurrence in the Baltimore nomination.[58]

The last days of Daniel Webster offered a spectacle of death as eloquent and sublime as his life. A man's death ought to epitomize his life. "The bed of death brings every human being to his pure individuality," he had himself said in eulogy of another. And so when his time came he made his own deathbed as deliberately and solemnly as if it were a public occasion.[59] His sickness worsened. Medicine, opiates primarily, when he was strong enough to take them, lost their effect. On September 20 he went to Boston to see the eminent Dr. John Jeffries, who offered no encouragement. A dinner for Thomas Baring, then on a visit to the United States, took place that day. Webster could not sit through it, but he made an appearance during the dessert course. "If a ghost had come among us, it could hardly have startled us more," Ticknor wrote. "He looked dreadfully, but he had his usual stately air and bearing."[60] For the next three weeks, while his condition steadily deteriorated, Webster maintained a curtailed schedule at Marshfield. Every morning he gave orders to the manager, Porter Wright, and attired in his rough blue overcoat and slouch hat, rode over his domain, often stopping to talk with his neighbors. He continued to entertain guests, presiding at dinner, conversing in his usual animated fashion, while confining himself to a diet of milk and lime-water, thin gruel, and diluted brandy. On October 10 Webster dictated to Ned Curtis a declaration of Christian faith for inscription on his tombstone. The Psalms, Watts's hymns, the verses of Milton were often on his tongue. On the eighteenth he consulted with George Curtis about his will. His estate was encumbered by debt, of course; in the final reckoning liabilities would exceed assets by approximately $100,000. Webster could do nothing about this; he was anxious, however, to preserve Marshfield in his blood and name, that is to bequeath it to Fletcher. The difficulty was that Caroline's marriage settlement gave her claim to the property. He proposed a cash settlement of her claim, suggesting that the subscribers to his annuity be asked to transfer it to her. Curtis went to Boston to arrange this and it was done to everyone's satisfaction.[61]

On the twenty-first Webster suffered an abrupt decline. Postmortem examination would disclose that he died of complications arising from a diseased liver, probably abetted by injury to the brain caused by the carriage accident. The latter was not evident—Webster's mind was clear to the end—but in a short time, had he lived, it would have caused decay of his mental faculties.[62] Often at his bedside, in addition to members of his immediate family, were Dr. Jeffries, both the Curtises, Peter Harvey, George Abbot, his relatives Mr. and Mrs. Paige, Caroline's brother, and of course his house servants. On the twenty-third, propped up in bed, Webster signed his will, then entered into a little sermon on the gospel of Jesus Christ. When evening came he called the entire household into his chamber and took leave of them one by one. He had, George Curtis observed, "an intense desire for a consciousness of the act of dying." The imposing scene would be captured, though not with strict fidelity, in Joseph Ames's spectacular painting, *The Last Days of Webster*. Falling in and out of sleep, scarcely knowing whether he was alive or dead, his mind wandering over literary passages but faintly remembered, Webster called out, "Poet, poetry; Gray, Gray." Fletcher picked it up, repeating the opening lines of Gray's *Elegy*, "The curfew tolls the knell of parting day," to which the dying man exclaimed, "That's it! That's it!" The book was brought and the poem read to him. So, in similar fashion, was the Twenty-third Psalm. Sometime after midnight, he burst out, "I still live!" But Webster died at 2:37 A.M., Sunday, October 24.[63]

The news reached Boston on a fine Sabbath morning. People awakened to the tolling of bells and the firing of guns and poured into the streets. Tributes to Godlike Daniel rang out from the pulpits. Robert Winthrop said he could have cried all day long. "Oh, what a man he might have been!" Winthrop sighed. "Yet let us not do injustice, or forget, what a man he was! Mighty in intellect, majestic in form, untiring in energy—the impress of greatness was upon him all over."[64] Emerson, who was on the beach at Plymouth, wrote in his *Journal:* "The sea, the rocks, the woods, gave no sign that America and the world had lost the completest man. Nature had not in our days, or not since Napoleon, cut out such a masterpiece."[65] At noon on Wednesday Boston held a memorial service in Faneuil Hall. The windows were darkened and the lamps lighted. Three thousand people came, yet not a sound was heard except the voices of the speakers, the sobs of the mourners, and the moaning "aye" to the resolutions offered by Everett for an appropriate monument. On the wall behind the podium hung G. P. A. Healy's grand picture of the Reply to Hayne, only recently installed and yet to be purchased by the city. George S. Hillard, one of the speakers, said "everyone looked as if he had been at the funeral of his own father." Boston's imposing funeral rites for the departed statesman did not occur until November 30.[66]

Webster was buried at Marshfield on the Friday after his death. It was a delicious hazy Indian Summer day. Marshfield was an out-of-the-way place, yet ten to twelve thousand people converged upon it for Webster's funeral. Classes were dismissed at Harvard and many students attended. In Boston hundreds boarded the Old Colony Railroad for Cohasset or Kingston, where it was necessary to transfer to a carriage for a drive of either fifteen or seven miles. Coaches, chaises, and wagons came by every crossroads until they formed a regular procession. "On looking over the country from the hill top [before the Webster place], they covered the land like grasshoppers," wrote Dana, who found little abolitionist company at the funeral.[67] Hillard, one of the mourners, wrote a touching account to his friend, Francis Lieber, in South Carolina: "The body was on a sort of bier or case, entirely exposed to view from head to foot, and draped as when alive in a blue coat and white trousers. It lay under an aspen whose yellow leaves trembled as if stirred with grief." Except for the crowd, it was a simple New England funeral, without display or ceremony. This was in accordance with the deceased's wishes.

He asked to be buried as the Farmer of Marshfield. "My heart swelled," Hillard wrote, "when I saw the eminent men all passed by and six plain men of Marshfield called out to be pall-bearers. Was that not beautiful?" The long file proceeded on foot a mile and a half to the family cemetery. After a prayer the body was laid to rest in Pilgrim earth.[68]

The following Sunday Theodore Parker, the Unitarian clergyman, reformer, and abolitionist, delivered a "Discourse on Webster" at the Melodeon, the Boston music hall where he had made his church. It was a tour de force. For three hours the congregation sat mesmerized by the preacher. At the outset, he evoked Godlike Daniel. Webster *was* a great man. He had impressed his massive intellect upon the nation. In New England he was an institution. His majestic brow was part of the natural landscape, like the great granite face in the New Hampshire mountains whence he came. Parker, like every other good Yankee, grew up honoring and loving him. He spoke affectionately of Webster's boyhood and youth. He recalled his early triumphs at the bar, on the platform, and in Congress, culminating in the Reply to Hayne. But as Parker turned the pages of his manuscript, it became apparent that he was weaving the web of an epic tragedy, of a fallen angel, like Whittier's *Ichabod;* and many in the congregation gasped. He spoke disparagingly of Webster as a legislator: "He looked only at the fleeting interest of his constituents, and took their transient opinions of the hour for his norm of conduct." The preacher thought no better of him as a diplomat. The Ashburton Treaty was a bad bargain, and the *Creole* Letter was wicked—the first sign of the colossal wickedness to come. Parker had not changed his mind about the speech of the 7th of March. Why had Webster made it? "He wanted to be President. That was all of it." He sold himself to the South. "Think of him!" Parker thundered. "The Daniel Webster of Plymouth Rock advocating the 'Compromise Measures.' . . . Think of Daniel Webster become the assassin of Liberty in the Capitol! Think of him, full of the Old Testament and dear Isaac Watts, scoffing at the Higher Law of God, while the mountains of Virginia looked him in the face!" To what end? Thirty-two votes and the nomination of Scott at Baltimore. Like a Lucifer, he debauched the conscience of the nation. "Truth fell prostrate in the street . . . the court house has a tarnish on its walls . . . the steeples point awry, and the 'Higher Law' is hurled down from the pulpit." The fatal flaw was one of character, Parker said, and he dwelled at length on Webster's public and private vices. As a public man, he had no religion, no philanthropy, no intellectual imagination, no political skill. As a private man, he had many popular qualities. "He was a farmer, and took a countryman's delight in country things." But his vices were notorious. A victim of low appetites, with a hunger for sensual pleasures, he was a debauchee as well as a spendthrift and a pensioner of rich capitalists. In the end, he fell and he died because he was an apostate against the New England conscience. And what a fall it was, Parker concluded, "the saddest sight in the Western world."[69]

In Boston, certainly, Parker's sermon was a public scandal. *De mortuis nil nisi bonum* was the rule. The other pulpits that Sunday morning adhered to it even to the point of insipidity and dishonesty. The praise of Webster as a Christian statesman, which his deathbed had invited, was an example. It was, therefore, refreshing, if also shocking, to hear or read something as honest, eloquent, and instructive as Parker's discourse. Eighty thousand copies of the *Commonwealth*, the Free Soil newspaper, which printed it, were sold; and this was followed by a pamphlet edition. Dana, with the image of the majestic man in his coffin still in his mind, and his heart still swelling for him, nevertheless felt that Parker had contributed the keen piercing truth of poetry to Webster's fame. "Strange that the best commendation, that has appeared yet," he wrote a week later, "the most touching, elevated, meaning eulogy, with all its censure, should have come from Theodore Parker! Were I Daniel Webster," said Dana, "I would not have that sermon destroyed for all that had been said in my favor."[70] As Pope said of Cromwell, "he was damned to everlasting fame." In December the flood of eulogy passed over the Senate of the United States. Cass, Butler, Davis, and others eulogized Webster; but again it was Seward who provided the only moment of interest to the historian. According to Massachusetts Senator Sumner, Seward had hoped he " 'might be spared any such day of humiliation,' " yet he rose in the Senate to speak in Webster's memory, to Sumner's deep regret. Parker, too, protested Seward's eulogy, to which the New Yorker replied that, while he concurred in much of the preacher's judgment (though he had no knowledge of alleged private vices), he "could not consent after the death of the Lion to seem unwilling to be generous to his memory."[71]

The last of the eulogies of Webster was delivered by Rufus Choate at Dartmouth College in July 1853. It was this discourse, with its great pulsations of rhetoric and its Ciceronian periods, that filled out the legend of the Dartmouth College Case, which Webster himself had considered the cornerstone of his fame. In some sense, the discourse was an answer to Parker. Choate lauded Webster not so much for his specific services but for elevating the whole tone of public thought and discourse in America and for preserving the Union and establishing nationality against powerful forces of disintegration. As to the charge that he had violated principle and conscience on the 7th of March, 1850, Choate declared, "the noblest politics [is] but an aspiring, an approximation, a compromise, a type, a shadow of good to come 'the buying of great blessings at great prices.' "[72] It was the answer of conservative wisdom to all the true believers.

EPILOGUE

"How are the mighty fallen!" resounded like a dirge across the land in 1852. For it was not only Webster who has passed away, but the last of "our second race of giants," the last of "the great lights of our generation." "Calhoun is dead. Clay is dead. And now Webster is dead . . . ," wailed Daniel Barnard, the American minister to Prussia in a memorial service at Paris. "It is time to mourn and sit in sackcloth. The bride hath lost her husband; the children are fatherless." Who could replace the Great Triumvirate in the councils of the republic? For some forty years each had been a host unto himself, and together they had triangulated the destiny of the nation. They seemed at the close of their lives, as the London *Times* remarked of Clay, "to be invested with something of antique greatness, and to represent the spirit of a wiser and severer age," which they had received from the American founders. They had failed, however, and the institutions had failed, to perpetuate or reproduce that greatness of statesmanship. They were, indeed, the last of the giants.[1]

Their shadows fell over the passage of events leading to the Civil War. The Kansas-Nebraska Act of 1854 reopened the controversy over the extension of slavery. Concerned with organizing two territories in the Louisiana Purchase domain north of 36° 30′, and therefore previously assumed to be covered by the historic restriction, the act boldly repealed the Missouri Compromise and left the slavery question to the decision of the settlers themselves. Authored by Stephen A. Douglas, who fraudulently contended that the same principle had been embodied in the territorial bill of the Compromise of 1850, the act wiped out the middle and drove politicians to the extremes. It destroyed the Whig Party, it gave birth to the Republican party, and it led to a little civil war between pro-slavery and anti-slavery settlers in Kansas. Three years later, in the case of *Dred Scott* v. *Sandford*, the Supreme Court followed its own line of reasoning to the conclusions earlier reached by John C. Calhoun. Congress had no power to legislate for the territories, the Missouri Compromise restriction was unconstitutional, and slaveholders could not be denied the right to carry their property to the territories. The remorseless course of events thus kept the names of Calhoun, Clay, and Webster in the public consciousness.

On January 4, 1859, the Senate occupied its new chamber in the enlarged Capitol—the same chamber it occupies today. Vice President John C. Breckinridge, in an address on that occasion, summed up a thousand reminiscences of the old chamber in a dramatic evocation of Webster, Clay, and Calhoun:

> There sat Calhoun, *the* Senator, inflexible, austere, oppressed . . . a man whose unsparing intellect compelled all his emotions to harmonize with the deductions of his rigorous logic. . . .
>
> This, was Webster's seat. He, too, was every inch a Senator. Conscious of his own vast power, he reposed with confidence on himself. . . . Type of his northern home, he rises before the imagination, in the grand and granite outline of his form and intellect, like a great New England rock, repelling a New England wave. . . . As a senatorial orator, his great efforts are associated with this Chamber, whose very air seems yet to vibrate beneath the strokes of his deep tones and weighty words.
>
> On the outer circle, sat Henry Clay, with his impetuous and ardent nature untamed by age. . . . Illustrious man!—orator, patriot, philanthropist—whose light, at its meridian, was seen and felt in the remotest parts of the civilized world; and whose declining sun, as it hastened down the west, threw back its level beams, in hues of mellowed splendor, to illuminate and to cheer the land he loved and served so well.[2]

The Civil War was a judgment on each of the departed statesmen. For Clay it offered grim proof of the limits of compromise. That there were limits he knew very well; no senator in 1850 had been more emphatic about the consequences of passing them. But his system of politics had raised conciliation and compromise to the level of high principle, higher, indeed, where the Union was at issue, than a strict regard for moral duty or for self-interest. No one seriously believed that Clay, any more than Webster, would ever have given in to the idea that civil war was irrepressible. He would have fought for compromise to the bitter end. Predictably, in 1860 Kentucky was one of three states—Virginia and Tennessee were the others—to give its presidential vote to the Constitutional Union candidate, John Bell. But unlike Virginia and Tennessee, Kentucky stayed with the Union in 1861. Was it not symbolic that the first shots fired in the Civil War were fired in Charleston harbor upon a ship named *Star of the West*, which President Buchanan sent to provision Fort Sumter? Clay had declared, if secession and war came, he would stand with the Union. Many years later a southern historian of the war attributed Kentucky's adherence to the Union to the influence of "the peculiar philosophy of Henry Clay, who left an impress upon his State, which it remained for future generations to attest."[3]

With respect to Webster, the war demonstrated the fragility of law and constitutions before moral and social forces he never truly understood. The man regarded by many as his natural successor, Edward Everett, who, in fact, succeeded him as secretary of state and in 1853 was elected to the Senate, sacrificed himself on the altar of the Union Webster, more than anyone, had raised, finally ending his political career as Bell's running mate in 1860. Yet the appeal to arms in defense of the Union was a confirmation and vindication of Webster's lifework. Lincoln, in writing his first inaugural address, had but four references before him: the Constitution, Andrew Jackson's Proclamation against nullification, Clay's great speech on the Compromise of 1850, and Webster's Reply to Hayne. Every Union cannon was shotted with the Reply to Hayne, it would be said; and in subordinating slavery emancipation to preservation of the Union, Lincoln was a faithful disciple of Webster and Clay.[4]

The war levied an awful judgment on Calhoun. In 1861 he appeared the better prophet, for secession, the formation of the Confederate States of America, and the South's rush to arms seemed a realization, not of his hope, for his hope was always the Union, but of his political vision during the last years of his life. When South Carolina seceded following Lincoln's election, citizens of Charleston unfurled a large banner bearing a pronounced image of Calhoun. Northern newspapers traced secession to his doctrine and influence.[5] The Confederacy stamped Calhoun's portrait on its currency and its postage, yet found his political legacy of state rights and sovereign conventions a mixed blessing at best. The devastation of the war did not reach South Carolina until 1865. Sometime earlier, when there were fears of invasion in Charleston, Calhoun's mortal remains were exhumed from their grave in St. Philip's churchyard and removed to a place safe from Yankee despoliation.[6] Near the end of the war, Walt Whitman, who nursed the wounded in Union hospital tents in Washington, heard one soldier say to another that he had seen Calhoun's monument in Charleston. The other, a veteran of much fighting, responded, "I have seen Calhoun's monument. That you saw is not the real monument. But I have seen it. It is the desolated, ruined South; nearly the whole generation of young men between seventeen and thirty destroyed or maimed; all the old families used up; the rich impoverished; the plantations covered with weeds; the slaves unloosed and become the masters; and the name of Southerner blackened with every shame—all that is Calhoun's real monument."[7]

The price of the war was paid, in some part, by the dead statesmen's children and grandchildren. Calhoun's only surviving son, Andrew, after a failed attempt to raise a volunteer regiment, continued at Fort Hill caring for the family plantation until his death 1865. His son, John C. Calhoun, rose to the rank of captain in the Confederate army. The Clemsons returned to South Carolina as the war began; their son, Lieutenant John Calhoun Clemson, became a prisoner of war in Ohio in 1863. Both soldiers survived the war but had nothing but the ashes of defeat to return to at home. Fletcher Webster, the last of the children and the bearer of the family name, died in the service of the Union army. James B. Clay, who had served briefly in Congress as an Old Line Whig, was a Confederate at heart and followed General Braxton Bragg's army out of Kentucky after the Battle of Perryville in 1862. Failing to obtain a commission, Clay went into exile in Canada, where he acted as a Confederate agent. Two of Clay's grandsons died of typhoid, one in the blue uniform, one in the gray.

The Calhoun Monument Association, started by a group of women in Charleston in 1854, led the effort to erect a fitting monument to the southern statesman. The cornerstone for a great statue was dedicated in 1858. The war brought things to a halt. When Sherman's army was at Columbia in 1865, burning the capital city, and Charleston was threatened, the treasurer of the association, it was said, stitched $75,000 worth of securities into her skirt, thus to preserve the means of erecting the monument after the war. Finally, in 1887, thirty-seven years after the statesman's death, a heroic bronze statue was unveiled in Marion Square. Unfortunately no one liked it, and it was later replaced.[8] Calhoun's family scrounged to survive at Fort Hill. The statesman's library was sold for $250 to pay debts. Fort Hill itself was lost and put on the auction block in 1872. Happily, it was purchased by Thomas Green Clemson, who had the dream of turning the property into a school or college. Believing that the young men of South Carolina, he wrote, "can have no greater, and better model set before them . . . than John C. Calhoun, it has long been my hope and desire to connect his name with our regeneration, or indeed I may say with our resurrection." And he left the property upon his death in 1888 to the state as the foundation of a mechanical and agricultural college.

Almost alone Clemson sought to promote Calhoun's teachings and reputation in the years after the war. Crallé's six volumes had been "a dead loss," he confessed sadly in 1880, and no biography of Calhoun had appeared.[9] Two years later one came out in Boston. Written by the German-born historian of the United States, Hermann E. von Holst, the work portrayed Calhoun as a tragic figure, all his great moral and mental powers devoted to a doomed and detestable cause, one which deprived him of any claim on the gratitude of his country. Under the reigning canons of nationalist historiography, there was not much else to say. Clemson, of course, wished for a southern biography of a southern statesman. In 1876 he prevailed upon Robert M. T. Hunter to undertake the work. Hunter agreed reluctantly, and trunk loads of papers were shipped to Richmond. He completed the manuscript for a slim volume and offered it to a New York publisher, but it was declined; and there was neither money nor press to publish the work in the South. Hunter gave it up in 1883, and the project was placed in the hands of William Pinckney Starke, a cultivated Carolinian of mature years. He discarded Hunter's work and started over. Alas, Starke died after completing little more than a fragment.[10]

Clay, too, was unfortunate in the way his literary remains were handled. His literary executor and official biographer, Calvin Colton, was a journalist with a facile pen so devoted to Clay that he was incapable of writing anything about him but panegyric. Well known as a Whig publicist and tariff advocate, Colton was appointed to a chair in Public Economy at Trinity College, Hartford, in 1852, and gave most of the five years remaining to him to Clay and his works. He published a volume that carried the *Life and Times of Henry*

Clay through the last seven years of the statesman's life. He published a volume of Clay's correspondence; and finally, *The Works of Henry Clay* in six volumes. The latter, while useful, presented Clay to posterity without the literary refinements—the care to tone and nuance, the improvement of infelicitous phrasings, the weeding out of excessive Latinity—that Everett provided Webster. Clay's speeches, in any event, were a poor measure of his power, eloquence, and intellect. That could only be conveyed by a discriminating and authoritative biographer. Happily Clay found one in 1887 in Carl Schurz, the many-sided American statesman and man of letters. His two-volume *Henry Clay* was published in the same "American Statesman" series with Holst's *Calhoun* and Henry Cabot Lodge's *Webster*, both single volumes and neither remotely equal to the scholarship, intelligence, judgment, and balance of Schurz's work. It would not be surpassed for half a century. Because Clay was the most national figure of the age, monuments to him were not confined to a single state or section. Even before the Civil War, they were raised in Pottsville, Pennsylvania; Richmond, Virginia; and New Orleans, Louisiana. And by 1860, according to James Parton, he had given his name to forty-two towns and counties in the United States, more than any other member of his generation except Andrew Jackson.[11]

With literary executors like Everett, Ticknor, and Curtis, with a host of aspiring Boswells who had hung around him while alive, and under the guardianship of the literary capital of the nation, Webster was secure in his fame. Several volumes of a biographical nature, long on reminiscence and anecdote, appeared in the years soon after his death. The authoritative work, Curtis's two-volume biography, was published in 1870. The cloud of obloquy of the 7th of March still darkened Webster's fame. As late as 1882, the year of the Webster centennial, which was generously observed in New England, Lodge held that speech against him. But the cloud broke up in the increasingly nationalist and conservative intellectual climate of late nineteenth-century America. Even the poet Whittier modified his judgment. In "The Lost Occasion" he regretted that New England's Olympian statesman had not lived to see the victory of Union arms!

> Redeeming in one effort grand
> Thyself and thy imperiled land!

Charles Francis Adams, the son and namesake of the man for whom Webster was the sum of State Street wickedness, voiced the dominant Yankee opinion inextricably linking Webster's fame with the achievement of American nationhood. "It was the mission of Daniel Webster to preach nationality . . . ," said Adams at the end of the century. "The names of Stein, of Cavour, and of Bismarck are scarcely more associated with this great instinctive movement of the century than is that of Daniel Webster. His mission was to preach to this people Union, one and indivisible; and he delivered the message."[12] Two years before the Civil War, over opposition both moral and aesthetic, a statue of Webster sculpted by Hiram Powers was placed before the State House in Boston. Twenty-seven years later another statue would be placed before the New Hampshire State House in Concord, for he was still the Granite State's favorite son. And there would be other monuments, including a larger-than-life bronze in New York's Central Park. It was not altogether surprising that in the initial balloting for the Hall of Fame of Great Americans, established at New York University in 1901, Webster finished second, just after Washington and tied with Lincoln. Clay finished fifteenth, and Calhoun so far down that he failed of election.[13]

If this was, in fact, the public perception—and allowance should be made for a certain bias in the selection process—it was scarcely an accurate measure of the historical stature and importance of the three men. But each generation remakes the reputations of the nation's great men. And so it has been with the Great Triumvirate. In these pages there can be no reckoning of their fame in the twentieth century. Near the end of the century they remain fixed figures in the American pantheon, and, unlike any others, their names and fame are irrevocably intertwined.

NOTES

Abbreviations

DWP   *The Papers of Daniel Webster*, Charles M. Wiltse and others, eds. (Hanover, New Hampshire, 1974–), 8 vols. to date. Where the reference is to this edition, volume and page numbers are given. Other references are to the previous microfilm edition.

HCP   *The Papers of Henry Clay*, James F. Hopkins and others, eds. (Lexington, Ky, 1959–), 8 vols. to date. References without volume and page numbers are to typescripts or other materials in the files of the project at the Univ. of Kentucky.

JCCP   *The Papers of John C. Calhoun*, Robert L. Meriwether, W. Edwin Hemphill and others, eds. (Columbia, S.C., 1959), 16 vols. to date. Other references are to typescripts and other materials in the files of the project at the Univ. of South Carolina.

Correspondence of Calhoun   *Correspondence of John C. Calhoun*, J. Franklin Jameson, ed. *Annual Report of the American Historical Association*, 1899, II (Washington, 1900).

Works of Calhoun   *The Works of John C. Calhoun*, Richard K. Crallé, ed. (New York, 1851–57), 6 vols.

Works of Clay   *The Works of Henry Clay*, Calvin Colton, ed. Federal Edition. (New York, 1904), 10 vols.

Writings   *The Writings and Speeches of Daniel Webster*, James W. McIntyre, ed. National Edition. (New York, 1903), 18 vols.

Chapter One: Paths to Power

1. *HCP*, I, 608.
2. To Dr. James McBride, Feb. 16, 1812, *JCCP*, I, 90.
3. *Ibid.*, 122.
4. Charleston *Courier*, Apr. 30, 1847.
5. Quoted in David P. Crook, *American Democracy in English Politics, 1815–50* (New York, 1965), 80.

1. "Star of the West"

1. Gilbert Imlay, *A Topographical Description of the Western Territory of North America* (London, 1797), 28; Thomas Hart Benton, *Thirty Years' View*, (New York, 1954), I, 418. See also Bernard Mayo, *Henry Clay: Spokesman of the New West* (Boston, 1927), ch. 2; Arthur K. Moore, *The Frontier Mind: A Cultural Analysis of the Kentucky Frontiersman* (Lexington, Ky., 1957).

2. For early Lexington, see Francois A. Michaeux, *Travels to the Westward of the Alleghany Mountains*, in Reuben Gold Thwaites, ed., *Early Western Travels, 1748–1846* (Cleveland, 1904), III, 99–206; Joseph M. Espy, *Memorandums of a Tour, in Ohio, Kentucky, and Indiana Territory, 1805* (Cincinnati, 1870), 8–24; Thomas Ashe, *Travels in America* (Newburyport, Mass., 1808), II, 146–58; Mayo, *Clay*, 58–60.

3. On statehood and the first constitutional convention, see Patricia Watlington, *The Partisan Spirit: Kentucky Politics, 1779–1792;* Joan Wells Coward, *Kentucky in the New Republic: The Process of Constitution Making* (Lexington, Ky., 1979); John D. Barnhart, *The Valley of Democracy: The Frontier Versus the Plantation in the Ohio Valley* (Bloomington, Ind., 1953).

4. Quoted in Calvin Colton, *The Life and Times of Henry Clay* (New York, 1846), I, 36.

5. *Ibid.*, 24, quoted from remarks in the House of Representatives. The passage, with minor variations, was often used to characterize Clay, e.g., by Theodore Frelinghuysen, *National Intelligencer* (Washington), Sept. 15, 1832; by a New York senator, in *Eulogies delivered in the Senate and House of Representatives* (Washington, 1853), 57. For an early use of "artificer of his own fortunes," see the *Address of the National Republican Convention of New York,* in *National Intelligencer,* Aug. 4, 1832.

6. Thomas F. Marshall, in a public letter, Louisville *Daily Journal,* Oct. 23, 1851.

7. To Calvin Colton, Sept. 16, 1845, *Works Clay,* V, 532.

8. Speech, Indianapolis, in *Niles' Weekly Register,* Oct. 29, 1842. On the Clay family, see Zachary F. Smith and Mary R. Clay, *The Clay Family, Filson Club Publications, Number 14* (Louisville, 1899). See also Mayo, *Clay,* ch. 1.

9. Mayo, *Clay,* 22.

10. *Ibid.,* 28.

11. William H. Channing, *Memorial of William Ellery Channing* (Boston, 1848), I, 96; Edward G. Parker, *The Golden Age of American Oratory* (Boston, 1857), 16; Raleigh *Register,* May 21, 1839.

12. Quoted in Colton, *Life,* I, 30.

13. Margaret Bayard Smith, *The First Forty Years of Washington Society,* Gaillard Hunt, ed. (New York, 1906), 84–85; "Lucretia Hart Clay. A Portrait by Her Contemporaries," typescript, Clay-Russell Papers, Univ. of Kentucky. See also William A. Leavy, "A Memoir of Lexington and Its Vicinity," *Kentucky Historical Register,* v. 40–42, (1942–44).

14. Joseph Story, "Progress of Jurisprudence" (1821), in *Miscellaneous Writings,* William W. Story, ed. (Boston, 1852), 219–221; Speech to the Virginia General Assembly, Feb. 7, 1822, *HCP,* III, 161–170.

15. Colton, *Life,* I, 96.

16. Mayo, *Clay,* 118, 119; Glyndon G. Van Deusen, *The Life of Henry Clay* (Boston, 1937), 24–25.

17. Lucius P. Little, *Ben Hardin: His Times and Contemporaries* (Louisville, 1887), 38–39.

18. Van Deusen, *Clay,* ch. 2; *HCP,* I, 526.

19. Quoted in Louisville *Journal,* July 12, 1844; Mayo, *Clay,* 73.

20. *HCP,* I, 22, 3–8; Asa E. Martin, *The Anti-Slavery Movement in Kentucky* (Louisville, 1918).

21. Coward, *Kentucky in the New Republic,* chs. 5 and 6.

22. Broadside (1806), quoted in Noble E. Cunningham, Jr., *The Jeffersonian Republicans in Power* (Chapel Hill, 1963), 279–80; George D. Prentice, quoted in Thomas D. Clark, ed., *Bluegrass Cavalcade* (Lexington, Ky., 1957), 263.

23. Robert Letcher to John J. Crittenden, Mar. 4, 1841, Crittenden Papers, Library of Congress. See also Mayo, *Clay,* 182–83, 204–5.

24. Mayo, *Clay,* 166, 162.

25. *Ibid.,* 171–77; Joseph H. Parks, *Felix Grundy, Champion of Democracy* (Baton Rouge, 1940), 20–29.

26. To Richard Pindell, Oct. 15, 1828, *Works of Clay,* 206–8.

27. *Ibid.;* William Plumer, *Memorandum of Proceedings in the United States Senate, 1803–1807,* Everett S. Brown, ed. (New York, 1923), 548–49.

28. *HCP,* I, 328–67.

29. James Johnson to Clay, Jan. 28, 1809, *ibid.,* I, 401. On the duel, *ibid.,* 397–400, Mayo, *Clay,* 337–43, and two letters: H. Blanton to T. M. Green, Mar. 15, 1889, Kentucky Historical Society, and James Hickman to William Scott, Feb. 1809, Missouri State Historical Society.

30. Plumer, *Memorandum,* 565, 608.

31. George Hoadly to Jeremiah Evarts, Aug. 23, 1807, Virginia Historical Society; Plumer, *Memorandum*, 595, 608; John Quincy Adams, *Memoirs*, Charles F. Adams, ed. (Philadelphia, 1874), I, 444.
32. *HCP*, I, 448–52.
33. *Ibid.*, I, 459–63.
34. *Ibid.*, I, 527–39.
35. Timothy Flint, *Recollections of the Last Ten Years* (New York, 1932), 70. See also John Melish, *Travels Through the United States, 1806–11* (Philadelphia, 1815), II, 208; *National Intelligencer*, Mar. 9, 1813.
36. Thomas F. Marshall, in *Louisville Journal*, Oct. 23, 1851.

2. "Young Hercules"

1. William Lowndes to his wife, Nov. 7, 1811, Lowndes Papers, Univ. of North Carolina.
2. Thomas P. Grosvenor of New York, quoted in Theodore Jervey, *Robert Y. Hayne and His Times* (New York, 1909), 51.
3. Calhoun's family background and early years are treated in Charles M. Wiltse, *John C. Calhoun Nationalist, 1782–1828* (Indianapolis, 1944), ch. 1, and in Margaret Coit's *John C. Calhoun, American Portrait* (Boston, 1950), ch. 1. Here and in what follows I have also drawn upon *The Life of John C. Calhoun* (New York, 1843), which I consider principally of Calhoun's authorship (see Gerald M. Capers, *John C. Calhoun, Opportunist* [Gainesville, Fla., 1960], app.); "Biographical Memoir of John C. Calhoun," attributed to Virgil Maxcy, in the *United States Telegraph* (Washington), Apr. 25–26, 1831; and the "Account of Calhoun's Early Life, Abridged from the Manuscript of Col. W. Pinckney Starke," pref. to *Correspondence of Calhoun*, II.
4. John H. Logan, *A History of the Upper Country of South Carolina* (Spartanburg, S.C., 1960), I, 9. (The book, by a native, was first published in 1859).
5. William A. Schaper, *Sectionalism and Representation in South Carolina*, in *Annual Report of the American Historical Association 1900* (Washington, D.C., 1901); David D. Wallace, *A Short History of South Carolina* (Chapel Hill, 1951), ch. 24.
6. See esp. Starke, "Early Life," 69. On upcountry farming, see D. Huger Bacot, "The South Carolina Up Country at the End of the Eighteenth Century," *American Historical Review*, v. 23 (1923), 682–98.
7. *Life of Calhoun*, 5; "Memoir," *U.S. Telegraph*.
8. Starke, "Early Life," 74.
9. *Ibid.*, 77–78; *Life of Calhoun*, 5–6.
10. David Ramsay, *History of South Carolina* (Charleston, 1809), II, 369–71; Augustus B. Longstreet, *Master William Mitten* (Macon, Ga., 1889), 107–08, 191; Starke, "Early Life," 78–80.
11. Reverend George Colton to Calhoun, [Feb. 3, 1819], *JCCP*, III, 539; George P. Fisher, *The Life of Benjamin Silliman* (New York, 1866), II, 98–99; *Life of Calhoun*, 6. For a detailed treatment of Calhoun at Yale, see Coit, *Portrait*, ch. 2.
12. The quoted passage is taken from the 1831 "Memoir," *U.S. Telegraph*, and was perhaps the original version; the prediction appears in *Life of Calhoun*, 6, and is repeated in Starke, "Early Life," 81, and in most biographies. Capers, *Opportunist*, 1–2, offers a different version. Still other versions have Dwight speaking his prophecy directly to Calhoun. In Mary E. Maragné, *A Neglected Thread: A Journal from the Calhoun Community, 1836–1842*, Della M. Craven, ed. (Columbia, S.C., 1951), 44, the following appears: "On being asked at College what was the extent of his ambition, he [Calhoun] replied: 'the Presidency of these United States.' " Coit, *Portrait*, 30, takes the ditty from Anson Phelps Stokes, *Memorials of Eminent Yale Men* (New Haven, 1914), II, 199.
13. Henry W. De Saussure to [Robert Goodloe Harper], May 13, 1805, Univ. of South Carolina.
14. To Horatio Seymour, May 9, 1822, *JCCP*, VI, 104–05.
15. Arthur W. Machen, Jr., ed., *Letters of Arthur W. Machen* (Baltimore, 1917), 47–48; "Memoir," *U.S. Telegraph*.
16. To Mrs. Floride Colhoun, Dec. 23, 1805, *JCCP*, I, 25; Starke, "Early Life," 84.
17. To Mrs. Floride Colhoun, Apr. 13, Dec. 22, 1806, Oct. 1, 1807, *JCCP*, I, 28, 33, 38; Ben Robertson, *Red Hills and Cotton: An Upcountry Memory* (New York, 1942).
18. See Walter L. Miller, "Calhoun as a Lawyer an Statesman," *Green Bag*, v. 11 (1899), 199–200; A. Bowie Letter, New York *Times*, Nov. 1, 1854.

19. William C. Preston, *Reminiscences* (Chapel Hill, 1923), 7–8; Mary Bates, *The Private Life of John C. Calhoun* (Charleston, 1852), 8–9.
20. To Mrs. Floride Colhoun, Apr. 6, 1809, *JCCP*, I, 41.
21. Starke, "Early Life," 85.
22. Letter on the Mode of Appointing Electors, Nov. 1846, *Works of Calhoun*, VI, 264.
23. Wallace, *Short History*, 359; see chs. 25 and 37 on changes in the state government. Schaper, *Sectionalism*, is invaluable. "Unification" is emphasized in George C. Rogers, "South Carolina Federalists and the Origins of the Nullification Movement," *South Carolina Historical Magazine*, v. 71 (1970), 17–32; and in Margaret K. Latimer, "South Carolina—A Protagonist of the War of 1812," *American Historical Review*, v. 61 (1956), 914–29.
24. W. H. Trescott, cited in Laura A. White, *Robert Barnwell Rhett* (Gloucester, Mass., 1965), 7.
25. *Life of Calhoun*, 5.
26. Starke, "Early Life," 84; Coit, *Portrait*, 34–36, accepts the story, though as she acknowledges it was rejected by Wiltse in *Nationalist*.
27. Speech, Dec. 19, 1811, in *Life of Calhoun*, 11. See the variant phrasing in Henry Adams, *History of the United States of America during the Administration of James Madison* (New York, 1890), II, 143.
28. Richmond *Enquirer*, Dec. 24, 1811; also quoted in *Life of Calhoun*, 9–10.
29. James H. Hammond, *Selections from His Letters and Speeches* (New York, 1866), 244.

3. *"Yankee Demosthenes"*

1. "Conversations with Charles Lanman," in *Writings of Webster*, XIII, 580. For the early life I have relied mainly on Webster's own writings. The principal biographies are George T. Curtis, *Life of Daniel Webster*, 2 vols. (Boston, 1870) and Claude M. Fuess, *Daniel Webster*, 2 vols. (Boston, 1930); also Maurice G. Baxter, *One and Inseparable: Daniel Webster and the Union* (Cambridge, 1984), used sparingly in this work.
2. See the brief account in Elizabeth F. and Elting E. Morrison, *New Hampshire: A Bicentennial History* (New York, 1976), 72–73.
3. To Jacob McGaw, Oct. 11, 1828, *Letters of Daniel Webster*, C. H. Van Tyne, ed. (New York, 1902), 137.
4. To Mrs. John M. Cheney, Aug. 29, 1845, *DWP*. See also Speech at the Festival of the Sons of New Hampshire, Boston, Nov. 7, 1849, *Writings*, IV, 196–213.
5. "Conversations," *Writings*, XII, 572.
6. "Personal Memorials of Daniel Webster," *National Intelligencer*, Nov. 27, 1851.
7. "Conversations," *Writings*, XIII, 578.
8. Claude M. Fuess, *Rufus Choate: The Wizard of the Law* (New York, 1928), 237.
9. To Richard Blatchford, May 3, 1846, *Private Correspondence of Daniel Webster*, Fletcher Webster, ed. (Boston, 1857), II, 228.
10. [Edwin D. Sanborn], "The Student Life of Daniel Webster," *Putnam's Monthly Magazine*, v. 1 (1853), 517–18.
11. See Edward Everett's biographical memoir originally appended to his edition of *The Works of Daniel Webster*, 6 vols. (Boston, 1851), hereafter cited in *Writings*, XVII.
12. To Richard Blatchford, May 3, 1846, *Private Correspondence*, II, 228–29; Curtis, *Life*, I, 18–20; Sanborn, "Student Life," and "Personal Memorials," in *National Intelligencer*.
13. Charles C. Coffin, *History of Boscawen and Webster, from 1733 to 1878* (Concord, N.H., 1878), 131; John J. Dearborn, *The History of Salisbury, New Hampshire* (Manchester, N.H., 1890), 435.
14. To the Reverend Merrill, Jan. 10, 1851, *Private Correspondence*, II, 412.
15. Quoted in Curtis, *Life*, I, 44. On curriculum, classmates, etc., see Herbert D. Foster, "Webster and Choate in College," in his *Collected Papers* (n.p., 1929), 213–49.
16. Amos Kendall, *Autobiography* (Boston, 1872), 67.
17. "Reminiscences of the Hon. Aaron Loveland," Scrap-Books, p. 123, Dartmouth College.
18. *Ibid*.
19. "Personal Memorials," *National Intelligencer*.
20. Edward G. Parker, *Reminiscences of Rufus Choate* (New York, 1860). For the denial, see Curtis, *Life*, I, 42, and Hiram Ketchum, *Eulogy of Daniel Webster* (New York, 1853), 11–12.
21. *Writings*, XV, 502.
22. Quoted in Curtis, *Life*, I, 60.

23. To James H. Bingham, May 18, 1802, *Private Correspondence*, I, 110–11.
24. To Mr. Cook, Jan. 14, 1802, *ibid.*, 131.
25. "Personal Memorials," *National Intelligencer;* Autobiography, in *Writings*, I, 18.
26. To James H. Bingham, Oct. 6, 1803, Ezekiel Webster to Webster, Nov. 6, 1802, *Private Correspondence*, I, 145, 124.
27. To Thomas Merrill, Nov. 30, 1804, *Private Correspondence*, I, 194.
28. Diary, in *ibid.*, 178–82. See also Samuel L. Knapp, *A Memoir of the Life of Daniel Webster* (Boston, 1831), 11–12, and Curtis, *Life*, I, 63–68.
29. Curtis, *Life*, I, 70.
30. William Plumer, Jr., "Reminiscences of Daniel Webster," in *Writings*, I, 546–47.
31. Quoted in Josiah Quincy to Josiah Quincy, Jr., Feb. 4, 1827, Quincy, Wendell, Holmes, Upham Papers, Mass. Historical Society.
32. Obituary, *Christian Examiner*, v. 5 (1828), 100; "Sketch of Mrs. Grace of F. Webster by Mrs. Eliza Buckminster Lee," *Private Correspondence*, I, 438–44.
33. *Ibid.*, 439.
34. To James H. Bingham, May 18, 1802, *Private Correspondence*, I, 112.
35. From the *Dartmouth Gazette*, in *ibid.*, 544.
36. *Writings*, XV, 564–74. On New Hampshire politics, see Donald R. Cole, *Jacksonian Democracy in New Hampshire, 1800–51* (Cambridge, 1971); Lynn Turner, *William Plumer of New Hampshire* (Chapel Hill, 1962), and *The Ninth State: New Hampshire's Formative Years* (Chapel Hill, 1983).
37. *Writings*, XV, 582.
38. *Ibid.*, 475–84.
39. *Ibid.*, XIII, 582.
40. To the Reverend Mr. Brazer, Nov. 10, 1828, *Private Correspondence*, I, 465. (Webster was paraphrasing Richard Whately.)
41. *Writings*, XV, 588, 547, 580, 589.
42. [Caleb Cushing], "Daniel Webster," *National Intelligencer*, Dec. 2, 1835. On the authorship, see Cushing to J. O. Sargent, Dec. 6, 1835, Sargent Papers, Boston Public Library.
43. *Writings*, XV, 594–95.
44. *Ibid.*, 609.
45. *Ibid.*, IV, 90.
46. N. P. Rogers, quoted in Peter Harvey, *Reminiscences of Daniel Webster* (Boston, 1877), 49.
47. Quoted in Morrison and Morrison, *New Hampshire*, 114; Robert Frost, *Collected Poems* (New York, 1939), 201.

4. War and Peace

1. To Samuel Bradbury, May 28, 1813, *DWP*, I, 141; to Moody Kent, Dec. 22, 1814, *Letters*, 69.
2. To Edward Cutts, Jr., May 26, 1813, *ibid.*, 33.
3. Timothy Pickering to John Pickering, June 5, 1813, Pickering Papers, Massachusetts Historical Society.
4. To Caesar Rodney, Dec. 29, 1812, *HCP*, I, 750–51; to Dr. James MacBride, Dec. 25, 1812, *JCCP*, I, 146.
5. *HCP*, I, 754–773.
6. John A. Harper, quoted in Irving Brant, *James Madison: The President* (Indianapolis, 1959), 134; Jonathan Roberts to Charles Jared Ingersoll, Jan. 1, 1813, Ingersoll Papers, Historical Society of Pennsylvania.
7. *Annals of Congress*, 13 Cong., 1 Sess., 169ff; Webster to Charles March, June 24, 1813, *Letters*, 44; William B. Grove to William Gaston, July 8, 1813, Gaston Papers, Univ. of North Carolina; Timothy Pickering to John Pickering, July 1, 14, 19, 27, 1813, Pickering Papers; *National Intelligencer*, June 22, 24, July 15, Aug. 5, 19.
8. Pickering to John Pickering, July 14, 19, 1813, Pickering Papers.
9. Quoted in the *Portsmouth Oracle*, June 29, 1813; *New Hampshire Patriot*, July 27, 1813.
10. Quoted in *Niles' Register*, July 5, 1845. (Webster was speaking at the New York Historical Society on the death of Andrew Jackson.)
11. *Writings*, XIV, 124.
12. *Annals*, 13 Cong., 2 Sess., 940–51, 994–1002.
13. *Writings*, XIV, 47–54; Webster to [Timothy Farrar], Oct. 30, 1814, *DWP*, I, 174–75.

14. *JCCP*, I, 131–32.
15. *Writings*, XIV, 42; Nathaniel Macon quoted in Adams, *History*, I, 377.
16. *JCCP*, I, 258–59.
17. *Portsmouth Oracle*, July 18, 1814; *New Hampshire Patriot*, July 5, 19, 1814.
18. *Patriot*, Aug. 2, 1814.
19. *Ibid.*, Nov. 15, 1814.
20. Webster to William Sullivan, Oct. 17, 1814 (2 letters), *DWP*, I, 170–71.
21. *Writings*, XIV, 69.
22. Charles Jared Ingersoll, in Congress, quoted in Boston *Courier*, Aug. 25, 1826.
23. Quoted in *Niles' Register*, Dec. 31, 1814.
24. Irving Brant, *James Madison: Commander-in-Chief* (Indianapolis, 1961), 240.
25. To Messrs. Bayard and Gallatin, May 2, 1814, *HCP*, I, 891.
26. Worthington C. Ford, "The Treaty of Ghent, and After," *Proceedings of the State Historical Society of Wisconsin* (1914), 90.
27. Adams, *Memoirs*, I, 101.
28. John Quincy Adams, *The Duplicate Letters, the Fisheries and the Mississippi* (Washington, 1822), 1–11.
29. On the negotiations, see Samuel F. Bemis, *John Quincy Adams and the Foundations of American Foreign Policy* (New York, 1949), 190–214; Bradford Perkins, *Castlereagh and Adams: England and the United States, 1812–1823* (Berkeley, 1964), ch. 4; Fred L. Engelman, *The Peace of Christmas Eve* (New York, 1962).
30. Quoted in *National Intelligencer*, Feb. 16, 1815.
31. See esp. the speech at Lexington, *HCP*, II, 68–71.
32. From the *Vermont Patriot*, in *National Intelligencer*, May 20, 1815.

Chapter Two: Dimensions of Nationalism

1. The term comes from John Pendleton Kennedy's *Defense of the Whigs* (1843), later included in his *Political and Offical Papers* (New York, 1872). For Madison's Seventh Annual Message, see J. D. Richardson, ed., *A Compilation of the Messages and Papers of the Presidents* (Washington, 1907), I, 547–54.
2. *National Intelligencer*, May 7, 1816.
3. Speech, Jan. 29, 1816, in *HCP*, II, 157.
4. Frederick Jackson Turner, *Rise of the New West, 1819–1829* (1906; reprint New York, 1962) and George Dangerfield, *The Era of Good Feelings* (New York, 1952), offer synthesis and broad interpretation.
5. Charles March, *Reminiscences of Congress* (New York, 1850), 54–55.
6. Theodore Parker, *Additional Speeches, Addresses, and Occasional Sermons* (Boston, 1867), I, 156.

1. Clay and the Disruption of Republicanism

1. The *Portsmouth Oracle*, quoting the *Columbian Centinel* (Boston), Mar. 22, 1817. See also Harry Ammon, *James Monroe, The Quest for National Identity* (New York, 1971), 367–68.
2. Armistead G. Mason, quoted in Leland W. Meyer, *The Life and Times of Richard M. Johnson* (New York, 1932), 172.
3. See George M. Blakey, "Rendezvous with Republicanism: John Pope vs. Henry Clay in 1816," *Indiana Magazine of History*, v. 62 (1966), 233–50; Orval W. Baylor, *John Pope Kentuckian: His Life and Times, 1770–1845* (Cynthiana, Ky., 1943), ch. 7; *Kentucky Reporter* (Lexington), June–Aug. 1816.
4. Quoted in *Niles' Register*, Dec. 20, 1823.
5. Joseph Story to Ezekial Bacon, Mar. 12, 1818, in *Life and Letters of Joseph Story*, William W. Story, ed. (Boston, 1851), I, 311.
6. Mary P. Follett, *The Speaker of the House of Representatives* (New York, 1904), ch. 3; Joseph Cooper, "The Origins of the Standing Committees and the Development of the Modern House," *Rice University Studies*, v. 56 (1970); Gerald R. Lientz, "House Speaker Elections and Congressional Parties, 1789–1860," *Capital Studies*, v. 6 (1978), 63–89; and James S. Young, *The Washington Community, 1800–1928* (New York, 1966), 131–35. For turnover in the House, see *Niles' Register*, Mar. 21, 1818.
7. *HCP*, II, 155–56, 289–92, 492–93. On the general subject, see Charles C. Griffin, *The

United States and the Disruption of the Spanish Empire (New York, 1937); Samuel Flagg Bemis, *John Quincy Adams and the Foundations of American Foreign Policy* (New York, 1949); and Randolph B. Campbell, "Henry Clay and the Emerging Nations of South America, 1815–1829," Ph.D. diss. Univ. of Virginia, 1966.

8. *National Intelligencer*, Oct. 21, 1817; Crawford to Albert Gallatin, October 27, 1817, *Writings of Albert Gallatin*, Henry Adams, ed. (Philadelphia, 1879), II, 55–56.

9. Crawford to Galatin, Mar. 12, Apr. 23, Oct. 27, 1817, *ibid.*, 26–27, 35–36, 55–56.

10. *Memoirs*, Charles Francis Adams, ed. (Philadelphia, 1874), IV, 28, 30–31, 70–71, 325–26; Adams to Thomas B. Adams, Jan. 14, 1818, in Adams Papers, Massachusetts Historical Society; Adams to Alexander H. Everett, Dec. 29, 1817, in *Writings*, Worthington C. Ford, ed. (New York, 1913), VI, 281–82.

11. *HCP*, II, 512–18.

12. Adams to Alexander H. Everett, Dec. 29, 1817, *Writings*, VI, 281–82.

13. *Annals of Congress*, 14 Cong., 1 Sess., 809–10.

14. *HCP*, III, 80–81.

15. Quoted from 1818 speech, in Calvin Colton, *Life and Times of Henry Clay* (New York, 1846), I, 221.

16. *HCP*, II, 857–58; see also, *ibid.*, III, 81.

17. Quoted from speech at Lexington, Ky., in 1820, in Colton, *Life*, I, 227.

18. *National Intelligencer*, July 28, 1818; Clay to Henry M. Brackenridge, Aug. 4, 1818, *HCP*, II, 590–91.

19. *Kentucky Reporter* (Lexington), Apr. 29, 1818; see also Jan. 12 and July 1, 1818.

20. Henry R. Storrs to M. S. Miller, Dec. 6, 1818, Misc. MSS, New York Historical Society.

21. Margaret Bayard Smith, *The First Forty Years of Washington Society*, Gaillard Hunt, ed. (New York, 1906), 145–56.

22. *HCP*, II, 658–59. Clay drew upon the sensational "Letters of Sidney" (by Benjamin Watkins Leigh) which appeared in the Richmond *Enquirer*, beginning Dec. 22, 1818.

23. "Memoirs of Jonathan Roberts," *Pennsylvania Magazine of History and Biography* (1938), v. 62, 399; *Kentucky Gazette* (Lexington), Feb. 19, 26, 1819.

24. Jackson to G. F. Preston, Feb. 2, 1819, in the Norcross Papers, Massachusetts Historical Society; Clay to Josiah Johnston, Oct. 6, 1827, *HCP*, VI, 1114–17.

25. Campbell, "Clay and South America," (150–52); Salma Hale to N. Silsbee, May 10, 1820, Hale Papers, New Hampshire Historical Society.

26. *Memoirs*, V, 290.

27. *HCP*, III, 81.

28. *National Intelligencer*, July 11, 1821.

29. To Caesar Rodney, Aug. 9, 1821, *HCP*, III, 106–7; Adams to Robert Walsh, July 10, 1821, *Writings*, VII, 113–18.

30. David Trimble, *Annals of Congress*, 17 Cong., 1 Sess., 1383.

31. Quoted in *The Autobiography of Martin Van Buren*, *Annual Report of American Historical Association*, 1918, II (Washington, 1920), 306; Glyndon G. Van Deusen, *The Life of Henry Clay* (Boston, 1937), 132.

32. *National Intelligencer*, May 9, 1823.

33. Bolivar to Clay, Nov. 21, 1827, in Colton, *Life*, 244.

34. "Latin America's Homage to Henry Clay," *Bulletin of the Pan American Union*, v. 61 (1927), 539–46.

35. Quoted in Dangerfield, *Era*, 306.

36. Richard Rush to Clay, June 23, 1827, *HCP*, VI, 714–15. See also [Alexander H. Everett], "Life of Henry Clay," *North American Review*, v. 33 (1831), 373.

37. *Annals of Congress*, 15 Cong., 2 Sess., 1175–1182; To Amos Kendall, Jan. 8, 1820, *HCP*, II, 752; George D. Prentice, *Biography of Henry Clay* (Hartford, 1831), 96.

38. The Boston Memorial, Dec. 3, 1819, is attributed to Webster and included in *Writings*, XV, 55–73. Jeremiah Mason, writing to Christopher Gore, Jan. 16, 1820, said the memorial was written by Justice Story, almost entirely from King's speech. *Memoirs and Correspondence of Jeremiah Mason*, George S. Hillard, ed. (Cambridge, 1873), 236. For the quotation, see Glover Moore, *The Missouri Controversy, 1819–1821* (Lexington, Ky., 1953), 69.

39. To Adam Beatty, Jan. 22, 1920, *HCP*, II, 766.

40. *Niles' Register*, Jan. 29, 1820; [George Watterston], *Wanderer in Washington* (Washington, 1827), 90–92; Glenn Brown, *History of the United States Capitol* (Washington, 1900), I, 66–68.

41. See Alfred Lightfoot, "Henry Clay and the Missouri Question," *Missouri Historical Review*, v. 61 (1967), 143–65, though I do not share his opinion that Clay "reversed" himself.
42. *Kentucky Reporter*, Mar. 1, 1820; see also *Kentucky Gazette*, Mar. 10, 1820.
43. *Annals of Congress*, 15 Cong., 2 Sess., 1222–40, 1272–82.
44. Quoted in Moore, *Missouri Controversy*; see his account of the passage, 94–105.
45. Carl Schurz, *Life of Henry Clay* (Boston, 1887), I, 181; *Annals of Congress*, 16 Cong., 1 Sess., 1587–94; Hugh A. Garland, *The Life of John Randolph of Roanoke* (New York, 1859), II, 128–30; Epes Sargent, *Life and Public Services of Henry Clay* (Auburn, N.Y., 1852) 39–42; John Randolph to J. M. Garnett, Feb. 23, 1820, Randolph Papers, Univ. of Virginia.
46. To Charles Tait, Oct. 26, 1820, *JCCP*, V, 412–14; *Writings of Webster*, XV, 55–72.
47. Moore, *Missouri Controversy*, 144.
48. To Caesar Rodney, Feb. 16, 1821, to Langdon Cheves, Mar. 5, 1821, *HCP*, III, 42, 58–59.
49. William Plumer, Jr., to William Plumer, Feb. 2, 1821, in Everett S. Brown, ed., *The Missouri Compromise and Presidential Politics, 1820–1825* (St. Louis, 1926), 32–33.
50. *National Intelligencer*, Feb. 13, 1821; *Argus of Western America* (Frankfort, Ky.), Mar. 8, 1821.
51. *Annals of Congress*, 16 Cong., 2 Sess., 1094; for the report, 1078–80.
52. *New England Galaxy* (Boston), Feb. 23, 1821; Frankfort *Argus*, Mar. 8, 1821; William H. Sparks, *The Memories of Fifty Years* (Philadelphia, 1870), 231; *Annals of Congress*, 16 Cong., 2 Sess., 1146.
53. *Ibid.*, 1160–63; *HCP*, III, 36–40.
54. In speech at Milledgeville, Georgia, Mar. 19, 1844, reported in *Niles' Register*, Apr. 20, 1844.
55. *Annals of Congress*, 16 Cong., 2 Sess., 1210–40; Moore, *Missouri Controversy*, 154–58; Plumer to Plumer, Feb. 26, 1821, in Brown, *Missouri Compromise*, 42–43; *Kentucky Gazette*, Feb. 29, 1821.
56. *Ibid.*; William Plumer, Jr., in Brown, *Missouri Compromise*, 43; *Kentucky Reporter*, Mar. 26, 1821; George D. Prentice, *Henry Clay*, 214–15; George Dangerfield, *The Awakening of American Nationalism* (New York, 1956), 136.
57. For an example of the confusion, see speech of Thomas J. Turner, Feb. 3, 1849, in the House, *Congressional Globe*, 30 Cong., 2 Sess., 388–89. See also James G. Blaine, *Twenty Years of Congress* (Norwich, Conn., 1884), I, 19.
58. *HCP*, II, 263–64.
59. Dangerfield, *Era*, 204.
60. Jefferson to John Holmes, Apr. 22, 1820, *The Portable Thomas Jefferson*, Merrill D. Peterson, ed. (New York, 1975), 568.
61. Adams, *Memoirs*, V, 324. See also Van Deusen, *Henry Clay*, ch. 9.
62. Bernard Mayo, "Lexington: Frontier Metropolis," in Eric Goldman, ed., *Historiography and Urbanization* (Baltimore, 1941), 21–42: Richard C. Wade, *The Urban Frontier: The Rise of Western Cities* (Chicago, 1959), 169–70; Charles Kerr, ed., *History of Kentucky* (Chicago, 1922), II, 600.
63. To Langdon Cheves, Feb. 10, 1821, *HCP*, III, 24–26. Clay later explained to the Senate his relations with the B.U.S., Dec. 23, 1833, *Register of Debates*, 23 Cong., 1 Sess.
64. *National Intelligencer*, June 27, 1821, excerpting the *Liberty Hall and Cincinnati Gazette*.
65. See the account in Francis P. Weisenberger, "A Life of Charles Hammond," *Ohio Archeological and Historical Quarterly*, v. 43 (1934), 356–58; and Clay's statement of the case, *HCP*, II, 114–15.
66. Story, *Life and Letters*, II, 423. See Paul W. Gates, "Tenants of the Log Cabin," *Missouri Valley Historical Review*, v. 69 (1962), 3–31.
67. To Martin Hardin, Jan. 4, 1819, *HCP*, II, 622–23.

2. The American System

1. For example, [Everett], "Life of Clay," *North American Review*, v. 33, 375.
2. *The Federalist*, No. 11, Modern Library Edition (New York, n.d.), 69.
3. See particularly his famous letter to Benjamin Austin, Jan. 9, 1816, *Portable Jefferson*, 547–50. Jefferson said much the same thing in other letters that also found their way into print. To the secretary of the American Society for Encouragement of Domestic Manufactures, in New York City, he wrote, on June 6, 1817, that as the last twenty years had taught us not to

look to Europe for "necesaries," he hoped the next twenty would "place the American hemi-sphere under a system of its own, essentially peaceable and industrious, and not needing to extract its imports out of the external fires raging in the old world." Here political economy and foreign policy were interrelated, as in Clay's thought. The editor of the *National Intelligencer*, reprinting the letter on June 3, 1830, suggested it was the origin of the idea and the phrase "American System."

4. *HCP*, III, 683.

5. *Ibid.*, 695; William B. Giles, *Political Miscellanies* (n.p., n.d.), 63.

6. There is no satisfactory study of the American System, but see Carter Goodrich, ed., *The Government and the Economy: 1782–1861* (Indianapolis, 1967), Daniel Walker Howe, *Political Culture of American Whigs* (Chicago, 1979), and Paul K. Conkin, *Prophets of Prosperity: America's First Political Economists* (Bloomington, Ind., 1980).

7. *HCP*, II, 828.

8. On "growth model," see James E. Winkler, "Henry Clay: A Current Assessment," *Register of the Kentucky Historical Society*, v. 70 (1972), 179–86; "inducement mechanism" comes from Albert O. Hirschman, *The Strategy of Economic Development* (New Haven, 1958), 10–11. See also R. C. Edwards, "Economic Sophistication in Nineteenth Century Congressional Tariff Debates," *Journal of Economic History*, v. 30 (1970), 302–38.

9. The idea and the phrase are first found in Richard Price, *Observations on the Importance of the American Revolution* (London, 1784), 62. Calhoun spoke of "a world of itself" in his Report on Roads and Canals, Jan. 7, 1819, *JCCP*, III, 465; and see the variation in *Niles' Register*, Oct. 3, 1812.

10. Adam Smith, *The Wealth of Nations*, Modern Library Edition (New York, 1937), 348–52, 422; Guy S. Callender, ed., *Selections from the Economic History of the United States, 1765–1860* (Boston, 1909), ch. 10.

11. *HCP*, II, 834.

12. A good statement of the idea is in the Report of the Committee on Commerce and Manufactures, House of Representatives, Feb. 13, 1816, in *Niles' Register*, Feb. 24, 1816. Another is Henry Baldwin, *Annals of Congress*, 16 Cong., 2 Sess., 1614. Douglas C. North, *Economic Growth of the United States, 1790–1860* (Englewood Cliffs, N.J., 1951), ch. 9, develops a model of the economy in similar terms of sectional specialization. It is disputed by Diane Lindstrom, *Economic Development in the Philadelphia Region, 1810–1850* (New York, 1978).

13. A general account of the tariff of 1816 may be found in Edward Stanwood, *American Tariff Controversies* (Boston, 1903), I, ch. 5. For the speeches of Clay and Calhoun and others see *Annals of Congress*, 14 Cong., 1 Sess., 1237 ff. See also Norris W. Preyer, "Southern Support of the Tariff of 1816," *Journal of Southern History*, v. 25 (1959), 306–22.

14. Quoted from the 1816 debate, in Alden Bradford, *History of the Federal Government . . . , 1789–1839* (Boston, 1840), 237–38.

15. See Baldwin's speech, *Annals of Congress*, 16 Cong., 1 Sess., 1916–46, and Stanwood, *Tariff Controversies*, ch. 6.

16. Quoted in Colton, *Life of Clay*, I, 146.

17. *HCP*, II, 836.

18. *Ibid.*, 835, 844.

19. *Annals of Congress*, 18 Cong., 1 Sess., 959–66.

20. *Ibid.*, 1548–49, 1560–63. See also Paul Gates, *The Farmers' Age, 1815–1860* (New York, 1960), 115–17.

21. *Annals of Congress*, 18 Cong., 1 Sess., 1923, 1916–46.

22. *HCP*, III, 701, 683–727.

23. Schurz, *Life of Clay*, I, 218; Webster's speech is in *Writings*, V, 94–149.

24. *Register of Debates*, 21 Cong., 1 Sess., 49.

25. William Plumer, Jr., "Reminiscences of Daniel Webster," in *Writings*, I, 550–51.

26. *Annals of Congress*, 18 Cong., 1 Sess., 1170–78; George T. Curtis, *Life of Daniel Webster* (New York, 1870), I, 203–5.

27. Quoted in Alexander Brady, *William Huskisson and Liberal Reform* (Oxford, 1928), 120. See also, J. H. Clapham, *An Economic History of Modern Britain*, 3rd ed. (Cambridge, 1950), 326. For Clay's opinion, see *HCP*, IV, 416–17, 529–30.

28. See the discussion in Robert L. Carey, *Daniel Webster as an Economist* (New York, 1929), ch. 4; and Curtis, *Webster*, I, 208.

29. To Mathew Carey, May 2, 1824, *HCP*, III, 745; to Joseph Story, Apr. 10, 1824, *Private Correspondence of Daniel Webster*, Fletcher Webster, ed. (Boston, 1857), I, 348–49.

30. *HCP*, III, 779.
31. *Niles' Register*, Feb. 24, 1816.
32. Carter Goodrich, "National Planning of Internal Improvements," *Political Science Quarterly*, v. 63 (1948), 16–44, and "The Virginia System of Mixed Enterprise. A Study of State Planning of Internal Improvements," *ibid.*, v. 64 (1949), 355–87. The best treatment of early national policy is Joseph H. Harrison, "The Internal Improvements Issue in the Politics of the Union, 1783–1825," Ph.D. diss., Univ. of Virginia, 1954.
33. *JCCP*, I, 401, 398–407.
34. *Ibid.*, 402, 403.
35. *Writings*, XIV, 92–100.
36. To James Madison, Mar. 3, 1817, *HCP*, II, 322, 485.
37. *Annals of Congress*, 15 Cong., 1 Sess., 1114ff.
38. *HCP*, II, 448–64, 467–89.
39. *Ibid.*, II, 474, III, 580.
40. *Ibid.*, II, 486–88. On the distinction see Carter Goodrich, "American Development Policy: The Case of Internal Improvements," *Journal of Economic History*, v. 16 (1956), 449–60.
41. *Annals of Congress*, 15 Cong., 1 Sess., 1386–89.
42. See Harriet M. Foster, "Memories of the National Road," *Indiana Magazine of History*, v. 13 (1917), 62; *HCP*, IV, 19–32.
43. This rests on inference, but see Thomas W. Cobb to C. W. Gooch, Jan. 7, 1828, Gooch Family Papers, Univ. of Virginia. Monroe's exposition, May 4, 1822, is in *Annals of Congress*, 17 Cong., 1 Sess., 1809–63.
44. *HCP*, III, 578.
45. *Ibid.*, 577.
46. In *Niles' Register*, July 12, 1828.
47. Report of the Secretary of Treasury, 1827, *Niles' Register*, Dec. 15, 1827.
48. Edward Gibbon Wakefield, *England and America* (New York, 1833), 226–27.
49. There is no full statement of Clay's views, but fragments may be found in several speeches, e.g., *Annals of Congress*, 16 Cong., 1 Sess., 883–84, and *HCP*, III, 718–19.
50. See the discussion in "Appropriation of Public Lands for Schools," *North American Review*, v. 4 (1821), 310–42.

3. *Calhoun at the War Department*

1. Langdon Cheves quoted in David D. Wallace, *A Short History of South Carolina* (Chapel Hill, 1951), 367.
2. *The Life of John C. Calhoun* (New York, 1843), 24–25; Charles M. Wiltse, *John C. Calhoun Nationalist, 1782–1828* (Indianapolis, 1944), 139–41.
3. *JCCP*, VI, 38.
4. [Watterston], *Wanderer*, 69.
5. Adams to Louisa Catherine Adams, Aug. 11, 1821, *Writings*, VII, 170–71.
6. William Plumer, Jr., in Brown, *Missouri Compromise*, 51–52.
7. Elijah H. Mills to his wife [1823], "Extracts from the Familiar Correspondence of the Hon. E. H. Mills," *Proceedings of Massachusetts Historical Society*, 1st. ser., v. 19 (1881–82), 37–38.
8. See the praise of Calhoun in Congress, *Annals*, 14 Cong., 1 Sess., 442, 555, 560, 840, 846–47, 909; and as quoted in *Life*, 23–24. See also DeWitt Clinton to General Van Rensselaer, Jan. 31, 1821, in Catherine V. R. Bonney, *A Legacy of Historical Gleanings* (Albany, 1875), I, 362; [George Watterston], *Letters from Washington* (Washington, 1818), 50–56.
9. *Memoirs*, IV, 36, V, 361.
10. "The Autobiography of William John Grayson," Samuel G. Stoney, ed., *South Carolina Historical and Genealogical Magazine*, v. 50 (1949), 136.
11. [Watterston], *Wanderer*, 69; Elijah H. Mills to his wife, Jan. 6, 1821, *MHS Proceedings*, 29; Charles Jared Ingersoll, Diary, 1823, Pennslyvania Historical Society; Wiltse, *Nationalist*, 266–67.
12. Josephine Seaton, *William Winston Seaton of the 'National Intelligencer,'* (Boston, 1871), 135; *Life, Letters and Journals of George Ticknor* (Boston, 1909), I, 349–51.
13. *Life of Calhoun*, 25. For a succinct account, see Leonard D. White, *The Jeffersonians: A Study in Administrative History, 1801–1829* (New York, 1951), 246–50, and *passim*; and Carlton B. Smith's essay in *America, The Middle Period*, John B. Boles, ed. (Charlottesville, 1973) 132–44.

14. Introduction, *JCCP*, II; Wiltse, *Nationalist*, 152.
15. See Calhoun's report to Congress, Dec. 11, 1818, *JCCP*, III, 374–86.
16. To Alexander Smyth, Dec. 29, 1819, *ibid.*, IV, 519–24.
17. To General Thomas A. Smith, Mar. 16, 1816, *ibid.*, II, 194–95.
18. Quoted in the *Kentucky Gazette*, Aug. 20, 1819.
19. The report, Jan. 1, 1819, is in *JCCP*, III, 462–72. For Clay's action see *HCP*, II, 630–63.
20. For a general view see Francis Paul Prucha, *American Indian Policy in the Formative Years* (Cambridge, 1962).
21. Report on the Indian Factory System, Dec. 5, 1818, *JCCP*, III, 341–55.
22. For the Senate debate, *Annals of Congress*, 17 Cong., 1 Sess., 317–43, 417–24. See also Thomas L. McKenney to Calhoun, Feb. 18, 1822, *JCCP*, VI, 704–6.
23. To the Speaker of the House, Jan. 15, 1820, *ibid.*, IV, 577.
24. "Regulations Concerning the Civilization of the Indians," Aug. 3, 1819, *ibid.*, 295–96: to James Monroe, Feb. 8, 1822, *ibid.*, VI, 679–83.
25. *Ibid.*, 682.
26. Andrew Jackson to Calhoun, Aug. 25, Sept. 2, 1820, *ibid.*, V, 336–37, 343–44.
27. See esp. Arthur J. DeRozier, Jr., "John C. Calhoun and the Removal of the Choctaw Indians," *Proceedings of the South Carolina Historical Association for 1957* (1958), 33–45, and *The Removal of the Choctaw Indians* (Knoxville, 1970).
28. The attack may be followed in Wiltse, *Nationalist*; see also Chase C. Mooney, *William H. Crawford* (Lexington, Ky., 1974), 156–205, and Norman K. Risjord, *The Old Republicans: Southern Conservatives in the Age of Jefferson* (New York, 1965), 175–200.
29. William Plumer, Jr., in Brown, *Missouri Compromise*, 64.
30. *Annals of Congress*, 16 Cong., 1 Sess., 1611.
31. To Jonathan Russell, Apr. 10, 1820, *HCP*, II, 819.
32. To Micah Sterling, Apr. 15, 1820, *JCCP*, V, 40–44.
33. Report, Dec. 12, 1820, *ibid.*, 480–90.
34. *Annals of Congress*, 16 Cong., 2 Sess., 728, 773, 777, 779, 787.
35. To Samuel D. Ingham, Dec. 17, 1820, to Andrew Jackson, Jan. 25, 1821, to the Rev. Moses Waddel, Mar. 6, 1821, *JCCP*, V, 500–2, 572–73, 661.
36. See intros., *JCCP*, VI and VII.
37. Quoted in *National Intelligencer*, Mar. 30, 1822.
38. Thomas L. McKenney, *Memoirs, Official and Personal* (New York, 1846), II, 53; De Rosier, *Choctaw*, 40.
39. *Life of Calhoun*, 27–28; *National Intelligencer*, Apr. 28, 1838, on the Indian portraits.
40. For example, in 1840: see the *Congressional Globe*, 26 Cong., 1 Sess., App., 442, and *ibid.*, 25 Cong., 3 Sess., 44.

4. *Webster at the Bar, on the Platform*

1. See Donald H. Cole, *Jacksonian Democracy in New Hampshire* (Cambridge, 1970), ch. 2.
2. Timothy Dwight, *Travels in New England* (New Haven, 1821), I, 365, 353–67; Claude M. Feuss, *Daniel Webster* (Boston, 1930), I, ch. 8.
3. Curtis, *Life*, I, 159; Maurice G. Baxter, *Daniel Webster and the Supreme Court* (Amherst, 1966), 14–15.
4. Irving Bartlett, *Daniel Webster* (New York, 1978), 71; Arthur B. Darling, *Political Changes in Massachusetts, 1824–48* (New Haven, 1925), 16; John Kasson, *Civilization and the Machine*, 68; Carl E. Prince and Seth Taylor, "Daniel Webster, The Boston Associates, and the U.S. Government's Role in the Industrializing Process, 1815–1830," *Journal of the Early Republic*, v. 2 (1982), 282–99.
5. George Ticknor's recollection appears in Curtis, *Life*, I, 161. See also Shaw Livermore, *Twilight of Federalism* (Princeton, 1962), ch. 3.
6. Webster to Joseph Story, May 25, 1823, *Private Correspondence*, I, 325.
7. Sydney Nathans, *Daniel Webster and Jacksonian Democracy* (Baltimore, 1953), 18–28.
8. "The Progress of Jurisprudence" (1821), in Story, *Miscellaneous Writings*, 227–28.
9. See MS, "Cases Argued by Daniel Webster in the Supreme Court of the U.S.," Dartmouth College; Pref. to Baxter, *Webster and the Court*.
10. I have relied mainly on Francis N. Stites, *Private Interest and Public Gain. The Dartmouth College Case, 1819* (Amherst, 1972) and Lynn Turner, *William Plumer of New Hampshire*

(Chapel Hill, 1962), chs. 13–15. See also John M. Shirley, *The Dartmouth College Causes* (St. Louis, 1879).

11. Chauncy A. Goodrich, quoted in Curtis, *Life*, I, 169.
12. *Ibid.*, 270.
13. *Writings of Webster*, X, 232.
14. *New Hampshire Patriot*, Mar. 24, 1818.
15. Curtis, *Life*, I, 69–71, extracts the only primary source, Chauncy Goodrich's letter of Nov. 25, 1852, to Rufus Choate, which the eulogist published in *A Discourse . . . at Dartmouth College, July 27, 1853* (Boston, 1853). See the general discussion in John W. Black, "Webster's Peroration in the Dartmouth College Case," *Quarterly Journal of Speech*, v. 23 (1937), 32–42.
16. [George Ticknor], "Webster's Speeches," *American Quarterly Review*, v. 9 (1831), 434–35.
17. To Jeremiah Mason, Apr. 23, 1818, *Private Correspondence*, I, 280–81.
18. Baxter, *Webster and the Court*, 97.
19. To Joseph Story, Apr. 28, 1818, *Private Correspondence*, I, 282–83.
20. Quoted in John T. Horton, *James Kent, A Study in Conservatism, 1763–1847* (New York, 1919), 287–88.
21. To Jeremiah Mason, Apr. 10, 1819, *Letters of Daniel Webster*, C. H. Van Tyne, ed. (New York, 1902), 80–81.
22. To Joseph Hopkinson, Mar. 22, 1819, *DWP*, I, 251.
23. Hopkinson to Francis Brown, Feb. 2, 1819, *Private Correspondence*, I, 301.
24. To Joseph Story, Mar. 25, 1819, *DWP*, I, 254.
25. For the contrast see William Pinkney, *The Life of William Pinkney* (New York, 1853), 383–85.
26. The argument is in *Writings*, XV, 261–67.
27. In Congress, Jan. 4, 1826, *ibid.*, 163, 177. A useful interpretation is R. Kent Newmyer, "Daniel Webster as Tocqueville's Lawyer," *American Journal of Legal History*, v. 11 (1967) 127–47.
28. George Ticknor quoted in Curtis, *Life*, I, 216–17.
29. Ticknor, "Webster's Speeches," 436; *Writings*, XI, 3–23.
30. See the report in the Boston *Courier*, Mar. 16, 1824.
31. *Writings*, XI, 29–40. For a brief sketch of national bankruptcy legislation, see Charles Warren, *Bankruptcy in United States History* (Cambridge, 1935).
32. [Caleb Cushing] "Daniel Webster," *National Intelligencer*, Dec. 2, 1835.
33. Quoted in Merrill D. Peterson, *Democracy, Liberty, and Property: The State Constitutional Conventions of the 1820's* (Indianapolis, 1966), 7.
34. *Writings*, V, 8–25. See also "The Law of Creditor and Debtor," published in the *North American Review* in July 1820, which is in above, XV, 74–86.
35. *Ibid.*, I, 179–226. See also William T. Davis, *Plymouth Memories of an Octogenarian* (Plymouth, Mass., 1906), 256–59, 260; Wesley Frank Craven, *The Legend of the Founding Fathers* (New York, 1956), 83–85.
36. In a case before the circuit court, *La Jeune Eugénie*, in 1821, Webster argued that the slave trade violated both the law of the United States and the law of nations.
37. Ticknor, *Life and Letters*, I, 330.
38. Adams to Webster, Dec. 23, 1821, *Private Correspondence*, I, 318. See also [Caleb Cushing], "Mr. Webster's Discourse," *North American Review* v. 5 (1822), 21–32.
39. Curtis, *Life*, I, 194–95.
40. Josiah Quincy, *Figures of the Past* (Boston, 1883), 47–48.
41. Quoted in F. O. Matthiessen, *American Renaissance* (New York, 1941), 17.
42. *The Heart of Emerson's Journal*, Bliss Perry, ed. (Boston, 1926), 2–3. The informant was probably Samuel Knapp.
43. Boston *Courier*, June 20, 1825; Quincy, *Figures*, 134–37; Ticknor, in Curtis, *Life*, I, 248–50; Elizabeth Peabody to Maria Chase, Sept. 3, 1825, in *Essex Institute Historical Collections*, v. 85 (1949), 362–65; Sarah Cunningham to June 20, 1825, in Clinch Papers, Massachusetts Historical Society.
44. *Writings*, I, 234–58.
45. Curtis, *Life*, I, 251. For a different version of the anecdote, see "Sketches of the Personal and Public Character of Daniel Webster," *National Intelligencer*, Aug. 24, 1839.
46. Quoted in Samuel G. Goodrich, *Recollections of a Lifetime* (New York, 1856), II, 412n.
47. *National Intelligencer*, June 28, Aug. 13, 1825; Curtis, *Life*, I, 250.

48. Everett, in *Works of Daniel Webster* (Boston, 1851), I, lxviii; Ticknor, *Life and Letters*, I, 378–79; Ticknor quoted in Curtis, *Life*, I, 275–767. See also Merrill D. Peterson, *The Jefferson Image in the American Mind* (New York, 1960), 3–14. The "Discourse" is in *Writings*, I, 289–326.
49. Ticknor, *Life and Letters*, I, 378.
50. *National Philanthropist*, Aug. 5, 1826. See also James S. Loring, *The Hundred Boston Orations* (Boston, 1852), 422.
51. *Writings*, I, 307–8. The passage was often excerpted in handbooks of oratory, e.g., Epes Sargent, ed., *The Standard Speaker* (Philadelphia, 1852).
52. Ticknor in Curtis, *Life*, I, 275.
53. *Niles' Register*, Jan. 7, 1826.
54. *National Intelligencer*, Dec. 2, 1835.

Chapter Three: The Political Crossroads

1. Rufus King to Christopher Gore, Feb. 3, 1822, *Life and Correspondence of Rufus King*, Charles R. King, ed. (New York, 1900), VI, 456.
2. To William Gaston, Sept. 8, 1824, *Letters of Daniel Webster*, C. H. Van Tyne, ed. (New York, 1902), 108.
3. *National Intelligencer*, Apr. 19, 1823.
4. To Joseph Hopkinson, Mar. 17, 1824, *DWP*, I, 355.
5. *Writings of Webster*, V, 76.
6. *Ibid.*, I, 560.
7. To Joseph Hopkinson, Nov. 13, 1822, *DWP*, I, 318; to Jeremiah Mason, Apr. 19, 1824, *Writings*, XVI, 84; George T. Curtis, *Life of Daniel Webster* (Boston, 1870), I, 187–88; *Writings*, I, 552.
8. To Jeremiah Mason, Jan. 15, 1824, *Memoir and Correspondence of Jeremiah Mason* (Cambridge, 1873), 282. See also Willie P. Mangum to Duncan Cameron, Dec. 10, 1823, *The Papers of Willie P. Mangum*, H. T. Shanks, ed. (Raleigh, 1950), I, 83.
9. See John Floyd to C. W. Gooch, June 9, 1824, C. W. Gooch Papers, Virginia Historical Society.
10. See George Ticknor's recollection in Curtis, *Life*, I, 176–77.
11. Martin Van Buren, "Memo," Dec. 30, 1826, The Papers of Martin Van Buren, Library of Congress; Ichabod Bartlett to John Kelly, Apr. 1, 1825, Bartlett Papers, New Hampshire Historical Society.

1. *The Election of 1824*

1. Quoted in Crawford's address, in *National Intelligencer*, Sept. 17, 1831.
2. *Memoirs of John Quincy Adams*, Charles F. Adams, ed. (Philadelphia, 1874–77), V, 326–27, VI, 43.
3. To Lewis Cass, Dec. 9, 1821, *JCCP*, V, 560.
4. *Ibid.*, 560–61; Crawford to Albert Gallatin, May 13, 1822, *Writings of Gallatin*, Henry Adams, ed. (Philadelphia, 1879) II, 242–44.
5. John M. Belahlavek, *George M. Dallas: Jacksonian Patrician* (Univ. Park, Pa., 1977), 19–21; Philip S. Klein, *Pennsylvania Politics, 1817–1832* (Philadelphia, 1940), 125–30.
6. To Virgil Maxcy, Dec. 31, 1821, *JCCP*, VI, 595–97; William Drayton to William Lowndes, Jan. 7, 1822, and D. E. Huger to Lowndes, Jan. 7, 1822, Lowndes Papers, Univ. of North Carolina.
7. Lowndes to Mrs. Lowndes, Jan. 6, 1822, to James Hamilton, Jr., Jan. 29, [1822], *ibid.*
8. James Hamilton, Jr., to Lowndes, Jan. 9, 1822, *ibid.*
9. To Ninian Edwards, Oct. 5, 1822, *JCCP*, VI, 295.
10. William Plumer, Jr., to William Plumer, Jan. 3, 1822, in Everett S. Brown, ed., *The Missouri Compromise and Presidential Politics, 1820–1825* (St. Louis, 1926), 72–73; Adams, *Memoirs*, VI, 477–78. Calhoun's biographers are divided on whether or not he actually sought the presidency. Charles M. Wiltse, *John C. Calhoun, Nationalist, 1782–1828* (Indianapolis, 1944), 242, 271, thinks he did not; Gerald M. Capers, *John C. Calhoun, Opportunist* (Gainesville, 1960), 77–79, thinks he did.
11. Adams, *Memoirs*, VI, 242–245; and for a summary judgment, VII, 446–47.
12. In addition to biographical accounts, see Thomas R. Hay, "John C. Calhoun and the Presidential Campaign of 1824," *North Carolina Historical Review*, v. 12 (1935), 20–44.

13. Crawford's comments, *National Intelligencer*, Sept. 17, 1831, are revealing. On the A.B. Letters, see Wiltse, *Nationalist*, I, 262–63; Calhoun to Ninian Edwards, Aug. 20 and Oct. 5, 1822, to Samuel Southard, Sept. 23, 1822, *JCCP*, VII, 247–49, 295–96, 277–78. See also Francis P. Weisenberger, *The Life of John McLean* (Columbus, 1837), 32–33.

14. The most damaging instance was the matter of the Mix contract. See Wiltse, *Nationalist*, 203–205, 253, 276, 344–46. For use of it during the campaign, see Calhoun to Virgil Maxcy, May 6, 1822, *JCCP*, VI, 97–98. The charges were later revived by Isaac Hill, *Register of Debates*, 24 Cong., Sess., 1874–76.

15. To Samuel Southard, Mar. 19, 27, 1823, *JCCP*, VI, 533, 546.

16. To Jeremiah Mason, Feb. 15, 1824, *Writings*, XVI, 80–81.

17. William Plumer, Jr., to William Plumer, Jan. 1, 1824, in Brown, *Missouri Compromise*, 94.

18. *New England Galaxy*, May 28, 1824.

19. Littleton W. Tazewell to John Randolph, Mar. 4, 1826, Tazewell Papers, Virginia State Library; Romulus M. Saunders to Thomas Ruffin, Dec. 29, 1823, *The Papers of Thomas Ruffin*, J. G. de Roulhoc Hamilton, ed. (Raleigh, 1919), I, 185–86.

20. To Joseph G. Swift, Aug. 24, 1823, *JCCP*, VIII, 243; to Robert Garnett, July 3, 1824, *Correspondence of Calhoun*, 231–33.

21. To Jacob Brown, Aug. 8, 1823, *JCCP*, VII, 215.

22. To Henry Wheaton, May 3, 1823, *ibid.*, 54; to Virgil Maxcy, Aug. 2, 1822, *ibid.*, VI, 232.

23. Quoted in Hay, "Campaign of 1824," 31.

24. William Plumer, Jr., to William Plumer, Nov. 24, 1820, Brown, *Missouri Compromise*, 56. For a different view, see Samuel Pleasonton to Caesar A. Rodney, Apr. 7, 17, 1820, Rodney Papers, Delaware Historical Society.

25. *National Intelligencer*, Dec. 12, 1822.

26. "Wayne" [Amos Kendall], "To the People of Ohio," *Kentucky Reporter*, Oct. 28, 1822, copying the *Cincinnati Gazette*.

27. To Peter B. Porter, Aug. 10, 1822, *HCP*, III, 273–74. See also Charles G. Sellers, "Jackson Men with Feet of Clay," *American Historical Review*, v. 62 (1957), 537–51.

28. Jonathan Russell to Clay, Oct. 15, 1815, "Letters of Jonathan Russell," *Proceedings of Massachusetts Historical Society* (1911) v. 44, 311.

29. John Quincy Adams, *The Duplicate Letters, the Fisheries and the Mississippi* (Washington, 1822).

30. Adams, *Memoirs*, VI, 49.

31. To Martin D. Hardin, June 23, to Jonathan Russell, July 9, 1822, *HCP*, III, 238–39, 252–57; to the *National Intelligencer*, Nov. 16, 1822, in *ibid.*, Dec. 17, 1822.

32. *Argus of Western America*, Feb. 2, 12, Mar. 19, Apr. 16, 1823.

33. *Kentucky Reporter*, June 21, 1824, copying the *Cincinnati Gazette*. See also *Observation on the Nomination of a Candidate for the Presidency . . . By a Citizen of Ohio* (n.p., [1822]); George Robertson, *Scrap Book on Law and Politics, Men and Times* (Lexington, Ky., 1855), 148–49.

34. Quoted in John Floyd to C. W. Gooch, June 9, 1824, Gooch Papers, Virginia Historical Society.

35. Peter B. Porter to Clay, Apr. 14, 1822, *HCP*, III, 191.

36. *Ibid.*, June 15, 1823, III, 433–34.

37. Henry R. Storrs to [——], Nov. 1, 1823, French Collection, Massachusetts Historical Society; Samuel Smith to Jonathan Russell, Sept. 15, 1823, Russell Papers, *ibid.*

38. Willie P. Mangum to Duncan Cameron, Dec. 10, 1823, *Mangum Papers*, I, 83.

39. Elijah H. Mills to his wife, Jan. 22, 1824, "Extracts from the Familiar Correspondence of the Hon. Elijah H. Mills," *Proceedings of Massachusetts Historical Society*, 1st. ser., v. 19 (1881–82), 41–42. See also Thomas Finley to James Findlay, Mar. 24, 1823, "Selections from the Torrence Papers," *Quarterly Publication of the Historical and Philosophical Society of Ohio*, v. 1 (1906), 68.

40. To Joseph G. Swift, Oct. 26, 1823, *JCCP*, VIII, 329. On Calhoun's change of tactics, see Charles Sydnor, *The Development of Southern Sectionalism, 1819–1848* (Baton Rouge, 1948), 162–65.

41. *Annals of Congress*, 18 Cong., 1 Sess., 850–66.

42. To Virgil Maxcy, Feb. 27, 1824, *JCCP*, VIII, 554–55.

43. Albert Gallatin to Albert R. Gallatin, Mar. 10, 1824 and to Walter Lowrie, Mar. 16, 1824, Albert Gallatin Papers, Library of Congress.

44. On the vice presidential nomination, see the memorandum of a conversation, Feb. 20, 1825, *Memoirs of John Adams Dix* (New York, 1883), II, 309–313.

45. To Francis Brooke, Jan. 22, 1824, *HCP*, III, 602–3.
46. Asher Robbins to Clay, Aug. 5, 1824, *ibid.*, 804.
47. Henry Shaw to Clay, Oct. 4, 1824, *ibid.*, 857–59.
48. Joseph T. Buckingham, *Personal Memoirs* (Boston, 1852), II, 5, 10–11; *Boston Courier*, Oct. 18, 1824; William Ingalls to Josiah S. Johnston, Aug. 6, 24, 1824, Ohio Historical Society.
49. *National Intelligencer*, Sept. 16, 23, 1824; Klein, *Pennslyvania Politics*, 171–75; Josiah S. Johnston to Clay, Sept. 22, 1824, *HCP*, III, 844–45.
50. *Ibid.*, and Sept. 11, 1824, III, 836–37.
51. See, e.g., Walter Lowrie to Albert Gallatin, Sept. 25, 1824, and Gallatin to Lowrie, Oct. 2, 1824, Gallatin Papers; Thomas Hart Benton to C. W. Gooch, Mar. 22, John Forsyth to Gooch, Apr. 25, Francis Johnson to Thomas Ritchie, June 5, Gooch to Forsyth, Sept. 14, 1824, Gooch Family Papers, Univ. of Virginia; Clay to Charles Hammond, Oct. 25, 1824, *HCP*, III, 870–72.
52. See esp. Roy F. Nichols, *The Invention of American Political Parties* (New York, 1967), ch. 17.
53. Thomas Hart Benton, *Thirty Years View* (New York, 1856), I, 49.
54. To Francis P. Blair, Jan. 8, 1825, *HCP*, IV, 9–10. See also Daniel Drake's statement on Clay's opinion before leaving Lexington, *National Intelligencer*, Apr. 5, 1825.
55. William Plumer, Jr., memo. of conversation, *Niles' Register*, July 5, 1828.
56. *Ibid.*; *HCP*, III, 893–94.
57. For Clay's account of the relationship, see his letter to Josiah S. Johnston, Oct. 6, 1827, *HCP*, VI, 1114–17. On Jackson's side, see William A. Butler, *Retrospect of Forty Years, 1825–65* (New York, 1911), 125–27, and James Parton, *Life of Andrew Jackson* (New York, 1960), III, 45–47.
58. Adams, *Memoirs*, VI, 444, 447, 457.
59. To Caesar Rodney, Aug. 9, 1821, *HCP*, III, 107.
60. To Benjamin W. Leigh, Dec. 22, 1824, *ibid.*, III, 901.
61. Louis McLane to his wife, Jan. 13, 1825, McLane Papers, Library of Congress; *Niles' Register*, Jan. 8, 1825.
62. Adams, *Memoirs*, VI, 464–65; Brown, *Missouri Compromise*, 131, 132–33.
63. "Reminiscence," *Writings*, I, 556; *HCP* IV, 19–32.
64. To Francis P. Blair, Jan. 29, 1825, *HCP*, IV, 46–48.
65. *Kentucky Gazette*, Jan. 6, 27, Feb. 3, 1825.
66. Calvin Colton, *The Life and Times of Henry Clay* (New York, 1846), I, 295–96.
67. *Ibid.*, 297–98.
68. See Richard R. Stenberg, "Jackson, Buchanan, and the 'Corrupt Bargain' Calumny," *Pennslyvania Magazine of History and Biography*, v. 58 (1934), 61–85.
69. See the analysis in William H. Riker, *The Theory of Political Coalitions* (New Haven, 1962), 150–55.
70. "Memorandum," Dec. 1824, in Fletcher Webster, ed., *Private Correspondence of Daniel Webster* (Boston, 1857), I, 364–73.
71. Shaw Livermore, Jr., *The Twilight of Federalism* (Princeton, 1962), ch. 9. The first—inaccurate—report, is in *Niles' Register*, Oct. 20, 1827.
72. Wiltse, *Calhoun, Nationalist*, I, 307.
73. William H. Crawford to Clay, Feb. 4, 1828, *Works of Clay*, III, 192; Colton, *Life*, I, 319.
74. Clay offered varying explanations of why he accepted the office; see, e.g., his letter to Francis Brooke, Feb. 18, 1825, and his "Address to the People of the Congressional District," Mar. 26, 1825, *HCP*, IV, 73–74, 143–65.
75. See the later reports by Branch and William H. Harrison, *Niles' Register*, Sept. 8, Dec. 1, 1827; Clay to Charles Hammond, Oct. 30, 1827, *HCP*, VI, 1202–3.
76. Jackson to William B. Lewis, Feb. 14, 1825, *Correspondence of Andrew Jackson*, John S. Bassett, ed. (Washington, 1926–1933), III, 276.
77. Jackson to Samuel Swarthout, Feb. 23, 1825, in *National Intelligencer*, Mar. 10, 1825; see also *HCP*, IV, 46n.
78. "Address," *ibid.*, IV, 143–65.
79. To Joseph G. Swift, Mar. 10, 1825, *JCCP*, X, 9–10.

2. Adams and Clay

1. To James Brown, May 9, 1825, *HCP*, IV, 336.

2. Webster to Clay, Apr. 7, 1825, *ibid.*, 230; Tyler to Clay, Mar. 7, 1825, in Lyon G. Tyler, *The Letters and Times of the Tylers* (Richmond, 1884), I, 360.

3. To Adams, June 28, 1825, *HCP*, IV, 489; *Niles' Register*, June–July, 1825 contains abundant material on Clay's travels and speeches.

4. Edward D. Mansfield, *Personal Memoir* (Cincinnati, 1879), 211; *Niles' Register*, July 30, 1825; *Papers*, IV, 529–30.

5. For a balanced view see Theodore E. Burton's contribution to Samuel F. Bemis, ed., *The American Secretaries of State and Their Diplomacy* (New York, 1928), IV, 115–60. See also, Van Deussen, *Clay*, ch. 12.

6. Horatio Greenough, quoted in Sylvia E. Crane, *White Silences . . . American Sculptors in Nineteenth Century Italy,* (Coral Gables, 1982), 30.

7. To James Erwin, Apr. 21, 1827, *HCP*, VI, 471.

8. Margaret Bayard Smith, *The First Forty Years of Washington Society*, Gaillard Hunt, ed. (London, 1906), 248–85; Josiah Quincy, *Figures of the Past* (Boston, 1883), 254–79.

9. Richardson, *Messages and Papers*, II, 299–317; Adams, *Memoirs*, VII, 59, 62–63, on the cabinet discussion. Adams's views on internal improvements are elaborated in his address at the ground-breaking for the C & O Canal, in *Niles' Register*, July 12, 1828.

10. *A Letter from the Secretary of the Treasury Enclosing the Annual Report on the States of the Finances* (Washington, 1825); Richard Rush to Clay, Dec. 29, 1825, *Papers*, IV, 955.

11. See, e.g., William Branch Giles, *Political Miscellanies* (n.d., n.p.); Thomas Cooper, *Consolidation . . .* (Columbia, S.C., 1824) and "Columbia Memorial," *Niles' Register*, Dec. 13, 1823.

12. Quoted in Robert Remini, *The Election of Andrew Jackson* (Philadelphia, 1963), 24.

13. To [S. L. Gouverneur?], Dec. 18, 1825, *JCCP*, X, 58.

14. Willie P. Mangum to Bartlett Yancey, Jan. 15, 1826, *Mangum Papers*, I, 234.

15. Copied in the *Courier*, Dec. 21, 1825.

16. *National Intelligencer*, Feb. 21, 1826.

17. G. H. Haynes, *The Senate of the United States* (Boston, 1938), I, 254.

18. To Micah Sterling, Feb. 4, 1826, *JCCP*, X, 72–73.

19. Fragment, [Oct.?, 1827], McLean Papers; Wiltse, *Nationalist*, 324.

20. *Writings*, V, 189.

21. To Poinsett, Mar. 26, 1825, *HCP*, IV, 166–77.

22. To Henry Middleton, Mar. 10, 1825, *ibid.*, 355–62; Bemis, ed., *Secretaries of State*, 135–36.

23. To Poinsett, Mar. 26, 1825, *HCP*, IV, 166–77; Poinsett to Clay, Sept. 28, 1825, *ibid.*, 699–700.

24. Van Buren, *Autobiography*, 200, 514. See also Samuel Bell to John F. Parrott, Feb. 11, 1826, Parrott Papers, New Hampshire Historical Society.

25. To John J. Crittenden, Mar. 10, 1826, *HCP*, V, 158.

26. To Jeremiah Mason, Mar. 27, 1826, *Writings*, XVI, 125–27; *Kentucky Reporter*, Mar. 13, 1826; Calhoun, *Life*, 31.

27. Webster, *Writings*, V, 178–217. For the Panama debate see *Register of Debates*, 19 Cong., 1 Sess., 1805–2514 *passim*.

28. Instructions to Anderson and Sergeant, May 8, 1826, *HCP*, V, 315–41. On the failure of the Panama Congress see Randolph Campbell, "Henry Clay and the Emerging Nations of Spanish America, 1815–1829," Ph.D. diss., Univ. of Virginia, 1966, chs. 11 and 12.

29. *Register of Debates*, 19 Cong., 1 Sess., 390–401; William C. Bruce, *John Randolph of Roanoke* (New York, 1939), I, 513–25; William P. Brobson, "Diary, 1825–1828," *Delaware History*, v. 15 (1972–73), 203–4; "Julius" [Richard Rush], *John Randolph, Abroad and at Home* (Washington, 1828).

30. John K. Kane, *Autobiography* (Philadelphia, 1949), 24–25.

31. *Annals of Congress*, 18 Cong., 1 Sess., 1297, 1311–17; Josephine Seaton, *William Winston Seaton of the "National Intelligencer"* (Boston, 1871), 152.

32. Lucius P. Little, *Ben Hardin: His Times and Contemporaries* (Louisville, 1887), 43–44; *United States Telegraph*, Mar. 27, 1826; to Francis T. Brooke, Apr. 19, 1826, *HCP*, V, 253; Beverley Tucker to Clay, Dec. 16, 1839, Henry Clay Papers, Library of Congress.

33. [Winslow M. Watson], *In Memorium: Benjamin Ogle Tayloe* (n.p., 1872), 220. See the account in Bruce, *Randolph*, I, 513–25.

34. Benton, I, 75–77; Joseph R. Rosenbloom, "Rebecca Gratz and Henry Clay," *Journal of the Southern Jewish Historical Society*, v. 1 (1959) 12.

35. Bruce, *Randolph*, II, 47.

36. See John J. Crittenden to Clay, Apr. 27, 1826, *HCP*, V, 277.
37. Edward Everett to Alexander H. Everett, Mar. 25, 1826, Edward Everett Papers (microfilm ed.), Massachusetts Historical Society.
38. The argument between "Patrick Henry" and "Onslow" may be followed in *JCCP*, X, 92–104 and *passim*. See also Haynes, *Senate*, I, 212–214; Calhoun, *Life*, 31–32; Adams, *Memoirs*, VII, 433; *Register of Debates*, 20 Cong., 1 Sess., 278–80.
39. Adams to Alexander H. Everett, Aug. 10, 1818, *Writings*, VI, 422–24. Anglo-American diplomacy is analyzed in George Dangerfield, *The Era of Good Feelings* (New York, 1952). See also F. Lee Benns, *The American Struggle for the British West Indian Carrying Trade, 1815–1830* (Indianapolis, 1923).
40. To Webster, Sept. 1, to Clay, Sept. 28, 1825, *HCP*, IV, 695–97. For Clay's view of Huskisson, see his speech at Cincinnati, July 13, 1825, *ibid.*, IV, 529–30.
41. To Albert Gallatin, Nov. 11, 1826; To Peter Force, Feb. 25, Mar. 25, 1827, *ibid.*, V, 895–915, VI, 239–40, 353–54; Dangerfield, *Era*, 370–79.
42. To Monroe, June 23, 1826, *JCCP*, X, 134.
43. To Levi Woodbury, Aug. 21, 1826, *ibid.*, X, 206–7.
44. *Niles' Register*, Apr. 28, 1827; *National Intelligencer*, Mar. 8, 1827. For Johnson's denial, see his letter to John McLean, May——, 1827, McLean Papers.
45. Joseph D. Lerned to Clay, Sept. 27, 1827, *HCP*, VI, 1079.
46. Carl Russell Fish, "The Crime of William H. Crawford," *American Historical Review*, v. 21 (1916), 546–56. The intent of the law was well explained in *National Intelligencer*, Jan. 1, 1822.
47. Adams, *Memoirs*, VII, 163.
48. *Ibid.*, 275; Thomas Smith to Clay, Oct. 7, 1827; Clay to Charles Hammond, Oct. 30, 1827, *HCP*, VI, 1122, 1204.
49. To Clay, Mar. 25, 1827, *DWP*, II, 175–77.
50. Benton, *View*, I, 80–82.
51. Culver Smith, *The Press, Politics, and Patronage: The American Government's Use of Newspapers, 1789–1875* (Athens, Ga., 1977), chs. 3–4; *Register of Debates*, 19 Cong., 2 Sess., 895–99, 923, 1182, 1388.
52. *U.S. Telegraph*, July 12, 1828.
53. *Courier*, Dec. 24, 1827.
54. William E. Ames, *A History of the National Intelligencer* (Chapel Hill, 1972), 110–11, 132–33.
55. Adams to the Rev. Charles Upham, Feb. 2, 1837, in Henry Adams, *The Degradation of the Democratic Dogma* (New York, 1949), 24–5.

3. *Bargain and Abominations*

1. To Charles Hammond, Nov. 1, 1825, *HCP*, IV, 780–83.
2. Quoted in James Parton, *The Life of Andrew Jackson* (New York, 1860), III, 97.
3. *Register of Debates*, 19 Cong., 1 Sess., 1957–58.
4. Quoted in Colton, *Clay*, II, 320. The letter was dated Nashville, Mar. 8, 1827, and was first published in the Fayetteville (N.C.) *Observer*, Mar. 27, 1827.
5. Colton, *Clay*, II, 323; *Niles' Register*, May 5, 1827.
6. Colton, *Clay*, II, 324–25.
7. *Ibid.*, 330–32; *Niles' Register*, July 7, 1827; to Charles Hammond, June 25, 1827, *HCP*, VI, 718–19.
8. "Lowndes," in *National Intelligencer*, Aug. 15, 1827.
9. *Kentucky Reporter*, Aug. 25, 1827; Jackson to Carter Beverley, July 18, 1827, in Colton, *Clay*, II, 337; John Sullivan, "Jackson Caricatured," *Tennessee Historical Quarterly*, v. 31 (1972), 39–44.
10. See Edward Everett's review, "Speeches of Henry Clay," *North American Review*, v. 25 (1827), 425–45.
11. To Francis Brooke, Aug. 14, 1827; Webster to Clay, Aug. 22, 1827, *Works of Clay*, III, 168–70. Buchanan's letter, Aug. 8, 1827, is in *ibid.* I, 263–67. See also Buchanan to Duff Green, Oct. 16, 1826, and to Samuel Ingham, July 12, 1827, *ibid.*, 218–19, 260; Philip S. Klein, *President James Buchanan: A Biography* (Univ. Park, Pa., 1962), 50–52, 56–59; Richard R. Stenberg, "Jackson, Buchanan, and the 'Corrupt Bargain' Calumny," *Pennsylvania Magazine of History and Biography*, v. 58 (1934), 61–85.

12. Jackson to Amos Kendall, Sept. 4, 1827, *Jackson Correspondence*, III, 380; *U.S. Telegraph*, Aug. 13, 15, 1827.
13. *Memoirs*, VII, 383.
14. Crittenden to Clay, Nov. 15, 1827, *HCP*, VI, 1265.
15. It was also widely copied in the press, e.g., *Niles' Register*, Jan. 5, 12, July 5, 1828.
16. Blair to Clay, Oct. 3, Nov. 14, Dec. 31, 1827, *HCP*. VI, 1106-7, 1261, 1403-5; William E. Smith, *The Francis Preston Blair Family in Politics* (New York, 1933), ch. 4; Albert D. Kirwan, *John J. Crittenden: The Struggle for the Union* (Lexington, Ky., 1962), 75-78; Orval W. Baylor, *John Pope Kentuckian* (Cynthiana, Ky., 1943), 286-94; *The Speech of Samuel Daveiss* [Feb. 6, 1828] (n.p., n.d.).
17. Powhatan Bouldin, *Home Reminiscences of John Randolph, of Roanoke* (Richmond, 1878), 289.
18. Jackson to Sam Houston, Dec. 15, 1826, *Jackson Correspondence*, III, 325.
19. Crittenden to Clay, Nov. 25, 1826, *HCP*, 951. See Arndt M. Stickles, *The Critical Court Struggle in Kentucky, 1819-1829* (Bloomington, 1929).
20. See Neils H. Sonne, *Liberal Kentucky, 1780-1828* (New York, 1939) and James H. Rodabaugh, *Robert Hamilton Bishop* (Columbus, Ohio, 1935), 41; Joseph Ficklin to John McLean, July 19, 27, 1826, McLean Papers; John H. Wright, *Transylvania: Tutor to the West* (Lexington, Ky., 1975).
21. Kendall to Clay, Oct. 4, 1825, Blair to Clay, Jan. 4, 1826, *HCP*, IV, 718-20, V, 56. See also, Smith, *Blair*, ch. 4; Kendall, *Autobiography*; Richard B. Latner, *The Presidency of Andrew Jackson* (Athens, Ga., 1979), 20-22, and "A New Look at Jacksonian Politics," *Journal of American History*, v. 61 (1975), 943-69.
22. *Argus of Western America*, Jan. 10, 24, 1827.
23. To Charles Hammond, Nov. 16, 1827, *HCP*, VI, 1270.
24. Van Buren, *Autobiography*, 514; Calhoun to James A. Hamilton, Mar. 2, 1828, *JCCP*, X, 355-56.
25. Thomas Worthington to John McLean, Aug. 29, 1826, McLean Papers.
26. To Samuel Southard, Oct. 11, 1825, to Levi Woodbury, Aug. 2, 1826, to James Monroe, June 23, 1826, *JCCP*, X, 27-8, 202, 206-7, 134.
27. See the suggestion in Thomas C. Grattan, *Civilized America* (London, 1859), I, 182.
28. To Samuel Ingham, July 23, 1828, *JCCP*, X, 40-42. See Alfred G. Smith, Jr., *Economic Readjustment of an Old Cotton State: South Carolina, 1820-1860* (Columbia, 1958), and William W. Freehling, *Prelude to Civil War: The Nullification Controversy in South Carolina, 1816-1836* (New York, 1966), chs. 1-3.
29. *Register of Debates*, 19 Cong., 2 Sess., 574-75; *U.S. Telegraph*, Jan. 5, 8, 13, Feb. 14, 1827; *Niles' Register*, Jan. 13, 1827; *National Intelligencer*, Feb. 15, 1827; Calhoun to James E. Calhoun, Feb. 14, 1827, *Correspondence of Calhoun* (1899), 239-40.
30. To James Brown, Dec. 14, 1826, *HCP*, V, 1001.
31. *Register of Debates*, 19 Cong., 2 Sess., 495.
32. To Littleton W. Tazewell, July 1, 1827, *JCCP*, X, 292-93.
33. To Tazewell, Aug. 25, 1827, *ibid.*, 300.
34. To James C. Calhoun, Aug. 26, 1827, *Correspondence of Calhoun*, 249-50.
35. In a letter to Green, July 1, 1828, in the *Telegraph*, July 12, and *Niles' Register*, Sept. 20, 1828. See also Calhoun to Samuel Smith, *JCCP*, X, 403-4.
36. *Courier*, Jan. 8, 11, 13, 22, 25, and *passim*, 1827.
37. *Writings*, XIII, 24-30; *The Letters of William Lloyd Garrison, 1822-1860*, Walter M. Merrill and Louis Ruchames, eds. (Cambridge, 1971), I, 39-40.
38. To John Barney, Apr. 13, 1827, *DWP*, II, 177-81.
39. John W. Davis to George Bancroft, Jan. 29, 1826, Bancroft Papers, Cornell Univ.
40. John C. Wright, quoted in Curtis, *Webster*, I, 301. See also Edward Everett to John W. Taylor, May 7, 1827, to Joseph E. Sprague, May 8, 19, 21, 1827, Everett Papers.
41. To Clay, May 7, 1827, Clay to Webster, May 14, 27, 1827, Levi Lincoln to Webster, May 24, 1827, *DWP*, II, 197-99, 200-2, 211, 206-8.
42. *Courier*, June 8, 9, 1827; Arthur B. Darling, *Political Changes in Masschusetts, 1824-48* (New Haven, 1925), 50-55.
43. Quoted in R. Kent Newmyer, "A Note on the Whig Politics of Justice Joseph Story," *Mississippi Valley Historical Review*, v. 48 (1961), 487. See also Gerald T. Dunne, *Justice Joseph Story and the Rise of the Supreme Court* (New York, 1970), and the trenchant comment in William W. Story, *Life and Letters of Joseph Story* (Boston, 1851), II, 408.
44. *Register of Debates*, 19 Cong., 1 Sess., 1576-77.

45. *Writings*, V, 163, 177.
46. *Ibid.*, XIV, 107–18; *Register of Debates*, 19 Cong., 2 Sess., 935–37, 1034–36, 1041–52.
47. To Story, May 8, 1826, *DWP*, II, 113; *Writings*, V, 150–77.
48. *Register of Debates*, 20 Cong., 2 Sess., 63.
49. *Writings*, VII, 250, XIV, 92–100; Quincy, *Figures of the Past*, 282.
50. Haynes, *Senate*, I, 232–33.
51. *Writings*, VII, 250.
52. Joseph Hopkinson to Webster, Apr. 13, 1827; Webster to Clay and Clay to Webster, Apr. 14, 1827, *DWP*, II, 188–99, 191–92; *Kentucky Reporter*, Aug. 5, 1827.
53. Note, *DWP*, II, 46–48; Walsh to Webster, Aug. 22, 1825 *ibid.*, II, 71; *National Advertiser* copied in *Courier*, July 13, 1825.
54. *National Intelligencer*, Oct. 17, 1827, May 13, 1828; Adams, *Memoirs*, VII, 46; Edward Everett to Alexander H. Everett, Dec. 16, 1827, Edward Everett Papers.
55. *Courier*, Nov. 7, 1826.
56. *Ibid.*, June 3, 1825.
57. Quoted in *DWP*, II, 159–60n.
58. To William Coleman, Feb. 23, 1827, *ibid.*, 160–63.
59. Curtis, *Webster*, I, 304–23; Bartlett, *Webster*, 91–96; Story to Jeremiah Mason, Feb. 27, 1828, *Memoirs of Mason*, 315–16.
60. *Register of Debates*, 20 Cong., 1 Sess., 2472.
61. For the traditional view of the Tariff of Abominations as only a party stratagem, see Dangerfield, *Era*, 405–9. It finds support in *Niles' Register*, Sept. 20, 1828. For the revisionist view, see Robert V. Remini, *Martin Van Buren and the Making of the Democratic Party* (New York, 1959), ch. 12.
62. *Writings*, V, 242, 228–47.
63. *Ibid.*, 320.
64. Abbott Lawrence to Webster, May 7, 1828; see also Samuel H. Babcock and Joseph T. Buckingham to Webster, both May 7, 1828, *ibid.*, 341, 342.
65. *Register of Debates*, 24 Cong., 2 Sess., 975–76.
66. *U.S. Telegraph*, June 4, 24, 1828.
67. *Niles' Register*, June 14, July 19, 1828.
68. See John Carter to Robert Y. Hayne, Oct. 28, 1828 (extract) and "Major Hamilton's Statement," James Hamilton, Jr. Papers, Univ. of North Carolina.
69. Everett to Alexander H. Everett, June 11, 1828, Edward Everett Papers; *Courier*, June 4, 7, 11, 1828.
70. *Writings*, II, 14–20.
71. See Henry Adams, ed., *Documents Relating to New England Federalism, 1800–1815* (Boston, 1877).
72. Everett to Alexander H. Everett, Nov. 15, 1828, Everett Papers.
73. Joseph H. Benton, *A Notable Libel Case* (Boston, 1904), 1; the report of the trial, *Courier*, Dec. 19, 1828; Theodore Lyman, Jr., to Francis Baylies, Nov. 19, 1828, Massachusetts Historical Society.
74. Ticknor, *Life and Letters*, I, 381; Adams, *Memoirs*, VII, 520–22.
75. Smith, *First Forty Years*, 285–86.
76. *Argus of Western America*, July 16, 1828.
77. *U.S. Telegraph*, Sept. 13, 1827; *Niles' Register*, June 28, 1828.
78. *U.S. Telegraph*, Aug. 2, 1827, Feb. 16, 1828; *Kentucky Reporter*, Sept. 22, 1827.
79. Quoted in *ibid.*, June 2, 1827.
80. *Enquirer*, Aug. 26, 1828.
81. *Niles' Register*, May 17, 1828.

Chapter Four: Liberty and Union

1. To Mrs. Ezekiel Webster, Mar. 4, 1829, *Private Correspondence of Daniel Webster*, Fletcher Webster, ed. (Boston, 1857), I, 473–74; to Ezekiel Webster, Feb. 23, 26, 1829, *Letters of Daniel Webster*, C. H. Van Tyne, ed. (New York, 1902), 141–42, 144–45; Memorandum, [Feb. 1829], *ibid.*, 142–43.
2. *A Compilation of the Messages and Papers of the Presidents*, J. D. Richardson, ed. (Washington, 1907), II, 436–38.

3. *Life and Speeches of Henry Clay*, Daniel Mallory, ed. (New York, 1843), I, 360–65; *National Intelligencer*, Mar. 10, 1829.

4. Norman Gash, *Sir Robert Peel* (London, 1972), 458–59.

5. J. J. De Graff to A. C. Flagg, Dec. 22, 1828, A. C. Flagg Papers, New York Public Library; Samuel Flagg Bemis, *John Quincy Adams and the Union* (New York, 1965), 156.

6. See, e.g., Clay to Webster, Nov. 30, 1828, and to Richard Brooke, Jan. 10, 1829, *HCP*, VII, 552–53, 594.

7. Clay to [Josiah S. Johnston], Apr. 1, 1829, *HCP*.

8. *Speeches*, I, 573, 564–81; *Kentucky Reporter*, June 3, 1829.

9. James Parton, *Famous Americans of Recent Times* (Boston, 1867), 41; Clay to [———], May 23, 1829, *HCP*.

10. *Kentucky Reporter*, July 8, *United States Telegraph*, Aug. 4, *Courier*, Aug. 11, Nov. 11, 1829.

11. *Kentucky Reporter*, Nov. 4, 1829; *Argus of Western America*, Oct. 21, 1829. Clay's travels may be followed in the pages of *Niles' Register*.

12. See, e.g., Clay to Samuel Southard, July 7, 1829, Southard Papers, Princeton Univ.

13. "Sketch of Mr. Clay," *American Monthly Magazine*, I (1829), 341–46. See the account by N. P. Willis, reprinted in the New York *Times*, Dec. 2, 1852. For contemporary comment on the article, see Frankfort *Argus*, Oct. 28, 1829.

14. *National Intelligencer*, Nov. 28; *Niles' Register*, Nov. 7, 1829.

15. Irving H. Bartlett, *Daniel Webster* (New York, 1978), 97.

16. George M. Dallas to Samuel Ingham, Dec. 30, 1829, Dallas Papers, Pennsylvania Historical Society.

17. Thomas H. Clay, "Two Years with Old Hickory," *Atlantic Monthly*, v. 60 (1887), 187–99; James A. Hamilton, *Reminiscences* (New York, 1869), 101.

18. Calhoun to William C. Preston, Nov. 6, 1828, in David R. Barbee, ed., "A Sheaf of Old Letters," *Tyler's Quarterly Historical and Genealogical Magazine*, v. 32 (1950), 91–92.

19. *Ibid.*

20. *Works of Calhoun*, VI, 1–59.

21. To John A. Dix, Jan. 2, to William C. Preston, Jan. 6, 1829, *JCCP*, X, 542, 545–46.

22. Robert P. Letcher to Clay, Dec. 21, 1829, *HCP*. See also *Life of John C. Calhoun* (New York, 1843), 37; Andrew Jackson to John Overton, Dec. 31, 1829, *Correspondence of Andrew Jackson*, John S. Bassett, ed. (Washington, 1926–33), IV, 109; Boston *Courier*, May 11, 1830.

1. *Webster and Hayne*

1. *Register of Debates*, 21 Cong., 1 Sess., 24. The entire debate may be followed in the *Register*. Rush's Report is in *American State Papers: Finance* (Washington, 1836–61), V, 630–42. See also *Niles' Register*, Dec. 15, 1827.

2. *Register of Debates*, 33.

3. See the discussion in Merrill D. Peterson, *Olive Branch and Sword—The Compromise of 1833* (Baton Rouge, 1982), ch. 1.

4. On the western interest in public lands policy, see Raynor G. Wellington, *The Political and Sectional Influence of the Public Lands, 1828–1842* (n.p., 1914). An interesting perspective on the cession proposal is William T. Hutchinson, "Unite to Divide; Divide to Unite: The Shaping of American Federalism," *Mississippi Valley Historical Review*, v. 46 (1959), 3–18.

5. Quoted in Wellington, *Public Lands*, 25; *Register of Debates*, 19 Cong., 2 Sess., 209–22; and 21 Cong., 1 Sess., 477–504.

6. *Ibid.*, 21–22; Robert Y. Hayne to Webster, Jan. 15, 1830, *DWP*.

7. In a speech, New York City, Mar. 10, 1831, *Writings*, II, 61.

8. Notes for Reply to Hayne, [Jan. 26, 1830], *DWP* (microfilm ed.); George T. Curtis, *Life of Daniel Webster* (Boston, 1870), I, 357.

9. *Register of Debates*, 39. The speech may also be found in *Writings*, V, 248–69.

10. *Ibid.*, 259, which may be compared with *Register of Debates*, 38, for slightly different wording.

11. *Ibid.*, 38–39; *Writings*, III, 260.

12. Nathan Sargent, *Public Men and Events* (Philadelphia, 1875), I, 171; Theodore D. Jervey, *Robert Y. Hayne and His Times* (New York, 1909), 265–66; Thomas D. Clark, ed., *South Carolina, the Grand Tour, 1780–1865* (Columbia, 1973), 177–78.

13. *Register of Debates*, 47–48; Jervey, *Hayne*, 238–39.

14. Sargent, *Public Men*, I, 173.
15. Everett to Charles W. March, Jan. 3, 1850, Everett Papers, Massachusetts Historical Society; Margaret E. White, *A Sketch of Chester Harding, Artist* (New York, 1970), 148–49.
16. Margaret Bayard Smith, *First Forty Years of Washington Society*, Gaillard Hunt, ed. (New York, 1906), 309; Lewis Machen to W. Slade, Jan. 30, 1830, *Letters of Arthur W. Machen*, Arthur W. Machen, Jr., ed. (Baltimore, 1917), 52–55.
17. Sargent, *Public Men*, I, 172; John W. Forney, *Anecdotes of Public Men* (New York, 1881), II, 127; John Fiske, *Essays Historical and Literary* (New York, 1902), I, 270.
18. To Warren Dutton, Mar. 18, 1830, *Private Correspondence*, I, 493–94.
19. Nicholas P. Trist to James Madison, Feb. 6, 1830, Trist Papers, Univ. of Virginia.
20. *Register of Debates*, 60. See also [Henry W. Hilliard], "Daniel Webster and the Constitution," *Harper's Magazine*, v. 54 (1876), 599–600.
21. *Register of Debates*, 62.
22. *Ibid.*, 64.
23. *Ibid.*, 68.
24. *Ibid.*, 70–71.
25. *Ibid.*, 72.
26. See the undated Memorandum on Nullification, [Dec. 31, 1830], DWP; Curtis, *Life*, I, 352–53n.
27. *Register of Debates*, 74.
28. Nathan Dane, *A General Abridgment and Digest of American Law*, Appendix (Boston, 1829), IX, 10–54 *passim*.
29. *Register of Debates*, 78–79.
30. William Rawle, *A View of the Constitution of the United States of America* (Philadelphia, 1825), 295–301. See also Kenneth Stampp, "The Concept of a Perpetual Union," *Journal of American History*, v. 45 (1978), 5–33.
31. *Register of Debates*, 78.
32. Quoted in Paul Nagel, *One Nation Indivisible: The Union in American Thought, 1776–1861* (New York, 1964), 145; "Daniel Webster," *Southern Literary Messenger*, v. 3 (1837), 759–60.
33. [Caleb Cushing], "Daniel Webster," *National Intelligencer*, Dec. 2, 1835; *Niles' Register*, Mar. 27, 1830; [George Ticknor], "Webster's Speeches," *American Quarterly Review*, IX (1831).
34. Henry S. Foote, *Casket of Reminiscences* (Washington, 1874), 36–37.
35. *National Intelligencer*, Mar. 20, 1841; Robert C. Winthrop, "Webster's Reply to Hayne," *Scribner's Magazine*, v. 15 (1894), 118–28.
36. Edward Everett to Webster, Feb.——, 1830, DWP; Curtis, *Life*, 364n.
37. Abbott Lawrence to Edward Everett, Apr. 4, 5, 13, 26, 1830, Everett Papers.
38. Joseph L. Williams to Webster, Apr. 4, 1830; A. M. Hughes to Webster, Apr. 29, 1830, DWP.
39. To Joseph E. Sprague, Mar. 16, 1830, *Letters*, 150.
40. *Register of Debates*, 449.
41. To Amos Lawrence, May 22, 1830, DWP, III, 72.
42. Joseph Story to Webster, Apr. 17, 1830, DWP.
43. Quoted in Howard A. Bradley and James A. Winans, *Daniel Webster and the Salem Murder* (Columbia, Mo., 1956), 68. See the account in Curtis, *Life*, I, 378–85.
44. Ralph Waldo Emerson, *Journals*, VIII, 296. For two contrasting views which agree that Webster accepted a fee in one case or the other, see Curtis, *Life*, I, 382–83, and Bradley and Winans, *Salem Murder*, 221–22.
45. Joel Parker, *Daniel Webster as a Jurist* (Cambridge, 1853), 52–53. The speech is in *Writings*, VI, 41–105.
46. *Niles' Register*, Oct. 16, 1830; Samuel L. Knapp, *A Memoir of the Life of Daniel Webster* (Boston, 1831), 178.
47. *Speeches and Forensic Arguments*, Charles B. Haddock, ed. (Boston, 1830), iv, v.
48. "Webster's Speeches," *American Quarterly Review*, IX, 420–56. There was also a pamphlet edition of this review.
49. William Wirt to Peachy Gilmer, Dec. 30, 1832, Wirt Papers, Library of Congress.
50. *Writings*, II, 43–44; *Niles' Register*, Apr. 2, 9, 1831.
51. Curtis, *Life*, I, 398–400.

2. *Calhoun and Jackson*

1. Jackson to John Coffee, Mar. 19, 22, May 20, 1829, *Correspondence*, IV, 13, 15, 38; James Parton, *Life of Andrew Jackson* (New York, 1860), III, 187, 189.
2. Reply to Major Eaton (1831), *Works of Calhoun*, VI, 439. See also "Peggy O'Neale at the Dawn of the Republic," *Southern Review*, v. 13 (1873), 213–31.
3. 5th edition (Boston, 1806), 182.
4. Parton, *Jackson*, III, 191.
5. Jackson to John Overton, Dec. 31, 1829, in *ibid.*, 294–95.
6. To Warren Dutton, Jan. 15, 1830, *Private Correspondence*, I, 483.
7. See the discussion in Richard P. Latner, *The Presidency of Andrew Jackson* (Athens, Ga.), 64–66.
8. Francis P. Blair to Mrs. Benjamin Gratz, Feb. 23, 1831, in Clay, "Two Years," 191; Washington *Globe*, Nov. 1, 1831.
9. *Works*, VI, 439.
10. "The Autobiography of William John Grayson," Samuel G. Stoney, ed., *South Carolina Historical and Genealogical Magazine*, v. 50 (1949), 85.
11. Thomas Hart Benton, *Thirty Years' View* (New York, 1856), I, 148–49. Benton is notably inaccurate, especially on his own role. See also *The Autobiography of Martin Van Buren*, vol. II of *Annual Report of American Historical Association* (Washington, 1920), 413–17; and Richard R. Stenberg, "The Jefferson Birthday Dinner, 1830," *Journal of Southern History*, IV (1938), 334–46.
12. *National Intelligencer*, Apr. 20, 1831; *United States Telegraph*, Apr. 23, 1831.
13. Johnston to Clay, Jan. 23, 1830, *HCP*.
14. Parton, *Jackson*, I, 299, 297–302.
15. To Clay, Apr. 18, 1830, *DWP*, III, 58–59.
16. On May 26, 1830. The entire correspondence is in *Correspondence between General Andrew Jackson and John C. Calhoun, President and Vice President of the United States, on the Subject of the Course of the Latter in the Deliberations of the Cabinet of Mr. Monroe on the Occurrences in the Seminole War*. It was first published in February 1831 as a 52-page pamphlet; it is also in Calhoun's *Works*, VI, 349–95. See also Parton, *Jackson*, III, ch. 25; Richard R. Stenberg, "A Note on the Jackson-Calhoun Breach of 1830–1831," *Tyler's Quarterly Historical and Genealogical Magazine*, v. 21 (1939), 65–69, and "Jackson's 'Rhea letter' Hoax," *Journal of Southern History*, v. 2 (1936), 480–96.
17. Grayson, "Autobiography," 82.
18. To James C. Coleman, Jan. 13, 1831, *Correspondence of Calhoun*, (1899), 280; *National Intelligencer*, quoting Albany *Argus*, Jan. 18, 1831.
19. Robert Y. Hayne to Stephen D. Miller, Jan. 26, 1831, Hayne Papers, University of South Carolina.
20. To James H. Hammond, Jan. 15, 1831, *JCCP*, XI, 301.
21. Joseph H. Parks, *Felix Grundy, Champion of Democracy* (Baton Rouge, 1940), 177–80; Van Buren, *Autobiography*, 376–79.
22. Marquis James, *The Life of Andrew Jackson* (Indianapolis, 1938), 269–70.
23. See Stenberg, " 'Rhea letter' Hoax."
24. Van Buren, *Autobiography*, 519, 751, 753, and ch. 27 *passim*; Washington *Globe*, Mar. 12, 1831.
25. Richard Frisby to Samuel Smith, Feb. 20, 1832, Smith Papers, Maryland Historical Society.
26. Jackson to John Coffey, Apr. 24, to John C. McLemore, June 27, 1831, *Correspondence*, 269, 304–6.
27. To Samuel Ingham, May 4, 1831, *JCCP*, XI, 377–80.
28. *Memoirs of John Quincy Adams*, Charles F. Adams, ed. (Philadelphia, 1874–77), VIII, 333, 337; Webster to Clay, Mar. 4, 1831, *DWP*, III, 107–8; Clay to Francis Brooke, Apr. 24, 1831, *HCP*.
29. *Life and Diary of John Floyd*, Charles H. Ambler, ed. (Richmond, 1918), 124–26, 104–11, 142.
30. *U.S. Telegraph*, Apr. 25, 26, 1831.
31. To Virgil Maxcy, Sept. 11; to Col. Nathan Towson, Sept. 11; to Samuel Ingham, Oct. 20, 1830, *JCCP*, XI, 226–28, 230–31, 250–51.

32. William J. Grayson quoted in William W. Freehling, *Prelude to Civil War: The Nullification Controversy in South Carolina, 1816–1836* (New York, 1966), 205.
33. To Virgil Maxcy, Sept. 11, 1830, *JCCP*, XI, 228–29.
34. *Works of Calhoun*, VI, 139.
35. To James H. Hammond, Jan. 15, 1831, *Correspondence of Calhoun*, 281–82.
36. Memo, Mar. 18, 1831, "Letters on the Nullification Movement in South Carolina, 1830–1834," *American Historical Review*, VI (1902), 744–45.
37. Frederic Bancroft, *Calhoun and the South Carolina Nullification Movement* (Baltimore, 1928), 102.
38. Edwin L. Green, *George McDuffie* (Columbia, S.C., 1836), 107–8; Freehling, *Prelude*, 221–23.
39. James Hamilton, Jr., to James H. Hammond, June 11, 1831, "Letters on Nullification," 746–47.
40. Duff Green to Calhoun, May 31, 1831, *JCCP*, XI, 398.
41. *Ibid.*; *U.S. Telegraph*, Apr. 9, 1831; *National Intelligencer*, Apr. 12, 1831.
42. To Samuel Ingham, June 16, 1831, *Correspondence of Calhoun*, 294.
43. *Works*, VI, 59–94. Dated July 26, the address was first published in the Pendleton (S.C.) *Messenger*, Aug. 3, 1831.
44. *National Intelligencer*, Aug. 17, 1831; Duff Green to Richard K. Crallé, Aug. 21, 1831, in Frederick W. Moore, ed., "Calhoun as Seen by His Political Friends," *Southern History Association Publications*, VII (1903), 167.
45. To Samuel Ingham, July 31, Sept. 8, 1831, *JCCP*, XI, 441–42, 468; to Samuel Gouverneur, Aug. 8, 1831, *Correspondence*, 288–89.
46. *Life of Calhoun*, 38.
47. See *The Calhoun Doctrine of Nullification Discussed by a Democratic Republican* (Charleston, 1831).
48. *Memoirs*, VIII, 332.
49. To Samuel Gouverneur, Aug. 8, 1831, *Correspondence of Calhoun*, 298–99.
50. Quoted in Charleston *Courier*, Aug. 23, in *U.S. Telegraph*, Aug. 27, 1831.
51. Duff Green to Col. A. Starrow, Sept. 3, 1831, Duff Green Papers; "Calhoun as Seen . . . ," 169; Alexander Hamilton to Virgil Maxcy, Oct. 3, 1831, Galloway-Maxcy-Markoe Papers, Library of Congress.

3. *Clay and Jackson*

1. Clay to James E. Conover, May 1, 1830, *HCP*.
2. Carter Goodrich, *Government Promotion of American Canals and Railroads, 1800–1890* (New York, 1960), 42; Eugene L. Schwaab, ed., *Travels in the Old South, 1783–1860* (Lexington, Ky., 1973), I, 269n; *Argus of Western America*, Dec. 9, 1829; *Kentucky Reporter*, Apr. 28, June 9, 1830; Andrew Kleinpeter to James Nielson, Jan. 23, 1830, Kleinpeter Papers, Louisiana State Univ.
3. *Messages and Papers*, II, 483–93. On Van Buren's authorship of the message, see Donald B. Cole, *Martin Van Buren and the American Political System* (Princeton, 1984), 326–27.
4. *National Intelligencer*, June 19, 1830.
5. Ebenezer C. Tracy, *Memoirs of the Life of Jeremiah Evarts* (Boston, 1845), 380.
6. Hugh McCulloch, *Men and Measures of Half a Century* (New York, 1889), 23. For the Lexington reaction, see *Kentucky Reporter*, June 9, 23, 1830.
7. To Adam Beatty, June 8, 1831, *Works of Clay*, IV, 276–77; to Webster, June 7, to James E. Conover, June 13, 1830, *HCP*; *Kentucky Reporter*, June 23, 1831; Jackson to F. P. Blair, Oct. 3, 1842, *Correspondence*, VI, 471–72.
8. To Francis Brooke, May 28, 1830, *Works of Clay*, IV, 272.
9. *Messages and Papers*, II, 508–17.
10. Farewell Address, quoted in Goodrich, *Government Promotion*, 42.
11. Carlton Jackson, "The Internal Improvement Vetoes of Andrew Jackson," *Tennessee Historical Quarterly*, v. 25 (1966), 261–79. See also George Dangerfield, *The Era of Good Feelings* (New York, 1952), 480–81n; Richmond *Enquirer*, July 10, 1832.
12. *National Intelligencer*, Aug. 7, 1830.
13. To Hezekiah Niles, Nov. 18, 1830, *HCP*; Samuel Gannon, Jr., *The Presidential Campaign of 1832* (New York, 1969), ch. 3.
14. George D. Prentice, *Biography of Henry Clay* (Hartford, 1831), pref.; Betty G. Congleton,

"Prentice's Biographies of Henry Clay and John Greenleaf Whittier," *Filson Club Historical Quarterly*, v. 37 (1963), 325–30. There are also several pertinent letters in the George D. Prentice Papers, New York Public Library.

15. Albert D. Kirwan, *John J. Crittenden: The Struggle for the Union* (Lexington, Ky., 1962), 88–91.
16. To Francis Brooke, June 23, 1831, *Works of Clay*, IV, 303–4; to Peter B. Porter, June 13, 1830, *HCP*.
17. Richard Rush to Clay, Sept. 25, 1830, June 1, 1831, *ibid*. For Thurlow Weed's view see his letter to William H. Seward, June 18, 1831, Seward Papers, Univ. of Rochester.
18. Richard Rush to Philip Fendall, May 19, 24, 1831, Rush Papers, Princeton Univ.
19. *Memoirs*, VIII, 368; Edward Everett to Francis Johnson, July 12, 1831, Everett Papers.
20. To Christopher Van Deventer, May 25, 1831, *Correspondence of Calhoun*, to Samuel Ingham, May 25, 1831, *JCCP*.
21. Duff Green to Richard Crallé, Sept. 11, 1831, in "Calhoun as Seen," 169; Alexander Hamilton to Virgil Maxcy, Oct. 3, 1831, Galloway-Maxcy-Markoe Papers.
22. John P. Kennedy, *Memoirs of the Life of William Wirt* (Philadelphia, 1849), II, 318, 330–31; Wirt to Dabney Carr, Oct. 5, to Robert Walsh, Oct. 24, 1831, Wirt Papers.
23. To James E. Conover, Oct. 9, 1831, *HCP*; Webster to Nathaniel Williams, Oct. 1, to Ambrose Spencer, Dec. 18, 1831, *DWP*; Boston *Daily Advertiser*, Oct. 14, Boston *Courier*, Oct. 4, 1831.
24. J. Q. Adams to Richard Rush, June 17, 1831, Gratz Collection, Pennsylvania Historical Society; Arthur B. Darling, *Political Changes in Massachusetts, 1824–1848* (New Haven, 1925), 101–3; *Memoirs of Wirt*, II, 330–31.
25. To Francis Brooke, Aug. 15, to Thomas Speed, Aug. 23, 1831, *HCP*.
26. J. J. Milligan to William P. Brobson, Dec. 12, 1831, Brobson Papers, Delaware Historical Society.
27. To Clay, Oct. 5, 1831, *Writings*, XVI, 212–14; to Charles Miner, Aug. 28, Miner to Webster, Sept. 8, 1831, *DWP*.
28. Kirwan, *Crittenden*, 88–91.
29. "Free Trade and the Tariff," *American Quarterly Review*, v. 10 (1831), 467, 44–474.
30. Richmond *Whig*, Nov. 23, 1831. See also Richmond *Enquirer*, Oct. 14, Nov. 22, 27, 1831, and Alexandria *Gazette* editorial repr. in *National Intelligencer*, Nov. 9, 1831.
31. To Francis Brooke, Oct. 4, 1831, *Works of Clay*, IV, 314–17.
32. Richmond *Enquirer*, Dec. 10, 1831.
33. *Messages and Papers*, II, 544–58.
34. Charles Francis Adams, "John Quincy Adams in the Twenty-Second Congress," *Proceedings of Massachusetts Historical Society*, 2nd Ser., v. 19 (1905), 509–10; J. Q. Adams to Richard Rush, Aug. 3, 1832, Rush Papers.
35. Diary, Dec. 28, 1831, Adams Papers, Massachusetts Historical Society.
36. Richmond *Enquirer*, Jan. 24, 1832; Charleston *Courier*, Jan. 21, 1832; Adams to Clay, Sept. 7, 1831, *Works of Clay*, IV, 311–14.
37. *Memoirs*, VIII, 446.
38. *Ibid.*, 447–48; Edward Everett to Alexander H. Everett, Jan. 17, 1832, Everett Papers.
39. *Speeches of Clay*, I, 581–98.
40. *Register of Debates*, 22 Cong., 1 Sess., 186–94.
41. Sargent, *Public Men*, I, 199–200; *Register of Debates*, 22 Cong., 1 Sess., 1319–33.
42. Van Buren, *Autobiography*, 520–27; Isaac Hill to Van Buren, Jan. 29, 1832, Van Buren Papers.
43. Benton, *View*, I, 219; John Randolph to Andrew Jackson, Mar. 28, 1832, Jackson Papers.
44. Washington *Globe*, Jan. 28, 30, 31, Feb. 1, 2, 1831; the Albany resolutions are in the Van Buren Papers.
45. Washington *Globe*, Feb. 1, Apr. 25, 1832.
46. *Speeches of Clay*, II, 5–55.
47. J. J. Milligan to William P. Brobson, Jan. 22 [?], 1832, Brobson Papers.
48. John J. Crittenden to Clay, Feb. 23, 1832, Crittenden Papers, Duke Univ.
49. To Samuel Ingham, Jan. 13, 1832, *JCCP*, IX, 543–44.
50. *Register of Debates*, 22 Cong., 1 Sess., 631–35, 638.
51. *Ibid.*, app. 112–18; *Speeches of Clay*, II, 56–85.
52. *Argus of Western America*, quoted in Wellington, *Public Lands*, 38.
53. *Register of Debates*, 22 Cong., 1 Sess., 1151.
54. *Speeches*, II, 64–65.

55. To Nicholas Biddle, June 14, Sept. 11, 1830, *The Correspondence of Nicholas Biddle Dealing with National Affairs, 1807–1844*, Reginald C. McGrane, ed. (Boston, 1919), 111–114.
56. Quoted in Thomas P. Govan, *Nicholas Biddle, Nationalist and Public Banker, 1786–1844* (Chicago, 1959), 117. For a different view, see Donald R. Cole, *Jacksonian Democracy in New Hampshire, 1800–51* (Cambridge, 1971), 109–32.
57. Nicholas Biddle to William G. Buckner, July 13, 1832, *Correspondence*, 195.
58. To Nicholas Biddle, Dec. 15, Samuel Smith to Biddle, Dec. 17, 1831, *Correspondence*, 140–45; Webster to Biddle, Dec. 18, John Cadwalader to Biddle, Dec. 25, 1831, Biddle Papers, Library of Congress.
59. Govan, *Biddle*, 172.
60. Charles F. Mercer to Biddle, Dec. 12, 1831, Biddle Papers.
61. Charles Jared Ingersoll to Nicholas Biddle, Mar. 6, 7, 1832, Biddle Papers; E. M. Carroll, *Origins of the Whig Party* (Durham, N.C., 1925), 64; Nicholas Biddle to R. M. Gibbes, Dec. 13, 1831, Biddle Papers.
62. Charles Jared Ingersoll to Nicholas Biddle, Mar. 6, 1832, Biddle Papers; Govan, *Biddle*, 185–86, 198.
63. *Writings*, VI, 124–48.
64. Robert C. Winthrop, *Memoir of the Hon. Nathan Appleton* (New York, 1969), 35.
65. *Register of Debates*, 22 Cong., 1 Sess., 3169–70.
66. To Peter B. Porter, May 3, 1832, *HCP*; William Drayton to Joel R. Poinsett, Apr. 5, 1832, Poinsett Papers, Pennslyvania Historical Society. The Treasury report and the subsequent report of the Committee on Manufactures may be found in the *Register of Debates*, 22 Cong., 1 Sess., App. 25–33, 79–93.
67. *Ibid.*, 3814; as quoted in Richmond *Enquirer*, May 13, 1832.
68. Boston *Courier*, June 15, 1832; Rufus Choate to Jonathan Shave, June 3, 1832, "Rufus Choate Letters," *Essex Institute Historical Collections*, v. 69 (1933), 81–82.
69. See the analysis in Peterson, *Olive Branch*, 34–39.
70. *Register of Debates*, 22 Cong., 1 Sess., 1217; Clay to Hezekiah Niles, July 8, 1832, *HCP*.
71. George M. Dallas to Henry Gilpin, July 13, 1832, Dallas Papers, Pennsylvania Historical Society.
72. J. Q. Adams to Louisa C. Adams, July 14, 1832, Adams Papers; speech by John Forsyth, Richmond *Enquirer*, Sept. 11, 1832.
73. Nicholas Biddle to Clay, Aug. 1, 1832, *Correspondence*, 196; *Messages and Papers*, II, 576–91.
74. Latner, *Presidency of Jackson*, 119.
75. George M. Dallas to Henry D. Gilpin, July 10, to Sophia Dallas, July 11, 1832, Dallas Papers.
76. To Nicholas Biddle, Aug. 25, 1832, *DWP*; *Writings*, VI, 149–81.
77. *Ibid.*, 167–68; *Speeches of Clay*, II, 104.
78. "Party," [Mar. 19, 1831?], John McLean Papers, Library of Congress.
79. Nicholas Biddle to Clay, Aug. 1, 1832, *Works of Clay*, IV, 341.
80. Washington *Globe*, Aug. 23; Boston *Courier*, Aug. 27, 1832.
81. Thurlow Weed, *Autobiography* (Boston, 1884), I, 372–73.
82. Quoted in Gabor S. Borit, *Lincoln and the Economy of the American Dream* (Memphis, 1978), 93.
83. Duff Green to Calhoun, Aug. 27, 31, and to John C. Spencer, Sept. 26, 1832, Green Papers.
84. Edward Everett to Josiah Johnston, Oct. 17, 1832, Johnston Papers, Pennsylvania Historical Society.
85. Thomas S. Allen to William Russell, Oct. 4, 1832, Clay-Russell Family Papers, Univ. of Kentucky.

4. *The Compromise of 1833*

1. To Francis Pickens, Mar. 2, 1832, *JCCP*, XI, 558.
2. To Waddy Thompson, July 8, 1832, *ibid.*, 604.
3. See Joel R. Poinsett to Andrew Jackson, Nov. 16, 1832, Jackson Papers. The Charleston *Courier* voiced approval of the new tariff on July 23, 1832. The exchange between Unionist William Drayton and Robert Hayne is interestingly discussed in the Richmond *Enquirer*, Sept. 11, 14, 1832.

4. Calhoun to James Hamilton, Jr., Aug. 28, 1832, *Works of Calhoun*, VI, 144–93.
5. Charleston *Courier*, Aug. 4, 6, 11, 1832; Webster is quoted from his speech in New York, Mar. 10, 1831, *Writings*, II, 60–61.
6. Jackson to John Coffey, July 17, 1832, *Correspondence*, IV, 462. On Jackson's outlook, see Richard B. Latner, "The Nullification Crisis and Republican Subversion," *Journal of Southern History*, v. 43 (1977), 19–38.
7. Richmond *Enquirer*, July 10, 1832.
8. See the article by Edwin A. Miles, "After John Marshall's Decision: *Worcester v. Georgia* and the Nullification Crisis," *Journal of Southern History*, v. 39 (1973), 519–44.
9. James L. Petigru to Hugh S. Legaré, Oct. 29, 1832, *Life, Letters and Speeches of James Louis Petigru*, James P. Carson, ed. (Washington, 1920), 102–3.
10. *Writings*, II, 87–128.
11. The important documents are collected in *State Papers on Nullification* (Boston, 1834).
12. *Messages and Papers*, II, 591–606; Report of the Secretary of Treasury, Dec. 5, 1832, in *Register of Debates*, 22 Cong., 2 Sess., 33–39.
13. Diary, Dec. 5, 1832, Adams Papers.
14. In Richmond *Enquirer*, Dec. 11, 1832.
15. *Messages and Papers*, II, 1203–09.
16. *Writings*, XIII, 40–43; *Autobiography of Van Buren*, ch. 36; Edward Everett to Josiah Johnston, Dec. 23, 1832, Johnston Papers. See also Sydney Nathans, *Daniel Webster and Jacksonian Democracy* (Baltimore, 1973), ch. 2.
17. Frederick Whittlesey to William H. Seward, Jan. 9, 1833, Seward Papers.
18. Report of the Ways and Means Committee, Dec. 18, 1832, *Register of Debates*, 22 Cong., 2 Sess., 39–41; John Munroe, *Louis McLane: Federalist and Jacksonian* (New Brunswick, 1973), 365–75; Robert W. July, *The Essential New Yorker: Gulian Crommelin Verplanck* (Durham, N.C., 1951). See also the suggestive comments in the New York *Evening Post*, Dec. 14, 31, 1832, and Jan. 4, 1833, and the Richmond *Enquirer*, Nov. 23, Dec. 18, 1832.
19. Hugh R. Garland, *The Life of John Randolph of Roanoke* (New York, 1859), II, 361–62. For rumors see Richmond *Enquirer*, Dec. 18, and C. C. Cambreling to Van Buren, Dec. 29, 1832, Van Buren Papers.
20. To Charles Hammond, Nov. 17, 1832, *HCP*.
21. To Francis Brooke, Dec. 12, 1832, *Works of Clay*, V, 345–46; to James Caldwell, Dec. 9, 1832, in Bernard Mayo, ed., "Henry Clay, Patron and Idol of White Sulphur Springs," *Virginia Magazine of History and Biography*, v. 55 (1947), 310.
22. James Brown to Clay, Nov. 5, 1832, James A. Padgett, ed., "Letters of James Brown to Henry Clay," *Louisiana Historical Quarterly*, v. 24 (1941), 1168; Alexander Porter to Josiah Johnston, Dec. 6, 20, 26, 1832, Jan. 16, 1833, Johnston Papers. See also Joseph G. Tregle, "Louisiana and the Tariff, 1816–1846," *Louisiana Historical Quarterly*, v. 25 (1942), 24–148.
23. Reported draft of Clay's first project, Huntington Library. The source and date of the document are unknown, but in light of Webster's later revelations it appears accurate as to Clay's original proposal. Clay reflected on the inception of the compromise, Feb. 25, 1837, *Register of Debates*, 24 Cong., 2 Sess., 968–69.
24. *Ibid.*, and Clay's speech at Milledgeville, Ga., Mar. 19, 1844, reported in *Niles' Register*, Apr. 20, 1844. Two general accounts of the Compromise Tariff are Glyndon G. Van Deusen, *Henry Clay* (Boston, 1937), ch. 16; and Frederick Nussbaum, "The Compromise of 1833," *South Atlantic Quarterly*, XI (1912), 337–49.
25. Speech in House of Representatives, July 5, 1842, reported in Boston *Courier*, July 9, 1842. See also Nathan Appleton to Abbott Lawrence, Feb. 15, 1841, Appleton Papers, Massachusetts Historical Society.
26. To Hiram Ketchum, Jan. 18, 1838, *Writings*, XVI, 293; Duff Green, in *U.S. Telegraph*, July 20, 1836; Richmond *Whig*, Feb. 2, 8, 1832.
27. To Francis Brooke, Jan. 17, 1833, *Works of Clay*, V. 347–48.
28. *National Intelligencer*, May 8, 1838.
29. *Writings of Hugh Swinton Legaré* (Charleston, 1846), I, 217; R. D. W. Connor, "William Gaston, A Southern Federalist," *American Antiquarian Society Proceedings*, New Ser., v. 43 (1934), 439; Richmond *Enquirer*, Jan. 3, 5, 1833.
30. To James E. Colhoun, Jan. 10, and to Bolling Hall, Jan. 12, 1833, *JCCP*, XII, 6–8.
31. *Messages and Papers*, II, 1173–95; William Drayton to Joel R. Poinsett, Jan. 13, 1833, and

[unknown] to Poinsett, Jan. 23, 18[33], Poinsett Papers, Pennsylvania Historical Society; Charleston *Courier*, Jan. 24, 1833.

32. To Armisted Burt, Jan. 16, to James Hamilton, Jr., Jan. 16, and to William C. Preston, Feb. 3, 1833, *JCCP*, XII, 15, 16, 37–38.

33. See, e.g., the Washington letter in the Richmond *Whig*, Jan. 22, 1833.

34. William T. Hammet to F. W. White, Feb. 4, 1833, Hammet Papers, Virginia Historical Society; Webster to William Sullivan, Jan. 3, 1833, *Private Correspondence*, I, 528–29, and to Joseph Hopkinson, Feb. 7, 1833, *DWP*.

35. Richmond *Whig*, Oct. 10, 1844, quoting James B. Rhett.

36. Thomas Ritchie to William C. Rives, Jan. 6, 1833, Rives Papers, Library of Congress.

37. *Autobiography of Van Buren*, 550–52; *The Autobiography of William H. Seward*, F. W. Seward, ed. (New York, 1877), I, 228–29; C. C. Cambreling to Van Buren, Feb. 5, 1833, Van Buren Papers.

38. See the detailed account in Norman D. Brown, *Daniel Webster and the Politics of Availability* (Athens, Ga., 1969), chs. 2–3.

39. *Congressional Globe*, 27 Cong., 1 Sess., 344. For eyewitness accounts of Calhoun's speech, see Henry Moore to Charles Sumner, Mar. 3, 1833, *JCCP*; Henry Barnard, "The South Atlantic States in 1833, As Seen by a New Englander," *Maryland Historical Magazine*, v. 13 (1918), 283, 308; Charleston *Courier*, Feb. 24, 1833.

40. *Works of Calhoun*, II, 197–262.

41. To Joseph Hopkinson, Feb. 15, 1833, *DWP*.

42. Pendleton *Messenger*, May 15, 1833, quoting the Charleston *Mercury*.

43. Quoted in Bartlett, *Webster*, 158.

44. "Ignatius Loyola Robertson" [Samuel Knapp], in *National Intelligencer*, July 17, 1830.

45. *Writings*, VI, 181–238; Barnard, "South Atlantic States," 306; Charleston *Courier*, Feb. 24, 1833.

46. Pendleton *Messenger*, quoting the Alexandria *Gazette*, and also the *Jeffersonian and Virginia Times*, Mar. 6, 1833. The quoted Randolph statement varies from the more common version, as in Charles M. Wiltse, *John C. Calhoun, Nullifier, 1829–1839* (Indianapolis, 1949), 194.

47. John Quincy Adams to Robert Walsh, Mar. 29, 1833, Adams Papers. See also William C. Preston to Virgil Maxcy, July 7, 1834, Galloway-Maxcy-Markoe Papers.

48. New York *Evening Post*, Jan. 26, 1833.

49. Michael Hoffman to A. C. Flagg, Feb. 4, 1833, Flagg Papers, New York Public Library; Silas Wright to N. P. Tallmadge, Jan. 27, 1833, Tallmadge Papers, Wisconsin Historical Society.

50. Silas Wright to A. C. Flagg, Jan. 14, 20, 1833, Flagg papers.

51. To Alexander Porter, Jan. 29, 1833, *HCP*.

52. To Thomas Speed, June 9, 1833, *ibid.*

53. To Joseph Hopkinson, Feb. 9, 1833, *DWP*. There are references to the meetings in Clay to Webster, Feb. 5, and to Nicholas Biddle, Apr. 10, 1833, *ibid.*

54. To Josiah Johnston, Mar. 15, 1833, *HCP*; Epes Sargent, *Life and Public Services of Henry Clay* (Auburn, N.Y., 1852), 141; Samuel F. Du Pont to John S. Wily, Mar. 4, 1833, Du Pont Papers, Eleuthurian Mills Library, and *Life of Eleuthère Irénée Du Pont from Contemporary Correspondence*, Bessie G. Du Pont, ed. (Newark, Del., 1923); Michael Hoffman to A. C. Flagg, Feb. 7, 8, 1833, Flagg Papers.

55. Benton, *View*, I, 242.

56. Josiah Johnston to [Alexander Porter?], Mar. 1, 1833, Johnston Papers.

57. Benton, *View*, I, 343. See the more detailed discussion in Peterson, *Olive Branch*, 67–70.

58. *Works*, III, 190.

59. The original bill (S 115), in Clay's hand, with related papers, is in the Senate Records, RG 46, National Archives. For the bill as passed see the *Statutes at Large*.

60. *Speeches of Clay*, II, 106–21.

61. William T. Hammet to F. W. White, Feb. 12, 1833, Hammet Papers.

62. On the significance of the election see especially the comments of "The Spy in Washington" [Matthew L. Davis], in the Albany *Evening Journal*, Feb. 17, 28, 1833.

63. *Niles' Register*, Feb. 16, 1833.

64. Boston *Courier*, Feb. 20, 1833.

65. C. W. Gooch to William C. Rives, Feb. 16, 1833, Rives Papers. See also Edward Everett to A. H. Everett, Mar. 13, 1833, Everett Papers, and John Quincy Adams to C. F. Adams,

Mar. 26, 1833, Adams Papers. For administration views: New York *Evening Post*, Feb. 14, and Washington *Globe*, Feb. 16, 1833.

66. George M. Dallas to Henry D. Gilpin, Feb. 19, 1833, Dallas Papers; Webster to Joseph Hopkinson, Feb. 15, to Nathan Appleton, Feb. 17, 1833, *DWP*.

67. Clayton's motives have been variously interpreted. See Sargent, *Clay*, 142–43, and Benton, *View*, I, 343.

68. *Register of Debates*, 22 Cong., 1 Sess., 694–97; Charleston *Courier*, Mar. 1, 1833. See also the account in Nathan Sargent, *Public Men*, I, 338–39.

69. *Register of Debates*, 22 Cong., 2 Sess., 723.

70. Notes of a Speech on the Compromise Bill, *Writings*, XIV, 586–87. The speech was never delivered. See the account in the New York *American*, Jan. 22, 1840.

71. *Register of Debates*, 22 Cong., 2 Sess., 722–25, 689. On the "dodge" charge see the exchange between Duff Green and "Vindex" [John M. Clayton] in the *U.S. Telegraph*, July 20, 29, 1836. See also Clay to P. R. Fendall, Aug, 8, 1836, *HCP*.

72. Notes for a Speech, Mar. 12, 1838, *DWP*.

73. *Register of Debates*, 22 Cong., 2 Sess., 137–38. For a slightly varying report, with comment on the audience reaction, see the Richmond *Whig*, Mar. 8, 1833.

74. *Register of Debates*, 22 Cong., 2 Sess., 731–32.

75. *Ibid.*, 1810.

76. Clay to James Barbour, Mar. 2, 1833, *HCP*; "The Spy in Washington," in Richmond *Whig*, Mar. 15, 1833.

77. John M. Clayton to E. I. Du Pont, Mar. 2, 1833, Eleuthurian Mills Historical Library. See also the report of Clayton's speech, June 15, 1844, in Boston *Courier*, June 21, 1844.

78. Silas Wright to A. C. Flagg, Jan. 24, 27, and Michael Hoffman to Flagg, Feb. 23, 1833, Flagg papers.

79. Boston *Courier*, Mar. 9, Charleston *Mercury*, Mar. 8, 1833; Clayton's 1844 speech, *Courier*, June 21, 1844.

80. Veto Message, Dec. 4, 1833, in *Messages and Papers*, II, 57–68.

81. See Peterson, *Olive Branch*, 82–84.

82. *Register of Debates*, 24 Cong., 2 Sess., 1365; Peterson, *Olive Branch*, ch. 3.

83. *Writings*, III, 131.

84. Notes for a Speech, Mar. 12, 1838, *DWP*; John Quincy Adams to C. F. Adams, Mar. 26, 1833, Adams Papers.

85. Quoted in Sarah M. Maury, *Statesmen of America in 1846* (Philadelphia, 1847), 172. For the Charleston ceremonies see Richmond *Enquirer*, Nov. 26, 29, 1833; *Niles' Register*, Dec. 7, 1833; Jervey, *Hayne*, 366–67.

Chapter Five: The Embattled Senators

1. Alexis de Tocqueville, *Democracy in America*, Henry Reeve, tr. (New York, 1904), I, 213–14; Edward Stanley, *Journal of a Tour in America, 1824–1825* (London, 1930), 317–18; Henry Jones Ford, *The Rise and Growth of American Politics* (New York, 1898), ch. 21; G. H. Haynes, *The Senate of the United States* (Boston, 1938), II, 1000–3.

2. Speech at Lexington, Ky., *Niles' Register*, July 25, 1835.

3. Quoted in Howard Lee McBain, *The Living Constitution* (New York, 1927), 2.

4. Harriet Martineau, *Retrospect of Western Travel* (New York, 1838), I, 144–45, 160.

5. Quoted by James H. Hammond in his oration on Calhoun, Nov. 21, 1850, in his *Letters and Speeches* (New York, 1866), 293.

1. The Bank War

1. *Writings of Webster*, XV, 106–7.

2. To Benjamin F. Perry, Apr. 27, 1833, *DWP*, III, 247.

3. To John Bolton, May 17, 1833, *ibid.*, 252–53. The letter was published in *Niles' Register*, June 29, 1833.

4. Irving H. Bartlett, *Daniel Webster* (New York, 1978), 139; Sydney Nathans, *Daniel Webster and Jacksonian Democracy* (Baltimore, 1973), 62–3.

5. Nicholas Biddle to Webster, Apr. 10, 1833; to Biddle, Apr. 21, 1833, *DWP*, III, 242, 244.

6. *National Intelligencer*, May 21, 1833.

7. To James Brooke, Mar. 11, and to Nicholas Biddle, Apr. 10, 1833, *HCP.*
8. To Biddle, Mar. 4; Biddle to Clay, Mar. 25, 1833, *ibid.*
9. *Examiner and Journal of Political Economy*, Aug. 7, Nov. 13, 27, 1833. See also *Autobiography of Martin Van Buren*, in *Annual Report of American Historical Association*, 1918, II (Washington, 1920), 693–97.
10. William T. Barry to Martin Van Buren, July 7, 1833, Van Buren Papers, Library of Congress.
11. Nathans, *Webster and Jacksonian Democracy*, ch. 2; Norman D. Brown, *Daniel Webster and the Politics of Availability;* (Athens, Ga., 1969), ch. 3; H. A. Dearborn to Webster, Aug. 12, 1833, *Private Correspondence of Daniel Webster*, ed. (Boston, 1857), II, 185; Rufus Choate to Webster, Aug. 12, 1833, *DWP.*
12. *Examiner and Journal of Political Economy*, Oct. 30, 1833; Joseph S. Jones to David Swain, Oct. 26, 1833, Swain Papers, Univ. of North Carolina; Robert C. Winthrop, *Memoir of Henry Clay* (Cambridge, 1880), 30–31.
13. William Plumer, "Reminiscences," *Writings*, I, 557.
14. Quoted in Calvin Colton, *Life and Times of Henry Clay* (New York, 1846), II, 97.
15. Andrew Jackson to Hugh Lawson White, Mar. 24, 1833, *Correspondence of Andrew Jackson*, John S. Bassett, ed. (Washington, 1826–35), V, 46.
16. Quoted by John M. Clayton, at Lancaster, Pa., Sept. 5, 1844, in *Niles' Register*, Sept. 14, 1844.
17. Nicholas Biddle to J. G. Watmough, Feb. 8, 1834, *Correspondence of Nicholas Biddle*, Reginald C. McGrane, ed. (Boston, 1919), 221. On Biddle, see *A Philadelphia Perspective: The Diary of Sidney George Fisher . . . 1834–1871*, Nicholas B. Wainwright, ed. (Philadelphia, 1967), 15, 154.
18. See Van Buren, *Autobiography*, 635–711 *passim* for a suggestive conjectural account.
19. To Nicholas Biddle, Dec. 21, 1833, *DWP.*
20. Willie P. Mangum to David Swain, Dec. 22, 1833, *The Papers of Willie P. Mangum* (Raleigh, 1950), II, 55–56. For a view of Webster's motives, see John W. Davis to——, Dec. 15, 1833, Davis Papers, American Antiquarian Society.
21. *United States Gazette*, repr. in Boston *Courier*, Dec. 20, 1833.
22. Edwin Croswell to N. P. Tallmadge, Dec. 20, 1833, Tallmadge Papers, Stephen White to Webster, Dec. 27, 30, 1833, Jan. 9, 1834, *DWP.*
23. John Rowan, in Lucius P. Little, *Ben Hardin: His Times and Contemporaries* (Louisville, 1887), 180. For the anecdote, see [Theodore N. Parmelee], "Recollections of an Old Stager," *Harper's Magazine*, v. 45 (1872), 604–5.
24. Charles Cotesworth Pinckney, "John C. Calhoun from a Southern Standpoint," *Lippincott's*, v. 62 (1898), 90.
25. *Register of Debates*, 23 Cong., 1 Sess., 59. Clay's speech follows. See also *Speeches of Henry Clay*, Daniel Mallory, ed. (New York, 1843), II, 145–90.
26. *Register of Debates*, 23 Cong., 1 Sess., 94; Pendleton *Messenger*, Jan. 15, 22, 1834; Webster to Nicholas Biddle, Jan. 4, 1833, *DWP.*
27. *Works of Calhoun*, II, 309–43.
28. *Life of John C. Calhoun*, (New York, 1843), 50–51.
29. Nathan Sargent, *Public Men and Events* (Philadelphia, 1875), I, 263–64. See also Thomas Hart Benton, *Thirty Years' View* (New York, 1856), I, 415–23.
30. *Ibid.*, I, 420.
31. *Ibid.; Kentucky Gazette*, Mar. 29, 1834.
32. The speech was inadequately reported at the time; it was later reconstructed for *Works of Daniel Webster* (Boston, 1853), VI, 265–69. See Horace Binney to Nicholas Biddle, Jan. 31, 1834, Biddle Papers, Library of Congress; Rufus Choate to William Palfrey, Jr., Jan. 31, 1834, in *Essex Institute Historical Quarterly*, v. 69 (1933), 86; Robert Winthrop, "Webster's Reply to Hayne," *Scribner's Magazine*, v. 15 (1894), 123–24.
33. Horace Binney to Nicholas Biddle, Jan. 31, 1834, Biddle Papers.
34. Clay to Nicholas Biddle, Feb. 2, 1834, *HCP.*
35. Willie P. Mangum to Duncan Cameron, Feb. 9, 1834, *Mangum Papers*, II, 75; Webster to Nicholas Biddle, Jan. 2, 1834, DWP, III, 298; James W. Webb to Biddle, Jan. 8, 1834, Biddle Papers.
36. *Register of Debates*, 23 Cong., 1 Sess., 984–96; Biddle to Webster, Mar. 15, 1834, *DWP.*
37. Samuel Jaudon to Biddle, Mar. 9, 12, 1834, and John Sergeant to Biddle, Feb. 17, 1834, Biddle Papers.
38. *Register of Debates*, 23 Cong., 1 Sess., 1057–74; John C. Calhoun to L. W. Tazewell, Feb.

9, Mar. 27, 1834, *JCCP*, 233–34, 273–74; *Life of Calhoun*, 54–55; Benton, *View*, I, 434–36.

39. Samuel Jaudon to Biddle, Mar. 9, 12, 1834, Biddle Papers.
40. Webster to Biddle [Mar. 25]; James Watson Webb to Biddle, Mar. 23, 27, 1834, *ibid*.
41. Philip Hone, *Diary . . . 1828–1851*, Allan Nevins, ed. (New York, 1927), 120–21, 125; Boston *Courier*, Apr. 18, 1834; *National Intelligencer*, Apr. 24, 1834.
42. Binney, *Life*, 120–21; Benton, *Thirty Years' View*, I, 422.
43. *Register of Debates*, 25 Cong., 1 Sess., 510; *National Intelligencer*, Oct. 21, 1837; Webster to Thomas G. Platt and Platt to Webster, Feb. 24, 27, 1836, *DWP*.
44. *Works of Calhoun*, II, 417.
45. *Register of Debates*, 23 Cong., 1 Sess., 1711–12.
46. Clay to John P. Kennedy, May 1, 1834, *HCP*.
47. See, e.g., Samuel P. Lyman to William H. Seward, May 23, June 8, 1834, Seward Papers, Univ. of Rochester.
48. For a good general account of Webster's candidacy see Nathans, *Webster and Jacksonian Democracy*, ch. 3.
49. *Register of Debates*, 23 Cong., 1 Sess., 960–78. See also Brown, *Webster and Availability*, 163–80.
50. To Samuel Jaudon, July 25, 1834, *DWP*, III, 357–59.
51. To Jaudon, Aug. 2, 1834, *DWP*, III, 358–59.
52. Michael Chevalier, *Society, Manners, and Politics in the United States* (New York, 1961), 177; George W. Erving to Andrew Jackson, Sept. 25, 1835, *Correspondence*, IV, 368–69. Two general accounts are Richard A. McLemore, *Franco-American Diplomatic Relations, 1816–1836* (Baton Rouge, 1941) and Henry Blumenthal, *A Reappraisal of Franco-American Relations, 1830–1871* (Chapel Hill, 1959).
53. *A Compilation of the Messages and Papers of the Presidents*, J. D. Richardson, ed. (Washington, 1907), III, 97–123; *Register of Debates*, 23 Cong., 2 Sess., App., 208–18.
54. Quoted in *National Intelligencer*, Mar. 19, 1835; Jan. 13, Mar. 17, 1835.
55. *Ibid.*; *Register of Debates*, 23 Cong., 2 Sess., 743–44.
56. *Ibid.*, 24 Cong., 1 Sess., 161–2.
57. To Jeremiah Mason, Jan. 10, 1835, *Writings*, XVI, 247–48.
58. Charles Francis Adams to Louisa Catherine Adams, Feb. 19, and Benjamin F. Hallett to John Quincy Adams, Feb. 20, 1835, Adams Papers, Massachusetts Historical Society. See also Samuel F. Bemis, *John Quincy Adams and the Union* (New York, 1965), ch. 26.
59. Adams to John Bailey, Mar. 30, 1835, Adams Papers.
60. *An Appeal from the New to the Old Whigs* (Boston, 1835).
61. *Writings*, VII, 205–29.
62. *Register of Debates*, 24 Cong., 1 Sess., 2270; Robert H. Goldsborough to Nathaniel F. Williams, Jan. 25, 1836, Maryland Historical Society.
63. To Caroline Webster, Jan. 24, 1836, *Letters of Daniel Webster*, C. H. Van Tyne, ed. (New York, 1902), 199. See the accounts in Sargent, *Public Men*, I, 310–15 and Parmelee, "Recollections," 751.
64. *Register of Debates*, 24 Cong., 1 Sess., 2414–35; Joseph P. Comegys, *Memoirs of John M. Clayton* (Wilmington, 1882), 119–25.
65. To Edward Everett, Mar. 12, 1836, *DWP*, IV, 91–2; to Samuel Lincoln, Jan. 15, 1841, *Writings*, XVI, 336–37.
66. *National Intelligencer*, Mar. 12, 1835.
67. To Samuel Southard, Apr. 28, to Nicholas Biddle, May 9, 12, 1835, *DWP*, IV, 42–5.
68. Tristram Burges, in *Niles' Register*, May 2; *National Intelligencer*, July 11, 1835.
69. Quoted in Brown, *Webster and Availability*, 113.
70. Clay to Samuel Southard, Apr. 12, to John Cabariess, June 12, 1835, *HCP*; Boston *Courier*, Aug. 27; *National Intelligencer*, Sept. 16, 1835; Webster to Robert Letcher, Oct. 23, 1843, *DWP*.
71. Edward Everett to Benjamin Hallett, Oct. 5, to H. Denny, Oct. 20, and Thaddeus Stevens, Nov. 2, 23, 1835, Everett Papers, Massachusetts Historical Society.
72. To William W. Irwin, Nov. 30, 1835; see also to the Antimasons of Allegheny County, Nov. 20, and to H. Denny, Nov. 20, 1835, *DWP*, IV, 64–5, 69–70.
73. Charles Miner to Webster, Dec. 17, 1835, *DWP*, IV, 73–74. See also Charles M. Snyder, *The Jacksonian Heritage in Pennsylvania Politics, 1833–1848* (Harrisburg, 1958), 67–70.
74. Robert Winthrop to Caleb Cushing, Feb. 25, 1836, Cushing Papers, Massachusetts Historical Society; Levi Lincoln, memo, Feb. 19, Webster to Henry Kinsman, Feb. 20, 29, to

John W. Davis, Apr. 7, to James Watson Webb, May 6, 1836, *DWP;* Richard Haughton to John W. Davis, [Jan. 1836], Davis Papers; *National Intelligencer,* Jan. 28, 1836.
75. To Caroline Webster, Jan. 10, 1836, *DWP.*
76. To Jeremiah Mason, Feb. 13, 1837, *DWP.*
77. In the Boston & Lowell Railroad Argument (1845), *Writings,* XV, 399.
78. To Lucretia Clay, Jan. 23, 1836; U.S. *Gazette,* Dec. 29, 1835, *HCP.*
79. Clay to Robert Letcher, Jan. 17, 1837, *ibid.*
80. Louisville *Journal,* Nov. 29, 1836.
81. *Speeches,* II, 278; Benton, *View,* I, 729.
82. *Register of Debates,* 24 Cong., 2 Sess., 417–18.
83. *Ibid.,* 504; Benton, *View,* I, 731.
84. *Works of Calhoun,* III, 140–41.

2. Calhoun and Abolitionism

1. *Works of Calhoun,* III, 399. See also two letters to Samuel Ingham, Dec. 31, 1834 and Dec. 21, 1836, *JCCP,* XII, 377–79, XIII, 246–48.
2. *Works,* V, 148–90. See also *Register of Debates,* 23 Cong., 2 Sess., 109, 249–51, and the ensuing debate, 360–660, *passim.*
3. Benton, *View,* I, 80–82, 556–67.
4. *Speeches,* II, 231–45.
5. On the railroad see Alfred G. Smith, Jr., *Economic Readjustment of an Old Cotton State: South Carolina, 1820–1860* (Columbia, S.C., 1958), ch. 5.
6. To Thomas Walker Gilmer and others, *Niles' Register,* Aug. 9, 1834.
7. To L. W. Tazewell, Jan. 24, 1836, *JCCP,* XIII, 48–49.
8. *Register of Debates,* 24 Cong., 1 Sess., 51.
9. *Ibid.,* 1810. For Calhoun's evolving thinking see his letters to James H. Hammond, Apr. 3, June 19, 1836, *JCCP,* XIII, 137–38, 243–45. For his major speech, *Works,* II, 534–69.
10. To Augustus C. Clayton and others, Aug. 6, 1836; speech at Pendleton, Aug. 12, 1836, *JCCP,* XIII, 263, 269. Both were reported in *Niles' Register,* Aug. 27, Oct. 1, 1836.
11. Edward G. Bourne, *The Surplus Revenue of 1837* (New York, 1885).
12. *Works of Calhoun,* II, 225.
13. Everett to W. H. Trescott, Dec. 17, 1855, Everett Papers.
14. Binney, *Life,* 314.
15. *Register of Debates,* 24 Cong., 2 Sess., 718–19.
16. Pendleton *Messenger,* Aug. 21, Sept. 11, Dec. 5, 11, 1835.
17. *Niles' Register,* Jan. 6, 1836. For the northern response and the South Carolina reaction see George McDuffie's message to the legislature, Nov. 28, 1836, in Henry D. Capers, *The Life and Times of C. G. Messenger* (Richmond, 1893), 548–68.
18. *Works of Calhoun,* V, 196–97; *Register of Debates,* 24 Cong., 1 Sess., 383–85.
19. Harold W. Thacher, "Calhoun and Federal Reinforcement of State Laws," *American Political Science Review,* v. 36 (1942), 873–80.
20. *Register of Debates,* 24 Cong., 1 Sess., 1145, 1148.
21. *Ibid.,* 72–74.
22. *Ibid.,* 479.
23. *Ibid.,* 482.
24. *Works of Calhoun,* 482–83.
25. *Ibid.,* 490.
26. *Register of Debates,* 24 Cong., 1 Sess., 805, 810; Boston *Courier,* Mar. 17, 1836.
27. To Armistead Burt, Feb. 15, 1837, *JCCP,* XIII, 435.
28. *U.S. Telegraph,* Feb. 10, 12, July 2, 1836; Pendleton *Messenger,* Apr. 1, 8, 1836; James Hamilton, Jr., to James H. Hammond, Feb. 10, 29, Thomas Cooper to Hammond, Feb. 12, Robert Hayne to Hammond, Feb. 18, 1836, in the Hammond Papers.
29. Charleston *Mercury,* Aug. 20, 22–25, 27, 30–31, Sept. 1, 1836.
30. *Ibid.,* Oct. 7, 8, 1836. See also Joel R. Poinsett to J. B. Campbell, Oct. 20, Dec. 9, 1836, in *South Carolina History Magazine,* v. 42 (1941), 150–53; James L. Petigru to Hugh Legaré, Sept. 6, to Mrs. Jane P. North, Dec. 9, 1836, in *Life, Letters and Speeches of . . . Petigru,* James P. Carson, ed. (Washington, 1920), 184–85, 187.
31. To ed. of Pendleton *Messenger,* Sept. 22; to an unidentified Tennesseean, Sept. 26, 1836, *JCCP,* XIII, 286–93, 293–94. A standard source is Samuel M. Derrick, *Centennial History*

of the South Carolina Railroad (Columbia, 1930), but see also Charles M. Wiltse, *John C. Calhoun, Nullifier* (Indianapolis, 1949), ch. 23.

32. Francis W. Pickens to James H. Hammond, Nov. 14, 1836, Hammond Papers; Joel R. Poinsett to J. B. Campbell, Dec. 9, 1836, *South Carolina History Magazine*, 152–53.
33. To Pickens, Nov. 16, to Armistead Burt, Nov. 8, 1836, *JCCP*, XIII, 302, 298.
34. To David Hubbard, July 15, 1838, *JCCP*. See also William H. and Jane H. Pease, *The Web of Progress* (New York, 1985), 173–77.
35. To Hayne, Oct. 28, and Hayne to Calhoun, Nov. 1, 1838, *JCCP*. See Theodore Jervey, *Robert Y. Hayne and His Times* (New York, 1909), 388–98.
36. *Register of Debates*, 24 Cong., 2 Sess., 710–11.
37. *U.S. Telegraph*, Nov. 18, 1836.

3. *War of the Giants*

1. Bray Hammond, *Banks and Politics in America from the Revolution to the Civil War* (Princeton, 1957), ch. 15, is critical of Jacksonian policy. A corrective, which stresses external causes of the Panic of 1837, is Peter Temin, *The Jacksonian Economy* (New York, 1969). See also Richard H. Timberlake, Jr., "The Specie Circular and Distribution," *Journal of Political Economy*, v. 68 (1960), 109–17, and Harry Scheiber, "Pet Banks in Jacksonian Politics," *Journal of Economic History*, v. 23 (1963), 196–214. On the general effects of the panic and political reaction to it, see John Bach McMaster, *History of the People of the United States* (New York, 1885), VI, 389–415.
2. "Remarks on the Condition of the Currency," *JCCP*, XIII, 493–95.
3. To Samuel Ingham, Feb. 5, to Willie P. Mangum, Mar. 8, 1837, *ibid.*, 384–85, 490–92.
4. Henry Slaven to Webster, Feb. 8; Webster to Robert Winthrop, Jan. 27, to Hiram Ketchum, Jan. 28, 1837, *DWP*.
5. Winthrop to Webster, Feb. 15; Webster to Winthrop, Feb. 23, to Ketchum, Feb. 24, 1837, *DWP*.
6. George T. Curtis, *Life of Daniel Webster* (Boston, 1870), I, 556. The reception is described in *Niles' Register*, Mar. 8, 25, 1837, and in Hone, *Diary*, 247–48; the speech is in *Writings*, II, 189–230.
7. Benton, *View*, II, 15. See also Washington *Globe*, Sept. 12, 1837.
8. To Biddle, May 24, 1838, *DWP*.
9. Peter W. Parish, "Daniel Webster, New England, and the West," *Journal of American History*, v. 54 (1967), 524–49; also John C. Parish, *George Wallace Jones* (Iowa City, 1912), 98–130; and Coleman McCampbell, "H. L. Kinney and Daniel Webster in Illinois in the 1830's," *Journal of the Illinois State Historical Society*," v. 47 (1954), 35–44.
10. *Writings*, 80, 82.
11. Francis Fessenden, *Life and Public Services of William Pitt Fessenden* (New York, 1907), 12–18.
12. New York press reports in the Boston *Daily Advertiser*, June 13, July 1, 1837, and Boston *Courier*, June 17, July 1, 1837; Robert Winthrop to John H. Clifford, June 9, 1837, Winthrop Papers, Massachusetts Historical Society. See also the account in Nathans, *Webster and Jacksonian Democracy*, 114–21.
13. *Ibid.*, 116; Weed to Willis Hall, July 28, 1837, Daniel Ullman Papers, New York Historical Society.
14. Clay to Matthew L. Davis, July 3, 1837, *HCP*.
15. Davis to Clay, July 15, 1837, *ibid.*, and Clay to a Committee of Gentlemen in New York, Aug. 6, 1837, *Works of Clay*, V, 415–17; Noah Cook to Willis Hall, Nov. 18, 1837, Ullman Papers; "Correspondence with Henry Clay," Boston *Courier*, Dec. 27, 1837, Jan. 1, 1838, and *National Intelligencer*, Dec. 28, 1837.
16. Jackson to Calhoun, Feb. 7, 1837, *JCCP*, XIII, 403–5; *Register of Debates*, 24 Cong., 2 Sess., 753–60; Calhoun to J. R. Mathews, Feb. 12, 1837, *JCCP*, XIII, 429–30.
17. *Register of Debates*, 24 Cong., 2 Sess., 975–76. The last sentence recalled Littleton W. Tazewell's remorseful line in 1828: "Sir, you have deceived me once—this is *your* fault— but if you deceive me again, it will be *mine*." See Richmond *Whig*, Mar. 3, 1837.
18. *JCCP*, XIII, 496.
19. E.g., John H. Pleasants to———, July 28, 1837, Ullman Papers.
20. Charleston *Mercury*, July 8, June 23, 29, Mar. 27, 1837.
21. To Duff Green, June 26, July 27, to James Iredell, July 31, *JCCP*, XIII, 516–18, 525–29.

The first of these letters was published in the newspapers. See also Francis W. Pickens to Richard Crallé, June 28, 1837, Pickens Papers, Duke Univ.

22. Preston to Willie P. Mangum, Oct. 14, 1837, *Mangum Papers*, II, 509; Remarks at Charleston, *JCCP*, XIII, 497; to Iredell, July 31, 1837, *ibid.*, 529.

23. To James E. Colhoun, Sept. 7, 1837, *ibid.*, 535.

24. *Ibid.*, 546–71.

25. James C. Curtis, *The Fox at Bay: Martin Van Buren and the Presidency, 1837–1841* (Lexington, Ky., 1970), 99–100. See also John M. McFaul, *The Politics of Jacksonian Finance* (Ithaca, 1972), ch. 7.

26. *Speeches*, II, 291.

27. *Writings*, VIII, 256.

28. *Ibid.*, 83.

29. *Works*, III, 233.

30. *JCCP*, XIII, 571.

31. *Register of Debates*, 25 Cong., 1 Sess., 276.; *JCCP*, XIII, 583.

32. Boston *Courier*, Oct. 10, and Washington *Globe*, Oct. 17, 1837.

33. *The Madisonian* (Washington), reported in Pendleton *Messenger*, Oct. 13, 1837. The editorial response of the Richmond *Whig* is particularly revealing on the dilemma of the southern Whigs.

34. John J. Crittenden to Willie P. Mangum, Oct. 11, 1837, *Mangum Papers*, II, 512.

35. To Anna Calhoun, Jan. 30, 1838, to James Lynch, Oct. 15, 1837, *JCCP*, XIII, 588, 623.

36. McDuffie to Calhoun, Nov. 29, 1837, *ibid.*, 631.

37. To J. Bauskett and others, Nov. 3, 1837, *ibid.*, 636–37. First published in the Edgefield *Advertiser*, Nov. 16, 1835, the letter was widely reprinted.

38. James Hamilton, Jr., as reported in *National Intelligencer*, June 30, 1838.

39. Charleston *Mercury*, Dec. 4, 14, 1837; Butler to Hammond, Dec. 27, 1837, Hammond Papers.

40. *Congressional Globe*, 25 Cong., 2 Sess., 39.

41. *Ibid.*, 55. Calhoun's speech is also in *Works*, III, 140–202.

42. *Congressional Globe*, 60, 72.

43. To William B. Porter, Jan. 10, 1838, *HCP*; to James Brooke, Jan. 13, 1838, *Works*, V, 424. On the "federal consensus," see William M. Wiecek, *The Sources of Antislavery Constitutionalism in America* (Ithaca, 1978), 187–90.

44. To Hiram Ketchum, Jan. 15, 1838, *DWP*. Calhoun did not comment directly, but see Francis Pickens to James H. Hammond, Jan. 15, Feb. 9, 1838, Hammond Papers; Charleston *Mercury*, Jan. 11, Apr. 13, 1838.

45. To George Bancroft, Apr. 14, 1838, *JCCP*.

46. *Speeches*, II, 310–49. Two standard accounts are Benton, *View*, II, 97–112, and Sargent, *Public Men*, II, 29–50. See also O. H. Smith, *Early Indiana Trials, and Speeches, Reminiscences* (Cincinnati, 1858), 245–50, and Parmelee, "Recollections," 758–60.

47. Washington *Chronicle*, Mar. 13; Smith, *Reminiscences*, 247; Benton, *View*, II, 98–99; John P. Richardson to James Chesnut, Mar. 14, 1838, Univ. of South Carolina.

48. *Works of Calhoun*, III, 244–79.

49. *Writings*, VIII, 152–237; Smith, *Reminiscences*, 248.

50. National *Intelligencer*, Mar. 16; Boston *Courier*, Mar. 17, 1938; John P. Richardson to James Chesnut, Mar. 14, 1838, Univ. of South Carolina; Levi Lincoln to H. A. S. Dearborn, Mar. 12, 1838, Lincoln Family Papers, American Antiquarian Society.

51. *Congressional Globe*, 25 Cong., 2 Sess., 264–65. The speech is in *Works*, III, 279–326.

52. *Ibid.*, 291.

53. See the reflections in *National Intelligencer*, Sept. 19, Oct. 6, 1840.

54. *Congressional Globe*, 26 Cong., 1 Sess., 96–98. There are eyewitness accounts in Boston *Courier*, Jan. 8, and Louisville *Journal*, Jan. 13, 1840.

55. To Harrison Gray Otis, June 26, 1838, *HCP*.

56. Boston *Courier*, Jan. 8, 1840.

57. To Armistead Burt, Apr. 19, 1838, *JCCP*.

58. For a general view, Ernest M. Lander, "The Calhoun-Preston Feud, 1836–1842," *South Carolina History Magazine*, v. 59 (1958), 24–37. See also Preston to Mangum, Apr. 7, *Mangum Papers*, II, 519, and Pickens to Hammond, Jan. 15, Feb. 9, 1838, Hammond Papers.

59. Calhoun to Joseph Black and others, July 24, to Duff Green, Aug. 10, 1838, *JCCP*.

60. Reports in *Niles' Register*, Sept. 22; Charleston *Courier*, Oct. 5; Pendleton *Messenger*,

Sept. 14, 1838. See also Henry D. Thompson, *Waddy Thompson, Jr.*, rev. ed. (n.p., 1929), and Benjamin F. Perry, *Reminiscences of Public Men* (Philadelphia, 1883), 297–98.
61. Pickens to Hammond, Feb. 19, 1840, Hammond Papers.
62. Quoted in Lander, "Calhoun-Preston Feud," 34.
63. Quoted in John C. Barnwell, *Love of Order: South Carolina's First Secession Crisis* (Chapel Hill, 1982), 31.
64. Grayson, "Autobiography," 87. At this same session of the legislature Calhoun was unanimously reelected to the Senate.

4. Webster, Clay, and the Whig Triumph

1. Binney, *Life*, 125.
2. *Speeches*, II, 304–9; *Congressional Globe*, 25 Cong., 2 Sess., 142–43.
3. *Writings*, VIII, 129–39.
4. Boston *Courier*, Feb. 7, 1838.
5. Clay to Harrison Gray Otis, July 7, to John M. Clayton, June 14, 1838, *HCP*.
6. *National Intelligencer*, July 31, 1838; *Writings*, II, 263–66, 277–82.
7. Boston *Atlas*, Sept. 14, 1838; see also July 17, Dec. 12, 1838.
8. Charles T. Congdon, *Reminiscences of a Journalist* (Boston, 1880), 67–69; E. M. Carroll, *Origins of the Whig Party* (Durham, N.C., 1925), 152–55.
9. Robert Winthrop to Edward Everett, Sept. 14, 1838, Everett Papers.
10. Boston *Daily Advertiser*, Sept. 26, Boston *Courier*, Sept. 21, Oct. 5, 1838.
11. Winthrop to Everett, Sept. 14, 1838, Everett Papers.
12. To Otis, Sept. 24, 1838, *HCP*. Otis had sent a copy of the *Atlas* editorial on the day it appeared; in William H. Smith Collection, Indiana Historical Society.
13. To Otis, Sept. 24, Dec. 13, 1838, *HCP*; see also Lexington *Intelligencer* editorial in Boston *Courier*, Oct. 9, 1838, and Carroll, *Origins*, 152–55.
14. To James Brooke, Nov. 3, 1838, *Works of Clay*, V, 429–31.
15. "A Friend of State Rights," Richmond *Whig*, June 12, 1838. This was the first article in a series. Authorship is identified by the scrapbook in the Nathaniel Beverley Tucker Papers, College of William and Mary.
16. See P. J. Staudenraus, *The African Colonization Movement, 1816–1865* (New York, 1961); David M. Streifford, "The American Colonization Society," *Journal of Southern History*, v. 45 (1979), 201–20.
17. *Speeches*, I, 515–27. See also the speeches in *HCP*, II, 263–64, 420–22, and the report in Louisville *Journal*, Sept. 9, 1836.
18. To W. H. Russell, July 18, 1835, to C. C. Baldwin, Mar. 8, 1838, *HCP*.
19. Louisville *Journal*, Sept. 9, 1836.
20. *U.S. Telegraph*, Sept. 13, 1836.
21. James G. Birney, Diary, Sept. 16, 1834, to Lewis Tappan, Jan. 7, 1836, *Letters*, Dwight L. Dumond, ed. (New York, 1938), I, 135n, 297. See also Theodore Weld, *American Slavery As It Is* (New York, 1839), 183.
22. John Greenleaf Whittier, *Letters*, John B. Pickard, ed. (Cambridge, 1975), I, 21n., 41n, 638–41.
23. Whittier to Clay, July 5, Clay to Whittier, July 22, 1837, and Whittier to Caleb Cushing, July 3, 1838, *Letters*, I, 241–2, 282.
24. Lewis Tappan to Clay, June 22, July 20, 1835, *HCP*.
25. *Ibid.*, May 1, June 5, and Clay to Tappan, July 6, 1838.
26. *Speeches*, II, 355–75. On the purpose see Clay to the Whigs of Nansemond, Virginia, *Niles' Register*, Aug. 17, 1839.
27. *Congressional Globe*, 25 Cong., 3 Sess., 177; Calhoun to Armistead Burt, Feb. 17, 1839, *Correspondence of Calhoun*, 423–24.
28. *Congressional Globe*, 25 Cong., 3 Sess., 168.
29. Richmond *Whig*, May 20, 1839; Benjamin Tappan to Lewis Tappan, Aug. 8, 1839, Ohio Historical Society.
30. Everett to Webster, Feb. 14, Webster to Biddle, Feb. 7, 1839, *DWP*.
31. Richmond *Whig*, Feb. 28; Washington *Globe*, Feb. 7; Pendleton *Messenger*, Feb. 22, Charleston *Mercury*, Feb. 12, 1839.
32. William Jay, *Miscellaneous Writings on Slavery* (Boston, 1853), 227.
33. "To the Pennsylvania Freeman," *Letters*, I, 334–38.

34. Diary, Feb. 7-12, 1839, Joshua R. Giddings Papers; *History of the Rebellion: Its Authors and Causes* (New York, 1864), 128.

35. "Remarks on the Slavery Question, in a Letter to Jonathan Phillips, Esq., 1839" and "A Letter to the Hon. Henry Clay, on the Annexation of Texas," *Works of William E. Channing* (Boston, 1841), V, 5-106, II, 181-260. See also Gerrit Smith, *Letter to the Hon. Henry Clay* (New York, 1839).

36. Washington *Globe*, Feb. 28, 1839; Franklin Elmore to Francis Pickens, Mar. [?], 1839, Pickens Papers; Clay to Preston, Apr. 24, 1839, in the Virginia Carrington Scrapbook, Library of Congress.

37. Richmond *Whig*, Mar. 19, 1839, which copied the *U.S. Gazette*, where Preston's speech was first reported. This was widely reprinted, e.g., Pendleton *Messenger*, Apr. 12; Louisville *Journal*, Mar. 21, 1839.

38. To Preston, Apr. 24, 1839, Carrington Scrapbook; Preston to Epes Sargent, Aug. 10, 1842, Sargent Papers, Boston Public Library.

39. *Congressional Globe*, 26 Cong., 1 Sess., 455, where it was said to be a New York circular. A slightly different version circulated in Illinois; see *Letters of Stephen A. Douglas*, Robert Johannsen, ed. (Urbana, 1960), I, 78.

40. Henry A. Wise, *Seven Decades of the Union* (Philadelphia, 1872), 165-66.

41. Hone, *Diary*, I, 415; *Niles' Register*, Aug. 31, 1839.

42. Winfield Scott to Benjamin Watkins Leigh, Oct. 29, 1839, Leigh Papers, Virginia Historical Society; Weed, *Autobiography*, 480-82.

43. *Memoirs and Letters of James Kent*, William Kent, ed. (Boston, 1898), 260.

44. *National Intelligencer*, May 23; *Niles' Register*, Aug. 24, 1839.

45. To Samuel Jaudon, Jan. 12, Apr. 15, 1839, *DWP*, IV, 338-40, 356.

46. Subscription for Webster, May 1, Receipt . . . , May 16, 1839, *ibid.*, 359-63; Thomas Wren Ward to Joshua Bates, Apr. 15, 1839, Ward Papers, Massachusetts Historical Society.

47. Washington *Globe*, May 31; *National Intelligencer*, May 28, June 1, 1839.

48. Edward Everett to Webster, May 13, Webster to Everett, June 12, 1839, *DWP*, IV, 370.

49. Edward Stanwood, *A History of Presidential Elections*, 3rd ed., rev. (Cambridge, 1892), 125-29; Robert G. Gunderson, *The Log Cabin Campaign* (Lexington, Ky., 1957), 59-60; Norman D. Brown, *Edward Stanley: Whiggery's Tarheel Conquerer* (Tuscaloosa, 1974), 58-59; Catherine V. R. Bonney, *A Legacy of Historical Gleanings* (Albany, 1875), II, 117; John J. Crittenden to Orlando Brown, Dec. 19, 1839, Brown Papers, Filson Club; Leslie Combs to Clay, Dec. [7], 1839, *HCP*.

50. Wise, *Seven Decades*, 171-72.

51. *National Intelligencer*, Dec. 10, 1839.

52. Wise, *Seven Decades*, 157-61; Lyon G. Tyler, *Letters and Times of the Tylers* (Richmond, 1884), I, 590-93; Robert Seager, *And Tyler Too: A Biography of John and Julia Gardner Tyler* (New York, 1963), 130-34.

53. *National Intelligencer*, Dec. 14, 1839.

54. *Works of Clay*, VIII, 195-214; to John M. Clayton, May 29, 1840, *HCP*.

55. The best general account is Gunderson, *Log Cabin Campaign*. See also McMaster, *History*, VI, 562-91.

56. New York *Herald*, Oct. 3, 1840.

57. *Works of Clay*, VIII, 215.

58. *Niles' Register*, Sept. 5; Louisville *Journal*, Aug. 24, 25, Sept. 26, 1940.

59. *Niles' Register*, July 20, 1839, quoting the London *Morning Herald*.

60. Claude M. Fuess, *Life of Daniel Webster* (Boston, 1930), II, 75-76; Henry Hallam to Mrs. Edward Ticknor, Jan. 21, 1840, Dartmouth College; *Letters of Sydney Smith*, Norvell C. Smith, ed. (Oxford, 1953), II, 687; *Correspondence of Emerson and Carlyle*, Joseph Slater, ed. (New York, 1964), 240.

61. Baring Brothers and Co. to Webster, Oct. 12, and Webster to Baring Brothers, Oct. 16, 1839, in *Niles' Register*, Dec. 28, 1839 (and in *DWP*, IV, 401-2, 404-7); Ralph W. Hidy, *The House of Baring in American Trade and Finance* (Cambridge, 1949), 283-85; George Bancroft to Martin Van Buren, Nov. 2, 1840, *Proceedings of the Massachusetts Historical Society*, v. 42 (1909), 387.

62. *Niles' Register*, May 9, 1840.

63. *Bay State Democrat*, repr. in Boston *Courier*, Feb. 11, 1840; J. P. Henly to Webster, Feb. 11; Webster to Edward Curtis, Feb. 17, 1840, *DWP*.

64. To Joshua Bates, Mar. 28, 1840, *DWP*.

65. See the speeches and reports in the New York *Herald*, Aug. 24, 28, Sept. 24, 25, 26, 30, 1840.

66. *Writings*, III, 30, 3–37; New York *Herald*, Aug. 24, 28, 1840; Louisville *Journal*, Sept. 4, 1840.

67. *Writings*, XIII, 114–42.

68. New York *Herald*, Sept. 24–26, 1840.

69. Niles' *Register*, Oct. 17, 1840.

70. *Ibid.*, June 27, Oct. 5, 1840; *Writings*, III, 94, 83–102.

71. Richmond *Enquirer*, Sept. 29, Oct. 6, 1840. See also Merrill D. Peterson, *The Jefferson Image in the American Mind* (New York, 1960), 109–10.

72. McMaster, *History*, VI, 590.

Chapter Six: The Whig Debacle

1. William Henry Harrison to Clay, Sept. 20, 1839, Harrison Papers, Library of Congress.

2. Louisville *Journal*, Dec. 15, 1841; Martin Beaty to J. J. Crittenden, Dec. 1, 1840, Crittenden Papers, Library of Congress; Freeman Cleaves, *Old Tippecanoe* (New York, 1939), 329–30; George R. Poage, *Henry Clay and the Whig Party* (Chapel Hill, 1936), ch. 2.

3. Washington *Globe*, Dec. 26, 1840; Louisville *Journal*, Dec. 10, 1840.

4. To Robert Brooke, Dec. 8, 1840, *Works of Clay*, V, 446–47; Louisville *Journal*, Nov. 10, 1842; Washington *Globe*, Dec. 22, 26, 1840; to John M. Clayton, Dec. 17, 1840, HCP.

5. Harrison to Webster, Dec. 1, and Webster to Harrison, Dec. 11, 1840; Julia Appleton to Webster, Dec. 11, 1840, DWP. See also Sydney Nathans, *Daniel Webster and Jacksonian Democracy* (Baltimore, 1973), 148–50.

6. Herman Cape to Webster, Feb. 10, 1840; "Property Settlement," Mar. 25, 1841; Richard A. Smith to Webster, Mar. 29, 1841, DWP. See also Thomas P. Govan, *Nichols Biddle, Nationalist and Public Banker, 1786–1844* (Chicago, 1959), 388–89.

7. *Congressional Globe*, 26 Cong., 2 Sess., 328–32; William A. Graham to Thomas Ruffin, Feb. 19, 1841, *Ruffin Papers*, J. G. de Roulhac Hamilton, ed. (Raleigh, 1918), II, 193; Niles' *Register*, Apr. 3, 17, 1841; Harold M. Hyman and William M. Wiecek, *Equal Justice Under Law* (New York, 1982), 101–102.

8. Quoted in Wilfred E. Binkley, *President and Congress* (New York, 1947), 89.

9. New York *Herald*, Feb. 23, 1841.

10. To Peter B. Porter, Jan. 8, Feb. 7, 1841, HCP; Philip R. Fendall Diary, Jan. 26, Feb. 8, 1841, Fendall Papers, Duke Univ.; Nicholas Biddle to Webster, Feb. 21, 1841; DWP; New York *Herald*, Feb. 25, 1841; Oliver Carlson, *The Man Who Made News: James Gordon Bennett* (New York, 1942), 205–7.

11. Ogden Edwards to J. J. Crittenden, Apr. 12, 1841, Crittenden Papers.

12. There are many sources, e.g., Charles Lanman, "Daniel Webster's Social Hours," *Harper's Magazine*, v. 13 (1856), 497; Ben: Perley Poore, *Reminiscences* (Philadelphia), n.d.), I, 250.

13. *Messages and Papers of the President*, James D. Richardson, ed. (Washington, 1896), III, 1860–76.

14. Millard Fillmore to Thurlow Weed, Feb. 6, 1841, Fillmore Papers, Buffalo Historical Society; Clay to Robert Letcher, Jan. 25, 1841, HCP; Albany *Journal*, Jan. 19, 1841; Boston *Courier*, Feb. 9, 1841; New York *Herald*, Feb. 23, Mar. 2, 3, 1841.

15. Clay to Harrison, Harrison to Clay, Mar. 13, 1841, HCP; Nathan Sargent, *Public Men and Events* (Philadelphia, 1875), I, 116.

16. Webster editorial, "The Call of Congress" [Mar. 25, 1841], DWP.

1. *Tyler Too*

1. Lyon Gardiner Tyler, *The Letters and Times of the Tylers* (Richmond, 1884), I, 360, 467, 590–93, II, 143–44, 464–65; Henry A. Wise, *Seven Decades of the Union* (Philadelphia, 1881), 157–61; Robert Seager, *And Tyler Too: A Biography of John and Julia Gardiner Tyler* (New York, 1963), 130–34.

2. "Mr. Wise's Speech in 1843," *William and Mary Quarterly*, 1st. ser., v. 18 (1909–10), 225.

3. To Maj. Charles Young, Jan. 4, 1841, JCCP; Charleston *Mercury*, Dec. 3, 29, 1840.

4. To Virgil Maxcy, Feb. 19, 1841, JCCP; Webster editorial [Dec. 4, 1840], DWP.

5. Samuel G. Townes to George F. Townes, July 25, 1841, Townes Family Papers, Univ. of South Carolina.
6. To C. H. Thomas, Apr. 11, 1841, *DWP*.
7. To John W. Davis, Apr. 16, 1841, *DWP*.
8. William C. Preston to Willie P. Mangum, May 3, 1841, *Mangum Papers*, H. T. Shanks, ed. (Raleigh 1950), II, 156.
9. Tyler, *Letters and Times*, II, 704.
10. Boston *Courier*, May 26, July 30, 1841; New York *Herald*, May 25, 1841.
11. *Messages and Papers*, III, 1889–92; Tyler to Clay, Apr. 30, 1841, *HCP*.
12. Clay to Thomas Ewing, Apr. 30, Ewing to Clay, May 8, 1841, *HCP*.
13. *Messages and Papers*, III, 1895–1904.
14. *Congressional Globe*, 27 Cong., 1 Sess., 22.
15. A. O. P. Nicholson to James K. Polk, June 14, 1841, *Correspondence of James K. Polk*, Herbert Weaver and Paul Bergeron, eds., (Nashville, 1893), V, 698.
16. *Congressional Globe*, 27 Cong., 1 Sess., 296–97, 318–19; Thomas Hart Benton, *Thirty Years View* (New York, 1856), II, 247–57; G. H. Haynes, *The Senate of the United States* (Boston, 1938), I, 394.
17. New York *Herald*, July 30, 1841.
18. Poore, *Reminiscences, I*, 271–72.
19. *National Intelligencer*, June 15, 16, 17; for drafts see *DWP*; Willie P. Mangum to Duncan Cameron, June 26, 1841, *Mangum Papers*, II, 182–83.
20. *Ibid.*, 183–85.
21. *Congressional Globe*, 27 Cong., 1 Sess., 79–81.
22. Mangum to Cameron, June 26, 1841, *Mangum Papers*, II, 185–87.
23. To Hiram Ketchum, July 16, 17, 1841, *Writings*, XVI, 344–51; Richard Frothingham, Journal, July 31, 1841 (Massachusetts Historical Society); Louisville *Journal*, July 20, 1841.
24. *Congressional Globe*, 27 Cong., 1 Sess., 210, 81–83.
25. Richmond *Whig*, July 30, 1841; Robert Winthrop to John H. Clifford, Aug. 9, 1841, Winthrop Papers, Massachusetts Historical Society; Peter B. Porter to William C. Preston, July 20, 1841, Virginia Carrington Scrapbook, Library of Congress; Porter to Clay, July 23, 1841, *HCP*; New York *Herald*, July 29, Aug. 11, 1841; Tyler, *Letters and Times*, II, 54–64.
26. New York *Herald*, July 29, 1841.
27. To Andrew P. Calhoun, July 31, 1841, *JCCP*; New York *Herald*, Aug. 5, 1841; Poage, *Clay and Whig Party*, 68–71.
28. *Messages and Papers*, III, 1916–21; Tyler, *Letters and Times*, I, 499.
29. Albany *Journal*, Aug. 18, Louisville *Journal*, Aug. 24, 25, 1841.
30. To Caroline Webster, Aug. 16, 1841, *DWP*; Winthrop to John H. Clifford, Aug. 22, 1841, Winthrop Papers.
31. "Diary of Thomas Ewing, August and September, 1841," *American Historical Review*, v. 18 (1912), 100–103; Benton, *View*, II, 331–47; "Memo Respecting the Banking Bill and the Vetoes," [1841], *DWP*.
32. Silas Wright to Martin Van Buren, Aug. 22, 1841, Van Buren Papers, Library of Congress; Ewing, "Diary," 103; *Speeches of Henry Clay*, Daniel Mallory, ed. (New York, 1843), II, 485–507.
33. Ewing, "Diary," 103.
34. Benton, *View*, II, 350; *Madisonian* (Washington), Aug. 27, 1841; Ewing, "Diary," 105; Webster to Edward Bates and Rufus Choate, Aug. 25, 1841, *Writings*, XVI, which appeared in the *Madisonian*, Sept. 9, 1841.
35. *Works of Calhoun*, IV, 13–43; see also III, 407–39, 560–83.
36. *Congressional Globe*, 27 Cong., 1 Sess., 348; Clay to Robert Letcher, Jan. 6, 1842, *HCP*.
37. Albany *Journal*, Aug. 10, 1841.
38. *Congressional Globe*, 27 Cong., 1 Sess., 344–45.
39. *Messages and Papers*, III, 1921–25; Robert J. Morgan, *A Whig Embattled: The Presidency Under John Tyler* (Lincoln, 1954), 43–45.
40. O. H. Smith, *Early Indiana Trials, and Speeches, Reminiscences* (Cincinnati, 1858), 594; Raymond C. Dingledine, Jr., "The Political Career of William Cabell Rives," (Ph.D. diss., Univ. of Virginia, 1947), 396.
41. Robert Winthrop to Webster, Sept. 13, 1841, *DWP*; *Memoirs of John Quincy Adams* (Philadelphia, 1874–77), XI, 13–14; Maurice G. Baxter, *One and Inseparable: Daniel Webster and the Union* (Cambridge, 1984), 310–12.
42. Tyler, *Letters and Times*, II, 122.

43. *Niles Register*, Sept. 18, 1841; Louisville *Journal*, Oct. 8, 1841; Charles H. Bohner, *John Pendleton Kennedy: Gentleman from Baltimore* (Baltimore, 1961), 148.
44. Boston *Courier*, Oct. 7, Boston *Daily Advertiser*, Oct. 7, 9, 1841.
45. Boston *Courier*, Sept. 17, Richmond *Whig*, Sept. 24, 1841.
46. To J. O. Sargent, July 29, 1843, *HCP*; Webster to Robert Letcher, Oct. 23, 1843, *DWP*.
47. To Virgil Maxcy, Sept. 13; Francis Pickens to Calhoun, July 18, 1841, *JCP*; to Andrew P. Calhoun, Sept. 12, 1841, *Correspondence of Calhoun*, 488–89; R. K. Crallé to Calhoun, Oct. 8, 1841, *Correspondence Addressed to John C. Calhoun, 1837–1849*, Chauncy C. Boucher and R. P. Brooks, eds., *Annual Report of the American Historical Association, 1929* (Washington, 1930), 161–62; Willie P. Mangum to Col. Webb, Dec. 6, 1842, Taliaferro Papers, Louisiana State Univ.
48. To Peter B. Porter, Jan. 16, 1842, *HCP*; J. J. Crittenden to Robert Letcher, Jan. 9, 1842, Crittenden Papers.
49. "The Exchequer," [Dec. 1841], *DWP*; Silas Wright to Martin Van Buren, Jan. 12, 1842, Van Buren Papers; Baxter, *Webster*, 313–14.
50. *Speeches*, II, 512–29.
51. *Works of Calhoun*, IV, 74–100.
52. Boston *Courier*, Apr. 21, *Daily Advertiser*, Apr. 6, 1842; John G. Tregle, "Louisiana and the Tariff, 1816–1842," *Louisiana Historical Quarterly*, v. 25 (1942), ch. 3; Malcolm R. Eiselen, *The Rise of Pennsylvania Protectionism* (New York, 1932), ch. 7; Clay to J. J. Crittenden, June 3, 1842, *HCP*; Merrill D. Peterson, *Olive Branch and Sword: The Compromise of 1833* (Baton Rouge, 1982), 113–20.
53. *Niles' Register*, May 7, 1842.
54. *Congressional Globe*, 27 Cong., 2 Sess., 372; *Works of Calhoun*, IV, 109–18, 171–201.
55. Clay to J. J. Crittenden, July 16, 1842, *HCP*.
56. Clay to James M. Berrien, Aug. 15, Sept. 9, 1842; Edward Stanwood, *American Tariff Controversies in the Nineteenth Century* (Boston, 1903), II, ch. 11.
57. *Life of John J. Crittenden*, Mrs. Chapman Coleman, ed. (Philadelphia, 1871), I, 177–79.
58. Silas Wright to Martin Van Buren, Apr. 2, 1842, Van Buren Papers; Charleston *Courier*, Apr. 4, 1842; Sargent, *Public Men*, I, 159–61.
59. *Ibid*; Alexander H. H. Stuart to———, [1842] Univ. of Virginia.
60. To Richard Hines and others, Mar. 21, 1842, in *Niles' Register*, Apr. 9, 1842.
61. To James Watson Webb, Apr. 30; W. J. Graves to Clay, Feb. 14, Clay to Henry A. Wise, Feb. 28, 1842, *HCP*; *National Intelligencer*, Mar. 22, New York *Herald*, Jan. 17, 31, Mar. 2, 1842; *Letters of John Fairfield*, Arthur G. Staples, ed. (Lewiston, Maine, 1922), 204; *Kendall's Espositor* (Washington), Mar. 5, 1844; John C. Parish, *George Wallace Jones* (Iowa City, 1912), ch. 5.

2. Webster at State

1. *Congressional Globe*, 25 Cong., 3 Sess., 259–60.
2. Webster to Henry S. Fox, Mar. 12, Fox to Webster, Apr. 24, 1841; Webster to J. J. Crittenden, May 15, *Writings*, IX, 247–66; S. O. Bloodgood to William H. Seward, Mar. 6, Seward to Webster, Mar. 22, to Christopher Morgan, July 26, 1841, Seward Papers, Univ. of Rochester.
3. To John Tyler, July———, to Ketchum, July———, 1841; Webster to Seward, Aug. 24, Seward to Webster, Sept. 3, 1841, *DWP*; "Notes of a Conversation, 1841," Massachusetts Historical Society *Proceedings*, 2nd. ser., v. 44 (1911), 337.
4. To Joshua Spencer, Sept. 21, 1841, *Diplomatic Papers of Daniel Webster* (Hanover, 1983), I, 146; to Joseph Story, July 16, [1841]; Henry S. Fox to Webster, Sept. 5, Tyler to Webster, Sept. 8, Webster to Joshua Spencer, Sept. 21, Spencer to Webster, Sept. 24, Seward to Webster, Sept. 12, 1841, *DWP*.
5. *Congressional Globe*, 27 Cong., 1 Sess., 14–18, 42–46.
6. Daniel Tallmadge, *Review of the Opinion of Judge Cowen* (New York, 1841); *Writings*, XI, 267–68; *Diplomatic Papers*, I, 705–6n.
7. *Congressional Globe*, 26 Cong., 2 Sess., 203–204; *Works of Calhoun*, III, 462–87.
8. Samuel Flagg Bemis, *John Quincy Adams and the Foundation of American Foreign Policy* (New York, 1949), 432–35; St. George L. Sioussat, "Duff Green's 'England and the United States,' " *American Antiquarian Society Proceedings*, n.s., v. 40 (1930); *Messages and Papers*, III, 2047–49.
9. To Edward Everett, Jan. 29, 1842, *Diplomatic Papers*, I, 178–85.

10. *Congressional Globe,* 28 Cong., 2 Sess., 255–56.
11. Samuel J. May to J. A. Collins, Feb. 28, 1842, May Papers, Boston Public Library, May to Webster, Mar. 29, 1842, *DWP.*
12. *Congressional Globe,* 27 Cong., 2 Sess., 342; George W. Julian, *The Life of Joshua R. Giddings* (Chicago, 1892), 117–19, 125.
13. *Complete Works of William Ellery Channing* (Boston, 1880), 853–907.
14. To Joseph Story, Mar. 17, Story to Webster, Mar. 26, 1842, *DWP.*
15. Clay to Epes Sargent, Sept. 25, 1843, *HCP.*
16. "Notes of a Conversation," 338; Jessie B. Fremont, *Souvenirs of My Time* (Boston, 1887), 18–19; Robert C. Winthrop, *Reminiscences of Foreign Travel* (n.p., 1894), 55–56.
17. Ashburton to Webster, Jan. 2, Webster to Edward Everett, Jan. 29, 1842, *DWP; Niles' Register,* Jan. 20, 1842.
18. "Edmund Ruffin's Visit to John Tyler," *William and Mary Quarterly,* 1st. ser. v. 14 (1906), 208–209; Seager, *Tyler Too,* ch. 7.
19. Webster to Hiram Ketchum, Mar. 1, 1843, *DWP.*
20. Boston *Courier,* July 29, New York *Herald,* Dec. 20, 24, 31, 1841.
21. Louisa Catherine Adams to J. Q. Adams, Aug. 8, 1841, Adams Papers, Massachusetts Historical Society; Nicholas Carroll to Willie P. Mangum, Oct. 28, 1841, *Mangum Papers,* IV, 247–48.
22. Henry E. Lawrence, Diary, Louisiana State Univ.; Leverett Saltonstall to Mrs. Saltonstall, Dec. 29, 1842, Massachusetts Historical Society.
23. "Extracts from the Diary of Lord Morpeth," MS copy (Library of Congress), 99, 103–104, 129; Morpeth (G. W. F. Howard, 7th. Earl of Carlisle), *Travels in America* (New York, 1851), *passim.*
24. Charles Dickens, *American Notes* (Boston, 1867), 62; *National Intelligencer,* Nov. 23, 1842.
25. See Webster's "Defense of the Treaty of Washington," 1846, *Writings,* IX, 78–150. See also Howard Jones, *To the Webster-Ashburton Treaty: A Study in Anglo-American Relations, 1783–1843* (Chapel Hill, 1977).
26. Ashburton to Aberdeen, Apr. 26, June 13, 1842, *Diplomatic Papers,* I, 545, 580.
27. F. O. J. Smith to Webster, July 2, Nov. 20, 1841, *DWP.* See also Frederick Merk, *Fruits of Propaganda in the Tyler Administration* (Cambridge, 1971) and Richard N. Current, "Webster's Propaganda and the Ashburton Treaty," *Mississippi Valley Historical Review,* v. 34 (1947), 187–201.
28. To Edward Kent, Dec. 12, 1841, to Ruel Williams, Feb. 2, Williams to Webster, Feb. 12, 1842; F. O. J. Smith to Webster, Apr. 16, Webster to John Fairfield, to John W. Davis, Apr. 11, 1842, *DWP.*
29. To Edward Everett, *Writings,* 120–24.
30. To Jared Sparks, May 14, 16, Sparks to Webster, Feb. 15, 1842, *DWP;* Herbert Baxter Adams, *The Life and Writings of Jared Sparks* (Boston, 1893), II, 400.
31. To Edward Everett, June 14, 1842, *DWP.* See also Jones, *Treaty,* ch. 6.
32. Adams, *Sparks,* II, 400–403; Jared Sparks to Webster, May 19, 1842, *DWP.*
33. *Niles' Register,* Aug. 6, 1842; Jones, *Treaty,* ch. 7; Baxter, *Webster,* 344–48.
34. John Tyler to Webster, Aug. 7, 1842, *DWP.*
35. Francis Lieber to Webster, Dec. 22, 1842, *DWP.*
36. *Diplomatic Papers,* I, 31–32.
37. To Edward Everett, Apr. 26, 1842, *DWP; Writings,* XV, 171–84.
38. Quoted in John P. Thomas, ed., *The Carolina Tribute to Calhoun* (Columbia, S.C., 1857), 30.
39. *Journal of the Senate,* 27 Cong., 2 Sess., App., 689–701; "The Treaty of Washington" [Aug. 22, 1842], *DWP.*
40. *Writings,* XIII, 143–49; Boston *Courier,* Nov. 7, 1842; *Diary of Philip Hone, 1828–1851,* Allan Nevins, ed. (New York, 1927), 628.
41. *National Intelligencer,* Apr. 20, 1843.
42. *Ibid.,* Apr. 22, 1843.
43. Ashburton to Charles Jared Ingersoll, Dec. 20, 1842, Ingersoll Papers, Historical Society of Pennsylvania; *National Intelligencer,* Feb. 16, 1843.
44. Ashburton to Webster, Jan. 2, 1843, *DWP.* See also Herbert C. F. Bell, *Lord Palmerston* (New York, 1936), II, 333–35.
45. Lewis Cass to Webster, Oct. 3, Edward Everett to Webster, Nov. 3, 1842, Webster to Cass, Apr. 25, 1842, *DWP; Writings,* XII, 17–20, XVI, 124–25. See also, Frank B. Woodford, *Lewis Cass, The Last Jeffersonian* (New Brunswick, 1950), 203–14.

46. *Writings*, XV, 171–84.
47. *Congressional Globe*, 29 Cong., 1 Sess., 344ff. See also William M. Meigs, *The Life of Charles Jared Ingersoll* (Philadelphia, 1900), 278–91.
48. To Edward Everett, Jan. 29, 1843, *Writings*, XVI, 393–96. See also Frederick Merk, *The Oregon Question* (Cambridge, 1967), 189–215.
49. *Congressional Globe*, 29 Cong., 1 Sess, 524–37; Robert Winthrop to Edward Everett, Apr. 11, 1846, Everett Papers, Massachusetts Historical Society; George M. Dallas to Mrs. Dallas, Apr. 7, 1846, *Pennsylvania Magazine of History and Biography*, v. 73 (1949), 375; Dallas to Richard Rush, Apr. 6, 1844, Rush Papers (microfilm ed., 1980).
50. *Congressional Globe*, 29 Cong., 1 Sess., 636–735 *passim;* Henry W. Hilliard, *Politics and Pen Pictures at Home and Abroad* (New York, 1892), 160–61.
51. *Louisville Journal*, Jan. 26, Feb. 14, Mar. 23, 1842.
52. George Bancroft to Martin Van Buren, Feb. 21, 1842, "Letters," *Massachusetts Historical Society Proceedings*, 2nd. ser. v. 42 (1909), 391; Webster to Edward Everett, Aug. 25, 1842, DWP.
53. To Thomas G. Clemson, Apr. 3, 1842, *Correspondence of Calhoun*, 508–509.
54. Webster to John Healy, Aug. 24, 1842, DWP. See also Robert Dalzell, Jr., *Daniel Webster and the Trials of American Nationalism, 1843–1852* (Boston, 1973), ch. 2.
55. Boston *Courier*, Sept. 15, 1842; to Charles P. Curtis, Sept. 15, 1842, *Writings*, XVI, 383. See also Willie P. Mangum to John M. Clayton, Mar. 16, 1844, Clayton Papers, Library of Congress.
56. Adams, *Memoirs*, XI, 256; Charles Sumner, quoted in Hamilton A. Hill, *Memoir of Abbott Lawrence*, 74–75; Charles Francis Adams, *Richard Henry Dana, A Biography* (Boston, 1890), I, 43–4. The report of the speech, *Writings*, III, 117–40, does not convey its extraordinary character.
57. George Ticknor, *Life and Letters* (Cambridge, 1909), II, 210–11; Sargent, *Public Men*, I, 191–92; George F. Hoar, *Autobiography of Seventy Years* (New York, 1893), I, 135; Richmond *Whig*, Oct. 4, 7, 1842.
58. Washington *Globe*, Oct. 3, 1842.
59. Benjamin W. Leigh to Willie P. Mangum, Mar. 28, 1844, *Mangum Papers*, II, 82.
60. To Edward Everett, Aug. 25, 1842, DWP.
61. To Waddy Thompson, June 27, 1842, *Writings*, XIV, 611–12; *Diplomatic Papers*, I, 826–31; Claude M. Fuess, *Life of Caleb Cushing* (New York, 1923), I, 411; David M. Pletcher, *The Diplomacy of Annexation: Texas, Oregon, and the Mexican War* (Columbia, Mo., 1973), 99–100; Merk, *Oregon Question*, 189–215.
62. *Diplomatic Papers*, I, 877–84; Fuess, *Cushing*, I, 400–401; Paul R. Frothingham, *Edward Everett, Orator and Statesman* (Boston, 1925), 227–34; *National Intelligencer*, May 2, 1843.
63. To Hiram Ketchum, Mar. 1, to Edward Everett, May 12, 1843, DWP; *National Intelligencer*, May 13, 23, 27, 1843.

3. *Calhoun, the Presidency, and Texas*

1. William C. Preston to Waddy Thompson, Dec. 17, 1842, Preston Papers, Univ. of South Carolina; Preston to William A. Graham, Dec. 4, 1842, *Graham Papers*, J. G. de Roulhac Hamilton, ed. (Raleigh, 1957), II, 386. See also Drew Gilpin Faust, *James H. Hammond and the Old South* (Baton Rouge, 1982), 232–36.
2. Dixon Lewis to Calhoun, Nov. 2, 1842, *Correspondence to Calhoun*, 181. See, in general, Matthew A. Fitzsimmons, "Calhoun's Bid for the Presidency, 1841–1844," *Mississippi Valley Historical Review*, v. 38 (1951), 39–60.
3. W. H. Roane to Martin Van Buren, Sept. 11, 1843, Van Buren Papers.
4. *Niles' Register*, Sept. 2, 1843; to Duff Green, June 7, 1843, *Correspondence of Calhoun*, 538.
5. Calhoun to Franklin H. Elmore, Jan. 16, 1844, JCCP; Diary, Oct. 25, 1844, James H. Hammond Papers, Library of Congress. See also *The Calhoun Text Book* (New York, 1843).
6. Hammond, Diary, Aug. 7, 1839.
7. *Ibid.*
8. *Niles' Register*, July 11, 1843.
9. George Kemple to Joel R. Poinsett, Oct. 10, 1842, Poinsett Papers, Library of Congress.
10. Quoted in *The History of Presidential Elections*, Arthur M. Schlesinger, Jr., and Fred Israel, eds. (New York, 1971), I, 755.

11. "Letter to the Hon. William Smith," July 3, 1843, *Works of Calhoun*, VI, 209–39; Dixon Lewis to Richard Crallé, May 30, 1842, "Calhoun as Seen by His Political Friends," F. W. Moore, ed., *Southern History Association Publications*, VII (1903), 357–58; Robert Banwell Rhett to Calhoun, June 22, Calhoun to Robert M. T. Hunter, Oct. 24, 1843, *JCCP*.

12. Quoted in Merrill D. Peterson, *The Jefferson Image in the American Mind* (New York, 1960), 171. See also *Works of Calhoun*, II, 597–611.

13. *Niles' Register*, June 17, 1843.

14. "Brook Farm," *U.S. Magazine of Democratic Review*, v. 11 (1842), 454. See also, "Popular Government," *ibid.*, v. 15 (1843), 281–96; and Thomas R. Ryan, *Orestes A. Brownson. A Definitive Biography* (Huntington, Ind., 1976), ch. 18.

15. To Orestes Brownson, Oct. 31, 1841, *JCCP*.

16. The contract, Jan. 23, 1843, is in the Galloway-Maxcy-Markoe Papers, Library of Congress. See Calhoun to Robert M. T. Hunter, Sept. 30, 1842, and J. F. Hutton to Hunter, Jan. 25, 1843, in *Correspondence of Hunter*, Charles H. Ambler, ed., *American Historical Association Annual Report, 1916* (Washington, 1918), II, 48–49, 58; Hunter to Mrs. Hunter [Jan. 1843], Hunter Papers, Univ. of Virginia. For the controversy about authorship, see Charles M. Wiltse's app., to *John C. Calhoun, Nationalist* (Indianapolis, 1944) and the app., to Gerald M. Capers, *John C. Calhoun, Opportunist* (Gainesville, 1960).

17. *Life of Calhoun*, 53, 61.

18. *National Intelligencer*, July 12, 15, 22, Aug. 5, 1843; Harper & Bros. to Virgil Maxcy, May 22, June 13, 1843, Galloway-Maxcy-Markoe Papers.

19. Summary in *JCCP*, XVI, 584–85; Laura A. White, *Robert Barnwell Rhett* (Gloucester, Mass., 1965), 62.

20. *Life*, 29.

21. Martin Van Buren to George Bancroft, Mar. 19, 1843, "Letters," 399.

22. See, e.g., Peter C. Manning to Robert B. Rhett, Jan. 26, 1843, Rhett Papers, Univ. of South Carolina.

23. John A. Stuart to James A. Seddon, Mar. 4, 1843, Seddon Papers, Virginia Historical Society; Charles H. Ambler, *Thomas Ritchie. A Study in Virginia Politics* (Richmond, 1913), 225–34.

24. Francis Pickens to Calhoun, July 19, 1843, *JCCP*; Robert B. Rhett to Calhoun, Mar. 10, 1844, *Correspondence to Calhoun*, 214.

25. To R. M. T. Hunter, May 16, Virgil Maxcy to Calhoun, May 27, 1843, *JCCP*; Hunter to Maxcy, Mar. 18, Franklin Elmore to Maxcy, May 2, Joseph Scoville to Maxcy, May 12, 1843, Galloway-Maxcy-Markoe Papers.

26. To R. M. T. Hunter, Sept. 30, to C. M. Ingersoll, Nov. 11, 1843, *JCCP*.

27. Dated Charleston, Sept. 23, 1843, in Hunter Papers, Univ. of Virginia; "The Baltimore Convention," *Democratic Review*, v. 13 (1843), 339–45.

28. *Niles' Register*, Sept. 23, 1843.

29. Hunter to Calhoun, Dec. 22, 1843, *Correspondence*, 556; Pickens to Calhoun, Dec. 27, 1843, Calhoun to Franklin Elmore, Jan. 16, 1844, *JCCP*.

30. *Works*, III, 239–54.

31. William Roane to Martin Van Buren, Feb. 3, Hugh Garland to Van Buren, Feb. 7, 1844, Van Buren Papers; Ambler, *Ritchie*, 235; Louisville *Journal*, Feb. 7, 1844.

32. Charleston *Mercury*, Jan. 27, 29, Feb. 16, 18, 1844; Pickens to Calhoun, Feb. 7, 1844, *JCCP*; James Gadsden to James E. Calhoun, Feb. 15, 1844, Gadsden Papers, Univ. of South Carolina.

33. To Duff Green, Feb. 10, to James H. Hammond, Mar. 5, 1844, *Correspondence of Calhoun*, 568–69, 571–72.

34. For contrasting views see Seager, *Tyler Too*, 216–17 and Charles G. Sellers, *James K. Polk, Continentalist, 1843–1846* (Princeton, 1966), 56n.

35. James G. Blaine, *Twenty Years in Congress* (Norwich, Conn., 1884), I, 27.

36. Francis Walker Gilmer to Calhoun, Dec. 13, 1843, *Correspondence to Calhoun*, 904–906; Benton, *View*, II, 581–82.

37. Duff Green, *Facts and Suggestions, Biographical, Historical, Financial and Political* (New York, 1866); Green to Calhoun, Jan. 24, 1842, *Correspondence* 841–44. See also Bernard Semmel, *The Rise of Free Trade Imperialism* (Cambridge, 1970) and Bruno Gujer, *Free Trade and Slavery: Calhoun's Defense of Southern Interests Against British Interference, 1811–48* (Zurich, 1971).

38. Abel P. Upshur to Calhoun Aug. 14, Calhoun to Upshur, Aug. 27, 1843, *JCCP*. See also Frederick Merk, *Slavery and the Annexation of Texas* (New York, 1972), 20–22.

39. George T. Curtis, *Life of Daniel Webster* (New York, 1872), II, 230–25.
40. Webster to Mr. Bigelow *et al.*, Jan. 23, 1844, *Letters of Daniel Webster*, C. H. Van Tyne, ed. (New York, 1902), 284–94; *Niles' Register*, Mar. 23, 1844; Kinley J. Brauer, *Cotton versus Conscience; Massachusetts Whig Politics and Southwestern Expansion* (Lexington, Ky., 1967), 65–66.
41. *Works of Calhoun*, V, 333–47.
42. See the convenient summary in William J. Cooper, Jr., *The South and the Politics of Slavery, 1828–1856* (Baton Rouge, 1978), App. A.
43. Washington *Globe*, May 6, 1844; Merk, *Slavery and Annexation*, 93; Benton, *View*, II, 589–91.
44. To John A. Mathews, July 2, 1844, *JCCP*.
45. *Congressional Globe*, 27 Cong., 1 Sess., 806.
46. To William R. King, Aug. 12, 1844, *Works*, V, 379–92; Josiah Nott, *Types of Mankind* (Philadelphia, 1854), 49–61.
47. To Henry W. Conner, July 3, 1844, *JCCP*; to Francis Wharton, Sept. 17, 1844, *Correspondence of Calhoun*, 616–17.
48. Hammond, Diary, Oct. 25, 1844; Charleston *Courier*, July 24, 1844. See White, *Rhett*, ch. 5; Chauncey S. Boucher, "The Annexation of Texas and the Bluffton Movement in South Carolina," *Mississippi Valley Historical Review*, v. 6 (1919), 3–33.
49. Charleston *Courier*, Aug. 14, 17, 1844.
50. Langdon Cheves, *Letter to the Editor of the Charleston Mercury, September 11, 1844* ([Charleston, 1844]), 8.
51. Calhoun to Armistead Burt, Aug. 7, to Franklin Elmore, July 30, 1844; Robert B. Rhett to Burt, Sept. 9, 1844, Burt Papers, Duke Univ.; John Barnwell, ed., "Hamlet and Hotspur: Letters of Robert Woodward Barnwell to Robert Barnwell Rhett," *South Carolina Historical Magazine*, v. 77 (1976), 252–53.
52. James H. Hammond to M. C. M. Hammond, Aug. 25, 1844; Diary, Oct. 25, 1844, Hammond Papers.

4. Clay and the Election of 1844

1. To J. Q. Adams, July 24, to J. J. Crittenden, June 13, 1842; mortgage deed, Nov. 29, 1842, *HCP*.
2. *National Intelligencer*, Mar. 19, 1844.
3. *Ibid.*, June 18, 1842; *Speeches*, II, 569–94.
4. Willie P. Mangum to Clay, July 4, 1842, *HCP*; *National Intelligencer*, June 21–July 4, 1842; William G. Brownlow, *A Political Register* (Jonesboro, Tenn., 1844).
5. Smith, *Early Indiana*, 136; *The Clay Minstrel*, John S. Littell, ed. 2nd ed. (Philadelphia, 1844), 267.
6. I have relied particularly on an eyewitness account, Charles F. and William Coffin, "Henry Clay at Richmond," *Indiana Magazine of History*, v. 4 (1908), 123–28. See also Leonard S. Kenworthy, "Henry Clay at Richmond in 1842," *ibid.*, v. 30 (1934), 353–58; Charles W. Osborn, "Henry Clay at Richmond," *ibid.*, v. 4 (1908), 117–23; *Niles' Register*, Oct. 22, 1842; *Speeches*, II, 595–600.
7. *Letters of James G. Birney*, Dwight L. Dumond, ed. (New York, 1938), II, 900; Ben Wade to Joshua Giddings, Giddings Papers, Library of Congress; "Historical News," *Indiana Magazine of History*, v. 17 (1921), 366–67; *Niles' Register*, Oct. 29, 1842.
8. *Ibid.*, Nov. 12, 1842.
9. Louisville *Journal*, Dec. 17, 1842; Webster to John P. Healy, Aug. 24, 1842, in Boston *Courier*, Nov. 29, 1842.
10. To John M. Clayton, Nov. 2, 1842, *HCP*.
11. To William L. Hodge, Aug. 10, 1843; Treagle, "Louisiana and the Tariff, ch. 3.
12. Richmond *Whig*, Jan. 20, 1843, copying the *New Orleans Tropic;* Alan S. Downer, *The Eminent Tragedian. William Charles Macready* (Cambridge, 1966), 266.
13. Robert Letcher to J. J. Crittenden, June 21, 1842, *Life of Crittenden*, 183.
14. To John M. Clayton, May 27, 1843, *HCP*.
15. John Neale to John Sartain, Nov. 15, 1842, Filson Club; *National Intelligencer*, Jan. 30, 1844.
16. John H. Hewitt, *Life and Speeches*, 2 vols. (Baltimore, 1877), 101–102.
17. Daniel Mallory, ed., *Life and Speeches*, 2 vols. (Boston, 1843); James B. Swain, ed., *Life and Speeches*, 2 vols. (New York, 1843). Still another volume of *Speeches* was edited by

Richard Chambers and published in Cincinnati in 1842. Epes Sargent also authored the memoir in the Mallory work. See Clay to Sargent, Aug. 20, 1842, *HCP*.

18. *Writings*, XIII, 150–57.

19. David Sears to Webster, Apr. 28, in Boston *Courier*, May 24, 1843; Sears to Robert G. Shaw, May 27, in *Courier*, June 6; *ibid.*, June 7, July 4, 8, 25, 1843; Boston *Daily Advertiser*, May 27, 31, June 20, 27, 1843; Louisville *Journal*, June 3, 17, 30, 1843; Nathans, *Webster*, 211; Robert Winthrop to Edward Everett, May 16, 1843, Everett Papers; George Bancroft to Martin Van Buren, July 18, 1843, "Letters," 411; Robert B. Rhett to Calhoun, Oct. 3, 1843, *JCCP*.

20. *Journals of Ralph Waldo Emerson*, Ralph H. Orth and A. R. Ferguson, eds., (Cambridge, 1971), X, 397; *Writings*, I, 259–83.

21. Adams *Memoirs*, XI, 381–84; Louisville *Journal*, June 27, 1843.

22. To John M. Clayton, May 27, to Robert Letcher, June 26, 1843, *HCP*.

23. William H. Seward to Peter B. Porter, Sept. 19, 1843, Porter Papers, Buffalo Historical Society; Porter to Clay, Sept. 25, 1843, *HCP*.

24. To Peter B. Porter, Oct. 3, to John Lawrence, Oct. 5, 1843, *HCP*.

25. John M. Berrien to Hamilton Fish, Oct. 26, 1843, Berrien Papers, Univ. of North Carolina; D. F. Bacon to Clay, Oct. 7, Peter B. Porter to Clay, Oct. 11, John W. Davis to Clay, Oct. 14, Clay to J. W. Webb, Oct. 27, 1843, *HCP*.

26. *Writings*, III, 159–85; Kinley J. Brauer, "The Webster-Lawrence Feud: A Study in the Politics of Ambition," *The Historian*, v. 29 (1966), 34–59; Adams *Memoirs*, XII, 214.

27. Webster to Edward Curtis, Jan. 11, 1844, *DWP*;——to William C. Preston, Feb. 9, 1844, Virginia Carrington Scrapbook; Willie P. Mangum to J. W. Webb, Jan. 20, 1844, *Mangum Papers*, V, 474; *Niles' Register*, Jan. 27, 1844.

28. John P. Kennedy, *Defense of the Whigs*, repr. in his *Political and Official Papers* (New York, 1872); *Niles' Register*, Aug. 19, 1843.

29. *National Intelligencer*, Oct. 21, 1843; Sargent, *Life of Clay*, 215–16.

30. Robert Toombs to John M. Berrien, Jan. 28, 1844, Berrien Papers; *Niles' Register* Dec. 19, 1843; Abbott Lawrence, *Letters . . . to the Hon. William C. Rives* (Boston, 1846). See also Arthur C. Cole, *The Whig Party in the South* (Washington, 1913), 95–101; Cooper, *South and Slavery*, 155–63.

31. *Ibid.*, 155; John W. Bear, *Life and Travels of "The Buckeye Blacksmith"* (Baltimore, 1873), 99–103; Louisville *Journal*, Dec. 21, 1843; Washington *Globe*, Mar. 11, 1844.

32. Albany *Journal*, Apr. 24, 1844, copying *Southern Miscellany*.

33. *Niles' Register*, Apr. 20, 1844.

34. Clay to J. J. Crittenden, Dec. 5, 1843, *HCP*.

35. Alexander H. Stephens to James Thomas, May 11, 1844, Stephens Papers; Stephens, *Recollections* (New York, 1910), 17; Clay to Crittenden, March 24, Apr. 17, 19, 21, to Mangum, Apr. 14, 1844, *HCP*.

36. Charleston *Courier*, Jan. 19, 184 and *passim*.

37. *Niles' Register*, Apr. 20, 1844.

38. *National Intelligencer*, Apr. 27, 1844.

39. To Crittenden, Apr. 17, 21, 1844; Albert D. Kirwan, *John J. Crittenden: The Struggle for the Union* (Lexington, Ky., 1962), 175; *National Intelligencer*, Apr. 27, 1844.

40. Marquis James, *Life of Andrew Jackson* (Indianapolis, 1938), 767–68.

41. *National Intelligencer*, May 2, 1844; Sargent, *Life of Clay*, 230–31.

42. Stephen Hess, *American Political Dynasties from Adams to Kennedy* (New York, 1966), 349–52.

43. Edward Stanwood, *History of Presidential Elections* (Boston, 1884), 155–56.

44. *Writings*, XIII, 196–202; Webster to Robert Winthrop, Apr. 28, 1844, *DWP*; William G. Brownlow to Clay, July 24, 1844, Indiana Historical Society; *Niles' Register*, May 25, 1844.

45. To James K. Polk, May 20, 1843, to Gales and Seaton, June 15, 1844, *HCP*.

46. *Niles' Register*, May 4, 1844; William Henry Sparks, *Memoirs of Fifty Years* (Philadelphia, 1870), 47–48; *Congressional Globe*, 25 Cong., 1 Sess., 550–51, 678–80, 777–84.

47. James Buchanan to Robert Letcher, June 27, 1844, *Works of Buchanan*, G. B. Moore, ed. (Philadelphia, 1908–11), VI, 59–60; Robert Letcher to Clay, July 6, Clay to B. W. Leigh, July 3, 20, Sept. 30, to J. Q. Adams, Oct. 26, 1844, *HCP*; to Willie P. Mangum, Sept. 11, 1844, *Mangum Papers*, IV, 192; Richmond *Whig*, Oct. 7, 1844.

48. *The Campaign of 1844*; Louisville *Journal*, Aug. 22, 1844; Sellers, *Polk, Continentalist*, 14.

49. Joshua Leavitt, *The Great Duelist* (n.p., n.d.).

50. *The Campaign of 1844*; M. M. Henkle, *Life of Henry Bidleman Bascom* (Louisville, 1854), 281–83; Louisville *Journal*, June 21, Sept. 17, 18, 20.
51. To William C. Rives, Aug. 19, 1844, *HCP*.
52. *Congressional Globe*, 28 Cong., 1 Sess., 662.
53. Francis Pickens, in Edgefield *Advertiser*, Aug. 17, 1859, Pickens Papers, Univ. of South Carolina; Sellers, *Polk, Continentalist*, 126–27.
54. *Madisonian*, Aug. 12, 14, 1844; Boston *Courier*, Aug. 17, 1844; Peterson, *Olive Branch*, 121–22.
55. Parmelee, "Recollections," 447–48.
56. *Congressional Globe*, 28 Cong., 1 Sess., 671; New York *Tribune*, Apr. 23, May 10, 1844; Clay to A. G. Henry, June 17, 1844, *HCP*.
57. Joshua Giddings to Clay, July 6, 1844, Giddings Papers; Giddings, *History of the Rebellion* (New York, 1864), 231–32; Lexington *Observer and Reporter*, Sept. 2, 1844; James B. Stewart, *Joshua R. Giddings and the Tactics of Radical Politics* (Cleveland, 1970), 93–98.
58. To Edward Curtis, Sept. 1, 1844, *DWP*; Sellers, "Election of 1844," 789; Clay to Joshua Giddings, Sept. 11, to Gales and Seaton, Sept. 23, 1844, *HCP*; *National Intelligencer*, Oct. 1, 1844; Poage, *Clay and Whig Party*, 145–50.
59. Cassius M. Clay, *Life* (Cincinnati, 1881), I, 96–101; Clay to C. M. Clay, Sept. 18, in *Niles' Register*, Oct. 12, 1844; to Joshua Giddings, Sept. 21, 1844, *HCP*.
60. To Theodore Frelinghuysen, May 22, to G. Davis, Aug. 31, J. Lee to Clay, Nov. 2, 1844, *HCP*; *Campaign of 1844*, 171, 185; Brownlow, *Register*, ch. 6; Hess, *Political Dynasties*, 352; Sellers, "Election of 1844," 793.
61. Stanwood, *Presidential Elections*, ch. 16.
62. Leslie Combs to W. W. Boardman, Nov. 28, 1844, Filson Club.
63. To John M. Clayton, Dec. 2, 1844; Horace Greeley, *Recollections of a Busy Life* (New York, 1868), 165–68; *Niles' Register*, Dec. 7, 1844.
64. Richmond *Whig*, Nov. 2, *Niles' Register*, Nov. 16, Louisville *Journal*, Nov. 23, 1844.

Chapter Seven: Private Lives, Public Images

1. Franklin Elmore to Calhoun, Nov. 18, John Barbour to Calhoun, Dec. 2, 18, 1844; Thomas Hart Benton, *Thirty Years View* (New York, 1856), II, 650–51.
2. Francis Pickens to Calhoun, Nov. 27, Dec. 18, 1844, *JCCP*; James H. Hammond to George McDuffie, Dec. 27, 1844, and Diary, Nov. 26, 1844 and *passim*, Hammond Papers, Library of Congress; *Selections from the Letters and Speeches of James H. Hammond* (New York, 1866), 99–104; Drew Gilpin Faust, *James H. Hammond and the Old South* (Baton Rouge, 1982), 250–54.
3. Charleston *Mercury*, Mar. 3, 1845; Calhoun to Francis Pickens, Mar. 1, 1845, *JCCP*; George M. Dallas to James K. Polk, Feb. 15, 1845, *Pennsylvania Magazine of History and Biography*, v. 73 (1949), 357–58. See also Joseph G. Raybeck, "Presidential Ambitions of John C. Calhoun, 1844–1848," *Journal of Southern History*, v. 14 (1948), 331–56.
4. To Francis Pickens, Apr. 1, 1845, *JCCP*.
5. To Robert Winthrop, Dec. 13, to Edward Everett, Dec. 15, 1844, *DWP*.
6. *Writings*, XIII, 245, 253–53.
7. Charles Francis Adams, *Richard Henry Dana, A Biography* (Boston, 1890), I, 174; Kinley J. Brauer, *Cotton versus Conscience: Massachusetts Whig Politics and Southwestern Expansion, 1843–1848* (Lexington, Ky., 1967), ch. 6.
8. *Writings*, XV, 192–212; Adams, *Dana*, I, 173–76; George F. Hoar, "Charles Allen of Worcester," *American Antiquarian Society Proceedings*, n.s., v. 14 (1901), 343–44; "Remarks by Mr. A. Goodall," *Massachusetts Historical Society Proceedings*, 2nd. ser. v. 12 (1899), 425–29.
9. Hoar, "Allen," 344–45. On the annuity, see esp. David Sears to Webster, Mar. 21, 1846, *Writings*, XVI, 445–56.
10. To David Sears, Mar. 26, 1846, *ibid.*, 446–47; Thomas Wren Ward to Joshua Bates, Jan. 30, 1845, Ward Papers, Massachusetts Historical Society; George Bancroft to Martin Van Buren, Jan. 22, 1845, "Letters," *Massachusetts Historical Society Proceedings*, v. 42 (1909), 434; *The Education of Henry Adams* (New York, 1931), 32.
11. Thomas W. Ward to Joshua Bates, Jan. 15, 1846, Ward Papers.
12. Calhoun to Francis Wharton, Sept. 17, 1844, *Correspondence of Calhoun*, 616–17.

13. Charleston *Courier*, Jan. 8, 1845; Louisville *Journal*, Nov. 23, Dec. 3, 12, 1844; Sarah L. B. French to Clay, Feb. 27, 1845, *HCP*.
14. Louisville *Journal*, Jan. 14, 1845; deed of emancipation, Dec. 9, 1844, *HCP*.
15. To John R. Thompson, Apr. 23, 1845, *HCP*.
16. To Octavia Le Vert, Apr. 20, 1845. See also Kelly and Connyham to Henry White, Jan. 15, 24, and D. M. Craig to John Adenhamer, Mar. 5, 1845, *HCP*; clipping from Lexington *Gazette*, Apr. 15, 1893, in Letterbook of Mrs. John Clay, Clay-Russell Family Papers, Univ. of Kentucky; *National Intelligencer*, May 10, 1845.

1. Clay at Ashland

1. James Parton, *Famous Americans of Recent Times* (Boston, 1867), 4. See especially "A Visit to Mr. Clay at Ashland," copied from New York *Tribune*, in *Niles' Register* June 21, 1845, and "Henry Clay at Home," *ibid.*, July 1, 1843; and "Extracts from the Diary of Lord Morpeth," MS copy (Library of Congress), 13–39.
2. To James A. Bayard, May 7, 1846, Bayard Papers, Delaware Historical Society. See also "Lucretia Hart Clay," typescript, Clay-Russell Family Papers, Univ. of Kentucky; James F. Simmons to Sarah Simmons, June 6, 1841, Filson Club.
3. Clement Eaton, *Henry Clay and the Art of American Politics* (Boston, 1957), 118–20; Paul Gates, *The Farmers' Age: 1815–1860* (New York, 1960), 115.
4. To John M. Clayton, Aug. 8, 1842, *HCP*.
5. To Francis Brooke, May 30, 1833, *Works of Clay*, V, 361; to S. S. Bennett, June 23, 1837, *HCP*; *National Intelligencer*, Mar. 15, 1842. See also James F. Hopkins, "Henry Clay, Farmer and Stockman," *Journal of Southern History*, v. 15 (1949), 91–95.
6. Sale announcement, Oct. 16, 1841; to William Prouther, Apr. 17, 1848, *HCP*.
7. To John M. Clayton, Aug. 8, 1842; Gates, *Farmers' Age*, 116–17, 326.
8. Leslie Combs to John L. Lawrence, Sept. 7, 1845, Univ. of Kentucky.
9. D. C. Craig to John Adenhamer, Mar. 5, 1845, *HCP*; Glyndon G. Van Deusen, *Life of Henry Clay* (Boston, 1937), 379–82.
10. J. Winston Coleman, Jr., *Henry Clay's Last Criminal Case* (Lexington, Ky., 1950).
11. To Lucretia Clay, 19, 1835, to Francis Brooke, Jan. 1, 1836, to Christopher Hughes, June 18, 1837, *HCP*; Sarah M. Maury, *Statesmen of America in 1846* (Philadelphia, 1847), 208. See also Zachary F. Smith and Mary R. Clay, *The Clay Family* (Louisville, 1899).
12. To Henry Clay, Jr., May 24, 1830; Richard Moody, *Edwin Forrest: First Star of the American Stage* (New York, 1960), 34; *HCP*, III, 83n.
13. "Dying Moments of Lieut. Col. Henry Clay, Jr.," *The Union Magazine of Literature and Art*, v. 1 (1847), 47.
14. *National Intelligencer*, Apr. 6, 1847; Rebecca Gratz to Ann B. Gratz, June 10, 1851, Univ. of Kentucky.
15. E. F. Berkley, "Henry Clay," clipping from St. Louis *Globe Democrat*, 1879, Missouri Historical Society; Thomas H. Clay to Samuel M. Duncan, 28, 1858, Filson Club; Calvin Colton, *The Last Seven Years of the Life of Henry Clay* (New York, 1856), 52–55.
16. Gamaliel Bradford, *As God Made Them* (Boston, 1920), 57.
17. J. Winston Coleman, Jr., *Slavery Times in Kentucky* (Chapel Hill, 1940), 76.
18. Eaton, *Clay*, 121–22; Joseph Sturge, *A Visit to the United States in 1841* (London, 1842), 83n; Clay to Lucretia Clay, Sept. 5, 1849, *HCP*.
19. *National Anti-Slavery Standard*, April 16, 1846.
20. *Ibid.*, June 11, 1846.
21. Coleman, *Slavery Times*, 279, 289.
22. Clay to James G. Birney, Nov. 3, 1838. See also Asa Earl Martin, *The Anti-Slavery Movement in Kentucky* (Louisville, 1918).
23. C. M. Clay to James S. Rollins, Sept. 5, 1845, Missouri State Historical Society; C. M. Clay to Clay, Sept. 9, 1945, *HCP*; *Life of Cassius Marcellus Clay* (Cincinnati, 1886), I, 168–74; David L. Smiley, *Lion of White Hall: The Life of Cassius M. Clay* (Madison, 1962), 130–32.
24. C. M. Clay to Rollins, Sept. 5, 1845; to William H. Seward, Oct. 24, 1850, Seward Papers, Univ. of Rochester; Louisville *Journal*, Apr. 21, 22, 24, May 6, 23, 1848.
25. To James B. Clay, March 3, to Richard Pindell, Feb. 17, 1849, *HCP*.
26. Quoted in Martin, *Anti-Slavery in Kentucky*, 127; *National Era* (Washington), Mar. 22, 1849.
27. Louisville *Journal*, Aug. 10, 1849.
28. *Diary of Philip Hone*, Allan Nevins, ed. (New York, 1927), 806–807.

29. Octavia Walton Le Vert, *An Address Upon the Laying of the Corner Stone of the Monument of Henry Clay* (n.p., n.d.); "Letter from Henry Clay to Madame Le Vert," Mrs. Thaddeus Horton, ed., *The Home Magazine* (June 1907), 18–20.

30. To Charles E. Lester, September 26, 1845, *HCP*; *Writings of Cassius M. Clay*, Horace Greeley, ed. (New York, 1848), 251–52; *Papers of Willie P. Mangum*, H. T. Shanks, ed. (Raleigh, 1950), V, 292.

31. Quoted in Lewis Collins, *History of Kentucky* (Covington, Ky., 1878), I, 64–65.

32. Marie De Mare, *G. P. A. Healy, American Artist* (New York, 1954), 134; George P. Healy, *Reminiscences of a Portrait Painter* (Chicago, 1894), 147–52.

33. *Speeches*, II, 31; Irwin G. Wyllie, *The Self-Made Man* (New York, 1966); Richard Hofstadter, *Anti-Intellectualism in American Life* (New York, 1962), 255.

34. *Louisville Journal*, Oct. 23, 1851.

35. C. M. Clay, *Life*, I, 49; O. H. Smith, *Early Indiana Trials, and Speeches, Reminiscences* (Cincinnati, 1858), 375; Tyrone Power, *Impressions of America* (Philadelphia, 1836), I, 270.

36. *Boston Courier*, Feb. 10, 1848.

37. *Memoirs of John Quincy Adams*, C. F. Adams, ed. (Philadelphia, 1874-77), V, 59.

38. *Charleston Mercury*, Sept. 23, 1839.

39. Harriet Martineau, *Retrospect of Western Travel* (New York, 1838), 174.

40. *Charleston Mercury*, Sept. 13, 1844, copying the *Madisonian*, which originally published the editorial without attribution; Hone, *Diary*, 532.

41. John W. Forney, *Anecdotes of Public Men* (New York, 1873), 9–10.

42. Constance Rourke, *American Humor* (New York, 1931), 105–106; Parton, *Famous Americans*, 5.

43. William Hazlitt, *Complete Works* (London, 1932), VII, 299.

44. "The Autobiography of William John Grayson," *South Carolina Historical and Genealogical Magazine*, v. 50 (1949), 136. See also Edward G. Parker, *The Golden Age of American Oratory* (Boston, 1857), 15–49; and Ernest J. Wrage's essay in *A History and Criticism of American Public Address* (New York, 1943).

45. Washington *Globe*, Aug. 28, 1838.

2. *Webster at Marshfield*

1. George T. Curtis, *Life of Daniel Webster* (New York, 1873), II, 216. See also *ibid.*, I, 220–21, 109–11, 216–18; Maurice G. Baxter, *One and Inseparable: Daniel Webster and the Union* (Cambridge, 1984), 282–85; Emeline S. Wortley, "A Visit at Mr. Webster's," *Harper's Magazine*, v. 3 (1851), 94–96; "Personal Memorials of Daniel Webster," *National Intelligencer*, Nov. 27, 1851; Henry C. Deming, in *Homes of American Statesmen* (New York, 1860), 473–84; Ben: Perley Poore, "Reminiscences of Marshfield," Boston *Journal*, Sept. 30, 1882, in "Scrapbook," Houghton Library, Harvard Univ.

2. Nathaniel P. Willis, *Hurrygraphs; or Sketches of Scenery, Celebrities, and Society, Taken from Life* (London, 1851), 18.

3. "Address," 1852, in *Letters of Daniel Webster*, C. H. Van Tyne, ed. (New York, 1902), 644–45.

4. "Personal Memorials," *National Intelligencer*, Nov. 27, 1851.

5. *Louisville Journal*, Nov. 30, 1843, copying New York *Commercial Advertiser*.

6. *Journal of Henry David Thoreau*, Bradford Torrey and F. H. Allen, eds. (Boston, 1901), IX, 262.

7. To John W. Davis, Oct. 2, 1838, *Writings*, XVI, 304.

8. Henry David Thoreau, *Works* (Boston 1893), VI, 138; Curtis, *Webster*, II, 664n.

9. To Millard Fillmore, July 23, 1851, *Writings*, XVIII, 454; Poore, "Reminiscences"; Curtis, *Webster*, II, 222.

10. Hone, *Diary*, 736, 737, 729, 689. See also Mary E. Sherwood, *An Epistle to Posterity* (New York, 1897), 20–22.

11. "Personal Memorials"; Wortley, "Visit," 94.

12. To Mrs. John M. Cheney, Aug. 29, 1845; Creighton Barker, "Daniel Webster and the Hay Fever," *Yale Journal of Biology and Medicine* (1937); E. B. White, *One Man's Meat*, new ed. (New York, 1944), 6–10; Curtis, *Webster*, II, 312.

13. *Writings*, IV, 109–10; Webster to Richard M. Blatchford, Aug. 30, 1849; to Millard Fillmore, July 17, 1852, *DWP*.

14. Curtis, *Webster*, ch. 34 *passim*; Deming, *Homes*, 482.

15. Quoted in Marvin Sadik, intro., *The Life Portraits of John Quincy Adams* (Washington,

1970). See also Charles Henry Hart, "Life Portraits of Daniel Webster," *McClure's Magazine*, v. 9 (1897), 619–30; James Barber and Frederick Voss, *The Godlike Black Dan* (Washington, 1982).

16. O. S. Fowler and L. N. Fowler, *Phrenology Proved, Illustrated, and Applied* (New York, 1883), 289–90; *A Sketch of Chester Harding, Artist,* Margaret E. White, ed. (New York, 1970), 158, 186.

17. Charles Edward Lester, *The Artist, the Merchant and the Statesman of the Age of the Medici and of Our Own Times* (New York, 1845), I, 66–70.

18. William Plumer, Jr., to Webster, Apr. 25, 1850, DWP.

19. Quoted in Barber and Voss, *Godlike Black Dan*, 20; *Register of Debates*, 22 Cong., 1 Sess., 1155.

20. Hone, *Diary*, 765–66; Barber and Voss, *Godlike Black Dan*, 40–41; De Mare, *Healy*, 109–11, 153–54.

21. *Ibid.*, 170–71; Healy, *Reminiscences*, 162–66.

22. *Congressional Globe*, 29 Cong., 1 Sess., 653. See also Irving Bartlett, *Daniel Webster* (New York, 1978), ch. 15; and for the apology, William L. Yancey to Webster, Aug. 1, 1850, DWP.

23. William Wetmore Story, *Life and Letters of Joseph Story* (Boston, 1851), II, 408–551; George S. Hillard to Francis Lieber, Dec. 30, 1851, Apr. 12, May 8, 1892, Lieber Papers, Huntington Library.

24. *Journals of Ralph Waldo Emerson*, Ralph H. Orth and A. R. Ferguson, eds. (Cambridge, 1971), IX, 380; Boston *Courier*, Apr. 28, 1846; Paul R. Frothingham, *Edward Everett, Orator and Statesman* (Boston, 1925), 272–73.

25. Francis Lieber to G. S. Hillard, Dec. 1852, *Life and Letters of Francis Lieber* (Boston, 1882), 256.

26. G. S. Hillard, in his eulogy, Boston *Courier*, Dec. 1, 1852. See also Fletcher Webster to Webster, Nov. 29, 1851, DWP; "Sketches of the Life of Daniel Webster," *National Intelligencer*, July 31, Aug. 17, 1839.

27. Boston *Courier*, Jan. 11, 1836. See also *ibid.*, Feb. 10, 1848; John Wentworth, *Congressional Reminiscences* (Chicago, 1882), 34–35; Horace Greeley, *Recollections of a Busy Life* (New York, 1868), 250–51.

28. Parton, *Famous Americans*, 100.

29. Martineau, *Retrospect*, 166, 147, 151. See also Parton, *Famous Americans*, 100; Henry Cabot Lodge, *Daniel Webster* (Boston, 1882), 196; Bradford, *As God Made Them*, ch. 1.

30. In William C. Wilkinson, *Daniel Webster: A Vindication* (New York, 1911), 176–79; *Diary of O. H. Browning*, T. C. Pease and J. G. Randall, eds. (Springfield, Ill., 1925), I, 593; G. S. Hillard to Francis Lieber, Apr. 12, 1852, Lieber Papers.

31. *Memoirs and Letters of James Kent*, William Kent, ed. (Boston, 1898), 261–62.

32. Francis Hull to William L. Stone, Sept. 25, 1843, Webster Papers, Dartmouth College; Wilkinson, *Vindication*, 114–15; Glyndon G. Van Deusen, *William H. Seward* (New York, 1967), 99–100.

33. Horace Mann to John W. Francis, Apr. 13, 1857, enclosure in Amasa McCoy to Francis, May 9, 1858, Webster Papers, New Hampshire Historical Society; Wilkinson, *Vindication*, 151, 171–72; Charles A. Stetson quoted in William C. Wilkinson, *Webster, an Ode* (New York, 1882), 50–51; Edward Everett Hale, *Memories of a Hundred Years* (New York, 1902), II, 41–42.

34. Bradford, *As God Made Them*, 32.

35. Among various versions, I have drawn mainly on three: John C. Parish, *George Wallace Jones* (Iowa City, 1912), 274–75; Henry S. Foote, *Casket of Reminiscences* (Washington, 1874), 9–10; Willis, *Hurrygraphs*, 192–93. The story came down to Willie P. Mangum's descendants that Webster rose in the midst of the performance and began singing "Hail Columbia" but Mrs. Webster grabbed his coattails and pulled him into his seat. *Mangum Papers*, V, 751. See also Rourke, *American Humor*, 105–106.

36. C. B. Butler, *A Sermon on the Death of Daniel Webster* (Washington, 1852), 21–22; Wilkinson, *Webster, An Ode*, 44–47, 110; Cortland Van Rensselaer, *New Jersey's Tribute to Massachusetts* (Burlington, N.J., 1852), 23–24; Isaac M. Wise, *Reminiscences* (Cincinnati, 1901), 185, 188; Peter Harvey, *Reminiscences of Daniel Webster* (Boston, 1877), 404–409; Parton, *Famous Americans*, 112; George J. Abbot to Edward Everett, Apr. 12, 1854, *Writings*, XV, 240–41.

37. *Writings*, I, 253–54; Paul C. Nagel, *This Sacred Trust* (New York, 1971), 90. See also Rufus Choate, *Addresses and Orations*, 6th ed. (Boston, 1891), 133–67.

38. *Writings*, IV, 208–11.
39. Webster's argument in *Luther* v. *Borden* is in *Writings*, XI, 217–42.
40. *Ibid.*, 221, IV, 90.
41. Story, *Story*, II, 469. The New York *Herald* reported the case: Feb. 14, 15, 16, 1844 and *passim*. See also Perry Miller, *The Life of the Mind in America* (New York, 1965), 198–202.
42. *Writings*, XI, 144, 132–84.
43. Story, *Story*, II, 469, 473. See *Vidal* v. *Girard's Executors*. 2 How. (43 U.S.) 127.
44. *Writings*, XI, 373–401.
45. *West River Bridge Co.* v. *Dix*, quoted in Leonard Levy, *The Law of the Commonwealth and Chief Justice Shaw* (Cambridge, 1957), 120n.
46. *Writings*, III, 206.
47. See the discussion in Baxter, *Webster*, 455–56.
48. To Fletcher Webster, Dec. 29, 1847, *Letters*, 603; *Writings*, XV, 403–404.
49. See esp. Melvin Dubofsky, "Daniel Webster and the Whig Theory of Economic Growth," *New England Quarterly*, v. 42 (1969) 551–72; and Arthur M. Schlesinger, Jr., *The Age of Jackson* (Boston 1945), 269–70, 280.
50. *Writings*, XIII, 278; XV, 381–83.
51. To James Brooks, Aug. 5, 1834, *Writings*, XVI, 241–42; to New Hampshire *Sentinel*, Feb. 27, 1843, in *Niles' Register*, Apr. 8, 1843; Rufus Choate to William Palfray, Jr., Jan. 31, 1834, "Rufus Choate Letters," *Essex Institute Historical Collections*, v. 69 (1933), 86; Robert C. Winthrop, "Webster's Reply to Hayne," *Scribner's Magazine*, v. 15 (1894), 123–34.
52. *Writings*, IX, 230; III, 175. See also Charles Mondale, "Daniel Webster and Technology," *American Quarterly*, v. 14 (962), 34–47.
53. *Writings*, XV, 385; IV, 109.
54. *Ibid.*, XIII, 63–78.
55. Richard B. Kimball to Webster, Dec. 13, 1851, DWP; see *ibid.*, Jan. 1846, for record of withdrawals, Library of Congress; Curtis, *Webster*, II, 670; George P. Fisher, *The Life of Benjamin Silliman* (New York, 1866), II, 121–23. See also Edwin P. Whipple, "Daniel Webster as a Master of English Style," *American Literature and Other Papers* (Boston, 1887), 139–332; and a recent estimate, Howard Mumford Jones, *Violence and Reason: A Book of Essays* (New York, 1969), 51–53.
56. Moncure Conway, *Autobiography* (Boston, 1904), I, 210; *Forty Years Familiar Letters of James W. Alexander*, John Hall, ed. (New York, 1870), II, 170.
57. James R. Lowell, *Anti-Slavery Papers* (New York, 1969), II, 35–43; Parker, *Golden Age*, 49–50; Josiah Quincy, *Figures of the Past* (Boston, 1883), 267; Lodge, *Webster*, 191–96.
58. Goldwin Smith, "America Statesmen," *Nineteenth Century*, v. 24 (1888), 262; Samuel G. Goodrich, *Recollections of a Lifetime* (New York, 1856), I, 419–21; [Francis Bowen], "Works of Daniel Webster," *North American Review*, v. 75 (1852), 90–93; Emerson, *Journals*, VIII, 359, IX, 374; Willis, *Hurrygraphs*, 19.
59. Winthrop, "Reply to Hayne," 124.
60. Quoted in Charleston *Mercury*, Feb. 3, 1847; Sargent, *Clay*, 111.

3. *Calhoun at Fort Hill*

1. Charles M. Wiltse, *John C. Calhoun, Nullifier* (Indianapolis, 1949), ch. 12; Margaret L. Coit, *John C. Calhoun* (Boston, 1950), 388–90; Harriet Hefner Cook, *John C. Calhoun, The Man* (Columbia, 1965).
2. [Joseph Scoville], "A Visit to Fort Hill," New York *Herald*, July 26, 1849.
3. *Ibid*; and see George W. Featherstonehaugh, *A Canoe Voyage up the Minnay Sotar* (New York, 1847), II, 267–71.
4. [Scoville], "Visit"; Benjamin F. Perry, *Reminiscences of Public Men* (Philadelphia, 1883), 43; Walter L. Miller, "Calhoun as a Lawyer and Statesman," *Green Bag*, v. 11 (1899), 197–98.
5. To Andrew Calhoun, Apr. 12, 1847; to Anna Clemson, July 16, 1842, *JCP*.
6. A. S. Salley, Jr., *The Calhoun Family of South Carolina*, (n.p., n.d.); Intro., *The Papers of John C. Calhoun*, Clyde N. Wilson, ed. (Columbia, S.C., 1981), XIV; Ernest M. Lander, Jr., *The Calhoun Family and Thomas Green Clemson* (Columbia, S.C., 1943).
7. *Ibid.*, ch. 2.
8. *Ibid.*, ch. 2–4; Calhoun to Abbott Lawrence, Apr. 9, Lawrence to Calhoun, Apr. 30, 1845; Henry W. Conner to Calhoun, Apr. 28, to Conner, May 2, 1845, Jan. 14, 1847, *JCCP*; J. Mauldin Lesesne, *The Bank of the State of South Carolina* (Columbia, S.C., 1870), 86. On

the purse, see Rosser H. Taylor, *Ante-Bellum South Carolina* (Chapel Hill, 1942), 48–9, and Louisville *Journal*, July 2, 1851.

9. Oliver Dyer, *Great Senators of the United States Forty Years Ago, 1848–1849* (New York, 1899), ch. 3; Maury, *American Statesmen*, 168–201; Elizabeth F. Ellet, *The Court Circles of the Republic* (Hartford, 1869), 400; Grayson, "Autobiography," 85; *Life*, 73.

10. "Mr. Calhoun's Portrait," Charleston *Courier*, Sept. 8, 1859.

11. Sylvia E. Crane, *White Silence . . . American Sculptors in Nineteenth-Century Italy* (Coral Gables, 1972), 181–82, 239; Harold F. Pfister, *Facing the Light: Historic American Portrait-Daguerreotypes* (Washington, 1978), 108; Caroline Le Roy Webster, "*Mr. Webster and I": Being an Authentic Diary . . . 1839* (n.p., 1942), 249; Charleston *Mercury*, May 8, 1850.

12. Charles Lanman, *Haphazard Personalities* (Boston, 1886), 303–33; "Clark Mills and His Equestrian Statue," *De Bow's Review*, v. 16 (1854), 39–42; Franklin Elmore to Calhoun, Apr. 7, 1845, *JCCP*.

13. Martineau, *Retrospect*, 229. See also Clement Eaton, *The Freedom of Thought Struggle in the Old South* (New York, 1964), ch. 6.

14. *The Letters of William Gilmore Simms*, Alfred T. Odell and T. C. Duncan Evans, eds. (Columbia, S.C., 1952–56), I, XCV; II, 206n.

15. Herman Melville, *Mardi: And a Voyage Thither* (Boston, 1923), 466. See the review in *Southern Quarterly Review*, v. 16 (1851), 261.

16. Dixon Lewis to Calhoun, May 6, 1845. See also the editorial "Chivalry alias Calhounism," Louisville *Journal*, Feb. 17, 1844.

17. Newspaper clipping, June 1902, Univ. of South Carolina; Perry, *Reminiscences*, 46–47; William C. Preston, *Reminiscences* (Chapel Hill, 1923), 7–8; Mary Bates, *The Private Life of John C. Calhoun* (Charleston, 1852), 10–11.

18. Calhoun to Anna Clemson, Mar. 7, 1848, *Correspondence*, 745.

19. "Subscription List for Building of Unitarian Church . . . ," September 1820, *JCCP*; Miller, "Calhoun as Lawyer," 330; Bates, *Private Life*, 26–27.

20. Martineau, *Retrospect*, 147–48.

21. *John C. Calhoun in His Personal, Moral and Intellectual Traits* (New York, n.d.), 6; Moore, ed., *Calhoun as Seen*, 355; Charles C. Pinckney, "John C. Calhoun from a Southern Standpoint," *Lippincotts*, v. 62 (1898), 83.

22. Wentworth, *Reminiscences*, 20; Brady's recollections, "Scrapbook," Houghton Library; Dyer, *Senators*, ch. 3.

23. Grayson, "Autobiography," 136–37; "Il Segretoria," in Louisville *Journal*, Aug. 30, 1850. See also James H. Hammond's eulogy, *Letters and Speeches*, 295, and Parmelee, "Recollections," 757.

24. "Bankruptcy and the Bankrupt Bill," *New York Review*, v. 17 (1840), 240–75; Edwin P. Whipple, *Character and Characteristic Men* (Boston, 1891), 155–56, and *American Literature*, 103.

25. Pinckney, "Calhoun," 87; "Works of Calhoun," *Southern Literary Messenger* v. 20 (1854), 327; [Lucian Minor], "A Few Thoughts on the Death of John C. Calhoun," *ibid.*, v. 16 (1850), 378.

26. *Ibid*; Louisville *Journal*, Aug. 30, 1850.

27. Grayson, "Autobiography," 84.

28. Charleston *Courier*, July 29, 1844; Edward G. Parker, *Reminiscences of Rufus Choate* (New York, 1860), 245; *Life*, 74.

29. N. B. Tucker to James H. Hammond, Mar. 13, 1847, Sept. 10, 1848, Tucker Papers, Duke Univ.

30. Quoted in Joseph Rayback, *Free Soil: The Election of 1848* (Lexington, Ky., 1970), 32n.

31. "John C. Calhoun of South Carolina," *United States Magazine and Democratic Review*, v. 12 (1843), 95; "Mr. Calhoun's Parliamentary Eloquence," *ibid.*, v. 14 (1844), 123–24; Parker, *Choate Reminiscences*, 245. For a modern view see the essay in Waldo W. Braden, ed., *Oratory in the Old South, 1820–1860* (Baton Rouge, 1970), 169–89.

32. William Mathews, *Oratory and Orators*, 12th. ed. (Chicago, 1896), 312. See also Whipple, *Character*, 157–58; Fairfield, *Letters*, 66.

33. Parmelee, "Recollections," 757.

34. *Works*, I. See also August O. Spain, *The Political Theory of John C. Calhoun* (New York, 1951), and Richard Current, *John C. Calhoun* (New York, 1963).

35. *Works*, II, 614.

36. *Ibid.*, IV, 81.

37. *Ibid.*, I, 359ff.
38. *Ibid.*, 1–6, 55–56 and *passim*; VI, 269–70.
39. Francis Lieber, *On Civil Liberty and Self-Government* (Philadelphia, 1853), ch. 22; *Works*, II, 613–14, VI, 269–70.
40. Redelia Brisbane, *Albert Brisbane* (Boston, 1892), 221–22.
41. *Works*, III, 180.
42. See Current, *Calhoun*, and particularly "John C. Calhoun, Philosopher of Reaction," in John L. Thomas, ed., *John C. Calhoun, A Profile* (New York, 1968), 151–63; and Richard Hofstadter, *The American Political Tradition and the Men Who Made It* (New York, 1948), ch. 4.
43. William Freehling, "Spoilsmen and Interests in the Thought and Career of John C. Calhoun," *Journal of American History*, v. 52 (1965), 25–42; appears also in Thomas, *Calhoun Profile*, 171–92.
44. Quoted in Edward B. Bryson, "The Political Philosophy of John C. Calhoun," *Southern Quarterly Review*, n.s., v. 23 (1853), 135; *Works*, II, 565–66.
45. *Ibid.*, II, 441.
46. *Works*, I, 390–95; VI, 388–93.
47. *National Intelligencer*, Nov. 13, 1851.
48. See Louis Hartz, "The Constitution: Calhoun and Fitzhugh," in Thomas, *Calhoun Profile*, 164–70.
49. Dixon Lewis to Calhoun, May 9, 1845, *Letters to Calhoun*, 293–94; Raybeck, "Presidential Ambitions of Calhoun."
50. J. S. Barbour to Calhoun, June 26, W. A. Harris to Calhoun, Aug. 4, 1854, *Correspondence to Calhoun*, 297–98, 301; Isaac Holmes quoted in *National Intelligencer*, July 6, 1848; Holmes to Calhoun, July 6, 1845, JCCP.
51. To Armistead Burt, Sept. 17, to Francis Pickens, Sept. 23, 1845, *JCCP*.
52. *Works*, VI, 273–84. See also St. George L. Sioussat, "Memphis as a Gateway to the West," *Tennessee Historical Magazine*, v. 3 (1917), 77–114.
53. Varina Howell Davis, *Jefferson Davis: A Memoir* (New York, 1890), I, 209–13.
54. Boston *Courier*, Dec. 3, 1845.

Chapter Eight: Ordeal of the Union

1. Norman Graebner, ed., *Manifest Destiny* (Indianapolis, 1969), 136. See also Albert K. Weinberg, *Manifest Destiny: A Study of Nationalist Expansionism in American History* (Baltimore, 1934) and Frederick Merk, *Manifest Destiny and Mission in American History* (New York, 1963).
2. James D. Richardson, ed., *Messages and Papers of the Presidents* (New York, 1896), III, 2242–48.
3. *Works of Calhoun*, IV, 245, 238–58.
4. *Ibid.*, 286.
5. To Francis Pickens, Aug. 21, Sept. 23, 1845, *JCCP*.
6. *Writings*, XIII, 310–18; *National Intelligencer*, Dec. 23, 30, 1845.
7. James K. Polk, *Diary During Presidency, 1845 to 1849*, M. M. Quaife, ed. (New York, 1910), I, 155.

1. *"The Forbidden Fruit"*

1. Polk, *Diary*, I, 131–32, 155, 159, 249–53. See also David M. Pletcher, *The Diplomacy of Annexation: Texas, Oregon, and the Mexican War* (Columbia, Mo., 1973), 319–32; Norman Graebner, *Empire on the Pacific: A Study in Continental Expansionism* (New York, 1955), 136–41; and in general, Charles G. Sellers, *James K. Polk, Continentalist, 1843–1846* (Princeton, 1966).
2. *Congressional Globe*, 29 Cong., 1 Sess., 109–110.
3. Duff Green to Calhoun, Mar. 18, Thomas G. Clemson to Calhoun, Apr. 27, 1846, *Correspondence Addressed to John C. Calhoun, 1837–1849*, Chauncy S. Boucher and R. P. Brooks, eds., *American Historical Association Annual Report, 1929* (Washington, 1930), 333, 343; Edward Everett to Calhoun, April 8, 1846, *Correspondence of Calhoun*, 1081.
4. *Writings*, IX, 63–69, 70–77; *Congressional Globe*, 29 Cong., 1 Sess., 567–68.
5. "Internal Improvements," *Southern Quarterly Review*, v. 9 (1846), 267.

6. *Works of Calhoun*, V, 246–93.

7. *Congressional Globe*, 29 Cong., 1 Sess., 30–33.

8. *Ibid.*, 742–46; *Works of Calhoun*, VI, 281–82.

9. See, e.g., the New York *Journal of Commerce*, as quoted in *Niles' Register*, Feb. 14, 1846; and Frederick Merk, *The Oregon Question: Essays in Anglo-American Diplomacy and Politics* (Cambridge, 1967).

10. Clay to——, June 5, 1846, *HCP*. For the legislative history, see Edward Stanwood, *American Tariff Controversies in the Nineteenth Century* (Boston, 1904), II, ch. 12.

11. Abbott Lawrence, *Letters . . . to the Hon. William C. Rives of Virginia* (Boston, 1846); Sellers, *Polk Continentalist*, 451–68.

12. The matter may be followed in Webster's correspondence with James K. Mills, beginning July 19, 1846, *DWP*; see also to Fletcher Webster, July 29, 1846, *ibid.* The Charleston *Mercury* reported, and denied, July 27, 1846, that Calhoun supported Webster's solution.

13. *Writings*, IX, 161–235; 226, 239.

14. To Fletcher Webster, July 29, 1846, *DWP*; John W. Davis to John M. Clayton, Aug. 22, 1846, Clayton Papers, Library of Congress.

15. *Congressional Globe*, 29 Cong., 1 Sess., 796, 302.

16. *Ibid.*, 29 Cong., 2 Sess., 411–12; to Andrew Calhoun, Apr. 25, James E. Calhoun, May 29, 1846, *Correspondence of Calhoun*, 690–91, 694.

17. To Henry W. Conner, May 15, 1846, *JCCP*; *Works*, IV, 338, 91, 371.

18. *Ibid.*, 308.

19. Charleston *Mercury*, Sept. 18, 1846.

20. *Ibid.*, June 9, 17, 20, 1846; J. Abney to Armistead Burt, July 23, 1846, Pickens Papers, Univ. of South Carolina.

21. To Mrs. Clemson, June 11, 1846, *Correspondence of Calhoun*, 696; to James E. Calhoun, Jr., June 29, 1846, *JCCP*.

22. To Thomas G. Clemsen, Aug. 9, 1846, Mrs. Clemsen to Calhoun, Dec. 25, 1848, *JCCP*.

23. To Henry W. Conner, Jan. 14, 1847, to Wilson Lumpkin, Dec. 13, 1846, *JCCP*; to Mrs. Clemsen, Dec. 27, 1846, *Correspondence*, 716.

24. Polk, *Diary*, II, 282–84, 293, 347, 371.

25. *Congressional Globe*, 29 Cong., 2 Sess., 368.

26. In Graebner, ed., *Manifest Destiny*, 166; *Writings*, IX, 253–56.

27. *Works of Calhoun*, IV, 396–425.

28. *Congressional Globe*, 29 Cong., 2 Sess., 396–97; *Works*, IV, 328–39.

29. *Congressional Globe*, 29 Cong., 2 Sess., 412–13; Washington *Union*, Feb. 9, 10, 13, 16, 1847.

30. *Ibid.*, Feb. 18, 1847.

31. William Gilmore Simms to James H. Hammond, Apr. 4, 1847, *Letters of Simms* (Columbia, S.C., 1952–56), II, 297. See also Joseph G. Raybeck, "The Presidential Ambitions of John C. Calhoun, 1844–1848," *Journal of Southern History*, v. 14 (1948), 331–51.

32. *Congressional Globe*, 29 Cong., 2 Sess., 142.

33. *Ibid.*, 182; Chaplain W. Morrison, *Democratic Politics and Sectionalism: The Wilmot Proviso Controversy* (Chapel Hill, 1967), 26–33.

34. *Works of Calhoun*, IV, 344–45, 339–49.

35. *Congressional Globe*, 29 Cong., 2 Sess., 244–47 (App.); Laura A. White, *Robert Barnwell Rhett* (Gloucester, Mass., 1965), 92; Robert H. Russel, "Constitutional Doctrines with Regard to Slavery in the Territories," *Journal of Southern History*, v. 32 (1966), 466–86.

36. Thomas Hart Benton, *Thirty Years View* (New York, 1856), II, 697; *Speech . . . to the People of Missouri*, May 26, 1849 (Jefferson City, Mo., 1849), 10–12; Charleston *Courier*, Mar. 1, Richmond *Whig*, Mar. 2, 1847.

37. *Works*, IV, 382–96; Charleston *Mercury*, Mar. 23, 1847.

38. Boston *Daily Advertiser*, Mar. 17, Charleston *Courier*, Mar. 20, *Mercury*, Mar. 23, Richmond *Whig*, Mar. 16, *National Era* (Washington), Apr. 1, May 13, 1947; Benton, *View*, II, 698–700.

39. *Ibid.*, 698, Philip Hamer, *The Secession Movement in South Carolina, 1847–1852* (Philadelphia, 1918), 9–10.

40. To Henry W. Conner, May 14, Aug. 25, to David Johnson, Nov. 5, 1847, *JCCP*.

41. To Duff Green, Mar. 9, Apr. 17, 1847, *Correspondence of Calhoun*, 719, 727; Franklin Elmore to Calhoun, June 29, Calhoun to Henry W. Conner, Dec. 16, 1847, *JCCP*. See also Morrison, *Wilmot Proviso*, ch. 3.

42. Boston *Courier*, Sept. 24, 1846; *Memoirs and Letters of Charles Sumner*, E. L. Pierce, ed.

(Boston, 1893), III, 123–29; Henry B. Stanton, *Random Recollections* (New York, 1887), 149–50. See also Robert Dalzell, Jr., *Daniel Webster and the Trials of American Nationalism, 1843–1852* (Boston, 1973), 117–22, and David H. Donald, *Charles Sumner and the Coming of the Civil War* (New York, 1960), 146–48.

43. Boston *Courier*, Feb. 20, 23, 1847.
44. Webster to Fletcher Webster, Apr. 24, 1847, *Writings*, XVI, 473–74.
45. Charleston *Courier*, Apr. 27, 29, 30, May 8, 10–13, 1847.
46. *National Era*, July 1, 1874.
47. Benjamin F. Perry, *Reminiscences of Public Men* (Philadelphia, 1883), 60–61, 64–65; *Life and Letters of Francis Lieber*, T. S. Perry, ed. (Boston, 1882), 210–11.
48. *Writings*, IV, 99–103; Richmond *Whig*, June 2, *National Era*, Aug. 19, 1847.
49. Boston *Courier*, June 8, 1847.
50. Kinley J. Brauer, *Cotton versus Conscience: Massachusetts Whig Politics . . . , 1843–1848* (Lexington, Ky., 1967), 212–18; Donald, *Sumner*, 156–59; Martin Duberman, *Charles Francis Adams* (Stanford, 1960), 126; Dalzell, *Webster*, 137–40.
51. *Writings*, XIII, 345–65.

2. *Three Statesmen and a "Frontier Colonel"*

1. Clay to Daniel Malloy. Oct. 12, Horace Greeley, Nov. 21, Thomas B. Stevenson, Dec. 19, 1846, *HCP*; F. W. Seward, *William H. Seward* (New York, 1891), I, 772–73; Louisville *Journal*, Jan. 25, Feb. 13, 15, 1847.
2. Albert D. Kirwan, *John J. Crittenden: The Struggle for the Union* (Lexington, Ky., 1962), ch. 11; James L. Crouthamel, *James Watson Webb: A Biography* (Middleton, Conn., 1969), 106–9; Betty C. Congledon, "Contenders for the Whig Nomination in 1848 and the Editorial Polities of George D. Prentice," *Register of the Kentucky Historical Society*, v. 67 (1969), 119–33.
3. Clay to John M. Clayton, Apr. 16, to Daniel Ullman, May 12, 1847, *Works of Clay*, V, 541–43. See also Holman Hamilton, "The Election of 1848," in Arthur M. Schlesinger, Jr., and Fred L. Israel, eds., *History of American Presidential Elections* (New York, 1971), 865–96.
4. *National Intelligencer*, Aug. 19, 26, 1847.
5. New York *Tribune*, Aug. 19, 23, Boston *Courier*, Aug. 18, 19, 23, 1847.
6. New York *Tribune*, Sept. 3, Oct. 11, *National Era*, Sept. 9, 1847.
7. Clay to John J. Crittenden, Sept. 21, 1847; Kirwan, *Crittenden*, ch. 11.
8. Washington *Union*, Aug. 12, Richmond *Whig*, Sept. 24, Boston *Courier*, Nov. 24, 1847.
9. *Ibid; National Era*, Dec. 30, 1847.
10. Tom Corwin to Thomas B. Stevenson, Oct. 16, 1847, Indiana Historical Society; *National Era*, Nov. 4, 1847.
11. Benjamin B. Thomas, *Abraham Lincoln* (New York, 1952), 114, 118.
12. *National Intelligencer*, Nov. 16, 1847. The resolutions are in Calvin Colton, *The Last Seven Years of the Life of Henry Clay* (New York, 1956), 67–9.
13. "Mr. Clay's Resolutions," *American Whig Review*, v. 6 (1847), 553–61; Frederic Hudson, *Journalism in the United States, from 1690 to 1872* (New York, 1873), 605; New York *Tribune*, Nov. 15, 24, 1847.
14. *Ibid.*
15. *Ibid;* Washington *Union*, Nov. 16, 26, *National Era*, Dec. 2, *National Intelligencer*, Nov. 30, Louisville *Journal*, Dec. 2, 1847; J. D. B. De Bow to Calhoun, Dec. 26, 1847, *Correspondence to Calhoun*, 414.
16. Joseph H. Parks, *John Bell of Tennessee* (Baton Rouge, 1950), 231; Seward, *Seward*, II, 57.
17. Louisville *Journal*, Nov. 30, Dec. 4, 1847; George Prentice to Clay, Aug. 13, 1848, *HCP*.
18. To H. W. Conner, Dec. 16, 1847, Jan. 7, 1848, *JCCP*; Ernest M. Lander, Jr., *Reluctant Imperialists: Calhoun, the South Carolinians, and the Mexican War* (Baton Rouge, 1980), 159–60.
19. *Works of Calhoun*, IV, 396–425; A. P. Butler to Franklin Elmore, Jan. 5, 1848, Elmore Papers, Library of Congress.
20. *National Era*, Jan. 27, 1848.
21. *Writings*, X, 3–33; *Congressional Globe*, 30 Cong., 1 Sess., 484–85; *National Era*, Mar. 30, 1848.
22. Boston *Courier*, Feb. 10, *National Intelligencer*, Jan. 11, 1848.
23. Boston *Daily Advertiser*, Jan. 21, 26, 1848.
24. John P. Frank, *Justice Daniel Dissenting: A Biography of Peter V. Daniel* (Cambridge,

1964), 239; Stanton, *Random Recollections*, 152; Boston *Courier*, Feb. 12, 1848; to Lucretia Clay, Mar. 13, to C. S. Morehead, Mar. 18, 1848, *HCP*.

25. To George W. Nesmith, [1848], *DWP*; New York *Tribune*, Jan. 26, 29, Feb. 7, 1848.

26. Robert Toombs to James Thomas, Apr. 16, 1848, *The Correspondence of Robert Toombs, Alexander H. Stephens, and Howell Cobb*, U. B. Phillips, ed., *Annual Report of American Historical Association* (Washington, 1913), 103-104; John Bell to W. B. Campbell, Apr. 13, 1848, *Tennessee Historical Magazine*, v. 13 (1954), 260; J. R. Giddings to J. A. Giddings, Apr. 15, 1848, Giddings Papers; Seward, *Seward*, II, 160-61; Salmon P. Chase to Charles Sumner, Feb. 16, 1848, *Diary and Correspondence of Chase, Annual Report of American Historical Association* (Washington, 1903), 130.

27. *Louisville Journal*, Feb. 15, 1848.

28. Robert Letcher to John J. Crittenden, [Feb. 1848], Thomas Metcalf to Crittenden, Feb. 20, 1848, Crittenden Papers, Library of Congress; Garrett Davis to John M. Berrien, Feb. 29, 1848, Berrien Papers, Univ. of North Carolina; Washington *Union*, Mar. 3, Richmond *Whig*, Mar. 8, *National Intelligencer*, Feb. 29, Mar. 2, 1848.

29. Kirwan, *Crittenden*, 212-13.

30. "To the Public," Apr. 10, 1848; first published in Lexington *Observer and Reporter*, Apr. 12, 1848.

31. John J. Crittenden to Clay, May 4, 1848, *HCP*; Richard Hawes to Orlando Brown, May 24, 1848, Brown Papers, Filson Club; Richmond *Whig*, Apr. 28, 1848.

32. James Russell Lowell, *The Biglow Papers* (Philadelphia, n.d.), 178; for the Allison Letter, dated Apr. 22, *Niles' Register*, July 8, 1948.

33. The letters were reprinted in the New York *Tribune*, Boston *Courier*, and elsewhere beginning in Mar. 1848; the address of the Massachusetts legislature is in the *Courier*, May 2, 1848.

34. James W. Webb to Webster, June 3, 1848, *DWP*.

35. George F. Hoar, *Autobiography of Seventy Years* (New York, 1903), I, 151; Sumner, *Memoirs*, III, 165n.

36. Horace Greeley to Clay, May 29, 1848, *HCP*.

37. Leslie Combs to Clay, June 10, 1848, *HCP*.

38. Hamilton, "Election of 1848," 876; Thomas B. Stevenson to Tom Corwin, June 29, 1848, in *Last Seven Years*, 467-68.

39. To Committee of Louisville, June 28, 1848, *Works of Clay*, V, 566-68.

40. [Theodore N. Parmelee], "Recollections of an Old Stager," *Harper's Magazine*, v. 45 (1872), 448.

41. "Joseph G. Baldwin's Reports on the Whig National Convention of 1848," M. C. McMillan, ed., *Journal of Southern History*, v. 25 (1959), 375-76.

42. New York *Tribune*, June 17, 22, 1848; Hamilton, "Election of 1848," 876.

43. James Erwin to A. T. Burnley, July 18, to———Anderson, July 27, 1848, Crittenden Papers; letter of Thomas Marshall in Louisville *Journal*, Nov. 27, 1851.

44. To Thomas B. Stevenson, Aug. 25, 1848, *HCP*.

45. James Russell Lowell, *Anti-Slavery Papers* (New York, 1969), I, 114; Charles Sumner to J. R. Giddings, Apr. 21, June 8, 1848, Giddings Papers; Hoar, *Autobiography*, 148; Ebenezer R. Hoar to Webster, Aug. 13, 1848, *DWP*; Oliver Johnson letter, Boston *Herald*, Feb. 5, 1882.

46. To Fletcher Webster, June 19, June———, 1848, *DWP*.

47. Frank O. Gatell, *John Gorham Palfrey and the New England Conscience* (Cambridge, 1963), 159; Boston *Courier*, June 24, 1848.

48. *Writings*, IV, 123-44; Winthrop quoted in Allan Nevins, *Ordeal of the Union* (New York, 1947), I, 210; Charles T. Congdon, *Reminiscences of a Journalist* (Boston, 1880), 133-34; P. Greeley to John W. Davis, Feb. 7, 1849, Davis Papers, American Antiquarian Society; "Largesses of D. Webster," undated memo, George F. Hoar Papers, Massachusetts Historical Society; *Papers of Millard Fillmore, Publications of the Buffalo Historical Society* (Buffalo, 1907), II, 136.

49. Robert Wickliffe to Robert Wickliffe, Jr., Nov. 10, 1848, Univ. of Kentucky; *National Intelligencer*, Nov. 18, 1848.

50. Seward, *Seward*, II, 82.

51. To Joseph Lesesne, July 15, 1848, July 19, 1847, Henry W. Conner, July 9, 1848, *JCCP*; Raybeck, "Presidential Ambitions," 349; Charleston *Mercury*, July 21, 1848.

52. *Works of Calhoun*, IV, 479-512; Hamilton, "Election of 1848," 907-8.

53. *Works*, IV, 511–12. See Arthur Bestor, "State Sovereignty and Slavery," *Illinois State Historical Society Journal*, v. 54 (1961), 117–80.
54. *Congressional Globe*, 30 Cong., 1 Sess., 932, 950, 953; Polk, *Diary*, IV, 19–23; "Journal of the Select Committee," Clayton Papers, Library of Congress.
55. *Congressional Globe*, 30 Cong., 1 Sess., 1074; *Works of Calhoun*, IV, 513–35; *Writings*, X, 34–44.
56. Charleston *Mercury*, Aug. 2, 1848.
57. James H. Hammond to William G. Simms, Sept. 11, N. B. Tucker to Hammond, Oct. 10, 1848, Hammond Papers, Library of Congress.
58. James H. Hammond to William G. Simms, Sept. 7, 1848, *ibid.*, White, *Rhett*, 97.
59. To Henry W. Conner, Oct. 18, 1848, *JCCP*; Charleston *Mercury*, Oct. 26, 1848.
60. Herman V. Ames, "John C. Calhoun and the Secession Movement of 1850," American Antiquarian Society *Proceedings*, n.s., v. 28 (1918), 26; Hamer, *Secession Movement*, 15–16, 28–29.
61. Cooper, *Politics of Slavery*, 270; Robert Toombs to John J. Crittenden, Sept. 27, 1848, *Correspondence of Toombs*, 139.
62. Henry W. Hilliard, *Politics and Pen Pictures at Home and Abroad* (New York, 1892), 199.
63. Boston *Courier*, Jan. 18, 19, Charleston *Mercury*, Jan. 22, 1849.
64. *Ibid.*, Jan. 23, 24, 1849.
65. Robert Toombs to John J. Crittenden, Jan. 22, 1849, *Correspondence of Toombs*, 141–42; New Orleans *Picayune*, Jan. 31, 1849; to Henry W. Conner, Feb. 2, 1849, JCCP.
66. In Rhett's oration on Calhoun, in *The Carolina Tribute to Calhoun*, J. P. Thomas, ed. (Columbia, S.C., 1857), 369.
67. *Works of Calhoun*, VI, 290–313.
68. *Congressional Globe*, 30 Cong., 2 Sess., 272–74; *Works*, IV, 535–41; *Writings*, XIV, 323–35; Benton, *View*, II, 730. See also Don E. Fehrenbacher, *The Dred Scott Case* (New York, 1978), 155–57.
69. *Congressional Globe*, 30 Cong., 2 Sess., 691; Benton, *View*, II, 732.

3. The Compromise of 1850

1. To Charles F. Mercer, Dec. 10, 1848, to James Harlan, Jan. 26, 1849, *HCP*; Reverdy Johnson to John J. Crittenden, Dec. 12, 1848, Crittenden Papers; Crittenden to John M. Clayton, Jan. 7, 1849, Clayton Papers.
2. To Mercer, Dec. 10, 1848, *HCP*.
3. Boston *Courier*, Feb. 9, 1849; M. K. Hall to Millard Fillmore, Jan. 8, 1849, Fillmore Papers; Alexander H. Stephens to John J. Crittenden, Dec. 5, John P. Kennedy to Crittenden, Dec. 22, William L. Dayton to Crittenden, Dec. 14, 1848, John M. Clayton to Crittenden, Jan. 23, 1849, Crittenden Papers; John Tyler to Webster, Feb. 21, 1849, *DWP*.
4. Truman Smith to Crittenden, Dec. 12, 1848, Crittenden Papers.
5. Quoted in Nevins, *Ordeal*, I, 230.
6. Clay to Reverdy Johnson, Mar. 7, to Zachary Taylor, May 12, Taylor to Clay, May 28, 1849, *HCP*.
7. William H. Seward to Mrs. Seward, Mar. 25, 1849, Seward Papers; Webster to R. M. Blatchford, Jan. 16, 1849, *Writings*, XVI, 504, to Blatchford, Feb. 25, *DWP*.
8. To Edward Curtis, Apr. 3, to Fletcher Webster, Apr. 6, 12, 16, 1849, *DWP*.
9. *National Intelligencer*, Oct. 9, 1849.
10. Boston *Courier*, Aug. 20, 1849.
11. New York *Herald*, Oct. 13, Nov. 8, 1849; Charleston *Mercury*, June 12, 1849.
12. To John H. Means, Apr. 13, 1847, *Correspondence of Calhoun*, 764–66; Ames, "Calhoun and Secession," 31–32.
13. Calhoun to C. S. Tarpley, July 9, 1849, quoted in Nevins, *Ordeal*, I, 248; David Wallace to W. R. Seabrook, Oct. 20, 1849, Seabrook Papers, Library of Congress; Calhoun to James H. Hammond, Jan. 4, 1850, *Correspondence*, 779. The extent of Calhoun's influence on the Mississippi proceedings is in dispute: see Hamer, *Secession Movement*, 43–44, and Thelma Jennings, *The Nashville Convention: Southern Movement for Unity, 1848–1851* (Memphis, 1980), 37–39.
14. *National Intelligencer*, Mar. 8, 1849, and *The Writings of Sam Houston*, A. W. Williams and E. C. Backer, eds. (Austin, 1938–43), V, 78–88.

15. *National Intelligencer*, July 21, 1849. See also Elbert B. Smith, "Thomas Hart Benton: Southern Realist," *American Historical Review*, v. 68 (1953), 795–807.

16. *National Intelligencer*, July 21, 1849; Samuel Trent to Calhoun, Aug. 22, 1849, *JCCP*.

17. To James A. Bayard, Dec. 14, 1849, Bayard Papers, Delaware Historical Society.

18. M. K. Hall to Millard Fillmore, Jan. 8, Mar. 10, Fillmore to Zachary Taylor, Apr. 5, 1849, Daniel Barnard to Fillmore, Dec. 17, 1848, Fillmore Papers; Sherry Penney, *Patrician in Politics: Daniel D. Barnard of New York* (Port Washington, N.Y., 1974), 100–103.

19. *Congressional Globe*, 31 Cong., 1 Sess., 69–74. For contrasting general accounts: Nevins, *Ordeal*, I, ch. 7; Holman Hamilton, *Prologue to Conflict: Crisis and Compromise of 1850* (Lexington, Ky., 1964), chs. 1–2.

20. Nevins, *Ordeal*, I, 257; Michael F. Holt, *The Political Crisis of the 1850s* (New York, 1978), 73–78; Cooper, *Politics of Slavery*, 290–95.

21. *Congressional Globe*, 31 Cong., 1 Sess., 202, 231.

22. *Ibid.*, 200–205.

23. To Leslie Combs, Dec. 22, 1849, to James B. Clay, Jan. 2, 1850, *HCP*.

24. Hilliard, *Politics and Pen Pictures*, 216–18; George T. Curtis, *Life of Daniel Webster* (New York, 1972), II, 397–98.

25. *Congressional Globe*, 31 Cong., 1 Sess., 225–27; Boston *Daily Advertiser*, Jan. 28, 1850.

26. Edward Coles to Clay, Mar. 15, 1850, Coles Papers, College of William and Mary; *National Intelligencer*, Feb. 20, 1951; Adrienne Koch, *Madison's "Advice to My Country"* (Princeton, 1966), 5.

27. *Congressional Globe*, 31 Cong., 1 Sess., 244–47.

28. New York *Tribune*, Feb. 8, 1850.

29. Colton, *Last Seven Years*, 305; *Congressional Globe*, 31 Cong., 1 Sess., 115–27 (App.).

30. Colton, *Last Seven Years*, 313.

31. *Ibid.*, 327–29. See R. Kent Newmyer, *Supreme Court Justice Story* (Chapel Hill, 1985), 370–74.

32. Salmon P. Chase to E. S. Hamlin, Feb. 2, 1850, *Chase Correspondence*, 200–201; New York *Tribune*, Feb. 18, 1850; *Congressional Globe*, 31 Cong., 1 Sess., 403.

33. Charleston *Courier*, Feb. 12, 1850.

34. New York *Herald*, Jan. 31, Feb. 8, 1850.

35. Cooper, *Politics of Slavery*, 295; Nevins, *Ordeal*, I, 271.

36. William E. Smith, *The Francis Preston Blair Family in Politics* (New York, 1933), I, 259, 261; Blair to Martin Van Buren, Mar. 24, 1850, Van Buren Papers, Library of Congress.

37. Richmond *Enquirer*, Sept. 6, 10, 1852.

38. *Congressional Globe*, 31 Cong., 1 Sess., 369; Colton, *Last Seven Years*, 207.

39. *Congressional Globe*, 31 Cong., 1 Sess., 365–69; Hamilton, *Prologue*, 62; *Records of the Columbia Historical Society*, v. 20 (1917), 179.

40. Joseph Scoville to James G. Bennett, Apr. 30, 1850, in New York *Herald*, May 3, 1850; New York *Tribune*, Jan. 3, 1854.

41. *Works of Calhoun*, IV, 542–73; John Wentworth, *Congressional Reminiscences* (Chicago, 1882), 23; Charleston *Courier*, Mar. 9, 1850.

42. *Carolina Tribute*, 134; New York *Herald*, Mar. 6, 7, 1850; Webster to———, March 1, *DWP*.

43. *Congressional Globe*, 31 Cong., 1 Sess., 517–18. For a sample of newspaper opinion: Richmond *Whig*, Mar. 8, Louisville *Journal*, Mar. 11, New Orleans *Picayune*, Mar. 9, 11, New York *Herald*, Mar. 7, 1850.

44. *Congressional Globe*, 31 Cong., 1 Sess., 461–64; *Works*, IV, 574–78.

45. To Franklin Haven, Jan. 13, to Charles A. Stetson, Feb. 15, 1850, *DWP*; New York *Herald*, Feb. 25, 26, 1850. See Herbert D. Foster, "Webster's Seventh of March Speech and the Secession Movement, 1850," *American Historical Review*, v. 27 (1922), 244–70; and Dalzell, *Webster*, ch. 5.

46. Webster to Charles Warren, Mar. 1, 1850, *Writings*, XVI, 535–36.

47. Mrs. Davis to John W. Davis, [Mar. 1850], Davis Papers; William H. Furness to Webster, Feb. 25, Benjamin Silliman to Webster, Mar. 5, 1850, *DWP*; Boston *Courier*, Mar. 2, 4, 1850; Robert C. Winthrop, *A Chapter of Autobiography* (n.p., 1872), 2–7; Oliver Johnson letter, Boston *Herald*, Feb. 5, 1882.

48. New York *Herald*, Feb. 24, 25, 26, Mar. 1, 4, 1850, and New Orleans *Picayune*, Mar. 7, 1850.

49. Waddy Thompson to Webster, Mar. 2, 1850, *DWP*.

50. Winthrop, *A Chapter*, 6–7.

51. George W. Julian, *Political Recollections, 1850 to 72* (Chicago, 1884), 86; New York *Herald*, Mar. 10, 1850.

52. *Writings*, X, 57–98.

53. Charleston *Mercury*, Mar. 11, Louisville *Journal*, Mar. 14, 1850, repr. in the Baltimore *Sun*. See also Richmond *Whig*, Mar. 11, Charleston *Courier*, Mar. 13, 1850.

54. Quoted in Foster, "Seventh of March Speech," 255, See also Ames, "Secession Movement," 40–41.

55. Winthrop, *A Chapter*, 9-10.

56. To Fletcher Webster, Mar. 21, Edward Curtis to Peter Harvey, Mar. 28, 1850, *DWP*; Curtis, *Webster*, II, 409–10n; Boston *Courier*, Mar. 25, 1850; Robert C. Winthrop, Jr., *A Memoir of Robert C. Winthrop* (Boston, 1897), 114.

57. "The Fugitive Slave Law," *Works of Emerson: Miscellanies* (Boston, 1891), 175. For a sample of the critical reaction in New England, see James Freeman Clarke, *Anti-Slavery Days* (New York, 1883), 135–47; Lowell, *Anti-Slavery Papers*, II, 177–94; Horace Mann, *Slavery: Letters and Speeches* (New York, 1969), Letters I and II.

58. Horace Mann to Mrs. Mann, Mar. 8, 1850, Mann Papers, Massachusetts Historical Society.

59. *Journals of Ralph Waldo Emerson*, Ralph H. Orth and A. R. Ferguson, eds. (Cambridge, 1971), XI, 345–46.

60. Theodore Parker, *The Slave Power* (Boston, n.d.), 218–47; Boston *Daily Advertiser*, Mar. 26, 1850.

61. John Greenleaf Whittier, *The Complete Poetical Works* (Boston, 1894), 186–87. The poem was first published in the *National Era*, May 2, 1850.

62. Boston *Daily Advertiser*, Apr. 3, 1850; Edward Everett to Abbott Lawrence, Apr. 29, 1850, Everett Papers.

63. Isaac Hill to Webster, Apr. 17, to Hill, Apr. 20, 1850, *DWP*; *National Intelligencer*, Oct. 26, 1850; Emerson, *Journals*, XI, 277.

64. Jane Grey Swisshelm, "The Indictment Against Daniel Webster," *The Independent*, v. 30 (Apr. 11, 1878), 2; Frederic H. Marbut, *News from the Capital* (Carbondale, Ill., 1971), 95–97.

65. *Congressional Globe*, 31 Cong., 1 Sess., 260–69 (App.); Glyndon G. Van Deusen, *William Henry Seward* (New York, 1967), 121–24; Thurlow Weed to W. H. Seward, Mar. 14, 26, 1850, Seward Papers.

66. *Congressional Globe*, 31 Cong., 1 Sess., 624–25; Edward G. Parker, *The Golden Age of American Oratory* (Boston 1857), 17–18; Wentworth, *Reminiscences*, 23–24.

67. To Fletcher Webster, Apr. 8, 1850, *DWP*.

68. Fredrika Bremer, *The Homes of the New World: Impressions of America* (New York, 1852), I, 301; Charleston *Courier*, Apr. 1, 2, 24, 27; and, in general, *Carolina Tribute*.

69. To Henry W. Conner, Mar. 18, 1850, *JCCP*.

70. Charleston *Courier*, Apr. 3, 1850.

71. N. B. Tucker to James H. Hammond, Nov. 15, 1850, Tucker Papers, Duke Univ.

72. Quoted in Steven A. Channing, *Crisis of Fear: Secession in South Carolina* (New York, 1970), 168n; *The Letters of William Gilmore Simms*, Mary C. S. Oliphant and others, eds. (Columbia, S.C., 1952–56), I, xcv-xcvi.

73. *Congressional Globe*, 31 Cong., 1 Sess., 662.

74. James S. Pike to James Schouler, Apr. 21, 1850, Schouler Papers, Massachusetts Historical Society; Boston *Courier*, May 15, 20, 1850.

75. Orlando Brown to John J. Crittenden, Apr. 19, Crittenden Papers; Crittenden to John M. Clayton, Apr. 6, 1850, Clayton Papers.

76. *Writings*, XIII, 386–89.

77. Edward Everett to Robert Winthrop, May 8, 29, 1850, Everett Papers.

78. "To the Citizens of Newburyport," *Writings*, XII, 225–37.

79. *Congressional Globe*, 31 Cong., 1 Sess., 944–48, 567–73 (App.).

80. *Ibid.*, 615, 1091 (App.); Boston *Courier*, May 22, Louisville *Journal*, May 28, 1850; Nevins, *Ordeal*, I, 319–20.

81. Salmon P. Chase to E. S. Hamlin, May 27, 1850, *Chase Correspondence*, 212, to Lucretia Clay, July 6, 1850, *HCP*; M. K. Hall to Millard Fillmore, May 1, 1850, Fillmore Papers; Seward, *Seward*, II, 134–35.

82. *Ibid.*, II, 140–41; *Congressional Globe*, 31 Cong., 1 Sess., 1210–11.

83. Wentworth, *Reminiscences*, 29; Hamilton, *Prologue*, 118–20.

84. *National Era*, July 18, 1850.

85. To Franklin Haven, July 4, 1850, *Writings*, XVI, 549.
86. Hilliard, *Politics and Pen Pictures*, 237; Nevins, *Ordeal*, I, 327–33.
87. Francis P. Blair to Martin Van Buren, July 15, 1850, Van Buren Papers; Seward, *Seward*, II, 147; Robert Winthrop to John H. Clifford, July 14, 1850, Winthrop Papers, Massachusetts Historical Society; Nevins, *Ordeal*, I, 324.
88. *Writings*, X, 144–70.
89. *Congressional Globe*, 31 Cong., 1 Sess., 1405–14 (App.); Francis P. Blair to Martin Van Buren, Aug. 1, 1850, Van Buren Papers.
90. *Congressional Globe*, 31 Cong., 1 Sess., 1413–14 (App.); White, *Rhett*, 108–109.
91. Nevins, *Ordeal*, I, 340; Hamilton, *Prologue*, 108–14; James A. Pearce to————, Aug. 5, 1850, Pearce Papers, Maryland Historical Society.
92. *Congressional Globe*, 31 Cong., 1 Sess., 1486–87 (App.).
93. Stephen A. Douglas to Charles H. Lamphier and G. Walker, Aug. 3, 1850, *Letters of Stephen A. Douglas*, Robert Johannsen, ed. (Urbana, 1960), 191–93; *Congressional Globe*, 31 Cong., 1 Sess., 1829–30.
94. To Franklin Haven, Sept. 12, to Peter Harvey, Oct. 2, 1850, DWP; E. P. Smith to Henry C. Carey, Nov. 28, 1856, E. C. Gardiner Collection, Pennsylvania Historical Society.

4. Last of the Giants

1. Richard H. Shryock, *Georgia and the Union in 1850* (Durham, N.C., 1926), 308–19; Nevins, *Ordeal*, I, 362–75.
2. *Carolina Tribute*, 330; *National Intelligencer*, Nov. 30, 1850.
3. *Carolina Tribute*, 370.
4. Quoted in Nevins, *Ordeal*, I, 373; White, *Rhett*, 132–33.
5. *Carolina Tribute*, 330–31.
6. Quoted in James Ford Rhodes, *A History of the United States from the Compromise of 1850* (New York, 1909), II, 353.
7. See, e.g., reviews in the *Southern Literary Messenger*, v. 20 (1854) and the *North American Review*, v. 76 (1853).
8. To Franklin Haven, Sept. 12, 1850, *Writings*; Curtis, *Webster*, II, 474.
9. To George Ticknor, January 16, 1851, *Writings*, XVI, 586; Paul R. Frothingham, *Edward Everett, Orator and Statesman* (Boston, 1925), 321–24; for the Webster-Hulsemann correspondence, *Writings*, XII, 162–80. See also Maurice Baxter, *One and Inseparable: Daniel Webster and the Union* (Cambridge, 1984), ch. 28, and Kenneth E. Shewmaker, "Daniel Webster and the Politics of Foreign Policy, 1850–52," *Journal of American History*, v. 63 (1976), 303–15.
10. *Congressional Globe*, 31 Cong., 2 Sess., 18–21; John W. Houston to John M. Clayton, Jan. 8, 1851, Clayton Papers.
11. *Congressional Globe*, 31 Cong., 2 Sess., 686–87, 694–701.
12. Edward Curtis, Diary, July 12, Oct. 2, 1852 (Dartmouth College). See also Curtis, *Webster*, II, 492–97.
13. Henry Cohen, *Business and Politics in America . . . : The Career Biography of W. W. Corcoran* (Westport, Conn., 1971), 85; "Some Notes from the Late Benjamin Ogle Tayloe," *Tyler's Quarterly*, v. 2 (1920–21), 82.
14. Baxter, *Webster*, 451; for contrasting views, *National Intelligencer*, Mar. 11, *National Era*, Mar. 6, 1851.
15. Dalzell, *Webster*, 218–22; Baxter, *Webster*, 484–85.
16. Webster to F. S. Lathrop and others, Oct. 28, 1850, *Writings*, XII, 252–53.
17. Harold M. Hyman and William W. Wiecek, *Equal Justice Under Law: Constitutional Development, 1835–1875* (New York, 1982), 149–50.
18. Wendell Phillips, *Speeches, Lectures, and Letters* (Boston, 1863), 64.
19. Richard Henry, Dana, Jr., *Speeches in Stirring Times* (Boston, 1910), 168.
20. Leonard Levy, *The Law of the Commonwealth and Chief Justice Shaw* (Cambridge, 1957), 90, 87–91; Webster to New York Committee, Feb. 20, 1851, *Writings*, XII, 263–64.
21. *Congressional Globe*, 31 Cong., 2 Sess., 596–97; Richardson, *Messages and Papers*, IV, 2637–42, 2645–46; Baxter, *Webster*, 479.
22. Levy, *Shaw*, 91–102.
23. To Francis Brinley, Apr. 19, 1851, in Curtis, *Webster*, II, 500; Claude M. Feuss, *Rufus Choate: The Wizard of the Law* (New York, 1928), 199; Boston *Courier*, Apr. 16–18, 22, 1851.

24. *Ibid.*, Apr. 23, 1851.
25. To R. M. Blatchford, May 11, 1851, in Curtis, *Webster*, II, 502–503.
26. *Writings*, IV, 242–62.
27. *Ibid.*, XIII, 408–21, 419.
28. *Ibid.*, IV, 267–90, 270.
29. *Ibid.*, XIII, 237–41.
30. *National Intelligencer*, Aug. 5, 1851; *The Speech of Mr. Webster at Capon Springs, Virginia* . . . (Washington, 1851); Curtis, *Webster*, II, 520–21. See also Boston *Courier*, July 2, Aug. 11, 1851; to George Abbot, July 23, 1851, *DWP*.
31. R. M. T. Hunter, "The Republic of Republics," *Southern Historical Society Papers*, v. 13 (1885), 344; Alexander H. Stephens, *A Constitutional View of the Late War Between the States* (Philadelphia, 1868–70), 387, 407.
32. To Franklin Haven, May 7, to Edward Everett, June 26, 1851, *DWP*; Boston *Courier*, June 11, 12, 1851. See also Dalzell, *Webster*, ch. 7.
33. To Franklin Haven, Dec. 14, 1851, *Writings*, XVI, 630.
34. Boston *Courier*, Oct. 25, 26, 1851.
35. E. Merton Coulter, "Downfall of the Whig Party, Kentucky," *Register of the Kentucky Historical Society*, v. 23 (1935), 162–64; William C. Davis, *Breckinridge: Statesman, Soldier, Symbol* (Baton Rouge, 1974), 51–56; Harry A. Volz, "Party, State, and Nation: Kentucky and the Coming of the American Civil War," Ph.D. diss. (Univ. of Virginia, 1982), chs. 1–2.
36. To Stephen Whitney *et al.*, Oct. 3, 1851, in *National Intelligencer*, Oct. 21, 1851; Carl Schurz, *Henry Clay* (Boston, 1887), II, 386–88.
37. Epes Sargent, *Life and Public Services of Henry Clay* (Auburn, N.Y., 1852), 367. Greeley carried Sargent's biography to Clay's death.
38. To Franklin Haven, Dec. 23, 1851, *DWP*; *Writings*, XIII, 452–62; Ben: Perley Poore, *Reminiscences* (Philadelphia, 1886), I, 403–406.
39. Colton, *Last Seven Years*, 223–24; *National Intelligencer*, Feb. 3, 1852.
40. To Edward Everett, Mar. 14, 1851, Everett Papers; Dalzell, *Webster*, ch. 7; Baxter, *Webster*, 486–90.
41. Fuess, *Choate*, 199; *Letters and Journals of Samuel Gridley Howe*, Laura E. Richards, ed. (Boston, 1906–09) II, 379; Curtis, *Webster*, II, 611–20; Boston *Courier*, May 24, 1851.
42. To Daniel Jenifer [June 19, 1851], *DWP*.
43. Boston *Courier*, June 25, 26, 1852; Claude M. Fuess, *Daniel Webster* (Boston, 1930), II, 188.
44. To Edward Curtis and George Ashmun, to Millard Fillmore, to Fletcher Webster, all June 21, 1852, *DWP*.
45. Poore, *Reminiscences*, I, 418; Poore memo, undated, Dartmouth College; Richmond *Enquirer*, June 30, 1852.
46. *Ibid.*, to R. M. Blatchford, June 22, 1852, *DWP*.
47. For a general account, John W. Coleman, *Last Days, Death and Funeral of Henry Clay* (Lexington, Ky., 1951). See also Joan S. Brown, "The Funeral of Henry Clay," *Antiques Magazine*, v. 112 (1977), 110–11.
48. *Eulogies Delivered in the Senate and the House of Representatives on . . . Calhoun . . . Clay . . . and Webster* (Washington, 1853), 24–26.
49. Quoted in Glyndon G. Van Deusen, *Life of Henry Clay* (Boston, 1837), 424.
50. Coleman, *Last Days*, 9.
51. *Report of the Committee of Arrangements of the Common Council of New York of the Obsequies of Henry Clay* (New York, 1852); George Templeton Strong, *Diary*, Allan Nevins and M. H. Thomas, eds. (New York, 1952), II, 101; Sargent, *Clay*, 422.
52. *National Intelligencer*, July 8, Louisville *Journal*, July 10, 1852.
53. *Ibid.*, July 7; Thomas H. Clay to Orlando Brown, July 19, 1852, Filson Club.
54. *Life of John J. Crittenden*, Mrs. Chapman Coleman, ed. (Philadelphia, 1871), II, 39–71; *Abraham Lincoln: His Speeches and Writings*, Roy P. Basler, ed. (Cleveland, 1946), 267–77.
55. A. H. Carrier, *Monument to the Memory of Henry Clay* (Cincinnati, 1858), 129–30. See also J. O. Harrison, "Henry Clay: Reminiscences of His Executor," *Century Magazine*, v. 11 (1886), 177–78.
56. To Fletcher Webster, July 6, to Edward Everett, Aug. 14, 1852, *DWP*; Edward Curtis, Diary, 44–45.
57. Curtis, *Webster*, II, 632–39.
58. To Moses Grinnell and others, Oct. 12, 1852, *DWP*. See also George T. Curtis to Alexander

H. Stephens, Aug. 13, 1852, Stephens Papers, Library of Congress; George Abbot to Edward Everett, Oct. 14, 15, 17, 18, Everett Papers.

59. Curtis, *Webster*, II, 702. In what follows I have replied primarily on ch. 38 of this work.
60. *Ibid.*, 671.
61. *Ibid.*, 689–92. The will, Oct. 21, 1852, and estate inventory, Nov. 1, 1853, are in *DWP*.
62. See "Verdict," Oct. 25, 1852, *DWP*; "Webster Record," *National Intelligencer*, Nov. 6, 1852; George S. Hillard to Francis Lieber, Nov. 2, 1852, Lieber Papers, Huntington Library; *Louisville Journal*, Nov. 2, 1852, Jan. 19, 1853.
63. "Last Moments of Daniel Webster," *National Intelligencer*, Oct. 28, 1852; Curtis, *Webster*, II, 701.
64. Robert Winthrop to John P. Kennedy, Oct. 25, 1852, Winthrop Papers; Boston *Courier*, Oct. 25, *National Intelligencer*, Oct. 26, 1852.
65. Emerson, *Journals*, XIII, 111.
66. Ticknor, *Life and Letters*, II, 284; George S. Hillard to Lieber, Nov. 2, 1852; Boston *Courier*, Oct. 25, Nov. 30, Dec. 1, *National Intelligencer*, Oct. 30, 1852.
67. *The Journal of Richard Henry Dana, Jr.*, Richard F. Lucid, ed. (Cambridge, 1968), II, 514–15; *Letters of Horace Howard Furness* (Boston, 1922), I, 8–10; *National Intelligencer*, Nov. 6, 1852.
68. George S. Hillard to Lieber, Nov. 2, 1852; Ticknor, *Life and Letters*, II, 283.
69. Theodore Parker, *Additional Speeches, Addresses, and Occasional Sermons* (Boston, 1867), I, 131–294.
70. Adams, *Dana*, 226.
71. William H. Seward to Theodore Parker, Dec. 27, 1852, Parker Papers, Massachusetts Historical Society; Sumner, *Memoirs*, III, 322.
72. Rufus Choate, *Addresses and Orations*, 6th ed. (Boston, 1891), 328.

Epilogue

1. "Editor's Table," *The Knickerbocker*, v. 40 (1852), 531; Boston *Courier*, May 15, 1852; Daniel D. Barnard, *Speech . . . 1852* (n.p., 1852), 9; New York *Times*, July 26, Oct. 25, 1952.
2. *Congressional Globe*, 35 Cong., 2 Sess., 203–204.
3. E. A. Pollard, *Southern History of the War* (New York, 1865), 610n.
4. Lincoln, *Speeches*, 589; Hoar, *Autobiography*, 230.
5. Rhodes, *History*, III, 93; H. C. Perkins, ed., *Northern Editorials on Secession* (New York, 1942), I, 168, 180.
6. "Exhumation of the Body of John C. Calhoun," *South Carolina Historical Magazine*, v. 57 (1956), 57–58.
7. *Prose Works 1892*, Floyd Stovall, ed. (New York, 1963), I, 109.
8. *A History of the Calhoun Monument Association* (Charleston, 1888) and *Appendix* (Charleston, 1898).
9. Thomas G. Clemson to Mary A. Snowden, Nov. 23, 1873, Snowden Papers, Univ. of South Carolina. See also Lander, *The Calhoun Family*, chs. 14–15.
10. See correspondence concerning Calhoun biography in the Clemson Papers, Clemson Univ., and in the R. M. T. Hunter Papers, Univ. of Virginia.
11. James Parton, *Life of Andrew Jackson* (New York, 1860), I, 236.
12. Whittier, *Poems*, 187; Charles Francis Adams, *The Sifted Grain and the Grain Sifters. An Address . . . 1900* (n.p., n.d.), 15.
13. Louis A. Banks, *The Story of the Hall of Fame* (New York, 1902).

INDEX

Abbot, George, 490

Aberdeen, Lord, 321, 322, 323, 326, 345, 346

abolitionism: and District of Columbia, 257–58, 259–62, 274–76, 322, 455, 470, 474; and U.S. mail, 258–59; and Clay, 286–87, 376–79; and *Creole* Affair, 322–23; in 1844 election, 365; and political parties, 416, 428–29; 237, 351

Adair, John, 14, 15

Adams, Charles Francis, 369, 370, 442

Adams, Charles Francis, II, quoted, 498

Adams, Henry, quoted, 370

Adams, John: 104, 105, 135, 140, 410; quoted on Webster, 107; Webster on, 110–11

Adams, John Quincy: quoted, 82–83; characterized, 86; quoted on Clay, 16, 45, 53, 201–2, 362, 381; on Calhoun, 86–87, 233, 406; on Webster, 224, 247, 332, 355; secretary of state, 50, 53, 55, 56, 57; presidential candidate, 113–29 *passim*, 162–64; president, 131–46 *passim*; and Federalism, 162; and Anti-Masonry, 199, 247; and nullification, 202, 216; mentioned, 44, 46, 188, 277, 333, 390, 438

Adams, Louisa Catherine, 133, 325

Adams-Onís Treaty, 56, 93, 115, 138, 359

Agg, Mrs. John, 393

Aiken, William, 368

Albany Regency, 198, 242, 336, 337, 384, 415

Alexander, Francis, 392

Allen, Charles, 346, 369, 370, 442, 479

Allen, William, 415

Allison, John S., 439

American Colonization Society, Clay and, 65, 121, 284–85, 286, 317, 437, 488

American Revolution: in Clay's heritage, 8–9; in Calhoun's, 19, 26; in Webster's, 27–28; and Latin America, 53; and American System, 73

American System, 68–84, 114, 122, 132–33, 147, 154, 165, 166, 170–71, 172, 176, 194, 197, 202, 203–4, 210, 216, 218, 238, 277, 357, 384

"American system" (hemispheric), 54, 57, 58, 68

Ames, Joseph, 491

Amistad Case, 323

Anderson, Richard, 139

Anti-Masonic party: 182, 193, 194; Clay and, 198–99, 211–12; Webster and, 247, 249–50

Appleton, Nathan: quoted, 219; 369

Arbuthnot and Ambrister, 55, 320

Archer, William S., quoted, 441

Arkansas, 61, 92

Army, U.S., reorganization of, 88, 93–95

Ashburton, Lord. *See* Baring, Alexander

Ashland, 12, 167, 318, 350, 372–74, 433

Ashmun, George, 431, 479

Astor, John Jacob, 90

Atchison, David R., 415

Austin, Benjamin, 161

Austin, James T., 104

Badger, George, 299, 312

Bailey, Gamaliel, 437

Baldwin, Henry, 72–73

Baldwin, Joseph G., quoted, 441

Bancroft, George, 331

Bank of Kentucky, 13, 17

Bank of South Carolina, 404

Bank of the United States, First, 17

Printed in the United States
135353LV00004B/9/A

6173590R0

Made in the USA
Lexington, KY
25 July 2010